UNDERSTANDING AMERICAN DEMOCRACY

LEON P. BARADAT

MiraCosta College

HarperCollins*Publishers*

For Elaine, my wife, and Pete, my father.

I have learned much from each.

Sponsoring Editor: Lauren Silverman
Project Editor: Diane Rowell
Design Supervisor: Dorothy Bungert
Text Design: Robin Hoffmann
Cover Design: Butler Udell Design
Cover Illustration: Butler Udell Design
Photo Researcher: Mira Schachne
Production Manager/Assistant: Willie Lane/Sunaina Sehwani
Compositor: Better Graphics, Inc.
Printer and Binder: R. R. Donnelley & Sons Company
Cover Printer: The Lehigh Press, Inc.

Understanding American Democracy
Copyright © 1992 by HarperCollins Publishers Inc.

Library of Congress Cataloging-in-Publication Data

Baradat, Leon P., 1940-
    Understanding American democracy / Leon P. Baradat.
       p. cm.
    Includes bibliographical references and index.
    ISBN 0-06-040478-7
    1. United States—Politics and government. 2. Democracy—United
States. I. Title.
JK274.B296 1992
321.8'042'0973—dc20   91-24512
                                                CIP

91 92 93 94 9 8 7 6 5 4 3 2 1

CONTENTS

PREFACE

The United States is a country of great accomplishment, but also one of paradox. It has the world's largest gross national product—greater than twice the size of the next largest national economy. We enjoy the greatest expanse of temperate, flat, well-watered land of any society, and we produce more food annually than it is possible for us to eat. We are about 5 percent of the world's population, yet we consume well over one-quarter of the world's annual production of resources.

Despite its wealth, however, the United States has the highest proportion of children living in poverty of all industrial societies, and 32 million of its people live below the poverty line. Our per capita income is second only to that of Switzerland, yet we give a smaller percentage of our national wealth to Third World countries than all but one of the other industrial states. Our tax rate is the lowest of all industrialized societies while our national debt and international trade debt are the highest in the world. We have the world's most advanced medical system, but the United States ranks eighteenth in infant mortality. We enjoy the world's most extensive educational institutions and in the past decade we produced five times as many Nobel Laureates as any other country. Even so, a full quarter of the nation's high school students drop out before graduation, and our students rank lowest in academic test scores among the industrial states. At the same time, our crime rate and our rate of teenage parenthood is greater than any other society.

The United States has one of the oldest, most admired democracies in the world, yet with the world's fourth largest population, we rank only seventeenth in newspaper circulation and our voter turnout rates are the lowest of any democracy. Our lack of interest and participation in public affairs is the most disheartening, and perhaps the most dangerous, because all of the features mentioned above—the successes and the failures—are vitally affected by government and by the political system. Indeed, the political process is the principal instrument by which we establish goals, and the government is the major vehicle by which we attempt to achieve them. Since our society is democratic, the people have a great deal to say—if they choose to—about society's objectives and how they will be reached. The most fundamental concepts of democracy imply that each of us has an obligation, to say nothing about an individual self-interest, to be conversant with the political system.

My purpose in writing this book, therefore, is to help you develop a more complete understanding of American politics. The organization of the text is clear and straightforward. It begins with an investigation of the writing of the Constitution and an analysis of the most important aspects of the Constitution's principles, including the civil liberties and the civil rights. The next several chapters introduce the important influences in the political process, including public opinion, the media, interest groups, political parties, and the electoral process. My greatest interest in discussing these phenomena is political rather than structural. While structure is important and is adequately explained, the greatest attention is given to how people—ordinary people like ourselves—and public officials interact with one another within the system so as to influence the course of public policy. The same approach is used in the presentations on the legislature, the executive, and the judiciary. Finally, the book turns to an analysis of the most pertinent issues of our time. Unfortunately, space limitations prevent exhaustive coverage of the national agenda. In an attempt to anticipate the issues that will dominate the political scene for the next few years, I have chosen to discuss economic policy, social policy, and foreign policy. By limiting the number of issues, I am able to examine the chosen areas in depth, and thus to demonstrate their substantive and political complexity. After a detailed examination of the

intricacies of particular issues and the almost endless variety of individual interests that relate to the issues, one can more easily appreciate the difficulty of crafting policy suitable for the nation as a whole. For example, the tragic absurdity of allowing millions of people to go malnourished in a country that produces food in abundance is obvious to all. But in a society composed of such social, ecnomic, and cultural diversity, deciding what to do about hunger and developing policies to reach whatever goals are sought can induce wrenching political controversies.

You are probably reading this book in connection with a required course. The requirement exists because society has determined that it is desirable for you to engage in a college-level analysis of the political process. But quite beyond studying American politics in satisfaction of a civic responsibility, I hope you will also find it to be intrinsically worthwhile. The study of American politics can be rewarding in its own right because it is replete with drama and pathos, triumph and failure, power and powerlessness. It is my hope that the following pages convey these features sufficiently to stimulate in you a desire to join your professors and me in a lifelong effort to better understand democracy in America.

Acknowledgments

A project of this scope cannot be completed alone: It requires the help and cooperation of many people. I am indeed fortunate to have friends and colleagues who generously gave of their time and expertise, helping to make this book a reality. My deepest debt of gratitude goes to my wife, Elaine, who shares the dedication of the book. She has spent untold hours typing and proofreading the manuscript, and offering innumerable suggestions for improvement. Elaine is uncommon in her willingness to give, and I am grateful to her beyond my abilities of expression. I also want to thank our sons Leon and René, who have cheerfully given up so many hours with us that might have been spent in pleasurable pursuits. Leon also did yeoman service in reviewing the manuscript, and he made numerous suggestions and criticisms for improvement. This book turned out to be a family project.

For taking care to correct my casual punctuation, eccentric spelling, and convoluted syntax, I thank Ms. Mary Murphy. I also wish to express my sincere appreciation to Professors Mohammed Rajah, Susan Critchfield, Paul Basart, William Colburn, James Stanton, and Dean Sharalee Jorgensen. Each made critical contributions to this book, as did Ms. Sherry Hiltz. The MiraCosta Learning Resource Center staff, including Director Leland Russell, Professor Gwendolyn Greene, and Vicki Krivoski, was always cheerful and helpful. Research librarian Janet Megill was especially resourceful, never hesitating to answer requests for sources and information. I also wish to thank Ms. Cathy Miller and Mr. Ellis C. Swadley of the San Diego county law library.

To my colleagues who reviewed the manuscript I extend my appreciation. Their insightful comments, criticisms, and suggestions were invaluable. They are Peter Bergerson, Southeast Missouri State University; Mary L. Carns, Stephen F. Austin State University; William Collins, Samford University; Larry Elowitz, Georgia College; James Hanley, Mott Community College; Richard Herrera, Arizona State University; Carl Lieberman, University of Akron; Patricia Caperton Parent, Southwest Texas State University; Pamela H. Rodgers, University of Wisconsin~La Crosse; John Roos, University of Notre Dame; and C. Alan Tarr, Rutgers University. Finally, the people at HarperCollins have done a wonderful job. I am particularly indebted to Lauren Silverman, Diane Rowell, Catherine Woods, Katherine Hieatt, and Harold Levinson.

Leon P. Baradat

Chapter 1

Interior View of INDEPENDENCE-HILL, Philadelphia.

BRITISH RULE AND SELF-GOVERNMENT

PREVIEW

Imbued with the British philosophical beliefs of natural law and the social contract, Anglo-American colonists established themselves on the North American continent in the early seventeenth century. The British colonial system differed from other imperialist states in its diversity, establishing three types of colonies: charter, proprietary, and royal. Serving as the model from which the written constitution, the presidential-congressional system, and the civil liberties developed, these colonies gradually flourished. The British policy of mercantilism relegated the colonies to subservient status, but the British were unable to govern the colonies as actively as they might have wished to—leaving the colonists to their own resources until 1763. Heartened by their success at self-government, the colonists began to chafe at British rule when the period of salutary neglect was ended.

For their part, the British expected the Americans to abide by the law, and when the colonists refused, the lines of confrontation were drawn. In 1775, beleaguered and oppressed, the citizens of Massachusetts confronted British troops at Lexington and Concord, with the result of starting a long, bloody war for independence, for which the Americans were only coincidentally prepared. During the war the states were governed on an ad hoc basis by the Second Continental Congress until the adoption, in 1781, of the Articles of Confederation, based on radical assumptions.

The critical period (1781–1789) marks a failed experiment, with the states becoming embroiled in petty jealousies, political ineptitudes, and economic crises. Fearing for the Union, conservative elements rallied and decided that tranquillity could be assured only by a stronger central government. To that end they gathered in Philadelphia in 1787 to hammer out a new government, based on unproven institutions. Many issues divided the delegates: The large states wanted to dominate Congress while the small states insisted on equal representation; the Northern states demanded that slaves be taxed and remain uncounted in determining congressional representation, but the Southern states held out for the opposite; the slave trade was challenged by the Northern states, and the Southern states were suspicious of giving Congress strong powers to regulate trade. Bargaining preferences and interests, the Constitutional Convention submitted a plan that balanced the states' interests against those of the greater good, and only with the utmost leadership, guile, and persuasion were they able to secure the ratification of the proposed constitution by the states.

The distinctions between Virginians, Pennsylvanians, New Yorkers, and New Englanders, are no more. I am not a Virginian, but an American.

Patrick Henry

The American political system is a complex synthesis of ideas and traditions developed over time. Sources for our system come from other societies, from experience, and from the creativity of our founders. Although other countries affected the development of our political system, without question the strongest outside influence was exercised by England. Indeed, the British colonial system and English political theory contributed heavily to our notion of good government.

British Political Theory

The philosophical principles most critical to our political system were those of **natural law** and the **social contract** as espoused by the venerable English philosopher **John Locke**. Locke opined that all people were subject to an absolute set of principles that governed right conduct. The natural law was superior to man-made laws; hence natural law could not be rightly ignored or contradicted by any human authority—including government. Further, since all people were equally a part of nature, the natural law applied to everyone in the same degree, and the **natural rights**, which Locke believed emanated from the natural law, applied to all people equally. Specifically, Locke reasoned that natural rights included *life, liberty,* and *property.*

Locke hypothesized that government was a conscious and deliberate contrivance of people to settle disputes judiciously among them, and that its principal obligation to the people was to pursue policies that extended their individual liberties. Hence the people were **sovereign**, or superior to government, and any government was illegitimate that did not advance the rights of people. The people, therefore, were justified in correcting or even overthrowing an oppressive government. The act of people creating government to further their liberties

John Locke (1632–1704)

was called the social contract, and it required that those who lived in society voluntarily obey the just rules of the contract.

We will see later that these ideas were critical to the development and adoption of the Declaration of Independence; indeed, in their time, these concepts were revolutionary. Locke's influence also played an important part in the foundation of the colonies themselves. Perhaps the clearest, most dramatic early example of the notion of the social contract is found in the **Mayflower Compact** of 1620, used to establish the basic law of the fledgling colony at Plymouth. The compact served as a constitution for the colony, and the colonists were pledged to obey the laws and rules established under its authority. Hence the Mayflower Compact represents, in a literal sense, a social contract forged by free individuals.

As significant as these ideas are, the American political system also evolved from phenomena much more empirical than political philosophy alone. The settlers' experience with British colonial government was an extremely important factor as well.

The British Colonial System

The British colonial system developed three different kinds of colonies—charter, proprietary, and royal colonies—and several important contemporary practices can be discovered by studying them. While the other imperialist countries established colonies that were founded and operated by royal patronage, the British system was more complex.

The first Anglo-American colonies to be established came to be called **charter colonies**. England, in the seventeenth century, was not yet a first-rate economic power. Hence, England's monarchs were necessarily frugal; they lacked sufficient interest and resources to develop their American territories. Consequently, it was left to private individuals to establish England's occupation of the North American continent. The motivation of these enterprising people varied: Some saw the colonies as commercial ventures where essential raw materials could be garnered, while others hoped to escape England's religious persecution and social stratification by relocating in America. In any case, these individuals formed companies for which they sought charters to legally authorize their enterprises.* The earliest charter colonies were Virginia, founded in 1607; Plymouth, founded in 1620; and Massachu-

setts, founded in 1629. Each of these colonies, however, failed commercially and was eventually taken over by the king. A bit later, the colonies of Rhode Island and Connecticut were established, and they continued to be governed by their charters until well after the American Revolution.

The charters are significant because they detailed the structure of the colonial governments and they also often included provisions that limited the companies' powers over the colonists. In short, the charters came to be regarded as constitutions—**written constitutions**—that conveniently listed, in a single place, the basic law of the colonies and the colonists' rights. In fact, the charters of Rhode Island and Connecticut afforded their citizens extensive rights and privileges that we now recognize as being among the civil liberties of Americans. The convenience of having the basic law of the land published in a single document was much appreciated by the early Americans, so when they severed their ties with Britain, the Americans quickly drafted the first written national constitution in history— the Articles of Confederation.

The **proprietary colonies** were of an altogether different character. These colonies were basically land grants given by the king, usually to his favorites. Unlike the charter colonies, whose governments were specified in the basic laws, the governments of the proprietary colonies were left to the proprietors themselves. In several cases, either in an effort to encourage settlers—as in the case of New Jersey—or in an enlightened attempt to avoid the repression that the proprietors had suffered in England—as with Pennsylvania and Maryland—these colonies afforded extraordinary political, religious, and social liberties to their settlers. Maryland (1632), New York (taken from the Dutch in 1664), New Jersey (1664), the Carolinas (1665), Pennsylvania (1681), and Georgia (1732) were created as proprietary colonies. In the long run, several of these en-

---

* Charters are legal documents that detail the existence, function, status, rights, and obligations of corporate ventures. The use of charters reaches far back into British law and continues to this day in both England and the United States.

terprises failed, and exercising **eminent do-main**,* the king asserted his control over them.

The third colonial model, the **royal colonies**, is similar to that employed by the other imperialist countries. By the time of the American Revolution, Georgia, Massachusetts, New Hampshire, New Jersey, New York, North Carolina, South Carolina, and Virginia had become royal colonies. Royal government tended to be stricter than the other models, and much of the trouble with England focused in these jurisdictions.

The most significant fact about the royal colonies for our purposes, however, is found in the structure of government they evolved. They are called royal colonies because they were ruled by the king through his designates. The king appointed a governor, who in turn appointed a council of prominent colonial citizens (usually landowners) to advise him. The interests of the commercial classes were addressed by an assembly elected by those who met the property requirement for voting. The laws passed by this two-house legislature (the council and the assembly) could be vetoed by the governor, and the governor nominated judges whose appointments were then ratified by the council. Hence, we see evolving the model structure used in the current national government and in most of the states. It is composed of a single executive, a bicameral (two-house) legislature, and an appointed judiciary. This system, known as the **presidential-congressional system**, is one of the major innovations in government developed in this country. It can be contrasted with the **parliamentary-cabinet system** used in England.

The British system employs a plural or col-lective executive—the cabinet—that is closely tied to the legislature because the lower chamber, the House of Commons, chooses the Prime Minister. In our system, by contrast, the executive is chosen separately from the legislature, and this separation of powers is enhanced by the checks and balances accruing from the veto and the ratification of appointments. The presidential-congressional system will be examined in more detail later, of course. For now, it is enough to point out that it and the written constitution, which evolved from the charter colonies, are two of the four great innovations in government developed in this country. The other two, **federalism** and **judicial review**, will also be studied later.

Revolution and Early Government

Two circumstances had overriding importance in the British colonial government of the American colonies: monopolistic mercantilism and salutary neglect. First, the British attempted to practice an economic system known as **monopolistic mercantilism**, which was detrimental to American interests. Giving favorites monopolies in certain aspects of trade and forbidding the colonies to trade with any country outside the British Empire, the king and Parliament attempted to control the imperial economy at the colonists' expense. The exploitive nature of monopolistic mercantilism grated on the Americans even though the British were never completely able to enforce the restrictions. Second, the period of **salutary neglect** (1607–1763*) ended when the French were vanquished on the continent. During this long era, the British, being distracted by domestic and foreign problems of their own, were forced largely to ignore the colonists. Thus, the colo-

---

* Eminent domain is a legal principle giving the government the right to appropriate private property for public use. This principle is used in United States law as well as in England. Present law, however, requires the government to justly compensate the private owner when land is appropriated.

* While historians differ about the year salutary neglect began, they generally agree that it ended in 1763.

nists learned to govern themselves and were imbued with the confidence that they could succeed without British tutelage if need be. Therefore when, after 1763, the British began to enforce the mercantilist laws with unaccustomed vigor, the Americans resisted, launching an inexorable course toward armed struggle with and independence from Britain.

When the fighting began in 1775, an assembly of delegates from the colonies, the **Second Continental Congress**, became the first government of the United States. It organized the war effort, appointing George Washington Commander in Chief of the army, and at the same time attempted to persuade the king that a change in British policy would see the colonies once again become contented and loyal subjects of the empire. Finally, after 15 months of armed struggle, the congress reluctantly concluded that independence was the only course left to it. A committee, headed by Thomas Jefferson, was created to draft a statement explaining that governments are created by people to enhance their liberties and that, since the British government had denied the colonists their liberties, the Americans were justified in breaking with the empire.

Upon receiving the document from the committee, the congress amended it in several respects but left its central theme untouched. The **Declaration of Independence** was signed on July 4, 1776. An unprecedented step, the vote for independence was won only with considerable difficulty, and it marked but the beginning of a trying and dangerous period. The worst of a long, brutal war still lay ahead, and there remained the other problem, the problem of self-government, now that the Americans* had crossed the Rubicon.

* It must be noted that while I refer to the "American" cause as opposed to the British, a large number of Americans remained loyal to the British Crown throughout the war and, indeed, many left the United States at war's end.[1]

THE ARTICLES OF CONFEDERATION

Having declared independence, the congress turned to the business of establishing a permanent government. At the same time, the colonies began to organize themselves into independent states.

Like the Declaration of Independence, the **Articles of Confederation** were founded on the ideas of John Locke: radical principles for the day.[2] You will recall that Locke believed the purpose of government was to maximize the liberty of the individuals in society. He reasoned that some amount of government was necessary so as to keep order, but that government should be as unobtrusive as possible. Echoing this sentiment, Thomas Jefferson paraphrased Locke, articulating perhaps the most deeply held political belief in the American mind: "That government governs best which governs least."

At odds with a centralized government that, from the American perspective, was dominated by an oppressive executive, the Americans resolved to assure individual liberty by creating a weak national government, one that would have difficulty governing and thus could interfere with the people's liberty as little as possible.

The fundamental principle of the Articles was state sovereignty—that is, the individual states were the highest legal authority within their territory. Hence the national government lacked the authority to enforce its law in the states. For example, if the national government made a treaty, it had no authority to punish a state for ignoring the protocols. Thus, the success of the national government, in most cases, depended upon the cooperation of the states. Such a condition becomes a serious problem since the colonies—now states—often did not trust one another. Indeed, **confederacy** suffers an inherent difficulty since the only reason for adopting this form of government, as opposed to a more authoritative and centralized structure, is that the individual participants do not completely trust their brethren and thus retain decisive power themselves.*

While the Articles created a unicameral (single-house) Congress, they provided no president or court structure. Hence enforcement, interpretation, and adjudication of national law was left to the individual states, resulting in a confusing lack of uniformity. Each state could send as many as seven delegates to Congress, elected by its state legislature, but each state had only one vote. Most important issues required a vote of nine states, while amendments to the Articles had to be adopted unanimously. Moreover, Congress lacked the power to tax, only being allowed to request money from the states—requests that were often ignored. The central government could not regulate interstate commerce (trade between the states), a serious omission. Congress was empowered to create a postal service, to borrow, to regulate Indian affairs, to make treaties, to raise an army and navy, and to make war and peace. Still, it must be remembered that the principle of state sovereignty precluded compulsory state compliance with any of these powers.

For their part, the states committed themselves to this "firm league of friendship." They were supposed to honor the judicial proceedings of other states and to afford the citizens of the other states free passage and the same rights and privileges that they granted to their own citizens. Since, however, there was no authority above the states to enforce actions within their own territory, little could be done if they

---

* The United States has had two confederacies in its history: The Articles of Confederation (1781-1789) and the Confederate States of America (1860-1865), neither of which was successful. Although history includes many attempted confederacies, they seldom succeeded. The longest-lasting and most successful confederation in history was the Swiss Confederation (1291-1806).

ignored these obligations. Furthermore, suspicious of executive power, most of the states emasculated the powers of their governors, making the governors subservient to the legislatures.[3]

THE CRITICAL PERIOD, 1781-1789

If liberty is, as Locke suggested, assured through the absence of governmental restraint, then the Americans were indeed free in such a political environment. But lax government also encouraged political and economic chaos, threatening the republic itself and resulting in what historians call the **critical period** (1781-1789).

During the Revolutionary War the states and the Second Continental Congress had issued huge amounts of paper money, causing severe inflation. After the war, the state governments retrenched economically with tight money policies. These policies, combined with a decline in European demand for American goods, launched a depression, causing the country's farmers to demand relief. Some states responded by granting credits to the farmers and issuing new paper money, whipping their economies back into inflation. Things became so bad in Rhode Island that debtors pursued creditors, some of whom fled the state rather than be forced to accept debt payments in worthless money.

At the other extreme, Massachusetts, controlled by merchants, steadfastly refused to grant farmers relief, thus causing many farms to be sold off. At the same time, tariff wars began between various states until interstate commerce was threatened with complete stagnation.

The chaotic financial situation alarmed the conservative elements, who began to look for ways to resolve their plight. Then in 1786, violence broke out in Massachusetts. To prevent further farm foreclosures, Western farmers intimidated the courts, including the Massachusetts Supreme Court. Led by Daniel Shays, a former officer in the Revolutionary War, the uprising wreaked havoc in Massachusetts until it was finally suppressed by elements of the state militia and volunteers, and the rebels were scattered and hunted down.

Hearing in France of **Shays' Rebellion**, Thomas Jefferson blithely shrugged it off, writing, "God forbid we should every twenty years be without a rebellion. . . . The tree of liberty must be refreshed from time to time with the blood of patriots and tyrants." But Jefferson's distant tranquillity about the situation was not shared by American conservative elements, who feared for the republic. Although usually calm, George Washington was shaken by the violence, exclaiming, "What, gracious God, is man! that there should be such inconsistency and perfidiousness in his conduct?" Washington went on to complain, somewhat hyperbolically, "We are fast verging to anarchy and confusion."[4]

Although debtors generally supported the ruinous inflationary conditions, and states' rights enthusiasts such as Samuel Adams, Patrick Henry, Richard Henry Lee, George Clinton, Elbridge Gerry, and George Mason preferred the anemic political situation, the conservative elements, including John Jay, Gouverneur Morris, James Wilson, Alexander Hamilton, George Washington, and James Madison, resolved that enough was enough, and set themselves a course that eventually led to the drafting of the Constitution of the United States.

The Constitution

Even before Shays' Rebellion, the problems encountered with the Articles had motivated attempts to ameliorate perceived difficulties. To address these matters, two meetings occurred: the first at Alexandria, Virginia, in 1785 and the second in Annapolis, Maryland,

in 1786. Little was resolved in these discussions, but the two people most responsible for the 1787 Constitutional Convention, Alexander Hamilton of New York and James Madison of Virginia, met and agreed that something had to be done about the Articles. The delegates at the Annapolis meeting passed a resolution, written by Hamilton, asking Congress to call for a convention to be held at Philadelphia in 1787 "to take into consideration the trade and commerce of the United States."[5]

Shaken by the faltering Articles and by Shays' Rebellion, but suspicious of the lengths to which such a convention might go if not restrained, the Congress called for a convention to meet on May 14, 1787,

> for the sole and express purpose of revising the Articles of Confederation and reporting to Congress and the several legislatures such alterations and provisions therein as shall when agreed to in Congress and confirmed by the states render the federal constitution* adequate to the exigencies of Government and the preservation of the Union.

The delegates, delayed by bad weather and financial problems, filtered into Philadelphia slowly. By the appointed day of the meeting, only Pennsylvania and Virginia delegates had arrived, and a quorum was not present until May 25. In the interim, representatives from Virginia and Pennsylvania met quietly among themselves. These meetings gradually evolved agreement between the two populous states about certain basic objectives. This *sub rosa* agenda proved to be the dominant element regarding a fundamental question: the proposal

---

* The term *federal constitution* here refers to the Articles of Confederation. Before the Constitution of 1789 gave a separate meaning to the word *federalism,* it was a synonym for confederation.

of an entirely new form of government, one in which, if the conspirators had their way, the populous states would enjoy control of Congress.

THE DELEGATES

Seventy-four people had been chosen by 12 states,* but only 55 delegates actually attended. The assemblage included a fair number of the prominent leaders of the republic, but it is also revealing to see who was not present. Thomas Jefferson was in France as the United States Ambassador, and John Adams was performing the same role in London. Thomas Paine was also in Europe, and Patrick Henry refused to attend. Sharing the qualms of the Rhode Islanders, he said he "smelt a rat." Henry's Virginia compatriot, Richard Henry Lee, the man who had introduced the resolution in the Second Continental Congress for independence from England, also demurred, claiming that as he had sat in Congress it was not proper for him to participate in the convention. Further, Samuel Adams and John Hancock failed to be chosen as delegates. Hence, particularly with the absence of Jefferson, Henry, Lee, Paine, Hancock, and Samuel Adams, the radical cause lacked its best leaders at the convention—a critical void.

The bulk of those who did attend represented more conservative views than those of the aforementioned. That said, their qualifications were remarkable indeed. Economically, all of the delegates were well to do, being merchants, lawyers, shippers, manufacturers, scholars, and large landowners. Only one delegate, William Few of Georgia, was a common farmer, while about one-third of the delegates owned slaves. Thirty-one of the 55 attendees

* Rhode Island, the most radical state at the time, refused to participate, correctly fearing that the convention would opt to increase the powers of the national government.

had college educations; 21 had served in the Revolutionary War; 39 had served in Congress; 8 had signed the Declaration of Independence; 6 had signed the Articles; and 3—Roger Sherman of Connecticut, Robert Morris of Pennsylvania, and Elbridge Gerry of Massachusetts—had helped draft the Declaration, the Articles, and later the Constitution. Two of them, Sherman and Morris, signed all three; 8 had helped to write their state constitutions; and 7 had been state governors. Equaling the stature of the absent radicals, although Jefferson called them "an assembly of demigods," the delegate list is replete with legendary people. Rivaling the delegate list of Virginia (George Washington, James Madison, Edmund Randolph, and George Mason), was that of Pennsylvania (Benjamin Franklin, Robert Morris, Gouverneur Morris, and James Wilson). From New York came Alexander Hamilton, and Massachusetts sent Rufus King and Elbridge Gerry. Roger Sherman, William Samuel Johnson, and Oliver Ellsworth represented Connecticut, while New Jersey sent William Patterson. John Dickinson, the author of the Articles, represented Delaware; and South Carolina sent John Rutledge, Charles Cotesworth Pinckney, and Charles Pinckney. While several other distinguished people were present, they played minor roles, with 6 delegates—William Blount of North Carolina, Jared Ingersoll of Pennsylvania, John Blair of Virginia, Nicholas Gilman of New Hampshire, Richard Bassett of Delaware, and William Few of Georgia—sharing the distinction of not uttering a single word in debate.[6]

Besides the radicals and the poor, other vast segments of the population were not represented at the convention, including African-Americans (slave or free), women, Indians, and the working class. While the delegates found themselves divided on many technical questions, they were remarkably united on fundamental philosophical assumptions. They were disposed to protect the propertied class;

THE FOUNDATION OF AMERICAN GOVERNMENT

The Constitution is signed—1787

they tended to hold a rather dim view of human nature, thinking people basically selfish and base; and most of them had little good to say about democracy, generally agreeing with Elbridge Gerry's description of democracy as "the worst of all political evils." The exceptions to this contempt of democracy should be quickly noted, however; George Mason, for example, was particularly supportive of popular participation, but such was not the dominant view, and the word *democracy* is nowhere to be found in the Constitution.[7]

THE DELIBERATIONS

Finally securing a quorum, the delegates convened on May 25, 1787. Meeting in the same hall where the Declaration of Independence had been signed, the delegates made two decisions almost immediately: George Washington was elected to preside, and the proceedings would be held in secret "so as not to disturb the public repose," as Washington explained.

Washington's selection as president of the convention went unopposed. His prestige was needed to encourage compromise among the participants. The matter of secrecy, however, was more controversial, with Jefferson upon hearing of it condemning the rule as an "abominable precedent." The reason given for privacy was that the participants wished to be free to speak their minds without fear of public interference or harassment. But also in the back of the delegates' minds was the desire to avoid alerting the radicals to their scheme for strengthening the central government.*

For three days the convention established the leadership and settled procedural questions. Then, on the fourth day, the Virginia delegation introduced a series of resolutions that transformed the meeting from a polite discourse on parliamentary procedure to an acrimonious debate over critical political questions. Rising to address the assemblage, Edmund Randolph, the leader of Virginia's delegation, introduced a set of 15 resolutions whose adoption would amount to the creation of an entirely new form of government. The resolutions, largely the creation of James Madison (often called the Father of the Constitution), had been massaged into final form in the preconvention meetings.

The **Virginia Plan**, as the resolutions came to be called, was a creative document that proposed unprecedented structure and offices, and would have the national government enjoy a new dominant relationship with the several states. Specifically, the plan provided for three branches of government: a legislature, an executive, and a judiciary. The legislature was to be bicameral (consisting of two houses) with state representation in each house to be apportioned according to the states' populations—a critical feature. Members of the lower house were to be elected directly by the voters, while upper-house members were to be elected by the lower house from candidates nominated by the states' legislatures. The executive was to be elected by the legislature to a nonrenewable term of unspecified length. Judges for a supreme court and

for several lower courts were also to be elected by the legislature, but for life terms. The Congress was to be given wide powers of legislation, including the power to tax. And the executive, together with selected judges, was to form a Council of Revision that could veto not only national statutes but also laws passed by the state legislatures.

Caught unaware, delegates representing the sparsely populated states did not at first object to the thrust of this plan, which would have given decisive power to the populous or large states. While they debated various minor provisions of the proposal, the significance of the proposal seemed temporarily to elude them. Then, during a brief recess in early June, they announced opposition to the Virginia plan, insisting upon equal representation for the states in the national legislature. Feverishly caucusing over the recess, the small-state representatives, led by William Patterson of New Jersey, drafted a counterproposal that is usually called the **New Jersey Plan**.

Lacking the time enjoyed by the large states to draft a proposal and not having the creative spirit of so close a student of government as James Madison, the small states' proposal is little more than a combination of some provisions in the Articles of Confederation and those of the Virginia Plan that they could support. While the New Jersey Plan accepted the three branches of government, it proposed important differences within that basic structure. The Congress was to be unicameral (one house), with its members elected by the state legislatures, and each state was to have only one vote. The proposal's only major innovation suggested that Congress elect a plural executive (its membership was not enumerated) for a nonrenewable term. The judiciary was to comprise only a supreme court, and its members were to be appointed by the executive to life terms. The legislature was given the power to pass statute in the same areas as could the

---

*Currently, it is generally thought that leftists favor a more powerful central government and that conservatives advocate states' rights. During our early history, however, leftists feared a strong centralized government, preferring that power be husbanded close to the people, while the conservatives wished to see the central government become more powerful.

Congress under the Articles, but it was also given the authority to assess some taxes and to regulate interstate trade. Further, the laws and treaties of the United States were to be supreme over the states, binding the states to their provisions.[8]

Now the lines were drawn. The large states insisted that they should have a greater say in national policy by virtue of their greater populations. The small states argued that each state was equal, regardless of population, and that that fact should be reflected in the legislature, the national policymaker. For a time, the two sides remained adamant and the convention seemed in jeopardy of collapse. Finally, in mid-July, a compromise was reached. The **Connecticut Compromise** was so named because it was worked out and advocated by Sherman, Johnson, and Ellsworth. The bargain provided that the Congress would comprise two houses: The lower house members (the House of Representatives) would be apportioned by population and be elected directly by the voters, while the states would receive equal representation in the Senate and its members would be elected by the state legislatures.* Further, to reassure the small states, the article dealing with amendments (Article V) was written to prohibit any state from receiving unequal suffrage in the Senate without its approval. Thus the most nettlesome problem at the convention was resolved: the question of representation.

Before leaving the issue of large versus small states, we must note that while the delegates became engrossed in controversy over the question of state representation in the national legislature, a much more fundamental issue evoked considerably less debate: the expansion of national government power at the expense of

*United States senators were elected by the state legislatures until 1913, when the Seventeenth Amendment provided for popular election of senators.

the states. The Articles of Confederation assured state sovereignty on the radical theory that personal liberty was enhanced when government power was impeded. The practical result of such "liberty," however, was political weakness and economic chaos, and the convention's delegates—conservatives for the most part—resolved very early that a stronger central government was essential for "domestic tranquillity." Hence, the Constitution explicitly provides that the national government is supreme over the states, so when the document was ratified, state sovereignty ceased to exist. The lack of great controversy among the delegates on this point does not mean that it was not a matter of deep concern to other Americans of the day, and it should not be assumed that the issue was unimportant. Indeed, it is the most fundamental change to the Articles, for it transformed the confederation into a new, unprecedented form of government, now commonly referred to as **federalism**. The proposal to change the essence of the government was indeed revolutionary, and it marked a movement in which the conservatives rose up to reassert their control over the country. Indeed, the Constitution of the United States, viewed in this light, represents a conservative counterrevolution to the American Revolution.[9]

In any event, the question of state representation was settled with the Connecticut Compromise, but that agreement led to another, more specific question of representation: If the states were to receive seats in the House of Representatives on the basis of their respective populations, who should be counted as people?

It is popularly believed that the founders were motivated by noble intent and that the Constitution was the product of a desire for "liberty and justice for all." To view the basic law in such idealistic terms is no doubt comforting, but such an assumption is terribly unrealistic. The founders shared no trait so completely as that of being pragmatic politicians. The constitutional founders, confronted with a serious political problem and an even more immediate economic emergency, saw their role clearly. They needed to find a new accommodation among the states or else see a chaotic situation progress into catastrophe. Hence, they were willing to compromise on the matter of state representation, and they also "cut a deal" on other, perhaps more compelling but certainly morally questionable issues.

The matter of awarding seats in the House in proportion to the states' populations immediately brought up the issue of slavery. About one-third of the people in the Southern states were slaves, and the delegates from these states expected that slaves would accrue to their benefit when apportioning House seats. The Northern delegates, however, objected to this scheme, thus launching a new, bitter debate and exposing a sad, yet delicious, irony.

The law held that the slaves were property, a position usually approved of in the South. But Northerners, except for those New England shipmasters who profited from transporting slaves from Africa to the Southern auction blocks, generally recognized slaves as people. Not necessarily keen on abolition, however, they contented themselves with the expedient that, while slavery may be immoral, it is a matter of states' rights if the people in the South wished to allow it. But, on the vital political question before the convention, the two sides exchanged positions.[10] Additionally, the Northern delegates wanted slaves to be counted in determining each state's contribution to a direct tax, while the South resisted such an assault on their cheap labor force. After lengthy, heated debate, the delegates finally settled on an ignoble but pragmatic compromise. The notorious **Three-fifths Compromise** provided that "free persons" would be counted as whole, "excluding Indians not taxed," but only three of every five "other Persons" (slaves) were to be counted.*

Slavery became an issue in yet another dispute at the convention. The commercial states of the North were intent upon giving the national government the power to regulate commerce between the states and international trade. The Southerners, however, were suspicious of such control since they feared that the North would soon enjoy a majority in both houses of Congress and pass laws contradictory to the South's interests. Specifically, they wanted to prevent laws that eliminated the slave trade (the brutal and deadly transport of slaves from Africa to America), and they also suspected that the North might practice taxing policies that would force the South to pay for Northern prosperity. To that end, a number of agreements were struck, which are collectively known as the **Commerce and Slave Trade Compromise**. The South relented on the issue of national government control of commerce, but in return, the North agreed to provisions prohibiting tariffs on exports and unequal national taxes on the various ports. Additionally, treaties would be ratified by a two-thirds vote of the Senate, and the slave trade would not be prohibited for 20 years.

Beyond these three major compromises, other issues had to be resolved by the process of give-and-take. Indeed, virtually every provision in the Constitution was the subject of some debate, from electing the president to determining who should vote (left to the discretion of the states), from the amendment procedure to the powers of the judiciary. But in the end, solutions were painstakingly hammered out, and the Constitution, the result of practical political deal-making, has been described as a "bundle of compromises."

---

*It is noteworthy that slavery was not mentioned by name in the Constitution.[11]

One of the questions constantly in the back of the delegates' minds was whether the states would ratify the proposed document, and many provisions were written not so much to reflect the wishes of the delegates as to successfully pass the scrutiny of those waiting to review the proposal. In this vein, it should be noted that ever the pragmatists, the founders did not create what they might have viewed as a perfect government; instead, they proposed the best system they thought could be ratified. No less a light than Washington himself stated the point in a letter to Patrick Henry. "I wish the Constitution," Washington reflected, "had been more perfect. But I sincerely believe it is the best that could be obtained at the time . . . and, if nothing had been agreed on by the Convention, anarchy would soon have ensued."[12]

Doubtless no delegate came away from the convention totally satisfied, and some were manifestly unhappy with it. Indeed, several delegates left the convention early, disillusioned with its work; and three delegates who stayed to the end—Gerry, Mason, and Randolph—refused to sanction it with their signatures. So it was that on September 17, 1787, the Constitution, which had been crafted into its completed form by the eloquent Gouverneur Morris, was signed by only 39 delegates and forwarded to Congress and to the states for ratification.

Ratification

Although the proponents of the Constitution tended to be centered along the Atlantic seaboard while its opponents were strongest in the interior, it is difficult to further generalize about the composition of the adversaries since rich and poor, merchant and landowner, slaver and non-slave-owner, Northerner and Southerner were divided on the issue. Historians generally agree that the opponents probably outnumbered the proponents among the general population, but this issue was not subject to a direct popular referendum. Receiving the proposed Constitution, the Congress of the Confederacy, meeting in New York since 1785, called for the states to create conventions for ratification.

The proponents of ratification, referring to themselves as **Federalists** and calling their adversaries **Antifederalists**, had a major task before them in overcoming the opposition. Still, they enjoyed some important advantages: They had spent the summer of 1787 developing their proposal and evolving arguments in its favor, they had a positive solution to suggest for remedying the failing Confederacy, and they benefited from a unified and distinguished leadership. Indeed, Washington and Franklin, the two most revered people in the country, were among them. Additionally, Federalist strength was centered in the cities, which proved to be easier to mobilize than the Antifederalist countryside.

The Antifederalists, who resented being tagged by their adversaries with so negative an appellation,[13] were forced to oppose the Constitution while being unable to develop any alternative save supporting an increasingly unpopular government. Their leadership, although composed of formidable individuals, was not coordinated or well organized. They did, however, benefit from a natural distrust of the unproven proposal; and they skillfully played upon provincial pettiness, fear of centralization, and claims that the Constitution represented a betrayal of the revolution. Most telling of all, however, was the Antifederalist observation that the Constitution failed to protect individual liberties. They demanded, at the least, that the document should be amended with a Bill of Rights, guaranteeing traditional rights against the new central government.[14]

Delaware and Pennsylvania were the quickest to take up the question of ratification. Brushing aside the opposition, Delaware was the first to embrace the Constitution, registering a 30–0 vote on December 7, 1787. Meanwhile, matters were less sanguine in Pennsylvania.

Pushed by Franklin and others, the Antifederalists in the state legislature balked at calling a ratifying convention. When it became clear that they would lose the vote calling for the meeting, the Antifederalists left the legislature in a bloc, thus denying it a quorum. Enraged at this dilatory tactic, a mob broke into the house where some of the Antifederalist legislators were sequestered, roughed them up, bodily carried two of them back to the floor, and physically restrained them in their seats. Thus, a quorum was present, although not altogether willingly, and the legislature voted to call a ratifying convention. The convention assembled in mid-November and James Wilson, who had made enormous contributions to the text of the Constitution, brilliantly led the Federalists in weeks of debate. Finally, on December 12, 1787, Pennsylvania voted 46 to 22 to ratify. Thus, Pennsylvania was the first of the four essential states to endorse the new government. By virtue of their population size and geographical centrality, Pennsylvania, Massachusetts, Virginia, and New York had to ratify if the new union was to succeed.

Three states followed Pennsylvania in rapid succession: New Jersey agreed on December 18 by 38 to 0; Georgia voted 26 to 0 in favor on January 2, 1788; and Connecticut ratified on January 9 by 128 to 40.

Now the action shifted to Massachusetts. This state, the cradle of the Revolution, found its great leaders divided on the question. Samuel Adams and John Hancock, governor of the state and president of the state ratifying convention, leaned against the question. They were joined by Elbridge Gerry who, although not a delegate to the ratifying convention, still exerted powerful influence. Supporting these legendary leaders were many Western delegates, several of whom had fought with Daniel Shays.

Arrayed on the other side was the indefatigable Rufus King, former governor James Bowdoin, George Cabot, and Francis Dana. Buttressing them was the considerable influence of John Adams, who from his ministry in London, lauded the Constitution as "the greatest single effort of national deliberation that the world has ever seen."

The debate was close and acrimonious at times, with the Antifederalists appearing to be carrying the issue at first. But the Federalists kept chipping away with arguments and guile. Knowing that Hancock was vain, the Federalists flattered him, suggesting that if Virginia joined the Union, Hancock was the logical choice to become Washington's vice president. What's more, they hinted that if Virginia did not ratify, the presidency would probably go to Massachusetts' leading citizen. The ploy succeeded and Hancock, perhaps the first American to be stricken with presidential fever, came out in support of the Constitution.

Although perhaps no less vain, Samuel Adams held out for more realistic concessions, becoming one of the leading advocates for inclusion of guarantees of the personal liberties in the Constitution. Upon securing Federalist support for this condition, Adams also swung over to support ratification. Accordingly, Massachusetts adopted a resolution that presaged the Bill of Rights, and on February 16, 1788, the convention voted 187 to 168 to ratify.

The debate then moved elsewhere through the spring and summer of 1788. Maryland voted 63 to 11 for ratification on April 26, South Carolina agreed by 149 to 73 on May 23, and New Hampshire became the ninth state to join the Union with a vote of 57 to 46 on June 21. Yet, although the number of states necessary to activate the Constitution had agreed to its provisions, two of the critical states remained uncommitted.

Like Massachusetts, Virginia enjoyed the leadership of titans, but alas, they too were divided. Nowhere was the Antifederalist leadership so sterling as in the Old Dominion. Spearheaded by Patrick Henry, they were also served by George Mason, Richard Henry Lee, Benjamin Harrison, John Tyler (father of the president), James Monroe, Edmund Ruffin, and William Grayson. These luminaries were fortified by the knowledge that, although intrigued by the feature of three branches of government, Jefferson (still in France) refused to support the Constitution unless a statement of the personal liberties was added.

Ranged against this distinguished host was an equally formidable group. Led by James Madison were Edmund Pendleton, George Wythe, John Marshall, George Nicholas, and Edmund Randolph. Randolph had been the person who introduced the Virginia Plan to the 1787 Convention but later decided not to sign the Constitution. By the time of ratification in Virginia, however, he had reconsidered and become an eloquent advocate of the proposal. Of course, George Washington favored ratification, and although not a delegate to the ratification convention, he corresponded closely with his compatriots.

Again the debate was heated and sharp. Henry, mustering the oratorical brilliance for which he is so rightly known, assaulted the proposal as an antidemocratic conspiracy of monarchists and aristocrats. But each of his assertions were met by the quiet but telling logic of Madison and his allies. After weeks of debate, during which the Federalists of Virginia, like those of Massachusetts, gradually agreed to embrace amendments enumerating the personal liberties, the convention put the issue to a vote on June 25, 1788; and it passed 89 to 79.

Alexander Hamilton (1755–1804)

The news that Virginia had ratified demoralized George Clinton, Robert Yates, John Lansing, and other Antifederalists in New York. Until then, they had enjoyed a clear advantage over the Federalists, including Alexander Hamilton, John Jay, and James Duane. In New York, the debate had been taken to the streets as well as to the ratifying convention. Madison, Hamilton, and Jay had written a series of newspaper articles, published under the pen name *Publius*. Collectively called the **Federalist Papers**, and later published in book form, this document is one of the most insightful political tracts ever written, and it is used as an authoritative document regarding the founders' attitudes on the issues of the day. At the time, though, the *Federalist Papers* had little impact on the New York public.[15]

Hamilton, contemptuous of the Constitution's weakness, nevertheless supported it because it was, from his point of view, far better than the Articles. Tireless in his efforts to persuade his colleagues at the convention, he spoke with eloquence, wit, and emotion. Not content to confine his campaign to the convention floor, he hosted an ambitious series of dinners and soirees, plying fellow delegates with food and drink in an effort to warm them to his cause. It is indeed ironic that this monarchistic genius should have played so great a role in calling the Constitutional Convention and in securing the charter's ratification.

Still, even such herculean efforts as Hamilton's had scant effect on the recalcitrant Antifederalists. The prospect of the Federalists' accepting assurances in the Constitution of personal liberties debunked their most convincing objections, and news that Virginia had ratified was another blow. But the most decisive factor of all was New York City's threat to secede and join the Union as a separate state, should ratification fail. Accordingly, on July 26, 1788, New York ratified by a narrow margin: 30 to 27.

While two states remained out of the Union (their absence was not critical), the Congress of the Confederacy scheduled elections, provided for the new government to take office in March of 1789, and then adjourned *sine die.* True to their word, the Federalists supported the adoption of the Bill of Rights; indeed, James Madison himself introduced it in the House of Representatives in the form of ten amendments, and it became effective on November 3, 1791. Meanwhile, North Carolina, having failed to ratify by a 75-193 vote on August 4, 1788, reversed itself by virtually the same margin (194 to 77) on November 21, 1789. Then Rhode Island, controlled for so long by radicals who refused to participate in writing the Constitution and who for three years prevented a ratifying convention from convening, finally voted ratification by 34 to 22 on May 29, 1790.[16]

Thus a new government with familiar principles but untested institutions was launched. It is to an examination of the specifics of the document that we now turn.

Summary

- The American colonists appropriated many ideas and institutions from the British colonial experience, including natural law, the written constitution, the presidential-congressional system, and the civil liberties.

- The British largely ignored the American colonies, and thus inadvertently prepared them for independence.

- The Articles of Confederation failed because of hard economic times and the weakness of state and national governments.

- The Constitution was drafted amid much debate and provided for Congress, an executive, and an independent judiciary. It also compromised the differences between the large and small states and between slaveholders and non-slaveholders.

- The ratification of the Constitution was hard fought, but eventually the Federalists carried the issue.

Notes

1. John Richard Alden, *The American Revolution* (New York: Harper & Row, Publishers, 1954), pp. 86–89.

2. Merrill Jensen, *The Articles of Confederation* (Madison: The University of Wisconsin Press, 1954), pp. 239–240.

3. Merrill Jensen, "The Myth of the Critical Period," in Nicholas Cords and Patrick Gerster, eds., *Myth and the American Experience,* Vol. 1 (New York: Glencoe Press, 1973), p. 108.

4. John A. Garraty, *The American Nation,* Vol. 1, 2nd ed. (New York: Harper & Row, Publishers, 1971), p. 188.

5. Catherine Drinker Bowen, *Miracle at Philadelphia,* 2nd ed. (Boston: Little, Brown, 1986), p. 9.

6. Bowen, p. 259.

7. Richard Hofstadter, *The American Political Tradition,* 3rd ed. (New York: Vintage, 1974), pp. 4, 7.

8. Carl J. Friedrich and Robert G. McCloskey, eds., *From the Declaration of Independence to the Constitution* (New York: Bobbs-Merrill Company, Inc., 1954), pp. 24–32.

9. Jensen, *The Articles of Confederation,* p. 245.

10. Winton U. Solberg, ed., *The Federal Constitution and the Formation of the Union of the American States* (New York: The Bobbs Merril Company, Inc., 1958), pp. 211–217.

11. Bowen, p. 95.

12. Bowen, p. 280.

13. Garraty, p. 191.

14. Solberg, p. 366.

15. Bowen, pp. 282–310.

16. Samuel Eliot Morison, Henry Steele Commager, and William E. Leuchtenburg, *The Growth of the American Republic,* Vol. 1, 6th ed. (New York: Oxford University Press, 1969), p. 259.

Suggestions for Further Reading

Barker, Ernest, ed. *Social Contract: Essays by Locke, Hume, and Rousseau.* London: Oxford University Press, 1947.

Beard, Charles A. *An Economic Interpretation of the Constitution of the United States.* New York: Macmillan, 1913.

Bowen, Catherine Drinker. *Miracle at Philadelphia* (2nd ed.). Boston: Little, Brown, 1986.

Corwin, Edward S. *The Constitution and What It Means Today,* rev. Harold W. Case and Craig Ducat. Princeton: Princeton University Press, 1981.

Farrand, Max. *The Framing of the Constitution of the United States.* New Haven: Yale University Press, 1962.

Friedrich, Carl J., and Robert G. McCloskey, eds. *From the Declaration of Independence to the Constitution.* New York: Bobbs-Merrill Company, 1954.

Garraty, John A. *The American Nation,* Vol. 1 (2nd ed.). New York: Harper & Row, 1971.

Ginsberg, Robert, ed. *A Casebook on the Declaration of Independence.* New York: Thomas Y. Crowell, 1967.

Hofstadter, Richard. *The American Political Tradition* (3rd ed.). New York: Vintage, 1974.

Hofstadter, Richard, William Miller, and Daniel Aaron. *The American Republic.* Englewood Cliffs, NJ: Prentice-Hall, 1970.

Jensen, Merrill. *The Articles of Confederation.* Madison: University of Wisconsin Press, 1954.

McCann, Michael W., and Gerald L. Houseman. *Judging the Constitution.* Glenview, IL: Scott, Foresman, 1989.

Morris, Richard B. *The Forging of the Union, 1781-1789.* New York: Harper & Row, 1987.

Morison, Samuel Eliot, Henry Steele Commager, and William E. Leuchtenburg. *The Growth of the American Republic.* London: Oxford University Press, 1969.

Morton, W. L. *The Kingdom of Canada.* Toronto: McClelland and Stewart, 1969.

Peltason, J. W., and Edward S. Corwin. *Understanding the Constitution* (10th ed.). New York: Holt, Rinehart & Winston, 1985.

Preston, John Hyde. *Revolution 1776* (2nd ed.). New York: Washington Square Press, 1961.

Rossiter, Clinton. *1787: The Grand Convention.* New York: Macmillan, 1966.

Solberg, Winton U., ed. *The Federal Convention and the Formation of the Union of American States.* New York: Bobbs-Merrill Company, 1958.

Ubbelohde, Carl. *The American Colonies and the British Empire, 1607-1763.* New York: Thomas Y. Crowell Company, 1968.

Van Doren, Carl. *The Great Rehearsal.* Harmondsworth, England: Penguin Books, 1986.

Wills, Garry. *Explaining America: The Federalist.* Garden City, NY: Doubleday, 1981.

Chapter 2

THE PRINCIPLES
OF THE CONSTITUTION

PREVIEW

While the precise meaning of the Constitution is open to wide interpretation, its basic principles are clear. By contrast with the case of a pure democracy, the people do not actually govern themselves directly; instead, they elect representatives to do so. While the founders expected the franchise to be severely restricted, today virtually every competent adult citizen may vote. This process is generally referred to as a democratic republic and is supported by the philosophy of John Locke.

The United States Constitution can be viewed as a social contract that limits the power of government vis-à-vis individual rights. Constitutionalism itself is taken to mean limitations on the powers of government. As a means of limiting the powers of government, the founders separated them among three branches: legislative, executive, and judicial. Then each branch was turned on the other as checks and balances against the possible excess of power.

The extraordinary powers enjoyed by the judiciary in our system are focused in the power of judicial review, which allows the courts to determine the meaning of the Constitution; all governments and their agents are held subject to the courts' opinions. Although judicial review is self-ascribed by the courts, its existence goes without serious challenge and serves as a stabilizing feature in our system.

Along with the separation of powers and the checks and balances, federalism is the third major structural feature in the Constitution. By dividing government's powers between the states and national governments, the founders hoped to prevent excessive centralization of authority. Time, political necessity, economic exigencies, and practice, however, have seen the erosion of state prerogatives and the expansion of national powers until today, only economic limitations and the Supreme Court remain as guardians of state powers. *Vertical federalism* refers to the relationship between the national government and the states, while *horizontal federalism* signifies the obligations among states.

Amendments to the Constitution can be accomplished in one of two ways. Formal amendments are achieved by following the provisions of Article V of the Constitution. Congress proposes amendments either by a two-thirds vote in each house or by calling a national convention upon the request of two-thirds of the states. Ratification is left to the states in a manner prescribed by Congress. Either three-quarters of the state legislatures must vote to adopt the proposed amendment, or three-quarters of the states ratify in state conventions.

Informal amendments are made by changes in our understanding of what the Constitution means. The agents of such change are the courts through judicial review, the president with executive interpretation, Congress through statutory enumeration, the functions of political parties, the acts of state governments, or the expectations of the body politic.

The United States is entirely a creature of the Constitution. Its power and authority have no other source.

Justice Hugo Black

Perhaps the least disputable thing that can be said about the Constitution of the United States is that its precise meaning is a matter of much controversy. Scholars and ideologues argue constantly about the intent of the founders and about the correct interpretation of the basic law. While there are many reasons for such quibbling, two factors rise above all others as stimuli for the conflict. First, the Constitution and the government it created is over two hundred years old. It was written to suit a nation of about four million people who were largely agrarian and illiterate. Yet the same document, with but 26 formal changes, is being applied two centuries later in a literate, urbanized, industrialized, cosmopolitan society of about 250 million. Given these circumstances, it would be strange indeed if no argument focused upon the application of its principles.

The second major reason for controversy about the Constitution's meaning is that the document was deliberately couched in vague terms. Unable to reach agreement among themselves about the particulars and concerned that a more specific proposal would not be ratified, the founders left the document open-ended in many critical areas. This ambiguity has, as it turns out, served the nation well. Not only was the document ratified, but its lack of specificity allows interpretation and applications to vary as the need is perceived. Hence, the Constitution breathes: expanding during times of optimism and confidence, contracting during more cautious eras.

The scholarly community has vacillated widely on the question of the founders' intent. The nineteenth century was dominated by theories suggesting that the Constitution was a prudent remedy for the economic and political woes of the Articles of Confederation and that the Constitution was adopted just in time to salvage a decaying situation. Early in this century, however, a quite different interpretation became prominent. Associated with historian Charles Beard, who addressed the question in his 1913 book *An Economic Interpretation of the Constitution of the United States,* revisionist theories suggested that the Constitution was written by elitists to protect the property interests in the young country. Contemporary historians have evolved more generous explanations, basically arguing that the founders were impelled by notions of the public good and convictions about just government.[1]

Addressing the subject in more polemical terms than the academics, contemporary ideologues (people with particular political views) see the question in other terms. People on the right of the political spectrum (the conservatives and reactionaries) question the validity of the evolution of democracy. Arguing that the founders intended the elite to rule a republic (defined in the next section) and the Constitution to give special protection to the propertied class, these critics lament the democratic and egalitarian trends in subsequent American history. On the left, the liberals and radicals do not necessarily dispute the rightists' claim about the founders' intent, but they advocate the continued evolution of our system to a democracy in which human equality is the guiding principle.

These arguments tend to be perennial and elusive of resolution. Still, the Constitution is composed of a number of features that can be considered basic principles. Hence, we shall now go to their examination.

Democratic Republic

The Constitution guarantees a republican form of government. By the term *republic*, Madison not only meant that the United States would not have a monarch (*republic* has traditionally meant a state without a monarch), but he also expected that the principal political officials would, in some way, be responsible to the electorate. Consequently, what he had in mind is more precisely called a **democratic republic**, a government of representatives who are elected to their positions by the public they serve.

It should quickly be observed, however, that the word **democracy** (rule by the people) is nowhere to be found in the Constitution. Indeed, the founders shared a rather dim view of democracy. Their reading of history and the experience of some states under the Articles of Confederation persuaded them that **direct democracy** (people making law themselves without benefit of a legislature) resulted in chaos or, even worse, in dictatorship. This skepticism is perhaps best reflected in a statement by Elbridge Gerry, who voiced frustration with certain popular but disruptive policies in the states by saying "the evils we experience flow from an excess of democracy."

Explaining his intentions for government, Madison wrote that a republic could

> refine and enlarge the public views by passing through the medium of a chosen body of citizens, whose patriotism and love of justice will be least likely to sacrifice it to temporary or partial considerations. Under such a regulation it may be that the public voice, pronounced by the representatives of the people, will be more consonant to the public good than if pronounced by the people themselves for the purpose.[2]

Thus, it is clear that Madison expected the people to be governed by their representatives in a benevolent fashion.

Yet, establishing this much, we still find ourselves confronted with the question of how democratic the system was supposed to be. Although the founders wished the government to be responsible to the people, it is indisputable that they permitted only a very low level of democracy to exist. For example, leaving the Constitution mute about the question of who

should be allowed to vote, the founders knew that state laws often imposed stringent gender, racial, religious, and property restrictions on the franchise (voting). Voting was, and remained for long after the Constitution was adopted, a privilege of the well-to-do, white male conformists. Indeed some historians believe that only about 10 percent of the population was allowed to vote during the early part of our history.

Quite beyond the limitations on *who* could vote, *what* the electorate was permitted to vote on was also severely limited. The electorate is not allowed to pass or to veto law. It is not empowered to recall elected officials or to vote on constitutional amendments. Indeed, the voters are allowed to elect only governing officials, and even then the Constitution originally prohibited the voters from directly electing any officials except the members to the House of Representatives. Senators were originally elected by state legislatures, and the president is still elected by an electoral college. Furthermore, the Constitution does not insist that the electors be elected by the people, leaving that question to the discretion of the states. And federal judges are chosen with no formal approval by the electorate at all.

Equally telling is the fact that while the founders made elected offices responsible to voters at election time, the officials are in no way formally bound to do the people's bidding while in office. The members of the electoral college are not required by the Constitution to vote for the candidate whom the people choose, and members of Congress are not legally compelled to vote as their constituents may direct. In each case, the officials are empowered to exercise their judgment irrespective of the popular will.

Thus, it is clear that while the Constitution grants a role to ordinary citizens, our government was not designed to be very democratic—yet democracy has come to be a treasured concept among the American people, and the system has evolved accordingly. The franchise has gradually been extended to virtually all adult citizens; each state has provided for popular election of presidential electors, and the expectation is that the electors will reflect the popular will with their votes. United States senators are, since 1913, elected directly by the people, and while members of Congress may still vote as they please, there is no question that the public can hold them accountable on election day. Hence, the system has been considerably democratized over the past two centuries.

DEMOCRATIC THEORY

The evolution of democratic government has been one of the signal developments in history during the past two centuries. Indeed, although viewed askance in earlier eras, democracy is perhaps the most popular political ideology of our time, for it has evolved not only in our own society but also in many other parts of the world. Indeed, it is so popular an idea that virtually every society gives at least lip service to its principles, and many of its fundamentals are reflected in basic documents of the United Nations and other international institutions.

Liberal democracy, which is now used in the United States, Western Europe, Japan, India, and many other countries, developed from the theories of seventeenth-century philosophers such as **John Locke** (1632–1704). Locke's essential theories were introduced in Chapter 1, so we need review them here only briefly. You will recall that Locke believed in the existence of a basic **natural law** that applied equally to all human beings. Thus, he concluded that all human beings were, in a fundamental way, equal. Once human equality is accepted as a given, one is confronted with the most fundamental of all political questions:

Why must I obey? or, What gives some people the moral right to govern their equals? Locke concluded, as have others, that government among equals is legitimate only when the ruled consent to being governed. Hence, the belief that legitimate political power comes from the consent of the governed gave rise to the **theory of popular sovereignty**, which holds that legitimate political power comes from no source other than the people themselves. And the theory of popular sovereignty becomes the fundamental base upon which our notions of democratic government rest.

The act of people exercising their sovereignty, you will recall, constitutes the **social contract**. That is, the social contract is forged when people create government. Accordingly, the opening phrase in the Constitution, "WE THE PEOPLE," is a clear expression of the founders' literal belief in popular sovereignty and the social contract.

But Locke was no more enchanted with pure democracy than were the constitutional founders who followed his advice about giving legislative power to elected representatives rather than directly to the people. Through the years, however, more confidence in popular government has evolved, and our expectations for popular involvement in government have expanded accordingly. Rejecting the limitations of the past, contemporary liberal democrats insist that all adult citizens have the *right* to vote, regardless of gender, race, national origin, religion, or financial status. Indeed, the only limitations now imposed are that people register to vote, be mentally competent, and be not currently under penalty of a felony (being punished for committing a serious crime). Furthermore, it is expected that each person's vote is equal to all others. We also hold it necessary that people be allowed to organize in order to win elections (form political parties); that they may petition the government and have a right to a response; and that each person, regardless of status, is held equal before the law and enjoys civil rights and certain individual liberties.

Quite beyond the political and legal rights supported by the early liberal democrats, most people today also include a measure of economic equality as necessary to democracy. Accordingly, we have recently also included equal opportunity for all citizens as a goal of democracy.

Thus, liberal democracy rests on the assumption that people are fundamentally equal and that they may therefore expect equal political rights, equal legal rights, and societal attempts to assure that all have a fair chance to prosper. Beyond that, as yet, we do not go.

Limited Government

Closely related to the concepts of popular sovereignty, social contract, and democratic republic is the notion of **limited government**. Since *sovereignty* means the highest legal authority within a given territory, democracy—which is based on popular sovereignty—demands that government serve the people rather than the reverse. Accordingly, government may not be all-powerful. Rather, as Locke would have it, the people are the source of power, and they create government to serve their needs and to further rights. Among their rights is liberty (the right to do as they wish), so long as they do not infringe upon the same right of others. Explaining the concept, Voltaire (1694–1778), the personification of the Enlightenment, said, "Your right to swing your arm ends at my nose."

Limiting government enough to maximize individual liberty is an honored principle of the Constitution. Indeed, it can be argued that *constitutionalism* and limited government are one and the same, and that the principal function of a constitution is to express the limits to the powers of government. For example, the Constitution of the United States prohibits government from holding a person in prison for an unreasonable period of time without preferring a charge and holding a trial. Other limits include preventing torture, forced self-incrimination, and unwarranted search and seizure.

Perhaps the most important limitation on the government, however, is the protection of **minority rights**. Democracy, in most people's minds, is far more than simply a process by which decisions are made. It is also a commitment to fair treatment of all people, and it subsumes the limitation that the majority may not legally deny to the minority their human rights, those liberties and rights accruing to them by virtue of their equality with all other human beings. Further, democracy compels those in power to assure the minority a reasonable opportunity to become the majority.

Separation of Powers and Checks and Balances

DISCRETE BRANCHES

The separation of powers is, by itself, one of the most severe limitations on the powers of government, or so it was intended by the founders. Madison wrote that the greatest difficulty in creating a constitution was "first enabling the government to control the governed; and in the next place obliging it to control itself."[3]

Accordingly, while the founders worked to create stronger government than was extant under the Articles, they provided that the three major elements of government—the legislature, the judiciary, and the executive—be *separated.* They accomplished this objective by creating discrete institutions to separately perform the major tasks of government. The legislative role was given to Congress, the executive function was dedicated to the president, and the judicial powers were delivered to the courts.

But in our Constitution the separation of powers is a much more expansive concept than a simple assignment of roles to discrete institutions. People are also included in the equation, since no person may legally hold office simultaneously in more than one branch. Furthermore, the method by which people rise to office, the period of time they hold office, and the constituency of each branch are unique. Judges are appointed by the president and confirmed by the Senate, and they serve for life, assuming good behavior. The President and Vice President are elected by the electoral college and each serves a four-year term. Compounding the equation further, the two houses of Congress are treated differently. Senators are now elected to six-year terms by the voters of their states, while members to the House of Representatives are elected to terms of two years by the voters of their districts.*

In all these ways—parceling out powers, limiting personal positions, creating several mechanisms by which to achieve office, providing various term lengths, and sculpting different constituencies—the founders hoped to so fractionalize power that tyranny would be avoided. Yet Madison's suspicion of power was so great as to encourage him to place a second great impediment in the way of potential authoritarians: checks and balances.

NEGATIVE EQUILIBRIUM

"Ambition must be made to counteract ambition," wrote Madison.[4] Thus, he advocated an intricate system of countervailing forces that have come to be called the **checks and bal-**

---

* The practice of electing representatives from electoral districts rather than in statewide elections is actually a matter that state law decides since the Constitution is silent on the issue. However, the use of congressional districts is a universal practice.

ances, and have become an inherent part of our political system and of the popular expectation for good government.

Madison's opinion of human nature was very skeptical indeed. He regarded human nature as fundamentally evil and aggressive. Hence, an ordered society needed government. But this conclusion presented Madison with a dilemma. If people were aggressive and needed government to restrain them, wouldn't the people in government use their power unjustly for their own purposes? The separation of powers is obviously an attempt to deal with the dilemma, but Madison was not content to rely on it alone. Rather, he compounded the limitation of powers with what he called "auxiliary precautions," turning government against itself and structuring society so that the people would find it difficult to forge a permanent majority. Accordingly, the Constitution embodies two systems of checks and balances: structural checks and balances, and popular checks and balances.

The *structural checks and balances* are the better known of the two. By Madison's formula, each house of Congress may negate the work of the other, and law can be passed only by each house's agreeing to identical legislation. Yet the president may check Congress through the veto power, which can be overridden only by a two-thirds majority in each house. The president executes the law, but his or her success is made dependent upon Congressional approval of spending. The courts have developed the power to negate law or executive acts that they find contrary to the Constitution, but the membership of the judiciary is determined by the president and the Senate—and, of course, Congress controls appropriations for the courts. Another check, albeit an awkward one, is that Congress and the states have the power to amend the Constitution should the courts adopt an unpopular interpretation of the basic law. There are many other examples of the structural checks and balances, but the foregoing are sufficient to make the point. An analysis of the practical political issues manifest by the checks and balances appears in a later chapter.

In their verve to prevent power abuse, the founders first separated government into three basic branches and then turned them against one another in the hope that government would police itself. In so doing, however, the founders deliberately created a contentious, inefficient government that engenders in the polity (the political public) frustration and aggravation.

"Why can't the Senate and the House ever agree? Why must the Congress constantly be at odds with the president, or vice versa?" Such complaints are frequently heard from a perplexed citizenry, and the tone of the remarks seems to imply that politicians, when they disagree, are failing to function as they should. In fact, the truth of the matter is the reverse. When the House contradicts the Senate, when the president and Congress conflict, and when the courts invalidate the work of the other two branches, the system is working precisely as it was designed to. The separation of powers and the structural checks and balances create a combative rather than a cooperative system. They encourage each branch to advance as far as it can while requiring the other branches to turn it back when it has gone too far. Conflict, collision, and discord are inherent features of the system. (See Figure 2.1.)

This deliberately created divisive phenomenon in our government is, at once, perhaps Madison's greatest genius and his most regrettable shortcoming. By engineering the separation of powers and the structural checks and balances, he managed to prevent the tyranny that could result from human aggression. Yet his system never asks our leaders to control their own aggressions. Rather, assured that they will be prevented by opposing institutions from transgressing too far, they are actually encouraged to reach to the limits of power, and thus create conflict within government.

Equally important as checking the people

Figure 2.1   *The Separation of Powers and the Checks and Balances*

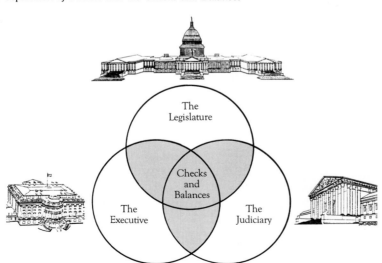

in government, however, was Madison's concern for checking the people out of government. Un-American though it may sound, Madison held a rather dim view of popular government, and he was especially concerned that a permanent majority should *not* be forged, because he feared that it might become tyrannical. Consequently, Madison led the founders in creating several *popular checks and balances.* To prevent the emergence of a national majority, he was content to allow the country to remain divided among several states, and he saw to it that no popular election would be national in scope. Thus, the people elect the members of Congress, and presidential electors, who are assigned to their respective states, elect the chief executive. Effectively, therefore, the country is divided into several electoral minorities, with no possibility of creating a single majority.

Although the original plan has since been changed, at first the people were allowed directly to elect only one body, the House of Representatives. The Senate was to be elected by the state legislatures, and the method for choosing electors was left to the states. The courts are created and staffed without reference to the franchise. To cap it all off, the Constitution originally left entirely to the discretion of the states the matter of who would be allowed to vote. Thus, we find the electorate poorly defined, fractured, and severely limited in power. But Madison went beyond even these restraints on popular rule. By staggering the terms for the House (two years), the Senate (six years), and the president (four years), he assured that a popular majority would have to be in power for several consecutive years if it wished to take control of the competing and contradictory political institutions. This, of course, says nothing about how long it would take a majority to get its partisans into controlling positions in the judicial branch.

Clearly, therefore, Madison's intent was not only to frustrate the politicians but also to deter the people. Thus, the separation of powers and checks and balances were designed to keep everybody off balance and to enhance individual liberty in the process. An efficient government was viewed by the founders as an oppressive government, so they designed a government that could not easily rule.[5]

Judicial Review

An integral part of the checks and balances and a fundamental principle of the Constitution is the power of **judicial review**. Yet, in describing the three basic governmental branches, the Constitution is most brief and least clear about the courts' powers and structure.

There is no question that the founders expected the judiciary to interpret (articulate the meaning of) the law, for that is in large measure an essential part of what courts do in any society. Furthermore, the founders clearly expected that all national law should be superior to all other laws and institutions in the society. This much is expressly provided for in Article VI of the Constitution. What was not provided in specific terms is the courts' power to impose its interpretation of the Constitution on the actions of the executive and the legislature. The power to declare unconstitutional an act by Congress or an action by the President—the power of judicial review—exists not because it is provided for in the Constitution but because the Supreme Court, under Chief Justice John Marshall, simply assumed the power.

Judicial review was self-assigned by the court in the most important case in our history: **Marbury v. Madison** (1803). John Adams was defeated by Thomas Jefferson in his 1800 re-election bid for president, thus ending 12 years of dominance by the conservative Federalist Party. Anxious to provide for his supporters and mistrustful of the "radical" Jeffersonian Republican Party (today's Democratic Party), Adams persuaded the outgoing Congress to enlarge the judiciary and to approve the Federalists he nominated for the posts. The Secretary of State, who is charged with delivering commissions of appointment to federal officers, was then John Marshall—himself appointed by Adams as the new Chief Justice of the Supreme Court.

But the feverish Federalist effort to pack the courts with their supporters before the dreaded Republicans took office was not completed by the time Adams's term ended on March 3, 1801 because Marshall was not able to deliver all of the "midnight appointments" before he had to vacate the Secretary of State office and assume his position on the bench. Therefore, he left the undelivered commissions to be handed on by the new Secretary of State, James Madison. Loath to see any more Federalists enjoy lifelong positions in government, President Jefferson told Madison to ignore the undelivered appointments.

William Marbury, one of the Federalists whose appointment was never forwarded, took his case to the courts, demanding that his appointment be consummated; thus, the contest of _Marbury_ v. _Madison_ was joined. Marbury asked that the Supreme Court issue Madison a writ of _mandamus_ (a court order requiring executive action), directing the Secretary of State to deliver his appointment. But this seemingly simple request embroiled Chief Justice Marshall in a complicated political dilemma.

Although Marshall was a distant cousin of Jefferson, the two men were political adversaries and personal enemies. Marshall knew that Jefferson would not miss an opportunity to weaken the Federalist-dominated courts, so the Chief Justice had to avoid giving his rival an invitation to do so. If the Court ordered Madison to deliver the appointment, the executive branch could simply ignore the Court's mandate, thus exposing the judiciary's inability to enforce its own judgments. On the other hand, if the Court did not issue the writ, it would be sanctioning the administration's arrogant refusal to honor the work of a previous president and Congress.

The predicament might have daunted a lesser person, but Marshall was a cunning politician as well as the most powerful jurist in our history. His solution not only embarrassed the executive branch but also vastly expanded the powers of the judiciary. He wrote that the president was duty-bound to award the appointment because it was legally made by his predecessor. However, he ruled that the Supreme Court could not issue the writ of _mandamus_ because section 13 of the Judiciary Act of 1798, which gave the Court the power to issue such writs, exceeded the limits of the Constitution and was therefore null and void. Thus, in a single stroke, Marshall denied the Supreme Court a rather insignificant power (issuing writs of _mandamus_) by appropriating an enormous power: assuming that the Court had the power to declare an act of Congress void because it violated Constitutional principles.[6]

The beauty of Marshall's decision is that because he vastly expanded the Court's powers by limiting one of its own minor prerogatives, no executive action was necessary to enforce it so Jefferson could not undo by default what Marshall had done by execution. Marshall, therefore, unilaterally expanded the Court's authority while his adversary, Jefferson, was powerless to interfere.

As clever as this maneuver was, Marshall's decision was not completely founded in his own considerable imaginative powers. In fact, there is evidence that judicial review may have been intended by the founders. To begin with, the Constitution designates itself the highest law in the land, and it clearly anticipated that the courts would interpret the law. Thus, it is not too great a logical leap to assume that the courts would presume to hold other elements of government to the strictures of the basic law. More specifically, Alexander Hamilton made clear at least his own intention that judicial review existed:

The complete independence of the courts of justice is peculiarly essential in a limited Constitution. Limitations can be preserved in practice *no other way* than through the medium of courts of justice, whose duty it must be to declare all acts contrary to the manifest tenor of the Constitution void. [Emphasis added][7]

Whatever the case, Marshall's decision established the power of judicial review; and although the Court did not declare another federal law unconstitutional until 1857, the power to do so has become deeply rooted in our political system and is a major feature of our constitutional government. Judicial review makes the courts a full partner in the dynamic of the separation of powers and the checks and balances, and the courts have used the power not only to check political institutions against themselves, but equally important, to protect the individual against excesses of the state.

Individual Liberties

The rights of the individual are also provided for in the Constitution. Perhaps the most fundamental provisions of the document, these rights and liberties are the subject of the next chapter, so further discussion of them will be postponed until then. For now, we shall focus on another major structural device in the basic law.

Federalism

Federalism joins the separation of powers and checks and balances as one of the most important structural features of the Constitution. Federalism divides the powers of government and strikes a middle course between the two other major forms of power distribution: the unitary system and the confederate system.

The **unitary system** vests all the powers of government in the central apparatus. The central government then delegates authority to more local levels for administrative convenience. For example, the state governments are unitary. The Constitution vests all state powers in the state governments, thus cities and counties have no constitutional imprimatur; their existence, powers, and functions are granted by the state governments, and they can be denied by the state governments.

By contrast, as we learned in Chapter 1, a *confederate system* is an association of several sovereign entities that agree to cooperate for purposes of trade, defense, and other common objectives. The constituent parts are sovereign, however. Hence, the central government has no real power over the several states. No good examples of confederacy currently exist. Canada claims to have a confederacy, but the sovereignty of its various provinces is questionable.

As mentioned above, the founders designed the federal system in an attempt to frustrate the consolidation of a single, permanent majority. Hence, the powers of government were divided between the central government and the 13 original states. The Constitution further provides that new constituent parts, which may be added to the union, should also join the whole as separate and distinct states.

DIVIDED POWERS

Federalism has often been referred to as the **division of powers**. That is to suggest that the Constitution parcels out authority between the central government and the several state governments. (Take care not to confuse the *division of powers* with the *separation of powers* among the three branches of the national government.)

The powers given to the national government (sometimes referred to as the federal government) are called the **delegated powers**. The delegated powers can be divided into three categories. The **express powers** are those stated, word for word, in the Constitution, and the bulk of them are to be found in Article I, section 8: for example, "The Congress shall have Power To lay and collect Taxes," "To borrow Money," "To regulate Commerce," "To coin Money," and "To declare War."

Less explicit but no less real than the express powers are the **implied powers**. The implied powers doctrine was laid down by Chief Justice John Marshall in *McCulloch v. Maryland* (1819), in which the state of Maryland challenged the national government's right to establish a national bank because no express authority appears in the Constitution. Citing the *necessary and proper clause* (sometimes called the *elastic clause*) in Article I, section 8, Marshall gave a sweeping endorsement of the national government's power to assume whatever authority was necessary in order to carry out the intent of the Constitution:

> Let the end be legitimate, let it be within the scope of the Constitution, and all means which are appropriate, which are plainly adapted to that end, which are not prohibited, but consist with the letter and spirit of the Constitution, are constitutional.

Hence, the federal government has vastly increased its powers over the years—not because the express powers have been increased, but because Congress and the president have inferred the right to do certain specific things in satisfaction of the express powers. For example, Congress has used the necessary and proper clause to expand the federal government's regulation of the economy, and the president has committed troops to armed engagements, without a congressional declaration of war, based on the commander-in-chief clause in Article II, section 2 of the Constitution.

It is, however, important to note that, broad as the implied powers are, they are de-

pendent powers. Marshall's mandate does not authorize every act in which the national government may wish to engage. To the contrary, the implied powers doctrine permits the exercise of only those additional powers that are necessary and proper to fulfill the letter and spirit of the Constitution. Hence, the implied powers are dependent on the express powers and the inherent powers.

The **inherent powers** is the third category of delegated powers. An inherent power is any attribute that is essential to the definition of an object. The inherent powers are those powers that are essential to a government. In other words, the term *government* is understood to mean an institution that has certain properties. Various governments may have different powers, but all governments hold certain powers in common, or they would not satisfy the definition of government. The common powers are the inherent powers. For example, it is understood that all national governments have the power to deal with other national governments—that they have the power to send and receive ambassadors, to make treaties, and to make war and peace. We also understand that governments can make laws and can enforce compliance with those laws. The procedure and the detail of each of these powers may differ from government to government, but the right to exercise these inherent powers is unquestioned. Thus, although many of the inherent powers are mentioned in the Constitution (e.g., to send or receive ambassadors, to make war, to make treaties, and to make law), they would belong to the national government even if they were not mentioned, because those are powers that a national government has by definition: They are inherent.

The states have **reserved powers**. This term, like the term *delegated powers.* is taken from the Tenth Amendment:

> The powers not delegated to the United States by the Constitution, nor prohibited

President Bush with Polish President Lech Walesa greeting workers at the Lenin shipyard in Gdansk, Poland. It is at this location where the famous Solidarity movement began that brought down Poland's communist government.

by it to the States, are reserved to the States respectively, or to the people.

Accordingly, any power assumed to be rightfully exercised by government but not mentioned in the Constitution is a state power. For example, marriage and divorce laws, education, public health and safety, and city and county government—which few question as legitimate powers of government—are not mentioned in the Constitution and thus are rightfully subject to state authority.

Another jurisdictional distinction is made between exclusive powers and concurrent powers. An **exclusive power** is one that may be exercised by one or the other level of government, but not by both. Most powers are exclusive. For instance, only the national government may engage in diplomatic relations with foreign governments, manufacture money, and regulate interstate trade: These powers are exclusive to the national government. By contrast, the powers that are exclusive to the states include education,

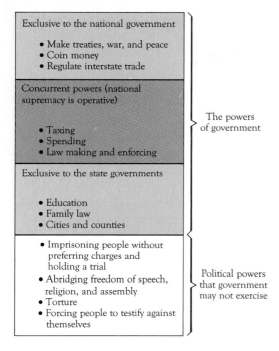

Figure 2.2   Exclusive and Concurrent Powers

The supremacy clause also answers another seeming contradiction. If education and the regulation of intrastate trade are state prerogatives, how can the federal government require the busing of children to integrated schools and the integration of restaurants and other public facilities? The answer rests in the fact that no government may legally use its powers in violation of the Constitution, and since the Supreme Court has ruled that segregation violates the individual liberty set forth in the Bill of Rights, segregation can be prohibited by federal authorities even when it involves a state power that is otherwise exclusive of federal involvement.

The question of relations between the national government and the states, to say nothing of the relations among states, however, is a more complicated matter than can be covered in this brief discussion of jurisdiction. A more complete examination demands consideration of the obligations and rights of the two levels of government.

establishing and empowering local government, and regulating intrastate commerce (trade within a state).

At the same time, however, each level of government may exercise some of the same powers. These **concurrent powers** include the police powers and the authority to tax and spend. However, a potential problem arises when two governments share powers: What happens if the laws of a particular state contradict the laws of the national government within a concurrent jurisdiction? Fortunately, the founders anticipated the difficulty and provided for it in the Constitution. Article VI contains the **supremacy clause**, which obliges the states to conform to national law when a contradiction occurs between the two levels. (See Figure 2.2).

VERTICAL FEDERALISM

Vertical federalism refers to the obligations of the national government to the states and vice versa. Article IV obliges the national government to defend the states against invasion and to answer a state's call for help in quieting domestic violence. Further, the national government must guarantee each state a "republican form of government"—a representative government, in other words. The national government is also charged with protecting the territorial integrity of the states, and while Congress can admit new states to the Union, the new states may not comprise the territory of extant states unless the states involved grant their permission. Moreover, other sections of the Constitution guarantee that each state shall have two, and only two, members to the United States Senate and that the same basic rules for awarding seats to the House of Representatives and to the electoral college will apply equally to each state. Effectively, therefore, the national government assures the relative political equality of the states.

For their part, the states are required to abide by the Constitution. This simple statement obliges the states to honor a profusion of mandates including submitting unsettled interstate disputes to the Supreme Court, refraining from imposing tariffs on imports and exports, passing no bills of attainder (legislating someone into prison without holding a trial), and awarding no titles of nobility. It also requires the states to respect the institution of the national government, to accede to its prerogatives, and to honor the principle of national supremacy.

HORIZONTAL FEDERALISM

Horizontal federalism refers to relations among the states. The states are obliged by the Constitution to extend to one another certain courtesies. We have already seen that Article III, section 2 requires states to take to the Supreme Court disputes that elude negotiated settlement. Article IV mandates that states give **"full faith and credit"** to the judicial proceedings of other states. For example, if a Pennsylvania court brings a monetary judgment against one of its citizens in a civil suit and the defendant moves to New Mexico, the state of New Mexico is supposed to enforce the judgment. Likewise the clause on **extradition** calls on the authorities of a host state to surrender a fugitive from another state upon the request of the state from which the criminal escaped. Article IV also requires that each state extend to citizens from other states the same **"privileges and immunities"** that they afford to their own cit-

izens. So if Florida, for instance, permits its citizens to drive up to 65 miles an hour through a certain section of the state, it cannot hold citizens from other states to stricter driving rules.

CONTEMPORARY FEDERALISM

Besides creating federalism to divide the public into local jurisdictions so as to frustrate the emergence of a permanent majority, Madison also hoped that the division of powers would discourage the national government from becoming too powerful. Soon after the Constitution was adopted, though, a struggle erupted between those who wanted to increase the power of the national government and those who wished to enhance the **states' rights**. This internal conflict has continued to the present day. At times the issue has been all-consuming—during the Civil War, for example—while at other times it has been eclipsed by other matters. But the controversy is irrepressible, rising to prominence at various junctures throughout our history; usually, the issue is ultimately joined in the courts because the political system lacks the authority to settle a dispute so fundamental to governance structure.

The earliest stages of constitutional history were dominated by the organization and consolidation of national and state government powers. It was not until late in the second decade of the nineteenth century that federalism itself became an issue. In 1819, you will recall, the Marshall Court was asked to decide the question of whether the federal government had the authority to create a national bank. *McCulloch* v. *Maryland* was a landmark decision. The Court not only found that the implied powers authorized the national government to establish the bank, but it also ruled that each level of government, state and national, enjoyed an equal right to exist and that neither had the power to dissolve or destroy the other. Just as it had presumed to overturn a national statute in *Marbury v. Madison* (1803), the Court now asserted its right to reverse a ruling of a state court. *McCulloch v. Maryland* revealed the Marshall Court to be a strong advocate of national government powers. Six years later, in the case of *Gibbons v. Ogden* (1824), the Marshall Court took a further step in support of national supremacy by negating a state law that contradicted the express power of federal regulation of interstate commerce.

So long as the indomitable nationalist John Marshall remained on the Court, the federal government's powers were secure from state intrusion. But Marshall left the Court in 1835, and during the next 30 years the issue of states' rights became ever more pervasive. The post-Marshall Supreme Court began to issue rulings focusing on the Tenth Amendment, and tended to view the area of public health and safety as exclusively state authority. During this period the Court ruled that the states could regulate trade in their jurisdiction—even interstate trade—when no national statute exists in the field. Furthermore, in the famous *Dred Scott* decision of 1857, although the case dealt solely with national law, the cause of states' rights was thought to be advanced when the Court ruled that Congress could not limit the extension of slavery. It was hoped that the *Dred Scott* decision would settle the issue of states' rights, but it actually helped propel the country into a terrible war between the states, in which while slavery was the emotional issue involved, the fundamental question was the nature of federalism itself.

Following the Civil War, the Court became very conservative and generally voided state and national laws that impeded business interests. Still, in the 1920s two important cases limited the state powers. In *Missouri v.*

Holland (1920), the court ruled that when a treaty between the United States and a foreign government is involved, the national government could impose regulations in areas where the states are usually the sole authority. Five years later, the Court ruled in **Gitlow v. New York** that the states were bound to the limitations of the First Amendment of the Constitution against limiting free speech.

With the Great Depression of the 1930s, the Court gradually backed away from its pro-business posture. The net result was that the powers of both the national government and the state governments were increased in the area of regulating business. But the post-World War II era saw the Court once again in a nationalistic mood. This time the controversy was joined in the field of civil rights. The landmark decision of **Brown v. The Board of Education of Topeka, Kansas** (1954) reversed the Court's previous support of state-mandated segregation established in *Plessy v. Ferguson* (1896): A number of rulings followed that unequivocally denounced racism, and later, gender discrimination, in public institutions.

During the late 1970s and early 1980s the Court vacillated on the issue of state prerogatives versus the powers of the national government. In *National League of Cities v. Usury* (1976), the Court seemed prepared to expand the powers of the states when it ruled that national minimum wage laws may not be imposed on state employees. Yet nine years later, the Court reversed itself on the issue in *Garcia v. San Antonio Metropolitan Transit Authority* (1985), once again increasing the federal powers. Indeed, the *Garcia* case was a sweeping nationalist victory because the Court went on to opine that the states could not challenge national laws that contradicted state powers.

As the Rehnquist Court has become decidedly conservative, however, it has begun to deemphasize the role of protecting the individual from government intrusion, and, as a result, it has strengthened the states. Although the conservative view has not prevailed on every decision, since 1989 it has dominated most cases. Hence, unless state laws contradict specific language in the Constitution, they have been allowed to stand. For example, states have been allowed to prohibit abortions in publicly funded hospitals,[8] make possession of child pornography illegal,[9] forbid corporate funding of political campaign ads,[10] and require clear and convincing evidence of a permanently comatose patient's wish to die before life support systems may be removed.[11] In a few cases, however, the liberals have carried the issue and have bound state law and practices to national norms. The Supreme Court has sustained lower court-mandated taxes to fund desegregation programs[12] and it has made most political patronage illegal.[13] In general, however, the Rehnquist Court seems intent upon leaving the question of the appropriate extent of state and national powers to the respective legislatures, and with the 1990 replacement of liberal William J. Brennan with conservative David H. Souter, this trend will probably increase in intensity.

Leaving the nature of federalism to the political process promises little chance of a definitive solution to the controversy. The issue has often been caught up in the turmoil of politics, and usually the courts have been asked to settle the matter. In the early period, the conservatives tended to favor a strong national government while liberals advocated states' rights. More recently, however, the antagonists have exchanged sides on the issue. Presidents John F. Kennedy and Lyndon B. Johnson pressed for state compliance with new national laws in civil rights and other fields that had previously been left to the states; Richard M. Nixon, Ronald Reagan, and George Bush each proclaimed a "New Federalism" that saw the federal government return to the states many responsibilities *and costs* that had previously been assumed by the national government, al-

though both Nixon and Bush also provided some additional revenues to the states for this purpose.

The conservative trend of returning power to the states is for the moment prevailing, but exactly where we are headed with regard to the division of powers between the national government and the states we shall have to wait to find out. No question exists for the moment, however, that the powers of the national government are vastly greater than the founders intended and that the states' prerogatives have been significantly reduced through time.

Besides the legal transfer of power from the states to the national level, another factor has been at play in this dynamic: economics.

THE ECONOMICS OF FEDERALISM

It has been said that "power follows money," and this maxim is evidenced in the evolution of our federal system. Access to larger amounts of revenue by the national government has given it an oblique entrée into many areas that previously were solely matters of state responsibility. Simply stated, beginning essentially with the 1930s **New Deal** policies of Franklin Delano Roosevelt, the national government has literally bought its way into the states' venue.

Before the Great Depression, federal financial assistance to the states amounted to a pittance. The prevailing attitude was that the national government should concern itself with matters of defense, interstate and international commerce, and other broad issues; the states were expected to focus on social concerns. But the Great Depression immersed the country in difficulties that rapidly outstripped state and private resources, so people turned to the national government for relief. The administration of Franklin D. Roosevelt responded with an unprecedented program involving the national government, as never before, in the daily

Single women demanding jobs at State Civil Works Administration Headquarters, 1933.

lives of American citizens. This new course was rife with controversy, however, and a national debate has ensued ever since over the appropriate level of federal involvement in the society. Consensus on the matter has emerged from time to time, but only temporarily, as the argument is taken up anew with the liberals usually advocating more national programs and the conservatives less.

A series of federal monetary grants to state and local governments has been employed as the vehicle for greater national government involvement in areas that previously involved the states exclusively. Many, indeed most, of these grants have included regulations and provisos as conditions for their award to the states. Consequently, if the states were to receive the additional revenue from the federal government, they were obliged to accept the federally imposed conditions for its use. In this way the national government has tended to impose upon state policy a measure of uniformity of which it was incapable before. The federal government has used three basic kinds of grants in its history: categorical grants, block grants, and revenue sharing.

Categorical Grants **Categorical grants** are the oldest form of federal assistance to state and local governments. They also account for the largest amount of grant money. These grants usually make funds available for specific purposes, and state and local governments are required to contribute matching funds to the program. These matching funds can be on a dollar-for-dollar basis, but often the receiver's contribution is significantly lower than the federal outlay. By providing money to state and local governments, the national government has often induced them to establish programs for their citizens that they had previously not offered. Some examples of items for which categorical grants supply money are welfare assistance, medicaid, and highway construction (which combine to account for about 40 percent of all federal money spent on grants), as well as employment training, pollution and toxic waste control, education, and rapid transit.

Unlike the usual categorical grants in which the state and local governments have little discretion about the use of the funds, one type—the **project grant**—provides funds for purposes that may be unique to the applicant. Even here, however, money is made available only for certain discrete areas such as community health. The exact use to which the money for community health is put may be determined by the terms of the project, but assistance given for a project in community health may not be spent for some other purpose.

Block Grants   More recently developed than the categorical grants, **block grants** are designed to give the receivers of aid more flexibility in disbursing the money according to the needs of the particular locale. These grants, which have sometimes been created from the combination of several categorical grants, give the receivers an amount of money to spend as they see fit within the specified area. This method tends to be favored by conservatives since it gives greater control to the local agencies. Liberals are suspicious of it, however, fearing that local elites may ignore the social programs that liberals wish to fund.

Revenue Sharing   The newest and most flexible of all grant programs is **revenue shar-**

ing, begun in 1972 by the Nixon Administration. Created when national government resources were perceived as sufficiently abundant to be used in relief of state and local agencies' crushing fiscal responsibilities, this program made grants of money to the receivers with few or no strings attached. Understandably popular with state and local governments, the program was, however, short-lived. Pressed by its skyrocketing deficits, the Reagan Administration advised that revenue sharing be phased out, and in 1986 the last vestige of this program was allowed to lapse.

As one can imagine, the federal largess represented by these grant programs has been a godsend to the fiscally beleaguered state and local governments. They have responded by aggressively pursuing federal funds. Most states and many cities employ lobbyists in Washington, and grant writers whose task it is to draft proposals to secure funds from the national government.

Unfortunately, however, the best of times for these programs has passed, at least for the foreseeable future. Driven by an ideological aversion to federal involvement in local affairs and impelled by unprecedented budget deficits, the Reagan Administration cut back severely on the federal aid package, and President Bush has not reversed that policy. Not only was revenue sharing abolished, but dozens of categorical and block grants were consolidated or dropped completely. From a high point of 16 percent in 1980, the share of the national budget spent in aid programs dropped to 6 percent by 1991. After adjusting for inflation, we find that all of the programs that survived are now receiving less in real dollars than they did before the Reagan era.

Even so, however, federal aid to state and local governments, while reduced, will likely continue because such programs address important economic, social, and political needs. Given the enormous task of state and local

A Midwestern factory belches smoke and contaminants that will eventually be deposited by the rain—acid rain—on New England.

governments in public health, welfare, safety, and education, their need for money is obvious, and little more need be said on this point. There are other reasons for continued federal aid, however. As industrialization, transportation, and communication continue to intertwine the various sectors of the country, we encounter problems that are now national in scope but that have heretofore been addressed only on a state or local basis. Consider the difficulties in dealing with acid rain, pollution, and toxic waste. In each of these areas, the activities in one state may very well affect the quality of life in other locales. Should Maine, Massachusetts, or New York pay for the damage caused by pollutants released into Ohio's skies and dumped by storms further east? Should the state of Wyoming or New Mexico become the dump site of nuclear waste produced in Califor-

nia or Colorado? And how are we to dispose of the mountains of refuse produced each day in states that are running out of landfills? Clearly these issues and many others are national in scope, and they demand national solutions and national funding.

Additionally, federal grants have proved an effective way of establishing national standards of health, nutrition, energy conservation, and so forth. Even Ronald Reagan, a commited opponent of national regulation of local governments, resorted in 1987 to the manipulation of federal highway construction money to force the states to set 21 years as the minimum age for legal drinking of alcoholic beverages.

Federal aid has also been credited with contributing to the solution of common problems without expanding the number of federal employees. It is seen as a mechanism to help states modernize their technological bases, and it is argued that federal aid has encouraged states to try innovative programs that might otherwise have gone unexplored. Yet, perhaps the most sobering legacy of the Reagan/Bush years is that additional government programs are not likely to be created soon. The budget deficit policies since the 1980s have forestalled dynamic new federal programs for the time being.

ADVANTAGES AND DISADVANTAGES OF FEDERALISM

There is little question that federalism has, during the last two centuries, become something different than the founders anticipated. The matter of evolution itself should not concern us since it would indeed be unusual for any institution to remain unchanged through time. But we should from time to time reassess the nature of our institutions in order to determine their continued utility in the society.

The structural aspects of federalism have a number of both positive and negative results. Federalism makes it easier for different and diverse cultures to exist together in a single nation. For instance, the people of the South can cultivate their social norms without interference from or to the people of the North. At the same time, however, this characteristic hinders developing a unified society. The division of powers affords society a measure of local control over its destiny, and it tends to bring home to large numbers of people the importance of public affairs and the ability to manipulate them. People are encouraged to take a keener interest in government because it is close to them and it clearly relates to their lives. Also, under federalism, local governments can more effectively respond to the needs and interests of the citizens. On the

other hand, federalism's local orientation tends to encourage provincialism in the body politic, even in the face of challenging national issues. However, by using semiautonomous state and local governments as frontline agencies in the effort to answer political and social needs, we create an environment in which experimentation is encouraged. State and local governments need not march lockstep with the national government on policy matters. When one locale develops an innovative way to address a problem, other state and local agencies are at liberty to profit from its ingenuity. Yet, all too often, state and local governments have tended to obstruct progress rather than encourage it; the civil rights problems in the 1950s and 1960s are a good example. Time and again in this century, the national government has had to prod and cajole the more local entities toward progressive solutions to outstanding problems. Local autonomy also tends to be redundant and wasteful, giving truth to the contention that federalism is costly and is affordable only for wealthy societies. National agencies—the Department of Agriculture, for example—are duplicated at the state and county levels. This subdivision increases the administrative cost of programs and swells the bureaucracy.

Many of the issues we face have rendered federalism a largely meaningless concept. Assuring safe toxic waste disposal, combating air and water pollution, housing the homeless, providing good education for all citizens, regulating large corporations, and dealing with many other issues exceed the resources of any single state. These problems and their solutions demand regional or even national solutions. Political necessity, economic exigencies, and court rulings have smudged, or even eliminated, a neat division of powers. In one area, however, the distinction between the state and national government remains as clear as ever it was: electoral politics. Every popular election (elections in which the public votes) is a state election. Seats in the House and Senate are awarded to states, and members of Congress are elected to office by the people in their states. Even members to the electoral college are apportioned to states, are chosen by the voters within their respective states, and never assemble outside their respective states. The interdependence of our electoral system and federalism is, by itself, so critical that any serious modification of federalism would surely cause a transformation in the political order—and should thus be considered long and hard before being undertaken.

Amendments

Before turning to an examination of individual liberties and rights, one last constitutional feature should be studied here: the question of amending the document. Essentially two kinds of amendments are made to the Constitution: formal and informal.

FORMAL AMENDMENTS

The *formal amendments* are those made according to the process set forth in Article V of the Constitution. There are two stages in this process: *proposal*, which is a national function, and *ratification*, which is left to the states. Within each stage, two alternatives may be used; Congress may propose an amendment by a two-thirds vote in each house, or Congress can call a national constitutional convention if two-thirds if the states request such a convention. Of these two methods only the former has been used. Since the 1791 adoption of the Bill of Rights, nearly six thousand amendments have been introduced in Congress, but only 23 have received the necessary vote to be sent to the

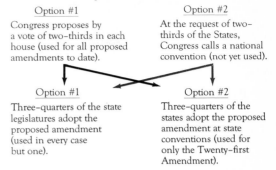

Proposal: A national function

Option #1	Option #2
Congress proposes by a vote of two-thirds in each house (used for all proposed amendments to date).	At the request of two-thirds of the States, Congress calls a national convention (not yet used).

Option #1	Option #2
Three-quarters of the state legislatures adopt the proposed amendment (used in every case but one).	Three-quarters of the states adopt the proposed amendment at state conventions (used for only the Twenty-first Amendment).

Ratification: A state function—Congress specifies the method

Figure 2.3   Formal Amendments of the Constitution

states, and only 16 of the 23 have been ratified.*

Ratification is accomplished when three-fourths of the states (38 states) vote to ratify. Congress specifies one of two methods for the states to ratify. Although it usually mandates ratification be executed by votes of the state legislatures, in one case—the Twenty-first Amendment, which repealed prohibition—Congress required ratification by conventions in each state. (See Figure 2.3.) Congress usually also specifies a maximum period of time (normally seven years) during which ratification must be accomplished. If the time limit expires before 38 states have voted to ratify, the issue is dead and must be reproposed to be considered further. Seven proposed amendments have failed ratification; none have yet been reproposed. The most recent issues to fail ratification are the Equal Rights Amendment (ERA) and a proposal to give Washington, D.C., members of Congress in the same manner as states of the Union are given them.

* Note that the president cannot veto a proposed amendment and enjoys no official role in the process of amending the Constitution.

It is generally agreed that a constitution should be difficult to amend if consistency is to be preserved and frivolous changes avoided. This said, however, the undemocratic nature of the formal amendment process should be examined. It must be remembered that extraordinary vote requirements (two-thirds or three-quarters) are deliberately created to protect against the *majority* and are therefore undemocratic on their face. Requiring a two-thirds majority of the House of Representatives means that representatives of just over one-third of the population can stop a proposed amendment. In the Senate it is worse. If 34 Senators from the country's smallest states vote against an amendment, Senators representing only about 13.2 million people in a country with about 250 million people (or only about 6 percent of the total population) can kill a proposed amendment. The ratification calculus is even more skewed. Since stopping a measure requires only 13 states to refuse ratification, states representing only 8.3 million people (4 percent of the total) could theoretically negate a proposed amendment. Conversely, if the 34 least populous states voted to ratify an amendment, they would represent only about 88 million people (or only 39 percent of the total). Looked at another way, since all states except Nebraska have two-house legislatures, only 13 houses out of 99 need oppose an amendment to cause it to fail, if ratification by state legislatures is mandated—which is usually the case.

INFORMAL AMENDMENTS

Informal amendments are modifications made to the meaning of the Constitution while the words remain unchanged. The Constitution has been called a living document because its meaning has tended to expand or contract according to the perceived need. The imprecise language of the Constitution, leaving the de-tails to subsequent interpretation, has been an important factor in this process. The sources of informal amendments are numerous and varied.

Judicial interpretation is perhaps the most dramatic and clearest example of informal amendments. The courts determine definitively what the Constitution means. Indeed, the very power of the courts to engage in judicial review is the product of an informal amendment. As you have seen, the Supreme Court has used its self-bestowed power of interpreting the Constitution to articulate the implied powers, to define federalism, to outlaw segregation, and so on. Indeed, it has modified the basic law in hundreds of other ways.

Presidential interpretations of the executive prerogatives have also fostered informal amendments. Over the years, presidents have assumed certain powers and authority that are not specifically stated in the Constitution. For example, Thomas Jefferson asserted his right as Commander in Chief to send the military into armed conflicts without a congressional declaration of war. Several presidents have claimed **executive privilege** (refusing to release information to Congress on the grounds of separation of powers), while others have made **executive agreements** with foreign countries as part of their right to make foreign policy.

Congress, too, has drafted informal amendments through *statutory enumeration.* By passing law in satisfaction of constitutional intent, Congress brings specific meaning to its abstract principles. Hence, Congress created the courts that are subordinate to the Supreme Court, it created the Cabinet to serve the president, and it created the independent regulatory boards and commissions (the National Labor Relations Board, the Securities and Exchange Commission, the Interstate Commerce Commission, etc.) to perform needed services in certain specific areas of public policy.

The **political parties** are not provided for

in the Constitution. Yet, their existence and the functions they perform amount to constitutional change. For example, they nominate people to run for federal office, and they select potential electors to elect the president. Indeed, the very fact of their existence causes the checks and balances to function differently. When the president is from one party and the Congress is dominated by another party (called divided government), the checks and balances are more keen than if the executive and the legislature are controlled by the same party.

State governments also modify the Constitution. State law determines that members to the House of Representatives are elected from congressional districts, that presidential electors are elected by the people, and that candidates for federal office are chosen by conventions or by primaries.

Finally, *public expectation* also plays a role in informally amending the Constitution. This phenomenon is perhaps nowhere as clear as when it relates to democracy. The word *democracy* does not appear in the Constitution. Yet, although there are reactionaries who argue that only representative government, not democracy, is mandated by the Constitution, and radicals who argue that true democracy is unknown in our system, the bulk of our citizens insist that the laws apply to all equally and that everyone who can reasonably be expected to do so be given the opportunity to choose our governors. In short, the masses demand of their Constitution a liberal democracy. Hence, public expectation has taken the meaning of the Constitution considerably further than was intended by the founders, and while the letter of the law has changed little in this regard, the spirit of the law has been modified mightily.

Summary

- The United States is a democratic republic in which the people elect representatives who govern them.

- The powers of government are separated among the legislative, executive, and judicial branches, whose powers are limited by the checks and balances and by the Constitution.

- Federalism, the division of powers between the states and the national governments, is another limitation on governmental power.

- The Constitution can be amended formally by Congress and the states, or informally by the courts and other institutions in the political system.

Notes

1. See John Fiske, *The Critical Period in American History, 1783–1789* (Boston: Houghton Mifflin, 1898); Charles A. Beard, *An Economic Interpretation of the Constitution of the United States* (New York: Macmillan, 1913); and Nicholas Cords and Patrick Gerster, eds., *Myth and the American Experience,* Vol. 1.

2. *The Federalist Papers,* #10.

3. *The Federalist Papers,* #51.

4. *The Federalist Papers, #*51.

5. See Duane Lockard, *Perverted Priorities in American Politics* (New York: Macmillan, 1971).

6. Dumas Malone and Basil Rauch, *The Republic Comes of Age, 1789–1841* (New York: Appleton-Century-Crofts, 1960), pp. 93–94.

7. *The Federalist Papers, #*78.

8. *Webster* v. *Reproductive Health Services,* 57 L.W. 5023 (1989).

9. *Osborne* v. *Ohio,* 110 S. Ct. 1691 (1990).

10. *Austin* v. *Michigan Chamber of Commerce,* 109 S. Ct. 1952 (1990).

11. *Cruzan* v. *Missouri,* 110 S. Ct. 2841 (1990).

12. *Missouri* v. *Jenkins,* 110 S. Ct. 1651 (1990).

13. *Rutan* v. *Republican Party of Illinois,* 110 S. Ct. 2729 (1990).

Suggestions for Further Reading

Bartholomew, Paul C. *Ruling American Constitutional Law* (Vols. 1 & 2). Totowa, NJ: Little, Adams & Co., 1970.

Elazar, Daniel J. *American Federalism: A View from the States* (3rd ed.). New York: Harper & Row, 1984.

Hale, George, and Marian Palley. *The Politics of Federal Grants.* Washington, DC: Congressional Quarterly Press, 1981.

Henig, Jeffrey R. *Public Policy and Federalism: Issues in State and Local Politics.* New York: St. Martin's Press, 1985.

Howitt, Arnold. *Managing Federalism.* Washington, DC: Congressional Quarterly Press, 1984.

Lockard, Duane. *Perverted Priorities in American Politics.* New York: Macmillan, 1971.

Malone, Dumas, and Basil Rauch. *The Republic Comes of Age.* New York: Appleton-Century-Crofts, 1960.

Murphy, Walter F. *Basic Cases in Constitutional Law.* North Scituate, MA: Duxbury.

Nathan, Richard P., and Fred C. Doolittle. *Reagan and the States.* Princeton: Princeton University Press, 1987.

Peterson, Paul E., Barry G. Rabe, and Kenneth K. Wong. *When Federalism Works.* Washington, DC: Brookings Institution, 1986.

Reagan, Michael D., and John G. Sanzone. *The New Federalism* (2nd ed.). New York: Oxford University Press, 1981.

Saffell, David C. *State and Local Government: Politics and Public Policy.* New York: Random House, 1987.

Wilson, Woodrow. *Congressional Government.* New York: Meridian Editions, 1908.

————. *Constitutional Government in the United States.* New York: Columbia University Press, 1908.

Wright, Deil S. *Understanding Intergovernmental Relations* (3rd ed.). Monterey, CA: Brooks/Cole, 1988.

Chapter 3

THE PEOPLE'S RIGHTS AND LIBERTIES

PREVIEW

Democracy is a complicated form of government, balancing majority rule against minority rights. The Bill of Rights has gradually been applied to the states as well as to the national government, and the Supreme Court tends to give it preferred status in constitutional interpretation because its provisions are central to the democratic system. The First Amendment guarantees each individual the right to believe as he or she chooses, and it sanctions any religious practice that does not threaten society or its people. The First Amendment also ensures that people may speak and publish their views as long as they do not endanger the national security and provided they do not defame others. Public officials and celebrities, while protected from malicious false statements, enjoy less protection from libelous comment than do ordinary individuals, however. Yet although we enjoy enormous latitude in expressing ourselves, particularly in our political statements, the Court refuses to see obscenity protected by the Constitution, although it has had an extraordinarily difficult time defining obscenity.

Our protections against government abuse in criminal matters are addressed in the traditions of the common law and in the Fourth, Fifth, Sixth, and Eighth amendments. We are most secure from search and seizure in our homes. The authorities must, except in unusual circumstances, secure court-issued search warrants to enter a home and to rummage through its contents. Restrictions are similar, but less strict, in street searches and searches of automobiles. A warrant is also required for an arrest, except when the police have probable cause to suspect the violation of law. After an arrest, the police must inform suspects of their right to obtain an attorney and to remain silent. Suspects are assured a speedy trial by an impartial jury that presumes innocence until proved otherwise, and evidence illegally obtained may not usually be used to win conviction.

Since 1968, the voters have tended to elect conservative presidents who have in turn appointed conservative jurists to the bench. This trend has resulted in increasingly narrow decisions regarding the individual's protection against the authorities, and some of the most expansive liberties have been curtailed in favor of greater police power. Perhaps the most latitude extended to the authorities has been in the apprehension and conviction of drug offenders.

Racial and gender discrimination are ancient traditions in our society. The abolition of slavery was followed by official and private policies of segregation until this was ruled unconstitutional in the mid-1950s. Seizing upon this change in public policy, African-Americans and other people of conscience launched the most dramatic domestic protest in this century: the civil rights movement. Court and congressional policy went beyond eliminating segregation to attempting to wipe out racial bigotry and discrimination in education, housing, public accommodations, and employment. Encouraged by the new social consciousness, people struck out at gender discrimination, demanding equal treatment for women in law, in the workplace, and in the schools. Heightened consciousness of women's rights and the Court's recognition of the right to privacy led to the legalization of abortion, but the recently created conservative majority on the Supreme Court has led to a more restrictive policy regarding this issue.

Besides African-Americans and women, other groups that have demanded fairer treatment by society include Native Americans, Asian-Americans, Hispanic Americans, the handicapped, the elderly, and homosexuals.

Among the areas most actively pursued in terms of social justice are fair employment practices. Launched by President Lyndon B. Johnson, affirmative action programs have been adopted in efforts to assure that women, ethnic minorities, and the handicapped are not wrongly relegated to menial, low-paying tasks. Firmly supportive of affirmative action plans, the Court has, however, stopped short of permitting quotas favoring racial minorities except where discrimination was blatant in the past. However, as with so many other areas in the civil liberties and the civil rights, the conservative Rehnquist Court has begun to place new limits on these programs as well.

A bill of rights is what the people are entitled to against every government on earth.
Thomas Jefferson

The Constitution goes far beyond the mechanical devices of separate powers and checks and balances. The United States is founded on principles that give very high priority to individual liberty and social justice. Those freedoms that come to us from our commitment to individual freedom are called the **civil liberties**, and the **civil rights** derive from our belief that all people are in essence equal and therefore have a right to the same fundamental treatment in society. These concepts are at the core of our societal aspirations and have grown in importance with the evolution of our political system. They are, in fact, the essence of democracy as we understand it. We shall examine the civil rights later. For now, we shall focus on the civil liberties, and we find that many of them are provided for in the Bill of Rights and other amendments.

The Bill of Rights and the States

The Constitution, as originally adopted, is primarily concerned with the structure of the national government and its relationship with the states. Precious little in the document addresses individual liberties and rights. Indeed, the only expression of individual rights and liberties in the unamended version are the **privileges and immunities** clause, **habeas corpus** (requiring a speedy trial), prohibition of a **bill of attainder** (a law making someone guilty of a crime without a trial), and prohibition of **ex post facto law** (law making an act a crime after it has been committed). Virtually all of the other personal liberties and rights including freedom of speech, religion, and assembly; the right to a defense; freedom from torture; equality before the law; and others appear in the amendments to the Constitution, particularly Amendments 1–9 and 13–15.

Not only were most of our rights and liberties afterthoughts to the original Constitution, but their applicability to the states was not required until more than one hundred years following the Constitution's adoption. The question was first broached in 1833. The City of Baltimore, by diverting a waterway, caused a privately owned wharf to become unusable.

The wharf owners sued the city claiming that it had violated the Fifth Amendment of the United States Constitution by denying them property "without just compensation." Although Chief Justice John Marshall usually stood for increased powers for the federal government, his reading of the Constitution exempted the states from the Bill of Rights. After all, the first ten amendments begin with the phrase "Congress shall make no law." It seemed clear that this explicit reference to the national legislature meant the states were not bound by the Constitution to the strictures of the Bill of Rights.[1]

The issue of state exemption from the Bill of Rights was thus settled for decades. Of course, many states adopted their own bill of rights, but little, save their own self-restraint, prevented them from denying their citizens what we now consider basic liberties. In 1868, however, the *Fourteenth Amendment* was adopted. Section 1 of this critical addition contains a **due process clause**, which was eventually used to require the states to abide by nearly all the provisions of the Bill of Rights. The clause reads:

> No State shall make or enforce any law which shall abridge the privileges or immunities of citizens of the United States; nor shall any State deprive any person of life, liberty, or property without due process of law.

Perhaps no provision in the Constitution, outside of the national supremacy clause, so limits the states in the exercise of power as does the due process clause of the Fourteenth Amendment. The Fourteenth Amendment, together with the Thirteenth and Fifteenth amendments, is one of the Civil War amendments that were designed primarily to abolish slavery and to secure fair treatment of African-Americans in the state and national law. Hence, the Fourteenth Amendment's full implications for federalism were not immediately

recognized. In time, however, the court applied the due process clause with almost revolutionary consequences.

After several cases in which the Supreme Court seemed unready to apply the due process clause to its full potential scope, it ruled in ***Gitlow v. New York*** (1925) that because of the due process clause, the free speech provisions of the First Amendment were unambiguously applicable to the states.[2] Since first applying that bank-shot kind of decision, the Court gradually applied the due process clause to most of the personal rights set forth in the Bill of Rights, thus requiring the states to honor its provisions. To date, the only provisions of the Bill of Rights not yet imposed upon the states are the following:

- The right to keep and bear arms (Second Amendment)
- The prohibition against quartering troops in private homes (Third Amendment)
- The requirement of a grand jury indictment for capital or infamous crimes (Fifth Amendment)
- The mandate that accused persons shall be tried in the venue where the crime occurred (Sixth Amendment)
- The right to a jury trial in civil cases (Seventh Amendment)
- The dictate to use common law rules in all trials (Seventh Amendment)
- The rejoinder against excessive bail and fines (Eighth Amendment)

All other requirements and strictures of the Bill of Rights are incumbent on the states, including the following:

- Freedom of religion, speech, press, assembly, and petition (First Amendment)
- Freedom from unreasonable search and seizure (Fourth Amendment)

- The requirement of search warrants issued only for probable cause (Fourth Amendment)
- The prohibition of double jeopardy (Fifth Amendment)
- The protection from self-incrimination (Fifth Amendment)
- The mandate against taking private property for public use without just compensation (Fifth Amendment)
- The right to a speedy, public trial by an impartial jury (Sixth Amendment)
- The right to be informed of the nature of charges of which one is accused, to be confronted with witnesses for the prosecution, to compel attendance of defense witnesses, and to have a defense attorney (Sixth Amendment)
- The restriction against cruel and unusual punishment (Eighth Amendment)
- All other rights retained by the people but not enumerated in the Constitution (Ninth Amendment)

All of these rights and more, which we will soon study, are guaranteed us by the Constitution. But to simply say they are ours by right is somewhat misleading; it reveals nothing about what exactly these rights mean, how extensive they are, in what manner they apply, and so forth. In our political system, these decisions are left to the interpretation of many people, from the police officer on the beat to the President of the United States. Ultimately, however, the final decisions about the meaning and extent of our liberties and rights are left to the courts.

The First Amendment

Congress shall make no law respecting an *establishment of religion,* or prohibiting the *free exercise thereof;* or abridging the *freedom of speech, or of the press;* or the right of the people *peaceably to assemble,* and to *petition the government* for a redress of grievances. [Emphasis added]

Without question, these provisions are among the most important, if not the most important, parts of the Constitution. They speak to freedom of conscience and to those liberties that must exist if we are to enjoy a democratic society. While Justice Hugo Black, who served on the Supreme Court from 1937 to 1971, believed that the phrase "Congress shall make no law" made absolute freedom of religion, speech, press, peaceable assembly, and petition, few other justices have afforded it such exalted stature. Yet because the First Amendment rights are so central to the democratic process, the Court has often applied the *preferred position doctrine* to the First Amendment. This approach gives special importance to these liberties, and only in the most extraordinary circumstances can they be modified. Accordingly, the most important features of the First Amendment should be examined.

FREEDOM OF RELIGION

"Separation of church and state" is commonly believed to be among the most inviolable principles of the Constitution. The importance of the concept is, of course, undeniable; however, there is much misunderstanding about it. To begin with, the phrase quoted above is nowhere to be found in the Constitution. It exists only in our understanding of the Constitution, not in its actual wording. Second, while freedom of religious worship was critical to many early Americans, it was looked at askance by some of our most prominent leaders. Thomas Paine publicly scoffed at the "absurdities of revealed religion," and Thomas Jefferson wrote that "freedom of religion also implies freedom from it."

Jesse Jackson and his family at a North Carolina rally where he announced his candidacy for the 1988 presidential election.

Third, the principle of "separation of church and state" is not symmetrically applied. So far as the Constitution is concerned, state is to be separate from church, but church is certainly not separate from state. There is no legal prohibition to the clergy serving in the government; indeed, many are politically active. For example, Father Robert Drinan, a Catholic priest from Massachusetts, served in Congress during the 1970s, and Reverend Jesse Jackson ran for president in 1984 and 1988, as did Reverend Pat Robertson in 1988. Quite apart from seeking public office, religious groups often become active in public affairs. They frequently mobilize on moral issues such as legalizing prostitution, abortion, or gambling, and banning pornography. Political activity by re-

ligious groups was sustained and protected as late as 1990 when the Supreme Court dismissed a challenge to the tax exemptions of the Catholic Church. The plaintiffs contended that the Church should pay taxes on its income because it used part of its funds to oppose abortion, which the plaintiffs saw as a violation of federal law prohibiting tax-exempt groups from using funds to influence legislation.[3]

During the 1970s and 1980s, the religious right, exemplified by the Moral Majority led by Reverend Jerry Falwell, stridently pursued a political agenda including banning the teaching of evolution in the public schools, allowing prayer in the public schools, and securing government financial support for religiously oriented schools. On the left, religious groups have mobilized in support of such causes as striking field workers and refugees from Central America. These are but a few examples of how the pulpit is often political, but what of the other half of the equation, the separation of state from church?

The United States has an extraordinarily high percentage of people who consider themselves religious. With about 60 percent of the population claiming to be members of a temple, synagogue, or church, the United States ranks first among the industrial nations in religious participants. Obviously, therefore, the question of the states' involvement with religion is important, and indeed, it presents the society with one of its most vexing and recurring problems.

The Establishment Clause The First Amendment contains two clauses regarding religion: the **establishment clause** and the **free exercise clause**. The establishment clause has to do with what the government may or may not do regarding the existence of religion.

Traditionally, the Supreme Court has relied upon Thomas Jefferson's famous dictum that a "wall of separation" should exist between state and church.* This means that the federal

---

* The Rehnquist Court gives indications that it may be preparing to modify the long-standing Court insistence on separation of church and state. Associate Justices Antonin Scalia, Anthony M. Kennedy, and Byron R. White have each called for the Court to allow more government support for religion, and Chief Justice William H. Rehnquist has long disputed the doctrine of separation of church and state. Although Sandra Day O'Connor has usually strongly supported church-state separation, Bush appointee David H. Souter seems to lean toward Rehnquist's view. While he has yet to announce a position from the high bench, as attorney general of New Hampshire in the 1970s he defended the state's attempt to require the Lord's Prayer in public schools and he supported a state order that public buildings fly the flag at half staff on Good Friday in commemoration of Christ's death.

government should do nothing to either encourage or impede the existence of religion in the society. Furthermore, it brought the state governments under the same stricture in *Everson* v. *Board of Education* (1947).[4]

But this neutral stance has never been used to prohibit government support that is seen as "incidentally" helpful to religion. If, for example, a government policy to educate children or to honor a particular national holiday has as its by-product the encouragement of religion, the courts have usually allowed this. Accordingly, while the Supreme Court ruled in the Everson case that the states were obliged to adhere to the establishment clause of the First Amendment, it also sanctioned a program of government-paid transportation of students to religiously oriented schools. The Court's reasoning in this apparently contradictory opinion was that the state was paying the costs of the education for children and that any religious training they might receive was only coincidental. More recently, in 1984 the Court approved of a nativity scene being erected on public property because it commemorated a public holiday and had only secondary religious importance.[5] The year before, the Court upheld the tradition of publicly paid chaplains being employed by public legislative bodies, a long tradition of the United States Congress as well as many state legislatures.[6]

On the other hand, the Court has consistently opposed practices that it perceived as direct government support of religion. In 1975, for example, the Court negated state purchases of educational services for use in parochial schools,[7] in 1989 struck down a state law allowing tax exemptions for religious publications,[8] and in 1990 ruled that states could assess taxes on the sale of Bibles and religiously oriented pamphlets and tapes.[9]

Since 1971, the Court has applied a test that it laid out in *Lemon* v. *Kurtzman*. This three-point test attempts to distinguish between laws and public practices that directly encourage religion and those that do so only secondarily. A disputed law or public practice must satisfy all three of the following points:

1. It is secular in purpose.

2. Its primary effect must be neutral with regard to religion.

3. It avoids excessive entanglement of government with religion.[10]

A law or public practice that is found to violate any part of the Lemon tests is rejected by the Court.

Among the measures found compatible with this formula are the following:

- Loans of public-owned textbooks to religiously oriented schools

- Grants of public money to construct buildings in private colleges, so long as the buildings have a secular purpose

- Publicly funded diagnostic and therapeutic services for parochial school students

Among the measures disallowed by the Lemon test are

- State tax credits for tuition payments to religiously oriented schools

- Public funds for salaries of teachers at parochial schools

- Loans of public school teachers to parochial schools to instruct on secular subjects

- Religious instruction in public schools by visiting teachers

Religion, the State, and the Schools   It is obvious that many of the most recent controversies over religious questions have involved schools. This is so because religious fundamentalist individuals and organizations have targeted the schools as forums in which to advance their political agenda. Although a number of issues have been joined in this venue, two major categories are of the greatest importance: curriculum and prayer in public schools.

Ever since the famous *Scopes trial* (sometimes called the *Monkey trial*) in 1925, in which a teacher was convicted of violating a Tennessee law forbidding teaching about the theory of evolution in public schools, the question of teaching in science classes about Charles Darwin's theory of natural selection has been controversial. The issue came to a head again in the 1960s when an Arkansas law proscribed teaching about evolution in its public schools. The law was negated in 1968 in *Epperson v. Arkansas*.[11] A later Arkansas law required science teachers to give equal treatment to both evolution and "creation science" (basically a "scientific" explanation for the Biblical version of the origin of the universe), and a Louisiana law was passed requiring essentially the same thing. Each of these laws was struck down on grounds that they were religiously inspired.[12]

Ever persistent, the religious right tried in the 1980s to have dozens of "godless" textbooks removed from the schools in Tennessee. The books, it was alleged, contained endorsement of "occultism, secular humanism, disobedience to parents, pacifism, and feminism." The offending books included *The Wizard of Oz, Cinderella*, and *The Diary of Anne Frank*. In 1988, the Supreme Court refused to hear an appeal from a lower court that refused to ban the books.[13]

The question of allowing organized prayer in the schools has been even more hotly contested. It is sometimes quipped that as long as there are mathematics exams, there will be prayer in the schools. Indeed, the courts have never actually forbidden prayer so long as it is done privately, at the instigation of the individual and not the state. What the Court has consistently ruled against are efforts by government to encourage religion through organized prayer in the public schools.

The landmark decision on this issue came

in 1962 when the Court struck down a New York state-approved nondenominational prayer that was required of all children. In *Engel* v. *Vitale* the Court ruled that the New York prayer violated the establishment clause by attempting to advance religious worship.[14] This case was quickly followed by a ruling against a Pennsylvania law that required daily Bible readings in public schools.[15]

In the 1980s, the fundamentalist movement, reinforced by a sympathetic president, Ronald Reagan, renewed its effort to reintroduce organized prayer to the public schools. A drive to amend the Constitution to this end failed to secure the necessary two-thirds margin in Congress; on the legal front the effort also met with frustration. In 1983, a Texas law permitting voluntary prayer was struck down,[16] and two years later an Alabama statute allowing a period of silence for "meditation or prayer" met the same end.[17] In 1990, however, the Court held that, as long as religiously oriented clubs were sponsored by students and not by school authorities, they could meet in school facilities and conduct prayer and Bible study sessions.[18] Also, in 1991 the Court agreed to decide whether public schools may include prayers in their graduation ceremonies. Some authorities are concerned that this move may signal the Court's willingness to permit a broader role for religion in the public schools.[19]

The Free Exercise Clause The question of free exercise of religion is, if anything, even more personal than any of the other issues orbiting freedom of religion. In a free society, is one at liberty to believe in what one chooses and to engage in any form of religious practices one wishes? The Court has consistently answered the first part of the question in the affirmative. We are absolutely free to believe in anything we wish.

The answer to the second part of the question is, however, much less incontrovertible. The Court has usually sustained the individual's right to religious practices so long as those activities cause no harm to others and do not affront the fundamental norms of society. For example, in 1943 the Court agreed that Jehovah's Witnesses do not have to salute the flag because such an act forces them to violate their religion's dictate against worshiping false idols.[20] The controversy over the Vietnam War brought up other questions of possible conflict between religious faith and patriotic values; one penetrating question was whether someone had to belong to an established religion in order to be exempt from combat as a conscientious objector. Indeed, the Court ruled in 1965 and again in 1970 that one's personal objection to warfare, even when quite divorced from religious scruples, was adequate to qualify one as a conscientious objector.[21]

At about the same time, the Court honored the religious objections of another minority cult. The Amish are religiously opposed to sending their children to school beyond the eighth grade, and they resisted doing so. Feeling that neither society nor the individuals in this tightly knit community would suffer by honoring such religious scruples, the Court supported the Amish claim in 1972.[22] More recently, in 1989 the Court unanimously sustained a person's right to collect unemployment benefits after refusing on religious grounds to take a job that required him to work on Sunday, even though he belonged to no particular religion.[23]

While these religious practices have been upheld because they were perceived harmless to the individuals involved or to society as a whole, the Court ruled differently when it found that religious practices constituted danger. When Bob Jones University racially discriminated against African-Americans in its student policies, the IRS denied it tax-exempt status. The university sued, claiming that its policies were consistent with its religious beliefs and that the government had no right to interfere. In 1983, however, the Court agreed with the government.[24]

In perhaps a more lamentable opinion, in 1989 the Court refused to restrain the National Forest Service from building a logging road in Northern California even though the land it crosses is considered sacred by the local Indians. Writing the opinion for the majority, Justice Sandra Day O'Connor said, "The First Amendment must apply to all citizens alike, and it can give to none of them a veto over public programs."[25] The next year the Court issued an even more sweeping opinion when it ruled that the Constitution did not protect taking peyote as a religious sacrament. Writing for five of the nine members, Justice Scalia declared that the Court would side with the government whenever religious rights clash with the government's need for uniform rules.[26] These opinions break with a 30-year trend of protecting free exercise of religion against the needs of government and may indeed give pause to the religious fundamentalists who campaigned for a more conservative Court.

In two other recent cases, the United States Supreme Court, by refusing to hear appeals from judgments of state courts, has affirmed that religious practice does not absolve people from personal liability for their actions. In one case the Court required the Unification Church, a sect headed by the Reverend Sun Myung Moon, to participate in a suit in which the plaintiffs were alleging that it used trickery and brainwashing techniques in recruiting membership.[27] In the second case the Court refused to prevent the prosecution of a Christian Science mother on charges of child endangerment and manslaughter. Although her daughter spent 14 days in agony and finally died of bacterial meningitis, Laurie Walker refused to take her child to a physician, resorting only to prayer for the child's cure.[28]

It is clear from these few pages that while freedom of religion in the United States is not absolute it is carefully restrained only in certain circumstances. While the government is not totally prevented from engaging in activities that may in some way benefit religion, it is prohibited from policy that either directly encourages or impedes it. The exercise of religion by individuals or groups remains unencumbered so long as the well-being of society or its individuals is not threatened. Hence, freedom of conscience seems relatively well protected— but what is the status of our ability to express our ideas?

FREEDOM OF EXPRESSION

United States Supreme Court Associate Justice William J. Brennan, Jr., wrote in a 1989 majority opinion,

> If there is a bedrock principle underlying the First Amendment, it is that the government may not prohibit the expression of an idea simply because society finds the idea itself offensive or disagreeable.

This simple but articulate statement speaks volumes about the nature of our democracy. It counsels tolerance and prudence in dealing with expression with which we may not agree. Indeed, an absolute prerequisite of democracy is tolerance for the ideas of others, for only by allowing the uninhibited flow of ideas can a society hope to remain free to find truth.

In the abstract, this proposition may sound reasonable and proper, but unfortunately, our national history is replete with examples of intolerance for unpopular ideas, even though our stated goal has been to achieve the ideal. For example, the **Alien and Sedition Acts** of 1798 made it illegal to publish or utter any "false, scandalous, and malicious" criticism of high government officials. The *Espionage Act of 1918* prohibited criticism of the government's involvement in World War I, and the McCarthy era of the 1950s became infamous for its persecution of people suspected of having Communist sympathies. Even today, foreigners can be refused visas to visit the United States or be deported because their ideas, while not imminently threatening to the security of the country, are unpopular,[29] and United States citizens who write letters to embassies of countries considered antagonistic to our national interests (e.g., the Soviet Union and Bulgaria) may suffer FBI investigations concerning their loyalty to the United States.[30]

Still, freedom of expression is a major goal of our society, and except during times of national hysteria, we have been able to afford ourselves an admirable degree of latitude regarding what we may say, publish, and broadcast. To learn the parameters of permissible expression, we shall consider each of these forums of free expression in their turn.

FREE SPEECH

Until 1919, the Court determined the limits of permissible speech by applying the **bad tendency doctrine**. This imprecise formula leaves it to the legislature to determine what kinds of statements may lead to illegal acts and can therefore be prohibited. Clearly, such a prescription leaves free speech not only to the whim of public opinion as expressed in legislation but also to the notion that a vaguely defined category of speech *may* lead to violation of the law and thus can be forbidden.

In 1919, the Supreme Court moved to give itself the authority to set the parameters of free speech and eventually to expand them beyond the narrow confines of the bad tendency doctrine. In *Schenck* v. *United States* the Court upheld the conviction of a member of the American Socialist Party who distributed literature encouraging young men to resist the draft during World War I; in doing so, it laid down the **clear and present danger doctrine**. This test holds that speech is permissible so long as it does not threaten imminent "substantive evils that Congress had the right to prevent. It is a question of proximity and degree." Justice

Oliver Wendell Holmes, who wrote the opinion, went on to give his famous analogy that "the most stringent protection of free speech would not protect a man in falsely shouting fire in a theater and causing a panic."[31] The ultimate point at issue between these two approaches is whether the state must be directly and unequivocally imperiled by someone's comments in order to stifle them, or whether it must justify state censorship by demonstrating someone's tendency to do civic harm. Although the bad tendency doctrine in 1919 was not immediately abandoned by all justices, the persuasiveness of Holmes's logic eventually prevailed. In the meantime, the Court brought state law under the restrictions of the First Amendment with *Gitlow* v. *New York* (1925).

During the 1950s McCarthy era, freedom of speech was briefly curtailed once again. The Alien Registration Act (the Smith Act), passed by Congress in 1940, forbade either advocating the forceful overthrow of the government or membership in an organization that advocated forceful overthrow, and the Supreme Court sustained convictions under the statute of a group of Communist Party members, even though it recognized that no clear and present danger to the society was threatened.[32] Fortunately, six years later the Court set aside 14 similar convictions of violating the Smith Act, claiming that a distinction must be made between the advocacy of an abstract idea that may prompt an unlawful act and active support for such an action being taken.[33]

The Court has not been so generous, however, with aliens. The *McCarran-Walter Act*, another product of the McCarthy era, is still on the books and is being used to "shield" the United States from unpopular ideas. Under its provisions, people with unpopular political views are regularly denied visitor's visas to enter the country, and, beginning with the Reagan Administration, the government has sought to deport legal aliens whose political views it finds offensive. Although in 1989 a United States

District judge blocked government attempts to deport some aliens by declaring portions of the McCarran-Walter Act unconstitutional, the Supreme Court has yet to rule on the law.[34] Congress also limited some of the McCarran-Walter Act provisions in 1990.

There are, of course, other restrictions to free speech beyond political objections. One is not free to berate or castigate another in such a way as to provoke a fight. When deliberately used to incite violence, such "fighting words" are placed beyond the pale of permissible speech by the Court.[35] This prohibition has usually been most strongly supported by liberals, but today the situation seems to be changing. For example, in an effort to combat growing tensions among students on college campuses, some 200 colleges and universities have adopted codes of conduct proscribing utterances on race, sex, religion, national origin, and sexual preference that might offend some students. Ironically, these new "speech codes" are supported by many liberal professors and students, while being opposed by conservatives. The Court has traditionally been very guarded about prohibiting speech—even fighting words—and it will be interesting to learn how it will rule on these new speech codes. The American Civil Liberties Union (ACLU) has come out against them and it will almost certainly challenge them in court.[36] The Supreme Court itself seemed to support limitations of free speech in 1991 when it sustained Reagan/Bush administrative regulations forbidding employees of federally funded family planning clinics from telling poor, pregnant women that abortion is an option for them.[37] This decision also appears to create a conflict between the law and medical ethics.

Freedom of speech, as it turns out, is not equally applied to all people in the society. There are certain forums in which the usual rules of free speech do not apply because of the nature of the environment. For example, military personnel can be limited in the exercise of free speech, as can prisoners in a penitentiary. But perhaps most pertinent, the Court has recently ruled that students in elementary and secondary schools may also be denied complete free exercise of speech. In *Widmar* v. *Vincent* (1981), the expulsion of a boy who, on school premises, made a speech that included sexual innuendo was upheld. In this decision the Court stated clearly that school authorities have the right to limit student speech to a greater degree than speech can be curtailed elsewhere.[38]

Yet, school authorities are not unlimited in their ability to regulate student speech. In *Tinker* v. *Des Moines Independent Community School District* (1969), the Court refused to sustain the suspension of several students who, in violation of school policy, wore black armbands to school in protest of the Vietnam War. The gesture, the Court found, was completely in keeping with the students' right to make political comment by *symbolic speech*.[39]

The extent of our right to exercise symbolic speech seems recently to have been expanded to a point approximating verbal speech. The flag, the most cherished symbol of the nation, has often been used to register symbolic political protest, and over the past 15 years the Court has sustained acts regarding the flag that are viewed as "desecration" by others. In 1974, it overturned a conviction of the Massachusetts courts of a man who had worn a flag patch on the seat of his pants.[40] And somewhat surprisingly, the increasingly conservative Rehnquist Court (although the Chief Justice did not support the decision) twice sustained burning the flag as a permissible political statement. When a Texas law prohibiting defacing the flag was struck down in 1989,[41] pressure built to make defacing the flag unconstitutional. Although President Bush pushed hard for an amendment, the Democrats in Congress parried by passing a statute protecting the flag, but this law too was voided by the Court as an unlawful restriction of free expression.[42]

FREEDOM OF THE PRESS

The Court is equally solicitous of freedom of the press, since it too is closely associated with the democratic process. The Court is perhaps most careful about *prior restraint* (i.e., censoring the printed word). In 1931, the Supreme Court established precedent forbidding prior restraint in most cases, ruling that newspapers could be closed down by the government only when what they publish may jeopardize national security.[43] If the publisher is guilty of deliberate untruth or malicious defamation of character, the injured party can pursue restitution in the civil courts afterward, but it would be dangerous for the government to decide what could and could not be published before the fact.

The issue was joined again when the government tried to prevent *The New York Times* and *The Washington Post* from publishing secret documents related to the Vietnam War. Daniel Ellsberg, an employee of the Pentagon, had given the newspapers stolen classified documents that he believed would expose gross government irregularities regarding the war in Indochina. The majority of the Court agreed that there could be circumstances under which the government could legally prevent the publication of classified documents, but that in this case the government had failed to persuade the Court that the national security was at imminent risk. The stolen **Pentagon Papers** were published.[44] The Supreme Court in 1980 did condone censorship, however, in a case of a CIA agent, Frank Snepp, writing a book on Vietnam. Because at the time of his employment Snepp had signed a document pledging to maintain confidence about his activities, the Court sustained the government's case.[45]

Just as with speech, however, freedom of the press is considerably less broad for students below the college level. A Hazelwood, Missouri, high school newspaper, expecting to publish an article on teenage sexuality, pregnancy, and divorce, suddenly found itself censored by the school principal who claimed that the article was "inappropriate and unsuitable" for teenaged readers. In an opinion very similar to that in the Widmar case, Justice Byron White wrote for the majority, "A school need not tolerate student speech that is inconsistent with its basic educational mission, even though the government could not censor similar speech outside the school."[46] There are signs, however, that the conservative Rehnquist Court is prepared to limit free expression for adult citizens more severely than past Supreme Courts have. Until late 1990, the Court had never formally upheld a lower court order barring the publication or broadcast of news and information. In November of 1990, however, in a 7-2 opinion, the Court ruled that Cable News Network (CNN) could be prevented from broadcasting tapes of government-recorded conversations between deposed Panamanian strongman Manuel A. Noriega and his attorneys.[47] In light of other conservative actions by the Court, civil libertarians worry that the Court may continue to reduce the right of free expression. With these major exceptions, however, the Court so far remains reluctant to allow prior restraint.

Responsibility of the Press To say that the press is given broad freedom is not, however, to suggest that it has no responsibility for what it publishes. For example, the Court has consistently upheld rulings requiring reporters and newspapers to surrender to authorities their information about crimes. In the most celebrated recent case, *Zurcher* v. *Stanford Daily* (1978), the Court even sustained a police search of the offices of the Stanford University student newspaper.

Libel is another area in which the press can

be held accountable for its publications. If the press maliciously defames an individual or deliberately prints mistruths, it can be sued for damages. But here again, the Court has been very careful to give the broadest possible protection to the press, and it gives much less consideration to public officials than it extends to private citizens. In *New York Times* v. *Sullivan*, the Court ruled that, in the interest of free political expression, public officials could not win a libel judgment against the press unless they proved that the offending statements not only were false but were printed with the knowledge that they were false and with the intent to do injury.[49] Only three years later the Court extended this stricture to all "public figures."[50] This should explain how "rags" such as *The National Enquirer* get away with the things they print.

More recently, the Court even added to the protection of the press. In its November 1983 issue, *Hustler* magazine published a full-page cartoon poking tasteless fun at Rev. Jerry Falwell, who was at the time the leader of the Moral Majority. The satirical attack pictured Falwell saying that his first sexual experience was with his mother in an outhouse. In the resulting decision, *Hustler Magazine Inc.* v. *Falwell*, a unanimous Court ruled that victims of satire, even when it is pornographic and "outrageous," could not win a libel judgment. Writing for the Court, Chief Justice Rehnquist said, "Were we to hold otherwise, there can be little doubt that political cartoonists and satirists would be subject to damage awards without any showing that their work falsely defamed its subject."[51]

In an even more recent instance, the Court struck down a judgment brought against a newspaper for publishing statements that, while true, were forbidden by state law. Florida law prohibits publishing the names of rape victims. The police mistakenly gave the name of a rape victim to a newspaper, and the paper printed it. The question at issue was whether the law could prohibit publication of information legally obtained, and the Supreme Court ruled that it could not do so.[52] Similarly, in 1991 a woman accused a nephew of Senator Ted Kennedy of raping her at a Kennedy family vacation home in Florida. In apparent violation of law and tradition, *The New York Times* and NBC News published the woman's name. What view the courts will take about this action remains to be seen. More clear, but no less unsettling, is a 1990 case in which the Supreme Court held that writers or speakers may be sued for statements expressed as opinion. This ruling negates the oft-used defense against libel charges that people are exempt from court judgments if they express opinions rather than facts. Some authorities fear that this judgment may have a chilling effect on critics, commentators, columnists, cartoonists, and people who write letters to the editor.[53]

Obscenity   Although the Court has never hesitated banning obscenity and pornography, it has had an extraordinarily difficult time defining exactly what kind of literature or films are sufficiently vile to be properly considered obscene. The landmark case on the subject, *Roth* v. *United States*, was decided in 1957. In this ruling, Justice Brennan laid down the first formula for determining whether something is obscene. Essentially he said that a production is obscene if "the average person, applying contemporary community standards," finds the material appealing to the "prurient" (lustful) interests.[54] Rather than settling the matter, however, the Court soon found itself deluged with cases on the question. Brennan's formula was far from objective in that it relied upon "the average person" and "community standards." After hearing several cases, Justice Potter Steward frustratedly quipped that he may not be able to define pornography, but "I know it when I see it."

By 1973, after seeing such material as Tar-

An *adult theater*.

zan books and *Lady Chatterly's Lover* banned as obscene in certain communities, the Court was prepared to lay down a more precise test. In *Miller* v. *California* a three-point measure was introduced. A work could be regulated by the government if it met the following criteria:

- Taken as a whole, it appeals to the prurient interests.
- It portrays sexual conduct in a patently offensive way.
- It lacks serious literary, artistic, political, or scientific value.[55]

Unfortunately, the Miller test has done little to clarify matters, as cases continue to come to the Court. It is clear, however, that the Court is willing to allow different standards to apply in different parts of the country because Miller also relies on "the average person, applying community standards." Hence, it is quite possible to prosecute someone for showing a film in one community that is well within the law elsewhere.

Still, the Court is unwilling to allow full reign to local communities, and it has acted several times to reverse unacceptable censorship. It objected to a Georgia community's refusal to allow the showing of the film *Carnal Knowledge* on grounds that it showed "a woman with a bare midriff,"[56] it set aside a New Jersey city's effort to censor topless dancing by manipulating its zoning laws,[57] and it prevented Los Angeles prosecutors from bringing criminal charges against merchants for selling X-rated films.[58] The Court also has recently overturned a 1989 federal law that banned dial-a-porn sales because it forbade all "incident" messages rather than only *obscene* ones.[59] On the other hand, the Court recently sustained a new approach to the problem. Responding to a call by then Attorney General Edwin Meese III's Commission on Pornography for a new crackdown on obscenity, the authorities have successfully prosecuted on antiracketeering charges bookstore owners who sell pornography.[60] Also, in 1990, the Rehnquist Court sustained a state law forbidding possession of child pornography, even though it was kept out of public view in a private home.[61]

Free artistic expression when funded by the federal government was severely reduced by Congress in 1989, although cases challenging it have not yet reached the Supreme Court. Responding to conservative objections that funds from the National Endowment of the Arts (NEA) was used to support art depicting sexual acts and other scenes considered by some to be obscene, Congress passed a prohibition on NEA funds for works "that may be considered obscene." The restrictions had a chilling affect on the art community, two dozen grants were rejected, artists were forced to sign a pledge not to display obscenity with funds from the NEA, and several lawsuits were joined challenging the law. Despite efforts to the contrary by Senator Jesse Helms and conservative groups, Congress rescinded the most objectionable clauses in 1990, after a public outcry about the limitations on free artistic expression.[62]

FREE EXPRESSION
IN THE ELECTRONIC MEDIA

The law is quite different as it pertains to the electronic media. The Federal Communications Commission (FCC) regulates radio and television transmissions, and it imposes stricter guidelines on the electronic media than are enforced on the press. The reason for this difference is that there are a limited number of bands over which to broadcast, so theoretically, those who are allowed to use the frequencies would have a monopoly on what could be said on them. This argument is subject to serious controversy since there are now far more radio stations in the country than newspapers, and with the introduction of satellite dishes and cable television, some critics question this exclusivity argument.

In any event, the FCC continues to impose limitations upon those in its purview. In the 1970s a New York radio station broadcast in the afternoon a recording by comedian George Carlin that featured "seven dirty words." The FCC disciplined the radio station and the controversy ultimately reached the Supreme Court, which sustained the FCC's right to keep offensive words off the air. Later, however, the FCC decided to allow such language in the late evening hours when children were unlikely to be tuned in. Currently, the most important limitation imposed is the *equal time* rule, which requires stations to allow all political candidates equal time on their broadcasts. The **fairness doctrine**, by which the FCC required broadcasters to give exposure to all sides of a particular issue, was recently abandoned by the FCC. In 1987, the FCC eliminated the fairness stipulation, claiming that it unnecessarily limited the First Amendment rights of the electronic media.[63]

Freedom is a complicated matter because the interests of the individual and those of society must be balanced. Generally speaking, we in the United States enjoy a remarkable degree of latitude. We can usually think what we like, read what we choose, and write what we wish. The law and its interpreter, the courts, protect us from undue interference in our political and legal endeavors. But they also protect those of us who find ourselves accused of violating the norms of society.

The Rights of the Accused

Anyone living in the United States must be impressed with the amount of crime with which it is afflicted. The crime rate is increasing by leaps and bounds. Between 1960 and 1985, violent crimes—including murder, forcible rape, robbery, and aggravated assault—rose by 290 percent, while crime against property—including burglary, larceny, and vehicle theft—rose by 372 percent. At the same time, the number of federal prisoners has more than doubled, while the number of state prisoners leaped by better than 300 percent.[64] Even more striking, ethnic minorities are most often the victims of crime and they are also most often the convicted perpetrators of crime. Recent studies by the Justice Department reveal that African-Americans are 29 percent more likely than whites to be victims of violent crime and an astounding 478 percent more likely to be murdered.[65] Furthermore, while 6 percent of all white males in their twenties are in jail, prison, or on parole, the figure is 25 percent for African-American youths.[66]

Undoubtedly the criminal justice system is a major institution in our society, and a large part of the Bill of Rights (specifically Amendments 4–8) is devoted to the rights of those who are accused of crimes. The Fifth Amendment requires that no one be denied life, liberty, or property without due process. There are actually two concepts of due process. *Substantive due process* holds the legislature to passing law that is fair. *Procedural due process*, on the other hand, requires that the executive and judicial branches apply the law correctly. Generally this means that searches and seizures, arrests, interrogations, trials, and punishments must conform to the Constitution as it is interpreted by the courts. However, these matters are complicated and subject to controversy, so a close examination of them is warranted here.

SEARCH AND SEIZURE

The Fourth Amendment governs search and seizure, and reads as follows:

> **The right of people to be secure in their persons, houses, papers, and effects, against *unreasonable searches and seizures,* shall not be violated, and no *Warrant* shall issue, but upon *probable cause,* supported by oath or affirmation, and particularly *describing the place to be searched* and the *persons or things to be seized.* [Emphasis added]**

Generally speaking, the Supreme Court has read this amendment to mean that unless one voluntarily gives the authorities permission for a search, one may be searched in only two very specific circumstances: (1) when a search warrant has been issued specifying what is being sought and where the search will occur, and (2) after an arrest.

As might be supposed, however, there are numerous qualifications and exceptions to these general principles. The most important protection against unlawful search and seizure is the **exlusionary rule** established by *Mapp* v. *Ohio* (1961). In this case, the Cleveland, Ohio, police entered the Mapp residence looking for a fugitive. The warrantless search produced pornographic material, and the unexpected evidence was used to prosecute and convict Mapp of violating an Ohio law against possession of pornography. The Supreme Court threw out the conviction, arguing that illegally obtained evidence cannot be used against a defendant. In other words, the Court insists that the law enforcers must also abide by the law.[67]

While this landmark case limited the police in search procedures, it has also begged a number of challenges in which the Court has gradually refined its mandate. In fact, the Supreme Court has significantly narrowed the parameters of the exclusionary rule since it was established. For example, the Court has allowed police, without a warrant, to stop and frisk suspects on the street if the police reasonably suspect them to be armed or dangerous.[68] It has allowed grand juries to question witnesses about illegally obtained evidence[69] and permitted illegally obtained evidence to be used to impeach defendants' testimony.[70] Furthermore the Court has allowed to be admitted evidence that might otherwise be considered illegally obtained, if it is taken as a result of police efforts to protect public safety,[71] and the Court has accepted evidence taken without a warrant from trash cans outside private homes.[72] The Court has also allowed illegally obtained evidence to be used if it can be shown that the evidence would "inevitably" have been discovered by a legal search,[73] if it has been obtained by an illegal search warrant which police believe to be valid,[74] or if it has been taken illegally but by an "honest mistake" by the police.[75]

Until 1967, the Court did not regulate electronic eavesdropping. But as technology made telephone tapping and long-distance listening easier, the Court finally held against electronic surveillance by the police unless they had a warrant.[76] The Rehnquist Court, however, recently let stand a lower court ruling that government agents may eavesdrop without a warrant on calls made from cordless telephones.[77]

The automobile receives less protection from warrantless searches than does the home or the telephone. The police may search any part of a car and any contents within it if they believe they have probable cause to suspect that evidence of a crime may be found.[78] Moreover, the Court decided that the same rules for searching automobiles apply to searching mobile homes.[79]

The growing concern about drug abuse, together with the emergence of an increasingly conservative Supreme Court, has led to broader interpretations about what constitutes lawful search and seizure where narcotics are involved, giving the police greater latitude in their investigations. The police can, without a warrant, enter a field where they can see marijuana growing.[80] Urine testing of employees entrusted with the public safety or of those who work with sensitive information may be required at the discretion of employers. These tests can be required of railway workers[81] and U.S. Customs Service employees,[82] and perhaps the rulings will also be applied to a myriad of other workers. Furthermore, authorities who have "reasonable suspicion" that travelers are carrying illegal drugs may search their luggage. Traveling between Honolulu and Miami, Andrew Sokolow fit the profile of a drug runner, catching the attention of the police. He was stopped and searched and was discovered to be carrying a large amount of cocaine in his bag. By approving of this detention and search, the Court went further than it had previously gone in upholding a search based on evidence that is not in itself criminal.[83]

As with several other kinds of liberties, schoolchildren enjoy fewer protections against being searched than do other people. In *New Jersey* v. *T.L.O.*, a high school student's purse was searched for cigarettes by school officials. The investigation revealed that the student was carrying marijuana as well as cigarettes. The Court ruled that school authorities need only "reasonable grounds" (less than probable cause) that school rules are being violated to search a student and the student's possessions on school property.[84] The Court has also ruled that juveniles can be questioned by police on less stringent grounds than would be necessary to interrogate adults.[85]

ARREST

A legal "bust" can occur in only a limited set of circumstances. Normally an arrest warrant must be issued before one can be taken into custody. But the police may also arrest a person during the commission of a crime or when they have probable cause to believe a suspect has committed a crime.[86] Beyond these guidelines, the Court has prohibited the police from making a routine arrest in a private home without a warrant.[87]

Once arrested, the suspect has certain rights. *Miranda* v. *Arizona* (1966) established that people do not enjoy their rights when they are denied them due to ignorance. Hence, the authorities must inform suspects, before interrogation occurs, that they have the right to remain silent, that any statement they make may be used in evidence against them, that they have the right to have an attorney present during interrogation, and that the state will provide an attorney if they cannot afford one. This *Miranda warning* must be read to any suspect before interrogation begins. Even if suspects waive their Miranda rights, interrogation must stop at any point that the suspect requests that an attorney be present.[88] This ruling is based on the self-incrimination clause of the Fifth Amendment: "No person . . . shall be compelled in any criminal case to be a witness against himself."

Since the Miranda decision, the Court has further modified the rules of interrogation, strengthening the original mandate in some cases but weakening it in others. In strengthening the rules, the Court has held that testimony by suspects that contradicted statements given immediately following their receiving the Miranda warning could be admitted in court,[89] that once a suspect requests counsel the police may not continue interrogation,[90] that statements obtained from suspects after the Miranda warning could not be admitted if they were obtained when no grounds for the arrest existed in the first place,[91] and that suspects have the right to an attorney being present during a psychiatric examination.[92]

The Court has weakened the Miranda protection in cases where it decided that statements made by a suspect before receiving the Miranda warning can be used to contradict the defendant's testimony given during a trial;[93] that a complete Miranda warning is not necessary in all cases;[94] that statements voluntarily made after a suspect has asked for an attorney, but before the lawyer arrives, can be admitted;[95] that when the public safety is imminently threatened, police may legally question suspects before informing them of their rights;[96] that videotapes of drunk drivers giving slurred answers to routine questions before the Miranda warning is given can be used as evidence in court;[97] and that police do not violate the Miranda rule if, at the time of arrest, they tell suspects that a lawyer will not be provided at public expense until they go to trial.[98]

Closely related to the Miranda doctrine is the question of whether a coerced confession can be used in evidence against a criminal defendant. For 94 years the Supreme Court held that any case in which a confession had been coerced by the authorities violated the Fifth Amendment rejoinder against self-incrimination. Such confessions were routinely thrown out of court and new trials were required. However, in 1991 the conservative majority on the Court ruled that a coerced confession may be introduced in evidence when other evidence independent of the confession fully supports conviction.[99] Supporters of this unprecedented opinion argue that it is foolish to throw out the conviction of an obviously guilty suspect just because the Court finds that the confession was coerced, while opponents of the opinion fear that the Court has issued an open invitation to the police to brutalize suspects in hopes of inducing them to confess. Ironically, the Court's opinion was announced within a week of Los Angeles police personnel being videotaped while savagely beating an African-American man they had stopped for speeding.

THE RIGHT TO AN ATTORNEY

The Sixth Amendment says: "In all criminal prosecutions the accused shall . . . have the assistance of Counsel for his defense." This provision was always read to guarantee that defendants could be represented by an attorney in criminal cases as long as they could afford to retain counsel. But what if one lacked the money to hire a defense attorney? Although since 1938 the Court had required the federal government to provide indigents with defense attorneys,[100] until 1963 it refused to compel the states to provide an attorney for indigent defendants. Finally, in *Gideon* v. *Wainwright* (1963) the Court, in effect, ruled that poverty was no reason in itself to go to jail.[101]

Clarence Earl Gideon, an itinerant, was arrested and charged with burgling a pool hall in Florida. Having only pocket change, he was forced to defend himself against a seasoned prosecutor. The result was predictable: Gideon was convicted and sentenced to five years in prison.

Although ignorant of the intricacies of the law, Gideon remained resolute that the Constitution guaranteed all people a fair trial, and he was equally adamant that he had not received one under the circumstances. After doing research in the prison library, he filed a "paupers' petition" with the Supreme Court, asking that the circumstances of his trial and conviction be reviewed. In the resulting case the Court ruled that the states must provide an attorney to all defendants who are accused of serious crimes and who cannot afford counsel.[102] In a case subsequent to this momentous decision, the Court went further, requiring that no person who had not waived the right to an attorney could be sentenced to prison unless represented by counsel.[103] Such protection, however, does not apply to persons on death row. Expressing impatience with the protracted process of appeals from the death sentence, the Rehnquist Court ruled 5 to 4 in 1989 that the states are not obliged to provide indigent death row inmates with attorneys to challenge convictions after the first appeal.[104] Furthermore, in 1991 the Court issued an order stating that it would no longer routinely accept "paupers' petitions," whose numbers—because of the growing size of the prison population—have sharply increased. In the future, the Supreme Court's law clerks will determine which paupers' petitions are "frivolous or malicious" and thus will not be reviewed by the justices.[105]

THE RIGHT TO A SPEEDY, IMPARTIAL TRIAL

Many factors obtain to the concept of a fair trial. Some of our most cherished rights are not found in explicit terms in the Constitution. Instead, they are incumbent in the traditions of the common law. The presumption of innocence, a jury of 12 citizens, and a unanimous verdict are all found in the common law. Even so, however, the Supreme Court has allowed states to use juries with less than a dozen persons, and it has sanctioned state judicial procedures allowing less than unanimity for conviction in criminal cases. Verdicts brought

by two-thirds of a jury have long been honored in civil cases as well.

The Fifth Amendment prohibits a second prosecution for a count on which the accused has been legally acquitted. This protection against **double jeopardy** does not prevent a retrial if the original jury cannot agree on innocence or guilt, of course.

Additionally, the Sixth Amendment requires that people accused of criminal violations receive speedy, public trials by impartial juries. Further, it requires that the trial be held in the venue where the crime occurred, that the accused be informed of the nature of the charges, that the accused be confronted with the witnesses against her or him, and that the accused be empowered to compel attendance at a trial of witnesses for the defense. Each of these mandates, except the one regarding venue, has also been imposed upon the states. Interestingly enough, only the provisions requiring a public trial and the right to know the nature of the charges of which one is accused were imposed upon the states before the 1960s. Among the many accomplishments of the Earl Warren Court, which sat during the 1950s and 1960s, were its efforts to assure defendants in state courts the same guarantees of a fair trial that the Bill of Rights imposes on federal courts.[106]

The Eighth Amendment assures defendants of a reasonable bail and prohibits excessive fines or cruel and unusual punishment. This provision, together with the Fifth Amendment's prohibition against denying people life, liberty, or property without due process, was generally understood to guarantee most people the right to be released on bail until the event of their conviction. However, in *United States v. Salerno* in 1987, the Supreme Court voted 6 to 3 that the right to reasonably priced bail does not guarantee the right to bail itself. In so voting, the Court upheld the *Federal Bail Reform Act* of 1984, which allows "preventive detention" of people who judges believe may be a threat to society. Although states have often denied bail to murder suspects and federal law allows judges to deny bail if a defendant is considered likely to flee prosecution or threaten a witness, the Court has never before upheld such a sweeping power to deny bail. Answering critics who contend that preventive detention punishes defendants without due process, Rehnquist wrote in the majority opinion, "The mere fact that a person is detained does not inexorably lead to the conclusion that the government has imposed punishment."[107] Between 1984, when the Bail Reform Act was passed, and May of 1987, over 2500 persons were denied bail by provisions of this law.[108] At the same time, the Court ruled that federal judges should take into account the safety of the community before releasing convicts who have appealed and won new trials. In an opinion that some critics charge is a violation of the principle of presumption of innocence, the Court voted 6 to 3 that convicts are not necessarily entitled to be free while a new trial is pending.[109]

Our judicial tradition prohibits torture, and it is usually agreed that justice demands that the penalty fit the crime. The most controversial issue relative to cruel and unusual punishment is the death penalty. Some people contend that the death penalty is barbaric and unnecessary, while others believe it is racially discriminatory, and still others argue that people who commit murder while they are minors should not be put to death. Some of those who favor the death penalty argue that some crimes are so heinous that their perpetrators deserve to forfeit their lives. Other supporters believe that the death penalty deters crime. If nothing else, they submit, at least executed persons will never again commit a crime. Opponents object on grounds that there is no conclusive evidence that the death penalty prevents heinous crime. Furthermore, they remind us that the death penalty is the only sentence that, once com-

pleted, cannot be undone. Hence, if an innocent person is executed, an irreparable injustice is done. Finally, they argue that given modern technology, many ways exist to protect society from egregious felons short of killing them.

The Supreme Court has been steadfast in its opinion that the death penalty is not cruel and unusual punishment and that it is therefore constitutional.[110] It has insisted, however, that the death penalty cannot be meted out capriciously; the penalty cannot intentially discriminate against minorities or the poor,* and juries must be given explicit instructions about the application of the death penalty before their deliberations.[111] Moreover, the Court ruled in 1977 that the death penalty can be exacted only in cases of murder or attempted murder.[112] Frustrated with the number and endurance of appeals from the death penalty, Chief Justice William H. Rehnquist not only presided over an opinion denying indigent death row inmates publicly paid appeals attorneys, but he presided over a 6 to 3 decision holding that prisoners who have failed in one habeas corpus appeal may not be granted another, unless they can give evidence of "a fundamental miscarriage of justice."[113] Thus the Court denied a second appeal to Warren Mc-

---

* Even so, statistics from state courts indicate that a much larger percentage of African-Americans are condemned to death for their crimes than the percentage of whites, and one is far more likely to get the death penalty for killing a white person than for killing an African-American. By February of 1991 there were 2,412 inmates on death row. Moreover, a 1991 study by Sentencing Project, a nonprofit organization, indicates that the United States incarcerates African-American males at four times the rate that black males are imprisoned in South Africa, and in the last decade, it has surpassed even the Soviet Union in the percentage of people sent to prison. Between 1973 and 1991, 143 persons were executed in the United States.

Cleskey, even though he was able to show that Georgia prosecutors falsely denied at McCleskey's 1978 trial for murder that they had worked with an informant who later testified against McCleskey. Incredulous at the decision, McCleskey's attorney, who requested the second appeal after discovering documents proving that the Georgia officials had lied about their involvement with the informer, said, "They are now saying it is our fault for having believed the state."[114]

Of the 37 states that currently employ the death penalty, 27 allow the execution of minors, and Indiana provides that people as young as 10 years old may be put to death. Partially settling the controversy of executing minors, at least for the time being, in 1989 the Court upheld the death penalty for a person who was 16 years old at the time of the crime.[115] Currently there are 30 people on death row who committed murder while they were under 18 years of age. The Court's decision clears the way for the United States to join only four other countries that, since 1979, have executed people who committed capital offenses under the age of 18 (the other countries are Pakistan, Bangladesh, Rwanda, and Barbados).[116]

The Civil Rights

Having studied our individual freedoms, or civil liberties, we now turn to an examination of our rights to equal treatment in society—our **civil rights**. Before going further, however, we should recognize the basic incompatibility of complete individual freedom and equality. That is to say, given the differences in individual material well-being, strength, talent, luck, intellect, and so on, it is patently impossible to allow individual liberty full reign and to enjoy an equal society at the same time. Conversely, to the extent that we insist on people's being treated and rewarded equally in society, we must deny a measure of individual liberty. The contradiction implicit in these two worthy goals involves us in a complicated balancing act in which we try to allow as much latitude to individual conduct as possible, while trying to ensure that no one is denied the basic human rights to which we are committed as a people.

While the authors of the Constitution were most concerned with advancing the cause of individual liberties, during this century equality had also become an important goal. The struggle to enhance the civil rights has been difficult and painful, and while we certainly have not yet reached our objective, few other societies have faced such a wrenching issue so squarely or publicly as have the American people.

AFRICAN-AMERICANS

While the concept of equality appears prominently in Jefferson's Declaration of Independence, it is not to be found in the original Constitution or even in the Bill of Rights. When these documents were adopted (the late eighteenth century), the overriding goal of our society was freedom from government oppression, or at least freedom for those fortunate enough to find themselves included in the number then thought deserving of it—principally white males. Women and Indians were, for the moment, only partially included in the privileged group at best, and many people, the slaves in particular, were wholly excluded. Hence, it is difficult to deny the basic truth of former Supreme Court Justice Thurgood Marshall—the Court's first and only African-American—who, reflecting on the long struggle for civil rights, said that the original government was "defective from the start" and required "two turbulent centuries" to set it right.[117]

As the social development of the country

proceeded, however, Jefferson's noble affirmation of human equality haunted the country. The grossest inequity in the land, slavery, became increasingly embarrassing to many, and finally, following the Civil War, three amendments (the Thirteenth, Fourteenth, and Fifteenth) were adopted largely to erase this wretched blight.

Section 1 of the Fourteenth Amendment ends with the enjoinder that no state shall "deny to any person within its jurisdiction the equal protection of the law." This phrase, adopted some 79 years after the Constitution became effective, marked the first and only specific mention of equality in the national charter. And although it was originally intended to address the condition of the former slaves, perhaps no other part of the Constitution has done as much to liberate from the fetters of injustices so many people in our society. The broad application of the equal protection clause, however, was not immediately forthcoming. Many years were to pass before the society was ready to confront the full implications of equality. Indeed, while slavery was eliminated after the Civil War, a new kind of injustice infected the land, and has not yet been altogether vanquished.

Racism in America Following the Civil War, Northern troops occupied the South and enforced the Civil War Amendments, which abolished slavery and mandated that African-Americans would be allowed to vote and would be treated as equal citizens. Congress followed these amendments with the **Civil Rights Acts of 1866 and 1875**, which gave the federal government regulatory power over the states' treatment of African-Americans and prohibited racial discrimination in situations of public accommodation, such as businesses open to the public and public transportation. Additionally, former slaves were elected to serve in the state governments. Unfortunately the bitterness among Southern whites over the war was exacerbated by the "foreign" occupation and the pro-African-American policies.

In 1877 these *reconstruction* policies ended. The Northern troops were brought home; the passion for aiding the former slaves abated, and the North focused its attention on expanding the industrial base it had created during the war. Southern resentment of the reconstruction combined with Northern complacency about social questions and a conservative Supreme Court set the stage for the introduction of the **Jim Crow laws** and the emergence of *segregation.*

In 1883 the Supreme Court ruled the 1875 Civil Rights Act unconstitutional. It argued that Congress had no right to forbid racial discrimination in private businesses since the Fourteenth Amendment addressed only the conduct of state governments and not that of private citizens.[118] This fateful decision was taken as a signal by many in the country that the federal government was relaxing its vigilance of racial discrimination, and there followed a number of practices and laws that relegated African-Americans to the status of second-class—or perhaps third-class—citizens. State laws were enacted that bound debtors (whites as well as African-Americans) to the land until they paid what they owed the landowner, making the poor farmers virtual serfs and condemning many African-Americans to perpetual economic dependence and squalor. At the same time, devices to deny the vote to African-Americans were employed throughout the South. *Literacy tests,* unfairly applied, were used; **poll taxes** kept the poor from voting; the infamous **grandfather clause** was invoked, which exempted anyone whose grandfather was eligible to vote in 1866 from the legal impediments to voting; and Texas conjured the **white primary**, which allowed only whites to vote in the Democratic primaries. Since, at that time, a Republican had little hope of winning an election in Texas, the Democratic candidate

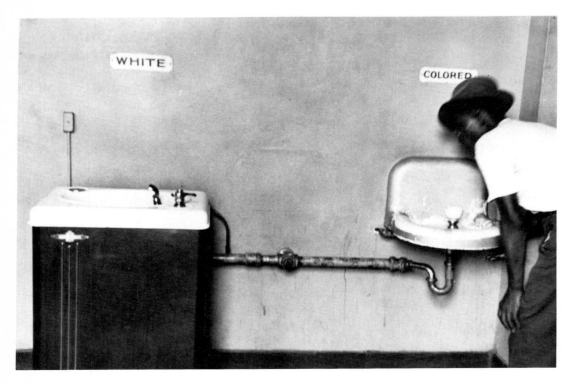

The way things used to be.

was assured success, and the white primary saw to it that African-Americans would play no part in selecting Democratic candidates.

Nonetheless, economic and political disenfranchisement was not enough to satisfy the race supremacists. As reconstruction ended, the white majority in the South began to construct the precursor to South Africa's present policy of **apartheid**, known in this country as segregation. Unwilling to associate with the African-American underclass more than was absolutely necessary, the segregationists passed laws forbidding interracial neighborhoods, hotels, apartments, hospitals, schools, cemeteries, restrooms, drinking fountains, restaurants, telephone booths, and elevators. In facilities that practicality demanded the races share, such as trains and buses, African-Ameri-

cans were required to sit in the back and to give up their seats should white persons be otherwise forced to stand.

Finally, in 1896, the legality of segregation was challenged before the Supreme Court. An African-American, Homer A. Plessy, took a seat on a railroad car reserved for whites only. After refusing to move, he was arrested, tried, and convicted of violating Louisiana's segregation law. The Supreme Court ruled in *Plessy* v. *Ferguson* (1896), that separate facilities for the races were allowable under the Constitution, provided that the facilities were equal. Hence, the *separate but equal doctrine* anointed segregation with legal respectability. The decision, however, was not unanimous. Recognizing the fraud that facilities for African-Americans were equal to those provided to whites, and denying the constitutionality of forced separation of the races in any case, Justice John Marshall Harlan, Sr.—himself a former slave owner—wrote a phophetic dissent:

> The white race deems itself to be the dominant race in this country. . . . But in view of the Constitution, in the eyes of the law, there is in this country no superior, dominant, ruling class of citizens. There is no caste here. *Our Constitution is colorblind,* and neither knows nor tolerates classes among citizens. In respect of civil rights, all citizens are equal before the law. The humblest is the peer of the most powerful. . . . In my opinion, the judgment this day rendered will, in time, prove to be quite as pernicious as the decision made by this tribunal in the *Dred Scott* case. It was adjudged in that case that descendants of Africans who were imported into this country and sold as slaves were not included nor intended to be included under the word "citizens" in the Constitution. [Emphasis added][119]

However, Justice Harlan was in the minority at the time, so by the close of the nineteenth century, racial discrimination was a well-established fact. Racism in America took even uglier forms than simple official discrimination, however. Organizations such as the *Knights of the White Camellia* and the *Klu Klux Klan* terrorized African-Americans, those who sympathized with their plight, Catholics, Jews, and anyone else the organizations viewed as un-American. Homes were burned down, businesses vandalized, people beaten and humiliated, and hundreds lynched. Incredibly, these practices continued throughout the country well into the twentieth century.

To struggle against the evil of racism, the **National Association for the Advancement of Colored People (NAACP)** was founded in 1909. Although it employed many different approaches to combat racism, its principal weapon was litigation, demanding justice in the courts. Slowly but surely, the efforts of the NAACP and other organizations began to bear fruit, and the bastion of segregation, racial superiority, and institutionalized bigotry began to crumble by judicial mandate. It should be noted that while some steps to combat racism were taken by Congress and the presidents in this century, until the 1960s those pursuing racial justice were forced to look primarily to the courts for solace.

The first major breakthrough came in 1915 when the Supreme Court struck down the grandfather clause in Oklahoma law, claiming that it violated the Fifteenth Amendment.[120] Then in 1938, the Court ruled that Missouri could not legally avoid admitting African-Americans to its law school through the device of paying their tuition to law schools in other states. The Court held that a state could satisfy its equal protection clause responsibility only within its own boundaries.[121] The white primary fell next: The Court ruled in 1944 that it violated the Fifteenth Amendment.[122] Only two years later, the Court also ruled that segregation of public carriers engaged in interstate commerce was forbidden.[123] Then in 1948, the Court sustained a Michigan law banning segregation on public carriers within its jurisdiction;[124] and the Court also ruled that *restricted covenants* (contracts providing that persons of designated races cannot buy certain property) were a violation of the equal protection clause of the Fourteenth Amendment.[125]

In the meantime, recognizing the contribution of African-Americans during World War II, President Harry S. Truman in 1948 ordered the integration of the previously segregated United States armed forces. Finally, in 1950 the Court held in *Sweatt* v. *Painter* that the University of Texas Law School had to admit an African-American because the Texas law school created especially for African-Amer-

Peaceful freedom marchers are confronted by Southern police—and their dogs.

icans was plainly inferior to the all-white University of Texas Law School. While this case certainly did not reverse *Plessy,* it at least tried to enforce the separate but *equal* doctrine.[126]

The Civil Rights Movement   The glacial pace at which society was progressing toward ending segregation quickened abruptly in 1954. In **Brown v. Board of Education,** the Supreme Court unanimously reversed *Plessy,* charging that in the public schools, separate is "inherently unequal" and thus violates the equal pro-

tection clause of the Fourteenth Amendment. In a subsequent hearing the next year, the Court ordered the integration of public schools be carried out with "all deliberate speed."[127] Unfortunately, after a decade and a half of resistance, little progress toward integrating the schools had been made, so in 1969 an impatient Court ordered immediate integration.[128]

In 1955, a small but determined young African-American woman, Rosa Parks, while returning home from work took a seat in the front of a Montgomery, Alabama, bus. When told to give up the seat to a white person, Ms. Parks refused. Her subsequent arrest for violating Montgomery's segregation ordinance led to an indignant reaction in the African-American community. Led by a young Montgomery Baptist minister, Dr. Martin Luther King, Jr., the African-American community initiated a long and bitter boycott of the municipal bus systems, and the **civil rights movement** was born. Over the course of the next decade and a half, the civil rights issue was carried to the streets, the schools, the lunch counters, and to the very steps of Congress, as well as to the serene chambers of the Supreme Court. Sympathetic whites, disgusted with institutionalized bigotry, joined their African-American compatriots in this century's most dramatic social movement.

Moved to respond to the public clamor for social justice, the politicians finally began to act. Presidents Dwight David Eisenhower and John F. Kennedy each enforced the integration of certain public schools, and Congress passed voting rights acts in 1957 and 1960. It was not until Lyndon B. Johnson entered the White House, however, that the country enjoyed a president fully committed to the civil rights movement. In 1964 the Twenty-Fourth Amendment was passed, outlawing the poll tax, and in the same year the **Civil Rights Act of 1964** was passed following a protracted debate in the Senate. The scope of this act is unequaled in the field of civil rights. It created the Equal Employment Opportunity Commission (EEOC) and sought to ban racial discrimination in employment, and it authorized the denial of public funds to programs in which racial discrimination was practiced. The following year the **Voting Rights Act of 1965** was passed, which caused a marked increase in the number of African-Americans who registered to vote in the South. Federal agents were authorized to register African-Americans in the Southern states most notorious for voter discrimination, and the act required that any sub-

stantive change in the voting laws of those states first be approved by federal authorities. Since that time, the number of African-American voters has more than doubled, and the number of African-Americans elected to public office in the South has catapulted. Several African-Americans have been elected to Congress, state legislatures, and city governments, including the mayors of Atlanta, Georgia, and Richmond, Virginia. Furthermore, in 1989, an African-American was elected to a governorship (Virginia) for the first time in history.

Following the decision on voting rights, in 1968 Congress acted again, passing the **Civil Rights Act of 1968**, which forbids discrimination in housing based on race, color, religion, gender, or national origin.

Court Tests for Discrimination Meanwhile the Court continued to find against racial discrimination. *Brown* v. *Board of Education* was understood to outlaw *de jure* segregation—in other words, segregation resulting from policy adopted by school authorities that is deliberately intended to keep the races separate. But many school districts are segregated *de facto,* or by the fact of demographics, with whites living in one section of a school district served by certain schools and African-Americans living in other sections with their own schools. Until 1979 de facto segregation was tolerated by the Court, but in that year the Court ruled that de facto segregation was probably also the result of official policy and ordered school districts in which the schools were not integrated to redraw the intradistrict lines and to bus children to integrated schools.[129] This opinion affected a much greater percentage of Northern schools than those in the South and served as clear notice that the problem of segregation is not limited to only one section of the country.

In applying the equal protection clause in challenges to the law, the Court resorts to certain presumptions and procedures. To begin with, the Court will not strike down all laws that discriminate among individuals; it will negate only those that authorize unfair or irrational distinctions. For example, while the Court would certainly strike down a law prohibiting African-Americans from attending college, it would not question a law that prohibited youngsters from drinking alcohol. The Court applies the **reasonable basis test** to questions of this sort; therefore, in normal circumstances, the Court will not strike down a law unless the plaintiff can prove that its purpose is to discriminate against certain people in an unreasonable way. On some issues, however, those that traditionally have been the object of unjust discrimination, the Court exercises a more rigorous or *strict scrutiny*. Predictably, these **suspect classifications** include race as well as religion and national origin. When the Court reviews laws dealing with the suspect classifications, it places the burden of proof on the government. The state must prove not only that the law is reasonable but that there is a "compelling public interest" for applying the questioned discrimination.

Civil Rights and a Conservative Court True to their campaign promises, Richard Nixon, Ronald Reagan, and George Bush appointed conservative jurists to the high Court, until today a majority of the Court is definitely situated on the right side of the spectrum. In consequence, while not completely backing away from the civil rights goals pursued for the last 35 or 40 years, the Court has dealt several blows to the aspirations of civil rights advocates.

Although in 1983 the Court sustained the revocation of tax-exempt status for religiously oriented schools that practice racial discrimination[130] and in 1988 ruled that a city could not prevent the building of apartments in a high-income neighborhood if the prohibition has the effect of encouraging racial segregation,[131] more recent Court opinions have been less sanguine for civil rights advocates. In an important

decision, *Patterson* v. *McLean Credit Union* (1989), the Court held that a person may not sue an employer for racial harassment under the provisions of the Civil Rights Act of 1866, a law that had been used for decades in such cases. The Court held 5 to 4 that the 1866 law covered only the contract stage in employer-employee relations; thus, one could not use it for protection against discrimination once one was on the job.[132] This blow to civil rights protection, together with the Court's recent rulings on affirmative action cases (to be discussed later), sent waves of alarm through the groups and individuals who have fought so long for civil rights.

In 1990, Congress passed a Civil Rights Act to restore many of the provisions the Rehnquist Court had struck down, but it was vetoed by President Bush. The next year, when Bush unveiled his own long-awaited civil rights proposal, civil rights advocates were shocked to find that the president included in it a provision that would allow employers to refuse employment to workers who would not sign a waiver of their right to sue the employer for discriminatory practices.[133]

Also, in 1991, the Supreme Court ended some federally imposed efforts to desegregate the schools, even if it results in "primarily one race schools." A lifelong opponent of required school integration, Chief Justice Rehnquist wrote that court-ordered desegregation was intended only "as a temporary measure." The 5-3 decision ruled that if a school board "has complied in good faith" with desegregation orders and has "eliminated to the extent practicable" the impact of discrimination, federal judges should drop further efforts to integrate the schools.[134] Civil rights advocates are concerned that this opinion will result in local school boards ignoring segregation in their jurisdictions. The Court's change of direction and the president's conservatism on civil rights promise to affect the fortunes of not only African-Americans but many other people as well.

On the other hand, in 1991 the Rehnquist Court augmented a 1986 ruling that prohibits African-Americans being systematically removed from a jury in a trial where an African-American is the defendant.[135] In its 1991 opinion, the Court said that African-Americans also cannot be systematically removed from juries when the defendant is white.[136] Only days later, however, the Court refused to hear an appeal from a case in which four civil rights attorneys were given heavy fines for having brought a "frivolous" civil rights suit to federal court. Civil rights advocates fear that conservative federal judges are using such fines to discourage legitimate civil rights cases. "It's bad enough to lose a case," said civil rights attorney George Cochran, "but now they can go after your bank account for having filed a lawsuit."[137]

WOMEN'S LIBERATION

Traditionally, women have been treated very paternalistically in this as well as in most other societies. The popular attitude that women should be protected and therefore kept apart from the dangers of the world—the man's world—was reflected in our political and judicial institutions as well. Indeed, as late as 1961, the Supreme Court rendered the opinion that women's place is in the home.[138]

Hence, it has been only with the greatest difficulty that women have managed to assert their rights under the Constitution. Early leaders such as Susan B. Anthony, Elizabeth Cady Stanton, and Victoria Woodhull, and others spoke out for women's right to vote and to be released from the stifling legal and social restrictions under which they were bound. After years of struggle, women's liberation achieved its first major forward goal: the right to vote.

Proposed in Congress just after the Civil War and many times afterward, the Nineteenth Amendment was finally adopted in 1920 and read, "The right of citizens of the United States to vote shall not be denied or abridged by the United States or by any state on account of sex." The right to vote, however, did not immediately lead to great improvement in the social conditions of women, so the struggle continued.

Helped by the growing efficacy of the civil rights movement, things began to change for women in the 1960s. Betty Friedan electrified the movement with her book *The Feminine Mystique* (1963), giving many people a fresh look at legal and social policies that unjustly discriminated against women, and in 1966 the National Organization of Women (NOW) was founded with Friedan's help to agitate for women's rights. Three years earlier, Congress passed the Equal Pay Act, requiring equal pay for equal work, a long advocated goal, and "gender" was included in the protected categories of the Civil Rights Act of 1964, largely due to the tireless efforts of Congresswoman Martha W. Griffiths (D-MI). Finally, in 1969, President Nixon mandated equal opportunity for women in federal employment, and in 1972, laws were passed to guarantee equal employment rights for women in publicly supported schools.

A year earlier the Court struck down an Idaho statute directing that men instead of women should be appointed administrators of estates when both genders were eligible.[139] Later in the decade the Court ruled that a state cannot establish different legal drinking ages for the genders,[140] that girls cannot be excluded from Little League,[141] and that arbitrary height and weight requirements cannot be used to deny employment.[142] The Court ruled in 1983 that women could not be given lower monthly retirement benefits than men, even though their average life expectancy is higher,[143] and in 1984 it struck down rules of the Junior Chamber of Commerce denying women membership.[144]

While the Court has sought recently to assure that the genders are treated equally where appropriate, it has stopped far short of insisting on complete equality. Although the Court has not included gender among the suspect categories, it has been careful to give gender special attention. In 1976 the Court laid down parameters for valid gender discrimination, arguing that it is permissible if it serves an important social purpose.[145] Accordingly, the Court permits single-gender schools so long as a school's quality is assured and enrollment is not compulsory,[146] laws against statutory rape by men but not by women,[147] and military conscription for men only.[148]

Although the women's liberation movement has made enormous strides in the past three decades, its most cherished goal has eluded it: an amendment to the Constitution specifically guaranteeing gender equality. The **Equal Rights Amendment (ERA)** was passed by Congress in 1971 and was referred to the states for ratification. Closely following the language of the Nineteenth Amendment, the ERA says simply, "Equality of rights under the law shall not be denied or abridged by the United States or any State on account of sex."

At first the proposed amendment seemed destined to pass, but by the end of the seven-year deadline, it lacked three states to secure ratification. The opposition to the ERA, led by author Phyllis Schlafly, included many women as well as men. It rejected the prospects of a "unisex" culture, objected to women being denied their "special status," and feared that the amendment would lead to compulsory military conscription and perhaps combat assignments for women, common bathrooms and dressing rooms, and other such phenomena. Feminists countered each argument, but to no avail. They argued that women do not want "special status"—they want equality. They held the "unisex" objections to be specious and absurd. Bathrooms and dressing rooms could easily be kept separate without denying women equality, and they held that women should not be exempt from the draft if men are conscripted, but that women should be given equal opportunity with men to advance through the ranks.

Another objective of women's liberation that has not yet come to fruition is **comparable worth**. While equal pay for equal work—that is, two people being paid the same amount for doing the same job—is fairly well established, a problem still exists concerning jobs dominated by women (e.g., clerical work and nursing). These positions tend to be paid less than jobs demanding no higher skill levels that are dominated by men (e.g., truck driving and firefighting). This apparent inequity is decried by the liberation movement, while more conservative voices aver that the market forces, not social policy, should set wage levels. To date, the drive for comparable worth has been successful only in a few local jurisdictions.

THE RIGHT OF PRIVACY

In 1965 the Supreme Court forged a previously unarticulated constitutional right: the *right of privacy*. A Connecticut statute forbidding the use of contraceptives by anyone, including married couples, was challenged; and in *Griswold* v. *Connecticut* the Court struck down the law, arguing that it violated the ancient right of privacy. Justice William O. Douglas, writing a controversial majority opinion, claimed that privacy has existed as an individual right since ancient times; that it is implied in the Third, Fourth, and Fifth amendments; and that the Court sanctioned it as one of the unmentioned rights guaranteed by the Ninth Amendment.[149] The Ninth Amendment, generally ignored until 1965, reads, "The enumeration in the Constitution, of certain rights, shall not be construed to deny or disparage others retained by the people."

Since Griswold, the Court has used the right of privacy to invalidate laws prohibiting interracial marriages[150] and to strike down laws forbidding possession of obscene materials;[151] in addition, it has refused to support the Reagan Administration's efforts to compel the use of life-support technology on severely handicapped infants.[152] However, the Court does not accept sodomy (oral and anal sex), even among consenting adults, as protected by the right of privacy.[153]

Perhaps the most controversial issue to date orbiting the right of privacy is the question of abortion. The Court first ruled abortion a private right in *Roe* v. *Wade* (1973). This decision struck down a Texas law forbidding abortion and the antiabortion laws of over 40 other states. Opining that the decision about whether to abort a pregnancy is an intensely private matter, one that the government has no right to regulate during the early stages of pregnancy, the Court divided pregnancy into three 12-week periods. During the first trimester the state has no right to prohibit or regulate an abortion decision; the matter is left entirely to the mother. During the second trimester the state may regulate abortion in order to protect the mother's health, and the state may regulate and prohibit abortion in the interest of the fetus during the third trimester.[154]

Ignoring the storm of controversy raised in opposition to *Roe* by religious and other groups loosely organized into the *Right to Life* coalition, for 16 years the Court remained steadfast, striking down state laws that violated the 1973 decision, although it has sustained legislation prohibiting the use of federal funds for abortion.[155] With the Court appointments of Ronald Reagan, a conservative majority was formed, and it has allowed the states new latitude in impeding abortions. In 1989 the Court upheld 5 to 4 a Missouri law proscribing abortions in publicly supported hospitals and forbidding public employees from assisting abortions in any way. *Webster* v. *Reproductive Health*

Services did not reverse Roe, but it did interrupt the long-standing Court policy of frustrating state efforts to impede abortions.[156] As mentioned earlier, two years later the Court upheld government regulations forbidding employees of federally funded family planning clinics to inform clients that they may terminate unwanted pregnancies by abortion.[157] Bush appointee David H. Souter voted with the majority in that case.

Obviously, the Court is in the process of changing its views, on the abortion issue at least. Whether it will at length completely reverse the right to abortion is, of course, a critical question. Even more basic, however, is whether this conservative Court will leave undisturbed the entire concept of the right to privacy as it has thus far been defined.

On the other hand, the Rehnquist Court handed down a victory to the feminist movement in 1991. It ruled that women could not be denied jobs solely on the grounds that the work may be harmful to a fetus, should a female worker become pregnant.[158] Almost 20 major corporations, including General Motors and Du Pont, had adopted such "fetal protection" policies.

OTHER UNDERREPRESENTED GROUPS

Of course, African-Americans and women are not the only groups that suffer the sting of bigotry and discrimination. The civil rights movement awakened the nation to the plight of many other people.

Native Americans The history of relations between the American Indians and the United States government is a sad one. The Indian population (in what is now the United States) in the 1500s, when the first white settlers arrived, is estimated to have been 10 to 15 million. Yet European disease to which the Indians had no immunity, callous policies, blatant disregard for Indian well-being, and open white hostility toward the "savages" combined to reduce the Native American population to about one-half million by the beginning of the twentieth century. Since that time the Native American population has increased by 300-fold, a substantial improvement. In fact, the growth rate of the Native American population in this century has been roughly the same as that of the population as a whole.

Still, today about half of the total Indian population lives on reservations, which are all too frequently squalid enclaves where disease and alcoholism are often prevalent. Never quite sure what to do about the Indians, the government did not even extend citizenship to them until 1924, and it took 22 years more for the United States to begin to settle the land claims certain tribes held against the government. In the 1960s and 1970s, stimulated by the civil rights movement, Native Americans pressed their claims for better treatment in society.

Today there are about 280 officially recognized tribes, and government aid and health programs serve them both on and off the reservation. Indians who live off the reservation are, of course, entitled to the same rights as other citizens, but until 1968, reservation Indians were treated more like wards of the government. With the passage of the *Indian Bill of Rights* in that year, however, reservation Indians began to enjoy the same liberties guaranteed others in the society.

Recently, the Court has also become more solicitous of Native American rights. Although it refused to honor the Indian request that a federal logging road not be allowed to trespass on sacred burial grounds, it has held that tribal courts have jurisdiction over the custody of orphaned Indian children, even when the parents had left the reservation.[159]

Asian-Americans   Although arriving in the United States much later than did the African-Americans and, of course, the Native

Americans, Asian-Americans have also suffered considerable prejudice in this country. Chinese coolies were imported into California in large numbers during the 1860s and 1870s to build the western end of the transcontinental railroad. In time, the Japanese followed, looking for a better life than was available in the old country. Relegated to farm labor and other menial tasks, Asians found themselves, for a time, excluded by state laws from owning land or voting.

Indeed, the prejudicial treatment accorded the Japanese in America served to heighten the tensions between the United States and Japan, which contributed to the Japanese attack on Pearl Harbor. During World War II, about 120,000 Japanese, many of them born in the United States and others of them naturalized United States citizens, were forced out of their homes and interned in *detention camps* without due process of law. The internees were allowed to take only the possessions they could carry and were given just 72 hours to sell their remaining belongings (houses, businesses, cars, furniture, etc.), usually at unconscionably low prices.

For years, the Japanese-American community turned its collective head from this indignity. They tried to forget the injustice done them, and to pick up their lives and carry on. A few persistent people sought restitution for their losses and an apology for the high-handed government policies, but to little avail. Then a former internee, Aiko Yoshinaga, discovered a long-suppressed document in the national archives that contradicted government claims that the internment had been executed solely out of military necessity. Instead, it said that "ties of race" made all Japanese-Americans suspect, no matter how much time was available to investigate them. In a subsequent trial, a Federal District Court found the government guilty of "concealment" and misconduct "of the most fundamental character." Following

A gay pride march.

this case, the Congress voted a public apology for the internment policy and approved a reparations payment of $20,000 for each internee.[160] Although this action hardly compensates for the enormous injustice done the Japanese-Americans, it finally closes a dark chapter in American history, and with luck its lessons will teach our generation and those that follow something about how fragile the cherished individual liberties are in the face of bigotry and mass hysteria.

Coming to the United States in large numbers after World War II, Filipino and Korean people have also established themselves in this country. Living mostly in California, they too suffered discrimination, but have recently also benefited from the tolerance accompanying the civil rights movement. At the close of the Indochina war large numbers of Vietnamese, Thais, and other Southeast Asians have also come to the United States. Often destitute *boat people*, these new arrivals are beginning to establish themselves, although many still find themselves living in poverty and squalor.

Hispanic Americans By 1985, Hispanic Americans constituted about 6.4 percent of the total population, just over half the size of the African-American population, our largest minority group. But the Hispanic Americans are the most rapidly growing minority. Comprising mainly Puerto Ricans who are concentrated in the Northeast, Cubans in Florida, and Mexican-Americans and Central American refugees in the Southwest, the Hispanic American population may overtake African-Americans in percentage of the population by the turn of the century if present growth trends continue.

Despite efforts to organize them by farm labor leader César Chávez and several political organizations, Hispanic Americans remain among the least politicized minority groups in the nation. Cultural proclivities, language difficulties, poverty, and bigotry among some whites continue to impede their progress toward political power and social justice. Hispanic Americans face enormous problems including labor exploitation in the nation's fields and sweatshops that suppresses wages and fringe benefits; for example, the farm labor force, of which Hispanic Americans constitute a large percentage, is poorly paid and often goes without social security, worker's compensation, unemployment insurance, and other economic protections. Much the same can be said about the sweatshops in which many urban Hispanic Americans toil. Such conditions make it difficult for Hispanic Americans to escape the rural poverty areas and urban barrios that they inhabit.

Exacerbating the problems encountered by Hispanic Americans is the massive influx into the United States of illegal aliens, most of them from Hispanic countries. Motivated by economic privation and political turmoil at home, thousands of people steal across the borders each year. Often the prey of callous smugglers, bandits, and exploitative American employers, these hapless people eke out an existence by working at menial tasks for paltry wages. Fearing detection by the authorities, they abide inhumane conditions at work and often find themselves living in makeshift shelters in thickets of trees or bush.

In an attempt to stem the tide of illegal aliens, Congress passed the *Simpson-Mazzoli Act* in 1986, giving amnesty to illegal aliens who can prove they have lived in the United States continuously since January of 1982, and exacting stiff penalties on employers who hire illegals. So far there is little evidence that this measure has had the desired effect, and shrill voices demand that the military be used to patrol the border with Mexico.

Other Aspirants   Besides women and ethnic minorities, other elements of the population have demanded fairer treatment from society. The disabled have asserted their right to enter the mainstream of American life, resulting in laws requiring special parking places, ramps replacing steps in public buildings, and other modifications to facilitate mobility. The

Americans with Disabilities Act of 1990 is a particularly noteworthy breakthrough in this regard.

The elderly, another long-ignored sector of our society, have also mobilized. Led by organizations such as the Gray Panthers and the American Association of Retired People, the elderly have become a significant political force, securing tax advantages, social programs, and antidiscrimination legislation to satisfy their needs. Less successful, but persistent nonetheless, homosexuals have demanded *gay rights* to liberate them from what they view as unenlightened prejudice in society. Their efforts to combat homophobia have recently been set back by some people's reaction to the AIDS epidemic.

Affirmative Action   Employment is the economic issue over which perhaps the most struggle has been waged concerning equal rights. Charging that job discrimination was a major problem in our society, President Johnson implored employers to go beyond passive efforts to assure equal job opportunity. Instead he called for **affirmative action** to seek out and employ the "underrepresented groups." In consequence, Congress passed laws directing that affirmative action programs be developed to assure equal employment opportunity to ethnic minorities, women, and the handicapped. Since the 1960s, the Court has heard many cases charging job discrimination or reverse discrimination, and it has attempted to establish appropriate parameters for these programs.

Regents of the University of California v. *Bakke* in 1978 confronted the Court with the first major charge of "reverse discrimination." Allan Bakke found himself twice denied admission to the University of California at Davis medical school, while minority students who had lower academic records were admitted under a university policy that set aside a fixed number of places for minority students. Bakke sued the university, alleging that he had been denied equal protection under the law. Although the Court was careful to express its support for affirmative action programs, it found in Bakke's favor, holding that strict racial quotas were inappropriate for most affirmative action programs.[161] Furthermore, in 1987, the Court sustained a policy that promoted a woman to a job in which women were underrepresented, even though a male colleague was better qualified for the position.[162] But while the Court allows gender and racial preference for hiring and promotion, it has repeatedly struck down layoff policies that ignored seniority in favor of racial and gender preference.[163]

Since 1989, however, the new conservative majority on the Court has in matters of job discrimination, as with so many other of the civil liberties and civil rights, begun to back away from the more liberal positions of its predecessors. Although it ruled in favor of a woman who had lost a promotion due to seemingly blatant sex discrimination—holding that in some cases firms must prove that promotion decisions are based on valid, nondiscriminatory criteria[164]—and it sustained a federal law giving ethnic minorities preference in the award of licenses for radio and television stations,[165] it has been less supportive of affirmative action in other circumstances. It reversed a previous position of sustaining municipal policies assuring that a certain percentage of city contracts go to minority firms,[166] and it denied a challenge to changed seniority calculations that were biased against women in a firm.[167] Even more serious, the Court ruled that white males may challenge affirmative action plans that have already been sanctioned by *consent decrees*. For decades, when plaintiffs challenged hiring practices, employers often settled by accepting court-approved employment and promotion policies. These consent decrees were considered final and not subject to further challenge. But in *Martin* v. *Wilks* (1989), the Court ruled that these agreements may now be challenged repeatedly.[168] Thus, it appears that affirmative action plans may never be completely safe from suit, raising the possibility that they will be made ineffective by constant court review. In the meantime, a 1991 study conducted by the Urban Institute found that widely suspected reverse discrimination does not exist in serious proportions, but that discrimination against African-Americans at the workplace is widespread. The study revealed that when closely matched pairs of white and African-American job seekers applied for work at the same firms, whites were hired over African-Americans by a ratio of 3 to 1.[169]

Summary

- The civil liberties are those freedoms that come to us from our commitment to individual freedom.

- Many of the civil liberties are found in the Bill of Rights, which guarantees that we may write, speak, and worship as we choose, so long as we do not harm anyone else.

- We are also protected against governmental abuse by the Bill of Rights, which strictly requires the authorities to use search and arrest warrants, to inform us of our rights before interrogation, and to afford us an impartial trial when we are accused of wrongdoing.

- In this century, the courts have expanded our civil rights—those that belong to us because of our belief in human equality. De jure segregation has been ended and discrimination based on gender, age, and disability have also been curtailed.

- Affirmative action programs have been initiated to combat the effects of centuries of discrimination against ethnic minorities and women.

Notes

1. *Barron v. Baltimore,* 7 Pet. 243 (1833).
2. *Gitlow v. New York,* 268 U.S. 652 (1925).
3. *Abortion Rights Mobilization v. U.S. Catholic Conference,* 110 S. Ct. 1946 (1990).
4. *Everson v. Board of Education of Ewing Township,* 330 U.S. 1 (1947).
5. *Lynch v. Donnelly,* 465 U.S. 668 (1984).
6. *Marsh v. Chambers,* 463 U.S. 783 (1983). This case involved a challenge of the practice in the Nebraska state legislature.
7. *Meek v. Pittenger,* 421 U.S. 349 (1975).
8. *Texas Monthly v. Bullock,* 108 S. Ct. 2842 (1989).
9. *Swaggart Ministries v. California Board of Education,* Slip No. 88-1374 (1990).
10. *Lemon v. Kurtzman,* 403 U.S. 602 (1971).
11. *Epperson v. Arkansas,* 393 U.S. 97 (1968).
12. *McLean v. Arkansas Board of Education,* 211 U.S. 539 (1982) and *Edwards v. Aguillard,* 482 U.S. 578 (1987).
13. *Mozert v. Hawkins County Public Schools,* 108 S. Ct. 1029 (1988).
14. *Engel v. Vitale,* 370 U.S. 421 (1962).
15. *School District of Abington Township v. Schempp,* 374 U.S. 203 (1963).
16. *Lubbock Independent School District v. Lubbock Civil Liberties Union,* 103 S. Ct. 800 (1983).
17. *Wallace v. Jaffree,* 105 S. Ct. 2914 (1985).
18. *Board of Education v. Mergens,* 110 S. Ct. 711 (1990).
19. David G. Savage, "Court May Ease Church-State Separation," *The Los Angeles Times* March 19, 1991.
20. *West Virginia Board of Education v. Barnette,* 319 U.S. 624 (1943).
21. *United States v. Seeger,* 380 U.S. 163 (1965) and *Welsh v. United States,* 398 U.S. 333 (1970).
22. *Wisconsin v. Yoder,* 406 U.S. 205 (1972).
23. *Frazee v. Illinois Employment Security Department,* 488 U.S. 814 (1989).
24. *Bob Jones University v. United States,* 461 U.S. 574 (1983).
25. *Lyng v. Northwest Indian Cemetery Protection Assn.,* 108 S. Ct. 1319 (1989).
26. *Employment Division, State of Oregon v. Smith,* 110 S. Ct. 2605 (1990).

27. *Holy Spirit Assn. for the Unification of World Christianity* v. *Molko and Leal*, 109 S. Ct. 2110 (1989).

28. *Walker* v. *Sacramento County Superior Court*, Slip No. 88-1471 (1989).

29. "Court Rejects Case of Writer Who Renounced Citizenship," *The Los Angeles Times*, June 20, 1989.

30. CBS Evening News, June 21, 1989.

31. *Schenck* v. *United States*, 249 U.S. 47 (1919).

32. *Dennis* v. *United States*, 341 U.S. 494 (1951).

33. *Yates* v. *United States*, 354 U.S. 298 (1957). Yates is sometimes called the Second Dennis Case.

34. Ronald L. Soble, "McCarthy-Era Law Suffers Blow in Deportation Case," *The Los Angeles Times*, Nov. 18, 1989.

35. *Chaplinsky* v. *New Hampshire*, 315 U.S. 568 (1942).

36. David G. Savage, "Forbidden Words on Campus," *The Los Angeles Times*, Feb. 23, 1991.

37. *Rust* v. *Sullivan*, Slip No. 89-1391 (1991).

38. *Widmar* v. *Vincent*, 454 U.S. 263 (1981).

39. *Tinker* v. *Des Moines Independent Community School District*, 393 U.S. 503 (1969).

40. *Smith* v. *Goguen*, 451 U.S. 566 (1974).

41. *Texas* v. *Johnson*, 488 U.S. 907 (1989).

42. *United States* v. *Eichman*, 110 S. Ct. 2404 (1990).

43. *Near* v. *Minnesota*, 283 U.S. 697 (1931).

44. *New York Times Company* v. *United States*, 403 U.S. 713 (1971).

45. *Snepp* v. *United States*, 444 U.S. 507 (1980).

46. *Hazelwood School District* v. *Kuhlmeier*, 108 S. Ct. 562 (1988).

47. *Cable News Network, Inc., et al.* v. *Manuel A. Noreiga*, Slip No. 90-767 (1990).

48. *Zurcher* v. *Stanford Daily*, 436 U.S. 547 (1978).

49. *New York Times Co.* v. *Sullivan*, 376 U.S. 254 (1964).

50. *Curtis Publishing Co.* v. *Butts*, 388 U.S. 130 (1967) and *Associated Press* v. *Walker*, 389 U.S. 997 (1976).

51. *Hustler Magazine Inc.* v. *Falwell*, 108 S. Ct. 876 (1988).

52. *Florida Star* v. *B.J.F.*, 108 S. Ct. 499 (1989).

53. *Milkovich* v. *Lorain Journal Co*, 110 S. Ct. 2695 (1990).

54. *Roth* v. *United States*, 354 U.S. 476 (1957).

55. *Miller* v. *California*, 413 U.S. 15 (1973).

56. *Jenkins* v. *Georgia*, 418 U.S. 153 (1974).

57. *Schad* v. *Borough of Mt. Ephraim*, 452 U.S. 61 (1981).

58. *California* v. *Freeman*, 488 U.S. 1311 (1989).

59. *FCC* v. *Sable Communications*, 488 U.S. 1003 (1989).

60. *Ft. Wayne Books* v. *Indiana*, 108 S. Ct. 2012 (1989).

61. *Osborne* v. *Ohio*, 110 S. Ct. 1691 (1990).

62. Allan Parachini, "Senate Defeats Attempts by Helms to Cut NEA Funding," *The Los Angeles Times*, Oct. 25, 1990.

63. Paul Huston, "FCC Repeals Fairness Rule for Broadcasters," *The Los Angeles Times*, August 5, 1987.

64. Harold W. Stanley and Richard G. Niemi, *Vital Statistics on American Politics* (Washington, DC: Congressional Quarterly, 1990), p. 373.

65. William J. Eaton, "Blacks Found More Likely to Be Major Crime Victims," *The Los Angeles Times*, Apr. 23, 1990.

66. David G. Savage, "1 in 4 Young Blacks in Jail or in Court Control, Study Says," *The Los Angeles Times*, Feb. 27, 1990.

67. *Mapp* v. *Ohio*, 367 U.S. 643 (1961).

68. *Terry* v. *Ohio*, 387 U.S. 929 (1967).

69. *United States* v. *Calandra*, 414 U.S. 338 (1974).

70. *United States* v. *Havens*, 446 U.S. 620 (1980).

71. *New York* v. *Quarles*, 467 U.S. 649 (1984).

72. *California* v. *Greenwood*, 108 S. Ct. 1625 (1988).

73. *Nix* v. *Williams*, 464 U.S. 431 (1984).

74. *United States* v. *Leon*, 468 U.S. 468 U.S. 897 (1984).

75. *Maryland* v. *Garrison*, 480 U.S. 79 (1987).

76. *Katz* v. *United States*, 389 U.S. 347 (1967).

77. *Tyler* v. *Berodt*, 110 S. Ct. 723 (1990).

78. *United States* v. *Ross*, 456 U.S. 798 (1982) and *Texas* v. *White*, 423 U.S. 67 (1976).

79. *California* v. *Carney*, 471 U.S. 386 (1985).

80. *Oliver* v. *United States*, 104 S. Ct. 1735 (1984).

81. *Skinner, Transportation Secretary* v. *Railway Labor Executives*, 109 S. Ct. 1402 (1989).

82. *NTEU* v. *VonRaab*, 482 U.S. 902 (1989).

83. *United States* v. *Sokolow*, 108 S. Ct. 2033 (1989).

84. *New Jersey* v. *T.L.O.*, 469 U.S. 325 (1985).

85. *Fare* v. *Michael C.*, 442 U.S. 707 (1979).

86. *United States* v. *Watson*, 423 U.S. 411 (1976).

87. *Payton* v. *New York*, 445 U.S. 573 (1980).

88. *Miranda* v. *Arizona*, 384 U.S. 436 (1966).

89. *Doyle* v. *Ohio* 426 U.S. 610 (1976) and *Wood* v. *Ohio* 110 S. Ct. 3279 (1976).

90. *Minnick* v. *Mississippi*, 110 S. Ct. 1921 (1990).

91. *Dunaway* v. *New York*, 442 U.S. 200 (1979).

92. *Estelle* v. *Smith*, 451 U.S. 454 (1981).

93. *Harris* v. *New York*, 401 U.S. 222 (1971).

94. *Michigan* v. *Tucker*, 417 U.S. 433 (1974).

95. *Oregon* v. *Hass*, 420 U.S. 714 (1975).

96. *New York* v. *Quarles*, 467 U.S. 649 (1984).

97. *Pennsylvania* v. *Maniz*, 110 S. Ct. 2638 (1990).

98. *Duckworth* v. *Eagan*, 109 S. Ct. 2875 (1989).

99. *Arizona* v. *Fulminante*, 110 S. Ct. 1528 (1991).

100. *Johnson* v. *Zerbst*, 304 U.S. 458 (1938).

101. For a fascinating account of this case, including a wonderful exposition of the inner workings of the Supreme Court, see Anthony Lewis, *Gideon's Trumpet* (New York: Vintage Books, 1966).

102. *Gideon* v. *Wainwright*, 372 U.S. 335 (1963).

103. *Argersinger* v. *Hamlin*, 407 U.S. 25 (1972).

104. *Murray* v. *Giarratano*, 109 S. Ct. 2765 (1989).

105. David G. Savage, "Supreme Court Curbs Appeals by 'Paupers'," *The Los Angeles Times*, March 30, 1991.

106. *Pointer* v. *Texas*, 380 U.S. 400 (1965), *Parker* v. *Gladden*, 385 U.S. 363 (1966), *Klopfer* v. *North Carolina*, 386 U.S. 213 (1967), and *Duncan* v. *Louisiana*, 391 U.S. 145 (1968).

107. *United States* v. *Salerno*, 429 U.S. 929 (1987).

108. David G. Savage, "Bail Denial Upheld by High Court," *The Los Angeles Times*, May 27, 1987.

109. *Hilton* v. *Braunskill*, 107 S. Ct. 2113 (1987).

110. *Gregg* v. *Georgia*, 428 U.S. 153 (1976).

111. *Furman* v. *Georgia*, 408 U.S. 238 (1972).

112. *Coker* v. *Georgia*, 433 U.S. 584 (1977).

113. *McCleskey* v. *Zant*, 110 S. Ct. 2585 (1991).

114. David G. Savage, "Supreme Court Limits Death Row Appeals," *The Los Angeles Times*, April 17, 1991.

115. *Stanford* v. *Kentucky*, 488 U.S. 906 (1989).

116. David G. Savage, "Executing Young Killers Is Upheld," *The Los Angeles Times*, June 27, 1989.

117. David G. Savage, "Marshall on Constitution: 'Defective From Start,'" *The Los Angeles Times*, May 7, 1987.

118. *Civil Rights Cases*, 109 U.S. 3 (1883).

119. *Plessy* v. *Ferguson*, 163 U.S. 537 (1896).

120. *Guinn* v. *United States*, 238 U.S. 347 (1915).

121. *Missouri ex rel. Gaines* v. *Canada*, 305 U.S. 337 (1938).

122. *Smith* v. *Allwright*, 321 U.S. 649 (1944).

123. *Morgan* v. *Virginia*, 328 U.S. 373 (1946).

124. *Bob-Lo Excursion Co.* v. *Michigan*, 333 U.S. 28 (1948).

125. *Shelley* v. *Kraemer*, 334 U.S. 1 (1948).

126. *Sweatt* v. *Painter*, 339 U.S. 629 (1950).

127. *Brown* v. *Board of Education*, 347 U.S. 483 (1954) and *Brown* v. *Board* 349 U.S. 294 (1955).

128. *Alexander* v. *Holmes County Board of Education*, 396 U.S. 19 (1969).

129. *Dayton Board of Education* v. *Brinkman*, 443 U.S. 526 (1979), and *Columbus Board of Education* v. *Penick*, 443 U.S. 449 (1979).

130. *Bob Jones University* v. *United States*, 461 U.S. 574 (1983).

131. *Starrett City* v. *United States*, 488 U.S. 946 (1988).

132. *Patterson* v. *McLean Credit Union*, 109 S. Ct. 2363 (1989).

133. David Lauter, "White House Backs Waivers of Job Bias Suits," *The Los Angeles Times*, March 2, 1991.

134. *Board of Education* v. *Dowell*, 396 U.S. 269 (1991).

135. *Batson* v. *Kentucky*, 471 U.S. 1052 (1986).

136. *Powers* v. *Ohio*, 110 S. Ct. 1521 (1991).

137. "Justices Let Stand Stiff Fines Against Civil Rights Lawyers," *The Los Angeles Times*, April 16, 1991.

138. *Hoyt* v. *Florida*, 368 U.S. 57 (1961).

139. *Reed* v. *Reed*, 404 U.S. 71 (1971).

140. *Stanton* v. *Stanton*, 421 U.S. 7 (1975).

141. *Fortin* v. *Darlington Little League*, 514 F. 2d 344 (1975).

142. *Dothard* v. *Rawlinson*, 433 U.S. 321 (1977).

143. *Arizona* v. *Norris*, 463 U.S. 1073 (1983).

144. *Roberts* v. *United States Jaycees*, 468 U.S. 609 (1984).

145. *Craig* v. *Boren*, 429 U.S. 190 (1976).

146. *Vorchheimer* v. *School District of Philadelphia*, 430 U.S. 703 (1977).

147. *Michael M.* v. *Superior Court*, 450 U.S. 464 (1981).

148. *Rostker* v. *Goldberg*, 453 U.S. 57 (1981).

149. *Griswold* v. *Connecticut*, 381 U.S 479 (1965).

150. *Loving* v. *Virginia*, 388 U.S. 1 (1967).

151. *Stanley* v. *Georgia*, 394 U.S. 557 (1969).

152. *Bowen* v. *American Hospital Association*, 476 U.S. 610 (1986).

153. *Bowers* v. *Hardwick*, 478 U.S. 186 (1986).

154. *Roe* v. *Wade*, 410 U.S. 113 (1973).

155. *Harris* v. *McRae*, 448 U.S. 297 (1980).

156. *Webster* v. *Reproductive Health Services*, 57 L.W. 5023 (1989).

157. *Rust* v. *Sullivan*, Slip No. 89-1391 (1991).

158. *International Union* v. *Johnson Controls*, Slip No. 89-1215 (1991).

159. *Mississippi Band of Choctaw Indians* v. *Holyfield*, 108 S. Ct. 1993 (1989).

160. Josh Getlin, "Redress: One Made a Difference," *The Los Angeles Times*, June 2, 1988.

161. *Regents of the University of California* v. *Bakke*, 438 U.S. 265 (1978).

162. *Johnson* v. *Transportation Agency, Santa Clara County*, 107 S. Ct. 1442 (1987).

163. *Firefighters Local Union No. 1784* v. *Stotts et al.*, 467 U.S. 561 (1984); *Sheet Metal Workers* v. *Equal Employment Opportunity Commission*, 478 U.S. 421 (1986); and *Wygant* v. *Jackson Board of Education*, 473 U.S. 932 (1986).

164. *Price Waterhouse* v. *Hopkins*, 109 S. Ct. 1775 (1989).

165. *Metro Broadcasting* v. *FCC*, 110 S. Ct. 2997 (1990).

166. *Richmond* v. *Croson Co.*, 108 S. Ct. 1010 (1989).

167. *Lorance* v. *AT&T Technologies*, 108 S. Ct. 1726 (1989).

168. *Martin* v. *Wilks*, 108 S. Ct. 2843 (1989).

169. Sam Fulwood III, "Hiring Study Finds Strong Anti-Black Bias," *The Los Angeles Times*, May 15, 1991.

Suggestions for Further Reading

Abernathy, Glen M. *Civil Liberties Under the Constitution* (rev. ed.). New York: Harper & Row, 1985.

Abraham, Henry J. *Freedom and the Courts: Civil Rights and Liberties in the United States* (4th ed.). New York: Oxford University Press, 1982.

Alley, Robert S., ed. *The Supreme Court on Church and State*. Oxford: Oxford University Press, 1988.

Edsall, Thomas B. *The New Politics of Inequality*. New York: Norton, 1985.

Freeman, J. *The Politics of Women's Liberation*. New York: Longman, 1975.

Klein, Ethel. *Gender Politics: From Consciousness to Mass Politics*. Cambridge: Harvard University Press, 1984.

Kluger, Richard. *Simple Justice: The History of Brown v. Board of Education and Black America's Struggle for Equality*. New York: Knopf, 1976.

Landry, Bart. *The New Black Middle Class*. Berkeley: University of California Press, 1987.

Lewis, Anthony. *Gideon's Trumpet*. New York: Random House, 1964.

McClosky, Herbert, and Alida Brill. *Dimensions of Tolerance: What Americans Believe about Civil Liberties*. New York: Russell Sage Foundation, 1983.

Mill, John Stuart. *On Liberty*. New York: Norton, 1975. (Originally published in 1859.)

Pritchett, C. Herman. *Constitutional Civil Liberties*. Englewood Cliffs, NJ: Prentice-Hall, 1984.

Prucha, Francis Paul. *The Great Father: The United States Government and the American Indians*. Lincoln: University of Nebraska Press, 1984.

Shapiro, Martin. *The Pentagon Papers and the Courts*. San Francisco: Chandler, 1972.

Sindler, Allan P. *Bakke, DeFunis, and Minority Admissions*. New York: Longman, 1978.

Spence, Gerry. *With Justice for None*. New York: Times Books, 1989.

Stanley, Harold H., and Richard Niemi. *Vital Statistics on American Politics* (2nd ed.). Washington, DC: Congressional Quarterly, 1990.

Chapter 4

PUBLIC OPINION, THE MEDIA, AND INTEREST GROUPS

PREVIEW

Public opinion is critical in any democracy, and it is closely watched by American politicians. Measuring public opinion has been refined during the past 60 years, until today it is fairly reliable and relatively inexpensive. Using cluster samples, pollsters are usually able to measure public opinion to within three or four percentage points, and with telephone interviews, pollsters are able to sample public opinion in a matter of hours. But some critics complain that the polls lead voters in their decisions, thus influencing elections.

As in any society, American public opinion is developed largely through socialization. People are influenced at various stages in their lives by family, school, peers, social class, occupation, ethnicity, gender, and a range of other stimuli. Although woefully ill-informed about certain basic facts, Americans have remained fairly stable in their political views over recent decades. Tending to be pragmatic rather than ideological, Americans opt for policy that they feel will meet their needs at the moment, rather than relying on long-range formulas for adopting policy options.

Another fundamental institution in any democracy is that of the media. Beginning in the 1830s and peaking in circulation in 1947, newspapers have since declined as a source of news among the population. As newspapers reached a smaller percentage of the public, the number of radios and more especially televisions has risen, until today virtually every home has both appliances.

The American news media enjoy an extraordinary degree of freedom, and they play an important role as watchdog of public officials. Public officials attempt to use the media to their own advantage, however, as news management has become a common practice in the society.

One of the most heated debates among American political scientists is whether our system includes enough public participation and control to qualify as a democracy. The elite theorists argue that the society is controlled by a small elite, and that democracy is only a pretense. The pluralists, on the other hand, take a more optimistic view. While they recognize the existence of a few powerful people, they believe that the elite's influence is checked by mass participation in interest groups. Whatever the case, the American people are joiners, uniting in groups to influence public policy. Although the poor associate with interest groups far less than do the middle and upper classes, interest groups have become a mainstay in the political system. Since the 1960s we have witnessed an immense growth in the number of interest groups and in the amount of their activity. At the same time, a larger variety of interests have become represented as people have organized to advance their particular causes. Interest groups pressure and cajole policy-makers, bringing them information and mobilizing their constituents. Lobbying and campaign finance, however, are the two most critical tools.

Lobbying occurs at every level of government, and along with the interest groups for whom they work, the number of lobbyists has skyrocketed. Successful lobbyists offer policy-makers information, strategy ideas, and support. They often coalesce with other lobbyists and with public officials and staff to achieve their goals. The federal laws regulating lobbyists are weak and ineffective, and most efforts to make the laws more stringent have not been successful.

Closely associated with lobbyists' efforts are the political action committees (PACs). These organizations raise funds for campaign contributions, and they too have increased in number and activity over the past two decades. Changes in election laws have permitted a tidal wave of money to deluge campaigns, raising their costs. The increase in campaign costs and the fact that PACs give far more to incumbents than to challengers mean that those holding office enjoy a significant advantage over people who might wish to unseat them. The need to get big money in order to stay in office also forces policy-makers to spend increasing amounts of time raising funds, and the sums they accept may jeopardize their independence.

Public sentiment is everything. With public sentiment nothing can fail, without it nothing can succeed.

Abraham Lincoln

The democratic process depends on the public's being able to formulate and express its opinion on matters of concern. Equally important is the ability to organize in order to influence the selection and decisions of policy-makers. The process by which public opinion is generated, manipulated, and publicized, as well as the means by which people attempt to influence policy-makers, is therefore fundamental to our study of the American political system.

Public Opinion

Public opinion is a vital factor in any political system. Indeed, no political leaders, be they dictators, oligarchs, or democrats, can afford to ignore the views of the governed. Yet public opinion is especially critical in a democracy. In fact, our national founders believed that the validity of the political system depended upon the people's right to formulate and voice their ideas. Expressing that sentiment, Thomas

Paine wrote, "Certain I am that when opinions are free, either in matters of government or religion, truth will fully and powerfully prevail."[1]

Important though it is, public opinion is a complicated subject. The public attitudes about anything are, in a general sense, public opinion. In this discussion, however, the term *public opinion* is limited to the public attitudes about political, economic, and social matters. Moreover, the term *public opinion* should not be thought about in the singular. Probably no idea has been universally accepted by this or any other society. Indeed, there are many public opinions—so many, in fact, that a majority opinion frequently does not exist, and the public is often divided into several minority opinions.

Public opinion is seldom constant; rather, it tends to fluctuate widely as events develop. This fluidity in public opinion can occur on even our most critical issues. For example, only a few days before the 1980 presidential election, polls showed that President Carter and challenger Ronald Reagan were almost even; yet on election day, Reagan won with a 10 percent margin. Since so many polls found the race to be a dead heat a week before the election, it is not likely that they were wrong. Rather, it seems that many more undecided voters chose Reagan and that perhaps some people leaning toward Carter changed their minds at the last moment. In another example, the public's attitude toward energy as a major issue has seesawed since 1974 depending on events and the availability of fuel.[2]

Regardless of how diffused, fluid, or contradictory public opinion may be, it is an essential element in American politics because it is the people's voice and because it, along with other factors, is used by policy-makers to determine action. Few contemporary American politicians can afford to be as contemptuous of the public as was Alexander Hamilton when he said to a colleague, "Your people, sir, are a great beast." Hence, the accurate measurement

of public opinion is important to the political system.

MEASURING PUBLIC OPINION

Politicians have always sampled public opinion, but only in this century has sampling been pursued with scientific precision. George Gallup pioneered scientific polling in the 1930s; since then the field has grown until now there are over 150 polling firms, and polling is used in commerce, in the media, in the social sciences, and by virtually every serious candidate for high public office. As a result, polling has been developed into a very accurate measure of public opinion. (See Figure 4.1.)

The first step in developing an accurate poll is to identify the *universe*. The universe is the group one wishes to sample, be it women, African-Americans, farmers, the citizens of Denver, or Republicans throughout the country. Pollsters generally agree that the most accurate polling model is a *random sample*, a poll

Figure 4.1 Accuracy of Public Opinion Polling, 1936–1988

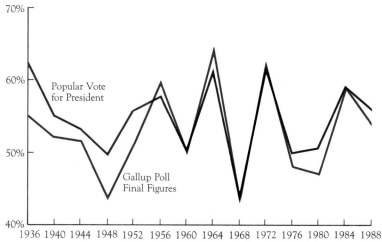

Source: Gallup Poll: Public Opinion, 1989, Scholarly Resource Inc., Wilmington, Del., May 1990.

taken at random throughout the entire universe. Yet given the enormity of the universe, such a poll would be difficult on a national basis, so pollsters resort to *cluster samples* instead. Using this model, pollsters divide the universe into groups of people (Hispanics, labor union members, born-again Christians, etc.) and randomly question people from each group or cluster.

The next step after identifying the universe and selecting the polling model is to write unambiguous but nonleading questions. If one truly wishes to get an accurate reflection of public opinion, the questions must be phrased in a clear but neutral manner, and the people performing the interview must be trained to conduct the poll in an unbiased fashion.

It is common to think of pollsters, clipboards in hand, personally questioning respondents on the street, at home, or in front of supermarkets. While face-to-face contact is still used, most broad-based major polls are now conducted on the telephone. Reduced long-distance telephone rates and advances in technology have seen the emergence of random-digit dialing as the most common form of polling. By comparison with the face-to-face method, it is fast and inexpensive.*

Using these techniques, a well-designed and properly conducted national poll can question only 1500 to 2000 people and yield results that are accurate to within three or four per-

centage points. Furthermore, if several hundred telephone lines are used simultaneously, a poll can be accomplished within an hour, as was done by the television networks immediately following the 1988 presidential debates.

Exit polling is perhaps among the most exotic samples. At each election, television viewers are amazed (and sometimes frustrated) when the networks project the outcome (with sometimes startling accuracy) before the voting booths are closed. Using fundamentally the same techniques as those described above, pollsters ask people as they leave the voting place whom they voted for. The results are tabulated, and the calculations are used to project who the winner will be before the official results are announced.

Polls are not always accurate, however. Mistakes in sampling can be made, as in the celebrated cases of the *Literary Digest's* falsely predicting a Republican victory over Franklin Delano Roosevelt in 1936, and the Gallup and Roper polls' erroneously forecasting Truman's defeat in 1948. In the 1936 case, the *Literary Digest* did a *nonprobability poll* (an unscientific sample with no attention to the proportions or characteristics of the people questioned) and concluded that Republican Alfred Landon (the father of Senator Nancy Kassebaum [R-KS]) would handily defeat President Franklin D. Roosevelt. The actual returns were the opposite. Similarly, in 1948 most polling organizations relied on nonprobability polls to forecast that Thomas E. Dewey would defeat President Harry S. Truman. In fact, however, Truman won the election by a comfortable margin. Interestingly, few but Truman himself believed that he would win. In other cases, polling data can be incorrectly interpreted or just plain falsely reported.[4] In 1989 the pollsters' projections for the elections of mayor of New York and governor of Virginia were woefully inaccurate, confounding most observers. Analysts agreed, however, that much of the problem was due to poor polling tech-

---

* Pollsters are not alone in their use of random-digit dialing. It is also used for commercial purposes and is becoming something of a problem, tying up essential telephone lines in hospitals and other sensitive facilities. Responding to complaints by private individuals who object to telephone intrusions of their privacy by electronic commercial messages and complaints from hospitals about needless obstructions of telephone lines, Congress is considering legislating regulation of random-digit dialing. What impact such regulations may have on polling is difficult to predict.[3]

niques.[5] When polls are done correctly, however, their accuracy can usually be relied upon.

Reputable pollsters claim nothing more about their findings than that they reflect the public attitudes at the time the polls are taken, yet considerable controversy surrounds the part that polling plays in American politics. Some critics suggest that polls can affect election results. There is the worry that a poll showing one candidate with a heavy lead might create momentum for her or him, thus dooming opponents. On the other hand, front-runners fret about commanding leads lulling supporters into staying away from the polls because the election is "in the bag." Another source of discord about the effects of polling on elections concerns the election-night projections. When it became obvious that he had lost his 1980 bid for reelection, President Carter conceded defeat hours before voting ended in the West. Critics, mostly disgruntled Democrats, complained that the early concession caused large numbers of voters to stay home, thus not voting on many other offices and issues that remained unsettled. This controversy has resulted in considerable pressure to ban election projections by the media before the voting places are closed.

SOURCES OF PUBLIC OPINION

The process by which people develop attitudes about society and their place in it is called **socialization**. Generally speaking, people derive attitudes from a large number of stimuli. Many of our attitudes are deliberately taught us at an early age. From the moment of awareness, family members, principally parents, teach children proper behavior and attitudes. The power of parents to mold personality during a child's formative years is immense, with the result that children normally adopt many of the ideas, values, and attitudes of their parents. This phenomenon is also true of general political attitudes, which often develop quite early in

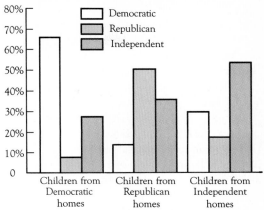

Figure 4.2 Partisan Identification of Children

Source: M. Kent Jennings and Richard G. Niemi, *The Political Character of Adolescence,* Princeton: Princeton University Press, 1974, p. 41.

a child's life.[6] Figure 4.2, for example, indicates that the majority of children identify with the partisan choices of their parents. As these data indicate, family tradition is an important factor in determining partisanship, although it is obviously not absolute.

School is another important vehicle for socialization. Emphasizing patriotism in the early grades, schools deliberately try to impart an appreciation for democracy, capitalism, our institutions of government, and our national heroes. Textbooks tend to emphasize the positive aspects of society and either gloss over or ignore entirely the negative factors. As students progress through school, they encounter increasingly sophisticated and objective analyses of the nation's history and contemporary political issues, but the initial positive attitude is rooted deeply in the student's mind, thus inhibiting later objective thought.

College-level offerings usually provide the most objective and critical inquiries into the social and political systems. Yet you may well be reading this book as part of a required class in American politics, and political socialization was probably a strong reason for exacting the requirement. Since a larger percentage of college graduates vote than does any other group and since most public officials are college graduates, the society feels obliged to school college students in the intricacies of the political system.

Although the inculcation of particular political attitudes in students may be seen as something of a paradox in a nation that sees itself as devoted to freedom of thought and inquiry, some degree of deliberate socialization is probably necessary. All people, from the most primitive to the most advanced, take pains to socialize their young. Societies are based on the cohesion of shared values and ideals, which would not necessarily exist unless they were intentionally taught.

We also acquire values from less formal sources. The world is full of lessons that we pick up without being deliberately taught. Peer groups are particularly influential socializers. Our customs, dress, language, and political beliefs are heavily affected by peer-group stimuli. We are also affected by matters of ethnicity, gender, religion, occupation, social class, authority figures, celebrities, art, music, technology, and a great many other factors. Among the most powerful informal socializers is television. School children spend more time before television sets than they do in school. They and each of us who watches television are powerfully influenced by the programs we see and the newscasts we watch.

Before leaving this discussion about the sources of public opinion, we should consider the question of human frailty: Human beings sometimes lack objectivity and openness to new ideas. We tend to filter information through previously conceived attitudes and beliefs. As a result, the practices of **selective perception** and **selective recall** occur. Each of us, to some extent, tends to assess new data in light of what we already believe. We are inclined to retain what reinforces our beliefs and to ignore contradictions. Similarly, we tend to remember things that sustain our attitudes and forget facts that might lead to other conclusions.[7]

AMERICAN VIEWS

Perhaps one of the society's greatest paradoxes is that the better educated we become, the less we seem to know. More people are in school now and more people are advancing to higher education than at any other time in our history, yet studies reveal an appalling absence of basic information among the public. A recent poll indicated that while the Reagan Administration supported the violent overthrow of the Nicaraguan government and spent hundreds of millions of dollars in support of the Contra rebels (or "freedom fighters"), fewer than half of the public knew where Nicaragua was.[8] Similarly, a Gallup poll revealed that fewer than half of the American people knew that freedom of the press was guaranteed by the First Amendment.[9] Perhaps even more alarming, a 1990 study showed that since 1970, young people (those between ages 18 and 30) have become indifferent about current affairs and are 20 percent less likely than their elders to know basic facts about political matters. This phenomenon contrasts sharply with findings from previous eras, when the difference in information among generations was only marginal.[10] Regardless how well or poorly informed the public, however, its opinion is essential to politicians, and they watch it closely.

Traditionally, the American people, as compared to people in other democracies, tend not to take firm ideological positions.[11] Instead, they are usually more *pragmatic*, preferring to support whatever policy option appears to make sense in a given situation, rather than holding dogmatically to a particular approach to political and social problems. Consequently, as Table 4.1 shows, at no time since 1974 have most people identified themselves as either liberal or conservative, preferring the moderate label instead. The data do reveal a slight shift

Table 4.1

AMERICAN IDEOLOGICAL SELF-IDENTIFICATION

YEAR	LIBERAL	MODERATE	CONSERVATIVE	DON'T KNOW
1974	29%	38%	28%	5%
1976[a]	27%	37%	30%	6%
1978	26%	36%	31%	5%
1980[a]	24%	40%	33%	2%
1982	26%	39%	31%	4%
1984[a]	23%	39%	35%	4%
1986	23%	39%	33%	5%
1988	27%	35%	34%	4%

[a] Presidential election years

Source: Developed from data in Richard G. Niemi, John Muller, and Tom W. Smith, *Trends in Public Opinion* (New York: Greenwood Press, 1989), p. 19.

away from liberal to conservative, but since 1986, the trend seems to have abated somewhat. Still, in spite of the huge popularity of conservative president Ronald Reagan, there has been remarkably little fluctuation in the people's ideological positions.

But knowing the ideological composition of the public is only of limited value since most Americans do not see the world in ideological terms; one might even question how specific their knowledge is of precisely what the terms *liberal* and *conservative* mean. More revealing are the public attitudes regarding specific issues.

The American people manifest an exceptionally high degree of pride in their country. A 1982 poll found 80 percent of the Americans questioned saying they were "very proud" to be citizens of the United States while much smaller percentages of West Europeans and Japanese were equally patriotic.[12] Even so, however, public confidence in the executive branch and in Congress has declined. In 1973, 79 percent of those polled said they had great or at least some confidence in the executive, but by 1988 the figure had fallen to 69 percent. Similarly, 83 percent had great or some confidence in Congress in 1973, but only 77 percent

responded positively in 1988. By contrast, the public has become more positive about the Supreme Court: In 1973, 81 percent had great or some confidence in the Court, but in 1988, the figure was 85 percent.[13]

On particular issues, the public (if college freshmen are any measure) has become more materialistic and less socially concerned. In 1967, 80 percent of the nation's college freshmen listed "developing a meaningful philosophy of life" as a major goal, but in 1990 only 43.2 percent registered the same objective. Similarly, in 1990, 73.2 percent of the entering

During the 1980s the United States spent more on defense than in any other peacetime period.

freshmen indicated that "being financially very well off" was important, while 20 years earlier only 44 percent cited that as a priority.[14] Also, the public attitude about government spending on such items as welfare, public health, drug abuse, environmental protection, and improving the conditions for African-Americans dipped between 1973 and 1980, but by 1987 it had returned to about the 1973 levels. Following the growing conservative trend of the late 1970s, the public support for defense spending leaped from 11 percent in 1973 to 56 percent in 1980, but by 1987 it had dropped to 15 percent. The public interest in government spending on crime prevention and foreign aid remained relatively unchanged between 1973 and 1987, while support for funds for education increased by 12 percentage points and approval of government spending on the problems in the cities decreased by 10 percentage points.[15]

As you can see from Figure 4.3, American public opinion has liberalized on some social issues while it has become more conservative on others. Public tolerance for women and African-Americans in high office has increased and a large majority consistently support gun control. On the other hand, support for the death penalty is on the increase and only a minority support abortion on demand.

Another recent poll demonstrates the same vacillation between liberal and conservative issues.[16] On the conservative side of the ledger, 51 percent of the public believe that books with "dangerous ideas" should be banned from public school libraries, 71 percent favor prayer in the public schools, 65 percent support mandatory testing of government employees for drug use, and 75 percent want tariffs to protect American jobs. At the same time, only 38 percent of the public favor a reduction in environmental protection control, 49 percent want defense expenditures reduced, and 48 percent of the public believe that it is all right for whites and African-Americans to date. Further, the ambivalence of public opinion among

issues also occurs within separate parts of the same issue. For example, while 55 percent of the people polled in 1987 believed that government regulation of business does more harm than good, half said that the government should do more to protect job safety, and 61 percent wanted more government regulation of the environment.[17]

The Media

Free media are a fundamental part of any democratic society, and as such they bear an enormous responsibility to the public. The accuracy and fairness of their reports are of paramount importance to the system, just as freedom of the press is central to democracy. Besides friends, the various groups with which we associate, the books we read, and other such sources, the media are our principal source of information about the events, issues, and personalities important to our political being. Indeed, the media are a major influence on public opinion. Media coverage of issues can arouse public concern, political careers can be made or demolished by the press, and public attitudes about the system itself can be influenced by the tone the media set.

CIRCULATION AND CREDIBILITY OF THE MEDIA

Daily newspapers began publishing in this country in the 1830s. By 1850 approximately 3.3 percent of the population received a newspaper, and by 1900 the figure had reached almost 20 percent. Newspaper circulation continued to increase until reaching a high point in 1947 of 36.7 percent. From that time, a period coinciding with the rise in popularity of television, newspaper circulation has declined, until in 1987 it had fallen to 25.9 percent of the population, nine-tenths of a percent below the mark it set in 1909. At the same time, the number of dailies reached a peak of

Figure 4.3   *Public Opinion on Certain Controversial Issues, 1957–1988*

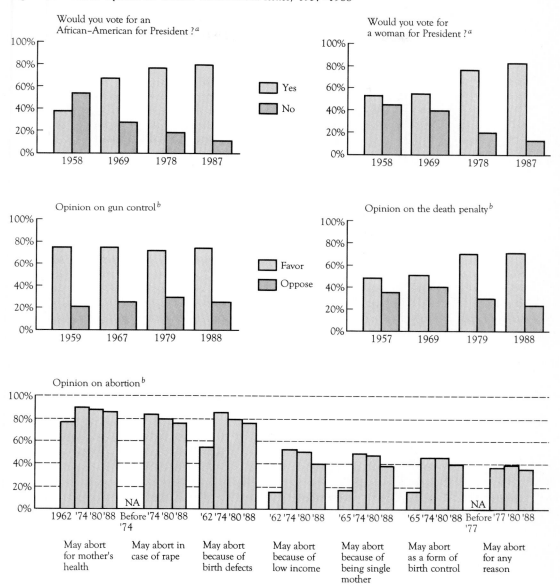

NA: not available

Sources: [a] Adapted from Gallup polls.
[b] *Vital Statistics on American Politics,* 2nd ed, pp. 31–33.

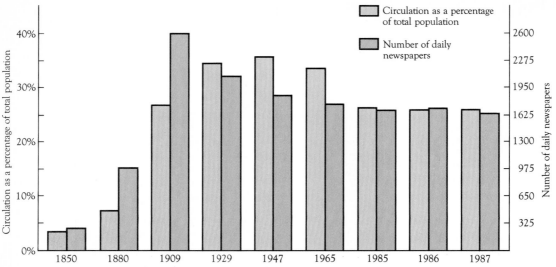

Figure 4.4   *Newspaper Circulation as a Percentage of the Total Population and Number of Daily Newspapers*
Source: Adapted from data in *Vital Statistics on American Politics*, 2nd ed., p. 51.

2600 in 1909 and has since declined by almost 1000. (See Figure 4.4.)

The disappearance of daily newspapers means that people increasingly find they have little selection among dailies. Of course, the broad area circulation of major papers such as *The New York Times*, *The Chicago Tribune*, and *The Los Angeles Times*, together with the emergence of national newspapers such as *The Wall Street Journal*, *The Christian Science Monitor*, and *USA Today*, affords some variety, but the sharp decline in the number of dailies is nonetheless regrettable. Furthermore, since most newspapers depend on a tiny number of wire services such as the Associated Press, United Press International, and Reuters, newspaper coverage beyond the local level has become somewhat homogeneous. Another major source of news in print are news magazines, but the three periodicals with greatest circulation (see Figure 4.5) account for a combined publication of just over ten million copies per week, enough to reach only about 11 percent of

the nation's households if each family subscribed to only one magazine apiece.

In contrast with the printed media, electronic media coverage has exploded in this century. Invented by Guglielmo Marconi in 1906, radio became a major source of entertainment by the 1930s, and regular news broadcasts were common by the 1940s. Today, 99 percent of American homes have radios—and radios come as standard equipment in most automobiles. At the same time, almost all radio stations feature news segments, and some are exclusively news broadcast stations.

Primitive experimental television broadcasts were made as early as 1926, but it was not until after World War II that commercialization began in earnest. In 1950, when almost 93 percent of American homes had radios, only 9 percent had television sets. But within a decade, 87 percent of the homes had sets, and television had come of age politically, with the broadcast of the first presidential debates, which many authorities believe was critical in

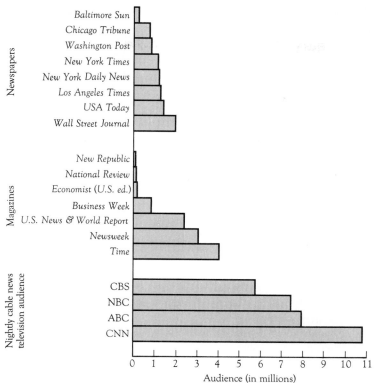

Figure 4.5 *Print Media Circulation and Nightly Cable Television Audience, 1990*
Source: *Newspapers:* Gale Directory of Publications and Broadcast Media, 1991; *Magazines:* Ulrich's International Periodicals Directory, 1990–1991; *Television:* "CNN is No. 1 in Ratings War," *The Los Angeles Times*, January 19, 1991.

John F. Kennedy's victory over Richard M. Nixon.

As the number of television sets increased in the country, the number of hours people spent before them also increased, until television has become one of the greatest single occupiers of American leisure time on a daily basis. At the same time, people began to rely increasingly on television news, until by 1986, 98 percent of American homes had at least one television set[18] and two-thirds of the population said that television was a major source of news. As you can see from Table 4.2, American reliance on the printed media has dropped precipitously over the past three decades, and radio, like the printed media, has become less popular as a news source. Only television has enjoyed an increase in use as a news source. Underscoring this point, a 1991 Roper poll revealed that 81 percent of those questioned said that television was their major source of news about the Persian Gulf War and 54 percent said that it was their *only* news source about the war.[19] Another study, however, indicates that, of people who follow presidential elections closely, about the same percentage rely on newspapers as on television for the news.[20] Thus, the greatest increase in televi-

Table 4.2
MAJOR SOURCES OF NEWS[a]

	1959	1968	1978	1988
Newspapers	57%	49%	49%	42%
Magazines	8%	7%	5%	4%
Radio	34%	25%	20%	14%
Television	51%	59%	67%	65%

[a] Respondents could list more than one item.

Source: Adapted from data in Stanley and Niemi, *Vital Statistics on American Politics,* 2nd ed.

Table 4.3
PUBLIC TRUST IN THE MEDIA

	1959	1968	1978	1988
Newspapers	32%	21%	23%	26%
Magazines	10%	11%	9%	5%
Radio	12%	8%	9%	7%
Television	29%	44%	47%	49%

Source: Adapted from data in Stanley and Niemi, *Vital Statistics on American Politics,* 2nd ed.

sion news watchers may be among those who follow the news only casually.

The data in Table 4.3 indicate that public trust in the media has followed the same course, with public confidence in the printed media and radio declining, even as it increased for television. One reason for low public confidence in the press is the perception that it is biased. Conservatives often attack the "liberal" television news departments, especially CBS, and liberals lament the "conservative" editorial bias of many major newspapers. For whatever reason, about 45 percent of the people believe reporters to be biased, while only 36 percent believe that they attempt to report the news fairly.[21]

Whether or not journalists are biased in reporting the news depends too much on individual journalists and upon the observers' perceptions to decide definitively. It is true, however, that 55 percent of journalists identify themselves as liberals, and even larger percentages list themselves in support of liberal approaches to social and political problems.[22] On the other hand, perhaps reflecting the difference between the press room and the board room, Figure 4.6 indicates a clear conservative tendency in many of the nation's editorial policies, although the trend is definitely toward a neutral stance since 1940. Note that only once since 1932 did more newspapers endorse the Democratic candidate for president than the

Republican candidate: That was in 1964, Lyndon B. Johnson versus Barry Goldwater, and even then, fewer than 8 percent more newspapers endorsed the Democrat. At the same time, more newspapers have usually remained neutral than have endorsed Democratic candidates, while only once, in 1988, have more newspapers remained neutral than have endorsed Republican candidates. Interestingly, newspaper endorsements do not seem to have much impact on the results of presidential elections since the voters have ignored the preponderance of endorsements in 7 out of 15 elections.

Another frequently logged criticism of the media is that they lack substance. While the printed media receive some blame in this regard, the harshest remarks are reserved for television news. Except for certain news programs such as "The MacNeil/Lehrer NewsHour," "Washington Week in Review," "Firing Line," "Face the Nation," and the like, some critics see television journalism as shallow; it tends to focus on photogenic subjects and seldom delves deeply into the issues. Hence, television news, from which the greatest number of people get information about public affairs, is little more than a series of headlines strung together with such action shots as the *intifada* throwing stones, trains crashing, and the public demonstrating.

The media perform a vital function in society, however, not only by reporting events as

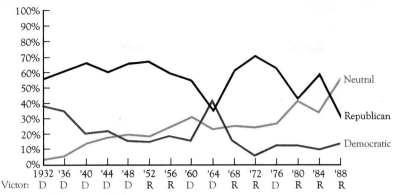

Figure 4.6   Percentage of Newspaper Endorsements in Presidential Elections, 1932–1988
Source: Editors and Publishers Yearbook, 1989.

they happen but also by serving as a check on those in power. At times the institutional checks and balances are not sufficiently alert to curb abuses. In those cases we benefit from "outside" sentinels: the media. Without the publication of the Pentagon Papers by *The New York Times* and the nightly television coverage of the Indochina war, United States policy in Southeast Asia might not have received much scrutiny. The ingenuity and persistence of investigative journalists Bob Woodward and Carl Bernstein of *The Washington Post* exposed the Watergate scandal as an unprecedented political subterfuge; media focus on the Iran-Contra arms-for-hostages scandal relentlessly brought home the arrogance and incompetence of a popular administration to a public that would rather have ignored the matter.

Although the public generally favors investigative journalism, controversy is never very far removed from the efforts of probing reporters. Perhaps the most serious question about journalistic tactics surfaced when in 1987 former senator Gary Hart, front-running candidate for the Democratic nomination for president, was photographed cavorting with Miami model Donna Rice on a yacht prophetically named *Monkey Business*. Whether the human foibles and personal peccadilloes of po-

litical candidates should be the focus of the media is a matter of considerable debate. Critics argue that such matters have little bearing on the candidate's ability to do the job, while supporters of the practice maintain that political leaders are, or should be, role models, that they personify public service, and that character is an essential factor in the choice of public officials.

MEDIA RELATIONS WITH GOVERNMENT AND POLITICIANS

No public media enjoy more freedom to know and to report than does the American press; even public officials, as we learned in Chapter 3, have little protection against castigation, innuendo, and allegations. Few governments make available to the press the breadth and depth of material that the American media can obtain. An important tool for the press is the **Freedom of Information Act** of 1966. This law requires federal agencies to provide citizens with access to public records upon request. The act exempts material relating to the national security, but it allows citizens to sue the government when disputes arise, thus giving the judiciary the decision about which contested documents shall be made public and which shall remain classified. Accordingly, the Supreme Court in 1989 sharply narrowed the scope of the act by ruling that information gathered by the government during routine operations may be kept secret if the information later becomes part of a criminal investigation.[23] In any event, by gaining access to previously classified documents, the press and many private citizens have uncovered cases of power abuse, attempted intimidation, and government harassment of private citizens.[24]

Formal procedures are, however, not the only sources available to journalists. Among the most controversial leads the press gets are **leaks**. A leak is information unofficially made available to the press. There are many reasons for people in the government to go to the press with information that is supposed to remain confidential. People who oppose the policies of superiors may make secrets public, as apparently was the case with "Deep Throat," the informant Woodward and Bernstein used to unravel the Watergate affair. Disgruntled employees may wish to embarrass superiors, bureaucrats may leak word of impending budget cut proposals so as to alert congressional allies, insecure functionaries may betray confidences to demonstrate that they have access to important information, or someone may just talk too much.

Anyone even casually acquainted with Washington D.C., knows that it thrives on rumor, innuendo, and leaks. The difficulty of keeping information and plans secret has plagued presidents from the beginning of the republic. Indeed, some presidents, such as Nixon and Reagan, became obsessed with the problem. Early in his administration, Reagan tried to place limits on the scope of the Freedom of Information Act and to stay the stream of unauthorized information hemorrhaging from his government.[25] Yet ironically enough, a large number of leaks come deliberately from the administration itself. When the president

Presidential press secretary Marlin Fitzwater at a March 1990 press conference avoiding a reply about the sexually explicit Indian doll Vice President Dan Quayle purchased during a recent trip to Chile.

wants something made public but does not wish to be associated with it, someone in the administration can leak it to the press with the proviso that the source of the item remain anonymous. These kinds of leaks are often referred to as **trial balloons**. By using unattributed leaks, the administration can test public reaction to a change in policy and later be able to deny association with the idea should the public respond negatively.

To this point, we have been examining the media as watchdogs of government, but the media are also often used by public officials to accomplish the officials' ends. **News management** has become an accepted fact of American public life. Any organization of reasonable size, probably including the college you are attending, has a public information office (PIO). A large part of the PIO's task is to feed the press positive stories about the organizations they represent and to practice **damage control** when a negative issue arises. Employed to put the "right spin" on the news, PIO officers are hardly committed to objectivity.

The same can be said about politicians. The president's press secretary, for example, is not only concerned with reporting the news to the press; he or she is openly engaged in presenting the administration's perspective and representing it as fact. In other words, politicians are engaged in conscious attempts to influence the media and thus indirectly manipulate public opinion.

Since President Franklin D. Roosevelt used his radio broadcast "fireside chats" to ally fear among the public caused by the Great Depression of the 1930s, each president has become heavily dependent upon the media to project his message and image, and each has made increasing attempts to control the media—to manage the news. But of all presidents to date, none has been so image-conscious or so adept at the use of the media as Ronald Reagan. Aware of his limited command of the facts and capitalizing on his speech-making talents, Reagan avoided direct contact with the press, preferring to go directly to the people via weekly radio addresses and occasional television speeches. Knowing that Reagan would often blunder if allowed to speak off-the-cuff, his staff carefully scripted his public remarks and painstakingly rehearsed him before they were uttered. Even his famous line, used in the 1980 Presidential debates to doom President Carter's bid for reelection, "Are you better off now than you were four years ago?" was written for him by a staff aid. Furthermore, in his recent book *Speaking Out*, Larry Speakes—former Reagan press secretary—admits to inventing comments himself, when Reagan had nothing to say on issues, and delivering the comments as though they had come from the President.

Reagan's staff devised other methods to insulate him from the press and to protect his image; the president would be brought out to make announcements that reflected positively on his administration, but when it was time to report bad news, staff aids or cabinet officials took the heat. Really bad news was often released on a Friday afternoon so that it would not hit the papers and broadcasts until Saturday, when fewer people were likely to see it,

and so that the negative fallout might be given a weekend to settle. Sometimes bad-news announcements would be timed to coincide with presidential flights to California for vacation, as when it was announced that the Marines were being pulled out of Lebanon in 1984. In other cases, reporters who were in disfavor for criticizing the administration would have difficulty getting the White House to return phone calls and staff aids would have the helicopter pilots turn up their rotors when the president walked from the White House to his helicopter, so he could not hear and, therefore, could not answer reporters' questions.[26]

At other times, when public comment could not be avoided on matters considered too sensitive for public knowledge, Reagan would deliberately mislead the press, as he did when he denied that the United States was planning to invade the island of Grenada in 1983. Although intentionally distorting the truth is considered a serious matter, it is sometimes seen as necessary—especially in the field of foreign policy—and President Reagan was certainly not the first politician to do so, nor is he likely to be the last. Equally serious, some presidents, including Lyndon Johnson and Richard Nixon, tried to intimidate the media, with Nixon even implying that some television networks might have trouble retaining their broadcasting licenses.[27]

Begun by Theodore Roosevelt, presidential press conferences have become an expected feature in American political life. As you can see from Figure 4.7, presidents have used them with varying frequency, but only Nixon and Reagan have held so few. Nixon distrusted the press, fearing that it was "out to get" him and that it liked to "kick him around." Reagan, on the other hand, enjoyed good relations with the press during most of his presidency, but his embarrassing ignorance of detail and sometimes even of generalities concerning his programs caused his aids to schedule very few press conferences, contradicting his promise to hold at

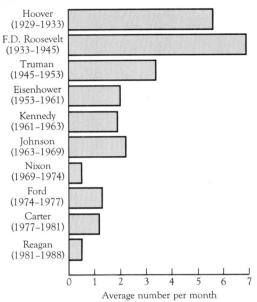

Figure 4.7   *Frequency of Presidential Press Conferences, 1929–1988*

Source: Adapted from *Vital Statistics on American Politics*, 2nd ed., p. 53.

least one press conference per month. So concerned was the staff that the president would muff his lines that each press conference was preceded by a thorough rehearsal, during which aids would pepper him with questions and then coach and critique his answers. The elaborate precautions were, however, not always enough to suppress incorrect statements, and press conferences were often followed by the staff's correcting the president's remarks.[28] For his part, President Bush is much more at ease with the press and has held press conferences almost once a week.

Presidents are not the only politicians who attempt to manipulate the media, however. As Hedrick Smith points out in his recent book *The Power Game,* the media has spawned a new breed of politicians. Unlike "insider" politicians who use traditional levers of power such

as seniority, personal contacts, and control of the political machinery, the new breed—or "outsiders"—have learned to increase their power by manipulating the media. Using press conferences, satellite dish television broadcasts to their districts, op-ed articles in the press, and other techniques, they have made themselves prominent in the public view and influential in politics.

Perhaps the most blatant attempts to use the media, however, occur during political campaigns. Campaigns will be dealt with in depth in later chapters; for now it is sufficient to note some of the techniques candidates use to procure favorable treatment from the media. Candidates mold their schedules, activities, and speeches around media needs. Campaign appearances are choreographed to exhibit enough color and movement to attract television editors; remarks are tailored to the media's penchant for 15-second "sound bites"; longer statements will be edited or cut altogether. Each campaign day is planned to the last detail: Advance people make sure a crowd is present to welcome the candidate; staff aides who have analyzed the scene suggest to television crews and press photographers the best spots and angles from which to shoot; and above all, the major campaign appearances of the day are carefully calculated so as to occur in plenty of time for reporters to make their deadlines.

Normally, candidates are warned not to argue with the press since it usually has the last word. George Bush, however, cleverly did exactly this during his 1988 campaign for president—and he did it so as to derive great benefit. Asked to participate in a CBS News interview with Dan Rather, Bush insisted it be broadcast live to avoid any editing. As Rather pressed Bush for details about his involvement in the Iran-Contra affair, Bush went on the offensive, with the result that he and Rather traded verbal blows for several minutes on national television.

Many of the freedoms enjoyed by the American press are suspended in time of war. The government has always assumed the right to censor the press in wartime so that the national security and safety of American troops is not jeopardized. However, during most of this century, the press has always been allowed to cover wars as it saw fit, provided it did not publicize troop movements or other such sensitive information. During the Vietnam War, for example, the press was allowed broad latitude of activity. Of course, the government gave daily briefings, which skeptical reporters called the *five o'clock follies* to reflect the often sanitized and self-serving accounts of the war's progress. Even so, the press was independently able to seek sources and information. Its activities during the war often embarrassed the military by publishing facts and analysis that contradicted the government's version of the war, and the military came to blame the press for the decline in public support for the war effort. Toward the end of the conflict, military officers joked that American service personnel had three primary obligations: "duty, honor, and hate the press." This antagonism subsequently resulted in a serious reduction of the freedom of the press to cover combat in which the United States is involved. For example, in the 1983 invasion of Grenada, the press was for the first time not allowed to accompany American troops. In fact, the press was deliberately told that rumors of such an invasion before it was launched were false. Similarly, the Bush Administration allowed only a small select group of American reporters to cover the Persian Gulf War, and they were forbidden to talk to American service personnel without an official present, or to travel wherever they wished. Errant reporters were sometimes arrested and treated roughly by the military.[29] Such tight control of the press is unfortunate because the American people have no independent observers to report events.

Whatever the case, the republic would be seriously weakened without a free press. It is a guardian against government misbehavior even as it informs us of the news. Indeed, its role in our political system is so critical that it deserves recognition, along with the electorate, as one of the principal checks outside the system. There is, however, a third element that exercises immense influence in society—the interest groups—to which we now turn our attention.

Interest Groups

Among the great debates in American politics is an argument about the nature of the political system. Is it democratic or not? If it is democratic, exactly how do the people relate to the government? How do they exercise control? Although this exchange reaches back to the earliest days of the republic, it was given new focus in the 1950s, and the dialogue as it was framed at that time continues to the present.

Being realistic, political scientists reject the notion that our political system is so simple that it can adequately be described as a democracy in which the political leaders respond directly to the needs of individuals. The reality is much more complex: If, in fact, the system is democratic, it operates in a much less direct fashion.

Essentially, the debate can be reduced to the positions of two major antagonists: **elite theorists** and **pluralists**. The elite theorists argue that democracy is but a pretense in the United States and that the government, while elected by the people, in reality responds to a different master—a group of extremely powerful people distributed throughout the society. Although elite theorism in one form or another can be traced back through the centuries, its most powerful statement as it relates to the

United States was advanced by sociologist C. Wright Mills.

Mills, in his book *The Power Elite*, claimed that the real rulers in the United States were to be found among the leading corporate heads, political figures, financial moguls, and so on; they share values and general objectives, and together they run the country.[30] Other elite theorists, including G. William Domhoff and Michael Useem, assert that popular government is an illusion. Instead, the country is run from the board rooms of corporations, universities, foundations, and the like. Marshaling evidence of elite control of the levers of power, political scientist Thomas Dye meticulously demonstrated that an enormous amount of the nation's wealth is concentrated in the hands of a tiny number of people, and that together only 7314 people command many of the nation's basic industries.[31] In addition, Robert Michels laid down the **iron law of oligarchy**, which suggests that in any organization the number of active people is tiny and that they therefore end up in control. In other words, most of us are too busy with ordinary concerns to take an active part in the management of most groups with which we are associated, be they the PTA, the associated student body, or the federal government; hence the elite of each group controls it.[32]

While the iron law of oligarchy may indeed be at work, critics of elite theorism aver that the elite in society obviously do not completely control the system; otherwise increased taxes for the major corporations could not have been passed in 1986, and reformers such as Franklin Delano Roosevelt and Lyndon B. Johnson would never have been allowed to implement the New Deal and the Great Society.

Pluralists, unlike elite theorists, generally believe that the system is democratic, albeit indirectly so. The demographic, ethnic, social, economic, and geographical diversity of the United States is so vast as to make impossible the ideal democratic situation in which a representative focuses on the needs of each constituent. Instead, people find it necessary to organize into groups to advance their interests collectively, hence the name **interest groups**. Thus, public policy reflects a melee of competing groups, each pressing for its point of view. Pluralists do not deny the existence of an elite, recognizing that some people enjoy much more power than others, but they suggest that the elite do not always get their way. Further, pluralists justify the dynamic they advance by citing James Madison's belief that "factions" among people are natural, and recounting his attempts to accommodate factions while at the same time preventing any single group from becoming dominant.[33]

The principal advocates of pluralism are political scientists David Truman and, especially, Robert Dahl. Truman argues that all societies tend to subordinate individual interests to those of subgroups and that, as Madison believed, this tendency is a natural human phenomenon.[34] This theme was taken up and made explicit by Dahl in *Who Governs?*, a case study of governmental decision-making in New Haven, Connecticut. Dahl concluded that the "majority rarely rules" in the simplistic sense, seldom rising to any particular issue. Instead, issues were usually addressed only by the minority of people who happened to have direct interest in them, and that those few tended to approach controversy through groups such as the Chamber of Commerce, labor unions, church congregations, neighborhood groups, and the like.[35]

Since the 1950s, the pluralist model has dominated American political science, but it has not gone without challenge. Some critics object to the pluralists' belief that the model they describe is democratic because, while many people's needs are indeed represented by interest groups, many other people often go unrepresented, such as farm labor, immigrants, the poor, the homeless, and consumers. Further, even though some views of a particular individual may be voiced, it is unlikely that every need of every individual is represented by the interest groups. Finally, while it may be correct to suggest that many different interests are represented by various groups, the consortiums are not necessarily evenly matched, some having more money, better leadership, and closer connections with policy-makers than others.

Theodore Lowi, a powerful critic of pluralism, argues that in a way pluralism works too well, that the pluralist process has become the objective of government rather than simply its procedural model. That is to say, government tries to accommodate each interest group and the result is a hodge-podge of very expensive and often contradictory legislation. For example, government-subsidized farmers successfully fight against regulation of their use of pesticides, while consumers make sure that billions are spent on treating poisoned ground water before it is deemed potable. Lowi further suggests that the close relationship between interest groups and government becomes almost symbiotic, with each seeing itself as the benefactor and protector of the other, leading to conservative policy that protects the establishment interests to the exclusion of others. In the process, the public interest is sometimes sacrificed.[36]

INTEREST GROUP STRUCTURE AND FUNCTIONS

Regardless of whether the pluralists are correct in their assessment of our political system, there can be little doubt about the centrality of interest groups in American politics. Indeed, in the early nineteenth century, a perceptive observer of American society, Alexis de Tocqueville, noted our unique proclivity to use group action in accomplishing tasks: "Whenever at the head of some new undertaking you see the government of France, or a man of rank in England, in the United States *you will be sure to find an association*"[37] (emphasis added).

As de Tocqueville observed, we are a "nation of joiners." Each of us has needs and desires we wish satisfied, and an extraordinary number of us belong to one or more groups that try to satisfy our interests. Of course, not everyone is a joiner. People in the middle class and above are more prone to associate with interest groups, just as they are more apt to be politically active than are people in the lower classes. While some people belong to no group at all, others belong to several—and they run the risk of seeing the policies of one group conflict with those of another. A person who enjoys driving in the wilderness could belong to both an off-road driving club and an environmental group at the same time. But clearly, these two groups could oppose each other over the appropriate use of the national forests.

In a formal sense, an interest group is an organization of people with shared interests that attempts to persuade government to adopt policy consistent with its wishes. Although interest groups used to be called pressure groups, they normally avoid that term now because it sounds manipulative, smacking of power politics. But, as political scientist Robert Huckshorn correctly insists, political "pressure is the stock-in-trade of interest groups."[38] Even so, we should not be myopic about the function of interest groups. Indeed, while our principal concern is in their efforts to influence government, they do several other things as well. Among the most important functions of interest groups is attempting to popularize issues; they keep their members informed of relevant issues and developments; they mobilize their members, giving them the opportunity to participate in government; they serve as watchdogs on government, assuring that the group's interests are not abused; and they often offer an array of benefits to members including insurance programs, financial programs, and discounts on consumer goods.

Perhaps the most striking fact about interest groups in the society is their phenomenal growth rate. Not only have they grown in number, but they have increasingly focused on Washington, D.C., and their scope has transformed. In his farewell address in 1981, President Jimmy Carter lamented the rising influence and the changing nature of the interest groups, and he warned of the impact on government and public policy:

> We are increasingly drawn to single-issue groups and special-interest organizations to ensure that whatever else happens our own personal views and our own private interests are protected. This is a disturbing factor in American political life. It tends to distort our purpose because the national interest is not always the sum of all our single or special interests.[39]

The growth of interest groups began to skyrocket in the 1960s and continued through the 1970s, but apparently leveled off in the last decade. The greatest increase in interest groups was among business and trade associations (industrywide associations). Not only have their numbers increased, but so have their advocacy activity and focus on the national government. Business interest groups with Washington, D.C., offices doubled in number between 1970 and 1980, and while the number of trade associations has not greatly increased, many of them have moved their headquarters to Washington, D.C., reflecting a significantly increased focus on lobbying. Between 1970 and 1986 the proportion of national trade associations headquartered in Washington rose from 21 percent to 31 percent. At the same time, 63

percent of the corporate departments that lobby for corporations augmented their professional staff; between 1961 and 1978, General Motors alone increased its lobbying staff from 3 to 28.[40] Meanwhile, there has been great growth in the number of public interest, single-issue, and ideological interest groups.

Many reasons are suggested for the leap in the number and focus of interest groups. The attention on social issues such as civil rights, the environment, the ERA, and prayer in the public schools, is partially responsible, together with the declining importance of political parties. Also, the increased involvement of government in the economy has caused people to mobilize. Further, changes in campaign finance laws and the decentralization of power in Congress have been factors. And as new groups arise to advance their interests, other groups mobilize to counter them.[41]

Although most interest groups are multifaceted and complex, it may be helpful to distinguish among them with regard to their focus. *Economically oriented interest groups* are among the oldest. They include organized labor, agriculture, and business interests. Labor is represented by specific unions such as the United Auto Workers and by the labor federations— the American Federation of Labor-Congress of Industrial Organizations (AFL-CIO), for example. Agriculture interests include large federations such as the American Farm Bureau Federation and more specifically focused groups such as the Cattlemen's Association. Business groups are also divided. Trade associations, such as the Chamber of Commerce and the National Cable Television Association, represent the general interests of their members or of an industry as a whole. More specifically, a large number of corporations have offices of government relations or public affairs departments that represent their corporation's specific interests. Another important business interest group is the Business Roundtable, comprising about 200 of the nation's leading corporate heads.

More recent arrivals on the political scene are the *public interest groups*. Responding to the growing trend of interest groups representing narrow self-interest, some people became concerned that the broader view was being lost in the shuffle. Complaining that "everyone is represented but the people," John Gardner, a liberal Republican and former cabinet secretary in the Johnson Administration, organized **Common Cause** in 1970 to advocate for good government practices. Since its founding, Common Cause has pressed for governmental reform, stricter regulations of lobbying, and election reform. A frequent ally of Common Cause, consumer advocate and government reformer *Ralph Nader* has created several groups that press for particular public concerns, including environmental protection, consumer protection, energy conservation, public health, government reform, and so forth.[42]

Public interest groups are organizations that advocate policy for the common good and not for the personal advantage of their members. Although they have developed in large numbers since the 1960s, some public interest groups existed before, including the League of Women Voters, the Sierra Club, the Audubon Society, and the Consumers Union.

The 1950s and 1960s also gave impetus to ethnic, gender, and lifestyle groups. Joining the National Association for the Advancement of Colored People (founded in 1909), the Southern Christian Leadership Conference and the Congress of Racial Equality (CORE) formed to advance the interests of African-Americans. Civil liberties and feminism are respectively advocated by the American Civil Liberties Union (ACLU) and the National Organization for Women (NOW).[43]

Responding to the social issues and to the gains made by some of the public interest groups, the *ideological groups* are among the most recent arrivals to the political scene. In the liberal column are the Americans for Democratic Action and People for the American Way (founded by Norman Lear, producer of "All in the Family" and other television programs). Much more numerous are the conservative groups, including the Conservative Union, Young Americans for Freedom, the Committee for the Survival of a Free Constitution, the Conservative Caucus, and Americans for Constitutional Action.

Another phenomenon associated with the increase in interest groups is the growth of single-issue organizations. These groups focus on one objective only and include the National Rifle Association (NRA), Mothers Against Drunk Driving (MADD), and ERAmerica. The single-issue orientation is growing among the public, and it is troublesome. An increasing number of people focus on one issue to decide their votes, be it abortion, crime prevention, drug abuse, the pledge of allegiance to the flag, or whatever. The problem with a single-issue orientation is that it neglects the vast array of other matters with which policy-makers must deal. In short, the single-issue approach, as President Carter said in his farewell address, tends to ignore the general social good.

Closely related to the single-issue groups are organizations based on *religious fundamentalism*. Religiously oriented interest groups such as the National Baptist Convention and the American Jewish Committee have existed for decades. Traditionally, these organizations have been interested in a broad range of issues. Recently, however, Christian fundamentalists have mobilized to combat *secular humanism* (the abandonment of biblical truth, as the fundamentalists see it, for focus on human morality without spiritualism) and the perceived decline of traditional American values. The most prominent of these groups was the *Moral Majority*.

POWER AND APPROACHES

The influence of interest groups with government has significantly increased. Interestingly, it appears that their power has elevated as voter turnout (which will be discussed in a subsequent chapter) has dwindled. Also, interest groups advocating specific issues have tended to become more powerful as political party loyalty among the public and party discipline in government have declined.

Interest groups employ several sources of power. Perhaps most important of all is *knowledge*. The legislation and administration of public policy is an extremely complicated process. Public officials and their staffs, while usually very knowledgeable, cannot possibly keep abreast of the intricacies of all the issues with which they deal. Interest groups, on the other hand, specialize and can thus offer policy-makers the benefit of their expertise. While policy-makers realize that interest groups have specific objectives, the information these groups possess is invaluable. Besides offering expertise on specific issues, interest groups can sometimes indicate to politicians the depth of public emotion on a particular issue, something any elected official is eager to know. Furthermore, such groups have valuable knowledge about how the system works. A good deal of time and energy can be wasted by people wishing to influence government but not knowing how to go about it. Working with government on a regular basis, interest groups know which legislator to ask to sponsor a bill, what kind of testimony is likely to have the greatest effect on a congressional committee, and what agency and personnel in the executive branch to approach about questions of policy execution and program administration.

Another important element in interest group influence is the amount of *money* it can bring to bear. Campaign contributions will be dealt with later, but money can also be used to employ the best staff; to maintain expensive Washington, D.C., offices; to do the most thorough research; to publicize the views of its clients; to wine and dine policy-makers; to pay them honoraria for speaking engagements; and to provide them transportation to conferences, tours of plants, and the like. *Membership size* can also be significant. If labor can persuade policy-makers that its millions of members will react negatively to an issue, its influence is increased. Other groups can maximize their power by mobilizing a large percentage of their members to contact policy-makers about issues. The National Rifle Association, with only three million members, can generate hundreds of thousands of letters from its constituents within hours, and it has been very successful at frustrating attempts to legislate gun control, although recently its power has waned a bit. Sometimes the type of membership is helpful. Groups composed of leading scientists, corporate heads, retired admirals, former diplomats, physicians, and prominent personalities enjoy automatic respect and authority that ordinary people may have to earn. The *integrity* of an organization is also important. Those groups noted for accuracy and candor in representing their constituents are appreciated by policy-makers who depend on them for information. Finally, of course, interest groups with personal contacts in government enjoy an advantage in satisfying their needs.

Besides hiring experienced lobbyists, one of the most notorious methods of getting contacts in government is the **revolving door**. Each year people from industry are appointed to government agencies that regulate or in some other way affect the industry from which they come. When their government service is ended, they often return to work for the same industry. In other cases, career government employees leave to take positions with industries that do business with the government, and the transferees can use their contacts to help their new employer. For example, in 1983 alone, 13,682 Pentagon officials left government service to work in defense industries.[44]

The methods used by interest groups to influence public policy vary enormously. Lobbying and campaign contributions are, of course, major approaches, but they will be dealt with later. In general, interest groups use direct and indirect methods to reach policy-makers. Many of the _direct approaches_ have already been discussed, including furnishing amenities to policy-makers, advocacy, and testimony. Some interest groups also attempt to influence elections by endorsing candidates and by publishing scorecards of incumbents' voting records. Others actively campaign to defeat unwanted officeholders. Perhaps the most successful recent effort of this sort occurred in 1980 when the National Conservative Political Action Committee (NCPAC) spent millions trying to defeat five United States senators whom they perceived as too liberal. Successful in all but one election, that of Alan Cranston (D-CA), NCPAC helped unseat Birch Bayh (D-IN), Frank Church (D-ID), John Culver (D-IA), and George McGovern (D-SD). Although some authorities question the importance of NCPAC's efforts in these defeats, most believe it was significant.[45] Since 1980, however, NCPAC has been less successful at affecting elections.

Other methods include trying to influence appointments of staff, cabinet officials, and even judges—for example, Judge Robert Bork's appointment to the Supreme Court in 1987. When efforts to influence the legislative and executive branches fail, pressure groups will often seek redress through litigation. As we have already seen in Chapter 3, civil rights groups such as the NAACP have been very successful in pressing court appeals—but economic, public interest, religious, and single-issue groups have also done so with effect. In fact, one study found that 63 percent of the most significant Supreme Court cases were brought by interest groups.[46]

Indirect approaches attempt to bring pressure on policy-makers through the voters. Using mass mailings, many groups alert their members to controversy and ask them to write their legislators. Other groups encourage their members to contact public officials personally in the community or by actually visiting the capital. Another technique is to organize public demonstrations to make a point. Public demonstrations reach beyond the membership of the interest group to the public at large. Pressure groups often resort to other techniques that manipulate public opinion for their benefit. Public utilities and banks have used billings and monthly statements to publicize their views on issues or even to encourage public action. Probably the most successful recent effort of this sort occurred in 1983 when the American Bankers Association and the U.S. League of Savings Institutions encouraged customers to protest a new law requiring taxes withheld from interest and dividends. About 22 million pieces of mail were sent to Congress in response to this effort, and the law was promptly repealed.[47]

Finally, corporations, trade associations, labor unions, and other groups spend vast sums on ads in journals and newspapers and on radio and television trying to popularize their views. Mobil Oil is probably the biggest participant in this field. Periodically it publishes in the major newspapers across the land articles about its view on the energy situation, taxation, and even lobbying itself. You may also recall ads calling upon you to "look for the union label" or "buy American." In 1989, the Northrop Corporation took out full-page ads in the major newspapers lauding the features of the B-2

Bomber (which it builds, of course) at a time when Congress balked at enormous production cost-overruns of the weapon, and when Northrop was under investigation for false billing on the project.

Although, as we have seen, the indirect approach can be effective, it is very expensive and is inconsistent in its effect since it relies upon the voluntary efforts of so many people. In most cases the direct approach is more fruitful, or at least more predictable. By far, the most effective tools in the direct approach are lobbying and money.

LOBBYING

Lobbying does not enjoy high esteem in American public opinion, usually conjuring visions of cigar-smoking fat-cats plying policy-makers with liquor, sexual partners, and bribes. While such stereotypes are sometimes valid, lobbying can be an honorable profession, and it is an important aspect of the American political system.

Lobbying exists at virtually every stage of American government, from the local level to the state, and finally to the federal government. Lobbyists ply their craft in the legislature, of course, but they also work closely with the administration, the bureaucracy, and the regulatory boards and commissions. Indeed, governments themselves spend considerable money and energy lobbying. Since the Eisenhower Administration, the president has had a staff assigned to congressional liaison, and by 1980 there were almost 700 lobbyists in the executive branch representing 32 cabinet and lesser agencies in the administration.[48] In addition, many cities, counties, states, schools and colleges, and other local public agencies maintain lobbyists in Washington, D.C.

As with the interest groups they represent, the number of lobbyists in Washington, D.C.,

has exploded in the past two decades. In 1961, only 365 lobbyists were registered with Congress, but by 1987 the figure had reached above 23,000, enough people to populate a fair-sized town, or 43 lobbyists for each member of Congress.[49] Since the only agents who must register as lobbyists are those whose principal purpose is to lobby Congress, many who lobby only as part of their function do not register. American business, trade, and professional associations account for a revealing 70.5 percent of all lobbyists, while foreign corporations have 6.5 percent, government 4.2 percent, citizens' groups 4.1 percent, unions 1.7 percent, and the poor 0.6 percent; all others make up 12.4 percent.[50]

The diffusion of power in Congress and the decline of party discipline (each to be discussed in later chapters) have meant that more and more lobbyists are needed to contact the ever-increasing number of officials who have influence over policy-making. Charles E. Walker, a long-time Washington lobbyist, put it this way: "With the decline of parties, the decline of leadership in the Congress, business lobbying groups have to cover the field. Many more bodies and much more time are needed to accomplish what we did [in the 1950s.]"[51]

Because most lobbyists are arms of the interest groups, they perform many of the same tasks as their employers. They are an important source of detailed information for policy-makers, they help keep policy-makers focused on issues in which their clients have interest, they can reflect public opinion on issues, and they make financial contributions to candidates. Additionally, lobbyists help legislators develop strategies and creative ideas for passing legislation, and they also provide a degree of personal friendship to the politicians. A good deal of the lobbyists' time is also taken up in simple *bill watching*. As you will see, the legislative and administrative processes are very complicated. Unless someone keeps a sharp eye on issues and bills, they can escape the notice of people whose interests are involved. Hence, lobbyists often publish legislative updates for their clients, identifying pending bills that touch on their interests and issues.

Lobbyists also organize the personal lobbying efforts of their clients. People who are affected by proposed legislation or policy execution can be good advocates. Hence, it is not uncommon for professional lobbyists to bring their clients to the capital and shepherd them through the maze in Congress or the administration to make their personal pitch on an issue. Organizations that employ lobbyists are becoming increasingly aware of the usefulness of their own people in persuading policy-makers, and many corporations are actively encouraging employees to lobby their legislators on behalf of the corporation.[52]

Among the traits commonly found in successful lobbyists are knowledge about the issues and about how the policy-making process works (most lobbyists have previous government experience), a reputation for candor and reliability, integrity, and the ability to compromise. Lobbyists rate personal contact, or "face time," with policy-makers as most important, but they also cultivate staff members. However it is done, lobbyists and the groups they represent must maintain high visibility among policy-makers if their interests are to be protected. "If you aren't up here," a state legislature staffer once told me about advocacy, "you don't count."[53]

An essential skill for lobbyists when working with elected officials is relating the issue to the well-being of the officials' constituency. "You go in there and talk to him about the specific program in his district," a lobbyist for the National Education Association said. "He isn't much interested in a national program. He needs to be able to take credit for doing something positive for the folks back home."[54] Public opinion is less a concern to the permanent bureaucracy, for which technical expertise is

the most desirable lobbyist trait. In either case, however, lobbyists work to make policy-makers dependent on their services.[55]

Lobbyists must also be good coalition builders. "Politics," it is often said, "makes for strange bedfellows," and this is certainly true of advocacy politics. Lobbyists must be willing to cooperate with other persons or groups if this will help the cause. Certain groups naturally share certain interests. Right-wing ideological groups are usually compatible with each other, for example, as are the environmental groups, and Common Cause normally sees eye-to-eye with associates of Ralph Nader. These groups often share information, swap mailing lists, and cooperate in lobbying efforts. But occasionally issues arise that produce different, less orthodox alignments. In 1974, for example, Ralph Nader, the Chamber of Commerce, the AFL-CIO, and the ACLU joined ranks in opposition to a bill sponsored by Common Cause to reform the 1946 Federal Regulation of Lobbying Act.

Team lobbying is also a technique used in major efforts. Here, a lobbying firm joins forces with public relations specialists, legal firms, and experts in grassroots politics to push for policy objectives. Yet another kind of coalition, the **iron triangle**, occurs when major lobbyists join with congressional committee members and their staff and with the personnel of administration agencies. These consortia occur frequently on defense issues, but they also form in other policy areas as well. These unions are powerful alliances—hence the term *iron triangle*.

Regulating Lobbying   Although lobbyists normally operate well within the law, scandals sometimes erupt in which lobbyists bribe officials, as in the Koreagate affair in 1977. More recently, several former Reagan Administration officials-turned-lobbyists, including Lyn Nofziger, Michael Deaver, and James Watt, were accused of unethically pulling government strings for clients, causing Senator Howard Metzenbaum (D-OH) to complain in frustration that "Washington has become a sinkhole of influence peddling." While most lobbyists are undoubtedly honest people, even those with a shady side have little difficulty staying within the law because the statutes regulating lobbying are vague and almost impotent.

Although there were some attempts to regulate lobbying in the early part of this century, they were half-hearted and ineffectual. Then, in 1946, the *Federal Regulation of Lobbying Act* was passed, requiring lobbyists to register with Congress and to itemize their income and expenditures. This law too, however, has disappointed those who wish lobbying to be kept on a shorter leash. Riddled with loopholes, the law allows each group or individual to define a principal function and to determine what expenditures should be reported. Further, indirect lobbying need not be reported,[56] nor is lobbying the administration, the bureaucracy, or the regulatory boards and commissions covered by the law. To round things off, no specific government agency is given the responsibility of enforcing the law, with the result that there have been only a handful of prosecutions since 1946.[57]

As pointed out earlier, efforts to toughen the law have been successfully opposed by almost every interest group and lobby. Only Common Cause has pursued rigorous regulation, but to little avail. Congress has, however, attempted to impede the mechanism of the revolving door—at least so far as members of the executive branch are concerned. The *Ethics in Government Act* of 1978 prohibits former members of the executive branch from representing clients to their former agency for one year after their departure from government. Further, the law proscribes former government employees from ever representing clients before their former agency on any matter in which they were involved while employed in govern-

ment. In 1988, former Reagan aid Lyn Nofziger was the first person convicted of violating this act, but the conviction was later overturned on a technicality. Also, Reagan adviser Michael Deaver was investigated for similar violations and convicted in 1988 for perjury. Reacting to the improprieties of numerous Reagan Administration officials, in 1988 Congress passed a law toughening the regulations on former government employees lobbying public offices, but it was vetoed by President Reagan.[58]

The laws regulating lobbyists are frail indeed and should be made stronger. But the major problem we face regarding lobbyists and pressure groups has a great deal more to do with the question of their *legal* use of money.

PACs

Perhaps the single most disturbing factor to have developed in the recent past in electoral and policy-making politics is the emergence of **political action committees (PACs)** as major sources of campaign funds. PACs are created by interest groups to funnel money to candidates for public office.

Since the mid-1970s the growth in the number of PACs and in the amount they contribute to federal campaigns has catapulted. In 1974 there were only 608 registered PACs, but by 1987 the figure had reached 4165. Of these, corporate PACs have increased from 89 to 1775; nonconnected PACs, including ideological groups, have risen from 110 to 957; trade association, membership, and health PACs have increased from 318 to 865; and labor PACs have jumped from 201 to 364.[59]

The reasons for such a dramatic increase in the number of PACs are complicated, but essentially the growth stems from passage of a series of election laws, Federal Election Commission rulings, and Court decisions. In 1974, the *Federal Election Campaign Act* was passed, amending previous election finance laws. The new statute provided for public financing of presidential elections, and it set limits on campaign expenditures for presidential and congressional elections. The law also set limits on the amount of money individuals and groups could contribute to candidates: $1000 per candidate for contributions by individuals and $5000 per candidate for contributions by groups for each primary, runoff, and general election. At the same time, however, the law repealed a previous prohibition against campaign contributions by corporations that did business with the federal government. Until 1974, corporations doing business with the government were proscribed from making campaign contributions, to prevent them from buying influence with policy-makers. The repeal of this provision was critical to the subsequent rise in the number of PACs.

The law was quickly challenged in court, and in 1976 the Supreme Court sustained much of it, but, importantly, it struck down the limitation on congressional campaign expenditures while allowing the limit on expenditures of presidential candidates who accepted public funds for their campaigns.[60] Meanwhile, the Federal Election Commission ruled that corporations could use their funds to administer their PACs and could raise money for campaign contributions from their employees and investors.[61] Since then, PACs of every possible description have emerged, especially in the corporate field. There is an Egg PAC; a Realtors' PAC; a Merrill Lynch, Pierce, Fenner, and Smith PAC; Fire PAC; and a Coca-Cola PAC. At least one group has a sense of humor about this otherwise serious business: The beer distributors have created a Six PAC.

Taken as a whole, these complicated factors have each contributed not only to the increase of PACs but to the immense expansion in the costs of congressional campaigns, which will be studied in a future chapter. The 1974 act allowing corporate PACs is obviously fundamental, but the limitation on individual contributions to candidates has also tended to funnel money to the PACs. Also, the new reliance of presidential candidates on public campaign financing, together with the limits on presidential candidate expenditures, has meant that more campaign contributions have gone to congressional races, thus driving up their costs.

Figure 4.8 shows that the amount spent by PACs for congressional campaigns has risen steeply in recent years, although it leveled off in 1990–1991. Further, the amount given to incumbents far exceeds the contributions to challengers. While business, trade associations, and nonconnected PACs give most to Republicans and labor focuses on Democrats, most interest groups give generously to candidates with whom they agree from each party, so as not to be left without influence in Congress no matter how the election turns out. Indeed, only a handful of members of Congress refuse PAC contributions; the number of members to the House who received half or more of all their campaign contributions from PACs rose from 63 in 1978 to 194 (45 percent) by 1986.[62] In the election of 1990 only four PACs contributed $22 million, or 13.8 percent of the total: The Teamsters' Democratic Republican Independent Voter Election Committee contributed $10.5 million, $5.8 million was given by the American Medical Association PAC, the Realtors' PAC gave $3 million, and the AT&T PAC contributed $2.8 million.[63]

Although most of the contributions from PACs come in the form of money, sometimes PACs give services instead. These services may be much more valuable to a candidate than just money, and they include campaign workers, mailing lists, specialists' advice on campaigning or public relations, and so on. While these services must be reported and count toward the $5000 maximum that PACs may give to any

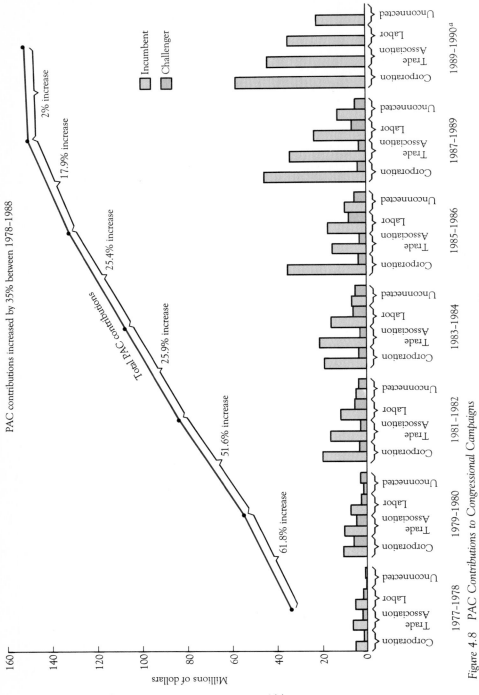

Figure 4.8 PAC Contributions to Congressional Campaigns

Note: [a] The amounts given to incumbents as opposed to challengers are not available.

Source: 1977–1989 adapted from data in *Vital Statistics on American Politics*, 2nd ed., pp. 167–168; 1989–1990 adapted from Sara Fritz and Dwight Morris, "Total of PAC Giving Election Fund Declines," *The Los Angeles Times*, March 31, 1991.

single candidate per election, other methods of contributions are not accounted toward this limit.

Bundling is a process by which PACs collect personal checks for a candidate. They then deliver these in a bundle, and since the contributions do not actually come from the PACs' own accounts, they do not count toward the $5000 limit. Also, the law places no cap on the amount that can be spent for a candidate by the PAC itself. It other words, PACs can themselves spend far in excess of $5000 on ads and literature for candidates without violating the law. The law limits only the amount of money given directly to a candidate's campaign organization. These *independent expenditures* (or soft money) have become an important factor in some congressional and presidential campaigns. Among the largest spenders of soft money in the 1990 congressional campaign were the Auto PAC, the National Realtors Association PAC, the National Abortion Rights Action League, and the National Education Association. Between them they spent almost $1.9 million on only ten candidates.[64]

The effect PACs have on American politics is difficult to measure. Some scholars suggest that PAC influence on congressional voting is only marginal, but others see indications that it has had a significant impact. For example, the Federal Trade Commission adopted a regulation requiring all used car dealers to display a statement about the mechanical difficulties on the cars they offered for sale. In response, the National Association of Automobile Dealers pumped money into the 1980 congressional campaigns, and Congress quickly repealed the regulation.[65]

While it would be unfair to imply that policy-makers sell out to big donors, they do admit that large contributions can buy interest groups access to them—and often this is enough to prevail. Most issues that legislators face do not bear directly on a large number of

their constituents, and even if they did, people not represented by interest groups, lobbyists, and PACs are unlikely to know when their interests are affected by a particular piece of legislation. The PACs and lobbyists do, however, and through their presence on the scene, their skills in advocacy, and their contributions, they are able to make their wishes known in a meaningful way. On the other hand, "There aren't any Poor PACs or Food Stamp PACs, or Medicare PACs," as Senator Bob Dole (R-KA) remarked wryly, even though in 1987 he led the list of senators who received funds from PACs. Thus, PACs empower those who can afford them, and they try to focus the policy-makers' attention on their particular interests, ignoring broader perspectives.

Some in Congress decry the prominence of PACs and call for reform. There have been suggestions that candidates be limited as to the total numbers of dollars they may accept from PACs, while raising the amount individuals can contribute to candidates. Senator David Boren (D-OK), one of the few congresspersons who does not take PAC money, has called for public funding of congressional campaigns. He complains that mounting campaign costs have driven members of Congress to spend so much of their time trying to raise money that they sometimes shirk their legislative duties, and that the size of the contributions they accept threatens their independence.[66] Whether any of these reforms, by themselves or as a group, can sufficiently combat the problems posed by the PACs is impossible to say. But certainly we should take a long, careful look at the question.

Over the past 30 years the American political system has been transformed in scope if not in kind. The explosion in the number and activities of interest groups, lobbyists, and PACs has been perhaps the most significant single recent development in the political system. The freewheeling activities of interest groups and lobbyists and the deluge of money available to policy-makers are matters of concern. Clearly the poor, the disaffected, and the politically inarticulate are less able to advance their interests than are the wealthy and the organized elements of society, and this imbalance deserves serious scrutiny. Money has come to play an enormous role in modern campaigns and in public policy-making, even as the political parties have become less prominent in our system. But we have not yet gotten a full perspective. For a more complete examination of our political system, we now turn our attention to political parties and elections.

Summary

- Public opinion, now subject to quick and accurate measurement, has become a staple of American politics.

- Public opinion is influenced by family, schools, peers, and the media; in America it tends to be reasonably stable and politically moderate.

- The media are extraordinarily free and provide an important "outside" check on the government.

- While elite theorists believe that the country is controlled by powerful leaders, pluralists believe that the people express their will through interest groups.

- Interest groups advocate their causes both by lobbying and by forming PACs, which gain access to public officials by making campaign contributions.

- The amount of money contributed to public officials for their campaigns has become a matter of concern, since it threatens to jeopardize their independence.

Notes

1. Quoted in Carl J. Friedrick, *The New Belief in the Common Man* (Boston: Little, Brown, 1943), p. 5.

2. M. E. Ahrari, "Congress, Public Opinion, and Synfuels Policy," *Political Science Quarterly* 102; 4 (Winter 1987–1988), 599–600.

3. Michael J. Yborra, "Up to Their Ears in Junk, Phone and Fax Users Say," *The Los Angeles Times*, Aug. 8, 1989; and William J. Eaton, "Curb on Phone, Fax 'Junk Mail' OKd by House," *The Los Angeles Times*, July 31, 1990.

4. Larry J. Sabato, "Misses and Mistakes: Sources of Error in Polls" in Larry J. Sabato, ed. *Campaigns and Elections* (Glenview, IL: Scott, Foresman, 1989), pp. 75–81.

5. Thomas B. Rosenstiel, "Inaccurate Poll Results Laid to Bad Polling," *The Los Angeles Times*, Nov. 9, 1989.

6. M. Kent Jennings and Richard G. Niemi, *The Political Character of Adolescence* (Princeton: Princeton University Press, 1974), p. 41.

7. James Burkhart et al., *Strategies for Political Participation* (Cambridge, MA: Winthrop Publishers, 1972), pp. 45–46.

8. National Geographic poll, 1988.

9. Gallup poll, 1986.

10. From a Times Mirror study reported in Thomas B. Rosenstiel, "Media Study Finds 'Age of Indifference,'" *The Los Angeles Times*, June 28, 1990.

11. Russell J. Dalton, *Citizen Politics in Western Democracies* (Chatham, NJ: Chatham House, 1988), p. 25.

12. Stichting European Value Systems Group, Tilburg, Netherlands, presented in Lewis Lipitz and David M. Speak, *American Democracy*, 2nd ed. (New York: St. Martin's Press, 1989), p. 182.

13. Richard G. Niemi, John Mueller, and Tom W. Smith, *Trends in Public Opinion* (New York: Greenwood Press, 1989), pp. 97–99.

14. Anne C. Roark, "Today's College Frosh as Liberal as Those of '60s," *The Los Angeles Times*, Oct. 31, 1986, and Larry Gordon "College Freshman More Likely to Join Protests, Survey Shows," *The Los Angeles Times*, Jan. 28, 1991.

15. From National Opinion Research Center General Social Survey, 1987.

16. Times Mirror poll, October, 1987.

17. Gallup poll, 1987; and NBC News/Wall Street Journal poll, 1987.

18. Stanley and Niemi, p. 45.

19. "Poll shows TV Main Source of War News," *Oceanside Blade-Citizen*, May 2, 1991.

20. Stanley and Niemi, p. 57.

21. Times Mirror poll, 1986.

22. William Schneider and I. A. Lewis, "Views on the News," *Public Opinion* (Aug.–Sept., 1985), 7.

23. *John Doe Agency and John Doe Government Agency v. John Doe Corp.*, 488 U.S. 1306 (1989).

24. Kim Murphy, "Surveillance Case Sheds Light on McCarthy Era," *The Los Angeles Times*, Oct. 18, 1987.

25. Hedrick Smith, *The Power Game* (New York: Random House, 1988), pp. 437–438, 442–446, and 580.

26. Smith, pp. 404, 408, 410, 413, 431, and 434.

27. Rowland Evans, Jr., and Robert D. Novak, *Nixon in the White House* (New York: Random House, 1971), pp. 315–317.

28. Smith, pp. 429, 432–433.

29. Douglas Frante, "Restrictions—MPs—Have Journalists on Defensive," *The Los Angeles Times*, Feb. 11, 1991.

30. See C. Wright Mills, The Power Elite (Oxford: Oxford University Press, 1956).

31. Thomas R. Dye, *Who's Running America?* (Englewood Cliffs, NJ: Prentice-Hall, 1983), p. 19.

32. Robert Michels, *Political Parties* (New York: Free Press, 1966). This volume is a reprint of the original from 1915.

33. See *Federalist Papers* #10 and Chapter 2 in this book.

34. See David B. Truman, *The Governmental Process* (New York: Knopf, 1951).

35. Robert A. Dahl, *Who Governs?* (New Haven: Yale University Press, 1961).

36. Theodore J. Lowi, *The End of Liberalism*, 2nd ed. (New York: Norton 1979), pp. 60–72.

37. Alexis de Tocqueville, *Democracy in America* (Garden City, NY: Doubleday, 1969), p. 485.

38. Robert J. Huckshorn, *Political Parties in America* (North Scituate, MA: Duxbury Press, 1980), p. 257.

39. "Prepared Texts of Carter's Farewell Address on Major Issues Facing the Nation," *The New York Times*, Jan. 15, 1981.

40. Jeffery M. Berry, *The Interest Group Society*, 2nd ed. (Glenview, IL: Scott Foresman/Little, Brown, 1989), pp. 20–21.

41. Huckshorn, p. 256, and Berry, pp. 31–33, 180, and 222.

42. Stephen Miller, *Special Interest Groups in American Politics* (New Brunswick, NJ: Transaction Books, 1983), pp. 113–114.

43. Graham Wootton, *Interest Groups: Policy and Politics in America* (Englewood Cliffs, NJ: Prentice-Hall, 1985), p. 193.

44. Smith, p. 173.

45. Richard F. Fenno, Jr., *The Making of a Senator: Dan Quayle* (Washington, DC: Congressional Quarterly Press, 1989), pp. 19–20.

46. Karen O'Connor and Lee Epstein, "The Role of Interest Groups in Supreme Court Policy Formation," in Robert Eyestone, ed., *Public Policy Formation* (Greenwich, CT: JAI Press, 1984), pp. 72–74.

47. Berry, p. 114.

48. Huckshorn, p. 293.

49. Smith, p. 29.

50. Kay Lehman Schlozman and John T. Tierney, *Organized Interests and American Democracy* (New York: Harper & Row, 1986), p. 67.

51. Quoted in Anne Colamosca, "The Trade Association Hustle," *The New Republic*, Nov. 3, 1979, p. 16.

52. Ralph Frammolino, "Big Business Taps Own for Lobbyists," *The Los Angeles Times*, Apr. 4, 1988.

53. Personal interview with William Chavez, consultant to a California state assemblywoman, 1980.

54. Berry, p. 145.

55. Lewis Anthony Dexter, *How Organizations Are Represented in Washington* (New York: University Press of America, 1987), pp. 87–101.

56. Wootton, p. 183.

57. Huckshorn, pp. 301–303.

58. Josh Getlin, "Landmark Ethics Bill Approved By Congress," *The Los Angeles Times*, Oct. 22, 1988.

59. Stanley and Niemi, p. 143. No PACs are listed for nonconnected groups before 1977.

60. *Buckley* v. *Valeo*, 424 U.S. 1 (1976).

61. Berry, pp. 118-120.

62. Berry, p. 122.

63. Sara Fritz and Dwight Morris, "Total of PACs Giving Election Fund Declines," *The Los Angeles Times*, Mar. 31, 1991.

64. Sara Fritz, "Car PAC Pumps Up 260 Hopefuls," *The Los Angeles Times*, Nov. 6, 1990.

65. Berry, p. 132.

66. David L. Boren, "A Way Off the Merry-Go-Round," *The Los Angeles Times*, Mar. 24, 1991.

Suggestions for Further Reading

Agee, Warren K., Phillip H. Ault, and Edwin Emery, eds. *Main Currents in Mass Communications*. New York: Harper & Row, 1986.

Asher, Herbert. *Polling and the Public: What Every Citizen Should Know*. Washington, DC: Congressional Quarterly, 1988.

Bagdikian, Ben H. *The Media Monopoly* (2nd ed.). Boston: Beacon, 1987.

Baradat, Leon P. *Political Ideologies: Their Origins and Impact* (4th ed.). Englewood Cliffs, NJ: Prentice-Hall, 1991.

Barnes, Samuel H., and Max Karse, eds. *Political Action*. Beverly Hills, CA: Sage, 1979.

Bennett, W. Lance. *News: The Politics of Illusion*. New York: Longman, 1983.

Berkman, Ronald, and Laura W. Kitch. *Politics in the Media Age*. New York: McGraw-Hill, 1986.

Berry, Jeffrey M. *The Interest Group Society* (2nd ed.). Glenview, IL: Scott Foresman/Little, Brown, 1989.

Burkhart, James, James Eisenstein, Theodore Fleming, and Frank Kendrick. *Strategies for Political Participation*. Cambridge, MA: Winthrop, 1972.

Chubb, John E. *Interest Groups and the Bureaucracy: The Politics of Energy*. Menlo Park: Stanford University Press, 1983.

Cigler, Allan J., and Burdette A. Loomis, eds. *Interest Group Politics* (2nd ed.). Washington, DC: Congressional Quarterly Press, 1986.

Dahl, Robert A. *Who Governs?* New Haven: Yale University Press, 1961.

Dalton, Russell J. *Citizen Politics in Western Democracies*. Chatham, NJ: Chatham House, 1988.

Dawson, Richard E., and Kenneth Prewitt. *Political Socialization* (2nd ed.). Boston: Little, Brown, 1977.

Domhoff, G. William. *Who Runs America Now? A View for the '80s*. Englewood Cliffs, NJ: Prentice-Hall, 1983.

Dye, Thomas R. *Who's Running America?: The Conservative Years* (4th ed.). Englewood Cliffs, NJ: Prentice-Hall, 1986.

Erikson, Robert S., Norman Luttbeg, and Kent L. Tedin. *American Public Opinion: Its Origins, Content and Impact* (2nd ed.). New York: Wiley, 1980.

Evans, Rowland, Jr., and Robert D. Novak. *Nixon in the White House.* New York: Random House, 1971.

Eyestone, Robert, ed. *Public Policy Formation.* Greenwich, CT: JAI Press, 1984.

Fenno, Richard F., Jr. *The Making of a Senator: Dan Quayle.* Washington, DC: Congressional Quarterly Press, 1989.

Friedrick, Carl J. *The New Belief in the Common Man.* Boston: Little, Brown, 1943.

Gleb, Joyce, and Marian Lief Palley. *Woman and Public Policies* (rev. ed.). Princeton: Princeton University Press, 1987.

Graber, Doris A. *Mass Media and American Politics* (3rd ed.). Washington, DC: Congressional Quarterly Press, 1989.

Greenwald, Carol S. *Group Power.* New York: Praeger, 1977.

Grossman, Michael Baruch, and Martha Joynt Kumar. *Portraying the President: The White House and the News Media.* Baltimore: Johns Hopkins University Press, 1981.

Halberstam, David. *The Powers That Be.* New York: Knopf, 1979.

Hallin, Daniel C. *The "Uncensored War": The Media and Vietnam.* Berkeley: University of California Press, 1989.

Harris, Louis. *Inside America.* New York: Vintage, 1987.

Hennessy, Bernard. *Public Opinion* (5th ed.). Pacific Grove: CA: Brooks/Cole, 1985.

Hochschild, Jennifer L. *What's Fair? American Beliefs About Distributive Justice.* Cambridge: Harvard University Press, 1981.

Holloway, Harry, and John George. *Public Opinion.* New York: St. Martin's Press, 1985.

Hrebenar, Ronald J., and Ruth K. Scott. *Interest Group Politics in America.* Englewood Cliffs, NJ: Prentice-Hall, 1982.

Huckshorn, Robert J. *Political Parties In America.* North Scituate, MA: Duxbury Press, 1980.

Iyengar, Shanto, and Donald R. Kinder. *News That Matters.* Chicago: University of Chicago Press, 1987.

Jennings, M. Kent, and Richard G. Niemi. *Generations and Politics.* Princeton: Princeton University Press, 1981.

―――. *The Political Character of Adolescence.* Princeton: Princeton University Press, 1974.

Kingdon, John W. *Agendas, Alternatives, and Public Politics.* Boston: Little, Brown, 1984.

Lichter, S. Robert, Stanley Rothman, and Linda S. Lichter. *The Media Elite.* Bethesda, MD: Adler & Adler, 1986.

Linsky, Martin, *Impact: How the Press Affects Federal Policymaking.* New York: Norton, 1986.

Lowi, Theodore J. *The End of Liberalism* (2nd ed.). New York: Norton, 1979.

MacFarland, Andrew S. *Common Cause: Lobbying in the Public Interest.* Chatham, NJ: Chatham House, 1984.

Malbin, Michael J. *Money and Politics in the United States.* Chatham, NJ: Chatham House, 1984.

Mansbridge, Jane J. *Why We Lost the ERA*. Chicago: University of Chicago Press, 1986.

Michels, Robert. *Political Parties*. New York: Free Press, 1986.

Mills, C. Wright. *The Power Elite*. New York: Oxford University Press, 1956.

Neuman, W. Russell. *The Paradox of Mass Politics: Knowledge and Opinion in the American Electorate*. Cambridge: Harvard University Press, 1986.

Niemi, Richard G., John Mueller, and Tom W. Smith. *Trends in Public Opinion* (2nd ed.). New York: Greenwood Press, 1990.

Norton, Philip, *The British Polity*. New York: Longman, 1984.

Patterson, Thomas E. *The Mass Media Elections: How Americans Choose Their Presidents*. New York: Praeger, 1980.

Prewitt, Kenneth, and Alan Stone. *The Ruling Elites*. New York: Harper & Row, 1973.

Sabato, Larry, ed. *Campaigns and Elections*. Glenview, IL: Scott, Foresman, 1989.

_____. *PAC Power: Inside the World of Political Action Committees*. New York: Norton, 1985.

Schlozman, Kay Lehman, and John T. Tierney. *Organized Interests and American Democracy*. New York: Harper & Row, 1986.

Smith, Hedrick. *The Power Game*. New York: Random House, 1988.

Speakes, Larry, with Robert Pack. *Speaking Out: Inside the Reagan White House*. New York: Scribner's, 1988.

Stanley, Harold H., and Richard Niemi. *Vital Statistics on American Politics* (2nd ed.), Washington, DC: Congressional Quarterly, 1990.

Sussman, Barry. *What Americans Really Think*. New York: Pantheon, 1988.

Truman, David. *The Governmental Process*. New York: Knopf, 1951.

Vogel, David. *Fluctuating Fortunes: The Political Power of Business in America*. New York: Basic Books, 1989.

Wootton, Graham. *Interest Groups: Policy and Politics in America*. Englewood Cliffs, NJ: Prentice-Hall, 1985.

Chapter 5

POLITICAL PARTIES

PREVIEW

George Washington, James Madison, and other founders of the United States were opposed to the existence of political parties, but parties inevitably developed anyway. The Federalist party organized first and was quickly followed by the Jeffersonian Republicans. The Federalist party lost popularity in the early 1800s, while the Republicans renamed themselves the Democrat-Republicans and finally the Democrats. The Whig party opposed the Democrats between the 1830s and 1850s, but it eventually declined and was replaced by the contemporary Republican party. Since the 1860s the Democrats and Republicans have dominated American politics, with each being strongest during different eras.

Essentially there are three kinds of party systems among the world's democracies. A single-party system exists when one party enjoys the overwhelming support of the public. A multiparty system has several powerful parties; thus the governing party usually does not enjoy the confidence of the popular majority. Coalitions are usually weak, and such a system is incompatible with the American presidential-congressional system of government.

The United States has a two-party system. Its government usually enjoys majority support, while a strong opposition checks the party in power. Third parties have not been very successful at winning elections in the United States, but they have managed to force the major parties to adopt issues that they popularize.

The principal functions of political parties are to nominate candidates and secure their elections. The winning party then forms a government and implements its policies, while the loyal opposition criticizes the majority party and offers alternative policies. Political parties also try to educate voters about the issues, and they attempt to hold their officials responsible to party platforms.

The two major parties are large amalgams of various social, ethnic, religious, and occupational groups. Being inclusive rather than exclusive, they attempt to appeal to the masses of voters. Thus the parties tend to be pragmatic and moderate rather than ideological and extremist. Each party is organized from the precinct to the national levels into a series of committees. Although the party structure is hierarchical, power does not usually flow to the top. Instead, power is decentralized, with local and state parties being largely in command of their own platforms, nominations, and elections. Once every four years, the parties gather in national conventions to nominate candidates for president and vice president, but these are about the only times the parties really function as united entities.

The Democratic and Republican parties are similar in many ways, but they also differ. A greater percentage of the Republican party, the smaller of the two, is white, well-to-do, college educated, and Protestant. The Democratic party is pluralist, trying to accommodate the needs of the discrete groups it comprises, while the Republicans are more concerned with party loyalty and are more unitary in structure. Republicans tend to be conservatives, favoring law and order, a strong defense, and property interests; they are supported by the monied elements of the country. As a group, the Democrats tend more toward the left of the spectrum, although they also have many conservatives in their midst. As liberals, they support civil rights, civil liberties, taxing the wealthy, and human understanding in foreign affairs; they are less successful than Republicans at raising money to fund campaigns.

The number of Independents is growing and currently stands at almost one-third of the population. No party enjoys majority status in voter identification, but the Democratic party remains the plurality party with broader public appeal. Accordingly, the Democrats win most elections; they have the majority of state governors, the majority in most state legislatures,and the majority in each House of Congress. But since 1968, they have won only one presidential election, meaning that we have had a divided government for most of the past generation. Seemingly, until the Democrats take a harder line on defense, crime, and fiscal policy, they will find it hard to capture the White House, and until the Republicans assume a more benevolent posture relative to the social issues and civil liberties, they will be hard pressed to win control of Congress.

Division of the republic into two great parties, each under its leader . . . is to be dreaded as the greatest evil under our Constitution.

George Washington

Early leaders of the American colonies and many of the founders themselves were opposed to the existence of political parties. George Washington warned in his farewell address of the "baneful effects of the spirit of party," and John Adams wrote of his "dread" that the republic would divide into parties. But no one was more articulate in opposition to political parties than James Madison, the principal author of the Constitution. He began a newspaper article advocating ratification of the proposed Constitution by asserting, "Among the numerous advantages promised by a well-constructed union, none deserves to be more accurately developed than its tendency to break and control the violence of faction," and he went on to complain that "the latest causes of faction are thus sown in the nature of man."[1] By *factions* Madison meant groups of people united to get their way from government, a definition certainly encompassing political parties. While Madison did not advise making factions illegal, he did hope to frustrate their

success through the institutions of the Constitution. Yet the early opposition to political parties could not prevent their development. In fact, within a decade of writing his indictment of factions, Madison himself joined with Thomas Jefferson to found a political party that took control of the government from the opposition.

Because they were not intended by the founders, political parties are not mentioned in the Constitution, and their development was evolutionary rather than planned. Hence their structure, characteristics, and functions are determined by the political environment in which they exist rather than by some grand design.

Although politicians and scholars have suggested many different definitions of political parties over the years, for our purposes, a straightforward description will do best. Political parties are groups of people united in efforts to gain control of government and to manage its policy.

Distinguishing between political parties and interest groups is important at this point. Political parties focus on getting their members elected to office, while interest groups are content with influencing the people who hold office. As a consequence, even though political parties are not mentioned in the Constitution, their role relative to government is formal; interest groups remain outside the formal structure of government. Interest groups tend to concentrate on small numbers of issues, but political parties, at least the most successful and long-lasting ones, address a broad range of issues. Political parties try to appeal to and relate with all people in society; interest groups, on the other hand, usually devote their attention to their members, relating with the general public only as a means to advance their particular causes. Still, there are many similarities between political parties and interest groups, and as we shall soon learn, the increased involvement of interest groups in popularizing issues and providing funds to candidates has weakened the political parties considerably.[2]

The History of Parties

True to his aversion to political parties, George Washington remained aloof from them during the early years of his administration. But as Madison foresaw, faction was inevitable, as Washington's principal advisers, Alexander Hamilton and Thomas Jefferson, struggled with each other over foreign and domestic policy. Hamilton's faction, calling themselves **Federalists**, advocated a strong central government, and policies that benefited the commercial elements. Ranged against the Federalists were the **Jeffersonian Republicans**,* who opposed

---

* Care must be taken not to confuse the Jeffersonian Republicans, which eventually became today's Democratic party, with the modern-day Republican party. The present Republican party was founded in 1854.

Hamilton's national bank and taxing policies, and supported **states' rights** at the expense of a strong central government.

John Adams, Washington's successor, was the only bona fide Federalist to become president. The election of 1800 brought the Jeffersonian Republicans to power and initiated a long period of Republican political dominance. By 1814, the Federalist Party had virtually disappeared, leaving the Republicans, by then calling themselves *Democrat-Republicans*, without opposition. This period, associated with the administration of James Monroe (1816–1824), is known as the **Era of Good Feeling**. Although the United States was dominated by a single party, the competition that previously had occurred between parties continued to take place within the Democratic-Republican party, which ran rival candidates for election.

EARLY REALIGNMENTS

A split in the Democratic-Republican party in the 1820s resulted in the first *realignment* (which occurs when people change party allegiance in such numbers as to create new coalitions within the parties[3]).* The conservative wing of the party broke away to form the Whig party. At the same time, the Democratic-Republican party, led by Andrew Jackson, dropped the term *Republican* from its name, becoming the *Democratic party*. Advocating more democracy in the form of universal manhood suffrage, the Democratic party became the first modern political party by encouraging mass membership. For their part, the Whigs were united largely in their probusiness policies and in their opposition to Andrew Jackson, the

---

* This view of realignments is most broadly accepted, but another interpretation suggests that realignments are much more profound than just changes in voting patterns and are also reflected in modifications in government and policy-making.[4]

dominant personality of the era. Usually unsuccessful at the polls, the Whigs won the presidency only twice and they were rarely able to gain control of the Congress.

Eventually the Whigs declined as a major party, being replaced by the *Republican party*—until then a minor party. Organized in 1854 in Ripon, Wisconsin, the Republicans galvanized a coalition of Northern industrialists and workers, free soilers (those who opposed the extension of slavery into free territory), freed slaves, antislave Democrats in the North, and former Whigs. Enjoying a meteoric rise to power, they won control of the House of Representatives in the elections of 1854 and 1858, and in 1860 they held the majority in both houses as Abraham Lincoln became president.

The Republican victory of 1860 represents the second realignment, and they dominated American politics throughout the rest of the century. During and immediately following the Civil War, with the exception of wanting to preserve the Union, the Republicans followed a liberal (some said radical) course. The slaves were liberated, the transcontinental railroad was built, federal aid to education was provided, the Homestead Act made free land available to family farmers, and in foreign policy Americans continued to avoid entangling alliances with foreign powers. By the 1870s, however, responding to the growing conservative mood among the public and to the industrialization of the country, the Republicans had turned to the right, pursuing probusiness policies, maintaining the gold standard for currency, and passing high protective tariffs.

Reflecting the mood of the country, the Democrats were conservative during this era as well, but they were able to win only two presidential elections (1884 and 1892). By 1896, however, a new challenge to Republican dominance was in the offing. The Democrats shed their conservativism and adopted the populist issues of free silver and governmental re-

form. The issues of the campaign, however, galvanized a new Republican alignment of Northeastern business people and urban workers, and William McKinley was elected president. This realignment ushered in 36 more years of Republican dominance. From 1896 to 1932 the Democrats elected only one president, Woodrow Wilson (1913–1921); they took control of the House in only 5 of 18 elections, and of the Senate in only 3.

From 1860 to 1932 the Republicans produced only two liberal presidents: Abraham Lincoln and Theodore Roosevelt. The remainder of the time the party was quite conservative and business oriented. In the 1920s, Republican presidents became even more probusiness, slashing taxes for the rich, levying heavy protective tariffs, and deregulating industry and finance. These policies combined with global economic trends to produce the 1929 stock market crash and the Great Depression (1929–1941).

THE CURRENT DEMOCRATIC ERA

The failed Republican economic policy of **laissez faire** (holding that government should not engage in economic activity), caused another realignment of the voters. The election of 1932 swept the Democratic **New Deal** coalition into office. Headed by Franklin Delano Roosevelt, the New Deal coalition was composed of the South, organized labor and other urban workers, white ethnics, African-Americans, Hispanic Americans, Jews, Catholics, and the poor. The New Deal initiated social security, public relief (welfare), collective bargaining, minimum wages, workmen's compensation, unemployment insurance, regulation of business, American leadership abroad, and the United Nations.

From 1932 to 1952 the Democrats monopolized the presidency and lost the majority in

South Carolina Governor (now United States Senator) Strom Thurmond expounds on his opposition to civil rights as a candidate for the Dixiecrat party in the 1948 presidential election.

the House and Senate only in 1946–1947. By 1948, however, the New Deal coalition had begun to weaken. In that year the Democratic party adopted a strong civil rights platform causing the Deep South (Louisiana, Mississippi, Alabama, and South Carolina) to defect, throwing its support to Governor Strom Thurmond and the *States' Rights Democratic party (Dixiecrats)*. Although the Democrats managed to win that election, the South showed itself increasingly uncomfortable with the New Deal coalition. In 1952 the Republicans, fielding the popular war hero Dwight D. Eisenhower, came to power, carrying every state in the North and West and winning Texas, Tennessee, Virginia, and Florida as well. Thus the South again showed its

independence from the Democratic party and, with the exception of 1976, it has not voted solidly Democratic since. In fact, of the former Confederate states, a majority voted for Democratic presidential candidates in but four of the last ten elections (1952, 1964, 1968, and 1976). In 1972, 1984, and 1988 no southern state voted Democratic and only one southern state voted Democratic in 1968 and in 1980. (See Table 5.1).

It should be noted, however, that while the Republicans are also winning more congressional seats in the South than they used to, the Democrats still control most of the seats. Indeed, the more local the election in the South, the more heavily Democratic the vote tends to be: some Southern state legislatures have almost no Republican representation at all. For example, in 1987 Alabama had only 21 Republican state legislators among a total of 140; in Georgia there were 37 out of 327; and in Mississippi there were 16 out of 174. Still, Republican strength is growing in the South.

DIVIDED GOVERNMENT

The Republicanization of the South is perhaps the most important development in presidential politics since the last realigning election in 1932, and it will be dealt with in more detail later. For the moment, however, we shall consider the tendency of **divided government** that is prevalent in the present era. Republican candidates have carried the White House in five of the past six elections, with the Democrats winning only a single term under Jimmy Carter in 1976. Yet in that time, the Democrats have monopolized the majority in the House, and they lost control of the Senate only between 1981 and 1986. In fact, since 1931, the Republicans have controlled the House for a total of only 4 years (1947–1948 and 1953–1954), while in the Senate they have dominated for

Table 5.1

SOUTHERN STATE PRESIDENTIAL VOTES

	1952	1956	1960	1964	1968	1972	1976	1980	1984	1988
Alabama	Dem	Dem	Rep	Rep	AIP	Rep	Dem	Rep	Rep	Rep
Arkansas	Dem	Dem	Dem	Dem	AIP	Rep	Dem	Rep	Rep	Rep
Florida	Rep	Rep	Rep	Dem	Rep	Rep	Dem	Rep	Rep	Rep
Georgia	Dem	Dem	Dem	Rep	AIP	Rep	Dem	Dem	Rep	Rep
Louisiana	Dem	Rep	Dem	Rep	AIP	Rep	Dem	Rep	Rep	Rep
Mississippi	Dem	Dem	Rep	AIP	Rep	Rep	Dem	Rep	Rep	Rep
No. Carolina	Dem	Dem	Dem	Dem	Rep	Rep	Dem	Rep	Rep	Rep
So. Carolina	Dem	Dem	Dem	Rep	Rep	Rep	Dem	Rep	Rep	Rep
Tennessee	Rep	Rep	Rep	Dem	Rep	Rep	Dem	Rep	Rep	Rep
Texas	Rep	Rep	Dem	Dem	Dem	Rep	Dem	Rep	Rep	Rep
Virginia	Rep	Rep	Rep	Dem	Rep	Rep	Rep	Rep	Rep	Rep

AIP = American Independent Party
Dem = Democrat
Rep = Republican

only 12 years (1931–1932, 1947–1948, 1953–1954, 1981–1986). With the landslide victory of Ronald Reagan and the Republican control of the Senate in 1980, the GOP* hoped that a new realignment was in the offing, with the Republicans to become the most popular party. The Democrats' gain of 26 seats in the House in 1982, however, dampened this ambition,[5] and even though Reagan won a second landslide victory in 1984, the predicted realignment has not occurred. The Democrats remained in control of the House, and the election of 1986 gave them back the majority in the Senate. The Republicans, with George Bush, won the presidency again in 1988, but they lost 5 seats in the House and 1 in the Senate. It is very uncom-

* *GOP* stands for *Grand Old Party*, an epithet adopted by the Republicans in the 1880s even though the Democratic Party is much older—but presumably not grander, from the Republican point of view.

mon for the party that wins the presidency to lose seats in Congress in the same election. On the other hand, although the Democrats picked up 9 seats in the House and 1 in the Senate in the 1990 congressional elections, these gains were unusually low. Normally the party not in control of the White House is expected to gain over 20 seats in the House and 3 or 4 in the Senate in elections when the presidency is not at issue.

It seems that as far as Congress is concerned, the New Deal coalition is still intact, albeit weaker than it once was. Why the voters have elected Republicans to the White House but Democrats to Congress in the present era is not completely understood. Some observers suggest that the Republicans have simply fielded more attractive candidates than Hubert Humphrey, George McGovern, Jimmy Carter, Walter Mondale, and Michael Dukakis, the losing Democratic candidates. Others maintain that the defection of the South to the Republican column in presidential elections combines with Republican strength in the Midwest and the West to give them a "lock" on the presidency. Still others advance that the people identify more with a Republican approach to national security and that they prefer conservatives handling the symbolic role of the president, while they prefer the Democrats in Congress solving their problems on a day-to-day basis. On the other hand, political scientist Everett Carll Ladd believes in what he calls a **cognitive Madisonianism** among the American electorate. Citing recent polls, Ladd concludes that the people currently believe it better for one party to control the presidency while the other controls Congress.[6] In other words, the voters are deliberately exercising the checks and balances by putting different parties in control of the executive and legislative branches.

Whatever the case, we are currently in the longest sustained period of divided government in our history, and party strength with the voters is more ambiguous than ever. The Democrats still appear to be the most popular party, controlling not only Congress but most state legislatures and governor seats, yet they cannot seem to capture the nation's most important office. By contrast, the Republicans have held the White House since 1969, with but one 4-year interruption, but they find themselves continuously frustrated in efforts to forge a new realignment and to again become dominant throughout the country. (See Figure 5.1.)

Two-Party System

A *two-party system* exists when there are only two major parties, each with the ability of winning control of the government. There may be any number of parties in existence, but there are only two major parties. This party system has the advantage of usually producing a majority for its winning candidates, while enjoying a strong opposition party that criticizes the "ins" and offers alternatives to the government's policies. The system also encourages compromise in that, in order to defeat the opposition, people must be willing to get along with others who do not share their exact views. On the other hand, the two-party system does not offer many alternatives. Politics is reduced to the establishment in-party and the establishment out-party, as if there were only two sides to each question. Instead, there are actually many different possible approaches to problems, and the enormous complexity of politics is not well represented in this system. Similarly, the two-party system offers the voters a limited number of candidates. "I'm not voting *for* candidate A," it is often lamented, "I'm voting *against* candidate B." The reason we are so often forced to vote against the greater of two evils is that there are only two viable candidates for each office and the chances are slim that the two major parties will be able to nominate candidates for each election that will stir positive feelings in most of the voters. A Franklin Delano Roosevelt, John F. Kennedy, or Ronald Reagan seems to be available only once in each generation.

The American Two-Party System

Except for the Era of Good Feeling, the United States has had a two-party system during its entire history. A glance at Figure 5.1, however, reveals that the major parties have not been equal in their appeal through time. Instead, the Democratic party won most elections from 1800 to 1860, the Republicans held sway from 1860 to 1932, the Democrats again came to prominence from 1933 to 1968, and since then we have usually seen divided government, with the Democrats usually controlling Congress while the Republicans occupy the White House.

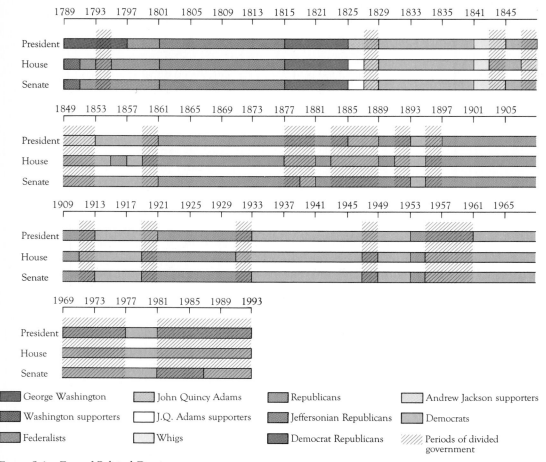

Figure 5.1   Eras of Political Dominance

Exactly why such a heterogeneous society as the United States should so consistently have a two-party system is unclear. Several different reasons have been advanced. One theory suggests that historically the United States has been bipolar in its approach to issues. The early leaders divided for or against adopting the Constitution, for or against high tariffs, for or against slavery, and so on until the tradition for two major parties was well established. Another view suggests that the American people have usually occupied the center of the political spectrum, with few people at the extremes. Thus, there has been little room for more than two parties, one leaning slightly left and the other slightly right. Additionally, it is argued that the high degree of social mobility traditionally enjoyed in the United States and the absence of a rigid social class structure explain why no more than two significant parties have emerged at the same time in our history: It is relatively easy for socially mobile people to compromise their views enough so that only two major parties are needed.

American electoral law has also been an important factor. Parties must register in each state to qualify for the ballot. The state laws governing party recognition are often quite difficult to satisfy. For example, a new party must obtain over 800,000 signatures of registered voters before its candidates can be placed on California's ballot. Few fledgling parties have the resources to satisfy such a strict requirement. Perhaps the most telling institutional restraint to the development of a multiparty system, however, is the single-member district.

A **single-member district** is an electoral jurisdiction with only one seat. Virtually all partisan offices (offices for which the parties nominate candidates) in the United States are single-member districts. A state with ten seats in the House of Representatives, for instance, will establish ten districts from each of which one member is elected. Each of the United States senators is elected separately by the state as a whole. Even the president is elected in single-member districts, since each state except Maine* awards all of its electors to the candidate who gets the most popular votes in the state.

The single-member district gives the two major parties a distinct advantage since the winner will be the candidate receiving the largest number of popular votes. Suppose three parties ran candidates for the House in a particular congressional district, and the vote broke down as indicated in Table 5.2. Clearly, the Republican candidate, with 42 percent of the vote, will go to Congress. In future elections the Democrats will almost certainly field candidates because they came very close in the last election and may indeed win next time. But the Libertarian party would have to more than double its vote to win, an unlikely prospect. Consequently, people will be discouraged from giving money, doing voluntary campaign work, or even voting Libertarian in the next election;

* Maine elects two electors at large and one elector from each of its two congressional districts, so it too elects electors from single-member districts.

Table 5.2
THE SINGLE-MEMBER DISTRICT

Party	Popular vote
Republican	42%
Democratic	40%
Libertarian	18%

thus the party will probably whither and disappear except for a tiny number of die-hards.[7]

A final reason for the existence of the two-party system in the United States relates to our political culture. Political scientist Robert Huckshorn avers that although we are a very diverse population, we are prone to compromise with one another in order to establish consensus. "Politics," the French statesman Georges Clemenceau said, "is the art of the possible." It is the product of people's trying to get what they want. But, since no individual is likely to get everything he or she wants, each of us must give up a little to get something back. Tolerance, in other words, is essential to the democratic process. The fact that most of the electorate has usually been willing to satisfy themselves with one or the other of the two major parties tends to indicate our willingness to compromise so as to enjoy stable government.[8]

THIRD PARTIES

Although the United States has a two-party system, there are in the country third parties seeking voter support—but minor parties have not enjoyed great success in the United States. Indeed, only one third party, the Republicans, has ever supplanted a major party (the Whigs); no other minor party has even come close to becoming a major party. From Table 5.3 you can see that only 11 minor parties have been able to win any electoral votes for president, and in two of those cases, the minor party

Table 5.3
THIRD PARTIES

	Party	Electoral vote (percentage	Popular vote (percentage)	Party	Electoral vote (percentage)	Popular vote (percentage)
1832	Anti-Masonic	2.4	7.8			
1848	Free Soil	0	10.1			
1852	Free Soil	0	4.9			
1856	Whig-American[a]	2.7	21.5			
1860	So. Democrat	23.7	18.1	Constitutional Union	12.9	12.6
1880	Greenback	0	3.3			
1884	Greenback	0	1.7	Prohibition	0	1.5
1888				Prohibition	0	2.2
1892	Populist	5.0	8.5	Prohibition	0	2.2
1896	National Democratic	0	1.0	Prohibition	0	0.9
1900	Socialist	0	0.6	Prohibition	0	1.5
1904	Socialist	0	3.0	Prohibition	0	1.9
1908	Socialist	0	2.8	Prohibition	0	1.7
1912	Socialist	0	6.0	Progressive[b]	16.6	23.2
1916	Socialist	0	3.2	Prohibition	0	1.2
1920	Socialist	0	3.4	Farmer-Labor	0	1.0

[a] Former President Millard Fillmore was the Whig-American candidate in 1856.
[b] Former President Theodore Roosevelt was the Progressive candidate in 1912.

candidates were former presidents who might have been expected to attract votes.

Table 5.3 also demonstrates another important point. Because the states award all their presidential electors to the candidate who gets the most popular votes, minor parties that are concentrated in only a few states tend to do better in the electoral vote tally than third parties whose supporters are spread throughout the country. For example, in 1948 the States' Rights Democratic party, a segregationist party in the South, got 1.169 million popular votes and 39 electors, while the Progressive party, a radical organization drawing support across the country, took 1.157 million popular votes, but did not win even a single electoral vote. More will be said about the electoral college in the next chapter, but for now it is enough to note that the number of votes a party receives is not the only factor to consider in running for president; the location of the voters is also critical.

Although more minor parties have fielded presidential candidates in the twentieth century than in the nineteenth century, the nineteenth-century electorate was twice as willing to vote for minor party candidates than has

Table 5.3 (Continued)

	Party	Electoral vote (percentage	Popular vote (percentage)	Party	Electoral vote (percentage)	Popular vote (percentage)
1924	Progressive	2.4	16.6	Prohibition	0	2.0
1928	Socialist	0	0.7	Communist	0	0.1
1932	Socialist	0	2.2	Communist	0	0.3
1936	Socialist	0	0.4	Union	0	0.4
1940	Socialist	0	0.2	Prohibition	0	0.1
1944	Socialist	0	0.2	Prohibition	0	0.2
1948	Progressive	0	2.4	States' Rights Democratic	7.3	2.4
1952	Progressive	0	0.1	Prohibition	0	0.2
1956	Socialist Labor	0	0.1			
1960	Socialist Labor	0	0.1			
1968	American Independent	8.6	13.5			
1972	People's	0	0.1			
1980	Libertarian	0	1.1	Independent Candidate	0	7.1
1984	Libertarian	0	0.3			

been true of the twentieth-century electorate. On average, in the 1800s minor parties won 9.6 percent of the popular votes in the elections they chose to enter, while they have won only 4.9 percent during this century. Thus, the country is even more firmly committed to the two-party system now than it was in the last century. And the trend continues: In the first ten elections of this century the minor parties were stronger than in the second ten elections. From 1900 to 1936 the minor parties averaged 7.2 percent of the vote in the elections in which they participated, while between 1940

and 1984 they averaged only 2.8 percent. Hence, as far as vote-getting capacity is concerned, the two-party system in this country is now stronger than ever, although the major parties themselves have been weakened, as will be discussed later.

While minor parties have been poor vote-getters in presidential elections, they have done better, albeit only marginally so, at the state and local level. Socialists have managed to elect a few mayors and in 1990 a socialist from Vermont was elected to Congress. The Farm-Labor party of Minnesota, the Liberal party of New York, the Conservative party of New York, and others have also managed to elect local officials, state legislators, members of Congress, and even some governors. Still, winning elections has not been the forte of the third parties. Their influence in American politics has come in other areas.

The greatest contribution of third parties has been in the area of generating and popularizing issues. The major parties tend to be hesitant to adopt new issues because they are afraid to alienate voters. This reluctance is sometimes too great, shunting aside issues that are truly popular. In such cases, minor parties have organized around the desired policy. When a minor party sufficiently popularizes an issue, however, one or the other of the major parties adopts it, thus causing the minor party to lose support and eventually disappear. The Anti-Masonic party, in its fear of secrecy, forced the major parties by its example to adopt the national nominating convention in the 1830s. The Free Soil party focused in the 1840s and 1850s on antislavery, thus creating an important plank for the newly emerged Republican party; the Populist party made sufficient headway with reforms such as the secret ballot, women's suffrage, popular election of United States senators, the progressive income tax, and regulation of business that the Democratic party adopted the issues as their own in 1896; and in the early twentieth century the Socialist party was the first advocate for social security, collective bargaining, welfare programs, and reform of prisons and mental hospitals—issues that the Democrats also eventually adopted.

Because of the prevailing conservative mood during most of our history, minor parties have normally come from the left. But since the New Deal, as the government began to reach out to the poor and the underrepresented, third parties such as Strom Thurmond's States' Rights party, George Wallace's American Independent party, and the Libertarian party have organized on the right to express their discontentment. In any event, third parties have played only a supporting role on the stage of national politics, and little evidence suggests that they will become more prominent.

Functions, Characteristics, and Structure of Major Parties

Beyond question, the most fundamental role played by political parties is to organize and execute campaigns for public office. A complicated process, this function requires recruiting candidates and nominating them. Indeed, many scholars consider the nominating process the parties' most important task. E. E. Schattschneider wrote, "Whatever else they may or may not do, the parties must make nominations."[9] The electoral function of the parties also obliges them to socialize conflicts (reach compromise among rivals) among interest groups, to identify and articulate the issues in which people are interested (among the most difficult tasks to do well), to raise money, to run campaigns, and to mobilize voters.

During the election the parties try to educate and politicize the electorate about their candidates and the issues they feel are important. Most people view elections simply as mechanisms by which democracies choose leaders, and indeed that is one of their important objectives. But a second goal of elections is to mobilize and politicize the public. Almost all countries—democracies, oligarchies, and dictatorships—hold elections. Even in societies where leaders are actually chosen by people other than the voters, elections are considered important for their educational content. Most people are apolitical most of the time. That is, while they may accept the government under which they live, they are largely too busy with personal matters to give much attention to public affairs. Elections tend to focus the attention of the masses on political issues. They serve as forums in which the issues of the day can periodically be debated or explained. Thus, virtually all societies hold elections as mechanisms by which to politicize and educate their people, and political parties play a major role in this process.

Once the election is over, the parties assume their governmental role. The winning party forms the government: Appointments are made, tasks are assigned, and legislation is drafted to translate the party's platform into policy. The "out" party has an equally important function; it must form the **loyal opposition**. Developed in England, the concept of the loyal opposition is a vital part of the democratic process. No system can be considered democratic unless it offers a reasonable opportunity for the minority to become the majority. The minority must be allowed to criticize the government and to offer alternative candidates and policy options to the electorate without being accused of treason or disloyalty. Put differently, although the party in power has the instruments to enforce its will, it must not use all the power available or else the democracy ceases to exist.

Quite beyond the accountability that occurs between parties, parties are also supposed to hold their own people responsible. It is expected that the parties will be true to their positions and that they will discipline their officials who do not support the party's cause. Additionally, the parties serve as conduits between the voters and the government, and among the national government, the state governments, and the local governments.

To describe the functions of political parties is not to suggest that they always perform each of the tasks well, however. Indeed, many of these roles are exceedingly difficult to perform, and their complexity may frustrate politicians. As we shall see later, many of the duties that the parties are to perform have been preempted by other individuals and groups, weak-ening the parties' role in American politics. Additionally, the public's attitude about political parties often prevents them from accomplishing their tasks, and there are also institutional obstructions that foul the works.

PARTY CHARACTERISTICS

The American two-party system has several characteristics, many of which are unique. To begin with, unlike most political parties in other countries, the Democratic and Republican parties are inclusive. There are no requirements for membership, no dues to pay, and no membership cards to carry. There are, of course, political clubs such as the Republican Women's clubs, and some states require people to specify their party affiliation when they register to vote, but the parties themselves want as many people as possible to identify with them, so they themselves impose no impediments to membership. In short, all one needs to do to be a Democrat or Republican is to believe oneself a member of the party.

Each party, then, is a mass organization and tries to appeal to the broadest possible spectrum of voters. Although the Democratic party is somewhat more successful in its mass appeal than the Republican party, each is composed of a large variety of socioeconomic groups, and each tries to appear open to all. Political scientist V. O. Key, a preeminent student of American political parties, wrote, "A party must act as if it were all the people rather than some of them; it must fiercely deny that it speaks for a single interest."[10]

In their attempt to appeal to all voters, the political parties mirror the American public remarkably, reflecting traits that exemplify the voters. For example, the American people tend to want quick-fix solutions to their problems. They are impatient with ideological approaches to problems, which may require time to accomplish, preferring instead "practical" policy that addresses the perceived problem directly. Accordingly, the parties usually try to evade labels such as *liberal* or *conservative* and try to approach politics pragmatically. They are reluctant to be perceived as institutions that offer only a single set of alternatives to the voter. Similarly, since the bulk of American voters are found in the middle of the political spectrum, neither leaning too far right or left, the major parties tend to be moderate as well.

Another characteristic of the American parties is that *they are weak*. Unlike the parties in most other democracies, American parties lack influence over their candidates, finding it difficult to discipline them when the need arises. There are several reasons for this unique impotence. Perhaps the most important is that the parties have lost a great deal of control over the nomination of candidates who carry their flags in elections. The *direct primary,* developed around the turn of the century, has been adopted in some form by virtually every state. Thus, party candidates are selected by votes cast by whoever decides to associate with the party in the primary election, and the party leaders have very little to say about it. Not being beholden to the party leadership for their nominations, party candidates often feel little obligation to follow party policy or dictates.

Campaign financing is another source of weakened parties. The parties have trouble raising money in their own right. Consequently, candidates are obliged to raise their own funds from individual donors, special interest groups, and PACs. Moreover, the parties are no longer the principal campaigners, as candidates rely more and more heavily on professional campaign managers, public relations firms, pollsters, fund-raisers, mass mailing specialists, political analysts, and the like.

Similarly, the parties used to be primary vehicles for distributing political information and analyses of current events. However, citizens now look to the media for information far more readily than relying on the political parties for cues. The public also has a rather jaundiced view of political parties. Public identification with the parties is in decline, and the public generally does not like the thought of a party disciplining errant officials. Indeed, politicians who flout the will of party leaders are often rewarded with increased public approval.[11]

A number of institutional factors also tend to weaken the parties. The creation and spread of the civil service has had the desired effect of insulating government employees from political pressure, but it has also reduced the amount of patronage (government jobs given to party loyalists) available for the parties to repay supporters. Federalism sees nominations and elections resting largely at the state and local level, frustrating attempts to unify party control. Further, the separation of powers assures independence among legislative and executive leaders, making it hard for presidents to demand the loyalty of their fellow party members in Congress. Indeed, few contemporary presidents have done very much to strengthen their parties, preferring to focus on their own political well-being instead.[12] For all these reasons, then, weakness is an important characteristic of the American two-party system. Indeed, the parties' presence in American politics has become so vitiated as to cause one scholar to suggest that they are often bystanders in elections. "They compete within the political process," writes William J. Keefe, "but do not dominate it. A great deal of contemporary politics, in fact, lies outside the parties and beyond their control."[13]

It should be noted that while most political scientists recognize these changes among the parties, they are not unanimous in the judgment that the political parties are in decline. Some scholars, including M. Margaret Conway, John Bibby, and Paul Herrnson, believe that the parties are going through an adjustment to changing political conditions. These observers point out that political parties are increasing their activities in areas of candidate recruitment and training, fund raising, research, and consultation. Hence, these authorities are more optimistic about the parties' status and argue that what others perceive as decline is actually a process of party modernization.[14]

Finally, reflecting both the federal format of government in the United States and the public's preference for keeping as much power as possible close to home, the parties tend to be structurally decentralized. That is, while a flowchart of the political party structure may be pyramidal, the reality of party power relationships is much less hierarchical. It deserves closer examination.

PARTY STRUCTURE

Essentially, American political parties are organized into a number of committees paralleling relevant electoral jurisdictions. The most fundamental political jurisdiction is the **precinct**. Each county, township, or parish is divided into precincts; residents who are registered to vote are assigned to a polling place within their

precincts. Precincts are created to facilitate voting by bringing the polls close to the voter. However, the reason the precincts are the basic campaign jurisidiction for the parties, or for anyone else running for election, is that the precinct lists include most of the information about the voters a campaigner needs. These lists include registered voters' names, addresses, telephone numbers, party affiliation, and occupations, as well as specifying whether they voted in the last election. A keenly organized political apparatus will mount its campaigns at the precinct level, but today the parties are seldom able to mobilize enough workers to sustain such grass-roots efforts.

Most states, however, do have elected county, township, or parish party committees (often called central committees). The county committee members are often elected by party members in the primaries, or sometimes they are appointed. The committee is responsible for the party effort within its jurisdiction, and its chairperson is often very powerful and courted by aspirants for party nominations. Some states also have legislative district committees or congressional district committees that focus on electing their party candidates to legislative seats.

Democratic National Committee Chairman Ron Brown exchanges pleasantries with First Lady Barbara Bush.

Republican National Committee Chairman Clayton Yeutter

Each party has a **state central committee** comprising either elected or appointed members. Almost all parties have permanent state committee headquarters and staffs; while some state committees are not very influential, others are, and the state committee chairpersons are usually significant, although they can be eclipsed by a powerful governor or legislator in their state party. The state committees have many of the same functions as lower-level committees, including raising funds, adopting party platforms, and organizing campaigns. Their power and effectiveness depend on several variables, including the partisan leanings of the people, the demographic mix within the state, and the leadership abilities of those involved.[15]

At the national level each party is capped by a **national committee**. Each national committee has a permanent headquarters and staff, although the Republican National Committee (RNC) is much better organized, more abundantly funded, and more active than is the Democratic National Committee (DNC). Besides raising funds, the national committees research issues and electoral data, and they are principally responsible for organizing and choosing the location for the quadrennial presidential nominating conventions. However, the national committees have very little to say about the nominations, campaigns, and elections of offices below the presidential and vice-presidential levels, since these are viewed as local matters.

Membership of the two national committees differs somewhat. The RNC has about 160 members drawn from the committee chairpersons, plus one man and one woman from each state, territory, and the District of Columbia. The DNC is more than twice as large and is composed of people selected both at large and by state, with careful attention to proportionate gender and ethnic representation. Each national committee has a chairperson who is often prominent, especially in the party that does not hold the presidency. Although the national committee chairpersons are technically elected by their respective national committees, they are actually chosen by the party's presidential standard bearer.

Recently, the Supreme Court gave the national committees more control over national convention delegates than they previously enjoyed. In 1974 the national party rules for selecting delegates to the national conventions were given precedence over state laws that might contradict them,[16] and in 1981 the Court ruled that national parties could refuse to seat convention delegates elected in open primaries.[17] (Open primaries are explained in the next chapter.) These opinions, together with Democratic reforms of the delegate selection process and successful fund-raising efforts of the RNC, have seen the national parties increase in authority, although the Democratic party is clearly more centralized than is the Republican party.[18] Yet, when one considers the totality of the intraparty relationships, the national parties remain weak. They have little control over the state parties and precious little authority even in the presidential campaigns.

Given the absence of firm national control of the parties, the profusion of committees within each state, and the fact that power is distributed differently within each state, the notion of a *two*-party system is something of an illusion. In reality there are hundreds of Republican and Democratic parties in the country. Each has a distinctive leadership and power base, and each responds to issues differently. For example, the Mississippi Democratic party is very conservative, while the New York Democratic party is liberal; the Republicans of Des Moines are concerned with urban renewal, while those of Sibley, Iowa, are focused on the government's price support for corn; the Cook County Democratic party is principally interested in matters that relate to Chicago's interests, while the DNC addresses questions of national and international scope; the Republican party of Oregon is relatively democratically organized and run, while the RNC tends to be leadership oriented; and the presidential candidates of both parties are closely bound to the party platforms, but their fellow party members in Congress, the state houses, or the state legislatures can ignore national party platforms with impunity. Viewing the parties through the prisms of federalism, one sees them refracted and disjointed. In fact, one might be tempted to conclude that there is no such thing as a two-party system in the United States, that at best what we have is a profusion of organizations that, like two herds of musk oxen, quadrennially draw together to meet each other as adversaries. Confronted by such ambiguity, one might wonder whether any consistency can be found within each party.

Democrats and Republicans

It should be noted at the outset that while the parties can be distinguished from one another in general terms, their differences are often subtle rather than dramatic. Each party has rich and poor members, men and women, minority and majority ethnic groups, labor and business persons, liberals and conservatives. Thus, each party has a wide range of members whose interests differ and sometimes conflict. To satisfy such diverse groups, the parties dare not develop overly specific programs. Trying to appeal to all people in society, each must assume broadly-worded positions because, in most cases, specificity will alienate more voters than it will attract. As a consequence of deliberate party attempts to be vague, many people (about one-third of the population) see little difference between them.

A second reason for the parties' appearing to be little different from one another is that their targets among the voters are largely the same. Figure 5.2 demonstrates a number of interesting things about the ideological preferences of the American people. To begin with, most people specify an ideological preference when asked, although there is no assurance that they clearly understand the difference between liberal and conservative. It is also obvious that there has been remarkably little fluctuation among the categories over the 14-year period the graph records. Third, the largest number of people consistently consider themselves moderate. While some fluctuation has occurred over the years, the change has not been severe and essentially the bulk of the voters have remained close to the center of the political spectrum. This unimodal distribution of voters (most voters being located at one general area on the spectrum) means that both parties must try to attract the same voters; thus each party will make similar appeals, neither varying dramatically from the other. When party candidates ignore the centrist location of the voters, going too far to the right as Barry Goldwater did in 1964 or too far to the left as did George McGovern in 1972, the result is crushing defeat. If the voters were distributed more evenly across the spectrum or if they formed a bimodal curve with large numbers on the right and large numbers on the left, the parties would probably focus their appeals on different parts of the spectrum, and their differences would be clear and dramatic. Such is the case in Britain, where no confusion exists about the differences between the Labour and Conservative parties.

The close similarities of the two major parties lead some people to believe that rather than having two parties, we actually have one party with two names. This generalization is incorrect, however, because there are funda-

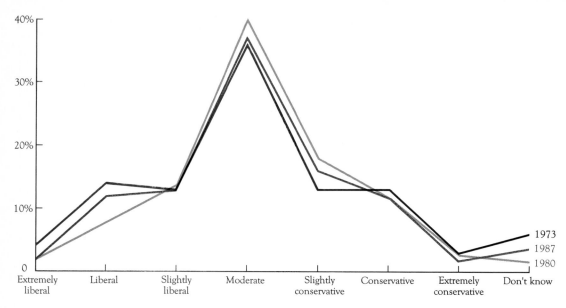

Figure 5.2   Ideological Self-Identification of American Public, 1973, 1980, and 1987
Source: General Society Survey, National Opinion Research Center.

mental, albeit subtle, differences between the two parties, and we shall examine the most important of them.

POLITICAL CULTURE

The **political cultures**, or the basic attitudes, assumptions, and psychology governing party behavior of the Democrats and Republicans are quite distinct. In 1986, political scientist Jo Freeman published a perceptive analysis of the political cultures of the two major parties. She found them different in significant respects.

The Democratic party, Freeman concluded, is pluralistic and polycentric in its outlook. The party tries to accommodate the interests of its constituent groups (ethnic minorities, women, labor, government employees, Jews, etc.) and believes that each group should have the opportunity to advocate its point of view within the party. By giving vent

to so many different interests, however, it is difficult for the Democrats to develop coherent policy statements, and because the party caters to each group, members often view themselves as African-American or union members first and Democrats only second; thus loyalty and unity are problems for the party. In 1991, the moderate-to-conservative wing of the party, calling itself the Democratic Leadership Council, began trying to insulate the party from the divisive impact of giving too much attention to the party's various special interest groups. To date, however, the success of this endeavor is far from complete.

Republicans, on the other hand, assume a more unitary attitude toward their party. Groups exist within the party, of course, but loyalty to the party is paramount, and constituency groups are primarily expected to expound the Republican message, rather than to press within the party for their individual interests.

Instead of trying to satisfy the individual needs of each group, the Republicans try to develop programs that will suit everyone to some degree, arguing that "all boats rise with the tide." This analogy should not be understood to suggest that the Republicans are concerned that everyone advance at the same pace. That position is more the Democratic view. Rather, Republican policy is oriented toward clearing the way of needless obstruction so that each individual can progress according to her or his luck, ability, background, and industry.

Freeman notes that the Republican party is modeled after the corporate structure where the leaders are at the forefront and power flows from the top down. When the leadership changes, the followers either line up behind the new policy-maker or suffer isolation from power. Democrats, on the other hand, are less leadership oriented. Regardless of who captains the party, the constituent groups continue to advocate their points of view. The leadership among Democrats is also very diverse culturally, while the Republican leaders are much more monolithic socially. This factor, Freeman suggests, makes it difficult for the Republicans to absorb new interest groups.

Since the diversity of the Democrats is magnified by their pluralistic approach and because the split between liberals and conservatives is more even among Democrats than Republicans, Democrats tend to engage in more public arguments than do Republicans. Remarking on the Democrats' proclivity for falling into rancorous debate, humorist Will Rogers once said, "I don't belong to any organized party, I'm a Democrat." But for the very reasons that loyalty and unison are not as greatly prized among the Democrats, Democrats are better able to ameliorate their differences after the battle, and although Republicans tend to fight among themselves less often, their splits are much more bitter and long lasting.[19]

The Democratic concern for letting everybody in the party have her or his say led to a number of significant reforms to its rules. In 1968, only 17 states used the presidential primary to choose delegates to the national nominating convention, while most other states used state conventions to choose delegates. Believing it desirable to open the system to more broad-based popular participation and that national convention delegates should reflect more closely the demographic variety of the country, the Democrats adopted major changes to their rules.

As Figure 5.3 indicates, the reforms have assured that the Democratic conventions are more proportionately balanced with regard to gender, ethnicity, and age. Presidential primaries were also encouraged, and by 1988, 35 states chose delegates by primary. Other rule changes provided that candidates would be awarded delegates in proportion to the votes they received in the primaries, and modifications were made to reduce the control over the convention previously enjoyed by the party leadership. The Republicans followed suit with a number of less drastic changes to their rules, but they remain less concerned than the Democrats with proportional representation.

Well-meaning though they were, the Democratic reforms have not had the effect anticipated by their sponsors. The voter participation figures you will see in the next chapter indicate that a more open convention system has not encouraged greater popular participation, and more representative conventions have not been able to nominate winning candidates.

PARTY FUND-RAISING

Another striking difference between the parties is their respective abilities to raise funds. The Republican party, with its ties to the corporate

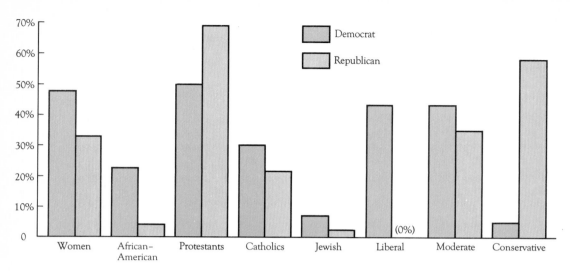

Figure 5.3   Profile of National Convention Delegates, 1988. (Median age: D, 46; R, 51.)
Source: Based on data in *Vital Statistics on American Politics,* 2nd ed., p. 135.

community, has always raised much more money than the Democrats, but in the 1960s it began mass mailing campaigns to encourage small donors to contribute, and these have been very successful. The Democrats, by contrast, did not begin serious efforts to tap their ordinary members until 1980. Instead, they relied on large individual or PAC contributions. Table 5.4 indicates that the Republicans usually raise twice to four times what the Democrats do, and their candidates receive much greater financial support from the party than do the Democrats. It should be kept in mind, however, that candidates must raise most of their funds themselves, and it is also worthy of note that the PACs usually give the greatest amount of support to incumbents. Hence, ironically, the Democrats, who purport to represent the "common man," depend more heavily than Republicans on PAC contributions because the Democrats have more congressional incumbents and enjoy less support from their party and other donors. Receiving little support from their party tends to make the Democrats less

beholden to their leadership than are the Republicans.

IDEOLOGICAL DIFFERENCES

Last in our discussion of the differences between the parties is the question of what they stand for. I have already mentioned that about one-third of the public finds little difference between the parties. But this perception is inaccurate, because there are discernible ideological traits in each party.

Both parties have members who consider themselves conservative and others who think themselves liberal, although the Republican party is preponderantly conservative while the Democratic party is more evenly split. The Republican party usually espouses "traditional American values" of the family, rugged individualism, private enterprise, and a strong national defense. Its attitude is that if people are allowed to compete "fairly" (meaning that people should not suffer encumbrance from gov-

Table 5.4
PARTY FUND-RAISING AND CONTRIBUTIONS TO CONGRESSIONAL CANDIDATES

	FUNDS RAISED (IN MILLIONS)			CONTRIBUTIONS TO CONGRESSIONAL CANDIDATES (IN THOUSANDS)			
	DEMOCRATS	REPUBLICANS	RATIO, R-D [a]		DEMOCRATS	REPUBLICANS	RATIO, R-D [a]
1977–1978	$ 26.4	$ 84.5	3.20	Senate	$ 467	$ 703	1.50
				House	$1262	$3621	2.86
1979–1980	$ 37.2	$169.5	4.55	Senate	$ 480	$ 677	1.41
				House	$1026	$3498	3.41
1981–1982	$ 39.3	$215.0	5.47	Senate	$ 579	$ 600	1.03
				House	$1052	$4721	4.49
1983–1984	$ 98.5	$297.9	3.02	Senate	$ 441	$ 591	1.34
				House	$1281	$4060	3.16
1985–1986	$ 64.8	$255.2	3.93	Senate	$ 583	$ 629	1.07
				House	$ 611	$1655	2.71
1987–1988	$127.9	$263.3	2.06	Senate	$ 489	$ 721	1.47
				House	$1198	$2651	2.21
Average ratio			3.71	Average ratio			2.10

[a] Republican dollars to every Democratic $1.

Source: Adapted from data in Stanley and Niemi, *Vital Statistics on American Politics,* 2nd ed.

ernment regulation), each individual will be able to accomplish whatever she or he can.

More sensitive to societal impediments to individual achievement, the Democrats dispute this, arguing that social institutions such as wealth, race, gender, and age biases interfere with the potential for individual accomplishment and that the government must be used to level the playing field. Thus, Democrats seek to use the government as a social arbiter and as an instrument of social justice, while Republicans resist government intrusion in the lives of individuals, and these philosophical discrepencies translate into different policy options. For example, Republicans tend to resist aggressive affirmative action programs in the workplace,

arguing that each person must openly compete for work so that the best candidate gets the job. Democrats, on the other hand, contend that social bias and inferior education for women and ethnic minorities make fair competition impossible. Consequently, the government should invoke policies that give previously underprivileged people an edge in the hiring process, until society no longer discriminates on the basis of sex or race.

Statements about Democratic and Republican differences on policy cannot be made in absolute terms, however, since each party includes both liberals and conservatives. The Democrats in the South are, for the most part, conservative and often find themselves more consonant with Republican policies than those of their own party. On the other hand, Republicans from the "Eastern establishment" (usually from the Eastern metropolises) and some Republicans from the Midwestern cities tend to be more moderate than their conservative fellows from the West and the rural sectors of the country. It is fair, however, to generalize by saying that Democratic officeholders, as a group, tend toward liberalism while most Republican politicians lean to the right.

There are two great arenas in politics— foreign and domestic—and each party has essentially the same objectives: peace and prosperity. The difference between them rests in how they define the objectives and how they believe the objectives can be reached.

Republicans tend to believe that people are essentially self-oriented and competitive, so in foreign affairs they are apprehensive about perceived adversaries. Conflict between opposing nations is to be expected unless it is deterred, and it can best be averted by maintaining a strong military establishment. "The way to preserve the peace," Republicans often say, "is to be prepared for war." Thus, Republicans tend to emphasize the military in foreign relations. They support large military budgets at home, and they negotiate defense treaties with friendly foreign governments, to which they send military aid. They are strong advocates of nationalism and patriotism, and they view communism as anathema. Accordingly, they will often support right-wing, authoritarian regimes, believing them necessary in order to stop the spread of communism, and they will go to considerable lengths to support anticommunist insurgencies such as the Contras in Nicaragua and the troops of Jonas Savimbi's National Union for the Total Independence of Angola (UNITA). More recently, President Bush and the vast majority of Republican members of Congress called for war in the Persian Gulf early in 1991, while most liberal Democrats insisted that the economic sanctions should first be given a chance to pressure Saddam Hussein into evacuating Kuwait.

Democrats are less suspicious than Republicans of people's intentions. They believe that human beings are not by nature combative and that conflict is caused by adverse circumstances (poverty, ignorance, disease, social inequity) and human misunderstanding. They will, therefore, pursue policies designed to ameliorate the causes of war, and they will establish mechanisms that bring people of different nations together to facilitate mutual understanding. The United Nations and the Peace Corps were created by Democratic administrations, as were the Marshall Plan and the Alliance for Progress. Democratic budgets tend to provide less military aid to foreign governments but much more social, economic, and technological assistance.

The assumptions about human nature that motivate foreign policy also determine the details of the Republican and Democratic domestic policies. Republicans support large police forces with fewer restraints on arrest and detention procedures. They advocate rigorous criminal laws and stern penalties, but they usually oppose gun control legislation. For their part, Democrats believe that the rights of the accused should be protected, many of them support gun control laws as a deterrent to crime, and they advocate training for the police in sociological and psychological skills, which they believe better enable law enforcers to deal with crime. Unlike the Republicans who believe that prison should be a punishment for crime, Democrats promote penal institutions designed and equipped to foster rehabilitation. Consequently, Republicans believe prison conditions should be rather harsh, and Democrats support psychological treatment, job training programs, and library and recreational facilities for inmates. "Some people are naturally bad," a conservative Republican might say, "and should be taught a lesson, or else they will misbehave again"; a Democrat is more likely to believe that "if you treat people like animals, they will behave like animals."

In social policy Democrats advocate individual freedom and equal rights. They support women's liberation, equal treatment for ethnic minorities, gay rights, public support for child care, programs for the physically and mentally disabled, medicare for the elderly, and education at all levels. They usually support what they believe to be women's right to abort pregnancy, but they oppose organized prayer in the public schools and tax deductions for private school tuition.

Republicans also support individual equality, but they define it differently. While the Democrats attempt to make people more equal economically, Republicans advocate policies that will remove government from what they see as undue interference in the individuals' lives. Accordingly, Republicans tend to resist government programs that tax some to provide for others, but there is also a strong impulse of traditional morality among Republicans, causing them to resist abortion and gay rights and to support organized prayer in the public schools. They also oppose the ERA because they feel that it would deny women their "special" place in the community and create a unisex society. Clearly, the Democrats and Republicans would both regulate and liberate people in different ways.

Republicans are most solicitous of individual liberties in the economic sphere. Believing that people will best be able to maximize their potential if each individual is free from government restraint, they oppose government regulation of business, social welfare programs, and heavy taxes. They also believe that, although the government should not restrain business except for criminal violations, it should be active in promoting a healthy industrial base. Consequently, they often support tax deductions for business and for income from capital investment, government financial incentives

for mechanization and resource development, government subsidies to business, and so on.

Democrats argue that suggesting people can compete fairly if the government stays out of their lives is specious since people are not at all equal economically. Freeing people from government restraint under these conditions liberates only those with money, allowing them to take advantage of the less fortunate. Furthermore, they argue that the free market espoused by Republicans would deal very cruelly with those who, for reasons of physical, mental, social, or personal impairment, cannot compete in the no-holds-barred environment the Republicans would create. Therefore, Democrats support government regulation of business for the public interest, social security programs, and social welfare programs, and they would tax the well-to-do citizens and corporations more heavily than would their counterparts.

It must be remembered that few people are absolutely consistent with these profiles, and the degree to which either party will pursue the policies described above depends on the international, political, social, and economic circumstances. But one can expect government to incline to the left during the Democratic administrations and lean to the right when the Republicans hold power. Indeed, as more and more Southerners gravitate to the Republican column, the ideological differences of the parties become more pronounced. Additionally, one can anticipate more ideologically based conflict between Congress and the White House over policy options during periods of divided government.

Voter Identification

A striking fact regarding public identification with the parties is that a growing number of people are choosing nonpartisanship instead of identifying as Democrats or Republicans. This trend extends throughout the entire population, but it is most pronounced among the youth. In 1940, about 80 percent of the public identified with one party or another, yet by 1990 the number of Independents had risen to about one-third of the people. Although increasing numbers of people express disenchantment with the major parties, they have not gravitated to other political parties, nor is there a reduction in public confidence that elections are the best way to choose political leadership.[20]

There are several reasons for the decrease in partisanship among the American public. Studies indicate a growing cynicism among voters, many of whom believe that politicians are interested only in getting votes and do not really care much about the public's opinions.* Furthermore, a growing number of people believe that government is failing to deal with society's mounting problems.[22] Also, a better-educated public, reinforced with information from the media, has less need for parties as cue-givers at election time.[23] Indeed, Austin Ranney argues that television has become so important in campaigns that it has "preempted many of the parties' traditional functions," among them that of being used by voters for cues in elections.[24] Yet, while declining in influence, partisan considerations remain one of the major criteria in voter preference, as about two-thirds of the public continue to identify with one party or other.

* Alan Monroe found in a study of party platforms between 1960 and 1980 that the parties closely followed the dominant public opinion most of the time, with Republican planks reflecting the majority opinion on about two-thirds of the issues and the Democratic rate being even higher, at about three-fourths. So if the politicians are indeed only interested in getting votes, at least they seem to reflect public opinion in the process. There is a fine line between simply pandering to the public will and representing the people.[21]

As mentioned before, the parties are actually coalitions of people, and people with certain common traits tend to associate with one party as opposed to the other. For example, the majority of people in each party are Protestant, but the percentage of Protestants in the Republican party is much greater than it is in the Democratic Party. Conversely, the percentages of Catholics and Jews in the Democratic Party are higher than in the Republican Party. People of national origins from Northwestern Europe, except for Ireland, (i.e., Britain, Scandinavia, and Northern Germany) are more apt to be Republican than Democratic, while people with national origins from Eastern Europe, Southern Europe, the Mediterranean, Africa, Asia, and Latin America tend to be Democrats. The greatest number of college graduates, business people, and professionals are Republicans, while Democrats tend to be dominant among the less well-educated and blue-collar workers. There used to be little difference in party identification between men and women, but in the 1980s women began to identify as Democrats in greater percentages than men. On the other hand, younger voters used to identify in greater numbers with the Democrats, but during the 1980s larger and larger numbers of the youths who stated a party preference saw themselves as Republicans. Republican strength is centered in rural areas, the Midwest, and the West; Democrats are strongest in the Eastern cities and in the South, although southern whites are rapidly becoming Republican. A recent Times Mirror study identified probusiness people and religious fundamentalists, totaling 30 percent of the likely voters, as core Republican groups, and it listed 1960s Democrats, New Dealers, and the poor, totaling 41 percent of the likely voters, as solid Democratic supporters. It positioned all others in between, able to vote for candidates from either party.[25] (See Table 5.5).

In terms of gross percentages, Table 5.6

Table 5.5
VOTER GROUPS

Republican core

Enterprisers: 10% of adult population, 16% of likely voters. Efficient, highly educated, 90% white, 60% male. Strongly opposed to government involvement in the economy.

Moralists: 11% of adult population, 14% of likely voters. Middle-aged, middle income, 90% white, heavily concentrated in the South. Favor prayer in public schools and social programs unless they are keyed to minority groups. Antiabortion and anticommunist.

Middle groups

Upbeats: 9% of adult population, 9% of likely voters. Young (yuppies) and very positive about America's future. 94% white. Generally lean Republican, but support the social programs.

Disaffected: 9% of adult population, 7% of likely voters. Middle-aged, middle-income, but alienated. Many live in the Midwest. Lean Republican, are antigovernment but also antibusiness. Strongly oppose gun control.

Followers: 7% of adult population, 4% of likely voters. Young, poorly educated, blue-collar workers. 25% African-American, 18% Hispanic-American, concentrated in the East and South.

Seculars: 8% of adult population, 9% of likely voters. Few religious commitments, mostly white, 11% identifying as Jews. Well-educated, heavily concentrated on the east and west coasts. Lean Democratic, favor personal freedom, pro-choice, oppose miliary spending and school prayer.

Bystanders: 11% of adult population, 0% of likely voters. Young, poorly educated, and totally uninterested in public affairs. 82% white, 13% African-American.

Democratic core

1960s Democrats: 8% of adult population, 11% of likely voters. Well-educated, upper-middle income, 60% female, 16% African-American. Strongly committed to peace, civil rights, and environmental protection. High tolerance for views and life-styles they do not share.

New Dealers: 11% of adult population, 15% of likely voters. Two-thirds are over 50 years of age. Largely blue-collar, union members, and middle-income. Religious, intolerant of differing views and life-styles. Favor most social spending programs except those targeted to minorities.

The Passive Poor: 7% of adult population, 6% of likely voters. Older group, concentrated in South, 31% African-American. Strong faith in America, favor all forms of social spending, and more supportive of increased taxes than any other group.

The Partisan Poor: 9% of adult population, 9% of likely electorate. Very low income, 37% African-American, concentrated in eastern cities and in the South. The most loyal Democratic group, favor school prayer and strongly favor increased social spending but oppose new taxes.

Source: Times Mirror Study published in the *Los Angeles Times*, October 1, 1987.

Table 5.6

PARTY IDENTIFICATION AMONG VOTERS

	1964	1968	1972	1976	1980	1984	1988
Democrats	52%	45%	41%	40%	41%	44%	35%
Republicans	25%	30%	23%	23%	23%	24%	28%
Independents	23%	25%	32%	37%	23%	30%	35%
Apolitical	1%	1%	1%	1%	1%	2%	2%

Source: Adapted from data in Stanley and Niemi, *Vital Statistics on American Politics,* 2nd ed.

indicates that the Democratic party was the largest until 1988. However, a 1991 Times Mirror survey indicated a startling reversal for the Democrats. This poll found that, for the first time in 60 years, more people identified as Republicans (36 percent) than as Democrats (29 percent).[26] If this shift is real, and if it is long-lasting, significant changes can be expected in future elections. Even in past elections, however, Republican party voting strength has been greater than the registration figures seem to warrant because its adherents are far more disciplined voters than are Democrats. Republicans not only vote more often than Democrats, but they vote a straight party ticket in greater percentages than their opponents. Although these factors increase the Republican chances at the polls, so far Democrats still win far more elections than do Republicans.

Indicating a consistent approval rate for the Democrats in all offices except president, voters have elected Democrats to the majority of Congress, state governorships, and state legislatures during most of the years since 1932. In 1987, for example, 26 of the 50 state governors were Democratic, and in 1990 the Democrats brought their total to 28. Interestingly, in 1990, two independent governors (in Alaska and Connecticut) were also elected—a rare occurrence—so the Republicans held only 20 state houses. In the state legislatures in 1988,

32 upper houses were controlled by Democrats and 17 were dominated by Republicans, while 37 lower houses were Democratic, one was evenly split, and 11 were Republican. Furthermore, 14 states had more than twice as many Democratic legislators as Republican, while only one state* had more than twice as many Republicans.[27]

Another perspective of the power relationship of the two parties can be seen in Table 5.7. In this study, John Bibby analyzed the electoral results of every partisan office except president in 50 states, and he ranked the states as to the consistency with which they voted for candidates from one party or another between 1974 and 1980. A state that elected only Democrats to the governor's chair and to state legislative seats would be given a score of 1.000, and 0.000 would be given to a state that elected only Republican officials. Scores in between these extremes represent states that to some extent split their votes between the major parties. As you can see, 8 states were ranked as "one-party Democratic," 19 states were "modified one-party Democratic" states, 22 states were divided between the two parties, 1 state was ranked as a "modified one-party Republican"

* Nebraska has a unicameral, nonpartisan legislature.

Table 5.7
PARTY COMPETITION, 1974~1980[a]

One-party Democratic 1.000~0.8500	Modified one-party Democratic 0.8499~0.6500	Two-party 0.6499~0.3500	Modified one-party Republican 0.3499~0.1500	One-party Republican 0.1500~0.0
Alabama (4)	California (6)	Alaska (6)	No. Dakota (6)	0
Arkansas (4)	Connecticut (5)	Arizona (6)		
Georgia	Florida (5)	Colorado (6)		
Louisiana (4)	Hawaii	Delaware		
Maryland	Kentucky (5)	Idaho (6)		
Mississippi (4)	*Massachusetts* (4)	Illinois (6)		
No. Carolina (5)	*Minnesota* (5)	Indiana (6)		
Rhode Island	Missouri (5)	Iowa (5)		
	Nevada (5)	Kansas (6)		
	New Mexico (6)	Maine (5)		
	New Jersey (6)	Michigan (5)		
	Oklahoma (6)	Montana (6)		
	Oregon (5)	Nebraska (6)		
	So. Carolina (5)	New Hampshire (6)		
	Tennessee (5)	New York		
	Texas (4)	Ohio (5)		
	Virginia (6)	Pennsylvania (4)		
	W. Virginia (4)	So. Dakota (6)		
	Wisconsin (4)	Utah (6)		
		Washington (4)		
		Wyoming (6)		
		Vermont (6)		

[a] See text for further explanation. The study examined state-level elections only. A state voting Democratic for all of its offices would have been given a 1.000 rating. For a complete perspective of party strength, boldface indicates the states that have gone Republican and italics indicates the states that have gone Democratic in at least four of the last six presidential elections.

Source: Based on data from John F. Bibby et al., *Politics in American States* (see note 28).

state, and no state was identified as "one-party Republican."[28] The original study, done by Austin Ranney in the 1970s, rated 7 states as modified "one-party Republican," 23 states as two-party, 13 as modified one-party Democratic, and 7 as "one-party Democratic."[29] Clearly, there has been a shift toward the Democratic party in nonpresidential partisan elections.

Some states are shown in boldface or italic to convey a different perspective of the parties' competition. No state voted Democratic all six times; only Minnesota did so in five elections, and the Democrats carried Massachusetts and West Virginia four times. Even more revealing, none of the eight states listed as "one-party Democratic" in nonpresidential elections supported the Democrats in more than three of the last six presidential elections. On the other hand, 21 states voted Republican in all six presidential elections, 13 went Republican five times, and 8 states voted Republican four times. Interestingly, only 2 of the 22 listed as two-party states voted Democratic as many as three times.

The major occupation of political parties is participating in the electoral process. Like our unique political party system, the American electoral system is unduplicated by other democracies. To understand the electoral system and how the political parties relate to it, we shall now turn our attention to nominations, elections, and voting behavior.

Summary

- Although many prominent early leaders of the United States opposed the creation of political parties, they quickly organized anyway, as James Madison expected.

- Political parties nominate candidates, raise campaign funds, execute elections, organize governments, and become the loyal opposition.

- During most of our history we have had a two-party system, with third parties playing peripheral roles.

- The major parties have been weakened by the adoption of direct primaries, independent sources of campaign funds for candidates from PACs, the loss of patronage through the creation of the civil service, and other factors.

- While the Republican party is conservative, relatively well-financed, and leadership oriented, the Democratic party is more liberal and pluralist.

- Party identification and straight-ticket voting are declining among the voters.

Notes

1. *Federalist Papers*, #10.

2. Robert J. Huckshorn, *Political Parties in America* (North Scituate, MA: Duxbury Press, 1980), pp. 258–260.

3. James L. Sundquist, *The Dynamics of the Political Party System: Alignment and Realignment of Political Parties in the United States* (Washington, DC: The Brookings Institution, 1983), p. 5.

4. Frank J. Sorauf and Paul Allen Beck, *Party Politics in America*, 6th ed. (Glenview, IL: Scott, Foresman, 1989), pp. 160–161.

5. Sundquist, pp. 43–46.

6. Everett Carll Ladd, "The 1988 Elections: Continuation of the Post-New Deal System," *Political Science Quarterly* 104 (Spring 1989), pp. 3–8.

7. Sorauf and Beck, pp. 43–46.

8. Huckshorn, pp. 45–48.

9. Elmer E. Schattschneider, *Party Government* (New York: Holt, Rinehart & Winston, 1942), p. 101.

10. V. O. Key, Jr., *Politics, Parties, and Pressure Groups*, 5th ed. (New York: Thomas Y. Crowell Company, 1964), p. 221.

11. William J. Keefe, *Parties, Politics, and Public Policy in America*, 4th ed. (New York: Holt, Rinehart & Winston, 1984), pp. 29–30.

12. William Crotty, "A Concluding Note on Political Parties and the Future," in Herbert M. Levine, ed., *Point-Counterpoint*, 3rd ed. (New York: St. Martin's Press, 1989), pp. 145–148.

13. Keefe, p. 184.

14. Paul S. Herrnson, *Party Campaigning in the 1980s* (Cambridge: Harvard University Press, 1988), pp. 4–5 and 42.

15. For a detailed study of the political party structures and functions in each state, see David R. Mayhew, *Placing Parties in American Politics* (Princeton: Princeton University Press, 1986), chaps. 2–6.

16. *Cousins* v. *Wigoda*, 419 U.S. 477 (1975).

17. *Democratic Party of the United States* v. *LaFollette*, 449 U.S. 897 (1981).

18. Leon D. Epstein, *Political Parties in the American Mold* (Madison: The University of Wisconsin Press, 1986), pp. 208–216; also see Nelson W. Polsby, *Consequences of Party Reform* (New York: Oxford University Press, 1983).

19. Jo Freeman, "Political Culture of Democrats and Republicans," *Political Science Quarterly* 101: 3 (1986), 327–356.

20. Keefe, pp. 7–8 and 171–172.

21. Alan D. Monroe, "Party Platforms and Public Opinion," *American Journal of Political Science* (February 1983), pp. 27–42.

22. James Burkhart et al., *Strategies for Political Participation* (Cambridge MA: Winthrop Publishers, 1972), p. 3.

23. Epstein, p. 265.

24. Austin Ranney, *Channels of Power* (New York: Basic Books, 1983), p. 110.

25. George Skelton, "Parties Nearly Even in 1988 Presidential Race," *The Los Angeles Times*, Oct. 1, 1987.

26. Jack Nelson, "GOP Popularity Greatest in 60 Years, Poll Reveals," *The Los Angeles Times*, Mar. 22, 1991.

27. *Statistical Abstract of the United States* (Washington, DC: U.S. Department of Commerce, 1990), p. 259.

28. John F. Bibby et al., "Parties in State Politics," in Virginia Gray, Herbert Jacob, and Kenneth N. Vines, eds., *Politics in the American States*, 4th ed. (Boston: Little, Brown, 1983), p. 67.

29. Austin Ranney, "Parties in State Politics," in Herbert Jacob and Kenneth N. Vines, eds., *Politics in the American States*, 3rd ed. (Boston: Little, Brown, 1976), pp. 51–92.

Suggestions for Further Reading

Burkhart, James, et al. *Strategies for Political Participation.* Cambridge, MA: Winthrop Publishers, 1972.

Crotty, William. *American Parties in Decline.* Boston: Little, Brown, 1984.

Eldersveld, Samuel J. *Political Parties in American Society.* New York: Basic Books, 1982.

Epstein, Leon D. *Political Parties in the American Mold.* Madison: University of Wisconsin Press, 1986.

Good, William. *The Party System in America.* Englewood Cliffs, NJ: Prentice-Hall, 1980.

Gray, Virginia, Herbert Jacob, and Kenneth N. Vines, eds. *Politics in the American States* (4th ed.). Boston: Little, Brown, 1983.

Herrnson, Paul S. *Party Campaigning in the 1980s.* Cambridge: Harvard University Press, 1988.

Huckshorn, Robert J. *Political Parties in America.* North Scituate, MA: Duxbury, 1980.

Jacob, Herbert, and Kenneth N. Vines. *Politics in the American States* (3rd ed.). Boston: Little, Brown, 1976.

Kayden, Xandra, and Eddie Mahe, Jr. *The Party Goes On.* New York: Basic Books, 1985.

Keefe, William J. *Parties, Politics, and Public Policy in America.* New York: Holt, Rinehart & Winston, 1984.

Key, V. O., Jr. *Politics, Parties, and Pressure Groups.* New York: Thomas Y. Crowell, 1964.

Lazarus, Edward H. *Third Parties in America: Citizen Response to Major Party Failure.* Princeton: Princeton University Press, 1984.

Levine, Herbert M., ed. *Point-Counterpoint.* New York: St. Martin's Press, 1989.

Mayhew, David R. *Placing Parties in American Politics.* Princeton: Princeton University Press, 1986.

Polsby, Nelson W. *The Consequences of Party Reform.* London: Oxford University Press, 1983.

Public Interest Profiles, 1988–1989. Washington, DC: Congressional Quarterly, 1988.

Ranney, Austin. *Channels of Power.* New York: Basic Books, 1983.

Riordon, William L. *Plunket of Tammany Hall.* New York: Dalton, 1963.

Sabato, Larry J. *The Party's Just Begun: Shaping Political Parties for America's Future.* Glenview, IL: Scott, Foresman, 1988.

Schattschneider, Elmer E. *Party Government.* New York: Holt, Rinehart & Winston, 1942.

Sorauf, Frank J., and Paul A. Beck. *Party Politics in America* (6th ed.). Boston: Little, Brown, 1988.

Stern, Philip M. *The Best Congress Money Can Buy.* New York: Pantheon, 1988.

Sundquist, James L. *The Dynamics of the Political Party System: Alignment and Realignment of Political Parties.* Washington, DC: The Brookings Institution, 1983.

Sundquist, James L. *Dynamics of the Party System* (rev.ed.). Washington, DC: Brookings Institution, 1983.

Wattenberg, Martin P. *The Decline of American Parties, 1952–1984.* Cambridge: Harvard University Press, 1986.

Chapter 6

THE ELECTORAL PROCESS

PREVIEW

Voter registration procedures used in the United States are often criticized for their tendency to discourage voting. State laws differ, but essentially citizens are either registered permanently or are periodically required to reregister.

Before elections can occur, candidates must be nominated. For local offices, people place their names on ballots either by self-announcement or by circulating petitions. Primaries are used by most states to nominate candidates for high office. Direct primaries use results of popular votes to determine who will be the candidates, while indirect primaries elect delegates who go to conventions to nominate candidates. Some states have closed primaries, in which only members of particular parties can vote, while open and wide-open primaries give voters greater choices. Nominating candidates by primary is, of course, democratic but it presents difficulties in that primary elections are expensive, the voters are often uninformed about the candidates, and the incumbents usually enjoy an advantage because they are better known and can raise funds more easily than can challengers.

While the convention system has largely been abandoned for nominating local, state, and congressional candidates, it is still used to nominate presidential and vice presidential hopefuls. Yet conventions have changed considerably in the past two decades. Since most delegates are chosen by state indirect primaries, little doubt exists before the conventions meet as to who will win the nominations. Brokered conventions, where party leaders horse-trade to choose candidates, have become a thing of the past. Still, conventions are needed to write party platforms and to formalize the nominations.

Elections have become extremely costly because they are now often run by professional staffs and they employ state-of-the-art technology. The special interest groups have become very influential with candidates since they supply a large part of the money needed for campaigns. Congress has tried to modify their influence with regulations, but so far to little avail. The mounting costs of campaigns also tends to accrue to the incumbents' advantage.

Only 537 people are elected to federal office. Members of Congress are elected in districts or in statewide elections, while the president and vice president are chosen by the electoral college. Using the electoral college, the people elect the executive officers indirectly. The voters elect the electors in November, and the electors gather at the state capitals in December to elect the president and vice president. The electoral college system is criticized for being complicated and undemocratic, but proposals for its modification also portend difficulties. The electoral college has not been abolished because it usually produces a clear winner and because the largest and smallest states enjoy advantages with it that would be lost otherwise.

As increasing numbers of people are allowed to vote, the percentage of people voting has declined dramatically. Voters are also less partisan than before, and while political party is still the leading factor determining voter choice, issues and personality are becoming increasingly important as deciding factors.

The people who vote most frequently are white, middle-aged, well-to-do, well-educated, and professional. Yet these people do not necessarily dominate elections, since their number is small compared with the total electorate. Women have begun voting in greater percentages than men, and most whites currently vote Republican, while African-Americans are wedded to the Democratic party.

Our political life is becoming so expansive, so mechanized and so dominated by professional politicians and public relations men that the idealist who dreams of independent statesmanship is rudely awakened by the necessities of election and accomplishment.

John F. Kennedy

The first step to voting is registration. Although North Dakota does not require its voters to register at all, most states use one of two kinds of registration: periodic registration and permanent registration. In **periodic registration** all people must reregister at specific intervals (before each presidential election, for example) or else they may not continue to vote. While this system helps to prevent election fraud because people who die or move away are periodically purged from the registration roles, it discourages voting. Most people are so busy with their day-to-day lives that they pay little attention to politics until shortly before election time. The deadline for registration in most states is about 30 days before the election, so it goes by before many people in periodic registration states realize that they must reregister. The **permanent registration** system allows people to remain registered as long as they live at the same address and continue to vote in the major elections.

In the past, some registration laws (literacy tests, grandfather clauses, etc.) were used to prevent African-Americans and others from voting. Although these unfortunate practices have been abolished, critics of contemporary voter registration processes argue that these still place unnecessary impediments in the way of

voters. Little effort is made to get people registered, they suggest. Someone wishing to register usually has to actively seek out a registrar of voters, fill out complicated forms, and meet deadlines. Since fewer than 70 percent of those eligible actually register to vote, organizations such as the League of Women Voters advocate relaxing the registration procedures and recommend that the government take active steps to see that people have a chance to register. Some steps that could be implemented are instant registration at the polls on election day, mail-in registration, placing registration forms in post offices and other government buildings and requiring functionaries to ask people whether they wish to register to vote when they apply for welfare, get drivers' licenses, enter college or adult school, register for the draft, and even pay their taxes. In 1990, the House passed a bill allowing some of these provisions but President Bush's threatened veto and a crowded legislative calendar prevented the bill from being taken to a vote in the Senate. As matters stand, except for in a few states such as Minnesota, which applies many of these techniques and enjoys one of the country's highest voter turnout rates, little concerted effort is made to encourage voter registration. The political parties often carry out registration drives before elections, but these efforts are frequently poorly organized, selective, and spotty in coverage.

Nominations

The next step in the electoral process is nominating the candidates. The process by which candidates are chosen is, of course, critical to elections. Reflecting this insight, New York City's Tammany Hall machine boss, William Marcy Tweed, once said, "I don't care who does the electin', so long as I do the nominatin'." As with voter registration and most other election rules, nomination procedures are determined by state law.

Basically, there are four nomination processes used today: self-announcement, petition, convention, and primary. For some of the most local offices, like school boards and city council, people who can prove they are at least 18 years old and that they reside in the district they wish to represent, can be placed on the ballot simply by formally applying for candidacy (**self-announcement**) or by securing a small number of signatures on a **petition**. Higher offices require more complicated nominating procedures.

Once the major means of nomination for important offices, the **convention system** has almost disappeared, except for presidential nominations. In the earliest days of the republic, candidates were nominated by **King Caucus**. Members of Congress from a given party would meet and decide whom they would support as their party's nominee for president. In the 1830s, complaining that this process was undemocratic and secretive, the Anti-Masonic Party popularized the national nominating convention, which was also adopted by the major parties. Delegates went to local conventions to adopt platforms for their parties for local elections, to nominate candidates, and to send delegates to the next higher convention. And

so it would proceed through the county and state levels, and finally to the national nominating convention itself. Some states such as Iowa still practice a form of this system, holding local *caucuses* where delegates are elected to attend their party's national nominating conventions.

PRIMARIES

By the turn of the twentieth century, however, the convention system itself was criticized as elitist, boss-controlled, and closed to the public. As a result, in 1904 the **primary system** was born in Wisconsin. Fundamentally, primaries are elections that in some way determine who the party candidates for office will be.* Since its origin, several different kinds of primaries have been developed. Based on the assumption that a partisan nomination is strictly a party matter, the **closed primary**, used in most states, allows only those people registered in a given party to vote to nominate that party's candidates. Advocates of this system believe it is absurd to let Republicans help decide who shall be the Democratic candidates.

The **open primary** also permits voters to vote in only one party's primary, but it allows voters to choose on election day the party whose primary they wish to participate in. Alaska, Louisiana, and Washington use the **wide-open** (or blanket) **primary**. Here, citizens receive a single ballot listing all candidates from every party who wish nomination for of-

---

* Care should be taken not to confuse **primary elections** with **general elections**. Primary elections nominate candidates who then run for election to office in the general election. General elections occur on the first Tuesday following the first Monday in November of even years. Primary elections, of course, occur sometime before the general election, with each state setting the date as it pleases.

fice, and the voter may cast one vote for each office. Accordingly, a person can vote to nominate a Republican for governor, a Democrat for United States Senator, a third-party candidate for a member to the House, and so on. The open and wide-open primaries give voters the greatest choice, of course, but they also encourage **raiding**. Let us say that a Democrat's favorite choice for governor is assured of getting the Democratic nomination. The Democratic voter in an open or wide-open primary state might then be tempted to temporarily abandon his or her party and vote to nominate the weakest Republican gubernatorial candidate, thus trying to assure that the Democratic aspirant will win when the two candidates oppose each other in the general election. Raiding may appear to be a clever ploy until one thinks about the implications of deliberately nominating someone who is thought to be undesirable for the office. That person could, indeed, win the election. (See Table 6.1, pp. 160–161.)

Most primaries are **direct primaries**, meaning that the people determine by their votes in the primary elections who will run for office. Presidential primaries, however, are **indirect primaries**. Because presidents are elected by voters across the country, it would be futile for states to independently choose which Democrat and Republican presidential hopefuls were to be placed on their ballots. When 1988 primary voters marked the ballot for George Bush, for example, they were not actually voting to nominate Bush directly. Instead, they were voting to send delegates to the Republican national convention who would then vote to nominate Bush.

In 1988, 35 states and Washington, D.C., selected most of their delegates to the national nominating conventions by indirect primaries. That is, the voters elected the delegates, who then went to the convention to nominate the party candidate. Thus the voters only indirectly

nominated the candidates. Most states require their convention delegates to vote for the person they have been elected to support, but in the last chapter we saw that —because of potential raiding—national conventions need not accredit delegates elected in open primaries. In such cases, the delegates are chosen in party caucuses, so the open presidential primary has become little more than a popularity contest. States that do not hold presidential primaries select delegates in caucuses or state conventions or by appointment by state party leaders. In 1988 about three-quarters of all delegates were elected in primaries.

Like the convention system and King Caucus before it, the primary system has become controversial. Supporters point out that primaries are democratic and open to the public. Accordingly, the nomination is available to any candidates who can persuade voters to support them, rather than being restricted to candidates who enjoy the confidence of party bosses. Also, the long primary campaigns weed out those who cannot withstand intense scrutiny. Democratic Senators Gary Hart and Joseph Biden, for example, each dropped out of the primary campaigns of 1988 because their personal failings were exposed during the long primary season.

But opponents of the primary system also make telling points. In primary states, candidates must run in not one but two elections, thus protracting the time and magnifying the costs of election campaigns. Election costs will be dealt with later, but the time required to secure the nomination can be intimidating by itself. It is not unusual for some candidates to begin seeking the presidential nomination three and even four years before the nominating convention meets. The emotional stress of such an endeavor is frightening. Consider these remarks by Walter Mondale, the Democratic candidate for president in 1984.

For four years, that's all I did. I mean, all I did. That's all you think about. That's all you talk about. That's who you're around. That's your schedule. That's your leisure. That's your luxury. That's your reading. I told someone, "The question is not whether I get elected. The question is can I be elected and not be nuts when I get there." It can twist people.[1]

The expense, length, and emotional stress of primaries often discourage politicians who otherwise would make good candidates.

Besides the grueling pace campaigning puts candidates through, they are often called upon to do silly things such as sport cowboy hats or team sweaters, cook pancake breakfasts, kiss babies, crown beauty queens, judge hog-calling contests, eat cold chicken and stale peas, ride in parades, shake hands until their joints ache, cut ribbons, inspect factories, ride on tanks, and hundreds of other crowd-pleasing but absurd tasks. Although campaigns for general as well as primary elections usually demand that candidates do inane things, primaries are particularly local, and thus particularly silly. One wonders, indeed, how we have done so well in choosing candidates, since the activities required to be elected have so little to do with the positions for which candidates seek votes.

We have already seen that primaries weaken the political parties by giving the nomination to whoever happens to choose to vote as a Democrat or Republican in a given election. Eric Uslaner laments, "No wonder American parties are in such dire straits. They cannot control their own nominating procedures."[2] Besides reducing party control, the aspect of peer review is lost by using the primary system. An advantage to having party leaders and activists choose candidates is that such people are most apt to know the qualifications of the aspirants and they also understand the office for which the nominations are sought. By contrast,

the voters are often ignorant of each of these factors. Few voters actually understand what a state controller or board of equalization does, but they have to vote for people to fill those offices. Moreover, there is a "Catch 22" in electoral politics: To win one must have money, but to get money one must first win. Thus during the primaries, challengers are often plagued by their inability to raise funds, since few people are going to give large amounts of money to candidates who have not yet proven that they stand a chance of winning the election. As a result, incumbents, who have little trouble raising money for reelection, are given an enormous advantage in the primary system.

Primaries often divide parties against themselves. For months, party candidates run against one another and sometimes engage in rancorous debate, and their respective supporters campaign hard for their choices. Then after the primaries have chosen the party candidates, the parties are supposed to unite behind the selected candidates. Putting the heat of the primary campaign behind them so as to win the general election is difficult enough for professional politicians, but it is even harder for some party members who become emotionally involved in the campaigns of losing party hopefuls. Thus, some disgruntled people may sit out the general election when the two parties face each other. The tendency for intraparty divisiveness usually works to the incumbents' advantage since they are least likely to have serious competition for the nomination; hence, their parties are not usually divided by the acrimony of the primaries.

Finally, there is a problem with the timing of the primaries. As matters now stand, the earliest primaries are in small states such as culturally monolithic New Hampshire. If candidates are to attract the funds necessary to survive until the larger states hold their prim-

Table 6.1

STATE REGISTRATION AND PRIMARY LAWS

	TYPE OF PRIMARY	REGISTRATION BY MAIL	MINIMUM RESIDENCY REQUIREMENT (DAYS)	CLOSING DATE FOR REGISTRATION BEFORE GENERAL ELECTION (DAYS)	AUTOMATIC CANCELLATION OF REGISTRATION FOR FAILURE TO VOTE AFTER ___
Alabama	closed	no	1	10	none
Alaska	wide open	yes	30	30	2 years
Arizona	closed	no	50	50	1 general election
Arkansas	closed	no	none	20	4 years
California	closed	yes	29	29	none
Colorado	closed	no	32	25	2 general elections
Connecticut	closed	yes	none	21	none
Delaware	closed	yes	none	third Saturday in October	2 general elections
Florida	closed	no	none	30	2 years
Georgia	closed	no	none	30	3 years
Hawaii	open	no	none	30	2 years
Idaho	open	no	30	10	4 years
Illinois	closed	no	30	28	4 years
Indiana	closed	no	30	29	2 years
Iowa	closed	yes	none	10	4 years
Kansas	closed	yes	1	20	2 general elections
Kentucky	closed	yes	30	30	4 years
Louisiana	wide open	no	none	24	4 years
Maine	closed	yes	none	Election Day	none
Maryland	closed	yes	30	29	5 years
Massachusetts	closed	no	none	28	1 year
Michigan	open	no	30	30	10 years
Minnesota	open	yes	20	Election Day	4 years
Mississippi	closed	no	30	30	4 years
Missouri	closed	no	none	28	none

Montana	open	yes	30	30	1 presidential election
Nebraska	closed	yes	none	Second Friday before Election Day	none
Nevada	closed	no	30	30	1 general election
New Hampshire	closed	no	10	10	10 years
New Jersey	closed	yes	30	29	4 years
New Mexico	closed	no	none	28	1 general election
New York	closed	yes	30	30	4 years
No. Carolina	closed	no	30	21[a]	2 presidential elections
No. Dakota	open	no voter registration	30	no voter registration	no voter registration
Ohio	closed	yes	30	30	4 years
Oklahoma	closed	no	none	10	8 years
Oregon	closed	yes	20	21	2 years
Pennsylvania	closed	yes	30	30	2 years
Rhode Island	closed	no	30	30	5 years
So. Carolina	closed	yes	none	30	2 general elections
So. Dakota	closed	yes	15	15	4 years
Tennessee	closed	yes	20	29	4 years
Texas	closed	yes	30	30	none
Utah	open	yes	30	5	4 years
Vermont	open	no	none	17	4 years
Virginia	closed	no	none	31	4 years
Washington	wide open	no	30	30	2 years
West Virginia	closed	no	30	30	2 general elections
Wisconsin	open	yes	10	Election Day	2 general elections
Wyoming	closed	no	none	30	1 general election

[a] Business days

Source: Adapted from data in Stanley and Niemi, *Vital Statistics on American Politics*, 2nd ed.

aries, they must first do well in states whose populations do not reflect the demographic diversity of the country as a whole. The problem could be solved if the large states scheduled their presidential primaries earlier in the year. Such manipulations, however, often do not have the desired effect. In 1988, hoping to focus more attention on the South and to force the parties to nominate conservative candidates, most southern states scheduled their primaries on the same day, March 8. For the Republicans, George Bush, who was not the party's most conservative choice, swept the primaries on "Super Tuesday," and among the Democrats, Jesse Jackson took the greatest number of votes.

Problematical though primaries are, it is not likely that we will abandon them and return to the boss-controlled conventions of old. Some critics suggest that the presidential primary system should be restructured, however. One proposal would have the regions of the country hold consecutive primaries: One regional primary would be held each month from March through July; their order would be decided by lot. A second proposal, first proposed by President Woodrow Wilson in 1913, would have a single presidential primary throughout the country. In each scheme, the elected delegates would finally settle on the nominees at the national conventions. Opponents of these proposals argue that the regional plan would focus too much on sectional problems and that the single nationwide primary would favor the well-known candidates because less well-known aspirants would lack time and resources to prove themselves.[3]

NATIONAL NOMINATING CONVENTION

Perhaps the greatest single hurrah in American politics, the quadrennial American national nominating conventions are duplicated no-

where else in the world. Thousands of delegates gather to parade their party on national television, cheer their side and ridicule the opposition, debate the issues and adopt platforms, forge alliances, listen to speeches, and participate in planned, timed, choreographed, "spontaneous" demonstrations—and, finally, to nominate candidates for president and vice president.

As indicated earlier, the national convention provides virtually the only time that the hundreds of local parties coalesce into national federations of Democrats and Republicans. Before the Democratic party reforms that caused so many states to adopt primaries in the early 1970s, most convention delegates were chosen in less democratic ways, and party leaders often controlled large blocks of delegates. Prospective candidates would bargain with the bosses in what was called **brokered conventions**, in which the result was often in doubt, necessitating several ballots to choose the candidates. The last convention to need more than one vote to select the candidate occurred in 1952, when Democrat Adlai E. Stevenson was nominated on the third ballot. Since then, the delegates' choice has been known before the balloting in all conventions except in 1960 when the Democrats nominated John F. Kennedy and in 1976 when the Republicans nominated Gerald Ford. Even in these conventions the candidates were each chosen on the first ballot.

The conventions also nominate the vice presidential candidates, but that too is a simple ratification, since the party's presidential candidate indicates whom he or she would like for a running mate. Vice presidential candidates are usually chosen with an eye to balancing the ticket: John Kennedy of Massachusetts chose Lyndon B. Johnson of Texas, Walter Mondale gave the nod to Congresswoman Geraldine Ferraro, and conservative Ronald Reagan picked moderate George Bush.

Today the national nominating conventions are essentially meetings where primary voters' choices are formally nominated as party candidates. Primary voters elect delegates who are pledged to certain candidates. At the conventions the delegates then vote, formally nominating the candidates. Democratic rules encourage states to award their delegates to candidates in proportion to the votes cast in the primary, while the Republicans usually give all a state's delegates to the candidate with the most primary votes. In any event, by the time of the convention, one candidate in each party usually has won enough delegates to be assured victory.

Although the 1988 Democratic convention was a model of decorum, usually their conventions are raucous affairs, with delegates staging "credentialing" and platform fights, often nominating their candidates late in the evening. Republican conventions, on the other hand, are much better organized. The platform struggles occur behind closed doors; on camera, Republican delegates exude unity, candidates are nominated according to schedule, and the presidential nominee makes his or her televised acceptance speech during prime time. Journalist David Gergen, who became a speech writer for President Richard Nixon and later worked in the Reagan Administration, described the 1972 Republican convention as follows:

> We had an advance script, even down to the applause lines worked into the script. . . . We figured that the importance of the convention was for show, for the people back home, and you had to run it like a TV production. So you were very conscious of television values in scripting it.[4]

Staged as they are these days, national conventions are still critical to the system. In case the primaries are indecisive, the conventions will finally decide who shall be the parties' candidates, and even when the primaries clearly anoint one person over all others, the conventions are needed to formalize the nominations, to adopt the party platforms, and to nominate a vice presidential candidate. Conventions also give the parties a chance to show off their talent and enthusiasm, to advertise their candidates and views, to criticize the opposition, to energize the party faithful, and to kick off the presidential campaign. In each of these ways the conventions, changed as they are from previous eras, perform vital tasks in the electoral process. Yet, although the conventions will undoubtedly continue to play an important part in the political process, the television networks have indicated that they may no longer devote so much prime time to them. Moreover, Ronald H. Brown, the Democratic national chairman—the first African-American to hold such an office in either party— announced that his party's 1992 convention may be shortened in an effort to reverse the flagging interest of television viewers.[5]

Elections

Americans elect more people to office than almost any other society. Each even year, when most elections occur, more than 500,000 public officials are elected to school boards, city councils, county offices, state legislatures, state executive positions, the House of Representatives and the Senate, and of course, every fourth year, the presidency. By contrast with other countries, our elections are drawn-out affairs. Campaigns for even the most local office can be protracted over two or three months and cost a considerable amount of money. Presidential campaigns, including the primary season, last for at least ten months, with some candidates beginning to seek support many months and, as noted earlier, even years before the election.

Elections have become a multi-billion dollar industry. Reflecting what Herbert Alexander calls the "professionalization of politics," any serious candidate employs a campaign manager, a media consultant, and pollsters. Additional money is spent on campaign headquarters, signs, media ads, bumper stickers, mass mailings, balloons, flags, pencils, hot pads emblazoned with the candidate's name, and all the other trinkets and dust catchers that accompany political campaigns.[6]

Presidential candidates employ legions of people, including campaign managers, fundraisers, legal counsel, public relations specialists, advance people, speechwriters, pollsters, consultants, researchers, policy advisers—the list is endless, and the cost is astronomical. The media, especially television, are used to reach the masses, as every candidate is consumed with the need to make the evening news for exposure.

Among the largest items in a campaign budget is media ads. As many as one-third of the voters make up their minds about candidates during the campaign, and a huge percentage of those who decide late are influenced by candidate ads, so it pays to advertise heavily until election day. Often the television ads and mailers are devoid of substance. Candidates who want to appear as pillars of society are pictured in a family photo, complete with shaggy dog and flanked by the American flag. Candidates trying to portray themselves as being environmentally concerned are pictured with their trusty golden retriever, skipping rocks at the beach. If the desired image is of someone involved with community development, the candidate will be photographed at a building site, festooned with a hard hat and pointing away knowingly with a roll of blueprints in hand. Leadership is conveyed by the candidate's appearing to be giving a visionary speech as onlookers of all races, ages, and gender look on admiringly. Each of us has seen

such ads. They say little of substance, but they are often powerful image communicators. Occasionally an ad addresses the issues, but such ads are reserved for topics with which the experts are sure few will disagree.

In recent years negative campaigning (campaign ads that focus on the faults, real or manufactured, of opponents) has become a serious problem. Laden with vitriol, these ads are decried by the public, yet at the same time, they are growing in number and in intensity because many campaign analysts believe that they accomplish their task. Furthermore, falsehoods and deliberate distortions in campaign ads seem to be on a sharp increase, so much so that in 1990 many newspapers began to include "truth boxes" in their pages, which contradicted false statements made by candidates in the media. Yet, although the "truth boxes" rankled some candidates and political consultants, the expensive but effective negative ads continued.[7]

Another area in which an increasing amount of money is being spent is high-tech electronics and computers. "We've come light-years in technology since the 1976 Jimmy Carter campaign," states Paul E. Maslin, a leading Democratic pollster. "Everybody knows everything, and they know it within 24 hours."[8] Computers and FAX machines have been incorporated into campaigns just as have satellite communications. Writers in Washington, D.C., can instantaneously relay speeches to candidates on late-breaking news events; candidates can rent satellite time and broadcast television programs directly to specific communities, saving time to campaign elsewhere; telephone surveys can measure public opinion on current issues within hours; new videotape editing techniques make it possible to piece together campaign footage for ads that feature candidates who never even participated in making the films; and computer programs sort voters by race, religion, occupation, and views on issues, so that personalized mailings can be done en masse. The computer is also used to store research, collate positions on issues, and feed candidates information about their opponents. Of course, all this sophisticated technology costs money, and for this reason, as well as others, the cost of political campaigns has skyrocketed in the past two decades.

MONEY

"We have the best Congress money can buy," lamented Senator Edward Kennedy. "Congress is awash in contributions from special interests that expect something in return." Kennedy's frustration is certainly understandable. In 1968 about $300 million was spent on elections at every level, but by 1988 about $3 billion was expended, which represents a 900 percent increase in 20 years! Restricted by the conditions for federal funding of presidential elections, the increase has not been as steep for the nation's highest office as it has for other elected positions. In fact, the presidential election of 1988, in which Bush and Dukakis each spent about $46 million, was the first presidential election to exceed the $91 million spent by Nixon and McGovern in 1972, the last election before public funds were provided to presidential candidates. It should be noted, however, that the 1988 figure includes only the amounts spent by the presidential candidates themselves. Millions more were laid out by PACs in independent expenditures ("soft money" spent to help candidates by individuals or groups unconnected to the candidates' campaigns).[9]

The major increase in campaign spending has occurred in congressional races. Currently, a serious candidate for the House of Representatives must expect to spend a quarter-million dollars, and many will spend much much more. Moreover, the average candidate for the Senate will spend almost $4 million to win. There is no evidence that the candidate who spends the most money will always win, but it is clear that anyone serious about winning an election must spend enormous sums. Before the money can be spent, however, it must be raised.

The major sources of campaign funds are individual contributions, loans to candidates, candidate contributions, and PACs, which are also important sources of funds for the parties themselves. In order to raise such staggering amounts for elections, which in the case of House members occur every two years, politicians must devote a large share of their time to fund-raising activities. Hedrick Smith reports that in contested districts nearly one-quarter of the legislators' time is consumed by fund-raising.

Obviously, few people give huge amounts of money to politicians for purely civic reasons, although some politicians have contended that this is so. Senator Alan Cranston (D-CA), for example, received for his campaign coffers almost $1 million from Lincoln Savings and Loan (now defunct) executive Charles H. Keating. Investigating Cranston's improper effort to pressure federal examiners to ignore the financial insolvency of Keating's S&L, the Senate Ethics Committee asked Cranston why a conservative Republican would give so much money to a liberal Democrat. The senator said it was because the financier "considers himself a patriot." No doubt Mr. Keating views himself as a loyal American, but previous to the Senate committee hearings he made it abundantly and publicly clear that he fully expected that his contributions to Cranston and four other senators would secure their influence in his case.[10]

What most large donors want from politicians is the chance to explain their points of view. Although occasionally the press reports that a politician has been on the take, such transgressions are rare; the problem is more complicated. Being forced to raise so much money for their elections, politicians become dependent on donors and, thus, attentive to their needs. Politicians are not usually "bought" in the sense that they pocket money given them under the table, but it is difficult to imagine a congressperson's not being sympathetic to the needs of someone who has contributed $5000 to his or her campaign and who will probably be good for another $5000 next time. In other words, the public need not worry so much about money *illegally* taken by politicians. Instead, our concern should be focused on the vast sums that are *legally* given to public officials.

Jana Weatherbee, a spokesperson for General Telephone Company of California, said a campaign contribution "doesn't buy you a vote. It buys you access."[11] The fact is, however, that most ordinary people do not enjoy the "access" the corporations and PACs can buy. Most issues congresspersons deal with do not directly affect their constituents, and most of those issues that do relate to their constituents' lives are apt to go through Congress without notice by many ordinary people. Thus, when a member of Congress is approached by a large donor about an issue in which his or her constituents appear to be uninterested, it is easy for the member to satisfy the donor and still appear true to the voters.

Congress is cognizant of the ethical dilemmas posed by high campaign costs, and it is responsible for legislation that regulates campaign funding. Its efforts to resolve the problem of "selling" access, however, have largely failed because of Congress's reluctance to restrict the flow of money to its own campaign coffers and because of the difficulties with the Constitution that campaign finance laws have encountered.

Federal law requires detailed information about any contribution that exceeds $100, limits PAC contributions to $5,000, and restricts individual contributions to $1,000 for each candidate in each election (primary and general). Further, individuals may not contribute more than a total of $25,000 annually, but the PACs have no such limitation. These regulations were designed to reduce the flow of money into political campaigns and to get a handle on influence-buying. Supreme Court rulings, however, have somewhat defeated the purpose by declaring three important restrictions unconstitutional: candidate contributions to their own campaigns,[12] independent expenditures toward the causes of candidates,[13] and political literature inserted in corporate mailings and billings.[14]

Abandoning their wish to legislate effectively against individual and PAC access-buying, some reformers propose that congressional campaigns be funded by the public treasury, as are the presidential elections. Since candidate spending in presidential elections has been held down by the public funding laws, a similar technique might suffice for Congress. We must keep in mind, however, that well-heeled individuals, corporations, and PACs could still exert their influence by making independent contributions (soft money), as they do in presidential elections.

In 1989, President Bush proposed campaign reforms that he believed would help the situation, and in 1990 the Democrats in the Senate passed their own bill. Neither proposal became law, however, because each side claimed the other's was biased. Bush's proposal would have eliminated most PACs while increasing the amount individuals and political parties could contribute to campaigns.[15] The Democratic measure would have eliminated PACs and sharply curtailed soft money. It also called for voluntary campaign spending limits in exchange for publicly funded campaign ads and mail discounts.[16] Although neither of these proposals succeeded in becoming law, each contained valuable ideas, and concerned citizens should demand a solution to the impasse.

COMPETITIVENESS

Incumbents have enormous advantages over challengers, as you can see from the reelection rate set forth in Table 6-2. Indeed, incumbency is apparently becoming an even greater advantage in the House. In 1984, 96.1 percent of the incumbents won reelection; in 1986, 98.5 percent were reelected; and in 1988, 97.7 percent succeeded.[17] In 1990, the incumbent victory rate slipped to 96.3 percent, but it still was higher than in 1984, and this figure was achieved in a year in which incumbents were supposed to suffer extraordinary losses.[18] Presidents also benefit from incumbency, as will be seen later.

Obviously, a great advantage for incumbents is their ability to raise campaign funds. Indeed, incumbents are so capable of raising campaign funds that often they accumulate huge war chests even when they are unopposed because the PACs and other large donors give money to buy access, an objective that has little relationship to whether the incumbent is opposed for reelection. The high cost of campaigning and the immense sums some incumbents have available often discourage potential challengers from running at all. When challengers do run, they seldom raise enough money to seriously contest the incumbent. In 1990, for example, only 51 of the 405 House incumbents were opposed by challengers who raised enough money to mount credible campaigns.[19] Even so, most of the well-financed challengers were defeated.

Other factors also give incumbents an important edge. Office-holders enjoy the prestige of their positions and can claim experience at the job. They have been in a position to help constituents, and they enjoy name identification. They can get their names in the media during campaigns through the legitimate exercise of their duties, and they have large staffs on the public payroll who can help in campaigns. The decline in straight-ticket voting (voting for all the candidates from a single party) also

Table 6.2

SUCCESS OF INCUMBENT CONGRESSIONAL CANDIDATES AT THE POLLS

	PERCENTAGE OF HOUSE INCUMBENTS REELECTED	PERCENTAGE OF SENATE INCUMBENTS REELECTED
1960–1968	93.0	86.9
1970–1978	94.7	76.7
1980–1988	95.3	79.6[a]
1990	96.3	96.9[b]
Average for Three Decades	94.8	85.0

[a] In the 1980 election, in which Reagan won the presidency and the Republicans took control of the Senate, only 55.2% of the Senate incumbents won reelection. This was by far the lowest percentage of incumbent victories in either house in the three decades between 1960 and 1988.

[b] The Congressional elections of 1990 were expected to be a bad year for incumbents. While 14 of 36 governor chairs did change hands and several states voted to limit the number of terms incumbent state legislators could serve, clearly the antiincumbent fever had almost no effect on the elections for Congress.

Source: Adapted from data in Stanley and Niemi, *Vital Statistics on American Politics*, 2nd ed., for the 1960–1988 data; *The Los Angeles Times*, Nov. 8, 1990, for the 1990 data.

seems to accrue to the incumbents' advantage. Of course, incumbents must defend their records, but House members in particular are usually not visible enough in their constituencies to be associated with their voting records. In short, provided they are not opposed by particularly well-funded, well-known challengers, members of Congress need only avoid making people angry to be relatively assured of being returned to office.

A final factor affecting the competitiveness in elections is the **coattail effect.** The popularity of ticket leaders such as presidential candidates often helps members of their party win seats in Congress. Normally, the winning president's party picks up seats in Congress in a presidential election year but loses some seats in nonpresidential years. Thus, the coattails of presidential ticket leaders are important during presidential election years, but being associated with the president's party in off years does not

seem to help. (See Table 6-3.) Interestingly, in 1988 George Bush won the presidency, but his party lost seats in both houses—a phenomenon that has not occurred since 1960, and in 1916 before that, and one that may reflect Ladd's theory of a cognitive Madisonianism growing among the American voters.

THE ELECTORAL PROCEDURE

Although state and local governments have thousands of elected officers, there are only 537 people elected to office in the national government: 435 members to the House, 100 senators, the vice president, and the president. The federal government assures only that people are not prevented from voting because of race, religion, national origin, gender, financial status, unreasonably long residency requirements, and age above 17 years. Almost

Table 6.3
PRESIDENTIAL COATTAILS[a]

PRESIDENT	PARTY	YEAR	HOUSE GAINS OR LOSSES FOR PRESIDENT'S PARTY	SENATE GAINS OR LOSSES FOR PRESIDENT'S PARTY
Franklin D. Roosevelt	Dem	1934	+ 9	+ 10
Franklin D. Roosevelt	Dem	**1940**	+ 5	− 3
Franklin D. Roosevelt	Dem	**1944**	+ 21	no change
Dwight D. Eisenhower	Rep	**1956**	− 2	no change
John F. Kennedy	Dem	**1960**	− 20	− 2
John F. Kennedy	Dem	1962	− 4	+ 4
Richard M. Nixon	Rep	1970	− 12	+ 2
Richard M. Nixon	Rep	**1972**	+ 12	− 2
Jimmy Carter	Dem	**1976**	+ 1	no change
Ronald Reagan	Rep	1982	− 26	no change
Ronald Reagan	Rep	**1984**	+ 14	− 2
George Bush	Rep	**1988**	− 3	− 1

[a] In all other elections between 1932 and 1988, the winning president's party gained seats in presidential election years and lost seats in off-year elections in each house. Boldface indicates presidential election years.

Source: Adapted from data in Stanley and Niemi, *Vital Statistics on American Politics,* 2nd ed.

everything else about voting is left to the states. As explained earlier, members to the House are elected from single-member congressional districts, and members to the Senate are elected in statewide elections. In each of these elections, the winner is the person who receives the largest number of votes (a **plurality**), which may be less than a **majority vote** (any number over half). Elections to Congress are **direct elections**, meaning that the results of the **popular vote** (the votes of the people) in the general elections determine who shall take office. But an entirely different system is used to elect the president and vice president.

THE ELECTORAL COLLEGE

The Constitutional founders were reluctant to give the ordinary people much control of government. You will recall that the states allowed only white adult males with property (about 10 percent of the population at the time) to vote, and the founders did not tamper with this dearth of popular participation. In addition, the authors of the Constitution permitted only the House to be directly elected by the people, while the Senate was elected by the state legislatures.* The founders also balked at allowing the people to directly elect the executives, so they ultimately settled on the **electoral college**.

The electoral college is an intricate procedure in which the electors are chosen in the states and a majority of electors is necessary to elect the president and vice president. The number of electors to which each state is entitled is equal to the total number of its seats in Congress, but the Constitution proscribes any member of Congress from serving as an elector. Thus, since Maryland has 8 members to the

---

* State legislatures elected United States senators until the Seventeenth Amendment was adopted in 1913, providing for the popular election of senators.

House and 2 senators, it is entitled to 10 electors. Ohio has 19 House seats and 2 in the Senate, so it has 21 electors; California, the biggest prize, has 52 House seats, so it has 54 electors. Because it is a federal district and not a state, Washington, D.C., originally had no electoral vote; but in 1961 the Twenty-third Amendment was ratified, giving it 3 electors. Consequently there are now 538 electors: one each for the 435 members to the House, one each for the 100 members to the Senate, and 3 for Washington, D.C., which has a population greater than that of Alaska, Delaware, Vermont, or Wyoming. (See Figure 6.1.)

The Constitution does not even provide that the presidential electors be elected by the people. Instead, it leaves the matter of selection to the states. In the early years, most of the electors were chosen by the states' legislatures, but gradually the legislatures provided that they

New York state electors gather in the ornate Senate chamber to cast their votes in 1988.

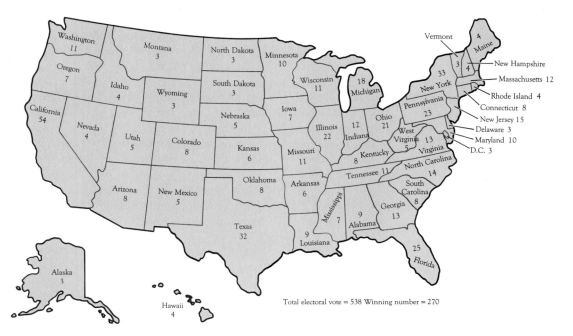

Figure 6.1   The Electoral Map of the United States

be elected by the people. The last holdout, South Carolina, did not allow its electors to be popularly elected until after the Civil War.[20]

Today, however, each state empowers the political parties running candidates for president to choose a slate of people as potential electors. (The people chosen as potential electors are usually longtime workers for or large donors to the party.) Each state except Maine* elects the party's electoral slate, which receives the largest number of popular votes in the state at large. So, as in the indirect primary, when voters placed an X behind the name of George Bush in the November general election, they were not actually voting for Bush. Instead, they were voting for the state electors committed to

cast their ballots for him. Then in December, the electors gathered at their state capitals and publicly cast one vote each for president and vice president, and forwarded the results to Congress. In January the House and Senate, presided over by the president of the Senate, met to tally the results of the electoral vote, and the winner was announced.* If no one receives a majority (270) of electoral votes, the president is elected by the House and the vice president is elected by the Senate. The House is to elect the president from the three candidates who received the greatest number of electoral votes. Rather than each member voting,

* Maine elects two electors at large and one from each of its two congressional districts. Several other states, including North Carolina and Connecticut, are considering adopting this system.

* An interesting sidelight: The vice president, who is president of the Senate, reads the results of the electoral vote. Thus, Richard Nixon, in 1961, and Hubert Humphrey, in 1969, each announced his own defeat for the presidency, while George Bush announced his own victory in 1989.

the Constitution directs that each state congressional delegation shall have one vote, and the winner must have a majority of the state delegations' votes. Currently 26 is the smallest number of states necessary to elect the president. In electing the vice president, each senator votes for one or the other of the two candidates with the highest electoral vote.[21] For a quick review of the procedure, see Table 6.4.

Criticisms of the Electoral College There are many criticisms of the electoral college. Indeed, the American Bar Association excoriated it, calling it "archaic, undemocratic, complex, ambiguous, and dangerous." Reduced to basic terms, the most often heard complaints are three. First—and this may come as a surprise—it is complicated. Few people understand the electoral college; in fact, many people are not even aware of its existence. Each presidential election year, it is explained in the media, and the electoral votes are counted on election night, but most people seem mentally to turn it off, like a bad television commercial.

Table 6.4
STEPS IN THE ELECTORAL COLLEGE PROCEDURES

1. The number of each state's electors is equal to the number of seats it has in Congress.

2. The parties each choose slates of electors.

3. The people vote in November, and the party's electoral slate with the most popular votes is elected in each state.

4. The electors vote for president and vice president in December in the state capitals.

5. The results are tallied in the United States Congress in January, and the winner is announced.

6. If no one receives a majority of the electoral vote, the House elects the president and the Senate elects the vice president.

Second, the state-adopted practice of giving *all* the electors to the person with the *most* popular votes disturbs some people. If a candidate takes only one more popular vote than his or her opponent in New York, for example, all of its electoral votes go to the popular-vote winner and none go to the candidate who got just one popular vote less than the winner. Theoretically, if a single candidate won one more vote than her or his opponents in each state, he or she would win 100 percent of the electors, while having gained only 50 more popular votes than the opponent. Moreover, it is possible to win a majority of electoral votes without winning a majority of the popular votes, thus becoming a **minority president**. This has happened 15 times in our history, as you can see in Table 6.5.

The easiest way for a minority president to be created is when more than two serious candidates split the popular vote, so that no one receives a majority. For instance, in 1968 Nixon got 43.4 percent, Humphrey 42.7 percent, and Wallace took most of the rest of the popular votes. Yet, because all of a state's electors go to the candidate who took the largest number of its popular votes, it is possible for a candidate to get fewer than a majority of the popular votes but a majority of the electoral votes, thus being elected president. This has happened 12 times. More disturbing, perhaps, is the possibility for one candidate getting the majority of the popular vote and still losing the electoral majority to the opposition, as occurred in the 1876 race between Tilden and Hayes, and in 1888, when, although no candidate won a majority of the popular vote, Cleveland won the most popular votes while Harrison took a majority of the electoral vote. This will happen when a candidate loses the large states narrowly and wins the small states by wide margins.

The third criticism of the electoral college is that the electors are not constitutionally bound to vote for the person to whom they are

Table 6.5
MINORITY PRESIDENTS

	CANDIDATE[a]	PARTY	POPULAR VOTE	ELECTORAL VOTE
1824	**J. Q. Adams**[b]	Nat Rep	30.9%	32%
	Jackson	Dem Rep	41.3%	38%
1844	**Polk**	Dem	49.5%	62%
	Clay	Whig	48.1%	38%
1848	**Taylor**	Whig	47.3%	56%
	Cass	Dem	42.5%	44%
1856	**Buchanan**	Dem	45.3%	59%
	Fremont	Whig	33.1%	39%
1860	**Lincoln**	Rep	39.8%	59%
	Douglas	Dem	29.5%	4%
1876	**Hayes**	Rep	47.9%	50.1%
	Tilden	Dem	50.1%[c]	49.9%
1880	**Garfield**	Rep	48.3%	58%
	Hancock	Dem	48.2%	42%
1884	**Cleveland**	Dem	48.5%	55%
	Blaine	Rep	48.2%	45%
1888	**B. Harrison**	Rep	47.8%	58%
	Cleveland	Dem	48.6%[c]	42%
1892	**Cleveland**	Dem	46.1%	62%
	B Harrison	Rep	43.0%	33%
1912	**Wilson**	Dem	41.8%	82%
	Taft	Rep	23.2%	2%
1916	**Wilson**	Dem	49.2%	52%
	Hughes	Rep	46.1%	48%
1948	**Truman**	Dem	49.5%	57%
	Dewey	Rep	45.1%	36%
1960	**Kennedy**	Dem	49.7%	56%
	Nixon	Rep	49.5%	41%
1968	**Nixon**	Rep	43.4%	56%
	Humphrey	Dem	42.7%	36%

[a] Boldface indicates the winner.
[b] Congress elected the President.
[c] The person with the most electoral votes *did not* win the most popular votes.

Source: Adapted from Stanley and Niemi, *Vital Statistics on American Politics,* 2nd ed.

pledged. One **faithless elector** bolted his or her party in each of the elections of 1948, 1956, 1960, 1968, 1972, 1976, and 1988. In 1988, a West Virginia Democrat cast his presidential vote for Texas Senator Lloyd Bentsen, the Democratic candidate for vice president.[22] The problem of faithless electors is a serious one. If the electoral vote margin is ever very close, say 272 to 266, one can imagine the "bargaining" that might go on behind the scenes before the electors voted in December. Consider these remarks by Senator Robert Dole, the 1976 Republican candidate for vice president. The election was so close in Ohio that it might have ultimately been decided for the Republicans, which would have given Carter 272 electors, only 2 more than the majority needed.

> We were looking around on the theory that maybe Ohio might turn around because they had an automatic recount.
> We were shopping—not shopping, excuse me.* Looking around for electors. Some took a look in Missouri, some were looking at Louisiana, some in Mississippi, because their laws are a little bit different. . . .
> We needed to pick up three or four after Ohio. . . . But it just seems to me that the temptation is there for that elector in a very tight race to really negotiate quite a bunch.[23]

Clearly, in a close election the possibility of electors changing votes threatens a major constitutional crisis, and the electoral college should be changed at least enough to deal with the potential problem of electors' selling their votes.

Changing the Electoral College Impatient with its complexity and unhappy with its undemocratic aspects, many people favor changing or even abolishing the electoral college. Among the proposals are requiring the electors to vote for the winner of the states' popular vote, keeping the electoral vote but abolishing the electors so that the winner of a state's popular vote would automatically receive its electoral total, awarding state electors to candidates in proportion to the popular votes they received, and abolishing the electoral college altogether.

Apart from the merits of each of these plans, changing the electoral college is very difficult since it involves amending the Constitution, which requires two-thirds majorities in the House and Senate and three-fourths of the states to ratify. To begin with, absent a Constitutional crisis, few people are concerned enough with the electoral college to muster the enormous majorities needed to change it. Further, far more than one-third of the states enjoy advantages in the electoral college system that would disappear if it is significantly changed. The largest states (California, New York, Texas, Florida, Pennsylvania, Illinois and Ohio), offering all of their electors to the winner of their popular votes, are not apt to sacrifice the prestige derived from being major electoral prizes since they receive an enormous amount of attention from presidential candidates. On the other hand, the smallest states (Delaware, North Dakota, South Dakota, Vermont, Idaho, Maine, Montana, New Hampshire, Nevada, and Rhode Island) have a greater proportion of the electoral college than the share they enjoy of the total population, so they would likely oppose eliminating the electoral college in favor of a direct popular election.

Direct popular election of the president would also cause other difficulties. The major parties, you will recall, offer candidates only a small portion of the money, services, and workers needed to run a campaign; the candidates must supply the lion's share themselves. At the national level, all the parties really offer candi-

---

* Senator Dole is known for his acerbic wit, so it is not unlikely that he deliberately made this slip of the tongue for effect.

dates is their name *and the electors*. If the electoral college were abolished, what motive would bring George Wallace and George McGovern into the same coalition? The party name could easily be pirated, with Dukakis leading the Democratic Party, Jackson the True Democratic Party, Richard Gephardt the First Democratic Party, and so on. Without the party electors we would suddenly have 10, 20, or more candidates for president. This is because the more candidates running, the smaller the vote necessary to win; hence, greater and greater numbers of candidates would run. If the electors were not necessary, Jesse Jackson, Gary Hart, Richard Gephardt, Robert Dole, Pat Robertson, Jack Kemp, and so on might well have continued in the 1988 race. Consequently, the two-party system might be forever shattered, and the United States could quickly evolve a multiparty system, with little chance of any presidential candidate ever being able to win a majority again. With such a profusion of candidates, the majority would certainly be lost, and the difference between the winner

and losers could be so slim that recounts would be demanded. Recounts on a national scale would almost certainly be indecisive, causing considerable consternation.

Another problem with close elections is that they may encourage cheating. The United States enjoys reasonably honest elections. Some fraud occurs, of course—but think what might happen if a big-city political leader thought she or he could make the difference in the presidential election with a little "creative" voter turnout.

Advantages of the Electoral College   Besides the disadvantages to changing the electoral college, its supporters suggest some other reasons for maintaining it. First, the electoral college has, except for the elections of 1800 and 1824, provided clear winners. While the popular vote has been close many times (1916, 1948, 1960, 1968, and 1978 in this century), the electoral vote is almost always one-sided. Only in 1916 was the electoral margin very close in this century. (See Table 6.6.)

Additionally, the electoral college encour-

Table 6.6
CLOSE POPULAR VOTES IN THE TWENTIETH CENTURY

	CANDIDATE[a]	PARTY	POPULAR VOTE	ELECTORAL VOTE
1916	**Wilson**	Dem	49.2%	52%
	Hughes	Rep	46.1%	48%
1948	**Truman**	Dem	49.5%	57%
	Dewey	Rep	45.1%	36%
1960	**Kennedy**	Dem	49.7%	56%
	Nixon	Rep	49.5%	41%
1968	**Nixon**	Rep	43.4%	56%
	Humphrey	Dem	42.7%	36%
1976	**Carter**	Dem	50.1%	55%
	Ford	Rep	48.0%	45%

[a] Boldface indicates the winner.

Source: Adapted from data in Stanley and Niemi, *Vital Statistics on American Politics,* 2nd ed.

ages the two-party system since it forces serious candidates to seek the nomination of one of the major parties in order to win its electors. Being reduced to a choice between two major party candidates, the election is most apt to end with a majority of the popular vote going to the winner. Finally, even when no candidate wins the majority of the popular vote, the electoral college usually gives victory to the person who got the most popular votes. Only in the elections of 1876 and 1888 did the electoral vote go to the candidates with the fewest popular votes.

As you can see, there are good reasons for keeping the electoral college, and there are also persuasive reasons for changing it. When considering its modification, however, we should bear in mind that no electoral system is flawless; any we may conjure will come with its own eccentricities.

By the way of a summary, study Figure 6.2. Here we see that in most primaries the voters directly nominate candidates who then run for office in the general elections, and the winner takes office in January. But the presidential primary is indirect; the voters elect delegates (other delegates are appointed or elected in caucuses) who go to convention to nominate the candidates. The parties field electors in the general elections, the winning electors then go to the state capitals to vote for president and vice president, and the winners of that contest take office in January.

Voter Behavior

E. E. Schattschneider wrote, "The outcome of every conflict is determined by the *extent* to which the audience becomes involved in it."[24] This statement perhaps more elegantly expresses the old bromide in political science that "in a democracy, the people usually get the kind of government they deserve." If so, the half of our population that does not vote had better hope that the half that does is benevolent.

Voter turnout in this century wavered until 1960 but is now in steep decline. In 1876, 85

Figure 6.2 The Electoral System at a Glance

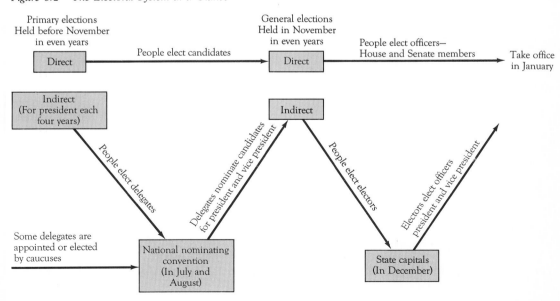

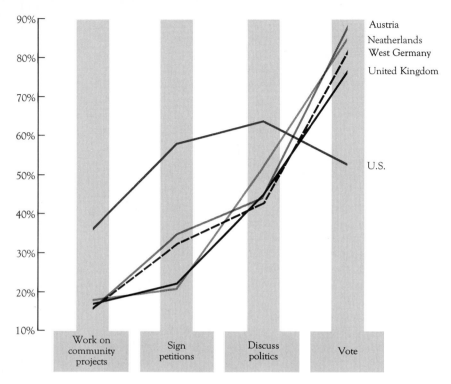

Figure 6.3   Comparative Political Activity

Source: Samuel H. Barnes and May Kaase (eds.), *Political Action,* (Sage, 1979) for
the data on nonvoting activities. David Gless et al., "Voter Turnout: An
International Comparison," in *Public Opinion* (Dec.-Jan. 1984) for voting data.

percent of the eligible voters cast ballots in the
presidential election, and voter turnout remained high to the end of the nineteenth century. It began to decline in the early 1900s,
reaching a low point in 1920, presumably because the newly enfranchised women had not
yet become politicized. After 1920, voter turnout improved, but dipped again in the 1940s,
only to rise anew, reaching a peak in 1960.
Since 1960, however, voter turnout has suffered a relentless decline. In fact, while a relatively high percentage of Americans engage in
other political activities, such as signing petitions, discussing politics, and working on com-

munity projects, a very low percentage of
Americans vote as compared with other democracies. (See Figure 6.3.)

Actually, American voter turnout is even
lower than it first appears. The highest voter
turnout is for presidential elections. It is considerably lower for congressional elections during presidential years, lower still in nonpresidential election years, and even worse for
local elections, which usually draw about 20 to
25 percent of the electorate. (See Figure 6.4.)

About 52 million eligible people (almost
30 percent) are not registered to vote in the
United States. Most democratic countries ac-

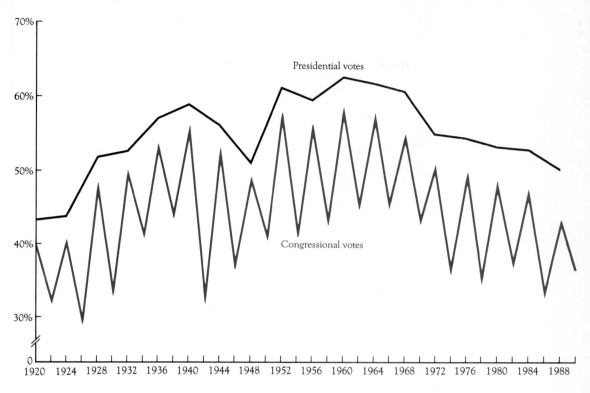

Figure 6.4   _Voter Turnout in Presidential and Congressional Elections, 1920–1990_

Source: U.S. Bureau of the Census, _Statistical Abstracts of the United States,_ for the years 1920–1928; _Vital Statistics on Congress 1987–1988_ for the years 1930–1986; _San Diego Tribune,_ November 9, 1988, for the 1990 figures.

tively encourage registration, and in many countries, people are automatically registered when they come of age.[25] Furthermore, some countries, including Australia and Uruguay, assess fines against people who do not vote. By contrast, American officials make little effort to encourage voting. The media release public service announcements, but the government takes few steps to reverse the dwindling voter turnout.

Some observers suggest that people may not vote because they are satisfied with the way things are going, but studies indicate other, less sanguine, reasons. Besides not being registered,

frequently given reasons for not voting include "too busy," "didn't like the candidates," "not interested in politics," "decided not to vote," and "never have voted." These responses betray a growing apathy among the public, a feeling that elections do not matter, or that "my vote doesn't count."

Another major reason for people's voting less these days seems to be associated with the declining popular attachment to the political parties. Besides discouraging voting, partisan ambivalence also tends to explain the growing trend toward **ticket splitting** (voting in the same election for one party's candidate for one

Advocates of each side of the issue demonstrate outside the Supreme Court building in Washington, D.C., as they await the Court's decison on a case dealing with abortion.

office and another party's candidate for a different office).[26]

In 1900, only 3.4 percent of the House districts were split, with voters choosing one party's candidate for president and another party's candidate for the House of Representatives. Split-ticket voting increased steadily throughout the century, but it never reached above 30 percent of the House districts until 1964. In the 20 years following 1964, a dramatic upturn in split-ticket voting took place, until 45 percent of the House districts produced split results in 1984. In 1988, however, split-ticket voting declined to only 34 percent.[27] (See Figure 6.5.) It is also important to note that partisan loyalty is greater among Republicans

than among Democrats. In every presidential election since 1952, with the exception of 1964 when Barry Goldwater was the Republican candidate for President, far greater percentages of Democrats voted for the opposition than did Republicans. In the aggregate, between 1952 and 1988 an average of 8.6 percent of Republicans voted for Democratic candidates for president, but 26.6 percent of the Democrats voted for Republican presidential candidates.[28]

Although party is still the greatest single determining factor in voting, as it becomes less important people use other criteria for deciding how to vote. Being better educated than before and having greater access to media information, voters rely less on the parties for advice

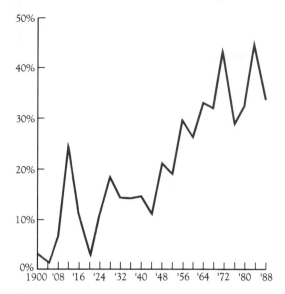

Figure 6.5   Split-Ticket Voting in This Century

Source: Adapted from *Vital Statistics on Congress 1989–1990*, p. 62.

ning for election. Clearly, by virtue of simple exposure, incumbents are most apt to be best known and thus benefit, at least usually, from the trend toward using personal characteristics as criteria for voting.

Who Votes? A large number of factors contribute to whether registered voters go to the polls or stay at home on election day. People who identify with a political party are more likely to vote than are nonpartisans. Whites vote more than do the minorities. Business and professional people vote more regularly than laborers and the unemployed. Property-owners vote more than renters. The most influential determiner, however, is education. Usually, the higher one's education, the greater the sense one has of political efficacy; that is, highly educated people are more apt to follow the news, to see political issues as relevant to their lives, and to believe that they can make an impact on government and on public policy. Accordingly, the higher people's educational achievements, the more likely they are to vote. Age also correlates closely: Younger people tend to vote far less than do their seniors. Interestingly, until the 1970s women usually voted in lower percentages than men, but recently women have turned out in greater numbers. A greater percentage of Jews and Catholics vote than Protestants, and Northerners turn out in greater percentages than Southerners, although the gap between sections of the country is narrowing. (See Table 6.7.)

A profile of a frequent voter might be a white, middle-aged professional who has a college education and owns property. The kinds of people who vote most frequently are also those who tend to identify with the Republican party. Yet their numbers are small by comparison with the rest of the electorate, so their impact is modified accordingly. (See Table 6.8.)

Besides the growing voter strength of the

and cues in deciding how to vote. Issues provide one criterion that has become important in the electorate's mind. In fact, **single-issue voting** has become quite prominent. Increasingly, people are voting for candidates solely based on their posture regarding a single issue such as abortion, defense, the ERA, gay rights, law and order, the environment, taxes, patriotism, and so on. While it is encouraging to see issue consideration becoming more important in determining votes, single-issue voting is problematical because it tends to ignore the complexity of politics.

Personality is also becoming more significant in voter determination. Consideration of candidates' qualifications and personal characteristics is, of course, important, but one might question how well acquainted voters can become with the personal traits of all people run-

Table 6.7
WHO VOTES?

	1972	1976	1980	1984	AVERAGE
Education					
8 years or less	47.4%	44.1%	42.6%	42.9%	44.3%
9–12 years	52.0%	47.2%	45.6%	44.4%	47.3%
More than 12 years	65.4%	59.4%	58.9%	58.7%	60.6%
Age					
18–20	48.3%	38.0%	35.7%	36.7%	39.7%
21–24	50.7%	45.6%	43.1%	43.5%	45.7%
25–34	59.7%	55.4%	54.6%	54.5%	56.1%
35–44	66.3%	63.3%	64.4%	63.5%	65.1%
45–64	70.8%	68.7%	69.3%	69.8%	69.7%
65 and over	63.5%	62.2%	65.1%	67.7%	64.2%
Race					
White	64.5%	60.9%	60.9%	61.4%	61.9%
African-American	52.1%	48.7%	50.9%	55.9%	51.9%
Gender					
Female	62.0%	58.8%	59.4%	60.8%	60.3%
Male	64.1%	59.6%	59.1%	59.0%	60.6%

Source: Federal Election Commission.

Republican party in the South, which has already been mentioned, two other trends regarding voter turnout should be noted. Until recently, there was no meaningful difference in candidate preference between women and men, but since the 1970s women have voted Democratic much more than men. For example, in 1980 only 47 percent of voting women voted for Reagan, while 54 percent of men did so. In 1984, 54 percent of women supported Reagan, and 62 percent of men voted Republican;[29] the same phenomenon occurred in 1988 when 50 percent of women voted for Bush, but Bush got 57 percent of the male votes.

Second, there is a clear dichotomy between the Republican and Democratic voters along racial lines. African-American voters comprise about a quarter of the total Democratic votes in national elections, while the Democrats have won the majority of the white votes in only one presidential election (1964) since 1944. The racial split is even more pronounced in the South. In 1988, 57 percent of the whites throughout the country voted for Bush, but 74 percent voted for him in the South.[30]

In this chapter we have studied the kinds of elections held in this country, who votes, and whom they vote for. It is now time to turn our attention to the institutions of government staffed by elected officials.

Table 6.8
PARTY IDENTIFICATION AND THE 1988 PRESIDENTIAL VOTE

	PARTISAN AFFILIATION			1988 VOTE	
	DEMOCRAT	INDEPENDENT	REPUBLICAN	DUKAKIS	BUSH
Gender					
Women	45%	26%	29%	49%	50%
Men	40%	30%	30%	41%	57%
Race					
White	38%	30%	32%	40%	59%
African-American	75%	17%	8%	86%	12%
Hispanic	51%	26%	23%	69%	30%
Age					
18–29	38%	30%	32%	47%	52%
30–49	43%	31%	26%	45%	54%
50 and over	45%	24%	31%	43%	53%
Education					
Non-H. S. graduates	54%	25%	21%	56%	43%
H. S. graduates	44%	28%	28%	49%	50%
Some college	39%	28%	33%	42%	57%
Bachelor's degree	34%	30%	36%	37%	62%
Graduate degree	34%	41%	25%	48%	50%
Income					
Below $25,000	43%	26%	31%	56%	43%
$25,000–$35,000	39%	35%	26%	44%	56%
Over $35,000	33%	23%	44%	37%	61%
Occupation					
Blue-collar	46%	29%	25%	50%	49%
White-collar	42%	31%	27%	42%	57%
Managerial & professional	37%	28%	35%	40%	59%
Religion					
Protestant	38%	30%	32%	33%	66%
Catholic	36%	39%	25%	47%	52%
Jewish	73%	17%	10%	64%	35%
Region					
Northeast	45%	25%	30%	49%	50%
Midwest	35%	34%	31%	47%	52%
South	46%	27%	27%	41%	58%
West	44%	26%	30%	46%	52%
Total Votes Received				47%	53%

Source: 1988 Gallup Poll for most of the data on party affiliation and 1988 *New York Times*/CBS News Poll for 1988 vote.

Summary

- Voter registration procedures are often complicated and are thought to discourage voter turnout at elections.

- Most states now use primaries to nominate candidates for high office, but, while democratic, primary elections are expensive and they usually work to the advantage of incumbents.

- Elections have become extremely costly, as candidates are now using large amounts of media ads and professional campaign consultants.

- While members of the House and Senate are elected directly by the people, the president and vice president are elected by the electoral college, after the people have elected the electors.

- Some states also allow voters to decide public policy by voting in initiative and referendum elections.

- Voter turnout is declining, with white, educated, well-to-do people voting most in proportion to their numbers.

Notes

1. Quoted in Paul Taylor, "The Way We Choose Presidents Is Crazy and Getting Crazier," in Robert E. DiClerico and Allan S. Hammock, eds., *Points of View*, 4th ed., (New York: Random House, 1989), p. 123.

2. Eric M. Uslaner, "Choosing Our Presidents: It Hasn't Always Been Crazy," in DiClerico and Hammock, p. 131.

3. William J. Keefe, *Parties, Politics, and Public Policy in America*, 4th ed. (New York: Holt, Rinehart and Winston, 1984), p. 79.

4. Hedrick Smith, *The Power Game* (New York: Random House, 1988), pp. 404–405.

5. Michael Oreskes of the New York Times News Service, "Democrats' Chief May Shorten Convention," *Escondido Times-Advocate*, July 12, 1990.

6. Paul S. Herrnson, *Party Campaigning in the 1980s* (Cambridge: Harvard University Press, 1988), pp. 22–24.

7. Thomas B. Rosenstiel, "Policing Political TV Ads," *The Los Angeles Times*, Oct. 4, 1990.

8. Quoted in John J. Goldman and Eileen Quigby, "High Tech Pushes Pace of Politics," *The Los Angeles Times*, Oct. 6, 1987.

9. Herbert E. Alexander, *Financing Politics*, 3rd ed. (Washington, DC: Congressional Quarterly Press, 1984), p. 7.

10. Sara Fritz, "Keating Contributed as 'Patriot,' Cranston Says," *The Los Angeles Times*, Nov. 30, 1990.

11. Robert W. Stewart and Tracy Wood, "Political Giving: Corporate Contributions Buy Access," *The Los Angeles Times*, Oct. 26, 1986.

12. *Buckley* v. *Valeo*, 424 U.S. 1 (1976).

13. *First National Bank of Boston* v. *Bellotti*, 435 U.S. 765 (1978).

14. *Consolidated Edison* v. *Public Service Commission*, 447 U.S. 530 (1980).

15. James Gerstenzang, "Bush Campaign Reforms Seek Curbs on PACs," *The Los Angeles Times*, June 30, 1989.

16. Paul Houston, "Divided Senate Approves Campaign Finance Cuts," *The Los Angeles Times*, Aug. 2, 1990.

17. Harold W. Stanley and Richard G. Niemi, *Vital Statistics on American Politics* (Washington, DC: Congressional Quarterly, 1990), p. 92.

18. For a more complete discussion of the rate of and reasons for incumbent victories in congressional elections, see Gary C. Jacobson, *The Politics of Congressional Elections*, 2nd ed. (Boston: Little, Brown, 1982), pp. 27–45.

19. Sara Fritz, "Campaign Cash Takes a Detour," *The Los Angeles Times*, Oct. 28, 1990.

20. Neal R. Peirce, *The People's President* (New York: Simon and Schuster, 1968), p. 76.

21. The particulars of the electoral college procedure are set down in Article 2, Section 1, of the Constitution; in the Twelfth Amendment; and in the laws of the states.

22. William J. Eaton, "Bush Follows Ancient Ritual, Declares Himself Victor," *The Los Angeles Times*, Jan. 5, 1989.

23. Given in testimony to Congress on January 27, 1977.

24. Elmer E. Schattschneider, *The Semisovereign People* (Hinsdale, IL: Dryden Press, 1975), p. 2.

25. For an excellent analysis of voter registration, see Richard A. Cloward and Frances Fox Piven, *Why Americans Don't Vote* (New York: Pantheon, 1988).

26. Martin Wattenberg, *The Decline of American Political Parties, 1952–1984* (Cambridge: Harvard University Press, 1986), pp. 17–23.

27. Norman J. Ornstein et al., *Vital Statistics on Congress 1989–1990* (Washington, DC: Congressional Quarterly, 1990), p. 62.

28. Percentages for 1954–1984 were calculated from data in Stanley and Niemi, p. 108. Data from 1988 is from an election day *New York Times*/ CBS News Poll.

29. Stanley Neisler, "Election Expected to Reflect Persistence of Gender Gap," *The Los Angeles Times*, Oct. 29, 1988.

30. Everett Carl Ladd, "The Elections: Continuation of the Post-New Deal System," *Political Science Quarterly* 104 (Spring 1989), p. 15.

Suggestions for Further Reading

Abramson, Paul R., John H. Aldrich, and David W. Rohde. *Change and Continuity in the 1988 Elections.* Washington, DC: Congressional Quarterly Press, 1990.

Alexander, Herbert E. *Financing Politics: Money, Elections, and Political Reform.* Washington, DC: Congressional Quarterly Press, 1983.

Asher, Herbert B. *Presidential Elections and American Politics* (4th ed.). Pacific Grove, CA: Brooks/Cole, 1988.

Brunham, Walter Dean. *Critical Elections and the Mainsprings of American Politics.* New York: Norton, 1980.

———. *The Current Crisis in American Politics.* New York: Oxford University Press, 1982.

Cloward, Richard A., and Frances Fox Piven. *Why Americans Don't Vote.* New York: Pantheon, 1988.

DiClerico, Robert E., and Allan S. Hammock, eds. *Points of View.* New York: Random House, 1989.

DiClerico, Robert E., and Eric M. Uslaner. *Few Are Chosen: Problems in Presidential Selection.* New York: McGraw-Hill, 1984.

Fiorina, Morris P. *Retrospective Voting in American National Elections.* New Haven: Yale University Press, 1981.

Flanigan, William H., and Nancy H. Zingale. *Political Behavior of the American Electorate.* Boston: Allyn & Bacon, 1983.

Herrnson, Paul S. *Party Campaigning in the 1980s.* Cambridge: Harvard University Press, 1988.

Jacobson, Gary C. *The Politics of Congressional Elections* (2nd ed.). Boston: Little, Brown, 1987.

———. *Money in Congressional Elections.* New Haven: Yale University Press, 1980.

Keefe, William J. *Parties, Politics, and Public Policy in America* (4th ed.). New York: Holt, Rinehart and Winston, 1984.

Ogden, Daniel M., Jr., and Arthur L. Peterson. *Electing the President* (rev. ed.). San Francisco: Chandler, 1968.

Peirce, Neal R. *The People's President.* New York: Simon and Schuster, 1968.

Sabato, Larry J. *The Rise of Political Consultants: New Ways of Winning Elections.* New York: Basic Books, 1981.

———. *Campaigns and Elections.* Glenview, IL: Scott, Foresman, 1989.

Schattschneider, Elmer E. *The Semisovereign People.* Hinsdale, IL: Dryden Press, 1975.

Sorauf, Frank. *Money in American Elections.* Boston: Little, Brown, 1988.

Teixeira, Ruy A. *Why Americans Don't Vote.* Westport, CT: Greenwood Press, 1987.

Verba, Sidney, and Gary R. Orren. *Equality in America: The View from the Top.* Cambridge: Harvard University Press, 1985.

Wallenberg, Martin. *The Decline of American Political Parties, 1952–1984.* Cambridge: Harvard University Press, 1986.

Watson, Richard A. *The Presidential Contest* (2nd ed.). New York: John Wiley, 1984.

Wayne, Stephen J. *The Road to the White House* (2nd ed.). New York: St. Martin's Press, 1984.

White, Theodore H. *The Making of the President.* New York: Atheneum, 1969.

Wolfinger, Raymond, and Steven J. Rosenstone. *Who Votes?* New Haven: Yale University Press, 1980.

Chapter 7

THE LEGISLATURE

PREVIEW

Congress is a dynamic institution that has changed significantly during its 200-year history. Although it has evolved from the most prominent branch to one that now often rests in the shadow of the president, Congress still performs vital tasks. Revitalizing itself in the 1970s, it has adopted reforms that diffuse power, thus giving more of its members influence over legislation but at the same time making party unity and leadership more difficult.

Members to the Senate are chosen in statewide elections, but members to the House are elected from gerrymandered congressional districts. Although gains have been made by minorities and women, Congress still is largely composed of middle-aged, white, incumbent males who come from middle-class or higher backgrounds. Members of Congress perform a multitude of roles. They are legislators, representatives, and ombudspersons trying to solve constituents' problems with the government. To accomplish their tasks, they employ staff and organize into caucuses, they elect leaders and form committees. Some committees, such as the standing, sub-, and conference committees, analyze legislation, while the select committees study issues of concern.

Without question, the most significant changes to occur in Congress recently are the decline in importance of seniority and the rise in influence of the subcommittees. These twin reforms have made the Congress a more vital body, spreading power out among greater numbers of members but making the leaders' roles more difficult. While the Senate has not changed as much as the House, even it has modified considerably. Another important change is the assertion of caucus authority, especially the House Democratic caucus, over committee action. This reform extends even to the powerful Rules Committee, which has been modified until now the once-independent group operates as an arm of the Speaker.

Passing a bill into law is a complicated and even delicate political task. To successfully carry a bill, supporters must lay the political groundwork carefully by clearing it with the leadership, the committee chairs, and other influential people. Sponsors must mobilize support outside of Congress as well, appealing to the executive branch, special interest groups, and their constituents. They must often spend valuable political capital rolling the log, extracting commitments from colleagues, and persuading committee chairs in order to get their bills passed. Even so, only a small percentage of all bills introduced ever become law. Bill opponents hold a distinct advantage because a bill may be killed at any of a number of stages along the way; yet if it is to pass, a bill must successfully negotiate every one of the potential booby traps. Specifically, a bill must pass through one or more standing committees and usually one or more subcommittees in each house. It must receive favorable treatment by the House Rules Committee and the Conference Committee, and of course it must pass the floor of each house. Even then, however, it can be vetoed by the president, and Congress is rarely able to override executive negation. Thus the legislative process is time-consuming, frustrating, and often disappointing: Successful legislation requires knowledge, imagination, compromise, patience, persuasion, and power.

> _All legislation . . . is founded upon the principle of mutual concession. . . . Let him who elevates himself above humanity, above its weaknesses, its infirmities, its wants, its necessities, say, if he pleases, "I never will compromise"; but let no one who is not above the frailties of our common nature disdain compromise._
>
> Henry Clay

Established by Article I of the Constitution, Congress is sometimes referred to as "the first branch." Its preeminence in the minds of the founders is indisputable. Not only did they give Congress first mention in the Constitution, but they also took pains to delineate controls on the powers of the legislative branch, imposing limitations to restrain the body they expected to be the dominant force in the government they were establishing.

True to the founders' expectations, except for the occasional terms of strong presidents, Congress remained the most powerful branch of government until the 1930s. Since the New Deal of Franklin Delano Roosevelt (1933–1945), however, the presidency has emerged as a powerful competitor for preeminence. The political attitudes in the country and the mettle of political leaders generally determine the precise relationship between the executive and legislative branches of government. Even when Congress is at its most submissive, however, it still exercises more independence from the executive branch than does any other national legislature in the world.

During the past two decades, the Congress has changed in a number of important respects. It has asserted its authority in foreign policy and budgetary matters; it has increased the power of the Speaker of the House even as it has reduced the authority of its senior members; it has revitalized its caucuses, enfranchised its

subcommittees, expanded its staff, disseminated its legislative powers among a large number of junior members; and it has attempted to address the delicate ethical issues brought to light by the illegal practices of some of its members. No longer the captive of aging and autocratic committee chairmen, the Congress is a more representative, more open, and more professional forum than it was a generation ago. It remains a dynamic organization and a vital force in the development of public policy in the United States.

Election and Membership

We studied escalating campaign costs in the last chapter, so a detailed discussion of that topic is not necessary here. Suffice it to say that in 1974 only 10 candidates for the House spent more than $200,000 on their campaigns, but in 1986, 370 did so, and 105 spent over $500,000. The average expenditure of House winning candidates in 1974 was $87,356, but in 1986 it was $358,992, a 310 percent increase in 12 years; in the Senate the average expenditure of the winners in 1974 was $510,026, while in 1990 it was close to $4 million.

The upward trend continued until in the 1990 election candidates raised a total of almost $500 million. Clearly the necessity for raising such huge sums takes valuable time and considerable energy, to say nothing about the ethical questions raised by the fact that public officials are obliged to PACs, corporations, and wealthy individuals for the lion's share of their campaign treasuries. As an illustration, in 1987, Senator Lloyd Bentsen (D-TX), the 1988 Democratic candidate for vice president, announced that he would have breakfast with any individual or group contributing $10,000 to his upcoming senatorial campaign. The resulting public outcry was so intense that Bentson quickly canceled his ham-and-eggs offer. But Senator Rudy Boschwitz (R-MN) continued to issue blue stamps to contributors of $1,000 or more until he was defeated in 1990. (He was the only incumbent senator to be unseated in that election.) Boschwitz's donors placed the stamps on their letters to him to assure his personal attention to their communications.

Assuming that on average a member of the House will spend about $400,000 in the next election, he or she must raise $3,846 each week of the present term, and the average member of the Senate who spends $4 million in the next election must raise $12,820 each week for his or her term. Decrying this state of affairs, former high-ranking Congressman Richard Bolling (D-MO) said,

> If we don't get something done about campaign finance, it could ruin us. It corrupts the system, if not the individuals, because somebody who is influenced by money can very easily pervert the system without appearing to have done anything.[1]

The amount of money given the candidates by the parties remains low, and although individual contributions are the largest source of revenue, PAC contributions are rapidly growing as a percentage of the total. In 1974, PACs contributed about 15 percent of the $75 million spent in congressional campaigns. But in 1988 the PACs paid for 32 percent of the $448 million spent in the general elections. Thus, while campaign costs increased almost sixfold between 1974 and 1988, the PACs more than doubled their share of the bill.[2] For the ten PACs that contributed most to the 1988 congressional campaign, see Table 7.1.

As mentioned in a previous chapter, PACs give the major portion of their contributions to incumbents; thus, seated lawmakers' access to PAC money helps assure their reelections. In fact, the number of safe seats in Congress is increasing. In 1956 only 59 percent of the House seats were won with a majority of 60 percent or more of the popular vote, but by 1988 the figure had risen to 88.5 percent of the seats.[3] The increase in the number of safe House seats, however, is due not only to the incumbents' greater access to campaign funds. Another important contributing factor is the method by which the congressional district lines are drawn.

APPORTIONMENT

Each state is entitled to two senators, and each senator is chosen in a statewide election. On the other hand, states are represented in the House in proportion to their populations, and are divided into congressional districts from which the representatives are elected. Each voter therefore may elect two senators and one representative.

Congressional district lines are drawn according to a complex process involving both federal and state authority. The Constitution requires that a census be taken each decade in the zero year (1980, 1990, 2000, 2010, etc.). Then Congress calculates the number of seats each state is entitled to, and it notifies the legislature of each state accordingly.

The first House of Representatives in 1789 consisted of 65 members, and the 13 states each

Table 7.1
TOP TEN PAC CONTRIBUTORS TO THE
1988 CONGRESSIONAL ELECTIONS

PAC	AMOUNT
National Association of Realtors	$3,040,969
International Brotherhood of Teamsters	$2,856,724
American Medical Association	$2,316,496
National Education Association	$2,104,689
National Association of Retired Federal Employees	$1,979,850
United Auto Workers of America	$1,953,099
Association of Trial Lawyers of America	$1,913,558
National Association of Letter Carriers	$1,737,982
American Federation of State, County & Municipal Employees	$1,663,386
International Association of Machinists	$1,490,780
Total	$21,057,533
Average	$2,105,753

Source: Federal Election Commission.

had two senators. Since that time, the number of senators has increased to 100, as the number of states in the Union has grown to 50. The House membership also grew with the population until 1913, when it reached 435 members. Since 1913 the House has remained at 435 members, which means that the number of people represented by each member has increased as the national population has grown. In 1959 the size of the House was temporarily increased to 437 to accommodate the admission of Hawaii and Alaska as states, but in 1962 the number was returned to 435, and these seats were apportioned among the 50 states. The House also hosts five nonvoting delegates: one each from American Samoa, the District of Columbia, Guam, Puerto Rico, and the Virgin Islands.

Dividing their states into the appropriate number of congressional districts, the state legislatures engage in a process known as **apportionment**. The districts must be equal in population and, being **single-member districts**

(see Chapter 5), each may elect only one House member.

When the state legislatures draw the congressional district lines, they also create the district lines from which they themselves are elected, and this process, done by partisan politicians, is usually a highly charged political affair referred to as **gerrymandering** (biased apportionment). Simply put, there are two main objectives in gerrymandering: to protect the incumbents and to give the advantage to the party that enjoys the majority in the state legislature. Accordingly, the district lines often take on odd shapes as the lines are drawn to isolate voters of the opposition party in the fewest possible electoral districts. Thus, the majority party tries to give itself and its incumbents the advantage in forthcoming elections.[4] For this reason gerrymandering is said to be done "of, by, and for the incumbent."

Regardless of the odd shapes that emerge when district lines are drawn, elections are held on a regular basis. House members serve two-year terms and thus must stand for reelection at each general election. Senators serve staggered six-year terms, with one-third of the Senate seats being subject to election every two years.

THE MEMBERS

The women and men who are elected to Congress have varied backgrounds, but some standard patterns emerge. Not surprisingly, incumbents have a great advantage. Because they enjoy name recognition, have a greater ability to raise funds, may take advantage of franking privileges (free postage for congressional business) and large travel budgets, have large staffs to help them, possess an intimate knowledge of the issues and of congressional procedure, and benefit from the stature of being an officeholder, the "ins" have a huge advantage in elections. Since 1954, no House election has seen more than 13 percent of the seats change party hands, while in the Senate as many as one-third of the seats up for election have changed parties.[5]

Just as these results are not unlike those of previous elections, the partisan split is also typical of recent elections. In the 100th Congress (1987–1988), House Democrats held a commanding lead over the Republicans (258 D to 177 R); and in the Senate, the Democrats recaptured their long-held lead (55 D to 45 R). In 1988, the Democrats gained three seats in the House and one in the Senate, and in 1990 the Democrats picked up one more seat in the Senate and eight seats in the House. Since 1933 the Democrats have held a majority in the House in every year except 1947–1948 and 1953–1954, and in the Senate except for 1947–1948, 1953–1954, and 1981–1986. As you can see, since 1933 the Republicans have enjoyed majorities in both houses during only two Congresses (1947–1948 and 1953–1954). (See Figure 7.1.)

Although Congress remains characteristically middle-aged, the average age has fluctuated recently. In 1977 the average was 53 years, by 1983 it had dropped to 47 years, and in 1987 it had climbed to 51.6 years. Presumably, in 1992 the average age will drop again because about 100 members of Congress are expected to retire in that year in order to take advantage of the last chance to convert surplus campaign funds to private use upon leaving Congress. These seniored members will probably be replaced by younger people.

The socioeconomic and gender composition of Congress also conforms to some interesting trends. Easily the most underrepresented group in Congress is women. In 1990 only 25 women served in the House and 2 in the Senate. Thus, women—who constitute more than half the total population—made up only 4.7 percent of the Congress. Although William Gray, the House majority whip until 1991 is black, African-Americans are also underrepresented in that they compose only 4.3 percent of the Congress while constituting about 12 percent of the population. Similarly, Hispanics hold only 2.2 percent of the seats in Congress while composing about 6.4 percent of the population. Of all the major minority groups in the country, only Asian-Americans enjoy greater representation in Congress (2.2 percent) than their share of the population (1.4 percent).

Occupation groups are also disproportionately represented, with lawyers being the greatest in number by far: 63 in the Senate and 184 in the House. After the legal profession, business persons and bankers rank second, with 28 in the Senate and 138 in the House. Other listed occupations—educators, farmers, journalists, public servants, and professional athletes (4 in the House and 1 in the Senate)—are represented at a rate far below lawyers and business persons. In 1990, not a single member of Congress listed a blue-collar field as a former occupation.[6]

From these data we can develop a profile of the typical congressperson: a middle-aged,

Figure 7.1   Party Representation in Congress, 1932–1988

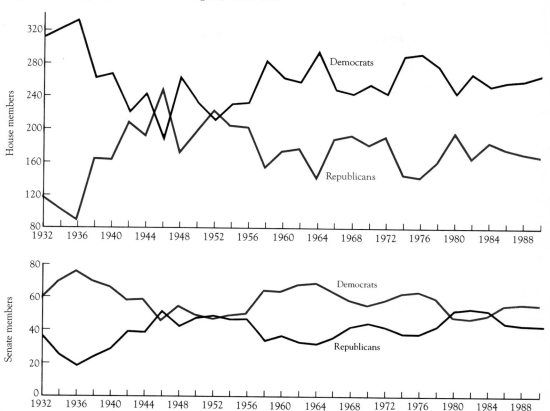

Source: Adapted from data in *Vital Statistics on Congress 1989–1990*, pp. 38–39, for 1932–1988; *The Los Angeles Times*, Nov. 8, 1990, for 1990 figures.

white male, professional. Hence, as a group, congress is whiter, more male, better educated, and better off economically than the population as a whole. Examining this information, females, ethnic minorities, blue-collar workers, and the poor may have some cause to worry about the representation their interests might receive on Capitol Hill.

Functions

Congress as a whole is responsible for a wide variety of functions, as are the individual members. While the two houses share most duties, a few functions are unique to each. The Con-

stitution stipulates that the House originate all bills raising revenue, and appropriations (spending) bills are also traditionally begun in the House. These bills must also be passed in the Senate, but the originating body has some advantage in the process. Additionally, the House is given the responsibility of bringing impeachment charges before the bar of the Senate and prosecuting the case. The Senate ratifies treaties by a two-thirds' majority vote, and it confirms presidential appointments by a simple majority. Further, the Senate tries impeachment cases, needing a two-thirds' majority vote for conviction. (Impeachment will be dealt with in detail in Chapter 10.)

By far the largest number of functions, however, are jointly performed by both chambers. Because Congress is the national legislature, public policy is adopted on Capitol Hill. Congress funds the government by taxing and appropriating expenditures, and it coins money. It alone may declare war, and it provides for the military services. It is heavily involved in foreign affairs through its legislative, consultative, and ratification roles. Further, it regulates international and interstate trade, and it establishes the federal court structure—the third branch—as well as confirming bench appointments. Congress plays a role in informing the public on matters of civic interest, and it exercises oversight of the bureaucracy as it checks and balances the powers of the judicial and executive branches.

Although the role of congresspersons is multifaceted, involving them in a vast array of duties, the bulk of their responsibilities can be reduced to three major areas: legislation, casework, and representation. The legislative role of congresspersons is complicated and time-consuming. Not only must they participate in activities on the floor, but they spend far more time serving on committees, attending party caucuses, doing research, reading reports, and discussing issues with a number of people—colleagues, constituents, staff members, bureaucrats, and lobbyists. Congresspersons must not only become expert in the subjects with which their committees deal, but they must also cast some 1000 votes per term on a bewildering variety of issues ranging from tax bills to price supports for sorghum, from public housing to the B-2 bomber, from banking practices to warning labels on cigarette packages.

Quite apart from their legislative duties, congresspersons are deluged with casework for their constituents. Members are bombarded by thousands of requests for services that may bear little on their legislative tasks. "Write your congressperson" is the often-heard advice to people who have problems with the federal government—and write they do.

Congressman Hamilton Fish, Jr. (R-NY) meets in his office with constituents.

Congressional intercession is requested by people seeking federal employment, citizens having problems with Medicare red tape, constituents who are at odds with the military, voters wishing to meet their legislator in Washington, students seeking appointments to the military academies, local officials needing assistance with the federal bureaucracy, educators wanting federal aid for schools, and even campaign supporters desiring tickets to the Kennedy Center during visits to the capital. Indeed, the casework load is increasing rapidly as constituents become more demanding of their representatives and as congresspersons are required to represent larger numbers of people. Between 1978 and 1987 alone, mail to congresspersons increased by 43 percent, leaping from 77.5 million to 111.1 million letters per year.[7] It is true, of course, that much of the casework can be handled by staff, but woe be it to the elected official who too often ignores the folk back home. As former Speaker Tip O'Neill cautioned, "All politics is local."[8]

The third major function of the members of Congress, representation, is closely related to legislation and casework. The question of representation confronts any publicly elected official, from congresspersons to school board members, with a very complicated question: Should the official represent the *will* of the constituents or their *interests*? The happiest circumstance obtains when the two interests are synonymous. But oftentimes the wishes of the voters are not compatible with what the congressperson judges to be in their best interest. In such cases, the representatives are faced with a delicate dilemma. The **tribunes** see their role as simple conduits for the decisions of their constituents. They can be applauded for remaining true to the views of the voter—but is it responsible to support an issue that appears deleterious of the people's interests even when they are not persuaded of the adverse effects? **Trustees**, on the other hand, believe that they

are elected to exercise their personal judgment on the issues. These representatives often cite James Madison's famous statement that calls upon those elected to Congress to use their own judgment on the issues because "under such a regulation it may well happen that the public voice, pronounced by the representatives of the people, will be more consonant to the public good than if pronounced by the people themselves."[9] But although the trustees might be content that they did the right thing regardless of public opinion, who among us can be so confident of his or her own superior judgment? A third group takes a middle position, trying to balance the two positions and attempting to develop consensus among constituents before taking action. These **politicos** can be complemented for efforts to bring compromise, but such behavior can also be used as a guise for inactivity or opportunism.

Philosophy of representation presents another quandary to members of Congress. Should the members vote to satisfy the interests of the districts they are elected to represent, or are they elected to vote for policy that is most compatible with the national interests, even though such a posture might contradict the best interests of the local constituency? Once again, the situation is most pleasant when the two interests are compatible. When they are at odds, however, the legislator has a problem. Edmund Burke, the great British parliamentarian of the late eighteenth century, once lectured his constituents on the subject, taking the nationalist view: "You choose a member, indeed, but when you have chosen him, he is not a member of Bristol, but he is a member of Parliament." The other point of view is also persuasive, however. Members of a national legislature could be found remiss if they sacrificed the interests of their electorate to other considerations, even if the legislators thought that the good of the whole was best served elsewhere. Otherwise, don't the representatives who knowingly vote against their constituents' interest thereby deny those people representation?

These perplexing questions are but examples of the many dilemmas encountered by conscientious politicians. There are no easy answers; each member must confront the issues and make decisions based on his or her conscience. Much more clear, yet perhaps equally perplexing, are the questions of life-style and ethics in Congress.

LIFE-STYLE AND ETHICS IN CONGRESS

Members of Congress live at a frantic pace. Compelled by increased casework and the persistent need to raise campaign funds, congresspersons spend Fridays and Mondays traveling, weekends politicking in their districts, and Tuesdays through Thursdays in session. In the districts they are seemingly always on the go—meeting with constituents, touring facilities, making speeches, visiting schools, and talking to campaign donors. In Washington, an average day sees them rising early to read the newspapers; attending two or three committee hearings and a floor session each day; meeting with constituents, lobbyists, colleagues, and the press; and telephoning campaign contributors. In the evening they often attend a fund-raiser or social event—where politics is often informally done; and finally they return home to finish the night reading legislation, committee reports, constituent mail, and other material for the next day.

As far as the workload in Congress itself is concerned, between 1950 and 1980 the number of standing committees and subcommittee meetings doubled. The number of bills passed, however, declined by about 36 percent, but the total number of pages of legislation jumped by 222 percent.[10] In other words, Congress is passing larger and larger bills. It is true

that some of these "megabills" are **pork barrel** legislation, which includes government spending in enough districts and states to be assured of passage. Members of Congress are anxious to return to their demanding constituents with proof that they are able to see to the districts' interests. It is also true that one person's "pork" is another person's necessity, and that these spending projects fund roads, bridges, schools, dams, and other projects desired by the locals. Also, with the Republicans in control of the White House, the Democratic majority in Congress tends to pass bills that each include many items so as to make it harder for the president to veto those policies he opposes. In any event, the legislative workload has grown since the 1950s and has become quite heavy by comparison.

Another factor to consider concerning the workload of Congress is intangible but important. Public policy is becoming increasingly complex even as the people are growing more assertive about their needs and perhaps unrealistic in their expectations. Norman Ornstein, a political scientist at the American Enterprise Institute who specializes in Congress, put it this way:

> One of the things that is happening here is that you have a public that is filled with contradictions itself. They want less government, but they want more government. They want the deficit to be cut through spending cuts rather than high taxes. But they also want increases in spending in the vast majority of programs.
>
> To whatever degree Congress doesn't get things done, it's because it is trying to cope with conflicting sentiments on the part of the public.[11]

Congressional Ethics   In exchange for their taxing and difficult job, members are afforded several amenities. Besides the power associated with their positions, they enjoy cut-rate dining, shoeshines, and haircuts; they have swimming pools, gymnasiums, and saunas on Capitol Hill. Their staffs are large, and they have adequate office and travel budgets. The question of salary, however, has become a significant problem. In 1988, congressional salaries stood at $89,500, about the same salary as middle-ranking business executives received and far below that of many other public employees such as school superintendents and college presidents. Between 1969 and 1989, congressional salaries failed to keep pace with inflation, with Congress members' purchasing power declining by 65 percent.

To augment their salaries, members resorted increasingly to the questionable practice of accepting honorariums for speaking engagements. Members could accept up to $2,000 for each appearance, to an annual maximum of $35,800 for senators and $26,850 for representatives. These engagements are usually all-expense-paid as well, and they often take members and their families to exotic resorts in the United States and even abroad. Indeed, sometimes members are paid an honorarium just for visiting a plant or for briefly attending a meeting. These practices have been referred to as "legal corruption" by Fred Wertheimer, president of Common Cause, and they raise the eyebrows of many congressional observers.[12]

In 1989, Congress proposed to make accepting honorariums illegal, in exchange for a 50 percent raise in salary, but the public outcry was devastating, and the bill failed. Trying again later in 1989, the House raised its salary by nearly 40 percent, but the law also prohibited House members from accepting honorariums to augment their salaries. The Senate balked at this huge increase, passing only a 9.7 percent salary increase. However, rather than prohibiting its members from accepting honorariums, it reduced the total amount they could accept in a year. In 1991, however, the Senate increased its salaries to equal those of the

House and it prohibited members from accepting honorariums. Annual congressional salaries are now $124,333.

Quite beyond their salaries, benefits, prerequisites, and expense-paid trips, members of Congress also benefit from campaign contributions. Although the law prohibits them from spending campaign funds for personal use, personal expenses and campaign spending are often divided by a thin line. Accordingly, members of Congress have used campaign money to purchase automobiles, clothing, portraits, Broadway show tickets, and numerous other items that might be seen as personal goods. One candidate for office even used campaign funds to pay for a member of the clergy to bless his campaign headquarters. Additionally, those members of Congress who were elected before 1980 may, until 1992, keep for personal use any excess campaign funds in their treasuries if they leave office before 1993.[13]

Although it is generally agreed that the ethical standards of Congress are higher than they have been in many previous eras, a few members have been found guilty of sexual indiscretion, financial improprieties, theft, bribery, and embezzlement. In 1989 the focus of public attention came to bear on congressional ethics as House Majority Leader Tony Coelho (D-CA) and Speaker Jim Wright (D-TX) were forced to resign from Congress when details of their private financial dealings were made public.[14] The Senate has also had its problems, as an unusually large number of its members came under scrutiny of the Senate Ethics Committee for financial irregularities and influence peddling. The "Keating Five"—Dennis De Concini (D-AZ), Alan Cranston (D-CA), John Glenn (D-OH), John McCain (R-AZ), and Donald W. Riegle (D-MI)—were called before the committee in 1991 in relation to the part they played in the savings and loan scandal. Never before have so many senators been brought before review of their peers at one

Speaker of the House Jim Wright (D-TX) became the first Speaker to be driven from office by public scandal.

time. While four senators were cleared of ethics violations, Cranston's case was forwarded to the full Senate, and disciplinary action is pending. Cranston, who is accused of having attempted to obstruct an investigation of a savings and loan failure after receiving almost $1 million in campaign contributions from the S&L owner, is only the second senator to be accused of wrongdoing by the Ethics Committee for behavior that did not involve personal gain.

Congressional Discipline Each house has a committee responsible for investigating charges of misconduct of its members. Upon the committee's recommendation the appropriate chamber can vote one of three kinds of punishment. **Reprimand**, the least severe, is a public resolution chastising a member for misconduct. Although no further disciplinary action accom-

panies the admonition, it is hoped that the chastised member will not run again or will be defeated by the voters. Barney Frank (D-MA) was reprimanded by the House in 1990 for misusing his authority for the benefit of a homosexual partner, but he was reelected. **Censure** is more serious. In this procedure a member can suffer the loss of seniority, be removed from committee assignments, or be otherwise disciplined. In 1990, Dave Durenberger (R-MI) was censured by the Senate for financial improprieties. Finally, **expulsion** can be voted by two-thirds of the appropriate house, unseating the member.

Traditionally, Congress has been reluctant to discipline its members, preferring instead to let the voters do so. The reasons given for such hesitance vary, but usually the members protest that they should not presume to contradict the electorate.[15] It is true that a constitutional question could be raised if Congress weakened or expelled a duly elected member, but there are other, more political, difficulties as well. Politicians usually try to avoid the rancor and negative publicity associated with such extraordinary procedures. Moreover, the members are not unmindful that they may suffer at the hands of a colleague whom they unsuccessfully try to discipline. Also, one wonders whether some members shun scrutinizing their colleagues for fear that they might be next in line for investigation. For example, when, after relentlessly pressing for the House Ethics Committee to discipline Speaker Wright, House Minority Leader Newt Gingrich found himself being investigated for alleged financial improprieties, a Republican House Ethics Committee member pointedly, but anonymously, told a *Los Angeles Times* reporter, "I am a firm believer that what's good for the goose is good for the gander. And he [Gingrich] is the gander."[16] Gingrich was later cleared of any wrongdoing.

It should be emphasized that although a few members are rightfully accused of misdeeds, the vast majority of congresspersons are honest, hard-working public servants. The work they do is central to our form of government, and understanding the structure of the institution in which they perform their tasks is important to comprehending how law is made.

Organization

The original Congress of 1789 had a budget of $374,000 and 6 employees. Today Congress spends over $2 billion; it has 31,000 employees, including those who work for such diverse congressional organizations as the Library of Congress, the Office of Technological Assessment, and the Government Printing Office. Congress has become a complicated body composed of caucuses, the leadership, staff, resource agencies, and committees. Basically, each house is structured much as the other is, but there are some significant differences that we will consider.

THE CAUCUSES

Each house divides itself into *party caucuses.* *
Members elected as independents or as minor party members also join one or the other caucus in their chamber—conservatives tend to ally with the Republicans, and liberals usually associate with the Democrats.

Hence, each house has two caucuses: the majority caucus, which decides most of the

* Currently, only the House Democrats continue to call their party organization a caucus. Senate and House Republicans and Senate Democrats now call their party organizations "conferences." I will, however, use the term *caucus* since that is the traditional term and also as an effort to avoid any possible confusion with the conference committee, which will be introduced later in this chapter.

procedural matters and actually determines how the chamber will function, and the minority caucus, which becomes the "loyal opposition," criticizing the majority and offering alternatives to its policies. By comparison with most other national legislatures, party discipline is weak in Congress, but still, about two-thirds or more of the members will vote their party's position on issues in which partisanship is a factor, and procedural matters are usually decided by strict party votes.

Party-line votes are usually defined as those issues on which a majority of one party voted aye and a majority of the other party voted nay. At the turn of the century, party-line votes were very common, but party discipline has since declined. By the 1950s only about 50 percent of the congressional votes were party-line decisions, and by the early 1980s the figure had fallen below 40 percent. By 1985, however, partisan splits became common again.[17]

The caucuses have varying importance depending on the party and house involved. Clearly, however, the House Democrats have fostered the strongest, most active caucus, and it has been used to modify the powers of the leadership in significant ways. Regardless of the power of any particular caucus, each party group elects its leaders and makes standing committee assignments—two very important functions.

THE LEADERSHIP

The principal leader in the House is the **Speaker of the House**. Each caucus nominates a candidate for Speaker, and invariably the candidate from the majority caucus is elected by the chamber. Since the House is a large body with strict rules, the Speaker wields considerable authority. Basically, the Speaker's powers include presiding over the floor, recognizing speakers, ruling on points of order, and referring bills to standing committees. In addition to appointing all House members to select committees and conference committees, when Democrats control the House, the Speaker also chairs the Democratic Steering and Policy Committee and appoints the chair and all of the Democratic members to the powerful Rules Committee. This authority gives the Speaker effective control over the scheduling of bills' arrival on the floor. These prerogatives, taken together, make the Speaker the most powerful member of the House.[18] (See Table 7.2.)

Each House caucus also elects a **floor leader**. The majority floor leader is second to the Speaker in the party. The majority and minority floor leaders perform similar functions in that they are responsible for developing and executing party policy and managing the party efforts on the floor of the House. They are limited in this task, however, by the fact that party discipline in Congress is not strong. Former majority floor leader Jim Wright articulated the delicate task of the floor leader as follows:

> The majority leader is a conciliator, a moderate, a peacemaker. Even when patching together a tenuous majority he must respect the right of honest dissent, conscious of the limits of his claims upon others.[19]

As the leader of the dominant party, the majority floor leader probably has a more satisfying legislative task than the minority floor leader, but since the Speaker is the principal spokesperson for the majority party, the minority floor leader carries the heavier burden in articulating the party position.

The **whips**, or assistants to the floor leaders, are also elected by the caucuses. These important officials do much of the legwork for the floor leaders. They are responsible for informing the members about the issues and the party's position on each, for getting members to commit to the party's position, for keeping track of the number of votes on each side of an issue, and for assuring that the caucus members attend important floor sessions. The whips are aided by a number of deputies and assistants, who are usually chosen on regional lines within their respective caucuses.

In addition to nominating a candidate for Speaker and electing floor leaders and whips, each caucus creates a committee of senior members and regional representatives called the Steering and Policy Committee to help the Speaker and floor leaders develop policy.

The Senate differs somewhat in its structure, both for constitutional reasons and because its members tend to be slightly more independent of party control than their House colleagues. The Constitution designates the vice president of the United States as the **President of the Senate**. Because of the adversarial relationship between the executive and legislative branches implicit in the separation of powers and the system of checks and balances, the Senate does not give its presiding officer great power. The vice president may vote only in case of a tie, and he or she may not make a speech except when invited to do so. Being a relatively small body, the Senate has few rules, and the tradition for collegiality among its members denies the presiding officer any substantive authority. Hence the vice president usually attends Senate meetings only for ceremonial occasions or for casting a deciding vote. But Vice President Quayle, a former senator, has become noted for his assiduous lobbying efforts among the senators for the president's programs.

The Senate elects a **President Pro Tempore** to preside in the absence of the vice president. But again, because presiding over the Senate is such an insignificant task, the office is honorarily given to the **Dean of the Senate** (the person from the majority party who has

Table 7.2
CONGRESSIONAL LEADERSHIP

| | PRESIDING OFFICER | FLOOR LEADER | | WHIP | |
		MAJORITY	MINORITY	MAJORITY	MINORITY
House	Speaker, Thomas S. Foley (D-WA)	Richard A. Gephardt (D-MO)	Robert H. Michel (R-IL)	William H. Gray* (D-PA)	Newt Gingrich (R-GA)
Senate	President, J. Danforth Quayle (R-vice president) President Pro Tempore, Robert C. Byrd (D-WV)	George J. Mitchell (D-ME)	Robert J. Dole (R-KA)	Wendell H. Ford (D-KY)	Alan K. Simpson (R-WY)

*Gray resigned from Congress in August 1991. At this point a successor has not yet been chosen.

been in the Senate the longest). The Dean of the Senate is usually a powerful person, but not because of this office. Seniority probably assures the Dean a committee chair, and the Pro Tem devotes most of his or her time to that task. Consequently, the actual duty of presiding over the Senate, except for important occasions, is shared by junior members of the majority party.

As in the House, the Senate caucuses elect floor leaders and whips. The most powerful person in the chamber is the majority floor leader, who presides over the caucus steering committee and has the right of first recognition on the floor. The majority floor leader, in consultation with the minority floor leader, schedules bills' arrival on the floor for a vote, and he or she can have an important impact on the fate of legislation.[20] Even so, perhaps history's most powerful Senate majority leader, Lyndon Johnson, remarked about the office's lack of tangible power, "the only real power available to the leader is the power of persuasion. There is no patronage; no power to discipline, no authority to fire Senators like a President can fire members of Cabinet."[21]

Since Johnson's time, however, the leadership's role in each house has been further complicated by the type of people elected to Congress. Escalating campaign costs and the increasing sophistication of campaign technology have seen a new breed of politician enter Congress. These "political entrepreneurs" are young, well educated, articulate, comfortable with the media, savvy about raising campaign funds, and independent of party. Although sanguine in many respects, these characteristics make the members difficult to lead, and developing coherent legislative policy objectives has become an arduous and often impossible task.[22] An eloquent example of this problem occurred in 1990 when, after months of negotiations over the budget, the president

and the congressional leadership of both parties in each house came forward with a compromise. Disgruntled that they were not allowed to be part of the negotiations, and wary about voting for major tax increases just before an election, House members from both parties rebelled, thus killing the legislation.

Some members of Congress recognize that exaggerated individualism is leading to legislative chaos and are beginning to call for a more centrally controlled legislature. For example, consider these remarks by Rep. Charles Schumer, a Democrat from Brooklyn:

> Congress has become atomistic. In the House we are 435 little atoms bouncing off each other, colliding and influencing each other but not in a very coherent way. There used to be much more structure. But now there is no bonding that holds the atoms together. . . . I think the pendulum has swung too far away from strong leadership.[23]

OTHER INFLUENTIAL FACTORS

Besides the caucuses and the leadership, a number of other people and institutions influence the course of legislation. Public opinion is, of course, a major factor on many issues. Most members are very solicitous of their constituency's wishes, and presumably will try to reflect these attitudes through their votes.[24] Often, however, there are other considerations at play besides the public will. Moreover, the wishes of constituents are apparent on only a small number of issues that Congress must decide.

Quite beyond public opinion, several other "cue givers" try to influence the vote. Reports from committees, pressure from lobbyists, colleagues requesting or reclaiming votes (vote swapping is called **logrolling**), the wishes of the president, and the momentum of the bureaucracy are all important influences. Some members have formed voting blocks on certain issues: The Hispanic, the Women's, and the African-American Caucuses are examples. There is a Steel Caucus, a Frost Belt Caucus, a Suburban Caucus, a Ball Bearing Caucus, and even a Mushroom Caucus in Congress. There are also ideological blocks, such as the liberal House Democrats' Democratic Study Group or the Conservative Democratic Forum (Boll Weevils). House Republicans have also mobilized into the moderate Gypsy Moths and the conservative Chowder and Marching Society. Perhaps the most powerful ideological block, however, is the **conservative coalition** composed of Republicans and Southern Democrats. One study finds that this influential group unites on about one-quarter of the major votes;[25] in the 30 years between 1957 and 1988, the House conservative coalition was victorious on 72.0 percent of the issues it joined, and in the Senate it was even more successful, winning on 75.2 percent of the issues on which it mobilized.[26]

Another very influential element, sometimes ignored, is the congressional staff. The Congress has afforded itself a very large and professional staff. Among the nonpartisan staffers are the **Congressional Budget Office (CBO)**, which analyzes proposed fiscal legislation, and the **General Accounting Office (GAO)**, headed by the Comptroller General of the United States, which is the fiscal watchdog for Congress, assuring that appropriated funds are spent according to law. The GAO also studies the efficiency of government agencies and is thus a major instrument in the congressional check of the other two branches. Another influential body, the **Congressional Research Service (CRS)**, which is attached to the Library of Congress, provides valuable information on issues and bills before the legislature. And, each house is served by *legislative counsel*, groups of attorneys who specialize in drafting legislation in such a way as to ensure that it says precisely what it is intended to convey—no more, no less—and that it will successfully stand constitutional challenge in the courts.[27]

A large partisan staff is employed by Congress as well. Each member of the House may employ 22 persons to work either in Washington or in the member's district. A senator's staff is generally larger, ranging between about 20 and 70, depending on the size of the state and its distance from Washington.

The staff of Congress has burgeoned in recent years. This "staff revolution" has become the topic of considerable controversy. First, staff members' growing influence over legislation causes some critics to question who is actually making the laws—the elected representatives or the appointed staff.[28] Indeed, staff members have enormous power. After Norman Dicks, a longtime staff aide to Senator Warren Magnuson, was elected to Congress in 1976, he said, "People asked me how I felt about being elected to Congress, and I told them I never thought I'd give up that much power voluntarily."[29] There can be little question that the staff influences congressional decisions, but that is exactly what it is designed to do. In this respect, Congress is no different from any other large government or private institution.

The sheer size of the congressional staff also causes considerable controversy. Between 1967 and 1977, the committee and personal staffers of Congress rose from about 7,000 to almost 13,000. At the same time, the cost of Congress increased from $300 million to $1 billion a year—a 300 percent jump.[30] By 1987 the congressional staff (not including employees of ancillary agencies) numbered about 18,000,[31] and the total cost of Congress was estimated at about $2.2 billion in 1989.[32]

Such an increase in both staff and expenditure is of course noteworthy, but one should resist the temptation to condemn it out of hand. Indeed, there is much to recommend a large congressional staff. The volume of casework and the growing complexity of the legislative process are considerations. Perhaps the most important factor, however, is that adequate staff furnishes members of Congress with a degree of independence from special interest groups that are only too anxious to "aid" them in their task.[33]

Committees

Not unlike any other large deliberative body, Congress divides itself into a number of committees in order to complete its work. Floor time is usually used for *pro forma* gestures and for formalizing decisions that have already been made informally elsewhere. In fact, the real work of Congress is done in committee.

STANDING COMMITTEES

By far the most important committees in Congress are the standing committees. Currently 16 standing committees in the Senate and 22 in the House receive the bills that are introduced in Congress. The standing committees are assigned subject-matter jurisdiction by the rules of their respective house, and their titles reflect their general area of expertise. Hence, we have the Senate Finance Committee, the House Agriculture Committee, the Senate Budget Committee, the House Judiciary Committee, and so on. The authority of the standing committees includes the power to study legislation, to subpoena witnesses or information, to remand bills to subcommittees, to vote bills dead, to table bills (putting them aside, thus allowing them to die quietly at the end of the congressional

term*), to amend bills, to write bills (amending a bill or writing an entirely new version of a bill is called **marking-up**), or to report the bill to the floor. Standing committees may report a bill to the floor with a negative recommendation, a rare occurrence since there is ample opportunity to dispose of unwanted legislation, or they can report it out (send a bill to the calendar) with a positive recommendation. In either case, the bill is accompanied by a report of the majority and sometimes also a minority report if dissidents wish to explain their views.[34]

Although standing committees are not all equally successful in persuading their colleagues, as a general rule the standing committees exercise an enormous amount of influence over legislation. Because as many as ten thousand bills and resolutions, totaling tens of thousands of pages, can be introduced in Congress each term, no member can be expected to read each of them, let alone become expert on the vast variety of subjects these bills encompass. Consequently, the members rely on one another to specialize in a limited number of areas and to recommend to their colleagues which bills should be passed. Herein lies the source of the committees' influence. Committee members are the experts in their fields, and their recommendations are given weighty consideration. Additionally, an element of logrolling is involved, for if Congressman Jones wishes his committee's recommendations to be taken seriously by Congresswoman Smith, he would be

---

* A congressional term is two years long, beginning in January of the odd-numbered year and ending in December of the following year. Thus Congresses are numbered by each term. The 100th Congress existed from 1987 to 1988, the 101st Congress sat from 1989 to 1990, and so on. If a bill is not passed during the term in which it was introduced, it dies at the end of the term and must be reintroduced in a subsequent term if its authors wish to try again for its passage.

well advised to return the courtesy. Understanding the power of these committees, those who wish to secure the passage of law—bill sponsors, lobbyists, bureaucrats, the president, and so on—must take care to satisfy the committees' problems on the bills before them.[35]

Yet the committee process is often considerably more complex than just satisfying one standing committee. A multifaceted bill may be assigned to more than one standing committee for review. Also, the jurisdiction of the standing committees is not as clear as might be wished. Indeed, several topics, including health, federal pensions, and energy, overlap into the province of several committees;[36] for example, over a dozen House and Senate committees share jurisdiction over President Bush's drug abuse program. The more committees a bill is referred to, the greater its chances of being eliminated since any standing committee can kill or table any bill with which it deals, thus preventing it from reaching the floor.

Indeed, most bills are stopped in committee. A bill rarely negotiates the congressional maze in its first attempt. In fact, rather than just having to pass on the floor of the House and Senate, bills must receive multiple majorities in each house before becoming law. A bill can be killed at any stage in the process, but to pass, it must win each contest confronting it. When a bill does make it through the committees and floor of each house, it has often been changed significantly during its time in the Cuisinart of congressional politics. In fact, while thousands of bills are introduced each term, only a small percentage ever become law. Between 1963 and 1988, the ratio of bills passed to those introduced in the House was only 0.124; in the Senate it was higher at 0.370.[37]

Committee Membership Few internal factors are as important to members' success as the standing committee to which they are assigned. The number of seats per standing committee averages about 35 in the House and somewhat fewer in the Senate. Committee assignments are made by the caucuses, with each caucus being entitled to roughly the same percentage of standing committee seats as the percentage of the floor it enjoys. Thus, the majority party will have the majority of seats on each standing committee, and the committee chairs will always come from the majority party. When the Democrats control the House, which they have consistently since 1955, they allow the Speaker to appoint each of their members to the Rules Committee, which is a standing committee of the House. The Democratic Speaker also appoints the Rules Committee chair. This gives the Speaker control of the House agenda.

Seniority is a common factor in making standing committee assignments, so once a member is on a standing committee, his or her continued tenure on that committee is assured. Seniority was first adopted in 1910, when the House took the power of making standing committee assignments away from the tyrannical Speaker, Joseph "Uncle Joe" Cannon. The rule not only applies to membership on the committees but also is usually the criterion for determining the standing committee chair. That is, the standing committee chair will usually be the person from the majority party with the longest continuous service on that committee. If a person changes committees, changes parties, or interrupts service in Congress, he or she loses seniority. For example, Senator Barry Goldwater (R-AZ) resigned from the Senate to run for president in 1964, and in the same year Senator Hubert Humphrey (D-MN) resigned to become vice president. Both were subsequently reelected to the Senate, but each seasoned politician reentered the chamber as a freshman member. Similarly, in 1964, Senator Strom Thurmond of South Carolina changed his affiliation from Democrat to Republican, thus sacrificing the seniority he had earned as a

Democrat and again becoming a junior member in a body in which he had already spent many years. In a more recent episode, Congressman Phil Gramm (D-TX) fell out with his congressional party because of his support for President Reagan's budget policies in 1981 so he resigned his seat in Congress and successfully ran as a Republican to succeed himself. Gramm has since been elected to the Senate and is one of that body's most influential members on budgetary questions.

Seniority is criticized in that it assures committee membership and usually the committee chair to people solely on the grounds that they have survived. Yet there are also compelling reasons for its use. Seniority is an objective criterion and thus discourages intraparty fights for valuable committee positions. When junior congresspersons are asked what they think of the seniority system, they often resort to the old aphorism, "The longer I'm in Congress, the better I like it."

Whatever its strengths, the seniority rule has not gone unmodified. Until the 1970s seniority was the only criterion applied, but in the early 1970s House Republicans and Democrats voted to temper seniority with other compelling considerations, and each caucus in the Senate has subsequently modified the seniority principle. Still, however, seniority is the most important factor in standing committee assignments, and each caucus tends to support the seniored members for privilege. On only three occasions have the House Democrats overridden the proclivity for favoring longevity. In 1975 they removed three powerful standing committee chairs on charges of incompetence and arrogance. In each case, however, the next seniored Democrat became the chair. A quite different, and perhaps more significant, episode occurred in 1985: Motivated by the responsibility to check and balance the president's power, the House Democrats unseated the chairman of the Armed Services Committee and replaced

him with Les Aspin from Wisconsin. It was hoped that Aspin, articulate and extremely knowledgeable on military affairs, would best be able to counter the Reagan Administration's martial policies. Significantly, however, Aspin was not second or even third in seniority: He was seventh. Thus the House Democrats ignored seniority in two ways: first by passing over the most seniored person, one who had been the Armed Services Committee chair for years, and second by reaching beyond five other more seniored members to pick the chair. In 1990 the Democratic caucus again removed two committee chairs because they were perceived to be out of touch with the rank-and-file of the party and too old to do the job effectively. In one case, the next seniored person was advanced to the chair, but in the other, the third seniored person was promoted.[38]

Several criteria are used by the caucus to determine which standing committee appointment each nonseniored member should receive. Foremost perhaps is the question of which committee assignment will enable the member to best serve her or his constituents, thus facilitating reelection. A member from New York City would probably be ill-placed on the Agriculture Committee, for example. Regionalism is another concern. The caucus usually tries to see that each section of the country is represented on the committees, although some areas may be more heavily represented than others. For instance, members from the Western states dominate the House Interior and Insular Affairs Committee because most of the public land is located west of the Mississippi.

A member's preference is of course another factor to be considered. Presumably this criterion is most true for members who wish to transfer from one committee to another. Committee transfers seldom are requested beyond the second or third term of office because of the resulting loss of seniority.[39] Still, at an oppor-

George Schultz, Secretary of State during the Reagan Administration, testifies before the House Standing Committee on Foreign Affairs in an early hearing on the Iran-Contra scandal.

tune time, a junior member may wish to transfer from a marginally important committee to a more powerful panel. In the Senate the most important committees are Appropriations, Armed Services, Finance, and Foreign Relations. To spread out the power base, each caucus assures each member a seat on one of these committees before giving any member a seat on two of them. Because the size of the Senate is limited, Senators hold seats on more committees than do House members. Currently, senators are limited to membership on no more than three standing committees and eight subcommittees, but this limit is not adhered to religiously.

In the House the most desirable committees, the so-called **exclusive committees**, are Appropriations, Rules, and Ways and Means. A member of an exclusive committee is precluded from membership on any other standing committee. House members on the nonex-

clusive committees are also limited, but less severely, as to the number of panels they may join, depending on how important their committee assignments are. The average number of House committee seats is 6.6 per member.[40]

Standing Committee Chairs Obviously, the most powerful members of the standing committees are the chairs. While their influence is still substantial, recent reforms in each house have reduced their power considerably. Prior to the caucus reforms of the 1970s, standing committee chairs, not so fondly called the "old bulls," were virtually unassailable masters of their committees. Entitled to the chair by dint of seniority, they had little to fear from a dissatisfied caucus. Their power over their committees was almost absolute. Hence, the legislative power of Congress was centralized in the party leadership and in the hands of the standing committees' chairs.

In the early 1970s, however, the House

Democrats, most of them liberals, revolted against alleged abuses of the standing committees' chairs, most of whom were conservatives. Following the House Republicans' lead, the House Democratic Caucus adopted a rule requiring caucus approval of their committee leaders—the chairs. As mentioned above, three chairs were promptly deposed and the remainder were put on notice that they too could be dumped if their performance became unacceptable to the caucus.

This reform sent shock waves through the Congress, but the Democratic House Caucus was not finished. It also limited the control that standing committee chairs had over the agenda, requiring that all bills be sent to the appropriate subcommittee promptly, unless a majority of the standing committee voted to keep a bill in full committee. Further, it reduced the chairs' control over the committee budget and staff. In short, this reform relaxed the chairs' grip on the subcommittees. Today, the House Standing Committee chairs remain very influential, and one is well advised to cater to their opinions if legislation is to navigate the committee system smoothly, but their powers depend much more upon their leadership ability and persuasive power than on brute force. The Senate followed suit and limited its Standing Committee chairs' power, but not to the same extent as in the House. Essentially, the Senate committee chairs have been forced to share staff appointments.

The House Rules Committee   Before we leave our consideration of the standing committees, one of their number is so unusual as to warrant special attention. The House Rules Committee exercises control over virtually every piece of legislation reaching the floor in that body. The Senate, with fewer members and with its tradition of collegiality, determines when bills come to the floor by agreements between the majority and minority floor leaders.

In the House, the process of scheduling bills for floor action is much more complicated. Under normal procedure, bills that are reported out of the standing committees go to one of four calendars, or waiting lists. The **Union Calendar** receives all fiscal bills, those reported out by the Appropriations (spending) and the Ways and Means (taxation) committees. The largest number of bills, those that are nonfiscal but controversial, go to the **House Calendar**. The **Private Calendar** is for bills that are written in the name of a private individual—a bill granting someone citizenship, for instance, or one settling an individual's claim against the government. Finally, the **Consent Calendar** receives all public policy bills that are expected to pass without dissent.

Except for bills on the Union Calendar, which may bypass the Rules Committee and be considered separately,[41] the Rules Committee is given the responsibility of determining which bills are most important and deserve priority. Members of this committee also decide, in light of the backlog on the calendars, how much time should be spent in debate on any particular bill. Accordingly, the Rules Committee establishes the date a given bill will reach the floor, how much time (usually one or two hours) will be allowed for debate, and whether the bill can be amended on the floor. These *special rules* are voted upon by the floor, but it is a rare occasion indeed when the recommendation of such a powerful committee is overruled.[42] By refusing to give a bill a set of special rules, and thus failing to report it out, the Rules Committee can effectively kill a bill; hence, this committee presents one more obstacle a bill must negotiate if it is to become law.

As powerful as it is, the Rules Committee has not escaped the reforms of the Democratic caucus. Once controlled by conservative chairmen who arrogantly frustrated the will of a more liberal majority, the committee has been tamed significantly. As mentioned before, the

Democrats now allow the Speaker of the House to choose all the Democrats on the Rules Committee and to appoint its chair. These appointments are subject to caucus approval, but the Rules Committee has effectively been reduced to an arm of the Speakership, giving the Speaker great control of the floor agenda. Additionally, under an extraordinary procedure, the Democratic caucus can force its members on the Rules Committee to adopt certain preferred rules for a given bill.[43]

There are several ways of circumventing the Rules Committee, but they are complicated, seldom attempted, and even more rarely successful. **Calendar Wednesday** allows standing committee chairs to bring bills to the floor on any Wednesday, but the bill must be passed on that day—a difficult requirement. Any bill can be brought to the floor from any calendar by suspending the rules, requiring a two-thirds' majority vote, or by unanimous consent.[44] The **Discharge Calendar** can be used, not only to flout the Rules Committee but to force any committee to report a bill to the floor. The Discharge Rule requires that a majority of the House (218 members) sign a petition demanding that a bill held in committee be surrendered to the floor. If the 218 signatures are obtained and if a majority of the floor votes its concurrence, the bill in question will be sent to the Discharge Calendar and then go to the floor.[45] Calendar Wednesday and the Discharge procedure, while they are sometimes invoked, are rarely successful, so the Rules Committee remains a formidable control valve through which virtually all House legislation must pass.

SUBCOMMITTEES

Perhaps the greatest beneficiaries of the caucus reforms in the 1970s were the subcommittees and the nonsenior members. In those reforms the House Democrats adopted a rule that any House standing committee with 20 or more members must be divided into at least four subcommittees. This rule was adopted to end the practice by the Ways and Means Committee of refusing to create subcommittees, thus centralizing taxing power in the hands of the chair. Accordingly, almost every standing committee now divides itself into a number of subcommittees.

In the 101st Congress, the House had 138 subcommittees and the Senate had 86. The subcommittees have few formal powers, but their influence has become enormous—so much so that some scholars now refer to the legislative process as "subcommittee government." The subcommittees can hold hearings, subpoena witnesses, and mark-up bills, but since the standing committees reserve to themselves the last word on bills and since only they can report bills to the floor, subcommittee work depends on their approval. Yet, this dependence is not as great as one may think, for the same principles that make the standing committees' recommendations influential on the floor work to the subcommittees' advantage in the full committee. The subcommittee is, after all, expert in the kind of legislation with which it deals, and logrolling is always a factor.

The most important event in the subcommittees' ascent to prominence occurred in 1973 when the House Democratic caucus adopted the **Subcommittee Bill of Rights**. This revolutionary rule constitutes the centerpiece in the limitations imposed on powers of standing committee chairs. Essentially, it provides that the Democrats on the standing committees are to create the subcommittees, elect their chairs (the chairs of the Appropriations Committee subcommittees must also be ratified by the Democratic caucus), establish the jurisdiction of the subcommittees, and provide the budget for the subcommittees. Additionally, it requires that the chairs of the subcommittees and the ranking minority member on each subcommittee be allowed to hire some of their own staffs, and it provides that the subcommittees may call their own meetings. These provisions made the subcommittees virtually autonomous and defused power to a considerable extent.

In a further effort to spread the power base among larger numbers of members, the Democrats allow their members to belong to no more than two subcommittees per standing committee on which they sit, and they limit any member to holding only one chair so that no standing committee chair may also chair a subcommittee and no senior committee member may monopolize the subcommittee chairs. This rule has, however, been relaxed: In the 101st Congress, 26 House Democrats chaired more than one committee. The Senate has also increased the prerogatives of its subcommittees, but here the standing committee chair remains much more in control of the situation. Still, because the Senate has so many standing and subcommittees, almost every majority member chairs at least two committees.[46]

The growth of subcommittees and the diffusion of authority have empowered many junior members who previously would have had to wait years before they could take a leading legislative role. The "old bulls" no longer enjoy their former monopoly on power, and the legislative process is more open than it was. Reflecting on the change, an experienced lobbyist said:

> In those days [the 1960s], if you could get the ear of the chairman, you could [count on] your case as being a victory. That isn't true today. Individual Congressmen contribute more. Today, other Congressmen have much more influence. Before, if the committee chairman didn't like your proposal, your chance for getting it through was over.[47]

But the changes in congressional structure and power distribution have also engendered difficulties. The profusion of subcommittees has caused multiple overlaps in jurisdiction, thus duplicating the number of committees a bill must visit on its legislative journey and increasing the number of committees to which the executive departments and agencies must report. Thus, passing legislation and administering policy has become much more complicated.

OTHER COMMITTEES

A number of other committees are important to our discussion. **Select committees**, also called special committees, are created for the length of a term to study special issues or problems that concern Congress. Only on rare occasion do they consider legislation; rather, they file reports with Congress on the results of their inquiries, although individual members may carry legislation on the subjects if they choose. Recent Congresses have had select committees study the Watergate affair, narcotics and drug abuse, and the Iran-Contra scandal.

Joint committees comprise members from each house. They usually exist to coordinate the work of the two houses in areas of mutual concern. These committees are often permanent, including the Economics Committee, the Library Committee, the Printing Committee, and the Taxation Committee. The most important joint committee, however, is a temporary body known as the **Conference Committee**. The function of this committee is to draft compromises on legislation passed in different forms in each house.

With the exception of revenue bills, which must originate in the House, any bill may be introduced first in either chamber. When the original house passes the proposed legislation, it is forwarded to the secondary house.* If the

---

* Actually, important legislation is often introduced simultaneously in both houses so that there will be time enough for it to become law within a single term.

bill is passed in identical form in the secondary house, it is sent on to the president. If, however, the bill is passed in a different form, it is returned to the original chamber for concurrence. If the original house accepts the secondary chamber's version, it is sent to the president. On the other hand, if it is not accepted by the original house, then a Conference Committee must be created.

Only about 10 percent of the bills passed in Congress must go to Conference, but, as you can imagine, these are usually the most important and most controversial bills. The membership of each Conference Committee differs. Usually, the chair of the standing committees or the subcommittees that have studied the bill in detail will be appointed, as will several other important members. The members from each house vote as a delegation, and the majority of each delegation must vote to approve the compromise for it to be returned to the Senate and the House. Upon receipt of a bill from Conference, each house must vote for or against the compromised form. No other amendments are allowed. If each house accepts the compromise bill, it is sent to the president, but if either house rejects the bill, it is dead. Hence, we see yet another potential roadblock through which some bills must pass in order to become law.

Because of their great power, the Conference Committees are sometimes called the "third house" of the Congress. They usually deal only with the most significant bills, legislation that has already been passed in some form in each house. Hence, the chances favor passage of the compromise bills, and the committees' authority to virtually rewrite legislation gives them enormous influence on the subjects with which they deal.

Each of these committees is designed to facilitate the work of Congress in passing legislation. Often, however, the committee system can obstruct the process. In any event, we now have the information necessary to study the path by which a bill becomes law.

The Legislative Process

The legislative process can be compared to a helicopter: When grounded, few vehicles look less airworthy, yet, seemingly in defiance of physics, if operated correctly the vehicle not only gets off the ground but can perform quite remarkably. So too with Congress. When seen on paper, with its complicated rules, committee systems, and calendar procedures, the legislative process just does not look as if it will fly, but when conditions are right and when the process is used correctly, it can perform very well indeed. Yet the process is complex and replete with potential surprises to an expectant bill sponsor. About the legislative process, a cynic once remarked, "Laws are like sausages. It is better not to know how they are made."[48] Given our purpose, however, we must enter the sausage factory and investigate its contents.

We should, however, keep one fact foremost in our minds during this examination. As Henry Clay reminded us in his statement at the head of this chapter, legislation is the product of necessary compromise among competing people and contradictory interests. No bill successfully negotiates the legislative process unless it is approved by many powerful people, and acquiescence in politics usually comes at a high price. Rather than producing the ideal, the legislative process—like politics itself—is an exercise in obtaining what is possible.

Although the houses have the same procedures in a fundamental sense, the two chambers are quite different in a number of specific ways. Upon visiting Congress, one is usually struck by the businesslike personality of the House and by the more leisurely and collegial atmosphere of the Senate. Being a much larger body, the House has stricter rules, and its power is more centralized in the hands of the leadership—especially the Speaker. The Senate, by contrast, has very few rules, and the members hold themselves more aloof from party leadership. Furthermore, the Senate tradition for unlimited debate remains a hallowed practice, both on the floor and in the committees, and this deliberative habit can be extended into a filibuster (talking a bill to death), which is one of the principal differences in the Senate procedure. Also, Senators are elected for terms three times longer than House members, and thus enjoy the luxury of being less consumed with reelection concerns during much of their term.[49]

Keeping the differences in temperament of each house in mind, we shall begin our investigation of the legislative procedure in the House.

INTRODUCTION

The first official stage in the processing of a bill is, of course, *introduction*. Before that step, however, a great deal of work must be done by the sponsor if the bill is to stand a chance of passage. Bills are seldom the direct product of the legislator. Rather, the idea for most of them originates outside of Congress. Constituents often request legislation, lobbyists seek sponsors, and, of course, the president has a large legislative package that must be carried. The choice of a sponsor is critical. Constituents tend, naturally enough, to ask their congressperson to introduce desired legislation. Insiders are more selective, however, preferring to seek the support of members who have special authority over certain issues. For example, the chair of the standing committee or the subcommittee to which the bill will be sent can be a powerful sponsor. Also, certain members have become respected authorities on specific kinds of legislation and are particularly influential in these fields.

Examples of people who have developed authoritative reputations in certain fields are Representative Henry A. Waxman (D-CA) on environmental matters, Senator Phil Gramm (R-TX) on the budget, and Senator Sam Nunn (D-GA) on armed services. Members who enjoy such respect can be said to have two constituencies, the voters in their districts and the people who are interested in their special fields. Hence, not only does Representative Patricia Schroeder (D-CO) serve the people of her congressional district, but she also presumes to represent the rights of women throughout the nation. Getting one or more of these people to sponsor legislation will help to assure its passage.

When a member consents to sponsor a bill, he or she will take the idea to the legislative council to be put into appropriate legalese. Toward assuring the bill smooth passage, the wise sponsor will also begin laying the necessary political groundwork before introduction. Supporters for the legislation must be mobilized. Party leadership and caucus backing for the measure are certainly desirable and co-sponsors must be found. Outside support is also essential. Securing the concurrence of the relevant executive department and agencies is very helpful. Citizens' groups and special interests who favor the bill should be brought on board. Finally, the sponsor should negotiate with the Speaker, trying to get a favorable committee assignment for the bill. Once the committee assignment is known, negotiations with the standing committee chair, the chair of the subcommittee, and the subcommittee membership are essential. All of this activity is time-consuming and laborious, but it must occur if the bill is to enjoy a chance of success.

When the bill is returned from legislative council, the sponsor drops it in the hopper on the House clerk's desk. (The clerk is an employee of the House, not a member, and he or she is the chief record keeper of the body.) The clerk assigns a number to the bill and announces its introduction at the next floor session. The Speaker, meanwhile, has given instructions about the bill's disposition, so it moves from the floor to the next stage: the committees.

THE COMMITTEE STAGE

The standing committee chair places the bill before the committee with a recommendation as to which subcommittee has jurisdiction over the bill, and the committee sends it to the appropriate subcommittee. If the sponsor has done the necessary legwork beforehand, it will pay off here. The subcommittee chair can have a substantial influence over the fate of the bill by orchestrating the hearings on the legislation. Enjoying complete control over the list of witnesses, the chair can stack the hearing in favor of or in opposition to the bill. About 90 percent of the bills introduced never leave committee, so getting a bill beyond this stage is a difficult task.[50]

Following the public hearing, the subcommittee turns to the task of marking-up the bill. When the subcommittee has completed its work, it returns the bill to the standing committee with its recommendations. At this point, the standing committee may hold additional hearings, and it may, if it wishes, mark-up the bill itself. We will assume that the bill we are following, while amended somewhat, was voted to the floor with a recommendation for passage and was accompanied by reports from the majority and minority on the committee. Now the bill has cleared its first major hurdles. From the standing committee the bill goes to the Rules Committee to be given special rules and calendar placement.

Our bill, like most, is a public policy bill and is placed on the House Calendar. The sponsor, and with luck the standing and subcommittee chairs that reported the bill out, should lay the groundwork for the Rules Committee hearing by lobbying its chair and some of its most influential members. Of course, the opponents to the bill will likewise lobby for their position. When the bill is heard by the Rules Committee, the chair of the committee that did the detailed work on the bill usually takes the lead in seeking the desired rules. Most important, of course, is that the bill be given a date for floor action. Also, the proponents would probably request that floor amendments be disallowed and ask for adequate time for debate to air the major features of the bill. At this point, the Rules Committee can refuse to report the bill out, seeing it die on the table at the end of the term, or the committee can give it a rule, in which case the bill goes to calendar and awaits its turn to come to the floor. Vetoed bills and Conference Committee compromise bills have privilege, coming to the floor without going through the Rules Committee.

FLOOR ACTION

When the bill reaches the floor, the Rules Committee's special rule is presented to the body, debated, and voted upon. Since the special rule is almost always adopted, the Rules Committee has much to say about the floor procedure. The merits of the bill will then be debated. The chair of the committee that reported the bill out usually acts as the floor manager of the bill, developing the strategy for floor action, getting votes committed, and arranging for those who will speak in its favor. The leader of committee opposition to the bill will do the same on the negative side. If floor amendments are allowed, they are proposed, debated (usually for no more than ten minutes each), and voted upon. Then one last round of debate on the amended bill occurs and the vote is taken on the bill itself.

Because of their busy schedules, members are able to give only limited attention to the thousand or so votes they must cast each term. Consequently, they rely on "cues" from trusted

sources. Members use a wide variety of cue-
givers for information about bills, but the major
ones include their colleagues, fellow members
whose judgment is trusted or who swap votes
(roll the log). The party leadership provides
direction on some bills, the various staffs in
Congress may have opinions about the issue,
the executive branch may have taken a position, the committee reports may be consulted,
the member may receive letters from constituents, and of course, lobbyists and special interest groups may be active on the issues. In any
case, if the bill is voted down, it is dead. But if
the bill is passed on the floor of the House, it is

sent to the Senate, where the House sponsor
has already arranged for a senator to carry the
legislation. (See Figure 7.2).

THE SENATE

The Senate procedure is much like that of the
House except that it is considerably less complex and includes a few possibilities not found
in the House. Introduction would be preceded
by the same back-scenes politicking that occurred in the House. In the Senate, bills are
referred to committee by a ruling of the Senate

Figure 7.2   The Legislative Process

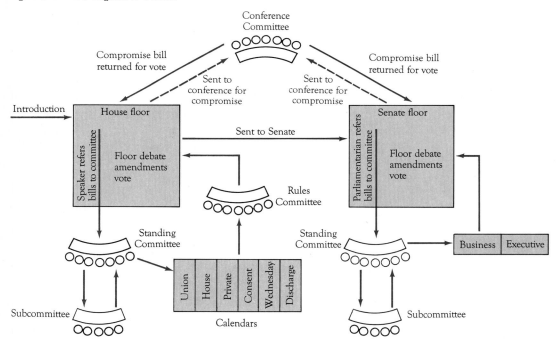

parliamentarian, who is an employee of the Senate. Members can challenge the ruling, but challenges are rare.[51] Senate standing committee chairs have more control over their committees and need not refer bills to subcommittees if they choose, but subcommittee work is becoming more and more important in the Senate, just as it is in the House.

The procedure and powers of the Senate committees are much the same as in the House, except that the Senate does not have a Rules Committee. Hence, bills and resolutions reported out of Senate standing committees go directly to the **Calendar of Business**. Proposed treaties and presidential nominations go to the **Executive Calendar**.

Negotiated agreements between the majority floor leader and the minority floor leader usually provide the Senate with much of the same discipline supplied to the House by the Rules Committee. Pursuant to these agreements, the majority floor leader moves to bring an issue to the floor from one of the two calendars by a unanimous consent vote of the floor.

The floor action in the Senate is usually similar to that in the House, but it can also differ considerably because of the Senate's dearth of rules. The House has two **germane rules**, which the Senate does not impose upon itself: All amendments in the House must be germane (related to) the bill in question, and all House debates must be germane to the issue on the floor. In the Senate, however, neither of these rules exist. Hence, the Senate can amend an unrelated bill (a **rider**) to another bill. If the Senate does so, the House may then vote on it since it comes to that body as part of a single bill. The Senate floor may attach a rider to another bill as a move to adopt an issue that one of its standing committees would not report out, or it may use a rider to circumvent a presidential veto. When the Senate wants a particular policy that it knows the president will veto, it sometimes amends the desired pol-

icy to an appropriations bill that the president needs for the conduct of government. Now the president is confronted with a dilemma. The chief executive may veto the bill, thus voiding the needed money, or sign the bill, accepting the unwanted policy so as to get the funds.

Second, unlike House members, Senators are not required to speak on the subject at issue when they take the floor. This liberty, together with the tradition of unlimited time for debate in the Senate, makes the **filibuster** possible. Reflecting the shrewd advice of constitutional founder Roger Sherman, who counseled, "When you are in the minority, talk; when you are in the majority, vote," a filibuster is a technique used by the minority side of an issue. Not having the votes to defeat an unwanted bill, the minority can take the floor and talk for hours, days, or even weeks, thus using up precious floor time until the majority is willing to either kill the bill or to remove from it the clauses found obnoxious by the minority. Long filibusters are usually done in relays. One dissident senator takes the floor and talks until an appointed time, when the Speaker yields the floor to a colleague who talks for a time and then yields to another colleague, and so on into infinity. They talk about the bill, the state of the union, the weather, their grandchildren, or golf strokes. They can recite Shakespeare and read constituent mail, the dictionary, or the phone book—all have been done. There have also been many one-person filibusters lasting hours. The present record is held by Strom Thurmond (R-SC), who held the floor for 24 hours, 18 minutes in opposition to a 1957 civil rights bill.[52]

It is very difficult to close debate in the Senate, which prides itself on being a forum of free speech. The **cloture rule** (to end debate) requires that 16 senators sign a petition moving cloture. After the 16 signatures are secured, the motion is not put to a vote for two working days. When finally the vote to close debate is held, it takes 60 senators in favor to pass. Even then, each senator may speak for an additional hour. Once cloture is voted, truly determined senators can prolong the agony with a **post-cloture filibuster**, in which numerous points of order and amendments are brought to the floor. These procedures can doom a bill desired by the majority, and even the threat of a filibuster can cause the majority to compromise on an issue.

The filibuster was rarely used before the late 1950s, but, determined to defeat civil rights legislation, Southern conservatives filibustered frequently during the Kennedy and Johnson administrations. Indeed, civil rights is still a target for extended debate. The Senate voted to end a filibuster on the Civil Rights Act of 1990, but the bill was later vetoed by President Bush. Since the 1960s, the filibuster has become even more widely used. New-breed independent senators such as Jesse Helms (R-NC) have filibustered a variety of bills to force their colleagues to back away from legislation they find offensive. The rising number of filibusters occasioned two reforms in the 1970s. One made cloture somewhat easier, resulting in a larger number of successful cloture votes. But the second, adopting a "two-track" agenda system that allows other business to be conducted while filibusters are in progress, seems only to have encouraged more obstructionism. This and other occluding techniques have grated on the members, encouraging some of them to support additional rule changes. For example, a recent study by the Center for Responsible Politics found that 77 percent of the senators favored limiting the filibuster and 62 percent supported limiting offering amendments on the floor.[53] Table 7.3 indicates the growing frequency of attempts to end filibusters.

However, back to our bill. Let us assume that it passed through the Senate, but with amendments. Now the bill must be returned to the House for approval. If the House accepts the Senate version, the bill is sent to the presi-

Table 7.3
SENATE CLOTURE VOTES, 1920–1986

	ATTEMPTED CLOTURES	SUCCESSFUL CLOTURES
1920–1960	23	5
1961–1962	4	1
1963–1964	3	1
1965–1966	7	1
1967–1968	6	1
1969–1970	6	0
1971–1972	20	4
1973–1974	31	8
1975–1976	26	16
1977–1978	13	3
1979–1980	21	10
1981–1982	26	8
1983–1984	19	11
1985–1986	23	10
1987–1988	43	11

Source: Ornstein et al., *Vital Statistics on Congress 1987–1988.*

dent. But, alas, the House would not accept some of the Senate amendments to our bill, so it must go to the Conference Committee. We are lucky, however (or we have done our political work well), for our Conference Committee is composed of the committee chairs who reported the bill out in each house, the sponsors of the bill, and other people from each house who are more interested in resolving the issue than in the "honor" of their respective chambers. Hence, an amicable compromise is reached and each house passes the compromise. Regrettably, however—*the president vetoed the bill!* Now an enormous amount of work must be done to generate the two-thirds' vote in each house necessary to override the president's veto. Unfortunately, since only about 3 percent of the president's vetoes are overridden, our bill fails to pass.[54] Better luck next time.

Cruel as its ending may seem, the foregoing description was designed to demonstrate how difficult, frustrating, and time-consuming the legislative process is. Yet, 5 to 8 percent of the bills introduced do become law. It is left to the president to administer the law and to interact with Congress. So at this point we leave the legislature and go to the executive branch for a different perspective of the American democratic process. We will return to the Congress when we review the relationship it holds with the president and the courts.

Summary

- While senators are elected at large in their states, members to the House are elected from state-gerrymandered districts.

- White, professional men predominate in Congress, and most of the important work of the institution is done in its many committees.

- The decline in importance of seniority, the rise in number and power of the subcommittees, and the increased activity of the caucuses are the most important changes in Congress over the past two decades, and the leadership finds it increasingly difficult to control its members.

- To pass, a bill must negotiate a complicated obstacle course of committee and floor action, and even then it can be vetoed by the president.

Notes

1. Marcus Stern, "Money Can Make the Wheels of Congress Go Round," *San Diego Union*, May 3, 1989.

2. Norman J. Ornstein et al., *Vital Statistics on Congress 1987–1988* (Washington, DC: Congressional Quarterly, 1987), pp. 92–93, and Norman J. Ornstein et al., *Vital Statistics on Congress 1989–1990* (Washington, DC: Congressional Quarterly, 1990), pp. 91–92, 105, and 108.

3. Ornstein et al. (1990), p. 59.

4. Gary C. Jacobson, *The Politics of Congressional Elections* (Boston: Little, Brown, 1987), pp. 10–16.

5. Ornstein et al. (1990), p. 42.

6. Ornstein et al. (1987), pp. 21–36.

7. William J. Keefe, *Congress and the American People* (Englewood Cliffs, NJ: Prentice-Hall, 1980), p. 97.

8. For a colorful analysis of recent American political history and the legislative process, see Thomas P. O'Neill with William Novak, *Man of the House* (New York: Random House, 1987).

9. *The Federalist* #10.

10. Calculated from data in Ornstein et al. (1987), p. 170.

11. Quoted in Marcus Stern, "Congress Is 200—And Under Fire," *San Diego Union*, Apr. 30, 1989.

12. Sara Fritz, "Firms, Lobbies Helped Pay for Wilson's Travels," *The Los Angeles Times*, June 21, 1989.

13. Sara Fritz, "Campaign Cash Takes a Detour," *The Los Angeles Times*, Oct. 28, 1990.

14. William J. Eaton, "Foley Becomes House Speaker," *The Los Angeles Times*, June 7, 1989.

15. Abner J. Mikva and Patti B. Saris, *The American Congress* (New York: Franklin Watts, 1983), pp. 357-363.

16. "Two Gingrich Aides Got Bonus After Campaign Stint," *The Los Angeles Times*, July 26, 1989.

17. Ornstein et al. (1987), p. 208.

18. Nelson W. Polsby, *Congress and the Presidency*, 4th ed. (Englewood Cliffs, NJ: Prentice-Hall, 1986), pp. 116-119.

19. *Congressional Quarterly Weekly Report* (December 11, 1976), p. 3293.

20. Polsby, pp. 108-113 and 128-134.

21. "Leadership: An Interview with Senate Leader Lyndon Johnson," *US News & World Report*, June 27, 1960, p. 88.

22. Keefe, pp. 69-70; and Barbara Hinckley, *Stability and Change in Congress*, 3rd ed. (New York: Harper & Row, 1983), pp. 138-140 and 159.

23. Quoted in Hedrick Smith, *The Power Game* (New York: Random House, 1988), p. 39.

24. Randall B. Ripley, *Congress: Process and Policy*, 2nd ed. (New York: Norton 1978), p. 119.

25. Keefe, pp. 93-95.

26. Calculated from data in Ornstein et al. (1990), p. 200.

27. Mikva and Saris, pp. 178-186.

28. Hinckley, pp. 83-84.

29. Quoted in Charles Peters, *How Washington Really Works* (Reading, MA: Addison-Wesley, 1980), pp. 114-115.

30. Keefe, pp. 84 and 99.

31. Calculated from data in Ornstein et al. (1990), p. 130.

32. Stern.

33. For an excellent analysis of the power of staff in government see Michael Malbin, *Unelected Representatives (New York: Basic Books, 1979).*

34. Hinckley, p. 136.

35. Hinckley, p. 138.

36. Mikva and Saris, pp. 150 and 205.

37. Calculated from data in Ornstein et al. (1990), pp. 151-157.

38. William J. Eaton, "House Democrats Oust Two Key Committee Heads," *The Los Angeles Times*, Dec. 6, 1990.

39. Keefe, p. 74.

40. Ornstein et al. (1987), p. 124.

41. Hinckley, p. 195.

42. Mikva and Saris, p. 217.

43. Keefe, p. 152.

44. Mikva and Saris, p. 219.

45. Hinckley, pp. 136–137.

46. Ornstein et al. (1990), pp. 121–122.

47. Quoted in Jeffrey M. Berry, *The Interest Group Society* (Glenview, IL: Scott, Foresman/ Little, Brown, 1989), p. 183.

48. Quoted in Mikva and Saris, p. 191.

49. Richard F. Fenno, Jr., *The United States Senate* (Washington, DC: American Enterprise Institute for Public Policy Research, 1982), pp. 26–29.

50. Mikva and Saris, p. 209.

51. Mikva and Saris, pp. 205–206.

52. Hinckley, p. 198.

53. Sara Fritz, "Congress—Too Many Free Agents," *The Los Angeles Times,* Jan. 1, 1988.

54. For a more detailed discussion of the legislative process, see Polsby, pp. 138–158.

Suggestions for Further Reading

Dodd, Lawrence C., and Bruce I. Oppenheimer, eds. *Congress Reconsidered* (3rd ed.). Washington, DC: Congressional Quarterly Press, 1985.

Fenno, Richard F., Jr. *The United States Senate.* Washington, DC: American Enterprise Institute for Public Policy Research, 1982.

Fiorina, Morris P. *Congress: Keystone of the Washington Establishment* (2nd ed.). New Haven: Yale University Press, 1989.

Henckley, Barbara. *Stability and Change in Congress* (3rd ed.). New York: Harper & Row, 1983.

Jacobson, Gary C. *The Politics of Congressional Elections.* Boston: Little, Brown, 1987.

———, and Samuel Kernell. *Strategy and Choice in Congressional Elections* (2nd ed.). New Haven: Yale University Press, 1983.

Keefe, William J. *Congress and the American People.* Englewood Cliffs, NJ: Prentice-Hall, 1980.

Maass, Arthur. *Congress and the Common Good.* New York: Basic Books, 1984.

Malbin, Michael J. *Unelected Representatives.* New York: Basic Books, 1980.

Mikva, Abner J., and Patti B. Saris. *The American Congress.* New York: Franklin Watts, 1983.

O'Neill, Thomas P., with William Novak. *Man of the House: The Life and Political Memoirs of Speaker Tip O'Neill.* New York: Random House, 1987.

Ornstein, Norman J., Thomas E. Mann, and Michael J. Malbin. *Vital Statistics on Congress 1989–1990*. Washington, DC: Congressional Quarterly Press, 1990.

Peters, Charles. *How Washington Really Works*. Reading, MA: Addison-Wesley, 1980.

Polsby, Nelson W. *Congress and the Presidency* (4th ed.). Englewood Cliffs, NJ: Prentice-Hall, 1986.

Ripley, Randall B. *Congress: Process and Policy* (2nd ed.). New York: Norton, 1978.

Sinclair, Barbara. *Majority Leadership in the U.S. House*. Baltimore: Johns Hopkins University Press, 1983.

_____. *The Transformation of the U.S. Senate*. Baltimore: Johns Hopkins University Press, 1989.

Smith, Hedrick. *The Power Game*. New York: Random House, 1988.

Smith, Steven, and Christopher Deering. *Committees in Congress*. Washington, DC: Congressional Quarterly Press, 1984.

Stern, Philip M. *The Best Congress Money Can Buy*. New York: Pantheon, 1988.

Wilson, Woodrow. *Congressional Government*. New York: Meridian Edition, 1908.

Chapter 8

THE EXECUTIVE

PREVIEW

The weakness of the political system under the Articles of Confederation persuaded the founders that a more powerful government was necessary and that it should include an executive. Less than a monarch but more than a clerk, the president was generally thought of as the head of the military and the implementer of congressional policy. With the exception of a few extraordinary personalities in the White House, the presidents of the nineteenth century were content to follow Congress's lead. The growing economic and political power of the United States and the resulting sociological changes, however, forced a transformation in the presidency, and when the Great Depression brought Franklin D. Roosevelt and the New Deal to Washington, D.C., the modern presidency was born.

From the time of the New Deal, the chief executive became increasingly strong until the eras of Lyndon B. Johnson and Richard Nixon. Critics complained of an imperial presidency that took on the trappings of royalty and exceeded its constitutional authority. The war in Vietnam, the Watergate scandal, and the resulting fallout from both saw a series of failed presidencies.

The president exercises a number of formal and informal powers. Among the formal powers are executing the law, managing foreign policy, commanding the military, appointing judges and executive officials, granting clemency, proposing law, and vetoing bills when necessary. The most important informal powers are being a moral exemplar, national spokesperson, party leader, and economic manager. The way these powers are exercised is of critical importance. Several political scientists have developed models of presidential leadership, including the centralized, collegial, and council models.

The much-maligned office of the vice president has become very important in the last half of this century. Constitutionally charged with presiding over the Senate and deciding tie votes, vice presidents have been peripheral and enigmatic characters in American history. Beginning in the 1950s, however, the vice presidency has grown in stature because presidents have given it important tasks to perform.

The president commands the executive branch, composed of about three million civilian employees. The executive branch can be divided into two parts: the administration and the bureaucracy. The administration is composed principally of appointed officials who head departments and agencies, and it in turn can be divided into several components. The Executive Office of the President (EOP), founded in 1939, includes the White House Office, the Office of Management and Budget, the National Security Council, the Council of Economic Advisers, and the Vice President's Office.

The Cabinet is another part of the administration. It is an extralegal body, principally composed of the heads of government departments (State, Justice, Defense, Transportation, and so on), and the president enjoys complete latitude over how the Cabinet is used. Before the founding of the EOP, presidents usually relied on the Cabinet as their principal advisors, but recently the president has tended to rely increasingly upon the advice of the EOP staff, and the Cabinet has become less important. Besides the EOP and the Cabinet, the administration includes a number of lesser agencies, including the independent agencies, the independent regulatory boards and commissions, government corporations, and a few foundations and institutes.

Together with the administration, the bureaucracy comprises the executive branch. Until about a century ago, presidents practiced the spoils system, replacing government employees with loyalists of their own. In 1883, the merit system was created, by which applicants qualify for government jobs or promotions by taking examinations, and now over 90 percent of all civilian government jobs are protected from partisan influence. However, the job security afforded by the merit system has created a dilemma. The bureaucrats are largely immune from discipline. Hence, the execution of public policy rests in the hands of unelected and sometimes unresponsive functionaries. Additionally, bureaucrats form alliances with congressional personnel and interest groups, thus increasing their power and independence. There are advantages as well as disadvantages to this state of affairs, but every modern president has had difficulty controlling the bureaucracy.

The powers of the presidency are often described. Its limitations should be occasionally remembered.

John F. Kennedy

The Presidency

Few American political institutions have changed so dramatically as has the presidency. In 1787 there was no precedent for an elected national executive: Monarchy was the only kind of executive extant. Few at the convention, however, save Alexander Hamilton, were interested in anything approaching a monarch for the new country. But beyond this consensus there was little agreement about the structure and powers of the office.

Some convention delegates preferred a plural executive, as proposed in the New Jersey Plan. Others wanted a weak executive who could be removed by the Congress at its discretion. Roger Sherman, for example, said he "considered the executive as nothing more than an institution for carrying the will of the legislature into effect."[1] On the other hand, Alexander Hamilton, George Washington, Governeur Morris, and especially James Wilson eloquently pressed for a strong president. In the end, confident that the trustworthy Washington would become the first president, the founders created a single executive elected to a four-year term, in whom all executive power was vested. The powers of the office, however, were only vaguely stated; thus time and circumstances were left to create the presidency as we now know it.

THE EVOLUTION OF THE PRESIDENCY

Being the first president, Washington established a precedent with virtually every official act. He set the tone for the office, he created the Cabinet, and he forged the relationship of his office with Congress: preferring to act as an executor of policy rather than its instigator. The role of a magistrate or executor of congressional policy was, after all, completely consistent with the ideas of John Locke and other political philosophers who had followings in the United States during that period.

Washington's deference to Congress and Congress's own assertiveness assured that the presidency would be a position of honor and prestige, but would bear relatively little political significance throughout most of the nineteenth century. There were, of course, important exceptions to the rule. Jefferson, the quintessential party leader, used this preeminence to pursue policies that expanded the powers of the presidency, and Jackson asserted his indomitable personality to do the same.

Between Jackson and Lincoln, however, the White House was inhabited largely by ineffectual persons. Abraham Lincoln, though, was made of stronger stuff. As he assumed office, the Southern states seceded and fired upon the colors of the United States. Refusing to call Congress into session for fear that it might recognize the South's right to sever from the Union, Lincoln took the executive powers beyond the point ever before or ever again equaled. Unilaterally he assumed dictatorial powers, raising an army and navy, spending unappropriated funds, and suspending *habeas corpus* (the constitutional requirement that suspects be brought to trial within a reasonable time). When he finally did call Congress into session, the country was irrevocably committed to the war.

Lincoln's strength as president alarmed legislators, and at his death Congress reasserted itself, missing by but one senator's vote to convict President Andrew Johnson on impeachment charges. Although Johnson was acquitted, his presidency was in shambles, and his successors returned to the compliant style of

their antebellum predecessors. From 1865 to 1901, only Grover Cleveland managed to assert himself sufficiently to be considered a strong president. Indeed, the preeminent congressional and presidential scholar of the era, Woodrow Wilson, wrote, "Our present government is simply a scheme of congressional supremacy. . . . [U]nquestionably, the predominant and controlling force, the center and source of all motive and all regulative powers, is Congress."[2]

With the new century, however, a new, more aggressive approach to the presidency evolved. Driven by clear purpose and boundless energy, Theodore Roosevelt led the government in foreign policy advances, trustbusting, and conservation of the wilderness. Roosevelt was also the first president to make a concerted effort to reach out to the general public, claiming that the presidency was a "bully pulpit."[3] Four years after Roosevelt left office, Woodrow Wilson himself, an equally strong if somewhat more sedate leader, became president. During his first term he initiated an unprecedented level of government regulation of industry and labor reform. Wilson also put into effect his theories about making the president a more powerful legislative leader by personally giving the State of the Union Address (something that had not been done since Jefferson's time) and working closely with congressional leaders. World War I, during his second term, involved his government in even more regulation and power over the lives of individuals. The last year of his presidency, however, saw him defeated on the Treaty of Versailles and saw a debilitating stroke rob him of vitality. In fact, for several months he was virtually incommunicado, and his wife, the former Edith Bolling Galt, in effect was the president during his long convalescence. The presidents of the 1920s (Harding, Coolidge, and Hoover) eschewed presidential activism, remaining content to allow Congress the lead again. Indeed,

Hoover, in many ways the most passive of the trio, believed that an active president threatened the liberty of the people.[4]

The Modern Presidency Although the development of the modern presidency can be traced back to the 1880s, it was not until the Great Depression, World War II, and the administration of Franklin Delano Roosevelt that the office took on the full measure of its present form and power.

Many factors contributed to the rise of the modern presidency. The growing complexity of American society, its industrialization and urbanization, and the interdependence of its citizens demanded that government have a greater role than before in the lives of individuals. The Supreme Court, with but few exceptions, sustained the growth of presidential power. Congress also surrendered power to the executive in 1921 by mandating that the president submit to it an integrated budget rather than receiving individual budget requests from each department, as was originally done. The new fiscal provision not only gave the president much more control over the administration, but it also enhanced the president's power over the cost and spending of government in general. Additionally, beginning in the 1930s, Congress gave the president several emergency powers that increased his independence from the legislature. Also, as the twentieth century opened, the United States emerged as a world power, thus augmenting the stature of its chief executive. The Spanish-American War (1898) ended in making the United States an imperial power as it took Cuba, the Philippines, and several lesser islands from Spain. The late but critical role that United States troops played in winning World War I and Wilson's leadership in establishing the format for the postwar world elevated the American position further. The subsequent American retreat from world affairs during the 1920s and 1930s was finally reversed by Pearl Harbor, the conduct of World War II,

the development of nuclear weapons, and the relative decline in power of England, Italy, France, Japan, and Germany. Following the war, a return to unilateralism in foreign policy was made impossible by the Cold War, and the president of the United States was thrust into the role of the leader of the Western nations. The exigencies of the Great Depression preceding World War II also vastly increased the president's role as a national policy-setter and leader.

Finally, the forceful personalities and competence of Theodore Roosevelt, Woodrow Wilson, and Franklin Roosevelt were essential ingredients in the recipe for the modern presidency. They were the necessary leavening agents facilitating the rise of the presidency to its present stature. Each of these men skillfully used partisanship, patronage, and mass appeal to lead the country into a new political era of executive dominance. Franklin Roosevelt's death brought to the presidency an ill-prepared but thoroughly competent man, Harry S. Truman. To him fell the task of leading the noncommunist world in the Cold War, but Truman also courageously gave impetus to the civil rights movement by desegrating the armed forces and calling for civil rights reforms throughout the society.

The election of 1952 brought to power a national war hero who eschewed party politics and insisted upon being a national leader instead. Dwight David Eisenhower's conservative politics and his tendency to delegate authority made him a less assertive president than his immediate predecessors, but the esteem he enjoyed with the public and his firm though somewhat reluctant efforts to enforce the Supreme Court's mandate to desegregate Southern schools assured that the presidency remained at the focal point of the political system.

John F. Kennedy's brief tenure earned mixed reviews. His legislative program was only marginally successful, but his youth, wit, and style established him as a popular leader of international stature. Kennedy's assassination shocked the world and brought to the presidency Lyndon Baines Johnson, already recognized as one of the most successful legislative leaders in our history. Johnson parlayed his legislative skills, a large liberal Democratic congressional majority, and the national sadness at Kennedy's assassination into another reform era. His **War on Poverty** and civil rights programs carried Kennedy's stalled legislative programs to fruition, and he went on to equal FDR's record for domestic reform. No president has matched his contribution to the poor and to civil rights. Yet, while many Great Society programs were successful, others had less sanguine effects, becoming mired in inefficiency, waste, and failure. Johnson's foreign policies were even less laudable. He was prone to seeking military solutions to international problems. In 1965 he sent the United States Marines to oust the leftist but legally elected government of the Dominican Republic, and at the same time, he dishonestly maneuvered Congress into voting him virtual carte blanche in Vietnam. Revelations of his duplicity in misleading Congress about the war in Vietnam caused the failure of his presidency.

Johnson's haughty approach to foreign policy was followed by the equally arrogant policies of Richard M. Nixon. Although Nixon's policies toward the Soviet Union and the People's Republic of China were brilliant successes, his conduct of the Vietnam War was as high-handed as Johnson's had been. Expanding the "Presidents' War" by secret bombings and invasions of other countries in Indochina, Nixon's war policies were almost completely bereft of meaningful congressional consultation. On the domestic side, Nixon supported additional federal aid to the aged poor and he returned money to the states through revenue sharing.

However, his paranoia and vengeful personality eventually resulted in developing "an enemies list"; establishing an unofficial secret police unit (the "Plumbers"); using the CIA, FBI, and IRS to intimidate people; burglary, serious violations of campaign finance laws, bribing witnesses, and obstructing justice. The denigration of the checks and balances by these two presidents led historian Arthur Schlesinger, Jr. to write of the emergence of an **imperial presidency.**[5]

The Watergate scandal, revealing Nixon's excesses, led to Congress's reasserting its authority over the presidency. Gerald Ford succeeded Nixon's resignation, but he found himself limited by two important factors besides an emphatic Democratic Congress: He lacked a popular mandate because he had been appointed vice president by the provisions of the Twenty-fifth Amendment, and he weakened himself with Congress and among the voters by pardoning Nixon for any crimes he may have committed while in the White House.

Jimmy Carter also had problems with Congress. Although his party held the majority in each house, Carter campaigned for the presidency as an outsider; indeed, he largely campaigned against the Washington establishment, a tactic offensive to Congress. Openly antagonistic to the personal aspects of politics, Carter remained aloof from his party's leaders and, as a result, lost their cooperation. Also, Carter found himself interested in the minutest details of his office. One of the brightest minds ever to hold the presidency, he delegated little authority, trying to make most of the decisions himself, an impossible task. Finally, Carter failed to limit his objectives to a small number of major issues; thus his administration became bogged down trying to accomplish things on too many fronts. Although, through patient but persistent diplomacy, Carter managed to improve relations between Egypt and Israel, another part of the Middle East vexed his last years in office. His failure to secure the release of American hostages in Iran, together with his inability to control Congress, conveyed the feeling among the American people that he was weak, and indeed, some critics were lamenting that the presidency itself was crippled.

Presidents Reagan and Bush Into this environment swept Ronald Reagan in the election of 1980. Reagan was ideologically committed, his election victory was convincing, and it also carried in a Republican majority in the Senate. An affable but tough-talking person with a clear agenda to cut taxes and social programs, increase defense spending, balance the budget, and pursue a hard line with the Soviet Union, Reagan cut an impressive figure in Washington. Like Carter, he was an outsider, but he worked at developing amicable relations with Congress and the press, even as he pursued policies that constituted a conservative revolution.

Caught off balance, the Democrats in Congress were unable to do more than moderate the impact of his cuts in the social programs. Reagan's legislative program of 1981 was as successful as that achieved by any previous president, and the presidency seemed restored to its pre-Watergate dominance. However, when the full gravity of the social programs' cuts came home and as the deficits catapulted to unprecedented levels and the country slipped into its deepest recession since the 1930s, Congress regained its feet somewhat, and the subsequent Reagan budgets were declared "dead on arrival."

In foreign policy, Reagan's truculence toward the Soviet Union and claims by his administration that we could survive a nuclear war alarmed many people. He also was more prone to use military force than was Carter. He invaded the tiny island of Grenada to prevent its becoming a military base for the Soviet Union and Cuba; he launched an air strike on Libya in an attempt to assassinate its leader, Muammar Qaddafi; he deployed the marines as peacekeepers in Lebanon; he sent the navy into the Persian Gulf to protect oil tankers during the war between Iraq and Iran; and he unsuccessfully tried to persuade Congress and the American people that the national interest justified sending United States forces into Central America to combat communism. Eventually, however, his foreign policy posture had to be modified. Few of the military adventures had sanguine results, the American people balked at being drawn into a Vietnam-like situation in Central America, and changes in the Soviet Union made the formerly tried-and-true- anti-Russian stance something of an anachronism. The end of his tenure found Reagan dealing amicably with the Soviets and signing an historic treaty to reduce nuclear warheads in Europe.

Reagan was also forced to moderate his domestic policy. The centerpiece of his second term, tax reform, was achieved only with the help of congressional Democrats as many Republicans refused to eliminate the capital gains tax advantages and other loopholes benefiting the moneyed interests. The most debilitating episode, however, was the Iran-Contra scandal, which revealed that Reagan's lax administrative style had allowed his aides to lie to Congress, engage in a secret foreign policy, sell arms to the Iranian government while Reagan and his administration publicly pledged never to deal with terrorists, and illegally divert public funds to the Contras in Nicaragua and to the coffers of private arms dealers.

Since Reagan's departure, the public has learned that his placid leadership style inadvertently encouraged broad-based mismanagement and corruption. News of unfolding scandals struck the public like thunderbolts as it became disillusioned with the Reagan years. At the same time, an unusually large number of kiss-and-tell books written by former highly placed Reagan Administration figures reveal internal squabbles and an uninformed and lackadaisical president.

What at first appeared to be a brilliant success is looking more and more like another failed presidency, and the Congress is again restive about accepting presidential leadership. George Bush, who entered the presidency with more governmental experience than any person since John Quincy Adams, has, in domestic policy, been very circumspect. With the exception of developing a savings and loan industry bailout policy, supporting a strong clean air act, initiating a relatively lackluster program to rebuild the nation's highways and bridges, and proposing resurrected conservative educational reforms, Bush has preferred not to address various domestic problems (e.g., public housing, poverty, crime, energy, etc.) with new initiatives. In foreign policy, an area Bush clearly enjoys, his policies have been more dramatic. Indeed, in 1991 *Time* magazine recognized Bush as its "*Men* of the Year" (emphasis added), arguing that he has displayed vision in foreign policy while displaying none at home.[6] While he has been cautious in his approach to changes in the Soviet Union, Eastern Europe, and China, he has been quick to employ dramatic efforts in some other regions. For example, in 1989 he launched an invasion of Panama to remove General Manuel Noriega from power, and American troops were also used to help suppress an attempted military coup in the Philippines. In 1990-1991 Bush sent the largest American troop deployment since the Vietnam War to the Arabian Peninsula. Eventually, he launched air strikes and a ground invasion in a successful effort to check the aggression of Iraqi President Saddam Hussein.

Bush's amicable personal relationship with Congress has led to a more cooperative atmosphere, but he still has to contend with the keen suspicions of presidential leadership in the Democratic Congress. As things currently stand, the relationship between Congress and the presidency remains in flux, but whatever the exact nature of contemporary presidential powers, they are certainly far greater than was anticipated by the founders.

PRESIDENTIAL POWERS

Clearly the early Americans were concerned about the potential powers of the presidency. It was hoped that Congress would check the office, but the balance of powers was an intricate one. As Gouverneur Morris warned, "Make him [the president] too weak; the legislature will usurp his power; make him too strong; he will usurp on the Legislature."[7]

The *formal powers* of the president (those stated in the Constitution) are not at all grand, and most of them are checked by Congress and limited in other ways. However, years of development have seen some presidential prerogatives become far more powerful than the founders imagined.

Executing the Law and Appointments The constitutional mandate to "take care that the laws are faithfully executed" is, of course, an important provision involving the president in a broad range of activities. In fact, presidents have used this authority to send police and even troops into the states to assure that federal law is honored. Eisenhower's use of federal troops to integrate Central High School in Little Rock, Arkansas, is an example.

Quite beyond law enforcement, however, is the broader question of implementing the law. To accomplish this function, the president relies on hundreds of thousands, even millions of people. Critical to this aspect is presidential appointments. Currently, the president appoints about 8000 nongovernment employees to federal office, but fewer than 10 percent of the offices carry significant political power. Eight thousand appointments may seem like a large number, but with about three million civilian people working for the government, it is clear that the president does not control the jobs of a very large percentage of government employees.

Most presidential appointees must be ratified by the Senate, but with only a few exceptions, the president may unilaterally remove appointees. The Congress from time to time has tried to require that the president seek its approval of removals from positions the Senate ratifies (the most celebrated case being the 1867 Tenure-of-Office Act, which Andrew Johnson was impeached for violating), but by and large, Congress has left the president free to manipulate the administrative offices as he or she sees fit.

Traditionally, presidents have used appointments for more than simply filling slots with competent people. They have used government jobs as leverage by which to influence someone or to repay campaign supporters. Most presidents have been sensitive to partisanship in selecting appointees, and others, especially Ronald Reagan, have been careful to appoint only those people who are compatible with their ideology. As you can see from Table 8.1, President Johnson was the least partisan in his appointments while President Reagan was the most.

Foreign Policy The president is perhaps least encumbered by the checks and balances in the field of foreign policy. The president is the country's chief diplomat and has the power to recognize other governments, without consultation with Congress, by receiving foreign ambassadors. The Senate must ratify presidential appointments of ambassadors, and the president must seek the advice and consent (by two-thirds' majority) of the Senate for treaties with foreign governments, but these limitations have not proved debilitating to the chief executive. As we will see later, the Senate rarely rejects a presidential appointment and the president has managed to circumvent Senate scrutiny of treaties by use of the **executive agreement**. An executive agreement is a bargain struck by the leaders of two governments of two

Table 8.1

PARTISAN APPOINTMENTS OF RECENT PRESIDENTS TO MAJOR POSITIONS[a]

PRESIDENT	FROM PRESIDENT'S PARTY	FROM A PARTY OTHER THAN THE PRESIDENT'S	UNAFFILIATED WITH A PARTY
Kennedy	63%	10%	27%
Johnson	47%	11%	42%
Nixon	65%	8%	27%
Ford	56%	8%	36%
Carter (1977–1978)[b]	58%	7%	35%
Reagan (1981–1984)	82%	3%	15%

[a] Major appointments include Cabinet and other major administrative positions and ambassadorships.

[b] The partisanship of most appointments is unavailable for the period 1979–1980 because the Carter Administration often did not list the party affiliation of its appointees in those years.

Source: Adapted from data in Stanley and Niemi, *Vital Statistics on American Politics,* 2nd ed.

countries. As a matter of practicality, the legal distinction between the two kinds of accords in unimportant, and the Supreme Court has generally ruled that executive agreements have the same effect as treaties.[8] However, because Senate ratification of an executive agreement is not required, the political difference between it and a treaty is critical. Thus, the president has an enormous loophole in the conduct of foreign affairs, becoming more independent in diplomacy than the founders anticipated. For example, in 1941, Britain was besieged by the Nazis. In an effort to help Britain, Franklin D. Roosevelt agreed to "lend-lease" 50 aging destroyers to England. Since this agreement was made without an official treaty, Senate ratification—which was unlikely—was not necessary. As you can see from Table 8.2, many more executive agreements than treaties have been adopted.

Military Power   Another major instrument of foreign policy, and potentially of domestic policy, is the president's role of commander in chief of the armed forces. When the founders wrote, "The President shall be Commander in Chief of the Army and Navy of the United States, and of the Militia of the several States, when called into actual Service of the United States," they had no idea of the full extent of the power they extended to the chief executive. Their view was that the power to commit troops to armed engagements rested with Congress because only it was allowed to declare war. Making the president commander in chief was important to the founders because it guaranteed civilian control of the military, but the president has vastly expanded the military power by assuming the right to deploy the armed forces, even in belligerent conflicts, solely on the authority of the commander in chief.

Beginning with the John Adams Administration, during which the United States fought a limited undeclared war with France, presidents have assumed they have the right to send troops into battle without requesting permission from Congress in the form of a formal declaration of war. Since Adams's time, presidents have committed United States troops to about 200 actions.[9] Most of these engagements have been small, but in this century the United States fought three major wars (Korea, Vietnam, and the Persian Gulf) and came to the brink of nuclear annihilation during the 1962 blockade of Cuba all without congressional imprimatur. While few question the president's authority to deploy troops without a declaration of war to defend against aggression, con-

Table 8.2

TREATIES AND EXECUTIVE AGREEMENTS

	NUMBER OF TREATIES	NUMBER OF EXECUTIVE AGREEMENTS	RATIO OF EXECUTIVE AGREEMENTS TO TREATIES
1789–1889	275	265	0.96
1890–1988	1,201	12,550	10.45
Total	1,476	12,815	8.68

Source: Adapted from data in Stanley and Niemi, *Vital Statistics on American Politics,* 2nd ed.

siderable controversy exists over whether a declaration of war is required for the president to begin a war when American troops and interests are not eminently threatened. Thus, President Bush's contention that he could order an invasion of Kuwait or Iraq without the formal approval of Congress became a serious constitutional issue in 1990. In 1991, however, Congress voted to approve Bush's military initiative, although it did not actually declare war, and the president subsequently launched air strikes and finally a ground invasion.

Judicial Powers Congress creates the federal court structure, and the president, with consent of the Senate, appoints federal judges, the U.S. Marshals, and the U.S. District Attorneys. The authority to pick the persons to staff the judiciary, a completely different branch of government, gives the president a good deal of influence over the law. More will be said about the president's influence on the judiciary in the next chapter.

The president also has the power to **reprieve** (postpone a sentence) and **pardon** (forgive) people or grant **amnesty** to groups convicted of federal crimes. This power of **clemency** is vested in the president alone, with no check against it by Congress or the courts. For example, in the late 1970s Jimmy Carter gave amnesty to the people who evaded the draft out of moral scruples about the Vietnam War. The clemency power also includes **commutation**: The president may commute (reduce) the sentence of any person convicted of a federal crime. The only major restriction on the president's power of clemency is that it cannot pertain to anyone convicted of impeachment charges.[10]

Legislative Powers In this century the president has become the nation's chief legislator, and bills from the administration occupy a great deal of congressional time. The Constitution directs that the president "shall from time to time give to the Congress Information of the State of the Union, and recommend to their Considerations such Measures as he shall judge necessary and expedient." During most of the eighteenth century, the president's State of the Union Address was sent to Congress and read by a congressional official. Hence, it did not have great influence on the congressional agenda. In 1913, however, Woodrow Wilson, who deeply believed that the president should become a legislative activist, personally delivered his State of the Union Address and then immediately adjourned to the President's Room in the Capitol to work with congressional leaders on strategy and tactics by which to pass his reform program. Since that time, presidents have personally presented their programs to Congress, and with the exception of Harding, Coolidge, and Hoover, they have been major players in the legislative arena.

The Constitution also gives the president the right to call Congress into special session, a rare event (the last special session was called by President Kennedy in 1962 to deal with the Cuban Missile Crisis). The president may adjourn Congress should the two houses fail to agree on a date of adjournment. Keen to prevent the president from interfering in their business, however, the leaders of Congress have always publicly announced the date of adjournment for each term so the president has never been given the opportunity to adjourn Congress. Neither of these powers has been very significant, but two other prerogatives have been very important to the president as a legislator.

The Constitution gives Congress the sole power to legislate, but in practice, the president or presidential designates now legislate much more often than does Congress. The executive's authority to legislate is called the **ordinance power**. The business of the United States has become extremely complicated, and

Congress could not possibly pass laws to cover every particular circumstance for which law is needed. Hence, the Congress passes laws that express its intent in general terms and authorizes the president or an executive designate to fill in the multitudinous details regarding the law's implementation. The president has the right to promulgate **executive orders** or *ordinances* only to the extent that they carry out the expressed intent of Congress. The executive may not legislate on matters that Congress has not first authorized. In any case, the rules and regulations established by the executive are voluminous, and they are as legally binding as is any law passed by Congress itself. For example, in 1970 Congress created federally funded family planning clinics with the caveat that "None of the funds . . . shall be used in programs where abortion is a method of family planning." In 1988 the Reagan Administration interpreted this provision strictly and promulgated regulations forbidding clinic employees to even mention abortion as an option to their patients. As pointed out in a previous chapter, although the regulations were challenged, the Supreme Court upheld them as an appropriate exercise of the ordinance power. It is clear, therefore, that the president and others in the executive branch have legislative power that affects the people as much as does legislation from the Congress.

The second major legislative power of the president, the **veto**, cannot be delegated to subordinates. As discussed in Chapter 7, the Constitution provides for two kinds of vetoes: the regular veto and the pocket veto. The **regular veto** applies when Congress is in session. When a bill passes in identical form in each house it is sent to the president for approval. The president has ten days (excluding Sundays) to sign the bill. If the president vetoes (blue-pencils) the bill, it is returned to Congress with a presidential message stating the president's objections and sometimes hinting at how Con-

President Lyndon B. Johnson gives Attorney General Robert Kennedy a pen at the ceremony for the signing of the 1964 Civil Rights Act. Presidents use several pens while signing important legislation and the pens are given to people who were important to the success of the legislation.

gress might pass a law on the subject that the president will sign. If two-thirds of each house votes to override the veto, the bill becomes law; otherwise it is dead.

Bills on which the president takes no action during the ten-day period, provided the ten days elapse while Congress remains in session, become law without the president's signature. In 1989, for instance, President Bush allowed a bill punishing defacing the flag of the United States to become law without his signature. He preferred a constitutional amendment to outlaw disrespect to the flag, but the Democratic Congress passed a statute rather than trifle with the First Amendment. Allowing the bill to become law without his signature enabled Bush to avoid vetoing a bill on an issue that was central to his 1988 campaign, while not backing down from his demand that the Constitution be modified.

If Congress adjourns during the ten days the president has to sign bills, the **pocket veto** becomes applicable. If the bill remains unsigned, it is vetoed, and since Congress is adjourned, the pocket veto cannot be overridden. Congress passes many bills late in the term, so a large number of them are subject to the pocket veto, as shown in Table 10.1 on pages 306–307, and several presidents have made ample use of the instrument.

Informal Powers   The presidential powers thus far discussed are formal powers in that they are in some way mentioned in the Constitution, or at least justified by constitutional language. However, the president also has a number of *informal powers*, which obtain because of the political environment rather than because of any specific constitutional provision.

The president has always been looked to as a *moral exemplar* and *spokesperson* for the society. People expect the president to represent the best qualities of the American character and to articulate the national mood. When tragedy strikes, the president is expected to express the national grief, and when triumph manifests, the president leads the nation in celebration. This function is nowhere found in the pages of the Constitution, but it is a critical part of the president's duties. When it is done well, as it was by presidents Franklin D. Roosevelt and Ronald Reagan, presidents enjoy great residues of public approval that support them even in trying times. When they do it poorly, however, as did Jimmy Carter, the president loses the commitment of the public. Style, therefore, is often as important as substance to the presidency. A recent example of this phenomenon can be found in President Bush's reaction to the 1989 opening of the Berlin Wall. Correctly not wishing to destabilize United States-Soviet relations by crowing at the demise of the most dramatic symbol of the Cold War, President Bush was restrained in his comments. An exuberant American people, however, were disappointed at the president's failure to express the national joy. Stung by criticism about his reserve, Bush was forced to turn up the volume of his approval.

Another important informal power of the president is *party leadership*. As was mentioned in Chapter 5, the president is the leader of his or her party and is the principal spokesperson for the party. The president's party has a national chair, of course, but he or she is hand-picked by the president and is largely relegated to second-rate status. Robert Strauss, normally a very powerful person in American politics, is reported to have lamented his subordinate role as the Democratic party chair during the Carter Administration with this colorful but succinct statement: "If you're Democratic party chairman when a Democrat is president, you're a goddamn clerk."[11]

It should be quickly noted, however, that the president is leader of only the national party. Typically, presidents have had relatively little influence with the parties at state and local levels. They do not control the nominations for congressional offices or for governor and other state offices, and presidents have often been rebuffed when they tried to influence state elections. Even such popular presidents as Franklin D. Roosevelt in 1938, Ronald Reagan in 1986, and George Bush in 1990 found that the people ignored their advice in electing members to Congress.

Nevertheless, the most successful presidents have been those who have executed strong partisan leadership. Thomas Jefferson, an unparalleled partisan leader, showed the way, and Abraham Lincoln, William McKinley, Theodore Roosevelt, Woodrow Wilson, and Franklin D. Roosevelt were all noted for their political skills within their parties. On the other hand, no president has been so secure that he could alienate the opposition and be sure of a successful term.[12]

The political tightrope the president must walk is becoming increasingly narrow as electoral politics change. Since the 1950s, most presidents have had to contend with divided government, in which the opposition controlled one or both houses of Congress. While legislators in the president's party usually want the president to succeed,[13] they cannot be taken for granted, especially if the interests of their constituents are directly involved.[14] Party loyalty has declined significantly due to the infusion of PAC money into congressional campaigns and a loss of dependence on local party bosses. As a result, Richard M. Pious tells us that the party structure has become "splintered" and "the small amount of party loyalty that exists provides precious little lubricant to prevent the clanking of gears in the machinery of government."[15]

The advent of the mass media and the emergence of the public president has also caused something of a diminution of partisan ties. Increasingly, presidents have tried to reach beyond the Congress and other traditional players to generate support among the masses. Although Woodrow Wilson and the two Roosevelts were noted in their day for appealing directly to the people, James W. Davis suggests that television has done more than anything else to create the modern presidency. "Television in modern politics," Davis writes, "has been as revolutionary as the development of printing in the time of Gutenberg."[16] Not only has television been critical in the elections of several presidents (Kennedy, Carter, and Reagan) but, when used skillfully by the president, it can be a powerful tool for advancing the president's policies. It can be used to persuade the public to support the president's programs and to pressure Congress to do the same. No better example of this phenomenon can be presented than Ronald Reagan, "the great communicator." Reagan's skills before the camera go unmatched in the history of the presidency. Exuding sincerity, strength, confidence, and competence, time and again in his prepared addresses he was able to mobilize public support for his proposals and his administration, encouraging Congress to adopt policies it might otherwise have resisted.

The public's relationship to the presidency has caused another transformation in its informal powers. Public expectations of the presidency have increased over the years, and nowhere have they become stronger than in the area of *economic leadership*. Before the New Deal, almost all economic policy was left to the state and local governments. Of course, the issues of tariffs, free silver, regulation of interstate commerce, and monetary control by the Federal Reserve System occupied the attention of presidents before the Great Depression, but the day-to-day concerns of economic life were not to be meddled with by the national government.

With the collapse of the economic system in the 1930s, however, came Franklin D. Roosevelt and a series of programs that involved the federal government deeply in the economy. Later, at the end of World War II, Congress passed the **Employment Act of 1946**, which recognized the permanent responsibility of the national government for economic prosperity—something previously acknowledged only in response to an emergency. Then, the **Great Society** of Lyndon B. Johnson involved the government even further in seeking to assure the material well-being of the individuals in the state. These developments have made the president the chief economist of the country. Ironically, however, although the president commands a huge array of agencies that seek to influence the economy, there are few fields in which the chief executive is more limited, as we shall see in a later chapter. Still, in the public's mind, the president is responsible for prosperity, and no other issue has as much effect upon whether the president is perceived by the public as successful.

The President's Leadership Style

It is clear that the powers of the presidency are enormous, but each president has approached the job differently and the success of presidents has often depended upon their styles of leadership. To better understand the office, some presidential scholars have tried to develop paradigms or models of presidential leadership styles.

The most useful analyses were developed by Richard T. Johnson[17] and Stephen Hess.[18] Each of these political scientists has produced models of the presidents' management styles which, while differing in several ways, can be consolidated into the generalization that most presidents have used one of two management styles: centralized or collegial. In the *centralized model* presidents empower their White House Office chief of staff to determine who shall see them, and what matters they shall deal with directly, rather than being referred to a lower level in the administration. The advantage to this system is that the lines of authority are clear and the policy-development process is highly structured. Problems can arise, however, if the chief of staff is too protective or if the president is too withdrawn, thus becoming isolated from political reality. Presidents who fit this description are Eisenhower, Nixon, Carter in his last year, and Reagan in his second term.

The *collegial model* has the president accessible to a great variety of people and a wide range of ideas. Obviously, this system demands that the president have a high energy level, and it tends to produce creative policy. Yet, unless care is taken, the policy-making process can become confused, staff members can attempt end-runs to the president, and coordination can be lost. Franklin Roosevelt, Kennedy, Johnson, Ford, and Carter in his first three years used this model.

During his first term Ronald Reagan employed a new approach, which might be called the *council model*, and it was extremely successful. Unlike Carter, who became involved in the minutest details of his administration, Reagan was detached and uninterested in administrative matters. Instead, he focused on broad policy goals and on public relations. This approach worked well as long as able and conscientious people were at the helm in the president's absence. During Reagan's first term, the White House and presidential policy were managed by a triumvirate in the White House Office, including James A. Baker, a Bush associate who became Reagan's Chief of Staff; Michael K. Deaver, a close friend of Mr. and Mrs. Reagan; and presidential counselor Edwin Meese III, a long-time political associate of the president. Meeting each morning for breakfast, these aides would schedule the president's appointments and appearances, organize political initiatives, shepherd the president's legislative agenda, and oversee the functioning of the administration. Although the administration was plagued with internal rivalry and acrimony, the president's staff received very high marks for efficiency and political savvy from all sectors, including Tip O'Neill, the Democratic Speaker of the House.[19] Most decisions were delegated to subordinates, and those matters that reached the president were explained by the staff, discussed, and usually brought to consensus.

At the beginning of Reagan's second term, however, things changed. Meese was appointed attorney general, Deaver returned to the private sector, and Baker exchanged jobs with Secretary of the Treasury Donald Regan, a former high-placed executive in a major stock brokerage firm. Regan was different in temperament and style from his predecessors. He was often curt and abrasive, he was not meticulous about administrative detail, and he enjoyed the power and publicity accompanying his new station. Without the watchful trio on the job, a detached president stood by while infighting within the administration increased, policy initiatives became disorganized, and subordinates began to operate on their own authority, eventually resulting in the Iran-Contra debacle. The Tower Commission sternly admonished both Regan and the president for their negligent management styles, and Regan, who had by then fallen afoul of Nancy Reagan, ultimately resigned. Howard Baker, a respected former Majority Leader of the Senate, succeeded Regan and managed to bring the White House staff and other elements of the Executive Office of the President back under control. The subsequent moderation of some of Reagan's foreign and domestic policies is also largely attributable to Baker's influence.

PRESIDENT BUSH

George Bush came to the presidency with more varied experience in the national government than any other president in this century. The son of a United States Senator from Connecticut, Bush made a fortune in the oil business in Texas. He served two terms in the House of Representatives, and later served as the United States Ambassador to the United Nations, Director of the CIA, Republican National Committee Chairman, United States envoy to the People's Republic of China, and Vice President. With only a few exceptions, he has proved an extremely cautious president, reluctant to commit early on issues. He is very sensitive to public opinion, a bitter political opportunist, conservative on domestic policy, moderate in relations with major foreign countries, but apparently quick to use military power in his dealings with lesser countries.

His management style seems to conform more to the collegial model than to the council

or centralized forms, although it is far from stereotypical. Bush has appointed a strong-willed chief of staff, John Sununu, but insists that people in the administration who want to see him should be allowed to do so. The most gregarious president since Lyndon Johnson, Bush consults widely among his staff, cabinet members, subcabinet officials, and members of Congress—including long-time friends among the Democrats. Yet, being a hands-on president, he delegates little authority, and he is criticized for relying on the advice of only a small cadre of people when major decisions may be made. So far, his principal confidants on foreign policy are Baker; Richard Cheney, Secretary of Defense; and Brent Scowcroft, National Security Adviser. In domestic policy Bush looks to his old friends Nicholas F. Brady, Secretary of the Treasury, and Robert A. Mosbacher, Secretary of Commerce, but especially influential are Sununu and Richard Darman, Director of the OMB. In fact, the influence of these two aides is very significant since Darman is conservative on fiscal matters, Sununu is conservative on social and moral issues, and both are ambitious and very bright.[20]

Ethics in the White House

Ethics, integrity, and honesty have always been a concern in Washington; and while no administration was completely free of scandal, most managed to acquit themselves with dignity. Except for the Grant and Harding administrations, none were shaken with debacles of catastrophic proportions until Richard Nixon's presidency. The Watergate scandal, leading to the resignation of the president, has already been mentioned, so it need not be examined again. President Ford's pardon of Nixon was greeted with public speculation that he was paying his debt for being appointed vice president, but no evidence has appeared to substantiate this suspicion. With the exception of the financial dealings of Director of OMB Bert Lance, the Carter Administration was also free of taint. Unfortunately, the same cannot be said for the Reagan Administration.

"Vast sums of money" are being spent, said Whitney North Seymour, Jr. in 1987, "to buy influence and favors." Seymour went on to exclaim that the "problem is too much loose money and too little concern in Washington about ethics in government." This statement might have been put down as a partisan attack except that Seymour is a Republican who, as independent counsel, successfully prosecuted Michael Deaver for perjury. "Leadership is the key," Seymour said indignantly. "So long as the White House and Cabinet members say, 'We're running an ethical Administration,' you're going to have ethics. If you don't have that at the top, it isn't going to work."[21]

As it turns out, Seymour's complaint was largely ignored, even though by that time more

Chief of Staff Donald Regan (left) and Attorney General Edwin Meese III look somber as they listen to President Reagan announce in 1986 the resignation of Admiral John Poindexter as National Security Advisor. Poindexter's resignation was necessitated by the part he played in the Iran-Contra scandal.

Reagan officials had been investigated and tried for ethics violations, fraud, and other infringements of the law than in any other previous administration. Not only did the Iran-Contra scandal erupt, but dozens of highly placed officials resigned in disgrace, some went to jail, and every few weeks a new scandal was made public.

In 1989, former Attorney General Edwin Meese was accused by the Justice Department staff itself of ethics violations that would have deserved discipline had he still been attorney general. The Justice Department report read:

> Based upon the facts that are available, we must conclude that Mr. Meese, in certain instances involving Mr. Wallach [an associate of Meese's who was later convicted of racketeering and fraud in connection with a project about which he had lobbied Meese], either did not understand, or did not appreciate, or simply did not care what impression could be left with the public about his own integrity and the integrity of those functions he oversaw.[22]

At the same time, of course, legal proceedings were being advanced against Oliver North and John Poindexter for their part in the Iran-Contra affair.

Meanwhile, it was revealed that officials in the Pentagon had sold information to corporations, giving them an advantage in bidding for government contracts. Several people have already been convicted, and investigations and prosecutions are continuing.[23]

One of the major improprieties was found in the Department of Housing and Urban Development (HUD). Giving great attention to its budget (HUD's funding was cut by 60 percent between 1981 and 1988) but apparently ignoring its management, Reagan's lax supervision allowed what funds remained in HUD to

be pillaged by unscrupulous officials and housing contractors. Billions of dollars in grants and
low-interest loans were given to people with
influence in the Republican party. The practice
of awarding HUD contracts to political allies of
the president goes back at least to the Carter
Administration and probably much further, but
at least HUD money was used for its intended
purposes in previous administrations. In the
1980s, however, large amounts of HUD money
intended for the poor were used to finance
luxurious apartment buildings, resorts, and golf
courses—and much of it was simply stolen.
The depth and breadth of graft are unprecedented.[24]

After discovering evidence of fraud and
corruption in HUD that implicated Samuel R.
Pierce, Jr. (Reagan's Secretary of HUD), James
G. Watt (Reagan's first Secretary of the Interior), and several lesser lights in the administration, Jack Kemp, Bush's Secretary of HUD and
a former Republican congressman, pledged to
Congress, "We're going to make it [HUD] work
for the poor and the needy. We're going to take
the greedy and the consultants and the Republican influence peddlers out."[25]

Honesty in government was an issue in the
1988 campaign, and candidate Bush pledged to
emphasize ethics. As president he has made
public efforts to assure that people in his administration are true to the public trust. However, deep concern lingers about his own
involvement in a suspected 1980 agreement
between Reagan/Bush campaign people and
Iranian officials to hold the American hostages
in Iran until after Reagan became president,
and Bush's culpability in the Iran-Contra scandal when he was vice president. There is growing suspicion that his administration is attempting to obstruct legal proceedings associated with
it.[26] Bush's Chief of Staff John H. Sununu's use
of military aircraft for personal trips, including
ski weekends and visits to his dentist, have
also tarnished the administration's record.[27]

Presidential Succession

While only one president resigned because of
ethical problems, several others have died in
office. For such cases, and in the event of the
president's disability, the founders provided
that the vice president would succeed, but the
founders left three questions unanswered: What
would happen if both the presidency and vice
presidency became vacant at the same time?
Should the vice presidency be filled if it becomes vacant? And, how is it to be determined
that a president is disabled?

Congress resolved the first problem by statute. Current law provides that if the presidency
and the vice presidency become vacant at the
same time, the Speaker of the House will succeed to the presidency, then the President Pro
Tempore of the Senate, and then the Cabinet
members in order of rank. The second and
third questions remained unresolved until the
Twenty-Fifth Amendment was adopted in
1967.

The Twenty-Fifth Amendment specifies
that the vice president shall become "acting
president" under two circumstances. First, if
the president sends Congress a written message
stating inability to discharge the duties of the
office, the vice president shall be acting president until the president sends a written message
to Congress certifying recovery. Second, when
the vice president and "a majority of either the
principal officers of the executive departments
or such other body as Congress by law provide"[28]
(emphasis added) transmit to Congress a written declaration that the president is incapable
of performing the duties of office, the vice president acts as chief executive. Again, the president will be reinstated when she or he sends a
written message to Congress stating that a disability no longer exists. If, however, the vice
president and a majority of the principal executive officers disagree about the president's ability to serve, Congress shall decide the matter by

a two-thirds' vote. The Congress has not yet exercised the option of designating a body other than the principal executive officers (the Cabinet) to join with the vice president in declaring the president disabled.

The disability clause of the Twenty-Fifth Amendment has been used only once, in 1985 when President Reagan was briefly incapacitated during surgery. The other provision, however, filling a vacancy in the vice presidency, has been used twice. Section 2 of the amendment provides that whenever a vacancy in the vice presidency occurs, the "President shall nominate a Vice President who shall take office upon confirmation by a majority of both Houses of Congress." In 1973 Vice President Spiro Agnew, who had committed fraud and income tax evasion while governor of Maryland, resigned to avoid possible impeachment. President Nixon, himself embattled over the Watergate affair, which ultimately ended in his own resignation to prevent impeachment, nominated Gerald Ford (R-MI), the House Minority Leader. Confirmed by Congress to replace Agnew, Ford succeeded to the presidency when Nixon resigned in 1974. Ford's succession left the vice presidency vacant again, so he also exercised the power given in the Twenty-Fifth Amendment: He selected New York Governor Nelson A. Rockefeller to become his vice president.

The Vice President

Perhaps no public office has been so maligned by its own occupants as the vice presidency, beginning with the nation's first vice president. "My country has in its wisdom," John Adams wrote plaintively to his wife Abigail, "contrived for me the most insignificant office that ever in the invention of man contrived or his imagination conceived."

Unlike many vice presidents, most people in the United States are comfortable with the vice presidency, but the office is really quite unusual. No other major democracy has an elected stand-in, and some leading citizens, including historian Arthur M. Schlesinger, Jr., believe that the office should be eliminated.[29] The founders originally intended to provide that the presiding officer of the Senate should fill a vacant presidency, but late in the convention, almost as an afterthought, they decided to create a second elected executive officer, and the office has been gradually evolving since.[30]

The vice presidency is unique among federal elected officials in that it is the only office allowed to violate the separation of powers; the vice president is constitutionally charged with presiding over the Senate. Indeed, presiding over the Senate is the only function the Constitution gives the vice president. In all other matters, the vice president is dependent on the president to assign tasks.

Although eight vice presidents have served two terms with the same president, only two (George Clinton and John C. Calhoun) served as vice president under two different presidents. Two vice presidents have resigned their office before their terms expired (Calhoun and Agnew), and the vice presidency has been left vacant 16 other times by either death (7) or succession (9). Although no vice president who succeeded to the highest office in the nineteenth century because of an untimely vacancy was elected president in his own right, all but one in the twentieth century (Ford) was elected to his own term as president. (See Table 8.3.)

Obviously, since the vice president may be called upon to became president, the office is critically important. Yet, because vice presidential candidates are chosen at campaign time, their ability to serve is regrettably often not the most fundamental issue when the choice is made. Rather, vice presidential candidates have usually been chosen with the

Table 8.3

PRESIDENTS AND VICE PRESIDENTS OF THE UNITED STATES

TERM	PRESIDENT	COMMENT	VICE PRESIDENT	COMMENT	LENGTH OF VACANCY OF VICE PRESIDENCY
1789–1793	Washington		John Adams	Announced own election as president in Senate.	
1793–1797	Washington		John Adams		
1797–1801	J. Adams[a]	First president to live in Washington, D.C. Adams was a Federalist.	Thomas Jefferson	Jefferson was a Republican, announced own election as president in Senate.	
1801–1805	Jefferson[a]	Elected by House.	Aaron Burr	Tried for and acquitted of treason in 1807.	
1805–1809	Jefferson		George Clinton		
1809–1813	Madison		George Clinton	Died in office.	10 months, 12 days
1813–1817	Madison		Elbridge Gerry	Died in office.	2 years, 3 months, 9 days
1817–1821	Monroe		Daniel D. Tompkins		
1821–1825	Monroe		Daniel D. Tompkins		
1825–1829	J. Q. Adams	Elected by House. Son of John Adams.	John C. Calhoun		
1829–1833	Jackson		John C. Calhoun	Resigned.	2 months, 2 days
1833–1837	Jackson		Martin Van Buren	Announced own election as president in Senate.	
1837–1841	Van Buren[a]		Richard M. Johnson	Elected by Senate.	
1841	W. H. Harrison	Died April 4, 1841.	John Tyler	Succeeded.	
1841–1845	John Tyler[a]				
1845–1849	Polk		George M. Dallas		
1849–1850	Taylor	Second cousin of James Madison. Died July 9, 1850.	Millard Fillmore	Succeeded.	3 years, 11 months

Table 8.3 (continued)

TERM	PRESIDENT	COMMENT	VICE PRESIDENT	COMMENT	LENGTH OF VACANCY OF VICE PRESIDENCY
1850–1853	Fillmore[a]				2 years, 7 months, 27 days
1853–1857	Pierce		William R. King	Died in office.	3 years, 10 months, 14 days
1857–1861	Buchanan		John Breckinridge	Announced own defeat for president in Senate.	
1861–1865	Lincoln		Hannibal Hamlin		
1865	Lincoln	Assassinated. Died April 15, 1865.	Andrew Johnson	Succeeded.	
1865–1869	A. Johnson[a]	Impeached/Acquitted.			3 years, 10 months, 17 days
1869–1873	Grant		Schuyler Colfax		
1873–1877	Grant		Henry Wilson	Died in office.	1 year, 3 months, 17 days
1877–1881	Hayes		William A. Wheeler		
1881	Garfield	Assassinated. Died Sept. 15, 1881.	Chester A. Arthur	Succeeded.	
1881–1885	Arthur[a]				3 years, 5 months, 13 days
1885–1889	Cleveland		Thomas A. Hendricks	Died in office.	3 years, 3 months, 7 days
1889–1893	B. Harrison	Grandson of W. H. Harrison.	Levi P. Morton		
1893–1897	Cleveland	Only president to serve nonconsecutive terms.	Adlai E. Stevenson	Grandfather of the 1952 and 1956 Democratic presidential candidate.	
1897–1901	McKinley		Garrel A. Hobart	Died in office.	1 year, 3 months, 11 days

Table 8.3 (continued)

Term	President	Comment	Vice President	Comment	Length of Vacancy of Vice Presidency
1901	McKinley	Assassinated. Died Sept. 14, 1901.	Theodore Roosevelt	Succeeded.	
1901–1905	T. Roosevelt[a]				3 years, 5 months, 18 days
1905–1909	T. Roosevelt		Charles W. Fairbanks		
1909–1913	Taft		James S. Sherman	Died in office.	4 months, 5 days
1913–1917	Wilson		Thomas R. Marshall		
1917–1921	Wilson		Thomas R. Marshall		
1921–1923	Harding	Died Aug. 2, 1923.	Calvin Coolidge	Succeeded.	
1923–1925	Coolidge[a]				1 year, 7 months, 2 days
1925–1929	Coolidge		Charles G. Dawes		
1929–1933	Hoover		Charles Curtis		
1933–1937	F. D. Roosevelt	Cousin of T. Roosevelt.	John N. Garner		
1937–1941	F. D. Roosevelt		John N. Garner		
1941–1945	F. D. Roosevelt		Henry A. Wallace		
1945	F. D. Roosevelt	Died April 12, 1945.	Harry S. Truman	Succeeded.	
1945–1949	Truman[a]				3 years, 9 months, 8 days
1949–1953	Truman		Alben W. Barkley		
1953–1957	Eisenhower		Richard M. Nixon		
1957–1961	Eisenhower		Richard M. Nixon	Announced own defeat for president in Senate.	
1961–1963	Kennedy	Assassinated. Died Nov. 22, 1963.	Lyndon B. Johnson	Succeeded.	

Table 8.3 (concluded)

TERM	PRESIDENT	COMMENT	VICE PRESIDENT	COMMENT	LENGTH OF VACANCY OF VICE PRESIDENCY
1963–1965	L. Johnson[a]				1 year, 1 month, 29 days
1965–1969	L. Johnson		Hubert H. Humphrey	Announced own defeat for president in Senate.	
1969–1973	Nixon[a]		Spiro T. Agnew		
1973–1974	Nixon	Resigned Aug. 9, 1974.	Agnew/Gerald Ford	Agnew resigned and Ford was later appointed. Ford succeeded Nixon after his resignation.	1 month, 26 days
1974–1977	Ford[a]		Nelson Rockefeller	Delay between Ford's succession and Rockefeller's appointment as VP.	4 months, 10 days
1977–1981	Carter		Walter Mondale		
1981–1985	Reagan		George Bush		
1985–1989	Reagan		George Bush	Announced own election as president in Senate.	
1989–	Bush[a]		J. Danforth Quayle		

[a]Presidents who were formerly vice presidents.

Source: Based on data in James W. Davis, The American Presidency, p. 415.

election in mind. Normally candidates are selected to balance the ticket geographically (Californian Richard M. Nixon chose Marylander Spiro T. Agnew), ideologically (moderate George Bush nodded to conservative Dan Quayle), or, in the case of Geraldine Ferraro, Walter Mondale's running mate in 1984, from the standpoint of gender.

THE MODERN VICE PRESIDENCY

In the role of President of the Senate, the vice president may vote only in the case of a tie. When the Senate was small, such an opportunity arose relatively frequently, but as the Senate grew, fewer occasions have presented themselves for the vice president to cast a deciding vote. Since the Senate allows its presid-

Democratic candidate for vice president Geraldine Ferraro during her 1984 campaign. The t-shirt says "A Woman's Place is in the White House."

ing officer little authority beyond breaking tie votes (even being allowed to speak requires an invitation from the body), most vice presidents visit the Senate only occasionally. The present era of divided government makes the vice president's role even less useful since the majority of the Senate is usually controlled by a party different from that of the administration, and hence, the vice president's influence as a lobbyist for the administration is muted. Dan Quayle has helped to keep conservative Republican senators in line with Bush's policies, however. Referring to his superfluous role in the Senate, Wilson's witty vice president, Thomas R. Marshall, once said,

> The Vice President is like a man in a cataleptic state. He cannot speak; he cannot move; he suffers no pain; and yet he is perfectly conscious of everything going on around him, but has no part in it.[31]

Presidents have used their vice presidents for administrative tasks increasingly since the Eisenhower Administration, however. The vice president's office is now located in the White House itself, and recent presidents have included the vice presidents among their most prominent advisers.[32] The importance of the vice president became especially prominent during the Carter and Reagan years. Both presidents were newcomers to Washington's politics, while their vice presidents, Mondale and Bush, were old hands at life inside the beltway (the environs of the capital).

The vice president is a statutory member of the National Security Council, and presidents often ask their vice presidents to serve on various boards, task forces, commissions, and committees; to engage in various diplomatic missions; and to become partisan agents during reelection campaigns while the presidents remain in the White House, ostensibly above the political fray. Even today, however, the vice president is often relegated to unwanted ceremonial roles such as attending state weddings and funerals. In fact, Vice President Bush attended so many funerals in the place of an aging president that a journalist quipped that Bush's slogan should be "You die, I fly."[33]

In 1988 George Bush selected J. Danforth (Dan) Quayle as his running mate amid great uproar and lingering doubt regarding Quayle's military record, experience, and intelligence. Since elected, Bush has given Quayle some minor administrative and diplomatic tasks, and late in 1989 the vice president acquitted himself well when, while the president was away from Washington at the Malta Summit with Soviet President Mikhail S. Gorbachev, Quayle directed the successful United States efforts to foil an attempted coup against Philippine President Corazon Aquino. To date, however, the vice president has yet to establish himself as a major player in the administration.

Perhaps in an effort to still distracting speculation about Quayle's fate, President Bush took the extraordinary step of saying in 1989 that he plans to include Quayle on the ticket in 1992.[34] Such an early commitment to a running mate is almost unprecedented. The nation does not share the president's confidence, however, since its approval rating of Quayle was even lower in the middle of his term than it was in 1989. Furthermore, the public was shaken when in 1991 the president suffered irregular heart rhythms, driving home the reality that Quayle could become president. Still, Bush remained firmly confident in the vice president.[35]

Regardless of what Quayle's ultimate performance as vice president turns out to be, it cannot be denied that the office has become much more important than it once was. In 1960, when Lyndon B. Johnson was considering whether to accept Kennedy's invitation to join the Democratic ticket, he called fellow Texan John Nance Garner for advice. Garner, who had stepped down from the powerful Speakership of the House to become vice president during Franklin D. Roosevelt's first two terms, told Johnson the vice presidency "isn't worth a pitcher of warm spit."* Johnson obviously ignored his mentor's advice, and he became president as a result. Perhaps the most thoughtful statement by a recent vice president about the enigmatic office was made by Gerald Ford:

> The Vice President is a Constitutional hybrid. Alone among federal officials he stands with one foot in the legislative branch and the other in the executive. The Vice President straddles the Constitutional chasm which circumscribes and checks all others. He belongs to both the President and Congress, even more so under the Twenty-fifth Amendment, yet he shares power with neither.[36]

The Administration

The president and the vice president are not alone in the executive branch, of course. Indeed, the executive is by far the largest of the three branches of government. The **administration** is of critical importance in helping the president formulate and execute policy.

A popular misconception of the administration is that it is primarily composed of the president and chief advisors in the Cabinet. Actually its structure is much more complicated. It comprises several distinct segments, each of which bears different responsibilities and enjoys a different relationship to the president. As Figure 8.1 indicates, the administra-

* Garner's colorful remark actually referred to liquid that comes from an altogether different part of the human anatomy.

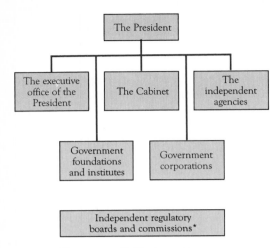

* Appointed but not controlled by the president.

Figure 8.1   The Administration

THE EXECUTIVE OFFICE OF THE PRESIDENT

Most presidents have had advisers who were not part of the administration—Jackson's Kitchen Cabinet, Wilson's Colonel Edward M. House, and Franklin D. Roosevelt's Harry Hopkins, for example; but before the time of FDR, presidents largely depended on the Cabinet for the bulk of their counsel. Indeed, the president was not afforded any publicly paid personal professional assistance until the late 1850s, and at the turn of the century the president was served by only a handful of domestics, three secretaries, and a few clerks. By the Hoover Administration the president's staff had increased only modestly, but in the mid-1930s, a Committee on Administrative Management (the Brownlow Committee) concluded that the president needed a major increase in staff assistance and advisors outside of the Cabinet. In response to the Brownlow Committee report the **Executive Office of the President (EOP)** was born in 1939, and it currently has a large complement of personnel, as displayed in Table 8.4. As you can see, the size of the EOP reached its peak in the era of the imperial presidency and has been significantly reduced since then.

tion includes the president, the executive office of the president, the Cabinet, the independent regulatory agencies, the independent regulatory boards and commissions, and the government corporations and institutes. The administration, the armed forces, and the bureaucracy (each dealt with later) constitute the executive branch of the government and total about 5.3 million people.

Table 8.4

EXECUTIVE OFFICE OF THE PRESIDENT PERSONNEL

PRESIDENT	YEAR	WHITE HOUSE OFFICE	OFFICE OF MANAGEMENT AND BUDGET	COUNCIL OF ECONOMIC ADVISORS	NATIONAL SECURITY COUNCIL	TOTAL EOP STAFF
Truman	1949	243	517	36	17	1,240
Eisenhower	1959	406	432	33	64	2,735
L. Johnson	1968	261	550	74	35	4,964
Nixon	1972	583	703	58	80	5,721
Carter	1979	418	638	36	73	1,918
Reagan	1988	366	552	29	60	1,554

Source: Adapted from data in Stanley and Niemi, *Vital Statistics on American Politics,* 2nd ed.

Today, the EOP has eclipsed the Cabinet as an advisory body, and comprises several agencies, each carrying out specific responsibilities. (See Figure 8.2.) Most of the EOP is housed in the Executive Office Building adjacent to the White House, but some of the most important agencies are located in the west wing of the White House itself. Being situated in close proximity to the chief executive, the EOP has become important to the president, but its influence also reflects factors related to internal politics within the administration. The people in the EOP are often most loyal to the president. Many of them served on the president's campaign staff, and unlike the Cabinet officers, they have no bureaucracy and government program responsibilities. Hence, the people in the EOP can be devoted to the president alone. The EOP staff is also often more politically attuned than the Cabinet members, who are frequently chosen for reasons other than their political acumen. Consequently, the EOP members' advice is especially valuable to the president, who above all else is a politician. However, there are important qualifications to the value of the advice presidents receive from the EOP staff. To begin with, being anxious to please "the boss," they may be encouraged to tell the president only what she or he wants to hear. "Presidents suffer from too much heel clicking from their staff,"[37] according to Charles Peters, a leading journalist with many years of experience inside the beltway. The temptation to please the president by giving compliant advice may be irresistible because there is usually intense competition within the EOP staff for the ear of the president, and thus for influence in the government.[38]

EOP personnel report directly to the president. Congress reserves few checks on its structure and function, except that the various agencies are created by law and most of the appointees are now subject to Senate confirmation. For the most part, however, the president is allowed to staff, organize, and use the EOP as needs dictate. To get a clear idea of the importance of the EOP, we shall examine some of its most important agencies.

The White House Office Closest to the president is the White House Office. Housed in the west wing of the White House, it is composed of about 100 domestic personnel and several hundred political aides. Each president has structured his White House staff a bit differ-

Figure 8.2   Executive Office of the President

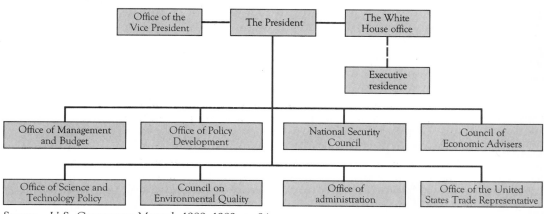

Source: U.S. Government Manual, 1988–1989, p. 84.

ently, but it usually includes a chief of staff, a press secretary, speech writers, media consultants, an appointments secretary, people who lobby Congress, the president's counsel (lawyer), a number of aides and advisers, and, of course, a small staff for each of them. Unlike most EOP personnel, White House Office staff are not subject to Senate confirmation.

Obviously, the chief of staff, who is responsible for coordinating the White House Office, is central to the administration. Indeed, some of the most important, and sometimes infamous, names in recent presidential history have occupied this office, including Sherman Adams under Eisenhower, H. R. Haldeman under Nixon, and Donald Regan under Reagan. Not surprisingly, these people are associated with the centralized model of presidential leadership, and they were extraordinarily influential. They controlled access to the president and determined what memos and reports came across his desk. Each of them was criticized for overcontrolling access to the president, thus denying him diverse points of view and causing him to lose touch with the public. President Bush's chief of staff, John M. Sununu, former governor of New Hampshire, ranks among the powerful presidential aides, and, although his abrupt style has alienated many people, he is credited with helping the conservative elements of the Republican party exert significant influence with the president.[39]

The Office of Management and Budget (OMB)   This agency was originally established in 1921 as an element of the Treasury Department and remained there until 1939. The largest agency in the EOP, the OMB has become central to the president's control of the huge federal bureaucracy. The OMB not only drafts the president's budget but also reviews the bureaucracy's structure and performance, and reports to the president on the efficiency and efficacy of the various institutions of government.

Long one of the most powerful positions in government, the directorship of OMB was given extraordinary influence by Ronald Reagan. David Stockman, then the director of OMB, was a veritable wizard with the budget and a shrewd strategist of congressional procedure. He became the architect of *Reaganomics*, the president's economic program. Drawing an analogy about the importance of his agency, Stockman told *New York Times* Washington bureau chief Hedrick Smith that "OMB is really the policy switchboard of the executive branch."[40] Although not equaling Stockman's power, Richard G. Darman, Bush's director of OMB, has emerged as a major player in domestic policy development.

The National Security Council   Created by the National Security Act of 1947, along with the Department of Defense and the CIA, the **National Security Council (NSC)** is authorized to advise the "President with respect to the integration of domestic, foreign and military policies relating to national security." The law lists the president, the vice president, the secretary of state, and the secretary of defense as members of the NSC, but the president may ask anyone thought appropriate to attend. The director of the CIA and the chairman of the joint chiefs of staff are frequently included, for example. The NSC also has a small staff housed in the west wing of the White House, which is directed by the assistant to the president for national security affairs (more commonly called the National Security Advisor).

Although President Truman opposed creation of the NSC and generally ignored it, subsequent presidents have made much use of it. Some national security advisors have become so powerful as to eclipse the secretary of state in the exercise of foreign policy. McGeorge Bundy, during the Kennedy and Johnson administrations, Henry Kissinger under Nixon, and Zbigniew Brzezinski, Carter's NSC head, were all extremely prominent.[41] The NSC assumed its greatest import, however, during the Reagan Administration.

John "Bud" McFarland and Admiral John Poindexter, successive NSC heads, together with NSC staff Lt. Colonel Oliver North, expanded the NSC's role from a policy analysis organization to an operative agency, engaging in several secret and ultimately illegal operations. The most celebrated of these missions was the sale of weapons to Iran and the diversion of part of the proceeds to the treasury of the Contra forces in Nicaragua. The exposure of these activities led to very critical remarks about the NSC by the Tower Commission, to congressional condemnation, and eventually to the criminal proceedings against North, McFarland, and Poindexter.

The Iran-Contra scandal redoubled Congress's concern about the exercise of presidential power, and it discredited the NSC. Admiral Poindexter was succeeded by General Colin Powell, a highly respected man who managed to lead the NSC through the rest of the Reagan Administration without further scandal. His place was taken in the Bush Administration by retired General Brent Scowcroft. Scowcroft was previously the national security advisor to President Ford, served on the Tower Commission, and is also highly regarded in Washington.

The Council of Economic Advisors The **Council of Economic Advisors (CEA)** was created by the Employment Act of 1946. It is composed of three presidentially appointed economists whose task is to study trends in the economy and to report their findings to the president. The Employment Act formalized the government's responsibility for assuring national economic prosperity, and the CEA's role is to provide the president the information needed to develop economic policy that combats inflation and recession.

The Vice President's Office The vice presidency has already been discussed, but it is important to observe here that the **Vice President's Office** has become a significant element in the EOP. Beginning in the 1970s, the Vice President's Office has been given a budget of its own and office space in the White House itself. Although the vice president's staff is sometimes engaged in rivalry with the president's staff, there seems little chance that the office will be denigrated: It has become an integral part of the EOP.[42]

THE CABINET

Although the Cabinet is not mentioned as such in the Constitution, Article II, Section 2 refers to the "executive departments," so it is clear that the founders expected there to be an executive establishment subordinate to the president. The first Cabinet was created by George Washington when he gathered together his department heads for consultation. What seemed a good idea in theory proved to be a source of considerable aggravation for Washington, however, as Secretary of State Thomas Jefferson and Secretary of the Treasury Alexander Hamilton bitterly argued with each other over policy questions. Since Washington's time, presidents have each used the Cabinet differently. Some have relied heavily on its advice, while others have largely ignored it. Lincoln's Cabinet, which he consulted frequently, was composed of powerful Republican party leaders, some of whom thought they should have been president instead of Lincoln. The department heads had little respect for Lincoln and pressured him to submit policy decisions to a Cabinet vote. Knowing that the Constitution gave all executive powers to the president, Lincoln bided his time, waiting for an opportunity to disabuse his advisors of their ambitions. When finally an issue arose upon which Lincoln knew his entire Cabinet disagreed with him, he put the matter to a vote. In announcing the results,

Lincoln said "Seven nays, one aye—the ayes have it," thus making clear that he had no intention of surrendering his constitutional authority.

Still, for most presidents, the Cabinet remained the principal advisory body until the creation of the EOP in 1939. Since then, only Eisenhower and Carter have used the Cabinet much; the others have relied more on the EOP for advice, and Carter himself became disenchanted with the Cabinet late in his term.

Currently the Cabinet is composed of the 14 department heads (see Table 8.5), and any other officials the president wishes to include. Recent presidents have included the United States ambassador to the United Nations, the director of the CIA, the director of the OMB, and the United States trade representative. Other officials are also invited to attend Cabinet meetings as need arises.

Protocol dictates that Cabinet members' rank is determined by the order in which the

Table 8.5
GOVERNMENT DEPARTMENTS

DEPARTMENT[a]	YEAR ESTABLISHED	NUMBER OF CIVILIAN EMPLOYEES
State	1789	25,634
Treasury	1789	160,516
Justice	1789	76,515
Interior	1849	78,216
Agriculture	1862	120,869
Commerce[b]	1913	52,819
Labor[b]	1913	18,178
Defense[c]	1947	1,049,619
Housing & Urban Development	1965	13,342
Transportation	1966	65,506
Energy	1977	17,031
Education[d]	1979	4,542
Health & Human Services[d]	1979	123,270
Veterans' Affairs	1988	245,467

[a] The Postmaster General has existed since the founding of the country, and in 1872 the Department of the Post Office was created. In 1971, however, it became a government corporation, independent of presidential control.

[b] The Department of Commerce and Labor was created in 1903, but it was divided into separate departments ten years later.

[c] The Department of War and the Department of the Navy were each established during the first years of the republic and were combined into the Department of Defense in 1947.

[d] In 1953 the Department of Health, Education, and Welfare was created, but in 1979 it was divided into the Department of Health and Human Services and the Department of Education.

Source: Adapted from data in Stanley and Niemi, *Vital Statistics on American Politics,* 2nd ed.

departments were created. Their actual relationship to the chief executive, however, is determined by each president, although the secretariats of state, treasury, defense, and justice are broadly recognized as major positions and usually go to very important people. These senior Cabinet officials usually play a significant part in policy development, although not always. President Nixon's first Secretary of State, William P. Rogers, was relegated largely to administrative tasks, while National Security Advisor Henry Kissinger joined with the president to formulate foreign policy and to execute the most sensitive diplomatic missions. The president appoints the department heads

as well as a number of undersecretaries, deputy secretaries, and assistant secretaries who compose the *subcabinet*. See Figure 8.3 for an example of subcabinet structure, in this case for the Department of Housing and Urban Development. All these appointments must be confirmed by the Senate, but the president has the right to remove them without Senate consultation.

Even though almost every modern president campaigned on the pledge to create a Cabinet government, none have succeeded. Each has, to one extent or another, found himself relegating the Cabinet to secondary status and relying on only a few favored secretaries

Figure 8.3   Department of Housing and Urban Development

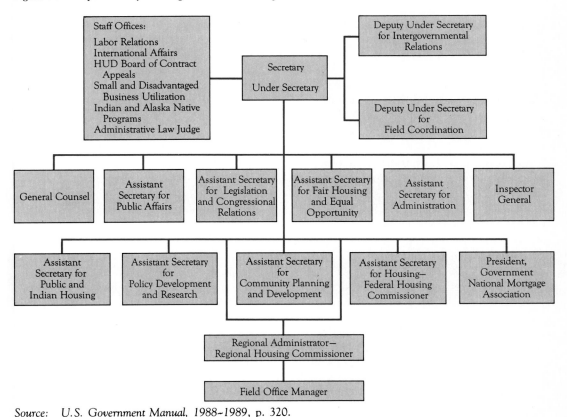

Source: U.S. Government Manual, 1988–1989, p. 320.

and on the EOP for advice. The reason for the decline of the Cabinet as a viable institution of government is to be found in the nature of the Cabinet positions and the political conditions within society. To begin with, Cabinet members find themselves divided between two often contradictory roles: They are to advise the president when asked, but they are also administrators of major departments within the government. Consequently, the quality of their advice to the president is suspect, since it would be very unusual for a secretary to recommend policy that would not benefit the department he or she administers. Increasingly, Cabinet members are seen more as spokespersons for their departments to the president than as messengers for the president to the departments. This means that the president governs a divided house with a multitude of conflicting interests.

Moreover, Cabinet members are not necessarily chosen because the president respects their opinions. While some secretaries are long-time associates and trusted advisors of the president (such as John Kennedy's brother Robert; Casper Weinberger for Reagan; and James A. Baker, Nicholas F. Brady, and Robert A. Mosbacher in Bush's Cabinet), often presidents do not know secretaries before appointing them to office. In one case, President Reagan did not even recognize Samuel R. Pierce, his Secretary of Housing and Urban Development, upon encountering him at a social function almost a year after his term began. The president mistook his secretary for a city mayor.[43] Cabinet secretaries are usually appointed for a variety of reasons. They are sometimes selected for their administrative prowess. More often, however, they are chosen for the political equilibrium they bring to the Cabinet. Because of the symbolic importance of the Cabinet posts, the president is obliged to pay close attention to factors of gender, ethnicity, religion, geography, and profession. It would be very damaging

politically, for example, if the Secretary of Commerce was not acceptable to the business community; the position of Secretary of the Interior is usually given to someone from the West, where most public lands are; the Secretary of Labor must not be obnoxious to organized labor; and the Secretary of Defense cannot be repugnant to the military establishment. Additionally, it is expected that African-Americans, Hispanic Americans, women, Catholics, and Jews will be seated on the Cabinet. With so many interests to please, the president has little latitude in selecting the Cabinet and only a few spots can be given to friends.

Cabinet members are people of considerable experience and accomplishment in their own right. Some of them have been corporate executives, governors, or members of Congress, and many have served in government on several occasions before. Hence, unlike most EOP staff, they are sometimes quite independent. Their expertise may induce them to offer advice a president may not wish to hear, or actually to oppose the president's policies, as did Walter J. Hickel, Nixon's Interior Secretary (currently the governor of Alaska); Joseph Califano, Carter's Secretary of Health, Education, and Welfare; and Alexander Haig, Reagan's first Secretary of State. In most cases, these dissident people eventually resign, but not before creating discord and controversy within the administration.

Finally, the rivalry between the EOP and the Cabinet is intense, each trying to gain the president's ear. The EOP usually prevails in these struggles, for several reasons. Its members are usually appointed by the president because of their loyalty; many of them come from the same section of the country as the president; they are assigned offices closer to the president and deal with the chief executive on a day-to-day basis; and finally, some presidents (Eisenhower, Nixon, and Reagan in particular, and Carter toward the end of his term) use the EOP, especially the White House Office staff, to screen their business appointments, even to the extent of isolating the president from the Cabinet officers.[44]

OTHER ELEMENTS OF THE ADMINISTRATION

As you can see from Figure 8.4, there are dozens of agencies and corporations that are subordinate to the president but not part of a government department. Essentially, these bodies can be divided into four categories. The **independent agencies** are often created to perform specific functions that could be housed in one of the departments, but for some reason are located outside of the normal government structure. They are called *independent* only because they are not part of a government department; they are subordinate and responsible directly to the president. As with the departments, the president appoints the top officials of the independent agencies, and they may be removed at the president's discretion. The Environmental Protection Agency (EPA) is such an institution. Created in 1970, it might have been attached to the Department of Interior or perhaps the Department of Agriculture, but instead, it was given separate existence so as to give emphasis to the government's efforts to protect the environment and also to prevent the new agency from being dominated, and perhaps inhibited, by an established bureaucracy.* Other such agencies are the Office of Drug Control, the Office of Personnel Management, and the Peace Corps.

---

* Reflecting his wish to emphasize environmental policy, President Bush asked that the EPA be given Cabinet status. The proposal easily passed the House in 1990 and will probably soon be approved by the Senate.

The **independent regulatory boards and commissions** are a second kind of agency. Because most of our economy is privately owned and operated, the need for government regulation of labor, industry, and finance is acute. Hence, over the years a number of regulatory bodies have been created. These organs, however, enjoy much more independence from the president than do the independent agencies. They are usually governed by a panel of commissioners appointed by the president with Senate confirmation to long, staggered terms. Commissioners may not be removed from office except for incompetence or malfeasance. These agencies span the breadth of the economy, and their regulations have much to do with working conditions, food and product quality, safety, truth in advertising (such as it is), fair competition, finance, and so forth. The list of these agencies includes the Federal Communications Commission, the Federal Reserve Board, the National Labor Regulation Board, and the Securities and Exchange Commission.

Enjoying similar independence from presidential control are the government corporations and government foundations. *Government corporations* are public agencies engaging in the production and sale of goods and services. The Tennessee Valley Authority (TVA), for example, provides flood control, recreation, and electricity to a vast area in the South that until the 1930s had few or none of these advantages. The Federal Deposit Insurance Corporation, the United States Postal Service, and the Resolution Trust Corporation are other examples of government corporations.

Congress has also created a small number of **government foundations** that are devoted to advancing cultural, educational, and scientific fields for the general benefit of society. The National Foundation for the Arts and the Humanities, the National Science Foundation, and the Smithsonian Institution are examples of such agencies. Although these organs are

Figure 8.4 The Administration in Detail

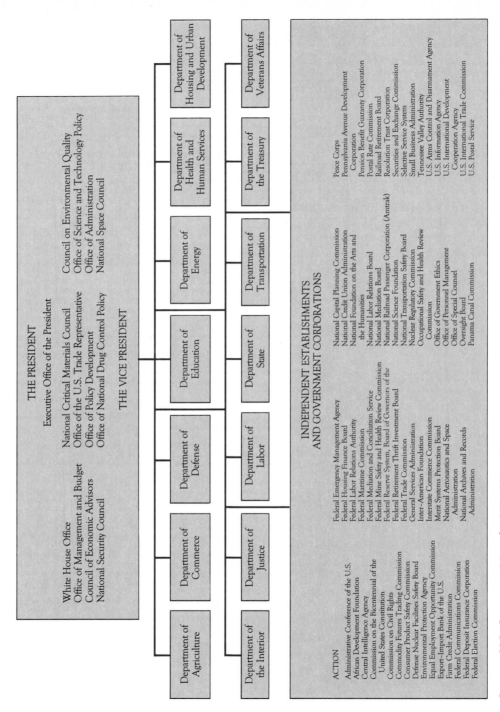

Source: U.S. Government Manual, 1990–1991, p.21.

designed to be free of politics, they do depend on funding from the government and are thus vulnerable. For example, in the 1980s budget cuts deeply slashed the money provided to the Foundation for Science, the Arts, and the Humanities, making its work more difficult. Then in 1989, the Congress passed legislation prohibiting the National Endowment for the Arts and the National Endowment for the Humanities from supporting art and programs considered "obscene." Although the legislation was not strong enough to suit Senator Jesse Helms (R-NC), it was condemned by Senator Edward M. Kennedy (D-MA) and others as the first time in history Congress had presumed to "censor" art.[45] In 1990, after considerable public criticism, Congress rescinded many of the limitations it had imposed the year before.

The Bureaucracy

Bureaucracy is a word that many people associate exclusively with government, but in fact, any large institution is likely to be bureaucratic, be it a business, an industry, a university (chances are that the educational institution you are attending is heavily bureaucratic), a religion, or a state or national association. Bureaucracies arise from the need to organize large institutions so that they efficiently conduct the function for which they exist. In doing so, any sizable enterprise is divided into specialties, people are placed in charge of them, and a staff is provided to help. Whenever such departmentalization begins, a bureaucracy is born.

Any large society such as the United States will be riddled with bureaucracies, and many of its citizens, including readers of this book, either already are bureaucrats (people who work in a bureaucracy) or will eventually become bureaucrats. The function of the federal bureaucracy is to carry out the policies of the government.

As you can see from Table 8.6, the number of federal employees has grown enormously over time, but so too have the functions and services of the government, especially since the New Deal and World War II. The number of federal employees peaked in 1945, the last year of World War II. Since then it has fluctuated, but it has not yet returned to the 1945 mark. Note too that the number of state and local government employees is included in the table and that currently only about 15 percent of all government employees work for the federal government. Also, to demonstrate the relative cost of government, a large part of which is salaries, Table 8.6 includes the federal budget as a percentage of the gross national product (GNP).

Approximately one-third of all federal civilian employees work for the Department of Defense, the nation's largest employer. The government employs people from virtually every walk of life, from typists to physicians, from clerks to scientists. Obviously, staffing the ranks of the federal establishment is a complicated job in itself, absorbing the efforts of a large number of federal employees.

THE MERIT SYSTEM

Until just over 100 years ago, virtually all federal employees were appointed by the president or by subordinates. It was standard practice for presidents to remove federal employees appointed by a previous administration and replace them with loyalists of their own. This practice became known as the **spoils system**. Rewarding party workers was always controversial, and when in 1881 President James A. Garfield was mortally wounded by a madman enraged about not being given a government

Table 8.6
GOVERNMENT EMPLOYEES, IN THOUSANDS

	NUMBER OF CIVILIAN FEDERAL EMPLOYEES	FEDERAL BUDGET AS A PERCENTAGE OF THE GNP	STATE AND LOCAL GOVERNMENT EMPLOYEES[a]	TOTAL NUMBER OF GOVERNMENT EMPLOYEES	FEDERAL EMPLOYEES AS A PERCENTAGE OF TOTAL GOVERNMENT EMPLOYEES
1816	4	NA	NA	NA	NA
1871	51	NA	NA	NA	NA
1901	239	NA	NA	NA	NA
1931	610	NA	NA	NA	NA
1942	2,296	22.1%	5,915	8,211	28.9%
1945	3,816	43.4%	NA	NA	NA
1952	2,601	19.3%	7,105	9,706	26.8%
1957	2,418	17.0%	8,047	10,465	30.0%
1962	2,514	18.6%	9,388	11,902	21.1%
1967	3,002	19.3%	11,867	14,869	25.3%
1972	2,608	19.0%	13,759	16,367	15.9%
1977	2,724	20.6%	15,459	18,183	15.0%
1982	2,733	23.6%	15,841	18,574	14.7%
1987	3,091	22.2%	16,933	20,024	15.4%
1988	3,123[b]	21.9%	NA	NA	NA

[a] Includes school employees. In 1987, 41.9 percent of all state and local employees worked in education.

[b] About 11 percent of all federal employees worked in Washington, D.C.; the rest are distributed throughout the country and across the world.

Source: Adapted from data in Stanley and Niemi, *Vital Statistics on American Politics,* 2nd ed.

post, public opinion galvanized to demand reform. Two years later the **Pendleton Act** was passed, creating a **civil service** based on the British model. The civil service originally applied to only about 10 percent of all government employees, but gradually more and more positions were brought under the civil service or some other kind of protective system, until now over 90 percent of all government civilian employees are covered by a **merit system**.

The merit system requires that applicants for government jobs or promotions take examinations administered by the **Office of Personnel Management (OPM)**. The three receiving the highest total scores (additional points are added to the test scores of veterans) are placed on a list, and the hiring agency may choose the candidate it prefers. It should be pointed out, however, that the merit system is not completely free from bias. In order to be able to hire people of proven ability, department heads are sometimes allowed to write job descriptions and qualifications statements in such a way as to assure that only one person can qualify for the position. When this prerogative is abused, civil servants are allowed to promote their friends. This practice is often referred to as "the buddy system."[46]

Government jobs are rated by a standard called the general service schedule, which has 18 levels. Applicants for jobs at the upper reaches of the general service schedule do not take examinations, however. Instead, they submit résumés of their experience and qualifications, and interview for the positions just as one would in the private sector. Most of these positions require technical skills and professional training, for example, as scientists, economists, physicians, or attorneys.

Only about 60 percent of the government jobs are subject to the OPM administration, however. The bulk of the others—postal service jobs, FBI positions, and foreign service posts, for example—are governed by merit systems run by those agencies. People protected by the merit system, after serving a brief probationary period, may be fired only for cause (incompetence, insubordination, or malfeasance), and strict rules of seniority protect them in cases of lay-offs.

The merit systems were augmented in 1939 and 1940 by the **Hatch Acts**. These laws prohibit federal government employees, and state and local employees whose salaries are paid by federal money, from engaging in most political activities except for voting. These limitations have long been controversial; in 1990 Congress passed a law relaxing some of the prohibitions on political activity by government employees. The law, however, was vetoed by President Bush. Hence, federal employees continue to be insulated from political pressure, but they are also severely restricted as to the political activities in which they may engage.

The merit system was designed to protect government employees from undue political pressure, and it has generally enhanced the professionalism of the bureaucracy by assuring that qualified people obtain and hold government jobs. These advantages have not come without cost, however. Protected workers are extremely difficult to fire even when they are unproductive, and it is said that government employees are like headless nails—once in, they cannot be gotten out. Indeed, only about one-seventh of 1 percent of all federal employees protected by the merit system are dismissed each year.[47] While it is desirable to protect government employees from political influence, this system also creates a dilemma in that the government is staffed by people who are largely independent of the president and the administration; thus they are sometimes not as responsive to the political leaders as might be wished.

POLITICS OF THE BUREAUCRACY

There is a natural tendency toward growth and permanence in all bureaucracies, government or private. Almost any job, Parkinson's Law tells us, can be so ordered as to consume all the time that people have to complete it. There is always one more source to read, interview to conduct, or report to write. Hence, bureaucracies are perpetually understaffed and constantly requesting more workers. Superiors share their subordinates' interest in increasing staff because often the importance of a given office, agency, or department is judged by its size. Furthermore, the larger the staff of a given department, the more people there are to advocate (lobby) for its perpetuation. It is very difficult to eliminate an agency when the result is large-scale unemployment.

The same dynamic causes bureaucracies to become top-heavy, and the ratio of chief to Indians tends to increase through time. The department head becomes more secure if the number of her or his assistants grows, and assistants become more secure when they supervise their own assistants, clerks, and clerical people. Also, bureaucracies tend to be expansionist or imperialist. Just as the number of staff employed tends to increase an agency's security, so too does the number of issues with which it deals. Hence, agency leaders are constantly on the lookout for ways to expand the role—and the staff—of the agency. This expansionism often results in duplication, with several agencies being involved in aspects of the same issue, thus causing confusion and defeating the particularization of role that is supposed to be the hallmark of bureaucracy in the first place.

Bureaucracies also tend to become increasingly conservative the longer they exist. Knowledge is power, and bureaucrats tend to try to increase their power by monopolizing information and procedures critical to the institution's function. Two basic phenomena result from this specialization: (1) Individual bureaucrats tend to refuse to do tasks that fall outside of their narrowly written job descriptions (how many times have you been frustrated by going to a large institution with a problem, and being sent from office to office in search of the person who handles such matters?); and (2) bureaucrats are resistant to proposed changes in their roles because change threatens their monopoly on the information and procedures that make their jobs secure. The same conservatism tends to discourage innovation in job performance, and CYA (cover your— "area") is the guiding principle for staff when controversy arises.[48]

Politics of the Federal Bureaucracy Each of the principles mentioned above applies equally to bureaucracies in the private as well as the public sectors. Several factors, however, are unique to government bureaucracies. Congress and the president often prefer creating new agencies to either adding roles to existing agencies or dissolving agencies altogether. When the political leaders wish to give special emphasis to an endeavor—space exploration, for example—it is often a better idea to create an independent agency such as the National Aeronautics and Space Administration (NASA) than to add the function to an established government department whose bureaucrats may be unwilling to give it the attention the politicians desire. Therefore, the tendency of bureaucratic growth is exacerbated in government. By the same token, eliminating an agency is difficult, and perhaps politically risky. So, once created, government agencies tend to endure. This is so because bureaucracies become wedded to certain members of Congress and constituent groups who have an interest in their preservation.

Federal bureaucrats naturally cultivate relationships with people who share their interest in their agency's preservation. Members of Congress whose constituents benefit from an agency's programs are prone to assuring the existence and funding of the agency. Similarly, private interest groups organize to support agencies that service them. Several departments in government (the Department of Defense, the Department of Veterans' Affairs, the Agriculture Department, the Department of Labor, and the Transportation Department, for example) are particularly close to clients among the population. You will recall that powerful alliances called **iron triangles** are forged among certain government agencies, certain pressure groups, and certain congressional personnel. These **subgovernments**, as they are also sometimes called, can be formidable in supporting legislation, budget requests, and appropriations.

An excellent example of the resilience of an agency long after it might have been expected to have dissolved is the *Rural Electrification Administration (REA)*. In the 1930s, only 12 percent of the rural population of the United States had electric or telephone services. The New Deal created the REA to bring these services to the farmers, and the REA did the work well since all rural areas have enjoyed electricity and phone service for decades now. Yet, the REA continues to exist and to receive generous appropriations. While it still helps poor farmers by giving low-interest loans to rural utility companies, many of the areas profiting from the REA subsidies are posh resorts and suburban locations that could well afford to pay the market rate for utilities.

Sustaining the REA is an alliance of powerful congressional personnel and private interest groups who fight fiercely for its appropriations. Telephone and electric companies servicing the areas with which the REA deals have well-oiled PACs and lobbyists who work with sympathetic members of Congress on behalf of the REA. Many congressional committee chairs are held by members representing rural districts; foremost among these is Jamie L. Whitten (D-MS), who represents largely rural northern Mississippi. Whitten is chair of the powerful Appropriations Committee of the House, and his support for the REA has been critical to its continued success.[49]

Alliances with Congress and clients also may make certain agencies virtually untouchable by the administration. That is to say, they enjoy such strong support that no president dares reduce their authority or funding. The FBI under J. Edgar Hoover was such an agency. In fact, Hoover himself, who headed the FBI from 1924* to 1972, had such personal power

that presidents were hesitant to remove him even though he had clearly abused his authority on a number of occasions. Obliquely alluding to the secret files containing embarrassing information about public officials that Hoover kept, President Johnson quipped, in response to a question about why he had not fired the FBI director, "Because I would rather have him inside my tent spitting out than outside spitting in."†

With elements in the bureaucracy enjoying such political support by people outside of the executive branch, the president's administration may have difficulty controlling them. Indeed, a number of factors make it difficult for the political leaders to control the bureaucrats. Their job security insulates them not only from political pressure but often also from administrative direction. Also, while the political leaders (presidents and appointees) come and go with the fortunes of electoral politics, the bureaucrats are permanent. Thus, they can frustrate an administration's policies by dragging their heels until a new president is elected whose policies might be more palatable. The transience of political leaders also makes it difficult for them to become knowledgeable enough about their agencies to control subordinates. Department secretaries, undersecretaries, agency directors, and so on, few of whom serve the full length of a president's term, may know little about the agencies they are appointed to lead. Even if they have some expertise in the fields with which their agencies are concerned, they cannot possibly know as much as do the full-time professional staffs who advise them. As a consequence, most political leaders rely upon their staffs for advice and recommendations.[50] This dependence, together with the tendency of agency heads to

---

* From 1924 to 1935 the national police agency was named simply the Bureau of Investigation. In 1935 the name was changed to the Federal Bureau of Investigation (FBI).

† As in Garner's remark about the vice presidency, Johnson actually referred to a different bodily fluid.

become boosters for their departments, causes some observers to question whether the heads are actually in charge. The old British adage expresses the idea well: "Do the ministers run the ministry or do the ministries run the ministers?"

Virtually every modern president has attempted to bring the bureaucracy to his will, but with little success. Most recently, Carter persuaded Congress to pass the *Civil Service Reform Act* of 1978. This bill created the **Senior Executive Service**, which is composed of about 7000 high-ranking bureaucrats who can be placed in or removed from agencies at the president's pleasure. It was hoped that this elite group of administrators would become disinterested and supremely professional bureaucrats whom the president could use to counterbalance other, less responsive, functionaries. The reform does not seem to have made a marked improvement in the bureaucracy's performance, however.

The Civil Service Reform Act also provided independent inspectors general to audit the conduct of government agencies. But this reform also has had disappointing results. Many departments were slow to fill the positions and, at least in the case of HUD, the inspector general was rather timid about calling Congress's attention to the massive improprieties in the department during the Reagan Administration.[51]

Ronald Reagan also tried to tame the bureaucracy. He pledged to reduce the number of government employees and to eliminate the Departments of Energy and Education. In reality, the number of federal employees increased by 341,000 people, and rather than reducing the departments by two, the Cabinet actually increased by one with the addition of the Department of Veterans' Affairs in 1988.

The principal tool of the president for controlling the bureaucracy is the Office of Management and Budget, which studies government agencies' productivity to determine what their budget allocations should be for the next year. Yet OMB's efforts are often frustrated. First of all, as Charles Peters points out, "The OMB might assign 6 or 7 employees to size up a cabinet-level department's budget, but the department will have 450 or 500 budget people whose job it is to keep the OBM from finding out the truth." If, on the other hand, Congress cuts an agency's budget, the bureaucrats may try to make reductions in areas that are most painful to the public, thus igniting political pressure to restore the funds.[52]

One should not, though, become too cynical about the federal bureaucracy. Although its political dynamic makes it ponderous, generally it is staffed with competent personnel who are dedicated to the goals of their agencies. If the wheels of government turn slowly, one can take solace that impetuous policy might be avoided thereby. If the bureaucrats balk at political leadership, consistency in policy may result. If government functionaries have secure jobs, they are at the same time highly skilled, experienced, professional, and immune from political pressure. Still, the difficulty presidents encounter in controlling their subordinates continues to be a problem—one not likely to be resolved to everyone's satisfaction soon. Presidents will have to take the bad with the good, and one might look at the bureaucratic political dynamic as something of an augmentation of the checks and balances.

Obviously, the executive branch is a large and powerful institution. Much smaller, but certainly no less powerful, is the judicial branch of the government, and we should now turn our attention to the courts.

Summary

- With only a few exceptions, until the time of Woodrow Wilson the presidency was dominated by Congress, and the modern presidency dates from the time of Franklin D. Roosevelt.

- Under presidents Lyndon B. Johnson and Richard M. Nixon the office became known as the imperial presidency, but since then Congress has reasserted itself to check the executive.

- Although the formal powers of the presidency are not impressive, Supreme Court support and the president's informal powers combine to make the office formidable. Yet even so, a number of failed presidencies have plagued recent times.

- The presidency has often fallen to the vice president and the Twenty-Fifth Amendment has been used, yet no occasion has arrived to dip further into the presidential succession lineup.

- While often held in contempt historically, the vice presidency has become an important office.

- The administration has greatly expanded since the 1930s, giving the president a large number of aides and organizations to assist in formulating and executing policy.

- As the major executors of policy, the bureaucracy has enormous power, and its independence and efficiency have long been matters of concern.

Notes

1. Quoted in Neal R. Peirce, *The People's President* (New York: Simon and Schuster, 1968), p. 32.

2. Woodrow Wilson, *Congressional Government* (New York: Meridian Edition, 1908), Vol. 1, p. 230. Originally published in 1885.

3. Quoted in Keith Melder, "Creating Candidate Imagery," in Larry J. Sabato ed., *Campaigns and Elections* (Glenview, IL: Scott, Foresman, 1989), p. 10.

4. William E. Binkley, *President and Congress*, 3rd ed. (New York: Vintage Books, 1962), p. 281.

5. See Arthur Schlesinger, Jr., *The Imperial Presidency* (Boston: Houghton Mifflin, 1973).

6. "A Tale of Two Bushes," *Time*, Jan. 7, 1991.

7. Quoted in Louis W. Koenig, *The Chief Executive* (New York: Harcourt Brace Jovanovich, 1960), p. 30.

8. *United States v. Belmont*, 348 U.S. 296 (1937).

9. David Gary Adler, "The Constitution and Presidential Warmaking," *Political Science Quarterly*, 103 (Spring, 1988), 35.

10. Article II, Section 2 of the United States Constitution.

11. Quoted in Joseph Califano, *A Presidential Nation* (New York: Norton, 1976), p. 153.

12. Austin Ranney, "The President and His Party," in Anthony King, ed., *Both Ends of the Avenue* (Washington, DC: American Enterprise Institute, 1983), p. 146.

13. Frank J. Sorauf, *Party Politics in America*, 5th ed. (Boston: Little, Brown, 1984), p. 377.

14. Ranney, p. 146.

15. Richard M. Pious, *The American Presidency* (New York: Basic Books, 1979), p. 134.

16. James W. Davis, *The American Presidency* (New York: Harper & Row, 1987), p. 107.

17. See Richard T. Johnson, *Managing the White House* (New York: Harper & Row, 1974).

18. See Stephen Hess, *Organizing the Presidency* (Washington, DC: The Brookings Institution, 1976). Also see James David Barber, *The Presidential Character*, 3rd ed. (Englewood Cliffs, NJ: Prentice-Hall, 1985), for analysis of the personality traits that affect the presidency.

19. Hedrick Smith, *The Power Game* (New York: Random House, 1988), p. 463.

20. Jack Nelson, "Conservatives Wielding Influence in the White House," *The Los Angeles Times*, Nov. 6, 1989.

21. Quoted in Robert L. Jackson, "Influence Peddling Grows, Deaver Prosecution Charges," *The Los Angeles Times*, Dec. 18, 1987.

22. Quoted in Ruth Marcus, "Meese Scored in Internal Report by Justice Dept.," *The Los Angeles Times*, Jan. 17, 1989.

23. Daniel M. Weintraub and Melissa Healy, "Scandal's Roots Traced to Basic Reagan Policy Goals," *The Los Angeles Times*, Aug. 4, 1988.

24. Douglas Frantz and Dan Morain, "Playing Favorites at HUD: Latest Twist on Old Game," *The Los Angeles Times*, July 30, 1989.

25. Quoted in Michael J. Ybarra, "Kemp Pledges to Halt GOP Influence Peddling," *The Los Angeles Times*, Aug. 9, 1989.

26. "Special Prosecutor Assails Thornburgh," *The Los Angeles Times*, Oct. 17, 1989.

27. David Lauter, "Sununu Travel Policy Violations Cited in Report," *The Los Angeles Times*, May 10, 1991.

28. Section 4 of the Twenty-fifth Amendment.

29. From a lecture given by Professor Schlesinger at MiraCosta College in May of 1987.

30. Joseph E. Kallenback, *The American Chief Executive* (New York: Harper & Row, 1966), p. 200.

31. Quoted in Davis, pp. 397–398.

32. Paul C. Light, *Vice Presidential Power: Advice and Influence in the White House* (Baltimore: Johns Hopkins University Press, 1984), p. 131.

33. William Safire, quoted in Davis, p. 409.

34. James Gerstenzang, "Bush Says He'd Keep Quayle on the Ticket in '92," *The Los Angeles Times*, Nov. 5, 1989.

35. David Lauter, "Focus Now Seen Shifting to Quayle," *The Los Angeles Times*, May 5, 1991.

36. Quoted in Davis, p. 404.

37. Charles Peters, *How Washington Really Works* (Reading, MA: Addison-Wesley, 1980), p. 124.

38. Peters, p. 123.

39. Nelson.

40. Hedrick Smith, *The Power Game* (New York: Random House, 1988), p. 352.

41. Davis, p. 218.

42. Davis, pp. 404–407.

43. Ronald J. Ostrow and Douglas Frantz, "FBI Once Planned to Push Pierce as Rival to King," *The Los Angeles Times*, Aug. 29, 1989.

44. Stephen Hess, *Organizing the Presidency* (Washington, DC: Brookings Institution, 1976), pp.16–17, and Smith, p. 307.

45. Sara Fritz, "Congress OKs Content Curbs on Arts Funding," *Los Angeles Times*, Oct. 8, 1989.

46. Peters, pp. 47–48.

47. Peters, p. 47.

48. Peters, pp. 5 and 36.

49. David Lauter, "REA's Tenacity Shows Why Some Government Programs Never Die," *The Los Angeles Times*, Oct. 1, 1989.

50. See Hugo Heclo, *A Government of Strangers* (Washington, DC: Brookings Institution, 1977).

51. William J. Eaton, "HUD Refused to Act on Abuses, Agency Official Says," *The Los Angeles Times*, July 1, 1989.

52. Peters, p. 40.

Suggestions for Further Reading

Barber, James David. *The Presidential Character: Predicting Performance in the White House* (3rd ed.). Englewood Cliffs, NJ: Prentice-Hall, 1985.

Barger, Harold M. *The Impossible Presidency.* Glenview, IL: Scott, Foresman, 1984.

Bernstein, Carl, and Bob Woodward. *All the President's Men.* New York: Simon & Schuster, 1974.

Binkley, William E. *President and Congress* (3rd ed.). New York: Vintage Books, 1962.

Bryner, Gary S. *Bureaucratic Discretion.* New York: Pergamon, 1987.

Burke, John P. *Bureaucratic Responsibility.* Baltimore: Johns Hopkins University Press, 1986.

Califano, Joseph. *A Presidential Nation.* New York: Norton, 1976.

Corwin, Edward S. *The President: Office and Powers.* New York: New York University Press, 1948.

Crispell, Kenneth R., and Carlos F. Gomez. *Hidden Illness in the White House.* Durham: Duke University Press, 1988.

Cronin, Thomas E. *The State of the Presidency* (2nd ed.). Boston: Little, Brown, 1980.

Davis, James W. *The American Presidency.* New York: Harper & Row, 1987.

Goodsell, Charles T. *The Case for Bureaucracy* (2nd ed.). Chatham, NJ: Chatham House, 1985.

Heclo, Hugo. *A Government of Strangers.* Washington, DC: Brookings Institution, 1977.

Hess, Stephen. *Organizing the Presidency.* Washington, DC: Brookings Institution, 1976.

Johnson, Richard T. *Managing the White House.* New York: Harper & Row, 1974.

Jordan, Hamilton. *Crisis: The Last Year of the Carter Presidency.* New York: Putnam, 1982.

Kernell, Samuel. *Going Public: New Strategies of Presidential Leadership.* Washington, DC: Congressional Quarterly Press, 1986.

King, Anthony. *Both Ends of the Avenue.* Washington, DC: American Enterprise Institute, 1983.

Knott, Jack H., and Gary J. Miller. *Reforming Bureaucracy: The Politics of Institutional Choice.* Englewood Cliffs, NJ: Prentice-Hall, 1987.

Koenig, Louis. *The Chief Executive* (4th ed.). New York: Harcourt Brace Jovanovich, 1981.

Lewis, Eugene. *American Politics in a Bureaucratic Age: Citizens, Constituents, Clients and Victims.* Cambridge, MA: Winthrop, 1977.

Light, Paul C. *Vice Presidential Power: Advice and Influence in the White House.* Baltimore: Johns Hopkins University Press, 1984.

Lowi, Theodore J. *The Personal President: Power Invested, Promise Unfulfilled.* Ithaca: Cornell University Press, 1985.

Mayer, Jane, and Doyle McManus. *Landslide: The Unmaking of the President 1984–1988.* Boston: Houghton Mifflin, 1988.

Mazmanian, Daniel A., and Paul A. Sabatier. *Implementation and Public Policy.* Glenview, IL: Scott, Foresman, 1983.

McConnell, Grant. *The Modern Presidency.* New York: St. Martin's Press, 1976.

Meier, Kenneth J. *Politics and the Bureaucracy* (2nd ed.). Monterey, CA: Brooks/Cole, 1987.

Neustadt, Richard E. *Presidential Power: The Politics of Leadership from FDR to Carter.* New York: Wiley, 1980.

Peirce, Neal R. *The People's President.* New York: Simon and Schuster, 1968.

Pious, Richard M. *The American Presidency.* New York: Basic Books, 1979.

Pressman, Jeffrey, and Aaron Wildavsky. *Implementation* (3rd ed.). Berkeley: University of California Press, 1984.

Reedy, George E. *The Twilight of the Presidency.* New York: New American Library, 1970.

Rossiter, Clinton. *The American Presidency* (Rev. ed.). New York: Harcourt Brace Jovanovich, 1960.

Rourke, Francis E. *Bureaucracy, Politics, and Public Policy* (3rd ed.). Boston: Little, Brown, 1984.

Schlesinger, Arthur, Jr. *The Imperial Presidency.* Boston: Houghton Mifflin, 1973.

Seidman, Harold, and Robert S. Gilmour. *Politics, Position, and Power* (4th ed.). New York: Oxford University Press, 1986.

Sickels, Robert J. *The Presidency.* Englewood Cliffs, NJ: Prentice-Hall, 1980.

———. *Presidential Transactions.* Englewood Cliffs, NJ: Prentice-Hall, 1974.

Sorauf, Frank J. *Party Politics in America* (5th ed.). Boston: Little, Brown, 1984.

Speakes, Larry, with Robert Pack. *Speaking Out: Inside the Reagan White House.* New York: Scribner's, 1988.

Thatcher, Charles C. *The Creation of the Presidency, 1775–1789.* Baltimore: Johns Hopkins University Press, 1922.

Wilson, James Q. *The Politics of Regulation.* New York: Basic Books, 1980.

Wilson, Woodrow. *Congressional Government.* New York: Meridian Edition, 1908.

Chapter 9

THE JUDICIARY

PREVIEW

The American legal system is based on the common law that developed in medieval England. Its major principles protect the individual from government abuse through the presumption of innocence and the grand and petit jury systems. The major governing authority in the common law is the power of higher courts to bind subordinate courts to their interpretations of law through establishing precedent. The criminal and civil laws are adjudicated through the adversarial system, which pits prosecution or plaintiff against defendant in the hope that justice will result.

The federal courts are distinguished by the auspices under which they were created by Congress: Legislative courts exercise authority under Article I, and constitutional courts are created pursuant to Article III of the Constitution. United States District Courts hear most cases under original jurisdiction, while the appellate courts review decisions from the lower courts. The Supreme Court has some limited original jurisdiction, but most of its time is spent on appeals cases. Most federal judges are appointed to life terms by the president with Senate confirmation. Although qualifications, gender, and ethnicity are considered in selecting nominees, partisanship is the most important criterion applied by most presidents. Filling seats on the bench probably constitutes the most important type of appointment in the government because the process creates an entirely different branch of government and because the appointments are for life terms.

The Supreme Court began its career rather timidly, but at the beginning of the nineteenth century, Chief Justice John Marshall made the Court a major player in the government by establishing the power of judicial review. Since that time the Court has exercised enormous influence over society, especially when taking an activist posture rather than a restrained stance.

In the 1950s and 1960s the Warren Court employed activist decisions in frontal assaults on racial bigotry, official abuse of individual rights, and unequal representation in the political system. Although the Burger Court limited somewhat the rights of people accused of crimes, it continued to protect the civil rights and it expanded the rights of women. The appointments in the 1980s gave the Court a distinct conservative cast, and the Rehnquist Court has begun to nibble away at several Warren Court opinions, even as it has become restrained relative to the actions of the other two branches.

The Supreme Court follows a rigorous tradition governing its procedure. Following the lawyers' arguments in court, the justices discuss the merits of the case in conference, write opinions, and then announce them in open court. The Court's interpretations are brought only after adherence to long-standing and rigorous standards. Regardless of how it makes decisions, however, the power and authority of the Supreme Court depends on its ability to produce opinions that are consistent with dominant forces in the society.

The Constitution will endure as a vital charter of human liberty as long as there are those with the courage to defend it, the vision to interpret it and the fidelity to live by it.

William J. Brennan, Jr.

The American Legal System

American law is based on the English legal tradition known as the **common law.** Reaching far back into Anglo-Saxon history, the common law is based on a series of rules and procedures established by judges over time. At first the judge-made law (**case law**) constituted the bulk of the jurisprudence in England, and its principles were set down by judges in treaties. Gradually, however, most of the principles of the common law were superseded by *statutes* (laws passed by legislatures), although the common law is still important in federal and state courts.*

The common law places special emphasis on individual justice and on protecting the individual from state abuse. In this regard two factors are most important. To begin with, someone accused of a crime is to be presumed *innocent until proved guilty.* Since the state prosecutes defendants in criminal law, the enjoinder of presumed innocence is a major check on the power of the government; because the burden of proof rests with the state, the defendant need not prove innocence. The second check against the state in favor of the individual is found in the *jury system.*

The common law developed two juries: the grand jury and the petit jury. In each case, a panel of ordinary citizens is interjected between the defendant and the state. The Constitution provides that defendants in federal criminal cases may not be brought to trial in a federal court unless they are indicted by a **grand jury.**[1] Federal grand juries are convened by the federal district court. The United States Attorney presents evidence to the jury and asks it to indict defendants. If the jury is persuaded that enough evidence exists that a defendant may be guilty of a crime, it hands down a true bill of indictment, thus authorizing a trial. The **petit jury** is the trial jury. Impaneled from a list of ordinary citizens, the jury hears the evidence and arguments presented by the attorneys for the prosecution and the defense, and then renders a verdict of guilty or not guilty. If the jury convicts the defendant, she or he is sentenced by the judge. Thus, defendants are protected from government abuse at two stages in the criminal procedure. Not only can the government not convict defendants unless the petit jury finds them guilty, but the government cannot even bring a defendant to trial unless the grand jury authorizes it. Of course, defendants may, if they wish, waive a jury trial, in which case the trial judge hands down the verdict.

It must be quickly noted that the grand jury system is controversial. Long since abandoned by the British legal system that spawned it, grand juries in this country are often accused of being pawns for prosecuting attorneys, bringing indictments against whomever they are asked to indict. In other instances, a "runaway" grand jury might ignore the counsel of its legal advisers and bring indictments not sought by

---

* All states except Louisiana recognize the common law to one extent or another. Louisiana uses a different system based upon the Napoleonic Codes, which is also used by most countries in Continental Europe and Latin America.

the prosecution. Furthermore, a person summoned to appear before a grand jury has no right to know the nature of the grand jury's investigation and no right to the presence of an attorney.[2]

Another critical feature of the common law is the principle of *stare decisis* (stand by the things decided) or **precedent**. Essentially, precedent gives discipline, stability, and historical control of the law. When a judge of a high court interprets the law in a particular way, precedent is established and all lower courts within the high court's jurisdiction must apply the law in the same fashion. When the United States Supreme Court, the nation's highest tribunal, establishes precedent (*Plessy* v. *Ferguson* approving segregation, and *Brown* v. *Board of Education* reversing it, for example), all other courts are bound to its interpretation.

Precedent gives consistency and a degree of certainty to common law systems. The precedents established in case law make clear what is legal and what is not. Indeed, "settled law" is of paramount importance to some judges. No less a light than Associate Justice Louis Brandeis held that consistency in the law was even more important than justice, if justice can be achieved through legislation:

> *Stare decisis* is usually the wise policy, because in most matters it is more important that the applicable rule of law be settled than that it be settled right. . . . This is commonly true even where the error is a matter of serious concern, provided correction can be had by legislation.[3]

The stability of the law, however, is also a matter of concern. Some critics argue that it is too rigid and resistant to change. Whatever the case, the common law system features precedent as one of its most fundamental principles, and a large measure of attorneys' work is to find precedents that sustain their clients' positions and to persuade judges that the favored interpretations should be used in adjudicating cases.

THE KINDS OF LAW IN SOCIETY

Essentially there are two kinds of law within the common law system: criminal law and civil law. **Criminal law** applies when someone is accused of violating the rights of society as a whole. In this case, the defendant is prosecuted by the government: society's agent. Serious crimes (rape, aggravated assault, armed robbery, murder) are called **felonies** and can bring heavy fines, imprisonment in a penitentiary, or even the death sentence. **Misdemeanors** (disturbing the peace, petty theft, traffic violations) are less serious crimes and are punishable by shorter periods of incarceration and lighter fines. **Civil cases** involve disputes between individuals in matters where the rights of society are not involved. Parties in civil cases can be persons, corporations, or governments, and civil cases take the form of lawsuits in which juries decide the matter. Among the most common types of civil suits are torts and cases in equity. A **tort** is a suit asking financial payment as remedy for a wrong. If someone damages the property or the person of another, for example, and the matter is not resolved privately, the **plaintiff** brings suit against the defendant, asking the court to award an amount to satisfy the aggrieved party.

A single act could result in both criminal and civil cases. If a building contractor is negligent about safety on the job and a crane collapses, killing people and damaging property, the contractor can be tried by the state for criminal negligence and sued by injured parties for the damage caused them.

The common law as developed in England was found unable to give remedy in certain cases, so justice was not always being done. Consequently, **equity** was developed to justly

Chapter 9 The Judiciary

settle disputes that the letter of the common law would not resolve adequately. For example, the common law is usually concerned with awarding remedy *after* damage has been done. Equity, on the other hand, can be used to secure satisfaction *before* damage actually occurs. Today, equity is used to dissolve contracts, including divorce, and also to petition the court to enjoin someone, thus halting an action that could do harm or to order recalcitrant individuals to do something that they are legally obliged to do.

The approach used to resolve criminal and civil disputes is called the **adversarial system**. The theory behind this format is that the truth will be best served if the lawyers on each side of a case present arguments and interrogate witnesses. Trial judges do not usually participate in the contest. Their task is to interpret the law, to assure that the rights of each party are protected, to instruct the jury as to the application of the law, and to issue the appropriate judgment or sentence.

The United States is a litigious society. In 1988 about 25 million cases were brought in the state courts, and almost 270,000 cases were filed in federal district courts.[4] Indeed, our reliance on court decisions is not new. It was recognized early in the nineteenth century by de Tocqueville when, in *Democracy in America,* he wrote, "Scarcely any political question arises in the United States that is not resolved, sooner or later, into a judicial question." As de Tocqueville noted, the courts are essential to the fabric of American political society. Understanding which courts serve society and what their interrelationships are is important to our understanding of the judiciary.

Structure of the Judiciary

In the United States the state governments and the national government each have complete court structures. Because of the supremacy clause in the Constitution,[5] state law and state courts are subordinate to the federal courts when the federal Constitution, federal treaties, or federal statutes become involved in the cases they hear. If a state court decides a case in which a federal law or treaty is involved, an appeal of that decision may be taken to the United States Supreme Court. The ability of the United States Supreme Court to be the final arbiter of state courts' interpretations of federal law is essential if cohesion and consistency are to be maintained within the country. Indeed, Justice Oliver Wendell Holmes held that such decisions are among the court's most critical functions. "I do not think the United States would come to an end if we lost the power to declare an act of Congress void," Holmes wrote. "I do think the Union would be imperiled if we could not make that declaration as to the laws of the several states."[6]

FEDERAL COURT STRUCTURE

Basically there are two sets of criteria that distinguish two categories of federal courts: constitutional and legislative courts, and courts of original and appellate jurisdiction. **Constitutional courts** are those established under the authority of Article III of the Constitution. Article III mentions only the Supreme Court by name, but it authorizes Congress to establish any other subordinate federal courts to exercise "the judicial Power of the United States." Besides the Supreme Court, the constitutional courts include United States Courts of Appeal and the United States District Courts. The **legislative courts** (or special courts) are established by Congress pursuant to its authority in Article I of the Constitution. While their rulings are as binding as those of the constitutional courts, their jurisdiction is limited to the fields in which Congress invests them. They include the United States Court of Appeals for the Federal Circuit, located in Washington,

D.C.; the United States District Courts for Guam, the Virgin Islands, and the Northern Mariana Islands; the United States Claims Court; the United States Court of International Trade; the United States Tax Court; the United States Court of Military Appeals; and the Administrative Law Judges.*

The second distinction among federal courts is based on their jurisdiction. Some courts, including the district courts and the court of claims, have **original jurisdiction**. This means that they are trial courts and hear cases when they are first brought to court. The Court of International Trade, the Tax Court, and the Administrative Law Judges also hear cases for the first time, but these cases are reviews of judgments made by administrative agencies. Cases decided in the courts of original jurisdiction may be taken for review to the courts with **appellate jurisdiction**, including the Courts of Appeal, the Court of Military Appeal, and the Supreme Court. The Supreme Court is primarily an appeals court, but it also has original jurisdiction over a small number of cases. This will be dealt with in detail later. (See Figure 9.1.)

COURT JURISDICTIONS

The legislative courts normally have very narrow fields in which they may function. The Court of Military Appeals is composed of 3 civilian judges and rules on military law in

* Actually, the Tax Court, the Military Appeals Court, and the Administrative Law judges are technically not part of the judiciary. Instead, the Tax Court is attached to the Treasury Department, the Military Appeals Court is found in the Defense Department, and over 1,000 Administrative Law judges are employed by various agencies such as the Department of Health and Human Services, the National Labor Relations Board, and the Occupational Safety and Health Review Commission.

reviews of cases from court-martials. The Tax Court, with 16 judges, hears cases arising from disputes over taxes. The 9 judges of the Court of International Trade hear cases involving tariffs and customs. The Claims Court, with 16 judges, tries cases arising over contract and damage disputes with the federal government.

Two kinds of legislative courts are unique because they deal with very broad varieties of law. The Territorial District Courts of Guam, the Virgin Islands, and the Northern Mariana Islands exercise the same function as other district courts over federal law, but they also hear cases arising from local laws within their territories. The United States Court of Appeals for the Federal Circuit hears appeals from the District Court of Washington, D.C.; it also hears appeals from rulings of the independent regulatory boards and commissions and challenges to rulings on trademarks, patents, and copyrights. This broad jurisdiction causes some observers to consider this court second in power only to the Supreme Court.

Unlike most legislative courts, the constitutional courts engage in a wide variety of legal cases. There are 89 district courts throughout the country, with each state having at least 1, and the largest states having as many as 5. There is also a District Court for Washington, D.C., and another for Puerto Rico. Several judges are assigned to each district court, and the president also appoints United States attorneys and marshals to serve in the courts' jurisdictions. The district court judges also appoint federal magistrates who perform many of the pretrial tasks, issue warrants and officiate at preliminary hearings. Additionally, Bankruptcy Courts, with judges appointed by the appellate courts, are attached to the district courts. Their judgments on bankruptcy proceedings may be appealed to the district court itself.

The district courts are the major federal trial courts in the country. Cases coming to them under original jurisdiction are presided

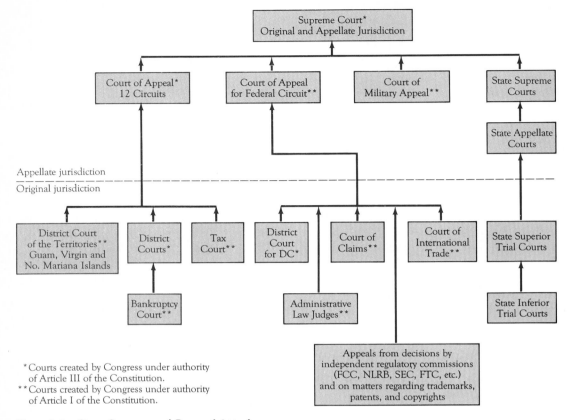

Figure 9.1   *Court Structure and Route of Appeals*

*Courts created by Congress under authority of Article III of the Constitution.
**Courts created by Congress under authority of Article I of the Constitution.

over by a single judge, and a jury is impaneled to decide the verdict. It is here that people get the first airing of their disputes in federal court.

There are 12 Circuit Courts of Appeal into which the 50 states are divided. Appellate court hearings are quite different from the trial court procedures. Appeals are heard by a panel of three judges; no juries, witnesses, or litigants are present. The ambience is subdued and the arguments are less dramatic. Usually the facts of the case are not discussed. Rather, precedent and the interpretation of the law absorb the lawyers and judges. When the court makes its decisions, it usually renders opinions explaining its reasoning in the cases. Appellate court

opinions are usually final. One may appeal a case to the Supreme Court, but only a small number of appeals are accepted by the nation's highest court. The procedure of the Supreme Court is unique and will be examined in detail later.

Appointing Judges

Judges in the United States are highly revered. Their positions are prestigious not only because of their responsibility to be just and scholarly, but also because the common law system entrusts judges with establishing precedents that may change the course of the law for all time. Unfortunately, the salaries offered federal judges have not kept pace with the salaries judges could earn in other pursuits. Hence, it is increasingly difficult to find qualified candidates for the bench, even as disgruntled federal jurists are resigning to enter lucrative private practices.[7]

Federal judges are appointed to life-long terms by the president, with confirmation of the Senate. There are no qualifications for federal judges listed in the Constitution, and although it is informally understood that judges must first have been attorneys, Congress has legislated no criteria for the occupants of the bench. A number of considerations go into choosing judges besides their qualifications. Several presidents have been interested in ethnicity, for example, but only Jimmy Carter was firmly committed to appointing minorities to the bench. Carter was also alone in the depth of commitment to appointing women to federal judgeships, since only 8 women were appointed to the federal courts before his time. Most federal judges are males, from white, middle-class, Protestant backgrounds, who practiced in medium (5 to 24 lawyers) to large (above 24 lawyers) law firms. Previous judicial experience is also a factor, especially for higher court appointees.

Perhaps the most important criterion for selecting judicial appointees, however, is partisanship. No president in this century has given more than 19 percent of his judicial appointments to people from parties other than his own, and most presidents have given more than 90 percent of their judicial appointments to people from their party. (For recent examples, see Table 9.1.) Presidents also usually try to appoint people to the bench who share their ideological convictions. Ronald Reagan was especially careful to appoint judges who agreed with his views on such issues as allowing prayer in the public schools and opposing abor-

tion. The effort to assure ideological conformity has not always been successful, however. Felix Frankfurter was more conservative than Franklin D. Roosevelt expected, Dwight D. Eisenhower was surprised by the liberalism of Chief Justice Earl Warren and Associate Justice William J. Brennan, and Harry Blackmun was much more liberal than Richard M. Nixon anticipated.

The data from Table 9.1 indicate that the five presidents included were partisan in making judicial appointments, with Ford being the least so and Reagan the most so. Carter was the least concerned about appointing people with prior judicial experience, perhaps in part because of his wish to elevate women and minorities to the bench. Republicans appointed greater percentages of whites and Protestants, while Jews, Catholics, ethnic minorities, and women had a better chance of being appointed by Democrats.

Presidents are very careful about appointing Supreme Court justices. Most Supreme Court justices have come from white, middle-class, Anglo-Saxon, Protestant backgrounds and have been graduates of the finest law

At work in her chambers, Federal Judge Norma Johnson is flanked by her law clerks.

Table 9.1
Characteristics of Appointees to the Federal Bench, 1963–1988

	L. Johnson (D)		Nixon (R)		Ford (R)		Carter (D)		Reagan (R)	
	Dist.	App.	Dist.	App.	Dist.	App.	Dist.	App.	Dist.	App.
Occupation										
Judiciary	31.1%	57.5%	28.5%	53.3%	34.6%	75.0%	44.6%	46.4%	37.2%	55.1%
Large law firm	2.5%	5.0%	11.2%	4.4%	9.6%	8.3%	13.9%	10.7%	17.6%	12.8%
Medium law firm	18.9%	17.5%	27.9%	22.2%	25.0%	8.3%	19.8%	16.1%	19.3%	10.3%
Political affiliation										
The president's party	94.3%	95.0%	92.7%	93.3%	78.8%	91.7%	92.6%	82.1%	93.4%	97.4%
Other party	5.7%	5.0%	7.3%	6.7%	21.2%	8.3%	4.4%	7.1%	4.8%	0.0%
Religion										
Protestant	58.2%	60.0%	73.2%	75.6%	73.1%	58.3%	60.4%	60.7%	60.0%	55.1%
Catholic	31.1%	25.0%	18.4%	15.6%	17.3%	33.3%	27.7%	23.2%	30.4%	30.8%
Jewish	10.7%	15.0%	8.4%	8.9%	9.6%	8.3%	11.9%	16.1%	9.3%	14.1%
Ethnicity										
White	93.4%	95.0%	95.5%	97.8%	88.5%	100.0%	78.7%	78.6%	92.4%	97.4%
African-American	4.1%	5.0%	3.4%	0.0%	5.8%	0.0%	13.9%	16.1%	2.1%	1.3%
Hispanic-American	2.5%	0.0%	1.1%	0.0%	1.9%	0.0%	6.9%	3.6%	4.8%	1.3%
Gender										
Women	1.6%	2.5%	0.6%	0.0%	1.9%	0.0%	14.4%	19.6%	8.3%	5.1%
Age										
Average age at nomination	51.4	52.2	49.1	53.8	49.2	52.1	49.7	51.9	48.7	50.0
Total appointments	122	40	179	45	52	12	202	56	290	78

Source: Based on data from Sheldon Goldman, "Reagan's Judicial Legacy: Completing the Puzzle and Summing Up," *Judicature* (April–May 1989), 321–325.

schools. President Carter is the only president in the twentieth century not to be able to fill a seat on the Court and the only president ever to serve a full term who did not do so.

Four justices were Jewish, including two of the "greats" (Louis D. Brandeis and Felix Frankfurter), but no current justice is Jewish.

There has long been at least one Catholic on the Court, but currently there are two (Antonin Scalia and Anthony Kennedy). President Johnson appointed Thurgood Marshall, the first African-American on the Supreme Court, and Ronald Reagan appointed the first woman, Sandra Day O'Connor. (See Table 9.2.)

Table 9.2

RATING OF SUPREME COURT JUSTICES AND A LISTING OF THE PRESIDENTS WHO APPOINTED THEM, THROUGH 1990

GREAT

JUSTICE	TERM	PRESIDENT
J. Marshall[a]	1801–1835	J. Adams
Story	1811–1845	Madison
Taney[a,b]	1836–1864	Jackson[c]
Harlan I[d]	1877–1911	Hayes
Holmes	1902–1932	T. Roosevelt
Hughes[e]	1910–1916	Taft[f]
Hughes[a]	1930–1941	Hoover[i]
Brandeis[g]	1916–1939	Wilson[c]
Stone[h]	1925–1941	Coolidge
Cardozo[g]	1932–1938	Hoover[i]
Stone[a,g]	1941–1946	F. Roosevelt[c,j]
Black	1937–1971	F. Roosevelt[c,j]
Frankfurter[k,l]	1939–1962	F. Roosevelt[c,j]
Warren[a]	1953–1969	Eisenhower

NEAR GREAT

JUSTICE	TERM	PRESIDENT
W. Johnson	1804–1834	Jefferson[c]
Curtis	1851–1857	Fillmore
Miller	1862–1890	Lincoln[c]
Field[g]	1863–1897	Lincoln
Bradley	1870–1892	Grant[m]
Waite[a]	1874–1888	Grant[m]
E. D. White[h]	1894–1910	Cleveland (2nd term)
E. D. White[a,g]	1910–1921	Taft[f]
Taft[a]	1921–1930	Harding[m]
Sutherland	1922–1938	Harding[m]

NEAR GREAT

JUSTICE	TERM	PRESIDENT
Douglas	1939–1975	F. Roosevelt[c,j]
R. H. Jackson	1941–1954	F. Roosevelt[c,j]
W. B. Rutledge	1943–1949	F. Roosevelt[c,j]

AVERAGE

JUSTICE	TERM	PRESIDENT
Jay[a]	1789–1795	Washington[c,j]
J. Rutledge[a]	1789–1791	Washington[c,j]
Cushing	1789–1810	Washington[c,j]
Wilson	1789–1798	Washington[c,j]
Blair	1789–1796	Washington[c,j]
Iredell	1790–1799	Washington[c,j]
Paterson	1793–1806	Washington[c,j]
S. Chase	1796–1811	Washington[c,j]
Ellsworth	1796–1800	Washington[c,j]
Washington	1798–1823	J. Adams
Livingston	1806–1823	Jefferson
Todd	1807–1826	Jefferson
Duvall	1811–1835	Madison
Thompson	1823–1843	Monroe
McLean	1829–1861	Jackson
Baldwin	1830–1844	Jackson
Wayne	1835–1867	Jackson
Catron	1837–1865	Van Buren
McKinley	1837–1852	Van Buren
Daniel	1841–1860	Van Buren
Nelson[g]	1845–1877	Tyler
Woodbury	1845–1851	Polk

Table 9.2 (continued)

AVERAGE		
JUSTICE	TERM	PRESIDENT
Grier	1846~1870	Polk
Campbell	1853~1861	Pierce
Clifford	1858~1881	Buchanan
Swayne	1862~1881	Lincoln
Davis	1862~1877	Lincoln
S. P. Chase[a]	1864~1873	Lincoln
Strong	1870~1880	Grant
Hunt	1873~1882	Grant
Matthews	1881~1889	Garfield
Gray	1881~1902	Arthur
Blatchford	1881~1893	Arthur
L. Q. C. Lamar	1883~1893	Cleveland (1st term)
Fuller[a]	1888~1910	Cleveland (1st term)
Brewer	1889~1910	B. Harrison
Brown	1891~1906	B. Harrison
Shiras	1892~1903	B. Harrison
Pekham	1895~1909	Cleveland (2nd term)
McKenna	1898~1925	McKinley
Day	1903~1922	T. Roosevelt
Moody	1906~1910	T. Roosevelt
Lurton[g]	1909~1914	Taft[f]
J. R. Lamar[g]	1910~1916	Taft[f]
Pitney	1912~1922	Taft[f]
J. H. Clarke	1916~1922	Wilson
Sanford	1923~1930	Harding
Roberts	1930~1945	Hoover
Reed	1938~1957	F. Roosevelt[c,j]
Murphy	1940~1949	F. Roosevelt[c,j]
T. C. Clark	1949~1967	Truman
Harlan II[d]	1955~1971	Eisenhower
Brennan[g,n]	1956~1990	Eisenhower
Stewart	1958~1981	Eisenhower
B. R. White	1962~	Kennedy
Goldberg	1962~1965	Kennedy

AVERAGE		
JUSTICE	TERM	PRESIDENT
Fortas[o]	1965~1969	L. Johnson
T. Marshall[p]	1967~1991	L. Johnson

BELOW AVERAGE[f]		
Justice	Term	President
T. Johnson	1791~1793	Washington[c,i]
Moore	1798~1804	J. Adams
Trimble	1826~1828	J. Q. Adams
Barbour	1836~1841	Jackson
Woods	1880~1887	Hayes
H. E. Jackson[g]	1893~1895	B. Harrison

FAILURE[q]		
JUSTICE	TERM	PRESIDENT
VanDevanter	1910~1937	Taft[f]
McReynolds	1914~1941	Wilson
Butler[g]	1923~1939	Harding
Byrnes	1941~1942	F. Roosevelt[c,i]
Burton[g]	1945~1958	Truman[r]
Vinson[a]	1946~1953	Truman[r]
Minton	1949~1956	Truman[r]
Whittaker	1957~1962	Eisenhower

NOT YET RATED		
JUSTICE	TERM	PRESIDENT
Burger[a]	1969~1986	Nixon
Blackmun	1970~	Nixon
Powell[g]	1971~1987	Nixon
Rehnquist[h]	1971~1986	Nixon
Stevens	1976~	Ford
O'Connor[s]	1981~	Reagan
Rehnquist[a]	1986~	Reagan
Scalia	1986~	Reagan
Kennedy	1988~	Reagan
Souter	1990~	Bush

Note: It is interesting to note that New York (13), Ohio (10), and Massachusetts (7) have produced the most justices. In fact, there have been only 24 years in which at least one New Yorker has not been on the

Table 9.2 (continued)

high court. Massachusetts has produced 4 great justices; New York, 3; and Ohio, none, while Alabama, California, Kentucky, Maryland, and Virginia have each produced 1 great justice. A majority of states have produced at least 1 Supreme Court justice, but 19 have not, including Alaska, Arkansas, Delaware, Florida, Hawaii, Idaho, Montana, Nebraska, Nevada, New Mexico, North Dakota, Oklahoma, Oregon, Rhode Island, South Dakota, Vermont, Washington, West Virginia, and Wisconsin. The only two justices appointed from Arizona (Rehnquist and O'Connor) are currently on the bench.

[a] Chief Justice.
[b] First Catholic justice.
[c] Rated as great presidents.
[d] John M. Harlan I was the grandfather of John M. Harlan II.
[e] Hughes was a Supreme Court Associate Justice. He resigned to run for president and was later appointed Chief Justice.
[f] Taft was the least partisan in his appointments. He appointed 3 Republicans and 3 Democrats.
[g] From a political party different from that of the appointing president.
[h] Later promoted to Chief Justice.
[i] Hoover, rated an average president, enjoys the highest marks for Supreme Court appointments. Two of his three appointees are rated as great justices.
[j] Washington appointed the most justices (11); F. Roosevelt was second with 9.
[k] An independent.
[l] First Jewish justice.
[m] Grant and Harding are rated as failed presidents, yet they each appointed two near-great justices.
[n] Brennan is now rated by some authorities as a great justice.
[o] Fortas was later unsuccessfully nominated by L. Johnson for Chief Justice.
[p] First African-American justice.
[q] All justices rated below average were appointed during the seventeenth and nineteenth centuries (6 of 57), while all justices rated as failures (8 of 48) were appointed during the twentieth century.
[r] Truman, an excellent president in many ways, has the worst appointment record. Three of his four appointees, including Chief Justice Vinson, are rated as failures.
[s] First, and as yet the only, woman justice.

Source: Adapted from data in Stanley and Niemi, *Vital Statistics on American Politics,* 2nd ed. Stanley and Niemi used Albert P. Blaustein and Roy M. Mersky, *The First One Hundred Justices* (Hamden, Conn.: Shoe String Press, Archon Books, 1978) for the Supreme Court rating and a 1985 poll by Arthur Schlesinger, Jr., for the presidential rating.

The president also appoints the solicitor general. Attached to the Justice Department, this officer is the government's chief trial attorney, and as such argues its cases before the Supreme Court. Created in 1870, this office has been held by such stellar personages as William Howard Taft (President of the United States and later Chief Justice of the Supreme Court), Charles Evans Hughes (Justice of the Supreme Court, presidential candidate, and Chief Justice of the Supreme Court), John W. Davis (a candidate for president and considered the best solicitor general in history),[8] Robert H. Jackson (later a Justice of the Supreme Court and United States prosecutor of Nazi war criminals at the Nuremberg trials), Archibald Cox (Harvard Law School professor and special prosecutor in the Watergate affair), Thurgood Marshall, and Robert H. Bork (unsuccessful nominee for the Supreme Court and a leading conservative jurist and legal commentator). The prestige of this office is such that the Supreme Court usually hears a case brought to it by the solicitor general.

The Supreme Court

In the early years of the republic, the number of Supreme Court justices was frequently changed by Congress, ranging between five and ten justices. In 1869, however, the membership was set at nine, and so it remains today. The history of the Court can be divided into four, and perhaps five, eras. In its earliest period (1789–1801), the court was a weak and largely ignored institution. In fact, several of its appointees refused to take office, and the first two chief justices resigned to take other, more important positions.

The situation was radically altered when John Marshall became Chief Justice. This second era of the Court lasted until the Civil War. This period was noted for a strong Court that supported a powerful central government and business interests. Setting the tone for the era, the Marshall Court (1801–1835) established **judicial review** (the power of the courts to declare laws and executive actions void when they violate the Constitution) with its landmark case of **Marbury** v. **Madison** (1803).[9] (See Chapter 2 and pages 285–288 in this chapter for a fuller discussion of judicial review.) In other cases, it delineated the relationship between federal and state governments, and supported property and business interests, often at the expense of government and the workers. Although the Court did not declare another federal statute unconstitutional between 1803 and 1857, the Court remained a powerful force in American politics by invalidating certain executive actions and striking down several state laws. In 1857, however, the Court unwisely tried to settle the slave issue by deciding in the **Dred Scott case** that Congress could not prohibit people from taking their slave property wherever they chose and by ruling that free African-Americans could not be citizens of the United States.[10]

Not only was the Civil War a national tragedy, it also represented a crisis for the Court, which stood rebuked by public opinion, and for decades afterwards it was relatively quiescent. While it did assert itself against President Lincoln's Civil War policy of denying *habeas corpus*,[11] it did so only after the war was over and Lincoln was dead. Moreover, the Court was careful not to contradict the Congress, which at the time was ascendant. During its third era (from the Civil War until 1937) the Court remained a minor player until toward the end of the nineteenth century when it once again became active in what Max Lerner called "the strategic link between capitalism and constitutionalism," striking down government regulations of business.[12]

The fourth era of the Court stretches from 1937 to the present. After several years of struggle against the economic policies of the New Deal, the Court switched, supporting the policies of Franklin D. Roosevelt by a narrow majority. It allowed more government regulation of business and, for the first time, became actively concerned for the rights of the individual, ultimately mandating state compliance with the Bill of Rights and using the Ninth Amendment to establish the right of privacy. (See Chapter 3 for a more complete discussion of the Court's advance of the individual liberties).

THE MODERN COURT

As late as the mid-1950s many states segregated schools, hotels, restaurants, housing, drinking fountains, transportation, and other facilities. Almost all states gave disproportionately large numbers of legislative seats to their rural areas, people could be tried and imprisoned without a lawyer if they could not afford one, state authorities could force confessions from hapless suspects, and evidence seized illegally could be used in state courts to obtain convictions. At the same time, women and minorities could be denied jobs because of their sex and race, and abortion and even contraceptive devices could be made illegal. In 1954, however, things began to change rapidly. The Warren Court (1953–1969), according to Archibald Cox, set in motion a "revolution in constitutional law" with its ruling in **Brown** v. **Board of Education.**[13] Suddenly the Court pounded on the walls of bigotry and injustice, and it received support in this endeavor from presidents Eisenhower, Kennedy, and Johnson as well as from a public recently awakened to poverty and social injustice in its midst. The Court required state compliance with the Bill of Rights, thus enlarging the protections of people accused of criminal violations and expanding individual liberties, even as it mandated that legislative districts be composed of equal numbers of people. (See Chapter 3 for a fuller discussion of the Warren Court's rulings.)

By the late 1960s, however, the public mood had shifted; Richard M. Nixon and Spiro T. Agnew were elected in 1968 on a law-and-order platform, with a pledge to appoint judges who would be tough on criminals. This turn of events is ironic since both Nixon and Agnew later resigned their offices in order to avoid impeachment for gross violations of the law. In the meantime, Earl Warren retired. Thus Nixon was able to appoint his own Chief Justice, Warren E. Burger, in 1969, and in the next two years he appointed three other justices: Harry A. Blackmun, Lewis F. Powell, Jr., and William H. Rehnquist. Gerald Ford succeeded Nixon and appointed John Paul Stevens in 1976 to replace William O. Douglas.

In the space of seven years, a majority of the Warren Court had been replaced by appointees of conservative Republican presidents, but the long-awaited reversal of the Warren era decisions did not materialize. Burger proved an ineffectual leader, Powell and Stevens took moderate positions on the Court, and Blackmun gradually became relatively liberal.

The Burger Court was not as sensitive to civil rights as was its predecessor, but it left in

place *Brown* v. *Board of Education* and the apportionment decisions. It was, however, less benign regarding the rights of those accused. While it did not reverse *Miranda* v. *Arizona, Gideon* v. *Wainwright,* or *Mapp* v. *Ohio,* it did create several exceptions to each, giving the police more latitude in dealing with suspected criminals. (See Chapter 3 for a more complete discussion of these issues.) On the other hand, the Burger Court not only sustained affirmative action programs but spoke out on the rights of women, particularly on the issue of abortion, something even the Warren Court had not done.[14]

The conservative mood of the country deepened during the 1970s, and in 1980 the public turned to a president who vowed to restore "traditional American values" and to appoint a judiciary reflecting them. Moderate Potter Stewart's 1981 retirement gave Reagan his chance to fulfill campaign promises to appoint a woman and a conservative to the Supreme Court. His choice, a Rehnquist suggestion, was Sandra Day O'Connor, a brilliant lawyer, politician, and jurist from Arizona. Even though O'Connor had graduated second-highest in her Stanford University Law School class (her friend, William Rehnquist, was at the head of the class), she could not find a job with a prestigious private law firm. After working as a state prosecutor she became an Arizona state senator, and finally a state judge, before being appointed to the United States Supreme Court.

Reagan's next opportunity to influence the Court came in 1986 when Burger retired. Turning to the most conservative member of the Court, Reagan appointed Rehnquist Chief Justice and filled Rehnquist's associate justice seat with Antonin Scalia, a scholarly and conservative professor at the University of Chicago Law School. Then, late in President Reagan's second term, moderate Lewis Powell retired from the bench, and after two failed nominations (to be discussed later), Reagan appointed

Anthony Kennedy, a conservative federal jurist from California.

Until Kennedy's appointment, Rehnquist found it difficult to command the Court. During his first years as Chief Justice, his doctrinaire conservatism frequently led him to the minority side of cases, thus surrendering control of the majority to more liberal justices. Since 1988, however, he seems in control of a rancorous yet conservative majority, and indications are that the Rehnquist Court may be inaugurating a new era of judicial restraint for the Supreme Court.

JUDICIAL RESTRAINT VERSUS JUDICIAL ACTIVISM

Among the most warmly debated issues about the Court is whether it should be restrained or activist in its power to void the laws and executive actions. Advocates of **judicial restraint** maintain that since judges are appointed to life terms and need not submit their records to periodic voter approval, they are aloof from the democratic process and pertinent social, economic, and political trends. Thus, they should be careful not to impose their individual wills on society by overinterpreting the Constitution. The Court, it is reasoned, should invalidate only such laws and actions as are clearly prohibited by the Constitution, and allow the political process to determine other, more ambiguous matters. Arguing for judicial restraint and against the undemocratic nature of judicial activism, Judge Learned Hand wrote:

> For myself it would be most irksome to be ruled by a bevy of Platonic Guardians, even if I knew how to choose them, which I assuredly do not. If they were in charge, I should miss the stimulus of living in a society where I have, at least theoretically, some part in the direction of public affairs. [15]

Judicial restraint has been advocated by some of the Court's most important members, including Oliver Wendell Holmes, Louis Brandeis, Harlan Fiske Stone, and Felix Frankfurter. A Court committed to judicial restraint not only gives the federal and state governments more latitude of action but also tends to refuse certain kinds of cases as being appropriate for political rather than judicial solution. Hence, a restrained Court will play a more subdued role in society than will its activist counterpart.

Advocates of **judicial activism**, on the other hand, assert that the Court should be concerned more with the *spirit* of the law than with its letter. They argue that the Constitution embodies certain paramount principles that the Court should protect from errant legislative or executive policy driven by the politics of the moment, and that the Court must assure that the Constitution be interpreted flexibly enough to accommodate the changing needs of society. Activist courts, therefore, tend not to avoid controversial issues, and they are often accused of overstepping the bounds of the judicial function by *making* policy rather than simply *interpreting* law. The Warren Court's assertion that *privacy* is a fundamental right, even though the word does not actually appear in the Constitution, is an example of judicial activism. [16]

Explaining his approach to the law, Supreme Court Associate Justice William J. Brennan, a leading judicial activist, said: "The genius of the Constitution rests not in any static meaning it might have had in a world that is dead and gone, but in the adaptability of its great principles to cope with current problems and current needs." [17] In addition to Brennan, the Court has had other prominent judicial activists, including John Marshall, Roger B. Taney, Hugo Black, William O. Douglas, and Earl Warren.

Because the liberal Warren Court, upon which Black, Douglas, and Brennan also sat, was the most activist recent Court, judicial activism is often mistakenly equated with liberalism. In fact, judicial activism is not specific to a particular ideology; it can be applied for any cause. There have been three eras in which the Court assumed an activist posture. The Marshall and Taney Courts (1801–1864) interpreted the Constitution in such a way as to enlarge the Court's power, expand the power of the federal government vis-à-vis the states, and protect the interests of business. Later, the Courts from roughly 1880 to 1937 were again activist in protecting business from government regulation. In that era the Courts also expanded the due process clause to include **substantive due process** and applied it against antitrust legislation, organized labor, and the New Deal reforms. These two eras were distinctly conservative, favoring the propertied classes. Only during the last era, 1937–1988, when the Court stood in protection of the individual against government and economic oppression, was judicial activism turned to liberal purposes. Interestingly, when judicial activism was used for conservative interests, liberals such as Louis Brandeis favored judicial restraint, while conservatives such as Robert Bork have advocated the same thing more recently in opposition to a liberal Court.[18]

THE REHNQUIST COURT

Besides Warren Burger, until 1986 only Rehnquist and Byron R. White, a John F. Kennedy appointee, were truly conservative. Harry A. Blackmun became more liberal the longer he was on the Court, and Stevens and Powell tended to vote in favor of civil rights, while they were more conservative about the rights of criminal defendants. When Sandra Day O'Connor and Antonin Scalia joined White and Chief Justice Rehnquist on the Court, the liberal/moderate majority narrowed considerably, but Brennan, the senior liberal, was often able to engineer majorities on his side of the cases.

In 1988, however, conservative Anthony Kennedy replaced moderate Powell, and his presence on the Court became critical. Not only did he join Rehnquist, White, O'Connor, and Scalia to create a conservative majority on the Court on most issues, but he also agrees with them that judicial restraint is the appropriate approach to the law; thus a new, less activist era for the Court may have begun. Like Scalia, who said the Court is not a "committee of philosopher kings" who can void a statute because it may not conform to the justices' opinion of what is right,[19] Kennedy has also been outspoken about the subject. Echoing Brandeis's statement that settled law may be more important than abstract notions of justice, Kennedy averred that it was wrong to "equate a just regime with a constitutional regime." Judges, he said, are supposed to faithfully interpret the language of the Constitution, which is not necessarily "a guarantee of every right that should inhere in an ideal system." He went further to suggest that the Constitution gives a state's legislators "the right to be wrong in matters not specifically controlled by the Constitution."[20]

In 1990, Associate Justice William J. Brennan, Jr. stepped down from the Court due to ill health. With his departure the Court lost its most articulate liberal spokesperson and skilled coalition builder. To fill the vacancy, President Bush quickly nominated David H. Souter, a man of unquestioned intellectual prowess but one whose views were unknown on most of the critical issues the Court must face. As his first term proceeded, however, it became clear that Souter was comfortable with the conservatism of the majority.

Meanwhile, the conservative majority on the Rehnquist Court is not altogether united. Although its 1989 and 1990 terms were more subdued, its 1988 term (October 1988–July 1989) saw considerable rancor surface among the conservatives, with Scalia and Kennedy attacking O'Connor for her opinions on abortion[21] and religious liberty,[22] and Rehnquist deriding Scalia and Kennedy for their dissent in the case striking down a Texas law against defacing the flag.[23]

The Court has executed an abrupt right turn, and although it may not be willing to strike down federal and state statutes, it is not expected to be so restrained where previous Court precedents are concerned. For example, the Court took a broad swipe at civil rights, negating a Virginia affirmative action plan,[24] rejecting statistics alone as proof of racial job discrimination,[25] narrowing the application of a crucial federal civil rights employment law,[26] and supporting discriminatory seniority policies.[27] In the field of criminal law enforcement, the Court was equally conservative, ruling that certain public and transportation employees may be tested for drug use without their consent,[28] that police may use low-flying helicopters to search neighborhoods for drugs,[29] and that police may stop and question persons simply because they look like drug couriers.[30] The Court also ruled that a defendant's *Miranda* rights were not violated by police who fail to provide lawyers for suspects undergoing questioning,[31] a defendant is not denied a fair trial when police lose evidence that might establish innocence,[32] drunk drivers do not have the right to a jury trial in some cases,[33] and, under certain circumstances, coerced confessions may be used by the authorities as evidence at trial.[34] States may execute murderers who were as young as 16 at the time that they committed the crime,[35] and they may execute murderers who are slightly mentally retarded.[36] Prisoners do not have a constitutional right to receive magazines in the mail[37] or to receive visitors,[38] and indigent death row inmates have no right to free legal

advice.[39] Most of these decisions were made by 5-4 majorities.

Conservative on civil rights and on the rights of the accused, the Court has been much less rightist on First Amendment questions. Although it allowed cities to display religious symbols on public property provided they did not appear to endorse religion,[40] it disallowed tax exemptions for certain religious expenditures,[41] and awarded unemployment benefits to a Christian who refused to work on Sundays.[42] The Court also struck down a state law prohibiting burning the flag,[43] and unanimously prohibited government bans on dial-a-porn[44] and seizing the contents of pornographic bookstores before a trial was held,[45] but it also upheld government regulations prohibiting people paid with federal funds from informing clients that abortion is among the options for dealing with unwanted pregnancies.[46] The Court prohibited reporters from using the Freedom of Information Act to obtain people's criminal records from FBI files,[47] but it ruled that a newspaper could not be punished for printing the names of rape victims when they are obtained from the police.[48]

Also untypical of conservatism is the Court's record regarding business interests. The Rehnquist Court has handed the business community a number of serious defeats. The Court ruled that a multimillion-dollar punitive damage award against a negligent corporation was not excessive,[49] a business that engages in fraud can be tried under racketeering laws and forced to pay triple damages,[50] a utility does not have the right to charge its customers for the costs of a failed nuclear power plant,[51] and the government may assess business user fees without Congress enacting a tax law.[52] In addition the Court validated the states' right to discourage hostile takeovers of corporations licensed by them.[53] Labor, however, fared no better with the Court than did business. The Court held that corporations may hire younger strike breakers in place of senior workers who went on strike[54] and that a union may not discipline dissident officers for exercising freedom of speech.[55]

The most controversial field in which the Court has ruled thus far, however, has been women's rights. In a 6-3 decision the Court held that a boss who made sexist remarks about a woman seeking a promotion had to prove that the company's promotion procedures were fair,[56] but in a 5-4 decision the Court ruled that a state may forbid abortions in public health facilities and may impose some regulations on abortion in order to protect human life.[57] The abortion decision, **Webster** v. **Reproductive Health Services**, not only nibbled at the fringes of **Roe** v. **Wade** and set major political movement in motion resulting in Republican losses of two governors' races (Virginia and New Jersey) and the mayoral contest in New York City, but it also put Sandra Day O'Connor in the hot seat. O'Connor joined the majority in *Webster* on the point of a state's being able to prohibit abortions in public facilities, but she refused to agree with Rehnquist, White, Scalia, and Kennedy that *Roe* v. *Wade* should be reversed altogether. Indeed, she has never publicly expressed an opinion on whether women have a constitutional right to abortion. Her hesitance in *Webster* moved Scalia to characterize her position as "perverse" and "irrational."[58]

O'Connor's attitudes on the issue, however, may have been revealed when she questioned an attorney during another abortion case in November of 1989. In that instance, she seemed to lean toward supporting abortion, at least in certain limited cases.[59] She also found herself opposed to the majority against allowing federally funded clinics to counsel patients about abortion. Whatever her position on abortion, on most issues O'Connor remains firmly with the conservative majority; hence, we can expect the Court to continue to restrict certain civil liberties and the rights of defendants in criminal cases, and to practice judicial restraint regarding federal and state laws. Thus the ideological course of the nation for more than the next few years will probably be set more by the state legislatures and Congress than by the Court, whose majority seems reluctant to strike down statutes that do not contradict explicit provisions in the Constitution. The right of privacy, therefore, which the Warren Court saw as implied in American tradition, may not be sustained if a state legislature chooses to pass laws abridging it. Moreover, since previous Courts' rulings on equality are based on a particular interpretation of the Fourteenth Amendment's relation to the Bill of Rights, we may see the present Court allow even more state legislative and congressional encroachment on the civil liberties and the civil rights. The rights to an education, privacy, equal populations in electoral districts, and separation of church and state, for example, are not provided in explicit terms in the Constitution. It is not difficult to see, therefore, that within the span of a few years the United States might become a considerably different place in which to live.

The rightward course of the Court may have been accelerated with the 1991 resignation of Thurgood Marshall. President Bush quickly nominated Clarence Thomas, a conservative, Catholic, African-American, to fill the seat.

SUPREME COURT PROCEDURE

While the judiciary has great power, the courts are also perhaps the most limited of the branches in the exercise of power. Tradition, procedural norms, the rules of evidence, and due process of law combine to fix strict guidelines governing how the courts do their work. Although the Supreme Court is the nation's highest, it too is bound by these narrow parameters. Therefore, a number of procedural matters must be satisfied for the Court to be able to decide a case.

Jurisdiction   Provided a case has exhausted all avenues in the lower courts, any litigant has the right to request a hearing before the Supreme Court, but in hearing and deciding between 250 and 300 cases per term, the Court accepts less than 10 percent of the issues brought to it for review. Hence, while the Supreme Court can be the court of last appeal, by default the lower courts finally decide most disputes.

A number of criteria must be satisfied before the Supreme Court, or any court for that matter, will hear a case. To begin with the case must be within the jurisdiction of the Court. Jurisdiction has to do with a great deal more than just the geographical area a court serves. The Supreme Court can hear cases from any part of the country or its territories. Unlike most lower courts, however, the Supreme Court has both original and appellate jurisdiction. Its original jurisdiction, although seldom exercised, covers cases involving foreign diplomats, cases between states, cases between the federal government and one or more of the states, and cases begun by states against people who are not citizens of that state.

The Constitution provides that the Supreme Court shall hear appeals "with such Exceptions, and under such Regulations as the Congress shall make."[60] Theoretically, therefore, the Congress could deny the Supreme Court appellate jurisdiction completely. Following the Civil War the Congress slightly limited the appellate jurisdiction of the Court, and it has made several other attempts to do so since, although none have passed. Until recently, Congress also required the Court to hear certain kinds of appeals, but since 1988 the Court enjoys total discretion regarding the appeals it hears within its jurisdiction.

Virtually any case involving federal law or the Constitution can be appealed to the Supreme Court. If a case is to be accepted by the Court, however, it must be satisfied that the case involves a "concrete controversy," meaning that the litigants must be trying to settle a real rather than hypothetical or moot dispute; that the litigants have "standing to sue" (that they have actually suffered by the imposition of a law, regulation, or judgment); and that the issue is "ripe" for settlement by the Court.

The Court must be satisfied that it is the appropriate body to settle the dispute rather than a lower court, an administrative body, or one of the two political branches (Congress and the president). Felix Frankfurter wrote, "Wise adjudication has its own time for ripening."[61] As mentioned before, the Court has sometimes refused to hear cases because it believed the issue was essentially a political matter. Currently, the area that the Court usually refers to the political branches is foreign policy. It refused to rule on the constitutionality of the Korean War and the war in Indochina.

Today, almost all cases reach the Supreme court by *writ of certiorari* (make more certain). The losers in a case at a lower level request that the Supreme Court issue a writ of certiorari ordering the lower court to forward to it the records of the case. Certiorari will be issued by the Supreme Court if at least four justices decide the case should be heard. The **rule of four** is not used simply because the justices believe an injustice has been done. Rather, the Court will hear cases only when questions of broad social importance are raised. Such cases usually involve a possible change of precedent or a matter of constitutional importance.

The Conference and the Courtroom
The Court's terms begin in October and end in late June or early July. They are titled by the year in which they begin, hence the term begun in October of 1991 is the 1991 term. The normal procedure is for the Court to hear argument during the first part of the week and to

meet in conference on Fridays. The conference is a critical stage in the process of each case. In conference the justices are completely unto themselves. Only they may attend these secret meetings. Tradition dictates that the justices begin by greeting each other with a handshake and then sit down around a huge table to discuss their views.

Reading the petitions for review provided by applicants (usually totaling about 4000 pages of complicated legal arguments each term) and researching the cases, the justices express their views about whether they think the court should hear certain cases. If four justices agree that a case should be heard (the rule of four) a date for argument is scheduled. Occasionally, however, a lower court decision is so far out of keeping with precedent that the Court does not schedule argument. In these rare instances, the Court issues *summary judgments* based upon the briefs submitted. Among the briefs submitted may be **amicus curiae** (friend of the court) **briefs**, which are added to the litigants' briefs by people or organizations not party to the suit but having an interest in the resolution of the issue.

If the Court decides to hear argumentation, it meets in the courtroom at the appointed time. The Chief Justice, at the center of the dais, is flanked by the associate justices in order of seniority. As with other appellate court hearings, no witnesses are called and presentations are given only by the attorneys for each side. As the attorneys present their cases (while Daniel Webster once took six days to present a case, today argument is usually strictly limited to one-half hour per side), the justices may interrupt with questions, engage the attorneys, and, not uncommonly, debate the issue among themselves. The justices are usually very demanding of pleading attorneys, expecting them to be concise and logical, and any attorneys who read their presentations find the justices becoming impatient and irritable. At the

end of the week, after hearing arguments, studying briefs, and researching the law, the justices gather again in conference.

Like the courtroom procedure itself, the conference is conducted with considerable formality and decorum. Discussion of a case is begun by the Chief Justice outlining the issue and giving his or her opinion and the reasons for the conclusion. The associate justices then all give their views on the case in order of seniority, with the junior justice speaking last. When the case has been fully reviewed (discussion of a particular case may extend over more than one conference), the positions of the various justices become clear, so formal votes on cases are no longer held in the conference.

The Chief Justice, although having no greater formal say in the discussions than the associate justices, can be very influential with the Court. He or she has three major opportunities to influence the Court. As "task leader," the Chief Justice can, through scholarship and argumentation, set the tone for the discussion and guide the deliberations. This, of course, is extraordinarily difficult because the Court is composed of many brilliant legal minds and, while the Chief Justice is technically considered senior on the Court, there might be several associate justices with longer service on the Court. Indeed, some of the justices may have participated in previous cases that established the precedent the Court is currently reviewing.

The Chief Justice is also the "social leader" of the Court. Members of the most exclusive club in the world, the justices work together for years, and their discussions and opinions can be laced with barbs and biting criticism of each other's ideas. Also, the ideological differences among the justices as well as personality incompatibility can, if care is not taken, drive a wedge between the justices, affecting their work.[62] If the Court is to operate smoothly and avoid personal animosity, the Chief Justice

Chief Justice Charles Evans Hughes, bedecked in his judicial robes, delivers a speech to a 1939 joint session of Congress. Seated behind Hughes on the left is Vice President John Nance Garner; to Hughes' direct left is President Franklin Delano Roosevelt, who also addressed the Congress as it celebrated the 150th anniversary of its founding.

must encourage comity. For example, the handshake with which each conference begins was originated by Chief Justice Melville W. Fuller (1888–1910) to remind the justices of the desirability of maintaining a degree of civility in their interrelationships.[63]

The third opportunity for the Chief Justice to influence the Court is at the opinion stage. Within a few days after the conference, the assignment for writing the majority opinion is made by memorandum. When in the majority, the Chief Justice assigns drafting the opinion. If the Chief Justice is in the minority, assigning the opinion falls to the senior associate justice in the majority. Authority to assign opinion writing can be critical since the assigner can pick the justice whose views on the case are most like her or his own. Obviously the senior member of the majority can take on the task of writing the opinion himself or herself, but time constraints and fairness demand that the workload be shared. Trying to tone down his liberal colleagues when they were in the majority,

Warren Burger sometimes voted in the majority on important cases so that he could write the opinion, thus moderating its tone. This ploy, however, simply evoked antagonism on the Court and elicited concurring opinions from justices who wanted the matter stated in less ambiguous terms.[64] Similarly, in 1986–1987, during his first year as Chief Justice, when Rehnquist's conservative dogmatism often forced him to the minority side of the issues, he thereby surrendered the power to assign opinions to Brennan, the senior associate justice. In his second term, however, Rehnquist was more sophisticated politically. He adopted Burger's technique of voting with the majority to control the writing assignments. His objective was clear since he deserted the conservative side of an issue only when it was in the minority.[65]

Opinion Writing   There are several other kinds of opinions besides the majority opinion. A **concurring opinion** is written by a justice who agrees with the majority vote but either has different reasons for agreeing or wishes to emphasize aspects of the case that the majority opinion ignores. Obviously, the more justices who endorse the majority opinion, the stronger the authority of the Court on the issue, so effort is made to avoid concurring opinions. **Dissenting opinions** are written by the minority on an issue. Those in the minority may agree among themselves who shall write the dissent for the group, or several justices may choose to write varying opinions explaining their reasons for disagreeing with the majority. Finally, a justice may write an opinion that concurs in part and dissents in part. In *United States* v. *Guest* (1966), for example, the Court unanimously agreed to sustain a conviction on a civil rights matter, but it was split four ways as to the reasons. Associate Justice Potter Stewart wrote the "majority opinion," but actually only he and Justice White endorsed it completely. Clark, Black, and Fortas agreed but thought the opinion should have gone further; Harlan concurred in part but dissented in part for certain reasons; and Brennan, Douglas, and Warren concurred in part and dissented in part for different reasons.[66] Obviously, in this instance, the case was decided but the law remained unsettled to a considerable degree.

Writing opinions is a laborious process, taking weeks or sometimes even months. When the author has completed the first draft, it is circulated to those who by their statements in conference seemed likely to endorse it. They then return written or verbal comments, suggestions, and critiques to the author, who reworks the opinion accordingly. This process continues until several drafts and refinements have been developed. During the process, the majority, concurring, and dissenting drafts are circulated among all the justices, and it is not uncommon for a justice to change his or her mind, which may cause a change in the majority on the issue. "I have had to convert more than one of my proposed majority opinions into a dissent before the final decision was announced," wrote Brennan. "I have also, however, had the more satisfying experience of rewriting a dissent as a majority opinion for the Court."[67]

Developing an opinion is a complicated process, accompanied by skillful negotiations. Justices exchange memos, meet together in their offices, debate over lunch, and exchange phone calls, all in efforts to sway one another on the issues. When it appears that the Court has decided the case, the opinions are printed. The matter is not final, however, until the decision is presented in Court. At that point, the decision is announced and the opinions are made public.

INTERPRETING THE LAW

The Supreme Court, or any court for that matter, interprets the law at two different levels. It may simply determine the meaning of the law,

or it may assess the validity of law or executive actions relative to the Constitution (judicial review). Laws are written in a political environment. They are the product of a process designed to satisfy, or at least obviate the objections of, a large number of competing and conflicting points of view. Consequently, most of the Constitution and many statutes were left vague so that a majority of the legislators could agree. Additionally, the Constitution is over 200 years old, and many statutes have been on the books for decades. They were written in the context of specific circumstances and events, few of which may be operative today. In interpreting the law, the courts must determine its meaning even though its language may be ambiguous, and they must apply the law to situations that may not have been anticipated by its authors. When a court interprets the law in this context, it performs a traditional function executed by judicial bodies across the globe. When, however, the American courts engage in judicial review, they are performing a unique function.

You will recall from Chapter 2 that the power of the courts to void unconstitutional statutes and executive actions is not expressly stated in the Constitution. The Court, led by Chief Justice John Marshall, was deeply embroiled in a power struggle with President Jefferson and a Republican (today's Democrats) Congress, and Marshall's opinion for a unanimous Court in *Marbury* v. *Madison* asserted, "It is emphatically the province and duty of the judicial department to say what the law is."[68] Interestingly, not only was this decision extraordinary, but it was brought to closure in unusual circumstances. Marshall, many will recall, had been the secretary of state who should have issued the judicial appointment that Marbury sought. Hence, being personally involved, Marshall should have removed himself from the case. Also, since the opinion of the Court was that it had no power to issue the *writ of man-*

damus that Mr. Marbury sought to force Secretary of State Madison to give him the appointment, the Court should not have ruled on the case at all, but simply refused to hear it because it lacked jurisdiction. Instead, the Court, led by the politically shrewd Marshall, used the opportunity to vastly expand its powers, while at the same time refusing to issue *mandamus* because it ruled the Congress did not have the constitutional authority to give the Court the power to issue such writs.*

Marshall's decision, however, was not completely outrageous since there was considerable precedent for the position and there is substantial evidence that it was intended by at least some of the founders. Before independence, the courts regularly reviewed colonial law against the colonial charters. After independence, several state courts voided state law on constitutional grounds, and one or two judges held minor acts of Congress unconstitutional before *Marbury*. Also, there had been several statements about judicial review in the Constitutional Convention, and it was referred to in several of the debates over ratification of the Constitution, including a clear reference to it by Hamilton in *Federalist #78*. [70] Beyond this documentation there lies the power of Marshall's logic:

> "The powers of the legislature are defined and limited; and that those limits may not be mistaken, or forgotten, the Constitu-

tion is written. To what purpose are powers limited, and to what purpose is that limitation committed to writing, if these limits may, at any time, be passed by those intended to be restrained?[71]

Marshall's argument is clear. If the powers of the Congress and the president are to be limited, the legislature and the executive can hardly be given the authority to define the limits of their own authority. This injunction, however, does not answer the question posed by Senator John Breckinridge (Jeffersonian Republican of Kentucky) when, in an 1802 congressional debate, he asked, if the courts are to check the powers of the other branches, "who checks the courts when they violate the Constitution?"[72]

Breckinridge presents an interesting dilemma, if one takes seriously the threat of judicial tyranny. However, since the courts have no police or armies by which to enforce their will on the public, their ultimate power rests upon the willingness of people to accept their wisdom, so they are checked by the political necessity of being reasonable and fair. It also makes considerable sense to leave the interpretation of the law to legal specialists whose life tenure insulates them from the political pressures of the moment. "The law," wrote Georgetown University law professor Eleanor Holmes Norton, "is not a value system. It is a system always in search of values."[73] Since, after all, stability in government demands that someone have the ultimate authority to interpret the law, society should take care to vest such subjective matters in politically independent, competent hands.

Charles Evans Hughes, bluntly echoing Marshall's proposition, said, "The Constitution is what the judges say it is." Although this is undoubtedly so, this oft-quoted statement suggests a degree of arbitrariness that the courts seldom exercise. Judges, as do other people, harbor preferences and biases, and these at-

---

* Jefferson and the Republicans of the early nineteenth century were not the only people to challenge the Court's power of judicial review. Indeed, questions about it persist even to the present, usually lodged by people who do not agree with the Court's opinions of the law. For example, Edwin Meese, President Reagan's Attorney General, inexplicably ignored almost two centuries of American jurisprudence and betrayed an abysmal ignorance of the principle of the separation of powers when, in 1985, he said the Supreme Court's rulings do "not establish a 'Supreme Law of the Land.'"[69]

titudes unquestionably affect their judgments of the law. "Judges' opinions," Max Lerner reminds us, "are not babies brought by constitutional storks." If the laws and the Constitution were absolutely clear and if the prejudices of jurists were not at play in reaching decisions, a lower court decision would never be overruled, and split decisions would never occur.

Yet jurists are constrained in arriving at their opinions by a number of external factors. Precedent is, of course, one of the major restraints. Judges are reluctant—some critics say too reluctant—to apply the law differently from the decisions of previous courts. Also, judges are constrained by professional norms to using four basic approaches to interpreting the law: the intent of the authors, the meaning of the words, logical analysis, and the adaptive approach. Using the *intent of the authors* approach, judges try to determine what the legislators had in mind when they passed a law. In their inquiry, judges not only research the law and precedent, but they also read the *Congressional Record* and other sources to ascertain the legislators' intentions.

President Ronald Reagan and Attorney General Edwin Meese urged the courts to follow exclusively what they called the *original intent* on constitutional issues. This formula is simple in theory. It suggests that judges should interpret the Constitution as the founders meant it to be.[74] As with many issues that on the surface seem simple, however, this proposition is much more complex than it appears at first glance. To begin with, no formal record of the Constitutional Convention was kept. The most authoritative exposition of what went on in the convention is Madison's notes, which are far from a complete coverage of the debates and which were not edited until years after the convention took place. Second, original intent assumes that there was agreement among a majority of the founders about the Constitution's meaning. This, unfortunately, is a simplistic expectation. Equally naive is the assumption

that the Constitution contained what the framers wanted. More likely, no one was completely satisfied with it, but they accepted it as the best compromise possible. It should also be pointed out that only 39 of the 55 delegates who helped draft the document finally supported its ratification. Moreover, the intentions of the founders is not the only important question here. What of the intentions of those citizens who voted to ratify it? Surely their views, if they can be learned, should be considered as well.

Clearly, original intent is unrealistic as an absolute principle. Furthermore, one could even question its relevance in certain circumstances. Problems arising from modern technology and changing social norms, such as nuclear weapons, genetic engineering, surrogate parenthood, electronic eavesdropping, and a raft of other issues, were unknown and even unimaginable to the founders, yet today they must be assimilated under the principles and institutions the Constitution provides. Relying upon the wisdom of the founders is comforting to some people since if we can persuade ourselves that they gave us all the answers, we need only look to history to determine justice; we need never actually confront the complex, bewildering problems of modern life ourselves. Obviously, studying what is known about the founders' intentions is helpful to our understanding of the Constitution, but absolute reliance on the original intent is not only illusionary and simplistic, it can also be dangerously escapist.[75]

A second method used by the courts to interpret the law is studying the *meaning of the words*. Similar to the authors' intent approach, this regime has the judges interpreting laws by studying their words as they were defined at the time the laws were written. This approach, however, causes difficulty because it imposes a literalist straitjacket on laws that were drafted in the freewheeling melee of practical politics, and it may thus lead to unfortunate distortions.

Flogging of errant seamen was commonly practiced at the time the Constitution was written, yet it is now considered cruel and unusual punishment. If the Constitution must be understood only in terms of the values of the era in which it was written, such barbarous punishment could not be deemed unconstitutional by the courts.

A third approach is the use of *logical analysis.* That is, the judges subject the law to logical scrutiny to determine its meaning and its application to particular circumstances. Marshall's argument in *Marbury*—that Congress would hardly be constitutionally limited if it was allowed to determine its own legal restraints—is an example of this approach. While this methodology is valuable, it also encounters problems since applying abstract logic to a law drafted in a politically charged atmosphere can result in interpretations that do not fit the purpose of the law. Oliver Wendell Holmes wrote:

> The life of the law has not been logic: it has been experience. The felt necessities of time, the prevalent moral and political theories, intuitions of public policy, avowed or unconscious, even the prejudices which judges share with their fellowmen, have had a good deal more to do than the syllogism in determining the rules by which men should be governed.[76]

Finally, judges also use the *adaptive approach.* John Marshall wrote that the Constitution is "intended to endure for ages to come, and consequently, to be adapted to the various crises of human affairs." Put another way, Jefferson said, "The Constitution belongs to the living and not the dead." Consequently, its meaning must be understood within the context of modern society. Judges try to apply the basic principles of limited government, separation of powers, individual liberty, and so forth in the context of contemporary realities. To do this well, the judges must be flexible yet true to the Constitution. Indeed, it may be that in adapting the Constitution to new situations, the judges must be truer to the Constitution than is necessary in the original intent doctrine, for in the face of changing social and political realities, interpretations of the Constitution must change if its principles are to be preserved.[77]

The Court does not take lightly its responsibility or ignore the practical limits of its powers. Even activist Courts are reluctant to tread on the prerogatives of the other two branches, or on public opinion. For example, while the Warren Court declared segregation illegal in 1954, thus reversing an 1896 Supreme Court opinion,[78] it waited a full year before ordering desegregation "with all deliberate speed,"[79] and it waited another 19 years before completely losing its patience on the subject.[80] In total, the Supreme Court has declared fewer than 130 federal statutes unconstitutional. It has stricken down more state statutes, but it has generally been cautious even in this field. (See Table 9.3.)

Table 9.3

NUMBER OF LOCAL, STATE, AND FEDERAL LAWS STRICKEN BY THE SUPREME COURT

YEARS	FEDERAL	LOCAL AND STATE
1789–1799	0	0
1801–1809	1	1
1810–1849	27	0
1850–1889	17	112
1890–1929	34	333
1930–1939	13	93
1940–1949	2	58
1950–1959	4	60
1960–1969	16	149
1970–1979	19	193
1980–1987	14	125
Total	120	1151

Source: Adapted from data in Stanley and Niemi, *Vital Statistics on American Politics,* 2nd ed.

THE POWER OF THE SUPREME COURT

The judiciary enjoys enormous respect in our society and wields great power. We refer to the chief executive simply as "Mr. President," but judges are called "Your Honor." Except for brides entering the church and presidents appearing at public forums, only judges are accorded the honor of all rising when they take the bench. No other single institution can affect the law with the finality of the courts. They not only interpret the language of the law but they can, and have, guaranteed individual rights and liberties that are barely hinted at in the Constitution. Integrated public facilities, the right of privacy, and the right to have an abortion were each created by the Supreme Court by extrapolation from its interpretation of the basic principles of the Constitution. That is to say, the Court presumes the power to make policy on matters that might otherwise have been decided in the political sphere. Regardless of how we might view any particular Court-created right, when the Court promulgates rights, it in fact circumvents the democratic process and thus should cause us to contemplate the nature of our system.

In some ways the courts are the weakest of the branches. They have no power to enforce their will; indeed, Alexander Hamilton pointed up the limitations of the courts when he wrote that the judiciary "has no influence over either the sword or the purse; . . . and can take no active resolution whatever. . . . [T]he judiciary is beyond comparison the weakest of the three departments of power."[81] On the other hand, if ours is a government of laws and if the laws are to be obeyed, the courts can be seen as the most powerful branch because, as Marshall and Hughes remind us, they are the instrument that ultimately decides what the law is.

Powerful though it is, the Supreme Court endures substantial limitations. Its precedents can be ignored or modified in application by the lower courts. Since the Supreme Court can review only a small number of cases each term, it depends upon the lower courts to voluntarily abide by its opinions. The Court is also dependent upon the acquiescence of the political branches. Remember that Congress can, if it chooses, completely deny the Court appellate jurisdiction and that the president can ignore its rulings, refusing to enforce them. Moreover, the Court depends upon the support of the public. That is, the legitimacy of the Court must be popularly recognized or else its status will be considerably reduced. "The power of the Supreme Court," wrote Archibald Cox, "to command acceptance and support not only for its decisions but also for its role in government seems to depend upon a sufficiently widespread conviction that it is acting legitimately, that is, performing the functions assigned to it, and only those functions, in the manner assigned."[82]

Although in most cases the Court has managed to carry off its role with aplomb, there have been critical decisions in which it did not prevail, at least immediately. In the 1857 *Dred Scott* case, rather than resolving the issue of slavery, its decision represented an important step on the path to civil war. Its rulings during the mid-1930s led to a withering presidential challenge to the judiciary. The decision in *Brown* was met with resistance that continues to the present, and most recently, *Roe* v. *Wade, Webster* v. *Reproductive Health Services* and *Rust* v. *Sullivan* ignited a wrenching political battle that will not soon be settled.[83] In essence, the Supreme Court's power is heavily dependent on both institutional support and public approval. As political scientists Mark Silverstein and Benjamin Ginsberg suggest, the influence of the judiciary depends heavily upon the political acumen of the Supreme Court. "The key to judicial power," they write, "has been the Court's success in linking constitutional interpretation with the needs of powerful social forces."[84] When it succeeds in doing so, it exerts vast influence in society, but when it fails, the Court is relegated to a secondary role. Thus, in the last analysis, even the meaning of the law is at the mercy of the political process.

The political interrelationship of the three branches of government is, of course, a matter of critical importance in our understanding of the political system. Hence, we will now turn to an examination of the checks and balances.

Summary

- The American judiciary is the strongest in the world, buttressed by the common law and constitutional authority.

- The constitutional courts are created to exercise the powers of Article III of the Constitution, while the legislative courts are created to adjudicate issues solely within the purview of Congress.

- Courts have both original jurisdiction, in which cases are heard for the first time, and appellate jurisdiction, in which higher courts review the decisions of lower courts.

- With its self-given power of judicial review, the Supreme Court has become a major player in the political system, expanding or contracting the civil rights and civil liberties as it sees fit.

- The Supreme Court's power, however, rests on the cooperation of lower courts, the Congress, the executive, and the support of the public.

Notes

1. Fifth Amendment of the United States Constitution.

2. Lewis Mayers, *The Machinery of Justice* (Totowa, NJ: Littlefield, Adams & Co., 1973), pp. 46–47.

3. *Burnet* v. *Coronado Oil & Gas Co.*, 285 U.S. 393 (1932).

4. Harold W. Stanley and Richard G. Niemi, *Vital Statistics on American Politics*, (Washington, DC: Congressional Quarterly, 1990), p. 281.

5. Article VI of the United States Constitution.

6. Oliver Wendell Holmes, Jr., *Collected Legal Papers* (New York: Harcourt, Brace and Company, 1920), pp. 295–296.

7. Sara Fritz, "Why a Judge May Leave the Bench," *The Los Angeles Times*, March 18, 1989.

8. See William H. Harbaugh, *Lawyer's Lawyer: The Life of John W. Davis* (New York: Oxford University Press, 1973).

9. *Marbury* v. *Madison*, 1 Cr. 137 (1803).

10. *Scott* v. *Sanford*, 19 Howard 393 (1857).

11. *Ex Parte Milligan*, 4 Wallace 2 (1866).

12. Quoted in Mark Silverstein and Benjamin Ginsberg, "The Supreme Court and the New Politics of Judicial Power," *Political Science Quarterly* (Fall 1987), 373-374.

13. Archibald Cox, *The Role of the Supreme Court in American Government* (New York: Oxford University Press, 1976), p. 57.

14. *Roe v. Wade,* 410 U.S. 113 (1973).

15. Learned Hand, *The Bill of Rights* (Cambridge: Harvard University Press, 1958), p. 73.

16. *Griswold v. Connecticut,* 381 U.S. 479 (1965).

17. David G. Savage, "After 33 Years, Brennan Is Still for Underdogs," *The Los Angeles Times,* Oct. 1, 1989.

18. Silverman and Ginsberg, p. 375.

19. *Wilkins v. Missouri,* 488 U.S. 887 (1989), or *Penry v. Lynaugh,* 109 S. Ct. 2934 (1989).

20. David G. Savage, "Kennedy: A Conservative Satisfied with Status Quo," *The Los Angeles Times,* Dec. 13, 1987.

21. *Webster v. Reproductive Health Services,* 488 U.S. 1003 (1989).

22. *Allegheny County v. ACLU,* 109 S. Ct. 3086 (1989).

23. *Texas v. Johnson,* 488 U.S. 907 (1989).

24. *Richmond v. Croson,* 488 U.S. 469 (1989).

25. *Wards Cove Packing Co. v. Antonio,* 110 S. Ct. 38 (1989).

26. *Patterson v. McLean,* 10 S. Ct. 2363 (1989).

27. *Lorance v. AT&T,* 488 U.S. 887 (1989).

28. *National Treasury Employees v. VonRaab,* 488 U.S. 886 (1989), and *Conrail v. Railway Labor Executives* 488 U.S. 815 (1989).

29. *Florida v. Riley,* 488 U.S. 445 (1989).

30. *United States v. Sokolow,* 109 S. Ct. 1581 (1989).

31. *Duckworth v. Eagan,* 488 U.S. 1002 (1989).

32. *Arizona v. Youngblood,* 488 U.S. 51 (1989).

33. *Blanton v. North Las Vegas,* 488 U.S. 810 (1989).

34. *Arizona v. Fulminante,* 110 S. Ct. 528 (1991).

35. *Wilkins v. Missouri,* 488 U.S. 887 (1989).

36. *Penry v. Lynaugh,* 109 S. Ct. 2934 (1989).

37. *Thornburgh v. Abbott,* 109 S. Ct. 1874 (1989).

38. *Kentucky v. Thompson,* 109 S. Ct. 98 (1989).

39. *Murray v. Giarratano,* 488 U.S. 923 (1989).

40. *Allegheny County v. ACLU,* 109 S. Ct. 3086 (1989).

41. *Hernandez v. IRS,* 109 S. Ct. 2136 (1989), and *Texas Monthly v. Giarratano,* 108 S. Ct. 2842 (1989).

42. *Caplin & Drysdale v. United States,* 488 U.S. 940 (1989).

43. *Texas v. Johnson,* 488 U.S. 907 (1989).

44. *FCC v. Sable Communications of California, Inc.,* 488 U.S. 1003 (1989).

45. *Ft. Wayne Books* v. *Indiana,* 109 S. Ct. 916 (1989).

46. *Rust* v. *Sullivan,* Slip No. 89-1391 (1991).

47. *United States* v. *Reporters Committee* (1989).

48. *Florida Star* v. *BJF,* 484 U.S. 984 (1989).

49. *Browning-Ferris* v. *Kelco,* 488 U.S. 980 (1989).

50. *J.C. Inc.* v. *Northwestern Bell,* 488 U.S. 826 (1989).

51. *Dusquesne Light* v. *Barasch,* 488 U.S. 299 (1989).

52. *Skinner* v. *Mid-America Pipeline,* 109 S. Ct. 1726 (1989).

53. *Amanda Acquisition* v. *Universal Foods,* 110 S. Ct. 367 (1989).

54. *TWA* v. *IFFA,* 109 S. Ct. 1358 (1989).

55. *Sheet Metal Workers* v. *Lynn,* 488 U.S. 347 (1989).

56. *Price Waterhouse* v. *Hopkins,* 109 S. Ct. 1775 (1989).

57. *Webster* v. *Reproductive Health Services,* 488 U.S. 1003 (1989).

58. See *Webster* v. *Reproductive Health Services.*

59. David G. Savage, "O'Connor Skeptical of Minnesota Consent Law," *The Los Angeles Times,* Nov. 30, 1989.

60. Article II, Section 2 of the United States Constitution.

61. Quoted in Herman Pritchett and Alan E. Westin, eds., *The Third Branch of Government* (New York: Harcourt, Brace & World, 1963), p. 14.

62. See Bob Woodward and Scott Armstrong, *The Brethren: Inside the Supreme Court* (New York: Simon & Schuster, 1979).

63. Alice Fleetwood Bartee, *Cases Lost, Cases Won* (New York: St. Martin's Press, 1984), pp. 45-46.

64. Woodward and Armstrong, pp. 21-32.

65. David G. Savage, "Liberals and Conservatives Uneasy as Rehnquist Veers Court to Center," *The Los Angeles Times,* July 5, 1988.

66. *United States* v. *Guest,* 383 U.S. 745 (1966); Bartee, p. 48.

67. William J. Brennan, Jr. "How the Supreme Court Arrives at Decisions," in Peter Woll, ed., *American Government: Readings and Cases,* 10th ed. (Glenview, IL: Scott, Foresman/Little, Brown, 1990), p. 588.

68. *Marbury* v. *Madison,* 1 Cr. 137 (1803).

69. Quoted in Lincoln Caplin, "For Lame Ducklings: Legal Difficulties," *The Los Angeles Times,* Jan. 10, 1988.

70. Cox, p. 15.

71. *Marbury* v. *Madison,* 1 Cr. 137 (1803).

72. Walter F. Murphy, "Why *Marbury* Matters," *Constitution* (Fall 1989), 65.

73. Eleanor Holmes Norton, "Equality and the Court," *Constitution* (Fall 1989), 19.

74. Philip Hager, "Stevens Assails Meese on Interpreting Constitution," *The Los Angeles Times,* Oct. 26, 1985.

75. For a thorough analysis of the efficacy of the original intent doctrine, see Leonard W. Levy, *The Peculiar Persistence of Original Intent* (New York: Macmillan, 1989).

76. Max Lerner, ed., *The Mind and Faith of Justice Holmes* (New York: Modern Library, 1943), pp. 51–52.

77. Harold J. Spaeth, *An Introduction to Supreme Court Decision Making*, rev. ed. (San Francisco: Chandler Publishing, 1977), pp. 47–54.

78. *Brown v. Board of Education*, 347 U.S. 483 (1954).

79. *Brown v. Board of Education*, 349 U.S. 294 (1955).

80. *Alexander v. Board of Education*, 396 U.S. 19 (1969).

81. *Federalist* No. 78.

82. Cox, pp. 104–105.

83. David E. Kyvig, "The Road Not Taken: FDR, the Supreme Court, and Constitutional Amendment," *Political Science Quarterly* (Fall 1989), 464.

84. Silverstein and Ginsberg, p. 375.

Suggestions for Further Reading

Abraham, Henry J. *Freedom and the Courts: Civil Rights and Liberties in the United States* (4th ed.). New York: Oxford University Press, 1982.

————. *The Judicial Process* (5th ed.). New York: Oxford University Press, 1986.

Baum, Lawrence. *American Courts: Process and Policy.* Boston: Houghton Mifflin, 1986.

————. *The Supreme Court* (2nd ed.). Washington, DC: Congressional Quarterly Press, 1985.

Carp, Robert A., and Ronald Stidham. *The Federal Courts.* Washington, DC: Congressional Quarterly Press, 1985.

Cox, Archibald. *The Role of the Supreme Court in American Government.* New York: Oxford University Press, 1976.

Forte, David F. *The Supreme Court in American Politics.* Lexington, MA: D. C. Heath, 1972.

Jacob, Herbert. *Justice in America: Courts, Lawyers and the Judicial Process.* Boston: Little, Brown, 1986.

Mayers, Lewis. *The Machinery of Justice.* Totowa, NJ: Littlefield, Adams, 1973

Murphy, Walter F., and C. Herman Pritchett. *Courts, Judges and Politics.* New York: Random House, 1974.

O'Brien, David M. *Storm Center: The Supreme Court and American Politics.* New York: Norton, 1986.

Spence, Gerry. *With Justice for None.* New York: Times Books, 1989.

Wolfe, Christopher. *The Rise of Modern Judicial Review.* New York: Basic Books, 1986.

Woll, Peter, ed. *American Government: Readings and Cases.* Glenview, IL: Scott, Foresman/ Little, Brown, 1990.

Woodward, Bob, and Scott Armstrong. *The Brethren: Inside the Supreme Court.* New York: Simon & Schuster, 1979.

Chapter 10

THE CHECKS AND BALANCES

PREVIEW

The American political system is based on the separation of powers and on the premise that each branch will check and balance the powers of the others. The Supreme Court interprets law by determining its meaning, but through judicial review it also determines when the president and Congress have exceeded the limits of the Constitution. The Court has been very careful, however, not to confront the other branches too often, or, for that matter, to alienate the public.

The Court has maintained the most cooperative relationship with the president, and it has usually enjoyed the support of the public. Early conflicts between the Court and presidents Jefferson, Jackson, and Lincoln were followed by long periods in which the Court generally sustained the expansion of executive powers. In this century, Franklin D. Roosevelt's confrontation with a conservative Court ended in the Court's retreat, and the Warren Court's activist policies were generally compatible with the presidents with whom it shared power. Yet the Court's positions were often more liberal than the mainstream of public opinion at the time, and considerable unrest resulted. The more moderate Burger Court was better received by the public, but the recent right turn of the Rehnquist Court in the face of growing ideological moderation among the public may result in another wave of social turmoil. Indeed, the abortion issue may be only the beginning phase of public frustration with the Court.

The Congress has great powers over the courts. It creates them, confirms their membership, sets their salaries, determines their jurisdiction, and may rewrite the law; with the states, it may also amend the Constitution, thus negating court opinions. Congress also impeaches; impeachment is seldom used and has focused primarily on federal judges, with two jurists being impeached in 1989 alone.

Congress and the president have also come into conflict, of course. Having different structures, constituencies, and timetables, the two political branches are bound to find themselves at odds on major issues. After dominating the presidency throughout most of the nineteenth century, Congress was eclipsed by the strong presidency of Franklin D. Roosevelt. Presidential power continued to grow until Lyndon B. Johnson and Richard M. Nixon were accused of administering arrogant, imperial presidencies.

Reacting to the Vietnam War and the Watergate scandal, Congress reasserted itself by legislating limitations on the president's foreign and domestic policies. Presidents Ford and Carter were each shackled by restive Congresses, but Ronald Reagan's popularity seemed to promise the reemergence of a strong presidency—until catapulting deficits and the Iran-Contra scandal again encouraged Congress to limit the presidency. President Bush's election has not settled matters, as the Congress continues to struggle with the president on executive privilege, vetoes, appointments, foreign policy, and various social issues.

A people deliberating in a temperate moment, and with the experience of other nations before them, on the plan of government most likely to secure their happiness, would first be aware, that those charged wtih public happiness, might betray their trust. An obvious precaution against this danger would be to divide the trust between different bodies of men, who might watch and check each other.

James Madison

In the preceding chapters, we have examined each of the three branches of government separately. Now we should briefly study the interplay among them so as to gain greater insight about how the government works.

Richard E. Neustadt described the American government as one of "separated institutions sharing power."[1] Unlike the British system, which centralizes power in the Parliament and asks its branches to cooperate and its officials to restrain their actions so as to protect the rights of individuals, our system diffuses power and expects each branch to guard against anticipated attempts at abuse by the other branches. The resulting intergovernmental struggles have been among the most dramatic and important clashes in American political history.

The Court and the President

The judiciary is in many ways the most exposed and dependent partner in this confrontational triangle. Insulated from the democratic process, it is the only branch dependent on the others for its existence and for its members, but it is also the only branch whose members enjoy life terms. Realizing their precarious position, the courts have been careful not to engage in prolonged disputes with either branch, and they are particularly careful not to find themselves at odds with both branches simultaneously.[2]

Perhaps because the Supreme Court has generally favored a strong national govern-ment, it has usually ruled in favor of increased presidential power and seldom acted to reduce it. Indeed, the judiciary and the presidency have traditionally enjoyed a closer relationship than either has exhibited with Congress.[3] In some cases, the Court has actually either ignored unconstitutional actions by the president or voided them only after the offending president had left office. Robert J. Sickles argues that the Court's reluctance to confront the president accounts, in large measure, for its successfully developing as much power as it currently enjoys.[4]

In the early years of the republic, Jefferson claimed that the Court had no legitimate right to limit the powers of Congress or the presidency. We have already examined the struggle between Jefferson and John Marshall in the Marbury case. Jefferson lost that encounter, but he remained defiant of the Court. Accordingly, he refused to honor a subpoena in the 1807 trial for treason of former vice president Aaron Burr. The strong-willed Andrew Jackson went even further, refusing to enforce a Court ruling regarding treaties with the Indians. "John Marshall has made his decision," Jackson said defiantly; "now let him enforce it." Lincoln's extraordinary power also ran afoul of the Court. Early in the Civil War the government arrested a southern sympathizer and held him without trial. The Court issued a writ of *habeas corpus* demanding the government to show cause for the prisoner's continued detention, but Lincoln ignored the order.[5] Five years later the Court ruled that martial courts must be "confined to the locality of actual war" and therefore, that the military trial and conviction of a civilian in an area where the civil courts preside is illegal.[6] Lincoln's action in this particular case was not voided, however, until after the war had ended and he was dead.

The most dramatic confrontation between the president and the Court, however, took place in the mid-1930s. Because the Court's members serve life terms, their views often lag behind the political mood and needs of the country. When the Great Depression struck, the Court was still dominated by jurists who followed the probusiness philosophy so prevalent in the era of 1880–1937. Accordingly, the Court struck down a number of New Deal policies designed to strengthen the president's hand in regulating industry and finance.[7]

Fresh from the 1936 elections, giving him the largest electoral victory in history, and frustrated by the intransigence of the conservative Court, Franklin D. Roosevelt resolved to manipulate the Court membership to create a more pliable bench. He decided to ask Congress to allow him to add a justice to the Supreme Court for every member who had not retired by age 70. While his proposal was legal, it was perceived by many as a blatant attempt to "pack the Court." Meanwhile, however, fearing the Court would ultimately lose in an open confrontation with so powerful a president, two Supreme Court justices changed their previous opposition to the New Deal, and most of Roosevelt's policies were sustained thenceforth.[8] In fact, Roosevelt's power was so great and the anti-Japanese emotions during World War II were so strong that the Court during the war closed its eyes to one of our history's most blatant denials of civil liberties: the Japanese-American internment.[9]

Although the Court ruled against President Truman's attempt to seize the steel mills where striking workers imperiled the country's efforts during the Korean War,[10] it usually supported the president's powers from the

Supported by his wife Pat, Richard Nixon says farewell to the White House staff on the day he resigned in disgrace from the presidency.

mid-1930s until the 1970s. The evolution of the **imperial presidency**, however, caused the Court to severely limit the powers of President Richard M. Nixon. In separate cases, the Court ruled that the government could not suppress publication of the *Pentagon Papers*,[11] that government electronic surveillance in the United States was unconstitutional unless a court had issued a warrant,[12] and that the president had to answer a court subpoena for material evidence in a criminal case.[13] President Reagan also had problems with the Court. In 1981 it ruled that an executive agreement by a previous president is binding on successors;[14] and in 1988, against Reagan Administration protestations that the position of independent counsel was unconstitutional, the Court upheld a law creating such a position to investigate alleged executive branch wrongdoing.[15] In 1990, the Bush Administration also found itself limited by the Court. Acting under the authority of a 1980 law permitting the executive to eliminate unnecessary paperwork required of private businesses, the Office of Management and Budget abolished regulations requiring businesses to warn workers and consumers of unsafe conditions in the workplace and dangerous features about products. The Court ruled that the OMB had overstepped its bounds, and ordered that it restore the warnings.[16]

Congress and the Court

Relations between Congress and the Court have been even more contentious, and the Supreme Court has negated almost 130 statutes and has frequently sustained the president in contests with the legislature. Still, the Court has been relatively careful not to anger a body that has so much power to inhibit its own authority. Not only does Congress determine the size and structure of the judiciary in general, but it has complete discretion about the size of the Supreme Court itself, and it may regulate the Court's appellate jurisdiction. Congress confirms the president's appointments to the courts; it sets judicial salaries; it decides how much the judiciary may spend each year, thus regulating its facilities and support staff; and it may mandate the procedure used by the courts.

On two occasions, when a determined Congress confronted a Court resolved to limit its powers, the Congress took steps to foil its opponent. In the political imbroglio that led to the *Marbury* decision, Congress repealed the Judiciary Act of 1801. Fearing that the Court would rule the repeal unconstitutional, Congress passed another act prohibiting the Court from holding its 1802 term.[17] In the second instance, the Court had held in *Ex Parte Milligan* that civilians could not be brought before military courts in places where the civil courts were open. Ignoring this injunction, Congress, controlled by the radical Republicans, established military courts in the defeated Southern states following the Civil War. A southerner who was tried and convicted in the military

courts appealed on grounds of the *Milligan* ruling. Congress, however, quickly passed a law denying the Court jurisdiction over the case.[18] When the case came before the Court, it demonstrated no willingness to press the matter and ruled that it could not issue an opinion since Congress had lawfully denied it jurisdiction.[19]

Of course, Congress also enjoys the authority to change statutes and the Constitution itself when the Court interprets them in unpopular ways. Many federal statutes ruled unconstitutional have subsequently been rewritten so as to circumvent the Court's objections. An example is the Civil Rights Act of 1990. Here Congress tried to put into statute certain rights for women and minorities the Rehnquist Court had struck from case law. President Bush vetoed the law, however, arguing that it established quotas in the workplace, so the struggle over this issue continues.

Congress, with state ratification, has also amended the Constitution to allow policy previously voided by the Court. The Sixteenth Amendment, for example, was passed in 1913 to exempt the progressive income tax from the prohibition in Article II, Section 8, that all taxes be "uniform throughout the United States." In 1895 the Court ruled the original income tax unconstitutional,[20] so Congress and the states changed the language of the Constitution.

IMPEACHMENT

The ultimate congressional authority over the courts, or so it is supposed, is **impeachment**. While impeachment has not been used often, most impeachment cases have involved jurists. The Constitution vests the House of Representatives with the "sole Power of Impeachment."[21] That is, the House brings charges (indicts and prosecutes) against an accused official. The Senate tries the case and convicts by a two-thirds' majority vote. The Chief Justice of the Supreme Court presides over an impeachment trial of the president or vice president; in all other cases the President of the Senate, the vice president, presides. The Constitution is vague about what offenses may be subject to impeachment. It says only that "all civil officers of the United States, shall be removed from Office on Impeachment for, and conviction of, Treason, Bribery, or other high Crimes and Misdemeanors."[22]

As daunting as it sounds, impeachment has not turned out to be the ultimate weapon it was intended to be. As early as 1797 Congress exempted its own members from impeachment.[23] The specter of the House prosecuting a Senator, or the Senate sitting in judgment of a member of the House grates at the perceived independence of the two houses, and each prefers to discipline its own members, as described in Chapter 7.

Congress has also been sparing in its approach to impeaching people in the executive branch. William W. Belknap, President Grant's third Secretary of War, was deservedly impeached for corruption, but his resignation forestalled trial and conviction in the Senate.[24] Before that episode, the post–Civil War Congress, controlled by the radical Republicans, impeached and tried President Andrew Johnson on highly questionable charges. While the House unanimously voted for 11 counts in the impeachment, the Senate failed by 1 vote to convict the hapless president.[25] More recently, Vice President Spiro T. Agnew resigned in 1974 to avoid impeachment for corruption, and later in the same year, President Richard M. Nixon did the same, after the House Judiciary Committee voted to recommend that the full House vote a three-count impeachment against him.

The cases of Belknap, Agnew, and Nixon illustrate that impeachment can be successful

in removing officers even when no trial is held. Actually, however, impeachment and subsequent trials have been very rare, and as already mentioned, most impeachment proceedings have been instigated not against the executive but against the judiciary. Of the 14 impeachment trials in United States history, 13 have involved federal judges, and there have been 7 convictions, all judges. In 1986, District Court Judge Harry Claiborne of Nevada was convicted for income tax evasion, and in 1989 two other District Court jurists were convicted within two weeks of one another, after proceedings lasting for over five years apiece. Alcee L. Hasting of Florida was convicted of conspiracy to receive a bribe and Walter L. Nixon of Mississippi was convicted of perjury.[26] No member of the Supreme Court has been convicted of impeachment charges; Associate Justice Samuel Chase was impeached in 1804, but the Senate acquitted him. In the 1970s there was a good deal of activity among Republicans in Congress to impeach Chief Justice Earl Warren and Associate Justices Abe Fortas and William O. Douglas. Fortas eventually resigned under pressure, but nothing came of the movements against Warren and Douglas.[27]

The procedures of impeachment and trial are time-consuming and fraught with turmoil and controversy, especially if the president is involved. It is difficult to imagine how the government could continue to function in this day and age should the House bring the president before the bar of the Senate. Congress is currently considering a constitutional amendment that would allow a panel of lawyers and judges to conduct impeachment investigations and trials, thus alleviating much of the burden on itself. Although this proposal may streamline matters for impeaching judges, many authorities still believe impeachment is not a viable option where the president is concerned.[28]

Congress and the President

When considering the relationship of Congress and the president, the basic differences of the two branches must be kept in mind. Members of Congress are elected from narrower constituencies than is the president. The people usually expect the president to address general concerns such as foreign policy and economic prosperity, while Congresspersons are asked to solve individual problems. There are structural differences as well. Congress is a body composed of hundreds of independent people, each with a different power base, and it is divided along partisan lines. Thus, it is difficult for Congress to act quickly or to project unity and clear policy statements. Power, while not absolutely centralized, is much more concentrated in the executive branch and when the president articulates policy, it is usually clear and easily discernible, while Congress, with its varied power bases, appears to be going in every direction at once. Also, Congress and the president work on different timetables. It is usually agreed that a president, who is limited to two terms, must introduce his or her initiatives in the first year of the term, taking advantage of the traditional honeymoon period with Congress* and because subsequent years are either dominated by elections or hindered by lame duck status. (*Lame ducks* are politicians who cannot be reelected to the positions they currently hold. The president is prohibited by the Twenty-second Amendment from being elected more than twice.) Congresspersons, on the other hand, have no limit on the number of terms they may serve. As long as they continue to maintain the confidence of their constituents, they may hold office. Consequently, they tend to view their positions as career-long occupations and feel little of the pressure to achieve early that affects most presidents.[29]

Other factors to keep in mind about the relationship of Congress and the president include the current tendency for divided government, the decline in party loyalty and strength discouraging cooperation between the two branches, and Congresspersons relying on their own ability to raise campaign funds instead of being provided them by the party, which makes politicians more independent than ever before. Also, Republican members of Congress are normally more prone to support their presidents than are Democrats, but the Republicans have not enjoyed a majority in both houses since 1953, even though they have held the presidency during most of that modern period. Moreover, the reforms of Congress since the 1970s, giving more power to junior members, have made it difficult to lead the organization and to keep it in line behind the president's policies.[30] For example, in Figure 10.1 we can see that the president has had a greater success rate with Congress when his party has held a majority in each house. Although presidents Eisenhower and Reagan each had high success rates in particular years, their average success rates fell below each of the Democratic presidents' average.

THE RISE OF CONGRESS

As mentioned earlier, the Congress deferred to the president increasingly after Franklin D. Roosevelt took office. The legislature gave the executive more and more power, until the imperial presidencies of Johnson and Nixon caused Congress to reassert itself. President Johnson seriously misled Congress on aspects of the war in Vietnam, and Nixon bombed and

---

* President Bush ignored conventional wisdom by introducing very few policy initiatives during his first three years in office. Whether he will be able to move Congress to action in the future or whether he has squandered the best time to accomplish his legislative program—which he was also slow to make clear—will be revealed in time.

Figure 10.1   Presidents' Success Rate in Congress, 1953–1988

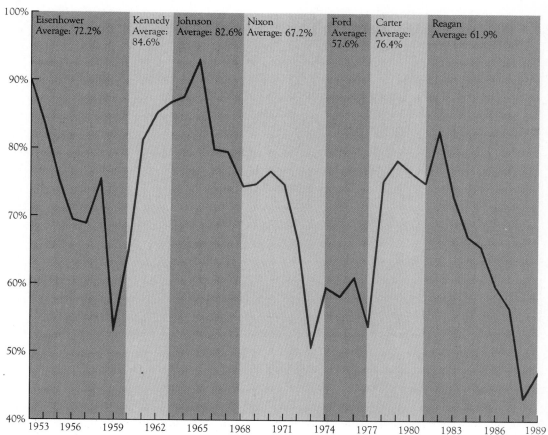

Source: Based on data in *Vital Statistics on American Politics*, 2nd ed., pp. 250–251.

invaded Cambodia, widening the war without informing Congress. Congress became increasingly restive as presidential duplicity became public, but it still hesitated to refuse financial support for the war even though the issue caused severe political and social repercussions at home. Another issue was needed to shake Congress from its acquiescence.

Finally, on June 17, 1972, a small group of people employed by the Nixon Committee to Re-elect the President (CREEP) was nabbed in

the midst of a burglary of the Democratic party headquarters at the Watergate, a fashionable office building in Washington, D.C. Although the president at first shrugged off the incident as a "third-rate burglary," gradually the issue unraveled, exposing the most disgraceful episode in the history of the presidency and wounding the office grievously. As the attempt to cover up the scandal became public, Richard Nixon, Attorney General John Mitchell, Chief of Staff H. Robert Haldeman, Presidential

Senator Sam J. Irvin (D-NC), Chair of the Senate Special Committee to investigate the Watergate scandal (center, left) raises his hand in a committee vote. Across the room seated at the near end of the witness table is John D. Ehrlichman, an aide to President Nixon and a principal participant in the attempted coverup.

Counselor John Ehrlichman, and numerous other high-placed officials in the administration were implicated for obstruction of justice; malfeasance in office; perjury; use of the IRS, CIA, and FBI to persecute and intimidate people on Nixon's "enemies list"; the creation and use of a secret police force; and many other outrages. Nixon's hold on public opinion was seriously weakened when, in the "Saturday night massacre," Archibald Cox, the special prosecutor investigating the matter; Attorney General Elliott Richardson; and Deputy Attorney General William Ruckelshaus were fired. Nixon wanted Cox removed because Cox insisted that the president turn over as evidence the tape recordings he had secretly made

of discussions in the Oval Office, but Richardson and Ruckelshaus refused to fire him—so Nixon dismissed them. Finally, Nixon was obliged by Solicitor General Robert Bork, who fired Cox. Eventually the Supreme Court unanimously ordered that the tapes be surrendered to the new special prosecutor,[31] and they revealed that Nixon himself had engaged in the coverup attempt, leading to his resignation in 1974 to avoid impeachment. Congress responded to revelations about the Vietnam War and the Watergate debacle with the admission that it had placed too much power in the hands of the president, and it moved to remedy the situation.

Acting even before Nixon left office, Congress passed the **War Powers Act** in 1973. This was the first serious attempt by Congress to limit the president's growing power to send troops to armed engagements without a declaration of war. Passed over Nixon's veto, the law requires the president to notify Congress before troops are sent into combat zones and, if prior notification is impossible, to inform Congress within 48 hours of giving the order to deploy troops. It further gives Congress the right to require the withdrawal of troops at any time by passing a concurrent resolution, and states that the president may not leave troops in harm's way for longer than 60 days without the express approval of Congress. The War Powers Act seems to conform to the intentions of the Constitution's principal author, James Madison, who wrote, "In no part of the Constitution is more wisdom found than in the clause which confides the question of war or peace to the legislature, not to the executive." Yet the law remains controversial and its effectiveness has been mixed. It intrudes Congress into matters of foreign policy more than at any other recent time, but every president since Nixon has claimed it is unconstitutional and has refused to comply completely with its provisions.[32] On the other hand, it has compelled presidents to keep Congress abreast of troop deployments, and it forced President Reagan to negotiate with Congress in 1982 in order to keep American peacekeeping troops in Lebanon beyond the 60-day limit.

For his part, President Bush was careful to notify Congress of his decision to invade Panama. The War Powers Act was also at issue in Operation Desert Storm, President Bush's deployment of over one-half million troops to the Persian Gulf war. In 1990 several important members of Congress from both parties asserted the legislature's right to approve or disapprove of the operation. Although Bush publicly disagreed with this position, he nevertheless asked for congressional approval. Finally, in January of 1991, Congress gave its approval for the president to take the nation to war if need be.

President Nixon also used highhanded techniques to manage the economy. Frequently, the Democratic Congress would vote more money for social programs than Nixon requested. Instead of vetoing the bills, thus losing the total appropriations, Nixon often signed the bills but spent only part of the money, placing the rest in impounded accounts; the money would eventually be returned to the Treasury. *Impoundments* are not unusual; they have been used since the early days of the republic. This scale of use, however, was unique to President Nixon. Indeed, Congress argued that Nixon's impoundment policies had the effect of giving the president the line item veto and was thus unconstitutional.

In 1974 Congress passed the **Budget and Impoundment Act**, which requires the president to inform Congress of all impoundments; unless within 45 days Congress approves a proposed recision (the return of money to the Treasury), it must be spent for its appropriated purpose. Also, the law provides that any presidential proposal to defer spending until the next year can be negated by a vote of one house of Congress. The Budget and Impoundment Act also established several other measures, including creating the Congressional Budget Office (CBO) to strengthen Congress' hand vis-à-vis the president in budgeting matters.[33]

Congressional investigations in 1975 revealed that Congress had been very lax about exercising *oversight* of the executive, especially in the area of intelligence operations. Since that time, although flaws persist, it has exhibited more care in reviewing the operations of the executive branch. It has also tightened up on the budgetary latitude of the Office of Management and Budget, and it created independent inspectors general to report to Congress on the operations of key executive agencies. Similarly, in 1976 Congress repealed a large number of emergency powers that had been given to the president since the 1930s, and the year before, it finally voted to cut off funds to the Vietnam War.

The Reagan and Bush Administrations The increased activity of Congress made the checks and balances keener than they had been for decades, and critics complained that congressional "micromanagement" had unduly weakened the presidencies of Ford and Carter. In 1980, Ronald Reagan was elected president, and then reelected in 1984 by a record margin. Committed to a platform promising to reduce taxes, roll back the social programs of the New Deal and the Great Society, legalize prayer in the public schools, forbid abortion, and build up defense with unprecedented peacetime military spending, Reagan overwhelmed congressional Democrats in 1981 and mobilized public support for many of his basic programs thereafter. However, the resulting skyrocketing deficits caused serious concern, and the Iran-Contra scandal once again moved Congress to assert itself, despite Reagan's and Bush's efforts to cultivate the legislature.[34]

Congress tried to get control of the "runaway" deficits in 1985 by passing the **Gramm-Rudman-Hollings Act**, which was supposed to gradually reduce government borrowing to zero by 1993.[35] Each side has blamed the other for the deficits, but unfortunately, nothing has yet succeeded in reducing them. Consequently, the budget process has become an increasingly contentious aspect in the relationship between Congress and the president.

Ordinarily, the budget process begins with the president establishing broad goals; then the Office of Management and Budget surveys the various government agencies to ascertain their needs and develops a budget, which is then laid before Congress. Meanwhile, Congress does its own studies, and when it receives the budget proposal, its budget committees hold hearings

and negotiations to develop the budget's final form. The implementing legislation is then written by the House Ways and Means, the Senate Finance, and the House and Senate appropriations committees.

In 1990, in an attempt to break a deadlock over the 1991 budget, this process was short-circuited. The OMB Director Richard Darman and Chief of Staff John Sununu negotiated for four months with congressional leaders from both parties. Their agreement was finally placed before Congress in the fall of 1990. Although the proposal enjoyed the backing of the president and most of the leadership in Congress, it went down to defeat because the chairs of the committees who usually develop final versions of the budget were not privy to the negotiations, and because—just before an election—it called for deep cuts in social programs and increased taxes on the middle class while leaving the wealthy virtually unscathed.

In the final few weeks before the 1990 elections, with the Republicans in Congress split and President Bush vacillating on the question of taxing the well-to-do, the congressional Democrats managed to pass a budget that protected most of the social programs, while raising the taxes of the wealthy. The net result was that the Congress insisted on using the traditional budget process and the president found the unity of his congressional party in shambles.[36] The 1990 budget agreement also included fairly rigorous new rules, however, binding Congress to reducing items in the budget by the same amount that other items are increased. So far this regime seems to be helping Congress and the president hold down spending increases.[37]

The president's Central America policy also created conflict. Toward the end of the Reagan Administration, the Iran-Contra scandal resulted in deep criticism of the president's management style, criminal convictions of several people in his administration, and lingering questions about then Vice President Bush's involvement in the affair. When Bush became president, the 1989 criminal trial of Joseph F. Fernandez, a former CIA operative in Central America with ties to Bush, might have shed some light on the matter, but the case was thrown out of court because President Bush's Attorney General, Richard Thornburgh, refused to submit evidence to the court on national security grounds. Claiming that the evidence Thornburgh withheld is commonly known (in part, it has to do with admitting that the United States has CIA stations in Central America, a fact that can be learned by reading the newspapers), Lawrence E. Walsh, independent counsel and prosecutor in the case, hinted that Thornburgh is covering up. Walsh claimed in 1989 that Thornburgh had violated the principle "that all persons are accountable to the law,"[38] and in 1990, he accused the Bush Administration of deliberately and unnecessarily delaying in providing information needed for his investigation.[39]

In a new area of potential conflict, President Bush has publicly spoken in support of establishing limits on the number of terms members of Congress may serve. As mentioned earlier, while the president may serve no more than two elected terms, there is no limit for congresspersons. In the elections of 1990, several states adopted limits to the number of terms their state legislators may serve, and many people have called for similar limits on Congress. By rising to this issue, Bush may have fired the first salvo of a new bitter controversy between the Congress and the presidency.

TRADITIONAL CONFLICTS

Congress did not responded to the Iran-Contra affair with the amount of corrective legislation that followed Watergate. It did, however, re-

double its efforts to check the executive in the traditional areas of interbranch conflict. The question of **executive privilege** is one of the areas over which Congress and the president have long been at odds. Since the earliest days, the president has refused to honor congressional requests for information when it was deemed to jeopardize the separation of powers or the national security. Congress, while not happy about the president's reluctance to share information, has usually acquiesced to the privilege. Following the Civil War, legislation was introduced to compel Cabinet members to respond to congressional inquiries, but none of it passed, and the issue remained dormant for many years.[40]

The question of executive privilege has recently been taken into the courts, however. Nixon's refusal to surrender secret tape recordings that could shed light on his involvement in the Watergate affair led to a unanimous Supreme Court opinion recognizing the principle of executive privilege but ruling that it could not be used to deny evidence in a criminal case.[41] Since then, Congress passed the *Classified Information Procedure Act* of 1980, giving the attorney general the power to decide what classified information may not be subpoenaed for national security reasons. Thornburgh is the first attorney general to use this power, and his denial of evidence in the Fernandez case led Walsh to recommend that Congress modify the law. In another case related to the Iran-Contra scandal, Admiral John Poindexter asked the court to subpoena the private papers of Ronald Reagan and George Bush because Walsh claimed that these papers prove that the former president and vice president knew about the diversion of funds to the Contras. District Court Judge Harold H. Greene ruled that Bush's notes were not sufficiently relevant to the case, but he did issue a subpoena for Reagan's papers because they were critical to Poindexter's defense. Reagan

Table 10.1
THE USE OF THE VETO AND OVERRIDES

President	Regular Veto	Vetoes Overridden	Percentage of Regular Vetoes Overridden	Pocket Vetoes	Total Vetoes	Pocket Vetoes a Percentage of all Vetoes
Washington	2	0	0.0%	0	2	0.0%
J. Adams	0	0	0.0%	0	0	0.0%
Jefferson	0	0	0.0%	0	0	0.0%
Madison	5	0	0.0%	2	7	28.6%
Monroe	1	0	0.0%	0	1	0.0%
J. Q. Adams	0	0	0.0%	0	0	0.0%
Jackson	5	0	0.0%	7	12	58.3%
Van Buren	0	0	0.0%	1	1	100.0%
W. H. Harrison	0	0	0.0%	0	0	0.0%
Tyler	6	1	16.7%	4	10	40.0%
Polk	2	0	0.0%	1	3	33.3%
Taylor	0	0	0.0%	0	0	0.0%
Fillmore	0	0	0.0%	0	0	0.0%
Pierce	9	5	55.6%	0	9	0.0%
Buchanan	4	0	0.0%	3	7	42.9%
Lincoln	2	0	0.0%	5	7	71.4%
A. Johnson	21	15	71.4%	8	29	27.6%
Grant	45	4	8.9%	48	93	51.6%
Hayes	12	1	8.3%	1	13	7.7%
Garfield	0	0	0.0%	0	0	0.0%
Arthur	4	1	25.0%	8	12	66.7%
Cleveland	304	2	0.7%	110	414	26.6%

refused to surrender them, however, claiming executive privilege. Although this matter was not settled, Reagan did agree to testify in the case when he was assured that, because his testimony was to be videotaped, no danger to the national security could be inadvertently done.[42] This concession, however, was not unprecedented since presidents or former presidents had given court testimony on six previous occasions.

The **veto power** is also the source of recurring controversy between the Congress and the president. The early presidents used the veto sparingly, only negating laws that they consid-ered unconstitutional. Indeed, several of them did not veto any laws at all. This early restraint, however, was ignored by Andrew Jackson, who not only vetoed more laws than all previous presidents combined but who also vetoed laws for policy reasons instead of just those deemed unconstitutional. Since then, the veto has been used increasingly, becoming a major instrument in the presidential struggle with Congress. No less a light than Woodrow Wilson, well before he became the chief executive, said the veto power made the president the "third branch of the legislature."[43] A recent analysis by political scientist David

Table 10.1 (continued)

President	Regular Veto	Vetoes Overridden	Percentage of Regular Vetoes Overridden	Pocket Vetoes	Total Vetoes	Pocket Vetoes a Percentage of all Vetoes
Harrison	19	1	5.3%	25	44	56.8%
Cleveland	42	5	11.9%	128	170	75.3%
McKinley	6	0	0.0%	36	42	85.7%
T. Roosevelt	42	1	2.4%	40	82	48.8%
Taft	30	1	3.3%	9	39	23.1%
Wilson	33	6	18.2%	11	44	25.0%
Harding	5	0	0.0%	1	6	16.7%
Coolidge	20	4	20.0%	30	50	60.0%
Hoover	21	3	14.3%	16	37	43.2%
F. Roosevelt	372	9	2.4%	269	635	42.4%
Truman	180	12	6.7%	70	250	28.0%
Eisenhower	73	2	2.7%	108	181	59.7%
Kennedy	12	0	0.0%	9	21	42.9%
L. Johnson	16	0	0.0%	14	30	46.7%
Nixon	26	7	26.9%	17	43	39.5%
Ford	48	12	25.0%	18	66	27.3%
Carter	13	2	15.4%	18	31	58.1%
Reagan	39	9	23.1%	39	78	50.0%
Bush[a]	20	0	0 %	1	21	4.8%

[a] As of June 1991.

Source: The presidencies of Washington through Reagan were based on data in Stanley and Niemi, Vital Statistics on American Politics, 2nd ed. The data on Bush's record is from The Los Angeles Times.

McKay, however, reveals that the use of a veto may be a sign as much of a president's weakness as of strength because recent Congresses have been more sucessful than in the past with veto overrides. Thus the veto is not as strong a weapon as it might be. McKay is quick to point out, however, that even the threat of a veto can still cause Congress to modify a bill so that the president does not void it.[44]

Table 10.1 indicates that the number of presidential vetoes has vastly increased since the early years of the republic and that every president since Chester A. Arthur has used it. Not only has the **regular veto** been employed, but the **pocket veto** is sometimes used even more frequently. Serving over three full terms, Franklin D. Roosevelt exercised the most vetoes, but Cleveland vetoed the most laws in a single term, and he is a close second to Franklin D. Roosevelt in total number of vetoes.

While Truman and Ford suffered the greatest number of regular veto overrides in this century, Ford, Nixon, and Reagan endured the highest percentages of overrides. Indeed, although Bush has yet to see one of his vetoes negated, the four presidents immediately preceding him suffered the highest aggregate percentage of overrides of any comparable grouping in this century. It seems, as McKay points out, that the veto power is becoming less resistant to congressional rejection. Also, we can see from the records of other recent presidents that normally presidents whose parties control the majority of Congress both veto fewer bills and have fewer bills overridden.

Not only the regular veto is controversial, however. Congressional authorities hold that the **pocket veto** is not applicable until after Congress has adjourned its term *sine die,* and most presidents have accepted this interpretation. However, Richard Nixon tried to pocket veto a law while Congress was in recess between sessions of a single term. An appeals court ruled that the congressional interpretation was correct and neither Ford nor Carter attempted another pocket veto except when Congress was actually adjourned. However, Reagan claimed to pocket veto two laws while Congress was in recess. Unfortunately, the matter is not yet settled as the Supreme Court refused to hear the case challenging Reagan's action because the case had become moot. Reagan did not try to use the pocket veto during a recess again after 1984, however.[45]

As mentioned earlier, although most state governors enjoy the power of the **line item veto** (permitting the executive to veto part of a bill while allowing the rest to stand), the president does not have that power—or at least, so it was assumed until 1989. Both presidents Carter and Reagan, trying to gain more control over federal spending, advocated that the Constitution be amended to give the president the line item veto, but Congress refused to so limit its own powers. President Bush, however, has taken a new tack. He instructed his staff to find a bill upon which he can exercise an item veto in order to test it in court. Bush argues that the founders intended Congress to pass single-subject bills, but over the years Congress has gravitated toward passing single pieces of legislation that cover a multitude of unrelated subjects.

Hence, Bush claims that Congress is operating contrary to the founders' intent and that the line item veto is therefore justified. Few constitutional scholars give Bush's interpretation much chance, however, and the aggressive move has angered the leaders of Congress.[46]

Between 1932 and 1983 Congress put its own slant on the veto power by passing over 200 laws that held executive action subject to its approval. This was called the *legislative veto.* If the executive took an action subject to these laws, Congress reserved the "right" to negate it by passing a resolution to that effect. The matter was taken to the Supreme Court in 1983, and it ruled that the legislative veto was unconstitutional because it gave Congress power to meddle in administrative affairs and thus was a violation of the separation of powers. With this decision, *Immigration and Naturalization Service v. Chadha,* the Court in one fell swoop voided parts of more federal laws than it had ever done before.[47]

The *appointment power* is yet another area of recurring conflict between Congress (or at least the Senate) and the president, although there is perhaps less controversy than one might imagine. There is one informal rule that no president can afford to ignore: **senatorial courtesy**. Because the Constitution gives the Senate the authority to confirm presidential appointments and because appointment to federal office is often a method by which to reward political supporters, the members of the Senate unite to force the president to share patronage with them. When the president is considering filling a position in an office whose jurisdiction is completely contained within a single state (United States Attorney, Marshal, District Court Judge, and sometimes Appellate Court Judge), the president is required to appoint a person whom the senator from the president's party in the state involved accepts. If both senators in a state are from the president's party, each must be consulted, although the senior senator usually enjoys the greater voice in the matter. If the president ignores this requirement, the senator from the president's party announces that the nominee is "personally obnoxious" and the Senate will not confirm the appointment. If neither senator is from the president's party, the president may consult state party leaders, powerful House members, or even senators from the opposition who represent the state in which the appointment is to be made, but the rule of senatorial courtesy does not demand it. Any attempt to make an appointment in violation of the rule, however, is doomed to failure. Interestingly, because nominations to the Supreme Court do not come under the rule, the president has the greatest latitude when filling the country's highest bench. Also, most administration positions do not come under the rule.

Over the years, the Senate has developed the policy of giving the president great latitude in selecting people for appointment provided senatorial courtesy is observed. Generally the

attitude has been that a president should be able to pick the people she or he wishes for federal appointments. As you can see from Table 10.2, only 25 nominees were rejected by the Senate between 1945 and 1988. Many more, however, were withdrawn or simply not confirmed by the Senate. Recently, however, the Senate has taken a harder look at major presidential appointments. President Reagan's commitment to a new social agenda (supporting prayer in schools, opposing abortion, and limiting civil liberties and civil rights) led congressional moderates and liberals to challenge several Reagan nominations. Controversial though Reagan's appointments were, however, all but two of his nominees were confirmed until 1986, when he nominated Robert Bork for the Supreme Court.

Throughout a distinguished career in academics, as Solicitor General, and on the federal appellate bench, Bork had challenged "settled law" and argued against many of the Supreme Court's opinions (civil rights, the right to pri-

Table 10.2

PRESIDENTIAL APPOINTMENTS AND SENATE ACTION, 1945–1988

President	Nominated	Confirmed	With-drawn	Rejected	Uncon-firmed	Percentage of Nominations Not Confirmed
Truman	237,849	224,412	260	11	13,166	5.7%
Eisenhower	349,300	345,468	165	4	4,663	1.4%
Kennedy[a]	102,849	100,741	1,279	0	829	2.1%
Johnson	365,440	359,297	243	0	5,900	1.7%
Nixon[b]	385,901	379,960	513	2	5,380	1.6%
Ford[c]	132,151	131,378	6	0	3,801	2.9%
Carter	292,301	279,395	84	0	14,171	5.1%
Reagan	472,964	466,638	98	8	11,665	2.5%

[a] Only nominees to the 87th Congress (1961–1962) are counted here. The nominees to the 88th Congress (1963–1964) are accredited to Lyndon Johnson's total.

[b] All nominees in the period 1969–1974 are counted in Nixon's total.

[c] Only nominees to the 94th Congress (1975–1976) are counted for President Ford.

Source: Based on data in Stanley and Niemi, *Vital Statistics on American Politics,* 2nd ed.

vacy, and the right to an abortion, for example). Bork's nomination to the highest court set off a firestorm of protest from minority and women's groups that ultimately led to his defeat in the Senate. Reagan's next nominee, Douglas Ginsburg, even ran afoul of conservatives when it became public that he had used marijuana in the 1970s. The withdrawal of his name forestalled a Senate defeat, but the conservatives had received a serious blow and a Democratic Congress was primed for future battles. Although Reagan's nomination of Anthony Kennedy and Bush's nomination of David H. Souter to fill vacancies on the Supreme Court were confirmed easily, the Senate withheld its approval of an important Bush nomination to the executive branch.

When President Bush came to office in 1989, he met a toughened Congress. Although the Senate confirmed several of Bush's appointments in the first months of his term, it balked

Surrounded by swarms of reporters, former senator John Tower (R-TX) campaigns in an unsuccessful bid to get Senate confirmation for his nomination as secretary of defense.

at John Tower for Secretary of Defense. Tower had served in the Senate for 24 years, his expertise on defense matters went unquestioned, and since the Senate rarely fails to confirm a Cabinet nominee and it had never before refused to give the nod to one of its own members, Tower's confirmation seemed at first assured. As the confirmation hearings progressed, however, the Democratic majority of the Senate became increasingly concerned about reports of Tower's flirtations and sexist habits. Perhaps more serious for one who was to know the deepest national security secrets of the country, the Senate was put off by his heavy drinking. After a bitter struggle, the Senate voted against Tower's nomination along party lines, with only three Democrats voting for him and one Republican voting against him. This stunning defeat marked the first time in history a new president's choice of a Cabinet officer was rejected and only the 12th time that a Cabinet nominee was not confirmed. (See Table 10.3.) Following Tower's defeat, Bush nominated Richard Cheney, a highly respected Republican member of the House from Wyoming, and he was quickly confirmed. Tower's rejection, however, gave impetus to Republican efforts in the House to unseat Speaker Jim Wright (D-TX).

Following the Tower episode, several other Bush appointees ran into trouble in the Senate in 1989. Senate critics complained that Bush was nominating for ambassadorships an inordinate number of people whose only obvious qualifications for the posts were that they had given generous amounts of money to the 1988 Bush campaign.[48] Also, after another bitter Senate battle, William Lucas was rejected as Assistant Attorney General for Civil Rights by the Senate Judiciary Committee because he was deemed unqualified. The confirmation of several other Bush nominees was also held up, forcing them to withdraw from consideration. The Senate seemed particularly concerned that

Table 10.3
CABINET NOMINEES NOT CONFIRMED

	NOMINEE	POSITION	PRESIDENT
1834	Roger B. Taney	Sec. of Treasury	Jackson
1843	Caleb Cushing	Sec. of Treasury	Tyler
1843	Caleb Cushing	Sec. of Treasury	Tyler
1843	Caleb Cushing	Sec. of Treasury	Tyler
1844	David Henshaw	Sec. of Navy	Tyler
1844	James M. Porter	Sec. of War	Tyler
1844	James S. Green	Sec. of Treasury	Tyler
1886	Henry Stanbery	Attorney General	A. Johnson
1925	Charles B. Warren	Attorney General	Coolidge
1925	Charles B. Warren	Attorney General	Coolidge
1959	Lewis L. Strauss	Sec. of Commerce	Eisenhower
1989	John Tower	Sec. of Defense	Bush

people with questionable records on environmental protection not be appointed.[49] Finally, in 1991, the Senate refused to confirm District Court Judge Kenneth L. Ryskamp for a seat on the Appellate Court because of Ryskamp's dismal record on civil rights cases.[50]

Bush entered office with the stated objective to end the conflict between the Congress and the president. "The American people," he said in his Inaugural Address, "did not send us here to bicker." Accordingly, he made several efforts to develop a good rapport with Congress, including making personal contacts with the leaders of both parties and the unprecedented gesture of "dropping by" on the Senate floor to greet his former colleagues. Although these efforts are commendable, they ignore the overriding factors dividing the two branches: partisanship, ideological differences, and the constitutional predisposition for conflict between the legislature and the executive. While Bush enjoyed the traditional honeymoon period in the first few months of his administration, inevitably he and the Democratic-controlled Congress fell to squabbling over the

important issues. Vetoing bills that would have provided government funds to the poor for abortions, advances for minorities and women in the workplace, and the first increase of the minimum wage in nine years, Bush further antagonized the Democrats by pushing a plan to reduce taxes on capital gains income, offering Poland and Hungary scant financial assistance for their efforts to shed the stagnation of Stalinist economics, insisting that the lion's share of the money used to bailout the ailing savings and loan industry be manipulated so that the increased debt would not be recorded on the federal deficit, and advocating an amendment to the Constitution (the first ever to change the Bill of Rights) in order to make it illegal to deface the flag. Hence, despite Bush's genuine efforts to create a better relationship with Congress—steps that congressional Democrats met with sincere attempts of cooperation—the realities of politics and the dynamics of the separation of powers and the checks and balances have not been overcome. The people's business is still decided in an environment of confrontation, and the president was reduced to complaining in frustration that his only recourse in attempts to lead Congress is to "veto and exhort."[51]

The nature of public policy and its administration are, of course, essential to our inquiry, so we shall now turn to their consideration.

Summary

- Although the courts can void the actions of the executive and the acts of Congress, they depend on the other branches for their very existence, so they have been careful not to unduly alienate either of the other two branches.

- Although the Supreme Court has been especially careful not to anger the president, it has on several important occasions held the president accountable to the Constitution.

- Congress controls the ultimate authority over the judges and the executive: impeachment. It has used impeachment sparingly, but most impeachment cases have been brought against judges.

- Congress and the president have frequently come into conflict, as attested by the current struggles over the War Powers Act and the budget.

- While throughout most of the century the president has dominated the political scene, since the 1970s the Congress has been especially assertive in combating the growing power of the president.

- Several areas have been subjects of traditional conflict between Congress and the president, including executive privilege, the veto power, and appointments.

Notes

1. Richard E. Neustadt, *Presidential Power* (New York: Wiley, 1960), p. 10.

2. Alice Fleetwood Bartee, *Cases Lost, Cases Won* (New York: St. Martin's Press, 1984), p. 2.

3. Robert Scigliano, *The Supreme Court and the Presidency* (New York: Free Press, 1971), p. 197.

4. Robert J. Sickels, *The Presidency* (Englewood Cliffs, NJ: Prentice-Hall, 1980), p. 138

5. *Ex Parte Merryman*, 17 Federal Case 9487 (1861).

6. *Ex Parte Milligan*, 4 Wall 2 (1866).

7. *Humphrey's Executor* v. *United States*, 293 U.S. 602 (1935); *Panama Refining Company* v. *Ryan*, 293 U.S. 388 (1935), the "hot oil" case; and *Schechter Poultry Corporation* v. *United States*, 295 U.S. 495 (1935), the "sick chicken" case.

8. David E. Kyvig, "The Road Not Taken: FDR, The Supreme Court, and Constitutional Amendment," *Political Science Quarterly* (Fall 1989), 465–466.

9. *Hirabayashi* v. *United States*, 320 U.S. 81 (1943), and *Korematsu* v. *United States*, 323 U.S. 214 (1944).

10. *Youngstown Sheet and Tube* v. *Sawyer*, 343 U.S. 479 (1952).

11. *New York Times* v. *United States*, 403 U.S. 713 (1971).

12. *United States* v. *District Court*, 467 U.S. 297 (1972).

13. *United States* v. *Nixon*, 418 U.S. 683 (1974).

14. *Dames & Moore* v. *Reagan*, 453 U.S. 654 (1981).

15. *Morrison* v. *Olson*, 487 U.S. 654 (1988).

16. *Dole* v. *United Steelworkers*, 110 S. Ct. 929 (1990).

17. Mark Silverstein and Benjamin Ginsberg, "The Supreme Court and the New Politics of Judicial Power," *Political Science Quarterly* (Fall 1987), 374.

18. Samuel Eliot Morison, Henry Steele Commager, and William E. Leuchtenburg, *The Growth of the American Republic* (New York: Oxford University Press, 1969), p. 754.

19. *Ex Parte McCardle*, 7 Wallace 506 (1869).

20. *Pollock* v. *Farmers' Loan and Trust Co.*, 158 U.S. 601 (1896).

21. Article I of the United States Constitution.

22. Article II, Section 4 of the United States Constitution.

23. Raoul Berger, *Impeachment: The Constitutional Problems* (New York: Bantam Books, 1974), pp. 224–225.

24. Richard Hofstadter, William Miller, and Daniel Aaron, *The American Republic*, (Englewood Cliffs, NJ: Prentice-Hall, 1970), p. 32.

25. John F. Kennedy, *Profiles in Courage* (New York: Cardinal, 1957), pp. 107–128.

26. William J. Eaton, "Senate Convicts Judge, Strips Him of Office," *The Los Angeles Times*, Oct. 21, 1989, and "Senate Convicts U.S. Judge on Perjury Counts," *The Los Angeles Times*, Nov. 4, 1989.

27. Harold J. Spaeth, *An Introduction To Supreme Court Decision Making*, rev. ed. (San Francisco: Chandler Publishing Company, 1972), pp. 8–10.

28. Michael J. Ybarra, "Senate Nearing Votes on Whether to Oust Two Impeached U.S. Judges," *The Los Angeles Times*, Oct. 10, 1989.

29. James W. Davis, *The American Presidency* (New York: Harper & Row, 1987), pp. 146–147.

30. Nelson W. Polsby, *Congress and the Presidency* (Englewood Cliffs, NJ: Prentice-Hall, 1986), pp 187–196.

31. *United States* v. *Nixon*, 418 U.S. 638 (1974).

32. James L. Sundquist, *The Decline and Resurgence of Congress* (Washington, DC: The Brookings Institution, 1981), pp. 254–272.

33. Norman J. Ornstein, *Vital Statistics on Congress 1987–1989* (Washington, DC: Congressional Quarterly, 1987), p. 137; also see Sundquist, pp. 209–215 and 236–237.

34. Hedrick Smith, *The Power Game* (New York: Random House, 1988), pp. 645–646.

35. Smith, pp. 290–291.

36. William J. Eaton, "Bush Apparently Outflanked on Budget Battleground," *The Los Angeles Times*, Oct. 27, 1990.

37. William J. Eaton, "Budget Agreement Having Positive Effect on Congress," *The Los Angeles Times,* Apr. 29, 1991.

38. Robert L. Jackson, "Walsh Assails White House on Case Dismissal," *The Los Angeles Times,* Dec. 12, 1989.

39. Ronald J. Ostrow, "Frustrated Walsh Held Set to Take Administration to Court to Get Data," *The Los Angeles Times,* Oct. 26, 1990.

40. Sundquist, pp. 18–19.

41. *United States* v. *Nixon,* 418 U.S. 368 (1974).

42. Norman Kempster, "Reagan Tapes Testimony for Poindexter Case," *The Los Angeles Times,* Feb. 12, 1990.

43. Woodrow Wilson, *Congressional Government* (Boston: Houghton Mifflin, 1985), p. 52.

44. David McKay, "Presidential Strategy and the Veto Power: A Reappraisal," *Political Science Quarterly* (Fall 1989), 448–449 and 460.

45. McKay, pp. 259–260.

46. David Lauter, "Bush Seeks to Fight It Out for 'Line-Item Veto' Power," *The Los Angeles Times,* Oct. 24, 1989.

47. *Immigration and Naturalization Service* v. *Chadha,* 462 U.S. 919 (1983), and Lawrence Baum, *The Supreme Court,* 3rd ed. (Washington, DC: Congressional Quarterly Press, 1989), pp. 114–115.

48. "3 Ambassadorial Nominations Squeak By in Senate Committee," *The Los Angeles Times,* July 26, 1989.

49. Rudy Abramson, "Forest Service Nomination Not Brought to a Vote in Senate, Is Dead," *The Los Angeles Times,* Nov. 18, 1989, and "Vote Delayed on Bush Nominee; 2nd Polls Name," *The Los Angeles Times,* Nov. 21, 1989.

50. David G. Savage, "Panel Rejects Bush Choice for Judgeship," *The Los Angeles Times,* Apr. 12, 1991.

51. David Lauter, "President Seeks to Downplay Abortion Issue," *The Los Angeles Times,* Nov. 8, 1989.

Suggestions for Further Reading

Abraham, Henry J. *Justices and Presidents: A Political History of Appointments to the Supreme Court* (2nd ed.). New York: Oxford University Press, 1985.

Berger, Raoul. *Impeachment: The Constitutional Problems.* New York: Bantam Books, 1974.

Cox, Archibald. *The Role of the Supreme Court in American Government.* New York: Oxford University Press, 1976.

Edwards, George C., III. *At the Margins: Presidential Leadership of Congress.* New Haven: Yale University Press, 1989.

Fisher, Louis. *Constitutional Conflicts Between Congress and the President.* Princeton: Princeton University Press, 1985.

Forte, David F. *The Supreme Court in American Politics.* Lexington, MA: D. C. Heath, 1972.

Johnson, Charles A., and Bradley C. Cannon. *Judicial Politics: Implementation and Impact.* Washington, DC: Congressional Quarterly Press, 1984.

King, Anthony, ed. *Both Ends of the Avenue.* Washington, DC: American Enterprise Institute, 1983.

Murphy, Walter F., and C. Herman Pritchett. *Courts, Judges and Politics.* New York: Random House, 1974.

O'Brien, David M. *Storm Center: The Supreme Court and American Politics.* New York: Norton, 1986.

Shuman, Howard E. *Politics and the Budget: The Struggle Between the President and Congress* (2nd ed.). Englewood Cliffs, NJ: Prentice-Hall, 1988.

Wilson, Woodrow. *Constitutional Government in the United States.* New York: Columbia University Press, 1908.

Chapter 11

ECONOMIC AND
SOCIAL POLICY

PREVIEW

For most of our history, American economic attitudes have been dominated by the concept of _laissez-faire,_ Adam Smith's advice, which discouraged government involvement in the economy. The Great Depression of the 1930s, however, brought Franklin D. Roosevelt's New Deal to government, and policies were adopted that saw the government become deeply involved in promoting and regulating the economy to assure that people would be spared the worst ravages of poverty.

Essentially, the government adopted policies consistent with the theories of John Maynard Keynes, which basically relied on fiscal policy to manage the economy. As the decades passed, however, new economic theories began to gain acceptance in certain quarters. The monetarists argue that the economy should be controlled by manipulating the price of credit and the amount of money in the economy, while the supply-side advocates believe that taxes should be lowered to stimulate economic activity. Both of these policies were applied in the 1980s, dramatically reducing inflation, unemployment, and taxes, but revenues fell while net government expenditures increased, which tripled the national debt.

The government has several fiscal means by which to manipulate the economy. Taxes both raise revenue and regulate human behavior. Interestingly, the income tax is not only a major revenue generator, it is also a favored mechanism for inducing desired behaviors and discouraging undesirable acts. The government fiscal policy uses borrowing and spending to manipulate the economy as well. In the 1980s, the level of borrowing became so great and the amount of interest paid so huge that Congress tried to control the annual deficits by passing the Gramm-Rudman-Hollings Act, attempting to gradually reduce the deficits, but they continue to mount.

Obviously the government buys goods and services with its expenditures, but it also increases employment and economic activity, and moves money from one place in the economy to another for the benefit of general economic prosperity. The government is also heavily involved in promoting and regulating the economy in a number of other ways, encouraging fair business and labor practices.

The Reagan Administration came to Washington with the same reluctance President Carter had to continue past regulatory practices. Accordingly, much government regulatory interference was eliminated, but at the cost of creating serious problems in some key areas. As a result, much of the nation's financial industry and some government agencies were mismanaged and looted by unscrupulous people, causing the loss of billions of dollars, which the government had guaranteed and now must repay.

The social policies of the government can be divided into social insurance programs and public assistance programs (welfare). The social security program is sustained by a high, regressive tax, and provides benefits to the aged, their survivors, and the disabled. Medicare pays a portion of the medical expenses for the elderly, and unemployment insurance can be collected by workers who have been laid off.

The largest public assistance program is Aid to Families with Dependent Children (AFDC). It is administered by the states, and the benefits and conditions for qualifying vary among the states. Medicaid pays many medical bills for AFDC recipients, and Supplemental Security Income (SSI) equalizes the incomes of indigent, disabled, and aged people. The government also has several programs to feed the hungry and to house the poor. The welfare programs have long been controversial and they were severely cut in the 1980s.

The bills for the 1980s excesses may be coming due.

Kevin Phillips, conservative social commentator

The government of the United States engages in several efforts to assure the general well-being of society. It manipulates the economy, promotes business and labor, regulates people and enterprises, and administers social programs. Although a complete examination of these efforts exceeds the reach of this book, we shall investigate the most important domestic policies here.

The Economic Policy of Government

Before the 1930s, the dominant economic view was that the government should do little to interfere with the economy. In his famous work, *The Wealth of Nations*, Adam Smith (1723–1790), the founder of capitalist theory, enunciated the principle of **laissez-faire**, by which he meant that the market should be left free to be guided by the "invisible hand" of supply and demand. Government was not to intrude in the economy because if it did, the natural forces of the market would become distorted and lead to reduced prosperity. Smith's ideas were perhaps most warmly received in the United States, but Smith's injunction was not completely endorsed in America. He op-

posed all forms of government involvement in the economy. The state was not to regulate or help commerce. While American entrepreneurs held firmly to the notion that government should not regulate the economy, they enthusiastically endorsed government policy designed to aid business. Thus tariffs, government subsidies to business, the Departments of Agriculture and Commerce, beneficial taxing policies, and many other devices created to advance the well-being of commerce were applauded.

The net result of these one-sided policies was that the United States became a major economic power, but that labor and consumers found themselves at the mercy of the financial, corporate, and commercial classes, and *caveat emptor* (let the buyer beware) became the guiding principle of the age preceding the Great Depression. The need for government regulation of the economy became a major political issue toward the turn of the century. Congress created the Interstate Commerce Commission (ICC) in 1887 to regulate the railroads, and three years later it passed the Sherman Antitrust Act to prevent the rapidly occurring monopolization of the basic industries. In the early 1900s another rush of regulatory legislation under President Woodrow Wilson created the

Clayton Antitrust Act and the Federal Trade Commission. These efforts, however, were largely frustrated by a conservative Supreme Court that treated capitalism as a constitutional principle, strictly curtailing government regulatory policy.[1]

In 1929, however, a depression struck that was of such magnitude that it could not be allowed to "bottom out" on its own. Billions of dollars' worth of credit evaporated as the stock market crashed and the banks closed. The gross national product (GNP)—an estimation of the dollar value of goods and services produced in a year—plummeted, until by 1933 it was only half of its 1929 mark. Fortunes disappeared, one-quarter of the labor force was out of work, wages fell precipitously, and farms were lost. Lines backed up for blocks at soup kitchens, and able-bodied workers sold pencils and apples on street corners. Confused and disoriented people struggled to make sense of their situation, and they cried out for the government to do something to set things right. President Herbert Hoover, a talented administrator and a well-meaning man, true to traditional *laissez-faire* dogma was convinced that government relief action would only make things worse. The people, on the other hand, seeing their

Unemployed farmers who, in the depths of the Great Depression, try to survive by selling apples in the city.

children starving, became impatient with such ideological intransigence and elected Franklin Delano Roosevelt in the landslide of 1932.[2]

Roosevelt's **New Deal** policies represented a fundamental change in notions about the government's appropriate role in the economy. Until the 1930s, economic and social policy were left almost entirely in the hands of state and local governments, and to individuals. By contrast, the New Dealers came to view economic and social well-being as a national concern to be addressed by the federal government in concert with state and local governments and the private sector. Accordingly, massive programs were implemented to regulate business and finance; public works projects created jobs and built dams, roads, bridges, and buildings; and personal financial security was stabilized by collective bargaining for labor, agricultural support schemes, unemployment insurance, social security for the aged and survivors, and welfare programs for the poor.

These policies, however, were only moderately successful in recovering from the Depression. Indeed, it was not until the stimulus of World War II that the economy managed to regain its pre-Depression vitality. After the war, Congress adopted a law that officially stated the policy upon which the New Deal was founded: It is the government's responsibility to pursue policies designed to assure the economic well-being of the country. This formal commitment took the form of the **Employment Act of 1946**, which not only acknowledged the government's responsibility to manage the economy, but also developed several instruments by which to do so. Thus, *laissez-faire* was abandoned and American capitalism was given a more human face by the infusion of a mild amount of socialism.

From the 1940s until the 1980s, few politicians opposed this basic policy change with more than rhetoric. The Democrats usually favored more government involvement in the economic and social systems, while the Republicans generally slowed the programs, but no one seriously attempted to reverse the policy. By the late 1970s, however, demands that government reduce its regulation of the economy had mounted. President Carter acceded to congressional pressure to deregulate the airlines, interstate trucking, and the railroads. Additionally, the Federal Trade Commission was limited in its regulatory powers in 1980.

These policies were redoubled by Ronald Reagan, who swept into office complaining that government was too heavily involved in the private sector, and that government regulations of business, finance, the stock market, and communications should be cut. He talked forcefully of an economic crisis in which taxes were oppressive, economic activity was sluggish, and the deficits were irresponsibly high. He averred that the federal government should focus on defense, which he said had been sadly neglected, and return to the states and to individuals the powers and freedoms in the economic and social realms denied them over the past half-century by an intrusive federal government. "For the first time," political scientist Hugh Heclo said, "Reagan brought an approach to Washington designed not so much to accomplish things but to stop them."[3]

Exuding self-confidence and certainty, Reagan deftly exploited the political opportunity his 1980 election victory offered by popularizing his supply-side philosophy (to be explained in the next section). Convinced that a cut in taxes would ignite an "explosion" of economic activity, he pushed through Congress a major tax cut in 1981, even as he secured immense increases in defense spending. Claiming that the anticipated tidal wave of economic activity would "raise all boats," thus improving the economic conditions of all people and making obsolete many of the government's social programs, he demanded that Congress slash domestic spending. Yet, although Congress cut deeply into the social programs, the huge increase in defense spending coupled with the fact that the economy actually plummeted into the deepest recession since the 1930s rather than skyrocketing, made the budget deficits that Reagan had promised to end jump to unprecedented levels. Actually, before the tax cut was passed, David Stockman, Director of the Office of Management and Budget, and other Reagan Administration officials recognized that the rosy economic projections they had advanced to justify the tax cut were badly in error. Indeed, they realized this early enough to warn Congress that a recession was developing, but since such information would almost certainly have killed the proposed 1981 tax cut, they said nothing.[4]

The overall economic record of the Reagan Administration is mixed. Inflation was reduced by almost two-thirds, unemployment fell to a 14-year low, and interest rates were much lower in 1988 than in 1980. The income tax was lower than it had been in decades and, following the recession of 1981-1982, Reagan presided over the longest peacetime economic recovery in history. But there are many negatives as well. While the economy expanded, the growth was sluggish and did not increase at anything near the rate predicted. Rather than balancing the budget as promised, the government borrowed almost twice as much money as had been borrowed in all previous administrations combined; although the size of government was supposed to be reduced, it actually increased; and by the end of Reagan's second term the federal government spent 24 percent of the GNP, 2 percentage points higher than in Carter's last year. At the same time, the United States fell from being the world's greatest creditor nation to becoming its greatest debtor in international trade. (See Figure 11.1.)

The immense cuts made in welfare, food stamps, public housing, job training, and edu-

cation have seen the gap between the rich and poor increase for the first time in almost 15 years. What's more, many analysts, including Bush OMB Director Richard Darman, suggest that the huge deficits will make it impossible to initiate any new social programs or to expand existing ones very much, so that the New Deal approach is permanently crippled by a heavily debt-burdened economy.[5]

Coming to office in 1989, President Bush faced formidable economic challenges. Industry was heavily mortgaged and uncompetitive; the plight of the poor, the homeless, and the hungry was obvious; and the environment and education were each in desperate need of attention. The nation's roads and bridges were in disrepair, our energy needs had to be addressed, and the financial system was in serious difficulty. Yet, government revenues were insufficient to the needs. The president's dilemma is perplexing, and so far, except for the savings and loan bailout, a clean air bill, and a few other proposals, he has done little to develop his own domestic programs.

No one in the Bush Administration mentions the supply-side approach any more, and "Reaganomics" has even gone out of fashion. What theoretical model Bush will use to try to pull the society out of its economic doldrums is as yet unclear, but there are several established formulas from which he can choose.

ECONOMIC THEORIES

The economic approach of the New Deal was based on **Keynesian economics**. John Maynard Keynes (1883-1946) was an English socialist and perhaps the most influential economist in this century. Keynes believed that the economy should be controlled by **fiscal policy**—the government's manipulation of taxes, borrowing, and spending. Depression, Keynes reasoned, came from people refusing to spend and invest

Figure 11.1   Reagan's Economic Performance

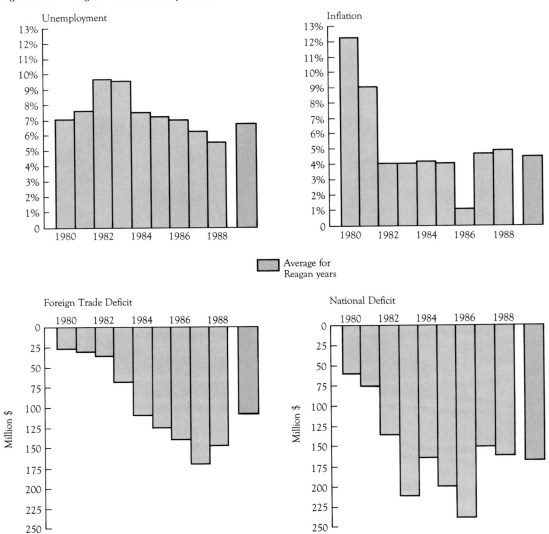

Source: Unemployment and National Debt, *Vital Statistics on American Politics,* 2nd ed., pp. 384–386; Inflation and Foreign Trade Deficit, Office of Management and Budget.

their money. In such cases, demand falls, so production is cut back, meaning that jobs and wages are reduced, resulting in even less spending and investment. If private sector spending falls, Keynes suggested that government should expand its expenditures, even if it must borrow money to do so, thus increasing the money in circulation and maintaining demand and employment. When people learn that the economy is not failing, they will begin to spend and invest again, and the government can back off. Inflation—when too much money is chasing too few goods, thus driving prices up—can be dealt with in the reverse. The government should tax and not spend, thus reducing the amount of money in the economy. Experience has taught that the Keynesian model works relatively well in averting depression but that it is less efficient, or even a failure, at combating inflation.

Two other theories have gained considerable followings in recent years. The **monetarists**, otherwise referred to as the **Chicago school**, led by Nobel Prize-winner Milton Friedman, argue that the health of the economy should be controlled by taking care that no more or less money is released into the economy than is justified by the growth of the economy. This model seems to be very effective at controlling inflation, but it is accused of leading to recession. For example, the rampant inflation of the late 1970s and early 1980s was tamed by the monetary policies of the Federal Reserve System under the leadership of Paul Volcker, but these policies also helped push the economy into the recession of 1981–1982.

The **supply-side** theory became popular in the 1980s. The key to this theory is that taxes should be reduced, because lower taxes will encourage private savings and investment as well as stimulate consumer spending and production. Producers will invest more because they have more money to venture, due to lower taxes, and the **Laffer Curve** (named for its creator, Arthur Laffer, Professor of Economics at the University of Southern California) projected that people would work harder to earn more because less would be taken out of their pockets for taxes. The increased economic activity would increase government revenues to compensate for the tax cuts, thus resulting in a win-win situation.

Implemented by the Reagan Administration, the supply-side theory proved a failure. Indeed, as early as 1981, Reagan's Director of the Office and Management and Budget and the principal architect of "Reaganomics," David Stockman, admitted that supply-side economics was a fraud. The disillusioned Stockman told *Atlantic Monthly* that supply-side rhetoric was only a ploy to reduce the taxes of the well-to-do. It was nothing more than a newly packaged "trickle-down theory" (the notion that the advantages given to the wealthy will eventually make their way to everyone).[6] Stockman's warning, which he soon retracted, was ignored by most people, so Reaganomics was allowed to run its course. Not surprisingly, the predicted "explosion of economic growth" did not materialize, and personal savings actually declined during the era, even as the budget deficits rose to unparalleled heights.

Disillusioned with the failure of Reaganomics, Stockman resigned from the administration and in a 1986 interview on the public television program "Front Line," he lamented, "We have conducted the greatest free-lunch fiscal policy of modern times." The current public disenchantment with the supply-side hypothesis is no surprise to the community of academic economists, who foretold its failure far in advance of the experiment.[7]

As can be seen from this or any other survey of economic theory, economists often disagree. Regardless of the theorem used, however, there are two principal formats in which politicians attempt to address the well-being of the economy: fiscal policy and monetary policy.

FISCAL POLICY

Fiscal policy refers to government taxes, borrowing, and spending, and it is largely controlled by the president and Congress. By manipulating these factors, the government can attempt to regulate the economy because it can take money from one sector and apply it elsewhere. If done correctly, the Keynesians believe that the government can prevent inflation and recession, thus assuring the economic well-being of the country.

Taxing Policy   Taxes come in three main varieties, flat, progressive, and regressive. A **flat tax** is a tax that falls evenly on everyone. For example, if all people were required to pay 20 percent of their income in taxes and if there were no tax deductions, the assessment would be a flat tax. Such a tax may seem fair at first glance, but since it does not take into account the ability of people to pay taxes, it could be devastating to people living at or below the poverty line. No federal tax is completely flat. **Progressive taxes** are those that tax most heavily those who have the greatest ability to pay. Using this model, in 1989 a person making $20,000 annually (the tax base) might be assessed a 15 percent tax rate, while a person making $200,000 annually might be expected to pay a higher rate, say 28 percent. The income tax is a progressive tax, but it also allows certain tax deductions which can be used to lower the tax base. If the tax base is reduced enough by using these deductions, the tax rate one must pay is also lowered. For example, say a person with a family of four made $40,000 per year. Without deductions the tax rate assessed would be 28 percent, or $11,200. But, if by

deducting for dependents, home mortgages, and tax shelters, the person could reduce the taxable income to $30,000, she or he would have to pay only 15 percent, or $4,500—a savings of $6,700.

It should be quickly pointed out, however, that the income tax schedule was not truly progressive at all in 1989. A glance at Table 11.1 reveals that the tax schedule was really "mid-gressive" in that the middle class paid a higher tax rate than did the poor or the wealthy. Also note that the government heavily subsidized married couples as opposed to single persons through the income tax schedule.

Regressive taxes are those that increase most rapidly for the poor as a percentage of total income. Interestingly, most taxes in the United States are regressive. It can be taken as a rule that taxes usually fall most heavily on people with the least political power because the politically powerful can always come up with reasons why someone else should carry a greater tax burden than themselves. An example of a regressive tax is the social security tax. Almost everyone pays the social security tax. The tax is roughly 8 percent, but in 1990 it was assessed only on the first $51,300 one earned. Accordingly, a person earning $20,000 per year paid 8 percent of total income toward the social security tax. By contrast, someone earning $200,000 per year paid only about 2 percent of income in social security tax. Because the social security tax asked the lower wage earner to pay 4 times as much of her or his salary as the $200,000-a-year person, the tax was sharply regressive. The 1990 budget agreement included an increase in the social security taxes paid by the rich, but the tax is still heavily regressive.

A recent report of the House Ways and Means Committee demonstrates that taxes in the 1980s became much more regressive than they had been before. It found that the effec-

Table 11.1
1989 PERSONAL INCOME TAX SCHEDULE

A MARRIED COUPLE FILING JOINTLY	A SINGLE PERSON	PERCENTAGE
0–$30,950	0–$18,550	15%
$30,951–$74,850	$18,551–$44,900	28%
$74,851–$155,320	$44,901–$93,030	33%
$155,321 and up	$93,031 and up	28%

Note: The middle-class paid a 33% tax rate while the wealthy paid only 28%. This phenomenon was known as the *middle-class bubble.*

It should also be noted that people pay taxes all the way through the tax schedule. Hence, a person making $93,030 in 1989 paid only 15% of the first $18,550 and 28% on income between $18,550 and $44,900. This person paid 33% only on income between $44,900 and $93,030, or 51.7% of his or her salary. By contrast, someone making $1,000,000 would have paid 33% on only 4.8% of his or her earnings, while paying only 28% on 95.5% of the total income.

tive federal tax rate—the total taxes paid on income and for social security/Medicare—rose for the poorest 20 percent of the population by 16.1 percent during the decade, while their real income increased by only 3.2 percent. This tax increase took place even though the 1986 tax reform bill removed millions of the poorest Americans from the tax rolls. Conversely, the taxes paid by the richest 20 percent dropped by 5.5 percent, even as their income rose by 31.7 percent. The income gain was highest among those who earned the most. The top 5 percent of American earners enjoyed a 46.1 percent increase in income during the 1980s.[8]

In a similar analysis, Kevin Phillips, the conservative social commentator quoted above, said of the 1980s, "In a nutshell, Middle America got the speeches; upper America got the bucks." Phillips points out that from 1980 to 1990 the top income tax bracket fell from 70 percent to 28 percent, while social security taxes shot up from 5.8 percent to 7.65 percent and the base for the tax doubled, from $25,900

to $51,300. Phillips also cited a Congressional Budget Office study showing that in 1977 the richest 1 percent of Americans owned 7.2 percent of the total wealth, but by 1990 their share had increased to 11.4 percent.[9]

Results of Taxation   Each tax has varied results and consequences, but all taxes do at least two things: raise revenue for the government, and regulate people. Revenue simply means income to the government, and the government has basically two kinds of revenue: **tax revenue** (the money it raises from taxes) and **nontax revenue** (money accruing to the government from sources other than taxes). Some examples of nontax revenues are gifts; fees and fines; and money earned by the United States Postal Service, the Tennessee Valley Authority (TVA), the Panama Canal, and the Government Printing Office. The largest single source of nontax revenue recently has been the annual deficits—the money government has had to borrow to meet expenses. While the nontax revenues total billions of dollars, they actually represent only a tiny percentage of the budget, except for the deficit, which was estimated to be 19 percent of the total revenue accumulated by the government in 1992.

Interestingly, although most government revenue comes from taxes, the federal government raises most of its tax revenues from only a small number of important taxes. The personal income tax is the largest single source of revenue, followed by the social security tax and the corporate income tax. Figure 11.2 indicates the proportion each major source of revenue represents in the total budget. Since the social security tax raises such a large share of the budget and is regressive, Senator Daniel Patrick Moynihan (D-NY) has recently charged that "the United States almost certainly has the most regressive tax structure of any Western nation." Indeed, about one-quarter of all wage earners in the country pay more in social security taxes than they do in personal income taxes, and if the employers' contribution is added to the calculation, the figure is increased to almost three-quarters of the taxpayers.[10] Furthermore, since 1981 the federal government has shifted many of the costs of government to the state and local levels, thus making the general tax burden even more regressive, since state and local governments are more sensitive than is Congress to the pressure exerted by the well-to-do for tax exemptions.[11]

Even so, however, the taxes paid by people in the United States are lower as a percentage of the gross national product (GNP) than in any other industrial society. (See Table 11.2.) This is primarily so because our government is not as socialist as most of its counterparts. Hence, we pay from the private purse for many things that other people pay for with taxes.

Regulation Through Taxes Taxes are used not only for economic purposes—to raise revenue—but also for political reasons—to *regulate people's behavior.* Many taxes are assessed for the sole purpose of regulating people, although they also generate revenue. Tariffs are used to artificially raise the price of foreign goods, thus encouraging Americans to buy domestic products. "Gas guzzling" taxes are levied against automobiles that do not meet govern-

Figure 11.2   Federal Revenue for 1992 as Estimated in President Bush's Proposed Budget

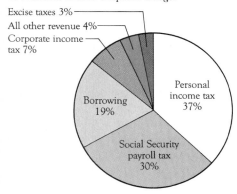

Excise taxes 3%
All other revenue 4%
Corporate income tax 7%

Borrowing 19%

Personal income tax 37%

Social Security payroll tax 30%

Total amount to be spent: $1.45 trillion.
Source: Office of Management and Budget.

Table 11.2

TAXES PAID AS PERCENTAGES OF THE GNP IN 1987

COUNTRY	PERCENTAGE
Sweden	56.7%
Netherlands	48.0%
Belgium	46.1%
France	44.8%
Austria	42.3%
W. Germany	37.6%
United Kingdom	37.5%
Italy	36.2%
Canada	34.5%
Switzerland	32.0%
Australia	31.3%
Japan	30.2%
United States	30.0%

Source: Statistical Abstracts of the United States, 1990.

ment standards for efficient fuel consumption. As with tariffs, the revenue this tax raises is inconsequential; it is important because it increases the cost of fuel-inefficient autos, thus discouraging their purchase.

Some taxes, however, are so versatile that they not only raise significant amounts of money but are also excellent regulators. The income tax is such a levy; indeed, it is almost a perfect tax—from the government's point of view, of course. A "good tax" from the administrative perspective should be easy to collect and should yield a high net amount (it should be inexpensive to collect). From the political standpoint, a tax should appear to be fair, it should make sense to the voters, and it should be able to induce desired behavior.

On all of these counts, the income tax performs well. It is collected by employers, for which service the government does not pay. Similarly, the individual accounts the tax (determines how much should be paid), and again the government pays nothing for the service. The Internal Revenue Service (IRS) receives the taxes and audits a tiny number of the returns, but beyond that, it does very little; hence the tax is both inexpensive and mechanically easy to collect.

Taxes can be assessed on anything. The government could, for example, tax the rate of growth of your fingernails. Such a tax, however, would be viewed as absurd and would thus be politically unacceptable. The income tax, however, is in most people's minds primarily a revenue tax. While few people like to pay it, they realize taxes must be paid if government services are to be sustained. Accordingly, a tax on income makes sense—at least to most people, even though few are happy to pay it. Also, the income tax appears to be fair. It taxes everyone who makes enough money to be expected to pay taxes. It also appears to tax people relative to their ability to pay because it is graduated or progressive.

In all these ways the income tax is a good revenue tax, but it can also be a good regulatory tax. That is, the government can use the income tax to encourage certain behavior by taxing it less than it taxes other endeavors.

Ours is a capitalist economy, which means that the bulk of money used to invest in increased productivity is private funds. If the government determines that more private capital is needed, it can encourage people to use their surplus wealth for investment by taxing proceeds from investment less than it taxes the earnings from work. Such was the case before January 1, 1987, when only 40 percent of the capital gains (the profits made from investment) were taxable, while 100 percent of money earned from work was subject to the income tax. Hence, people who made their living by work were much more susceptible to paying taxes than were people who made their money from investments. If, for example, a married couple filing a joint return made a taxable $20,000 from work and another person made $20,000 from capital gains, the workers would have paid 11.87 percent of the $20,000 in taxes, or $2,375. The investor, on the other hand, would have paid taxes on only $8,000, reducing the tax rate to 6.25 percent, for a total tax bill of $500. Obviously, it would have made more sense to earn money from investments than from work—but one first needed the *capital* to invest, and as long as workers were taxed more than investors, it was difficult for workers to accumulate the capital to invest. One might suggest that the investor risked capital, making the tax break justifiable, but we should remember that most capital losses were and remain deductible so that the investor was protected at both ends, while the worker enjoyed neither advantage.

This tax policy was eliminated by the tax reform of 1986, but in 1990 President Bush managed to get a moderate cut in the capital gains tax. He will almost certainly continue to press for greater reductions in the future, since cutting capital gains taxes was one of his major campaign promises.

How can such a tax advantage for the wealthy be justified? It is argued that there is not enough voluntary private capital to sustain our economy. Since prosperity depends on private investment to create new jobs and improve productive efficiency, the government must—by this and a large number of other incentives—encourage people to invest their money.

During the past decade the changes made in the current income tax system were the most dramatic since its founding in the early years of this century. The two world wars and the growth of the social programs since the New Deal caused the income tax, which was originally designed as a mere augmentation of federal revenue, to become the government's primary source of funds.[12] As the levies on both personal and corporate income taxes became heavier, advocates for the well-to-do pressed for tax shelters, exemptions, and other loopholes. Following World War II the shift in taxes from the well-to-do accelerated. In 1953, families with incomes at the national average paid 11.8 percent of their incomes in federal income tax, but by 1980 the proportion had effectively doubled, to 22.7 percent.[13] Yet during the same period, the proportion of the federal budget derived from corporate income taxes declined from 25 to 12 percent.

Ronald Reagan was elected on a pledge to reduce taxes and thus stimulate the economy. The tax cuts of 1981, however, went largely to the wealthy and aggravated the widening gap between rich and poor. Indeed, by 1989, the gap between rich and poor was greater than at any other time since 1947, when such calculations were first made.[14] The growing disparity of wealth and taxes eventually led to a public demand for a more equitable tax structure.

The 1986 tax reform reduced the number of tax brackets from 14 to 4 (see Table 11.1), and although the new system still included loopholes for certain special interests, it required profitable entities that previously legally paid no federal income taxes to do so. For example, in the first four years of the 1981 tax reform (1982–1985), 42 of the 250 largest American corporations tallied $59 billion in profits but paid no federal income taxes at all. Indeed, they actually received a total of $2 billion in tax refunds. At the same time, another 130 of these profitable corporations managed to pay no federal taxes in at least one of the years under study. In aggregate, these companies paid 14.9 percent taxes on profits of $338 billion. That tax percentage was only slightly higher than one would have paid making $45,000 and supporting a family of four. One hundred of the companies surveyed paid less than 10 percent.[15] (See Table 11.3 for more detail.)

A follow-up study in 1988 revealed that the 1986 tax reform had improved matters. In the 1982–1985 period, between 34 (in 1982) and 72 (in 1984) corporations paid no taxes. In 1987, however, only 16 profitable corporations managed to pay no income taxes. Among these, General Motors, International Business Machines (IBM), and Aetna Life & Casualty also received substantial tax refunds. Further, the 250 leading profitable corporations paid an average of 22.1 percent in taxes.[16] However, in the same year, a married couple filing a joint return would have needed to make only $60,000, and a single person would have needed to make only $35,000, to be required to pay 23 percent in taxes.

The persistent annual budget deficits and growing discontent about the *middle-class bubble*, requiring the upper middle class to pay a 33 percent tax rate while the wealthy paid only 28 percent, forced Congress and President Bush to reform the tax structure yet again in 1990. Revenues had to be increased and expenditures

Table 11.3
TEN OF THE PROFITABLE AMERICAN CORPORATIONS WHICH, BETWEEN 1982–1985, PAID NO FEDERAL TAXES YET RECEIVED TAX REFUNDS[a]

CORPORATION	REFUND (IN MILLIONS)
America Telephone and Telegraph (AT&T)	$636
DuPont	179
Boeing	121
General Dynamics	91
Pepsico	89
General Mills	79
Transamerica	73
Texaco	68
International Paper	60
Greyhound	54
IC Industries	54
Total	$1504[b]

[a] These and other corporations were able to receive income tax refunds while paying no income taxes because the law allows corporations to "carry back" deductions. That is, when the deductions accrued in a given year are so great that they exceed the amount necessary to exempt a corporation from paying income taxes, the surplus deductions can be used to secure refunds from taxes paid in a previous year.
[b] These ten corporations earned an aggregate profit of $39.7 billion during this period, with AT&T alone earning almost $25 billion.

Source: A study done by Citizens for Tax Justice as reported in *The Los Angeles Times*, July 18, 1986.

contained if the budget deficits were not to go spinning completely out of control.

The negotiations were protracted over a four-month period, with the Democrats and Republicans each posturing for their favorite programs and tax targets. Eventually, Bush was forced to withdraw his "no new taxes" pledge and the Democrats agreed to accept reduced spending on Medicare and other programs.

Ultimately the debate focused on taxes and who would be asked to pay more. Bush was unable to sell his proposal for reducing taxes on capital gains to 19.6 percent. Instead, capital gains will be taxed at 28 percent. This lowers the tax rate paid on capital gains by the upper middle class but holds steady the rate for the wealthy. For their part, the Democrats backed away from their insistence on increasing the tax rate for the wealthy to 33 percent. Instead, Congress and the president agreed that the tax bracket for the upper middle class and the wealthy would be the same: 31 percent. Thus the middle-class bubble was eliminated.

Some other minor adjustments were made to raise the income tax rates on the wealthy, but the less well-to-do were also required to pay more. Federal taxes on cigarettes, alcohol, wine, beer, gasoline and airplane tickets were increased. Hence, while the personal income tax was made more progressive, the other taxes, since they fall most heavily on the less well-off, were made more regressive.

Spending Policy   Just as taxes are used for political as well as economic reasons, government spending is manipulated to influence the economy and the society. In 1991 the federal budget was well in excess of 1 trillion dollars. The federal government is the largest spender in the country, and it is the greatest single customer for almost every major American industry, as well as being the nation's largest employer. In practical terms the government is an immense enterprise, and its spending policies have an important impact on the society.

Although millions of people receive government spending in one form or another, the bulk of its annual outlay is confined to only a small number of budget categories. (See Figure 11.3.) Clearly, close to half of all government spending is devoted to payments for individuals, including social security, Medicare, federal retirement programs, unemployment insurance, and public assistance programs. Defense takes another giant bite out of the budget, and recently, the interest payments on the national debt have also become enormous.

Much of the budget is fixed by legal commitments the government has incurred in the past. These items—for example, social security, Medicare, salaries, federal retirement programs, and interest on debt—can be modified only by changing the law, and at considerable political and economic cost. If, for example, the government were to precipitously reduce social security, the political uproar would be significant. On the other hand, if the government refused to pay the full measure of interest it owes, few investors would be willing to loan it money again. The portion of the budget that falls under this nondiscretionary umbrella has increased steadily. In 1970 it accounted for 61.5 percent, by 1980 it had reached 70 percent, and in 1990 it was esti-

mated to constitute 78.4 percent.[17] In practical terms, therefore, Congress and the president actually can manipulate only a bit over 21 percent of the budget.

The spending priorities Congress and the president agree on will have enormous influence on the future. There are at least four dimensions to government spending that should be considered. First, goods and services that the government needs are purchased. Second, government spending creates jobs. When the government buys in quantity, it creates demand, which attracts resources and skills, fueling the economy.

These two dimensions of government spending are usually appreciated by most people. The next two apsects, however, are less well understood, but they are at least as important over the long term. When the government channels large sums in one direction or another, it is not only buying employment, goods, and services for the present, but it is also determining the future. If the government decides to cure cancer, reduce global warming, develop solar energy, or build the Strategic Defense Initiative (SDI), or "Star Wars," it buys enormous amounts of valuable talent and resources, which, of course, will not be available for other objectives. Presumably, most readers of this book are preparing for the marketplace, and many will be attracted to fields in which the government, through spending, has created jobs. Therefore, the government is indirectly determining where many of us will work and what we will learn, but quite beyond this phenomenon, government is also instrumental in determining what information is available to learn.

The United States government pays for over 90 percent of all the pure research done in the country. Hence, its decision about what it wishes to know is critical in determining what information will be available to society and what will not. Interestingly, the by-products of government-purchased research and develop-

Figure 11.3   The Federal Budgets for 1980 and 1992

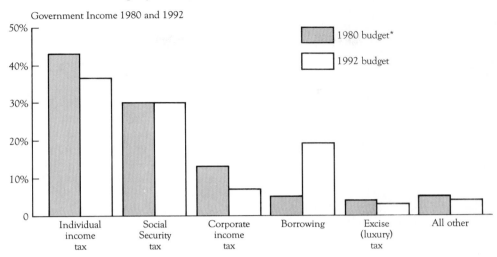

Government Income 1980 and 1992

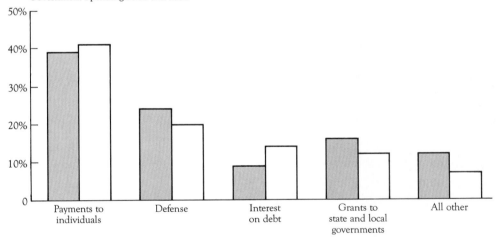

Government Spending 1980 and 1992

* The 1980 figures are included to give perspective about the shift of taxes
  and budget priorities during the Reagan and Bush Administrations.

ment are sometimes as important as are the purchases themselves. For example, President Kennedy committed the country to landing people on the moon. The obvious objectives of the government were to gather scientific data, and, most important, to score heavy public opinion victories in the race in space. The by-products of the lunar effort, however, were much more far-reaching in their effect than either of the primary objectives, and they have heavily influenced the world in which we live today. The information-rich, computer-driven, cybernetically controlled world in which we live today was made possible primarily because of the money the government devoted to developing the technology necessary to accomplish the moon landing. Similarly, decisions the government makes today about which research projects should go forward and which will not be funded will have the same impact on the near future.

Finally, when the government spends, it often does so in a Keynesian effort to influence the flow of money in the economy. When a particular sector of the economy is perceived to be slowing down, thus threatening to become an impediment to the economy as a whole, one thing the government can do to improve the situation is to spend money in the failing sector to encourage recovery. Spending can be executed either actively or passively. If, for example, an industry that is fundamental to the economy—say housing—begins to fall on hard times, eventually the problems encountered will spread throughout the economy. To help buttress the housing industry, the government could increase its appropriations for public housing. This would be an example of the active spending approach. An alternative, passive approach, however, would be for the government to reduce taxes associated with owning a home, thus encouraging more people to buy housing. Either of these techniques could be used to reduce a housing shortage, but in the example just suggested, the major objective was not housing at all; rather, it was to shore up a lagging sector of the economy in an attempt to maintain prosperity. Government spending, however, often exceeds its income, and in such cases the government must borrow the difference.

The National Debt   When the government must borrow money to cover its expenses, it runs a deficit. (See Table 11.4.) Long controversial in national politics, the annual budget deficits, the national debt, and their consequences have recently become the focus of heightened concern.

Actually, the United States, along with most countries in the world, has had a national debt for its entire existence. Until recently the government borrowed only in response to a national emergency, like a war or the Great Depression. Since 1946, however, the govern-

Table 11.4

IMPORTANT TERMS RELATED TO THE NATIONAL DEBT

Balanced budget: When government income and spending are equal. If the government balances the budget, it has not paid off the debt; it has simply not added to it by borrowing more.

Surplus budget: When government income exceeds its expenditures. The surplus funds could be used to avoid a deficit in a following year, or they could be used to reduce the debt.

Deficit budget: When government income is lower than its expenditures. Unless the government has a surplus from a previous budget to make up the shortfall, it must borrow money.

Annual deficit: The amount of money the government must borrow to cover expenditures. When the annual deficit is reduced, the debt is not reduced. All that happens is that the amount borrowed this year is lower than what was borrowed in the past, so the rate of growth of the debt has been reduced.

The national debt: The total of unpaid deficits through history. Each new deficit adds to the debt. A balanced budget means that no new borrowing occurred but none of the debt was paid off. If, however, the government used money from a surplus budget to pay off a portion of the debt, it would be reduced by that amount. The government borrows money by selling government bonds and securities to private individuals and corporations or to government agencies.

ment has used borrowing in an attempt to encourage prosperity. The period from 1946 to 1981 marked the apex of Keynesian economic application: an era in which cyclical deficits were incurred. Here the deficits were used as an economic control mechanism to regulate the well-being of the economy. In 1981, however, because revenues were reduced by tax cuts while expenditures continued to grow, the government necessarily switched from a cyclical to a structural deficit policy.

A **cyclical deficit** is based on the potential productivity of the country. No more money would be borrowed in a given year than the government could raise in revenues if everyone was employed. Thus the debt did not grow beyond the potential of the economy. It was hoped that the borrowed money would be used

to stimulate the economy, thus increasing the GNP at a rate greater than that of the mounting debt. A **structural deficit**, on the other hand, has the government borrowing far more than could be equaled in revenues even if full employment existed. Thus, the government is borrowing so much that it would have deficits even in the best of economic times. This is a dangerous practice because it means that the government is living far beyond its optimum means. (See Figure 11.4 for the deficits incurred since 1946.) As a consequence, the burden of servicing the national debt has also increased heavily. In 1980, the interest payments on the national debt consumed 9 percent of the budget. In the 1992 budget, the figure had increased by over one-third, to 14 percent.

The national debt has always been a matter

Figure 11.4 Annual Deficits by President, 1946–1989

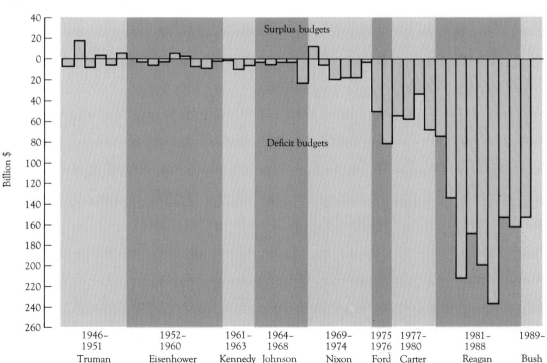

Source: Extrapolated from data in *Vital Statistics on American Politics,* 2nd ed., pp. 391–392.

of controversy. Opponents argue that it betrays moral weakness and that the government should set the good example of not buying things it cannot afford. Furthermore, it is argued that we are buying things for which we are condemning our children to pay and that the immense amount of capital demanded by the annual deficit drives interest rates up, suppressing economic growth. Supporters of deficit funding divide into basically two groups. The Keynesians argue that a cyclical deficit, if used correctly, prevents recession and strengthens the economy. Even they, however, are critical of the structural deficits because the debt has grown much faster than has our GNP, which is the most reliable measure of our ability to repay it. Also, the Keynesians point out that much of the money borrowed in the 1980s was applied toward rebuilding the military, an investment that may have been politically appropriate but did little to increase economic growth. As mentioned, Reaganomics was supposed to create an explosion of economic activity; the reality was disappointing. While the average economic expansion during Reagan's two terms was 3.2 percent, higher than Ford's 1.8 percent, Nixon's 2.4 percent, and Eisenhower's 2.4 percent, it was only marginally higher than Carter's 3.1 percent, and it is much less than Johnson's 4.8 percent and Kennedy's 4 percent.

The second group of supporters of deficit financing are new converts: the supply-siders. Vehemently opposed to deficits before 1980, these observers now suggest that the growing debt is actually a healthy sign, demonstrating how much confidence investors have in our economy.[18]

Whether deficit financing is good public policy is a matter each person must decide individually because there is no scientifically verifiable answer. The debt as a factor on the economy can be measured accurately, however. Debt, like all other things, is a relative matter. The degree to which one is in debt should be measured against one's ability to repay it.

Hence, economists plot the debt as a percentage of the GNP to gain insight about its magnitude. Table 11.5 illustrates the performance of the debt as measured against the GNP.

These data indicate that during World War II, the debt was rapidly increased as a percentage of the GNP, but a 35-year period followed during which the debt, although it increased, rose much more slowly than did productivity. Hence, we were better than four times as able to pay the debt off in 1980 than we were in 1945. This happy state of affairs reflects, to some extent, the successful employment of Keynesian economics. However, since structural deficits have been used, the debt has grown much faster than the GNP, with the result that in 1990 we were no more able to pay it off than we had been in 1963, and we continue to lose ground on the debt's relation to the GNP. This is not a healthy state of affairs, since the debt should not be allowed to grow relative to the GNP for a sustained period. Moreover, most of the deficits incurred since 1981 have been during times of economic prosperity, a period when we should actually borrow less, not more. Consequently, the major reason the government is doing so little to reduce the suffering of the unemployed during the 1991 recession is that it is so heavily in debt that it cannot afford to do more.

Almost two of every three persons who express a view on the debt want the government to balance the budget.[19] Why, then, do politicians continue to borrow with such evident abandon? The politics of the national debt are relatively simple. The public suffers from unrealistic expectations: It wants government spending reduced, but it does not want higher taxes or cuts in the major government programs. David Stockman pointed out in *The Triumph of Politics* that everyone wants to cut big government, but there is no line item in the budget entitled big government. Big government is social security, agriculture, education, the military, public housing, and so forth, and

Table 11.5
THE NATIONAL DEBT AS A PERCENTAGE OF THE GNP

	SIZE OF DEBT (IN MILLIONS)	PERCENTAGE OF GNP
1940	$42,772	44.6%
1945	$235,182	110.7%
1950	$219,023	82.1%
1955	$226,616	58.6%
1960	$236,840	46.7%
1965	$260,778	38.8%
1970	$283,198	28.6%
1975	$394,700	25.9%
1980	$709,291	26.6%
1985	$1,499,362	37.9%
1990 est.	$2,285,014	41.7%

Source: Based on Stanley and **Niemi,** *Vital Statistics on American Politics,* 2nd ed.

each of these line items has constituencies demanding to be served. Hence, the politicians—the representatives of the people—kept government expenditures high and taxes low, while they borrowed the difference,[20] until the 1988 deficit was greater than the total income taxes paid by all the people west of the Mississippi River, and the interest payment alone exceeded half of all personal income taxes paid in 1989.[21]

Gramm-Rudman-Hollings Act Mounting frustration over the rising national debt caused a number of attempted solutions. President Reagan, while sharing with Congress responsibility for almost tripling the debt, stridently called for a constitutional amendment requiring a balanced budget. Realizing that public resolve to balance revenue with expenditures is the only realistic way to solve the problem, Congress refused to resort to such a legal Band-Aid.

In 1985 a legislative approach was developed by Congress, but its success is far from certain. The **Gramm-Rudman-Hollings Act**

(the Balanced Budget and Emergency Deficit Control Act) established a schedule of reduced deficits until in 1993, the budget is supposed to be balanced. As the law stands now, if a given deficit exceeds the projected limit the Director of the Office of Management and Budget is to make equal cuts in domestic and defense programs until enough money is saved to reach the limit. (Social security, interest payments on the debt, and a few other accounts were exempted from the cuts.)

Through some savings and tax increases the deadlines have been reached. A major aspect of these efforts, however, is "smoke and mirror" gimmicks, such as delaying payment of certain bills a few days at the end of the fiscal year so that the books would not record the expenditures for that year, using unrealistic economic forecasts to make it appear that the deficit would be within the statutory limit, authorizing additional expenditures after the deadline for calculating the Gramm-Rudman-Hollings limit had passsed, calculating the bulk of the savings and loan bailout "off-budget" so that the borrowing for that program is not accounted as part of the national debt, and so on. The richest gimmick yet used, however, is involved with the growing surplus from social security taxes.

By the early 1980s, the projections for the social security program showed a major shortfall in the early 21st century as the baby boom generation (those born between 1946 and 1964) begins to retire. To meet this potential crisis, Congress passed a series of reforms that reduced benefits and increased taxes. This policy would build a surplus in the social security trust fund that could be used when the baby boom generation retired. The surplus social security funds are invested in Treasury bonds and thus become part of the national debt. Because the government does not have to borrow that money from the private sector, however, the social security surplus loans are not computed in the deficit. Hence, in fiscal year 1990, the social security surplus was $70 billion, which was loaned to the government. The government borrowed an additional $169 billion from the private sector, for a total of $239 billion, but recorded a deficit of only $169 billion. Many critics complain that this process is inherently dishonest since it leads the public to believe that the annual deficit is much lower than it really is. Further, they argue that paying for government operations with money from the regressive social security tax, while the wealthy are given many loopholes to reduce their income tax payments, places an unfair burden on the middle and lower classes.[22] Even with all the gimmicks, however, it is impossible to reach the Gramm-Rudman-Hollings goal of balancing the budget by 1993.

Reviewing the national debt can leave readers with a mild funk, but one should not become too depressed about the economic prospects. While our circumstances are serious, they are not yet grave; and a glance at Table 11.5 reveals that it is possible to reverse current trends and once again increase the GNP more

rapidly than the national debt rises. To do so, however, requires a more realistic attitude among American voters. They must be prepared to bring government expenditures more closely into line with receipts, and this will necessitate sacrifice. Long-term failure to do this courts disaster.

Fiscal policy—taxing, spending, and borrowing—is only one part of the government's control over the economy, however. The second aspect is monetary policy.

MONETARY POLICY

Monetary policy refers to the controls the government exercises on the amount of currency in circulation and the price of credit. As indicated earlier, the *Chicago school* of economists, led by Milton Friedman, believes that the economy is best managed by monetary policy.

The principal tool for controlling the money supply is the **Federal Reserve System**, called the *Fed*. Established in 1913, this institution is headed by a seven-member board of governors appointed by the president to 14-year, staggered, nonrenewable terms. The chair of the Federal Reserve Board is appointed to a four-year renewable term, and all appointments must be ratified by the Senate. Federal Reserve Board members, however, may be removed only for cause (malfeasance or incompetence), so any policy of the Fed is quite independent of the president and Congress; indeed, it may actually be opposed to them from time to time.

The Federal Reserve System is composed of 12 banks with several branches throughout the country, and over 6000 private banks have become members of the system. The member banks must allow Fed audits of their books and are subject to Fed regulations, which include being insured by the **Federal Deposit Insurance Corporation (FDIC)**. The FDIC is a government corporation that insures individual deposits in member banks up to $100,000.

The major advantage of being a member of the Federal Reserve System is that private banks in the system may borrow capital from the Federal Reserve Banks. Through its loans to member banks and by its regulation of them, the Fed (the bankers' banks) is able to control the amount of currency and the price of credit on the market, thus regulating the volume of financial activity in the economy.

There are three major mechanisms used by the Fed to regulate the economy. It can raise or lower the amount of money member banks are required to keep on deposit. Banks usually loan out or invest the money they receive in deposits, but the Fed requires that they keep a certain percent on hand. If the Fed raises the required reserve, it reduces the amount of money available to be loaned. The scarcity of capital will probably drive interest rates up and fewer dollars will be borrowable. Conversely, the Fed can increase the number of borrowable dollars, thus forcing interest rates down.

When member banks borrow money from the Fed, the rate of interest charged, the *discount rate*, determines the member banks' overhead and thus influences the interest rates they charge for loans to their customers. The Fed manipulates the amount of currency in circulation by buying and selling government bonds and securities. If it buys bonds and securities, it releases more money into the economy, but if it sells them, it takes money out of circulation.

When the economy is inflated, the Fed can increase its discount rate, raise the reserve requirement for its member banks, and sell government bonds and securities. These policies will reduce the amount of money in circulation, drive interest rates up, and make less money available for loans, thus reducing inflation. Some of these techniques were used to tame the double-digit inflation that developed during the Carter Administration. Paul Volcker, the Fed Chairman at the time, is widely credited with manipulating the monetary policy to reduce inflation. However, he is also blamed for the profound recession of 1981–1982.

When the economy turns down, however, the Fed can reverse gears, causing money to flow more freely and averting a recession. For example, in 1990–1991, encouraged by the government's effort to control future deficits and wishing to soften a developing recession, the Fed reduced its discount rates several times and lowered the required reserve that banks must keep on hand, thus making credit cheaper and more available to private citizens. Also, the Fed can play a major part in stabilizing the stock market. When the price of stocks plummets, the reflex is for loaners to raise interest rates and call in all loans. This reaction soaks up capital and tends to aggravate the crash. However, in 1987 when the market lost over 500 points on a single day, the Fed announced it was freeing up money, thus creating capital and perhaps averting a very serious financial crisis.

The fiscal and monetary policies of the government are important mechanisms for regulating and promoting the general well-being of the economy. There are, however, a multitude of other ways in which government policy affects our economic and social lives.

Government Promotion and Regulation

The government attempts to promote economic well-being through a number of direct and indirect ways. For example, the Weather Bureau provides information critical to farmers and shippers; the Small Business Administration grants loans to people trying to establish themselves commercially; government tariffs, import quotas, and other trade policies protect American business and labor from foreign competition; and federal funds for highways, railroads, air travel, and merchant shipping are important. We have already seen how tax policies can affect business. The government subsidizes some industries, such as shipbuilding, by flat grants of money. Lucrative contracts have kept defense industries in the black when they might have found more competitive pursuits impossible. The government has refinanced and consolidated railroads, guaranteed loans for major corporations such as Lockheed and Chrysler, and even engaged in owning and operating a few corporations itself.

All of these endeavors are socialist in that they involve the government in the economy, contradicting the principle of *laissez-faire;* but most of them have been wholeheartedly supported by the business, industrial, and financial communities. Other efforts—specifically, regulatory policies—have not been so favored.

Capitalism is driven by competition, yet competition tends to defeat itself: In this economic "king-of-the-mountain," eventually someone wins, eliminating competitors and monopolizing a segment of the market. The tendency of capitalism to monopolize and thus self-destruct was recognized in this country late in the last century. Hence it was concluded that in order to be preserved, competition must be regulated. In 1890 the **Sherman Antitrust Act** was created, but as mentioned earlier, the Supreme Court interpreted it in such a way as to make it ineffective. In 1914 Congress passed the **Clayton Antitrust Act** and also created the **Federal Trade Commission (FTC)**, which gave teeth to the government's efforts to outlaw restraint of trade. Then, the New Deal ushered in a new age of business regulation, which has already been discussed.

Besides reigning in business, the New Deal gave organized labor an unprecedented degree of support. Until the 1930s the **individual contract theory** was used in the United States. This concept saw each worker and corporation as equal individuals and insisted that they should arrive at an agreement about wages and working conditions without benefit of the workers' collectively bargaining with employers through their unions. The absurdity of this arrangement is clear if one considers the bargaining position of an immigrant worker in negotiations with General Motors or United States Steel. The **Wagner Act** (the National Labor Relations Act) of 1935 recognized for the first time in this country—far later than in most industrial countries—the right of labor to bargain collectively and to strike. It created the National Labor Relations Board (NLRB), which prevents company unions (unions created by management to control workers), settles disputes between management and labor over contract disputes, and supervises union elections. Hence, labor rights were strongly protected.

In the late 1940s, however, Congress passed several reforms that labor has been fighting ever since. In 1947 the **Taft-Hartley Act** (the Labor-Management Relations Act) was passed over President Truman's veto. This bill was designed to eliminate many of the privileges that from management's point of view labor unduly enjoyed. Among the most important provisions of this critical law, **closed shops** were forbidden, and states were allowed to adopt so-called **right-to-work laws** outlawing **union shops**. The law also forbids **jurisdictional strikes** and **secondary boycotts,*** and it provides that when the national security is at risk, strikes can be enjoined by the government for an "eight-day cooling-off period." Further,

---

* A closed shop is one in which the employer may hire only employees who belong to a given union. A union shop contract requires that new employees join the union within a certain period after getting the job. Twenty states have adopted right-to-work laws, and their elimination remains a major objective of labor. Jurisdictional strikes are work stoppages brought on by disputes *between unions* over whose members are to do certain work for an employer. A secondary boycott is a kind of double-team technique. Say Union A is striking against employer X. Union B may boycott its employer, Y, hoping that Y will then pressure X to settle with union A.

Taft-Hartley makes it illegal for a union to refuse to bargain with its employer, and provides that the two parties may sue each other in federal court over contract disputes.

Taft-Hartley focused upon the relations between employers and the unions, but during the 1950s Congress began to investigate the influence of organized crime with the unions. In an attempt to reform the internal practices among unions, Congress passed the **Landrum-Griffin Act** (the Labor Reform Act) in 1959. While the law strengthened some of the Taft-Hartley prohibitions, basically it focused upon the relationship of the unions to their members. It prohibits convicted felons from becoming union officers, mandates secret ballots for union elections, and requires that unions file with the Labor Department their constitutions, rules of procedures, and statements declaring their financial status.

Predictably, organized labor membership rose during the era of its greatest successes. By 1953 approximately 30 percent of all American workers belonged to unions, and they were a potent political force. After the 1950s, however, the fortunes of the American labor movement began to wane. Its support with the general public declined, and its membership by 1984 barely included 20 percent of working Americans, most of whom were affiliated with the **American Federation of Labor-Congress of Industrial Organizations (AFL-CIO)**. Aggravating the reduced union popularity has been the decline in industries where unions are traditionally strong, and the feeling among workers that union protection is no longer necessary.[23]

The 1980s have been particularly hard on unions. Beginning with President Reagan's dismissal of over 10,000 striking air-traffic controllers in 1981, unions suffered defeat after defeat in struggles with management. Although the majority of workers voted for Reagan in 1980 and 1984, he repeatedly vetoed increases in the minimum wage and other bills important

to organized labor, including the 1988 foreign trade bill because it included a provision requiring major American employers to give their workers 60 days' notice before closing their plants. This position became so controversial, however, that presidential candidate George Bush persuaded Reagan not to veto it again when it returned to his desk during the 1988 presidential campaign. The negative attitude toward labor was also manifest in the Supreme Court. In a critical 1989 decision, the Court ruled that although the law prohibits employers from firing striking employees, they can give permanent jobs to strikebreakers at the expense of more seniored striking employees.[24] Clearly this ruling will have a chilling effect on labor when pressing its rights with employers in the future.

Another area in which the well-being of workers has been compromised is in regulating the administration of private pension plans. Private pension plans have long been the targets of unscrupulous managers. Before 1974, only an estimated 3 percent of retired workers received the full benefits promised by their private pension plans. Congress addressed this disgraceful record in 1974 by passing the *Employee Retirement Income Security Act (ERISA)*, which established federal regulations for the administration of private pension plans and directed the Pension and Welfare Benefits Administration of the Labor Department to monitor the plans. The law also provided for both criminal and civil prosecution of management personnel who defrauded private pension plans. Until 1981, thousands of reviews and investigations of these plans' administration resulted in criminal prosecution of law violators. When the Reagan Administration came to Washington, however, its aversion to government regulation of business caused a precipitous fall in the number of investigations, until by 1988 they had declined by 269 percent, although the number of pension plans increased by 54 percent during his term and the accumulated value of the funds had shot up by 275 percent. (See Figure 11.5.) Furthermore, the option of criminal prosecutions was almost completely abandoned. Of the 5000 investigations between 1986 and 1988—fewer than the number in only a single year of the Carter Administration—just 95 were criminal inquiries. Such reluctance to threaten unscrupulous businesspersons with prison for defrauding the pension plans they control has bred a "new generation of racketeers," according to George Hohol, a worker who found his pension plundered by his former employer. Since 1981 the number of pension plans to fail has skyrocketed, causing the government agency that insures them (the Pension Benefit Guarantee Corporation) to develop a deficit of $4 billion, and threatening the bankruptcy of the agency by the year 2000. However, in 1990 the Supreme Court held that corporations in bankruptcy can be required to continue funding pension plans, thus averting a possible fiscal disaster even greater than the S&L failure.[25] Even so, government insurance of private pension funds remains in serious financial jeopardy.[26]

THE SAVINGS AND LOAN BAILOUT, BANKS, AND HUD

The recent debacle in the savings and loan industry is another excellent example of what can happen when government ceases to regulate an industry and yet continues to guarantee deposits of its customers. The **Federal Savings and Loan Insurance Corporation (FSLIC)** was created in the 1930s to insure deposits in the savings and loans (savings institutions that, until 1982, were strictly restricted to loaning money under regulated conditions to local people for building homes). The high interest rates of the 1970s however, threatened the S&Ls because most of their money was out in relatively low-interest, long-term loans. As a partial solution to the industry's problems, the S&Ls were deregulated, allowing them to be-

Figure 11.5   Private Pension Plans

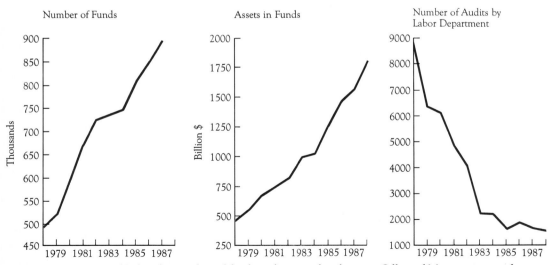

Source: Department of Labor for number of funds and accumulated assets. Office of Management and Budget for number of Labor Department audits.

come much more speculative in their financial dealings, while the government continued to insure their depositors.

What followed was a combination of bad economic times in the Southwest and "an orgy of mismanagement, miscalculation, greed, and outright theft," which culminated in the collapse of over 400 S&Ls in 1989–1991 and the possibility of even more closings, costing the government an estimated $300–$600 billion in deposit guarantees, costs that will drive up future budget deficits. It should be remembered that many S&Ls closed because of hard economic times, and at least one-third of the S&Ls in the country are sound and managed well—but many more are headed for disaster, and much of it could have been avoided had the government been more vigilant in protecting the public's interests. (See Table 11.6.) Of the 4000 S&L's that existed in 1980, 1000 had

Table 11.6

FORECLOSURES OF THE SAVINGS AND LOANS BY MARCH 1989 (IN MILLIONS)

STATE	IN MILLIONS OF ASSETS REPOSSESSED	STATE	IN MILLIONS OF ASSETS REPOSSESSED
Texas	$15,849	Minnesota	$143
California	$3,490	Utah	$143
Arizona	$1,228	Mississippi	$114
Florida	$1,207	Tennessee	$111
Oklahoma	$756	South Carolina	$82
Colorado	$753	Rhode Island	$79
Louisiana	$646	Indiana	$76
Arkansas	$576	Nevada	$67
Illinois	$496	Wyoming	$62
Kansas	$491	Michigan	$62
Missouri	$479	Massachusetts	$46
New York	$370	West Virginia	$44
Ohio	$346	Alaska	$42
New Jersey	$339	Kentucky	$38
Nebraska	$313	North Dakota	$37
Pennsylvania	$309	Hawaii	$23
Iowa	$301	South Dakota	$19
Virginia	$299	New Hampshire	$18
New Mexico	$270	District of Columbia	$16
Alabama	$202	Montana	$16
Washington	$176	Delaware	$9
North Carolina	$167	Connecticut	$8
Georgia	$167	Idaho	$4
Oregon	$164	Maine	$3
Wisconsin	$160	Vermont	$0
Maryland	$156	Total	$30,975

Source: The Los Angeles Times, Aug. 11, 1989.

closed by 1989, another 1000 are expected to collapse by the mid-1990s, and there could be as few as 1000 left by the end of the decade.[27]

To liquidate the hundreds of billions of dollars in assets of the S&Ls that have so far collapsed, Congress created the **Resolution Trust Corporation (RTC)**, which instantly became the largest real estate firm in the country. Its task is to sell the buildings, homes, businesses, and other assets left from the defaulting S&Ls. Much of this will be sold with little difficulty, but an estimated $100 billion of assets includes such properties as a syphilitic racehorse, condominiums overlooking Louisiana oil rigs, shopping centers ten miles from the nearest housing, played-out gold mines, and other such white elephants.[28]

Meanwhile, the Justice Department is prosecuting S&L officials who are suspected of larceny, and several have already been convicted. Even President Bush's son, Neil, was punished for his role in the collapse of a Denver S&L. The biggest alleged offender so far, however, has yet to be tried. Charles H. Keating, Jr., who owns the holding company controlling failed Lincoln Savings and Loan, is suspected of purchasing influential congressional support with political contributions totaling $1.3 million. As mentioned before, Senator Alan Cranston (D-CA) has already been accused of improper conduct in this regard by the Senate Ethics Committee.

Although the S&Ls have dominated public attention, the nation's banks are also in poor financial shape, jeopardizing the *Federal Deposit Insurance Corporation (FDIC)*, which insures bank depositors up to $100,000. While not as foolhardy with their investments as were

The sign comes down on a failed bank.

some of the S&Ls, intense competition and unfavorable economic conditions caused over 1200 banks to fail between 1987 and 1990. By contrast, only 198 banks closed between 1942 and 1980.[29] The recent failures have seen FDIC reserves fall to their lowest level since the corporation's founding in 1933. The greatest problem rests in the "too big to fail" doctrine, by which FDIC usually rescues large failing banks by arranging for their sale. This complex process results in the government insuring 100 percent of the banks' deposits—even those that exceed the $100,000 limit. To deal with this crisis, President Bush is considering a change in policy that would deny government protection to large bank depositors, with the hope that bank executives would be more cautious in their business decisions.[30] However, the plan also calls for allowing banks to become involved in selling insurance, stocks, and bonds and in other activities previously prohibited to them. Critics warn that the Bush plan is dangerously close to the 1980s policies that saw the S&Ls go bankrupt. Whether this change will be enough to avert a collapse of FDIC remains

to be seen. As things now stand, many of the country's largest financial institutions are in serious trouble. (See Table 11.7.)

Not at all unclear is the scandal at the Reagan *Department of Housing and Urban Development (HUD)*. Samuel R. Pierce, Jr., the only Cabinet secretary to serve the full eight years of Reagan's presidency, claimed not to be a hands-on administrator at HUD. The day-to-day decisions at HUD, according to Pierce, were left to a group of young assistants, including Deborah Gore Dean, Pierce's executive secretary; Deputy Assistant Secretary DuBois L. Gilliam; and Thomas T. Demery, Assistant Secretary for Housing. In the September 1989 congressional hearings on the HUD scandal, Pierce elected to remain silent by invoking the Fifth Amendment protections against self-incrimination; he is the first Cabinet secretary to do so since the Teapot Dome scandal of the Harding Administration.

Although the full extent of the scandal has yet to become public, the broad outlines are now clear. As the HUD budget was slashed from $30 billion in 1981 to $12 billion in 1988,

Table 11.7

FINANCIALLY TROUBLED BANK HOLDING COMPANIES
IN DECEMBER 1990

HOLDING COMPANY	NONPERFORMING LOANS (IN BILLIONS)	PERCENTAGE FALL IN STOCK VALUE FROM 1989
Citicorp	$6.1	61%
Chase Manhattan	$2.9	75%
Security Pacific	$2.5	60%
Chemical	$2.2	70%
First Interstate	$1.8	63%
Manufacturers Hanover	$1.3	52%
BankAmerica	$1.2	33%
Bankers Trust	$1.2	24%
J. P. Morgan	$0.2	9%

Source: Prudential-Bache Securities; New York Stock Exchange.

high-placed politicos plundered the funds that remained. HUD "was set up and designed to be a political program," Deborah Gore Dean told the media, "and we ran it in a political manner."[31]

Congressional hearings revealed that prominent figures such as James G. Watt, former Reagan Interior Secretary, and Edward Brooke, former Republican senator from Massachusetts, took fees totaling hundreds of thousands of dollars for making "a few phone calls" to HUD for real estate developer clients. HUD funded projects of questionable merit for former Reagan Administration officials,[32] campaign strategists for Reagan[33] and for President Bush,[34] Republican National Committee persons,[35] Republican city mayors,[36] Pierce's personal associates,[37] and so forth. In some cases, developers would secure millions in HUD loan guarantees without committing any of their own capital;[38] they would grossly inflate the value of projects to get higher HUD grants;[39] they used money for low-income housing to build luxury apartments along golf courses;[40] and they developed "equity skimming" scams in which they would buy homes with HUD grants, rent them out, and then fail to pay the mortgages.[41] As it turns out, people at HUD were not only on the giving end: Some of them also took. Former HUD employees became consultants, commanding high fees for using their influence with the agency; and Marilyn Louise Harrell, a HUD escrow agent, embezzled over $5 million for her personal use. Her claim to have given much of the illicit money to charity prompted the press to refer to her as "Robin HUD," but the prosecuting attorneys said little evidence existed that she had used most of the money for any but personal expenses.[42] Even President Reagan, it seems, became caught up in the manipulation of HUD funds for unintended purposes. In September 1982, Reagan ordered HUD to fund a New Jersey housing project in an effort to secure the election of a Republican candidate for the

United States Senate. Campaigning with candidate Millicent Fenwick in New Jersey, Reagan jokingly told an audience, "If you don't elect her as senator, we'll take [the project grant] away." The candidate did not win and the funds were not revoked, but a memo to Secretary Pierce authorizing the grant leaves no doubt as to the reason for its approval.[43]

It is important to note that the use of HUD funds to help politicians in their district and to reward campaign supporters far predates the 1980s, but never has the scope of favoritism been so great, and HUD funds were never so systematically used for the well-to-do rather than for the poor, for whom they are intended. Further, the scale of influence-peddling and outright fraud during these years is unprecedented. During hearings on the scandal, Rep. Henry B. Gonzalez (D-TX), Chair of the House Banking Committee, said with disgust, "as the Reagan Administration swung the wrecking ball at every facet of HUD, there was an army of quick-buck artists—looters—picking through the wreckage for their personal gain. The HUD scandals prove just how dangerous it is when programs are turned over to their enemies."[44]

To deal with the crisis, Bush's Secretary of HUD Jack Kemp laid before Congress a series of proposed reforms that will, it is hoped, together with his own careful administrative supervision, make impossible the kind of crass pecuniary abuse HUD has suffered in the past. The reforms, which were passed by Congress in November 1989, include plugging loopholes that gave developers enormous tax advantages while they misused HUD funds and creating oversight agencies to monitor the use of HUD monies. The Congress also expressed its confidence in Kemp's energetic and forthright efforts to clean up the mess.[45] On another level, Attorney General Richard Thornburgh acted to create an independent counsel to investigate the conduct of Pierce, Dean, Gilliam, Demery, and other former HUD officials.[46]

The HUD scandal, the collapse of the S&Ls, the looming problems with the nation's banks, and the threat to private pension programs all provide examples of how costly it can be when people who are elected and appointed to office are negligent. The full cost of these debacles has yet to be calculated, but already we know that it will easily reach over $500 billion dollars, which the taxpayers will have to make up. On the other hand, when government programs are efficiently managed, they can render valuable services to society. Even the government's insurance of S&L deposits, as poorly managed as it was, served its intended role. As news of the impending bankruptcy of so many savings institutions hit the press, no panic among depositors ensued because they were confident that their money was guaranteed by the government. If, however, a wider collapse of the nation's financial institutions occurs, or if the private pension plans go under, the government may not be able to cover the shortfall. Consequently, voters must insist that government redouble its efforts to assure the efficacy and viability of these programs. Finding that single-minded aversion to government involvement in the economy courts disaster, the people have learned a costly and embarrassing lesson.

The government's efforts to deal with the country's financial and economic issues are critical to the society, but the measures just discussed often seem remote and obscure to ordinary people. The social programs the government engages in, on the other hand, are immediate, and in this regard the government often comes into direct contact with the public it is trying to help.

The Social Programs

Dealing with the less privileged people in our midst has always been a source of controversy in this wealthy and generous, yet individualistic, society, and among the industrial states, we have been the slowest to adopt government programs to aid the poor. Before the Great Depression there was no federal social welfare program. Some states had retirement programs and some had relief programs, but the matter of caring for the aged and indigent was largely left to the individual or to private charities. With millions hungry during the 1930s, however, Franklin D. Roosevelt's New Deal moved to give the federal government a role in the lives of individuals —a role never before known in this society, although such programs had long been implemented in other industrial countries.

The *Social Security Act* of 1935 created two basic programs that still exist today and serve as points of continuing controversy. Basically, the government created a *social insurance program* for the aged, dependents, the disabled, and the unemployed. It also created an *assistance program* to help those who cannot help themselves. The insurance programs are funded by taxes paid by people who later, when they are eligible, collect the benefits according to prescribed schedules. Public assistance, on the other hand, is paid for from the general revenues, and people can collect it regardless of whether they have ever paid taxes. These programs are what is generally referred to as **welfare.** Although not without controversy, the social insurance programs are among the most popular government endeavors, and few politicians could survive an attempt to destroy them. The politics of welfare, on the other hand, are fraught with argument.

SOCIAL INSURANCE PROGRAMS

Originally created only to serve as a financial buffer for the aged who paid into the fund, in 1939 **social security** benefits were extended to cover the survivors (widows and children) of employees, and in 1956 it was made available to disabled people, becoming the **Old-Age Sur-vivors and Disability Insurance (OASDI).** In 1965, another major change was made to the program. In that year **Medicare,** a program to pay a portion of the medical costs of the elderly, was passed. In 1977, social security was indexed, meaning that social security benefits automatically increase as the consumer price index goes up; it has done a great deal to insulate today's aged from the poverty many of them once suffered, yet it also contributed greatly to the program's increased costs. Finally, in 1988, Congress passed a law providing Medicare recipients with protection against catastrophic illness. The program, however, was to be paid for by a surtax on the social security recipients themselves, the first time the recipients were asked to pay the entire cost of their benefits. When the tax bills came due, a loud outcry was heard, primarily from the nation's most affluent retirees, and Congress quickly repealed the law, fearing that its attempt to improve conditions for the elderly might ironically result in the loss of their votes.[47]

Social security is administered directly by the federal government. Almost all income earners are required to pay social security taxes; only some government employees who have their own publicly funded retirement programs are exempt. In 1991, employees paid 7.65 percent of all earnings up to $51,300 toward the tax, and their employers paid a like amount, for a total of 15.3 percent; 2.90 percent of the total is for Medicare. The money goes to a trust fund from which only social security and Medicare payments can be made; any surplus is invested in government bonds. When a contributor is at least 65 years old and retired, she or he collects benefits according to a schedule. The disabled and dependents who survive social security recipients are also eligible for benefits. In 1990, 110 million workers paid social security/Medicare taxes, while 40 million were collecting benefits.

As the benefits increased and the average life span lengthened, a greater and greater strain on social security resources developed. The original social security tax was about 2 percent and now exceeds 15 percent. The tax has gone from a relatively low portion of most peoples' budgets to a significant expenditure, and the budget category "payment for individuals," of which social security/Medicare is the lion's share, has become the largest single item in the budget. (Refer to Figure 11.3.)

Until 1983, social security was funded on a pay-as-you-go basis. That is, the contributions made by workers in 1970, for example, were added to a trust fund from which the recipients of benefits at the time were paid. As has already been explained, by the early 1980s it became obvious that by 2015, the numbers of retirees would be so great that the workers at that time would have to pay exorbitant social security taxes to maintain benefits for those retired. Accordingly, in 1983 Congress adopted its proposal to increase social security taxes and to reduce its benefits so as to build a surplus in the social security trust fund sufficient to accommodate the expected increase in demand for social security benefits in the coming century.

As the social security surplus built from 1984 into the 1990s, it was invested in government bonds—a prudent investment since no savings are safer. That means, however, that the money paid through the regressive social security tax was funding government borrowing. Senator Daniel P. Moynihan (D-NY), long an expert on social problems, thought it unfair that middle- and lower-income people should be asked to pay higher taxes—money used to defray the deficit—while the wealthy enjoyed a tax decrease. (See Table 11.8.)

The annual social security surplus, which in 1990 had reached $70 billion, was scheduled to total about $3 trillion by 2015, which would accrue some $9 trillion in interest in 30 years. When the baby boom generation begins to re-

Table 11.8
1990 TAX RATES FOR VARIOUS PERSONS

If Worker A, filing a single tax return, made $51,300 in taxable income:

Her income tax rate would be	23.9%	or $12,272
Her social security/Medicare tax rate would be	7.65%	or $3,924
Her total federal tax rate would be	31.6%	or $16,196

If corporate executive B, filing a single return, made $1,000,000 in taxable income:

His income tax rate would be	28%	or $280,559[a]
His social security/Medicare tax rate would be	0.4%[a]	or $3,924
His total federal tax rate would be	28.4%	or $284,483

In this example, although Mr. B earns 94.9% more than does Ms. A, he will pay only 89.9% as high a tax rate as she. This illustrates why Senator Moynihan believes that United States taxes are among the most regressive in the world.

[a] The 7.65% social security/Medicare tax is assessed on only the first $51,300. Hence, Mr. B would only pay 0.4% of his total income toward the tax.

Source: 1990 federal income tax schedule, the 1990 OASDI tax schedule, and President Bush's proposed tax cut for long-term capital gains.

tire, the $12 trillion surplus would gradually be reduced until in about 2050 it would be exhausted. (See Figure 11.6.) The problem, as Moynihan sees it, is that not only are the lower-income groups being forced by regressive taxes to fund more than their share for current expenditures and deficits, but for the same reason they will also pay disproportionately the $9 trillion in interest earned by the social security surplus. It is, in other words, a double-whammy tax.

As an alternative, Moynihan proposes reducing the OASDI tax to 6.55 percent, which would eliminate the social security surplus and reduce the amount people paid in regressive federal taxes. The problem with the proposal is that it would put social security back to square one—a pay-as-you-go system with no allowances for the huge drain on social security coming when the baby boomers begin to retire. To cover the shortfall, the social security tax would have to be raised beginning in 2015, and it would peak at 9.05 percent for workers and

18.1 for self-employed people in 2025. Such a heavy tax burden carried by workers to pay for the benefits of retirees who had refused to defer the costs of their own retirement while they were working is not likely to go down well. Moynihan's strategy seems to be to frame the quandary we face so that a meaningful debate about regressive taxes can be held before the capital gains tax is cut further by a Congress representing an anesthetized public. President Bush, on the other hand, opposes the tax cut—an embarrassing position for a Republican—arguing that it will eventually increase taxes and reduce benefits. It is in the politician's interest to build the social security surplus since, as already explained, it makes the annual budget deficits appear to be lower than they actually are.[48]

Medicare   The United States enjoys what some believe to be the best medical services in the world, and no one disputes that they are the most expensive in the world. In 1989, Americans spent almost $600 billion on health

Figure 11.6   Projected Social Security Surplus

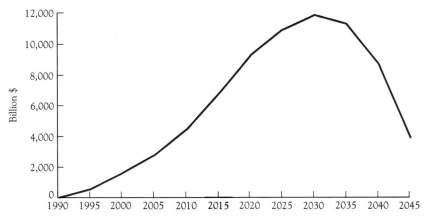

Source: Social Security Administration.

services, or 11.5 percent of the GNP, up from 8.5 percent in 1976. Government spending on health—including research, Medicare, Medicaid, veterans' hospitals, and so forth—accounts for 3.1 of the 11.5 percent.

Medicare expenditures amount to the bulk of the goverment's spending on health. This plan pays a large share of the hospital expenses of the almost 33 million aged people on the program, and a low-cost supplement can be purchased to help defray doctors' bills. These coverages, however, are limited and do not pay for extended illnesses. It was to cover these catastrophic illnesses that in 1988 Congress passed a reform that, because of objections among the aged, was repealed only 16 months later.

The present program covers only the aged; the rest of the population depends on either private insurance coverage or welfare benefits in the form of **Medicaid**. In 1990, however, a government study found that 37 million people, 15 percent of the population, had no health insurance whatever and 60 million more had inadequate coverage. In a 1990 *Los Angeles*

Times national poll, one-quarter of all respondents said they delayed seeking medical attention because of its costs, and over half believe that they would not be able to afford medical treatment if they became critically ill. Seventy-two percent said they favored creation of a comprehensive national health plan, and 66 percent favored a mandatory employer-based program for health insurance.[49]

In the same year, a badly split congressional commission, the Pepper Commission, called for an $86 billion program to provide health insurance for all people in the country. The plan calls for $66 billion in increased government spending and $20 billion financed by private employers who currently do not provide their workers with health insurance. With the Congress divided on the issue along partisan lines and the president opposed, the proposal seemed to have little chance of passage. In 1991, however, the American Medical Association (AMA) usually a conservative group, decried the lack of medical insurance among so great a proportion of the population, and threw its support behind adopting a national health insurance program. Ironically, the AMA had been the most vociferous opponent in 1965 to adopting Medicare.[50]

UNEMPLOYMENT INSURANCE

Another social insurance program created by the Social Security Act is **unemployment insurance**. This program, however, is funded by state as well as federal assessments on employers. The states, within federal guidelines, establish the eligibility conditions, the amount paid, and the length of time benefits can be collected. Obviously these factors vary widely from state to state, although all states require that people have first held steady jobs before becoming eligible for benefits when they are laid off. Approximately 90 percent of all American workers are covered by some form of unemployment insurance.

PUBLIC ASSISTANCE

Poverty   Poverty was widespread and obvious during the Great Depression, but with World War II and the economic growth of the 1940s and 1950s, a myth developed that little poverty existed after the war. In 1962, however, Michael Harrington, soon to become the nation's most prominent socialist, published *The Other America,* graphically documenting poverty in America and explaining that it went largely unrecognized by the public. Coming at a moment of growing social awareness in the country and a mounting commitment to address the problems of civil rights and the environment, the book struck a responsive chord and is credited with giving impetus to President Johnson's **War on Poverty**. The War on Poverty, however, became one of the early casualties of Johnson's own Vietnam War policies, and poverty, although reduced from 22.2 percent of the population in 1960 to 12.1 percent

in 1969,[51] continued in the country. Regrettably, it has increased significantly since 1981.[52]

The passage of Medicare in 1965 and the indexing of social security benefits in 1977 have combined to stabilize the conditions of the elderly, previously the largest single group among the poor. In 1970, one in four of the elderly lived in poverty, but by 1986 only one in eight lived on incomes below the federal poverty line,[53] and today, although many older people are still living below the poverty line, the elderly are the nation's most affluent age group. The economic conditions of the 1980s, however, caused poverty to rise among people at the opposite end of the generational spectrum: young adults and especially children.

As has been pointed out, the gap between rich and poor grew in the 1980s. By 1988, the unemployment rate was at 5.3 percent, the lowest in 14 years, but half of the net increase in jobs was in positions that paid below the poverty line. Most poor adults work, but they do not make enough to reach subsistence. The minimum wage, for example, was not raised during the entire Reagan presidency because of his repeated vetoes. In 1988, with approximately 8 percent of the labor force working for minimum wages, a 40-hour-a-week job at the minimum wage for a breadwinner with three dependents earned only 60 percent of the poverty-line mark.[54] In 1989, President Bush also vetoed a proposed increase in the minimum wage from $3.35 per hour to $4.55 because of fears that such a large increase would be inflationary. Later that year he signed a bill advancing the minimum wage to $4.25 per hour for adults by 1991, but with the proviso that youngsters 16–19 years could be employed for a 90-day training period at only $3.35 per hour. Even if the $4.25 figure had taken effect in 1989, a 40-hour job at the minimum wage would have earned $8,840 in a year, only 73 percent of $12,100, the federal poverty line for a family of four.

While overall family incomes kept pace with inflation during the 1980s, the median income of families headed by people of 30 years or less dropped by 30 percent, and the figure was 50 percent for young African-American families. At the same time, young people left the housing market as the percentage of their income needed to pay for housing rose from 23 percent in 1973 to 51 percent in 1986. Home-ownership sharply declined among young people for the first time since the Great Depression. In 1981, 61 percent of young families owned their homes;* in 1987 the figure was 53 percent.[55] Although the drop for all ages is less severe, the United States Bureau of the Census reported in 1991 that home ownership fell to 63.9 percent in 1990 from 65.6 percent in 1980. Interestingly, while young people as a whole, especially single mothers, declined economically, women overall, especially those with college educations, made gains during the 1980s.[56]

As noted earlier, the saddest economic decline in the 1980s occurred among children. The proportion of children living in the poorest homes increased by 25 percent, and almost all lived in families headed by single women. Al-

most half of all children born in America today will live for a period of their youth in poverty. One-fifth of all American children and one-fourth of all preschoolers live in poverty; they are the single largest group of poor people in the country. Thirteen million children live in desperately poor homes, where the breadwinners cannot pay the rent and buy adequate food at the same time.[57]

A greater percentage of African-Americans suffer poverty in America than do any other ethnic group members. Probably the largest single social condition in which poverty has grown recently is in single-parent families, and the increase in single-parent African-American families has been striking. In 1960, three-quarters of all black families were composed of two parents. By 1985, however, the figure had dropped to half, and it is in these families where two-thirds of the poor African-American youngsters reside. John E. Jacob, President of the National Urban League, sees a strong parallel between unemployment among African-American males and the dissolution of their families. Indeed, he argues that there is a direct correlation in the percentages of male unemployment and broken families.[58]

As the tax policies of the 1980s gave great advantages to the wealthy, budget cuts in the social programs made life increasingly difficult for the growing number of poor people. (See Table 11.9 for facts about the gap between rich and poor.) Not only were programs reduced, however; the criteria for qualifying for public assistance were also toughened, resulting by 1989 in 299,000 families receiving reduced benefits, and 408,000 families losing all benefits completely.[59] (See Table 11.10 for examples of cuts in the social programs.)

The conservatives who politically dominated the 1980s had a deeply felt suspicion that welfare was replete with freeloaders and cheats, and that it made people permanently dependent. Therefore, welfare recipients should be

---

* It should be kept in mind that by owning rather than renting a home not only do people accumulate equity that can be used to improve their standard of living, but also they get an important tax advantage. Owning a home is the greatest single tax loophole for most people since the government allows home owners to deduct the mortgage interest from their income before calculating their taxable income. In other words, they lower their tax base. In effect, the government is helping people buy their homes. Renters, on the other hand, get neither advantage. If the economic conditions deny the opportunity of home ownership to increasingly larger percentages of young people, they are impoverished, penalized by the tax structure, and denied an important aspect of the American dream. Any society that impoverishes its youth risks serious social problems.

Table 11.9
GROWING POVERTY IN AMERICA

In 1988 the gap between rich and poor was the worst since World War II. After adjustments for inflation, the richest 20% of American households earned $9109 a year more in 1988 than in 1978, while the poorest 20% of American households earned $576 less.

The poorest of the poor in 1988 were at the lowest level in 15 years. Eleven million people, about 5% of the population, lived in families earning less than one-half of the poverty line.

During the 1980s the working poor increased by 2 million to a total of 16 million people.

In 1988, the average wage, after being adjusted for inflation, was the lowest in 25 years.

In 1988, 32 million people—more than one in eight—were members of families living below the poverty line. That was an increase of 6 million over 1978.

In 1988, almost 12.5 million children—one in five—were poor.

In 1988, the United States spent less of its GNP on social programs than any other industrial country except for Japan, and it spent less of its GNP on elementary and secondary education than any other industrial country in the world.

Source: Adapted from Stanley Meiser and Sam Fulwood III, "Economic Gap Bodes Ill for U.S.," *The Los Angeles Times,* July 15, 1990.

Table 11.10
SOCIAL PROGRAM REDUCTIONS 1981–1988
(IN MILLIONS OF DOLLARS, ADJUSTED FOR INFLATON)

PROGRAM	FY[a] 1981	FY 1988	PERCENTAGE DECLINE[b]
Training and employment	$9106	$2887	68%
Energy assistance	$1850	$1162	37%
Health services	$856	$814	5%
Legal services	$321	$232	28%
Compensatory education	$3545	$3291	7%
Housing assistance for elderly	$797	$422	47%
Funds for local antipoverty agencies	$525	$290	45%

[a] Fiscal year.

[b] These cuts were made in the face of an increase in the percentage of people living below the federal poverty line from 11.7 percent in 1979 to 13.5 percent in 1988.

Source: Center on Budget Priorities as reported in the *Los Angeles Times,* Jan. 20, 1989.

weaned from it whenever possible, and the welfare frauds should be abruptly rooted out. There was also a very strong belief that poor people do not prosper because they are basically lazy. In 1981 George Gilder, a supply-side economist, published *Wealth and Poverty,* in which he articulated these views in unambiguous terms: "In a society of rapid social mobility, . . . the poor know that their condition is to a great degree their own fault *or choice.*" (Emphasis added.) Going on to decry government programs to alleviate poverty, he wrote,

> The only dependable route from poverty is always work, family, and faith. The first principle is that in order to move up, the poor must not only work, they must work harder than the classes above them.[60]

Many of Gilder's sentiments are echoed by a small number of African-American scholars. They argue that the poor cannot expect to be helped by government programs, and indeed, that these programs tend to mire them deeper in poverty. Encouraging African-Americans to do more to help themselves escape poverty, Harvard political scientist Glenn C. Loury wrote, "No people can be genuinely free so long as they look upon others as responsible for their deliverance."[61]

People on the other side of the issue argue that often the social and economic conditions of the country create poverty and that government is obliged to pursue policies that mitigate the suffering of society's unfortunates and attempt to eliminate poverty as much as possible. If, they argue, we can afford to subsidize the logging industry, guarantee loans for the Lockheed and Chrysler corporations, and bailout the savings and loan industry, surely we have a duty to tend to the needs of our poor. Furthermore, they argue that federal programs to help the poor have been historically successful (a matter contested by opponents) and that when

the government relaxes these efforts, as it did in the 1980s, the numbers and suffering of the poor increase tragically. They also suggest that capitalism tends to write off those who cannot compete and that society must act to soften this inhumane treatment of human beings. As to the allegations that welfare is fraught with cheaters, they argue that the greatest fraud against the government is committed by the defense industry, by Medicare and Medicaid over billings, by real estate developers, and so on.

The Hungry and the Homeless   The rise of poverty during the past decade was manifested in an increase of people who are hungry and homeless. Between 1980 and 1989 over 3 million additional people fell below the poverty line. It was estimated in 1989 that there were between 2 and 5 million people suffering from hunger, and another 8 to 10 million on its cusp. At the same time, school lunch programs were cut back, and 1 million fewer people were allowed to use food stamps in 1989 than were using them in 1980.[62]

Homelessness became a critical problem during the same period. Increased poverty, together with the release of mentally ill people from institutions, bureaucratic foul-ups with social security checks, the rise in use of crack cocaine, and reduced federal spending on housing for the poor (between 1980 and 1988, federal spending on low-income housing declined by 77 percent), combined to send skyrocketing the number of people with no home. Some estimates place the number at 3 million people who sleep on the streets, in parks, in parked cars, and in public shelters.

Although accurately counting the homeless is difficult, and their exact number is a matter of considerable debate, the trends are fairly well known. In the early 1980s, the major growth in the homeless population came from the "mainstreamed" mentally ill. By 1983, however, a large number of able-bodied young adults found themselves on the streets, having lost their homes in the recession of 1981-1982. Finally, the mid-1980s saw whole families who had become impoverished looking for a declining supply of housing. Children, for the first time in our history—perhaps as many as 1 million of them—joined the ranks of the homeless.[63] Indeed, Robert M. Hayes, counsel for the National Coalition for the Homeless, paraphrasing a study on the homeless, wrote that "entrenched poverty" assured that "skid row became more democratic in the 1980s."[64]

This view was questioned by the government, which slashed its public housing and food budgets, and some of its spokespersons challenged suggestions that the number of poor people was growing. In 1983, presidential counselor—soon to become Attorney General—Edwin Meese III said in the face of volumes of evidence to the contrary,

> Well, I don't know of any authoritative figures that there are hungry children . . . . I think some people go to soup kitchens because the food is free and that's easier than paying for it.[65]

Five years later this attitude still pervaded the Administration—even at the top. When asked by David Brinkley in a 1988 ABC News interview about the number of homeless, President Reagan replied, "Doesn't that go back—that there are always going to be people—they make it _their own choice_ for staying out there."[66] (Emphasis added.)

In spite of the public's apparent growing frustration with homeless people, studies indicate that Americans have not lost their concern for the less fortunate, and support more government spending on certain programs for the poor. Generally, Americans support programs that they perceive to be designed to help the poor help themselves: aid to education, job training, and workfare programs (ones in which

people receiving assistance from the government are required to work if they are able). They remain suspicious, however, about "handout" programs in which the poor are given money after having proven the need for it, because they believe such programs encourage laziness.[67]

WELFARE

A national responsibility for the basic well-being of all of our people was first recognized in the 1930s. The Social Security Act created not only social insurance policies for those who could afford them but also a public assistance program for those who could not see to their own basic needs. Although public assistance programs for the indigent aged and the blind were established, the most extensive and expensive welfare program was **Aid to Families with Dependent Children (AFDC)**, and it remains the country's most costly and most controversial welfare program. Funded by federal and state matching funds in which the federal contribution is the heaviest, AFDC is administered by the state and local governments. Like all public assistance programs, AFDC is a means-tested program (people must demonstrate the need for public assistance), and state-employed social workers make regular visits to recipients' homes to verify the continued need for government help. As with unemployment insurance, the criteria for qualification for AFDC and the amount paid are established by state policy according to the amount of state resources they wish to devote to their programs. Hence the benefits available to the poor vary widely from state to state.

Being an unpopular program, AFDC is subject to a great deal of criticism, some accurate and some not. Among the most persistent myths about welfare is that people receive princely sums. In fact, the government has never come close to providing poor families with enough to reach the federal poverty line. (See Table 11.11.) Federal welfare programs have been gradually increased to cover more people, however. In 1950, AFDC benefits were extended to disabled persons, and in 1965 the Medicare bill also provided for *Medicaid*. This program pays the medical expenses for most illnesses for people receiving public assistance. In 1974, the **Supplemental Security Income (SSI)** program was established to bring the incomes of the indigent blind, disabled, and aged up to uniform minimum federal levels; states could offer greater benefits if they chose, but they could not fall below the legal minimums. Finally, in 1988 a reform of AFDC was passed requiring able-bodied adult recipients who are not needed at home for child care to either work toward a high school diploma, receive job training, or become employed (called *workfare*). It is hoped that this reform will encourage people to find jobs and leave the welfare rolls.

The federal government also maintains a public housing program whose origins reach back to the Great Depression. Basically the government housing programs are of two kinds. One builds public low-cost housing projects, which are often administered locally, and the second defers a percentage of the housing costs of people who meet the means test. As you have already learned, the cuts in funds for public housing during the 1980s have seriously aggravated the problems of poor people's finding affordable housing. President Bush has proposed a policy to give tax credits and government grants totaling $6.8 billion to help low-income families buy homes. Also, in a proposal virtually identical to Michael Dukakis's 1988 campaign proposal, Bush would allow moderate-income people to apply part of their savings from Individual Retirement Accounts (IRAs) toward the first-time purchase of a home or toward the cost of a college education.[68]

For the hungry, the government maintains a number of programs including food stamps and subsidized school lunches. The **food stamp**

Table 11.11
AID TO FAMILIES WITH DEPENDENT CHILDREN

PRESIDENT	YEAR	AVERAGE POVERTY THRESHOLD FOR A FAMILY OF FOUR	AVERAGE ANNUAL BENEFIT PER FAMILY	PERCENTAGE OF POVERTY THRESHOLD REACHED BY BENEFITS
Eisenhower	1960	$3,022	$1,269.00	42.0%
Kennedy	1963	$3,128	$1,442.28	46.1%
Johnson	1965	$3,223	$1,598.40	49.6%
Johnson	1968	$3,553	$2,020.92	56.9%
Nixon	1970	$3,968	$2,197.56	55.4%
Nixon	1974	$5,038	$2,451.24	48.7%
Ford	1976	$5,815	$2,833.20	48.7%
Carter	1977	$6,191	$2,955.24	47.7%
Carter	1980	$8,414	$3,360.36	39.9%
Reagan	1981	$9,287	$3,384.48	36.4%
Reagan	1985	$10,989	$4,105.80	37.4%

Source: Extrapolated from Stanley and Niemi, *Vital Statistics on American Politics,* 2nd ed.

program also has its origins in the New Deal, but the current program began in 1977. Administered by the Department of Agriculture, the program makes coupons available to people on public assistance that can be redeemed in food purchases at local grocery stores. The amount of food stamp aid given to people is in inverse proportion to the welfare checks their states authorize, so people living in states that pay lower welfare subsidies receive proportionately higher values in food stamps. (See Table 11.12 for a comparison of state AFDC and food stamp programs.)

In other programs the government subsidizes school breakfasts, milk, lunches, and summer feeding programs for poor children. In some cases, these might be the only well-balanced, hot meals the children will have for the day. Child-care food programs and nutrition programs for expecting mothers are also funded. Additionally, during the Reagan Administration the government distributed surplus cheese, butter, and powdered milk to the poor.

The food stamp program was fairly successful at addressing the problem of hunger until the past decade.[69] In 1981, however, it suffered seriously from budget cuts. Between 1980 and 1987, the program was cut by 15 percent; 1 million people were removed from the food stamp rolls, and millions more saw their monthly food stamp allotment reduced. At the same time, 3 million more people were added to the ranks of the poor. In 1989 the food stamp program fed 19 million at an annual cost of $13 billion.[70]

Other food programs were also slashed. Between 1982 and 1985, funds for child nutrition were cut by 27.7 percent, 750,000 poor children were dropped from school lunch programs, and 500,000 were cut from summer lunch programs.[71] Frustrated by these cuts, a homeless mother complained, "Hungry kids don't learn.

They stay stupid."[72] The "silent erosion of the school lunch program" has recently been aggravated by the reduction in government surplus dairy products and beef. These once-plentiful reserves were given to schools to subsidize the cost of school lunches, but now schools are having to pay for them, thus forcing up the cost of the lunches and reducing the number of children who can afford them.[73] Similarly, the reduced government surpluses of food have eliminated the free food packages that were distributed to the poor by local authorities. Ironically, while the program was in operation, the sight of lines of poor people queued up to receive blocks of cheese did a great deal to bring home to the American people the problem of hunger, the existence of which the government denied.[74]

Although suffering dramatic reductions in support, the welfare programs managed to survive the conservative onslaught of the last decade. They remain meagerly financed, but most of them are intact, awaiting a more generous era. Even so, however, some authorities claim that large numbers of deserving people have fallen between the cracks of public assistance. John E. Jacob asserts that one-quarter of the poor, mostly children, do not receive AFDC benefits, one-third of the aged poor do not qualify for SSI, *most* eligible women with infants do not receive adequate assistance, almost 10 million eligible people do not get food stamps, only one-fifth of the children in need of Head Start programs are able to take advantage of this vital program, and just a tiny percentage of those who should receive job training do so.[75] Also, the Mental Health Law Project, a private organization, estimates that because of antiquated bureaucratic regulations, about 75 percent of all disabled children are deemed ineligible for SSI benefits.[76] With luck, this omission will soon be corrected: In 1990 the Supreme Court ruled that the regula-

Table 11.12
1988 Benefits in AFDC and Food Stamps by State

	Maximum AFDC Grant per Month	Percentage of Poverty Threshold[a] AFDC Grant Reaches	Food Stamp Benefit per Month	Value of Combined Benefits	Percentage of Poverty Threshold Combined Benefits Reach
Alabama	$118	15.7%	$228	$346	46%
Alaska	$779	82.7%	$201	$980	104%
Arizona	$293	38.9%	$219	$512	68%
Arkansas	$202	26.8%	$228	$430	57%
California	$633	83.5%	$117	$750	99%
Colorado	$356	47.3%	$201	$557	74%
Connecticut	$601	79.3%	$127	$728	96%
Delaware	$319	42.0%	$212	$537	70%
District of Columbia	$379	50.2%	$194	$573	76%
Florida	$275	33.9%	$225	$500	66%
Georgia	$263	34.8%	$228	$491	65%
Hawaii	$515	59.8%	$308	$823	95%
Idaho	$304	40.3%	$216	$520	69%
Illinois	$342	45.2%	$210	$552	73%
Indiana	$288	37.9%	$221	$509	67%
Iowa	$381	50.5%	$193	$574	76%
Kansas	$409	54.2%	$195	$604	80%
Kentucky	$207	27.6%	$228	$435	58%
Louisiana	$190	25.0%	$228	$418	55%
Maine	$416	54.9%	$183	$599	79%
Maryland	$359	47.4%	$217	$576	76%
Massachusetts	$510	67.6%	$154	$664	88%
Michigan[b]	$528	70.2%	$171	$669	93%
Minnesota	$532	70.4%	$148	$680	90%
Mississippi	$120	15.8%	$228	$348	46%

Missouri	$282	37.4%	$223	$505	67%
Montana	$359	47.6%	$200	$559	74%
Nebraska	$350	46.3%	$202	$552	73%
Nevada	$325	43.1%	$210	$535	71%
New Hampshire	$486	64.5%	$162	$648	86%
New Jersey	$424	56.1%	$188	$612	81%
New Mexico	$264	34.1%	$228	$492	65%
New York[c]	$539	71.5%	$162	$701	93%
No. Carolina	$266	35.0%	$228	$494	65%
No. Dakota	$371	49.1%	$196	$567	75%
Ohio	$309	41.0%	$219	$528	70%
Oklahoma	$310	40.1%	$214	$524	69%
Oregon	$412	54.9%	$219	$631	84%
Pennsylvania	$402	53.3%	$187	$589	78%
Rhode Island	$503	66.3%	$195	$698	92%
So. Carolina	$200	26.6%	$228	$428	57%
So. Dakota	$366	48.7%	$198	$564	75%
Tennessee	$159	21.0%	$228	$387	51%
Texas	$184	24.6%	$228	$412	55%
Utah	$376	50.1%	$195	$571	76%
Vermont	$603	80.2%	$126	$729	97%
Virginia	$354	47.2%	$201	$555	74%
Washington	$492	65.0%	$174	$666	88%
W. Virginia	$249	32.9%	$228	$477	63%
Wisconsin	$517	68.5%	$152	$672	89%
Wyoming	$360	47.7%	$199	$559	74%

[a] The poverty threshold is that set for 1987.
[b] Wayne County only.
[c] New York City only.

Source: Computed from data in Stanley and Niemi, *Vital Statistics on American Politics*, 2nd ed.

tions violated the intent of the law and that thousands of disabled children previously denied benefits are entitled to them.[77] Even so, Richard Darman, Director of the Office of Management and Budget, warns that the United States may not be able to continue its commitment to social programs. He added that the expense of the savings and loan bailout, the mounting interest on the national debt, the projected costs of cleaning up the nuclear weapons production plants, and growing environmental safety costs are "hidden pac-men" that eat up government revenue and may make its long-term social welfare commitments too costly.[78]

It seems that we stand at a crossroads in social policy. The worst-case projections are grim. The temptation for some is to cut further the social expenditures to relieve the budget of its seemingly impossible commitments. Before we take this drastic step, however, we should consider a few mitigating factors. The food and housing programs were begun in an effort to aid the construction industry, the agriculture industry, and the finance industry and to reduce government agricultural surpluses at least as much as they were intended to help the poor.[79] What impact might the future curtailment of these programs have on the overall economy? Additionally, rather than going down an economic black hole, welfare payments are spent in local economies for groceries, clothing, and other necessities. It is also important to contemplate what depredations might plague local merchants if these funds are not spent. In a secondary sense, the local grocer and haberdasher are almost as much recipients of welfare benefits as are their customers. Also, if an economy cannot employ a large percentage of its work force at a livable wage and no social programs exist to alleviate their misery, one might wonder about the social and political consequences.

Summary

- The United States practiced Adam Smith's *laissez-faire* policies until the Great Depression of the 1930s forced it to adopt fiscal and monetary policies to foster general economic prosperity.

- Fiscal policy manipulates taxes, borrowing, and spending, while monetary policy adjusts the price of credit and the number of dollars in circulation.

- Government also regulates and promotes business and labor through a number of programs.

- Even though spending on social programs was cut during the 1980s, the increased spending on defense and the reduction of taxes caused unprecedented annual budget deficits.

- At the same time, government policies caused a decline in services and wages for the less well-to-do, while the wealthy became richer.

- Government regulation of financial institutions also relaxed until problems of near-crisis proportions arose.

- Society finds itself frustrated by a regressive tax structure and a declining standard of living for the lower classes.

Notes

1. *Lochner* v. *New York*, 198 U.S. 45 (1905); *Wolff Packing Co.* v. *Court of Industrial Relations*, 262 U.S. 522 (1923); and *Adkins* v. *Children's Hospital*, 261 U.S. 525 (1923).

2. See Arthur M. Schlesinger, Jr., *The Crisis of the Old Order* (Boston: Houghton Mifflin, 1956).

3. Quoted in Tom Redburn, "Budget Deficits to Restrict Social Programs for Years," *The Los Angeles Times*, Aug. 26, 1988.

4. See David Stockman, *The Triumph of Politics* (New York: Harper & Row, 1986).

5. Frances Fox Piven and Richard A. Cloward, "Capitalism Against Democracy," in George McKenna and Stanley Feingold, eds., *Taking Sides*, 4th ed. (Guilford, CT: Dushkin Publishing Group, 1985), p. 244; and Art Paine, "Darman Likens Long-Term Federal Commitments to 'Hidden Pac-Men'", *The Los Angeles Times*, Jan. 30, 1990.

6. William Greider, "The Education of David Stockman," *Atlantic Monthly*, Dec. 1981, pp. 46–47.

7. See Arjo Klamer, *Conversations with Economists* (Lanham, MD: Rowan and Littlefield, 1984).

8. "Tax Report Says Rich Gained, Poor Lost During '80s," *The Los Angeles Times*, Feb. 6, 1990.

9. Kevin Phillips, "When Politics Come to Push & Shove," *The Los Angeles Times*, Jan. 28, 1990.

10. William J. Eaton, "Moynihan Urges Social Security Tax Cut, Return to Pay-As-You-Go Benefits System," *The Los Angeles Times*, Dec. 30, 1989.

11. Piven and Cloward, p. 243.

12. Piven and Cloward, p. 244.

13. Everett Carl Ladd, "The 1988 Elections: Continuation of the Post-New Deal System," *Political Science Quarterly* (Spring 1989), 8.

14. William J. Eaton, "$25 Billion Tax Hike Urged to Cut Deficit," *The Los Angeles Times*, Dec. 29, 1989.

15. "Study Lists Firms Not Paying Taxes," *The Los Angeles Times*, July 18, 1986.

16. "Fewer Healthy Firms Legally Escape Taxes," *The Los Angeles Times*, Sept. 23, 1988.

17. Harold W. Stanley and Richard G. Niemi, *Vital Statistics on American Politics*, 2nd ed. (Washington, DC: Congressional Quarterly Press, 1990), pp. 389–390.

18. Kevin Phillips, "When Debt Is Respectable the GOP Heads for Trouble," *The Los Angeles Times*, Dec. 31, 1989.

19. Stanley and Niemi, p. 396.

20. See David Stockman, *The Triumph of Politics*.

21. The McNeil/Lehrer NewsHour, KPBS, Oct. 6, 1989, and Jan. 22, 1990.

22. Marlene Cimons, "Foley Urges Caution on Payroll Tax Cut," *The Los Angeles Times*, Jan. 22, 1990.

23. Jeffrey M. Berry, *The Interest Group Society*, 2nd ed. (Glenview, IL: Scott, Foresman/ Little, Brown, 1989), p. 23.

24. *TWA* v. *IFFA*, 103 L. Ed. 2d 456 (1989).

25. *Pension Benefit Guarantee Corporation* v. *LTV Corp.*, 110 S. Ct. 2668 (1990).

26. Douglas Frantz and Robert L. Jackson, "Pension Plans Looted as Safeguards Weaken," *The Los Angeles Times*, Oct. 29, 1989.

27. Tom Furlong, "Bailout Seen as Eliminating Many S&Ls, Inviting Abuse," *The Los Angeles Times*, July 29, 1989.

28. Robert A. Rosenblatt and James Bares, "Agency Hold $400 Billion Fire Sale," *The Los Angeles Times*, Aug. 11, 1989.

29. Robert A. Rosenblatt and James Risen, "U.S. Banks: A Crisis in the Making?" *The Los Angeles Times*, Apr. 14, 1991.

30. James Risen, "Bush to Seek Cuts in Soft Net for Banks," *The Los Angeles Times*, Dec. 2, 1990.

31. Quoted in Ronald J. Ostrow and William J. Eaton, "Areas Most in Need May be Real HUD Scandal Victims," *The Los Angeles Times*, July 2, 1989.

32. William J. Eaton, "Panel Says Pierce OK'd $27 Million Award for Builder After Short Talk," *The Los Angeles Times*, July 2, 1989.

33. Marlene Cimons, "Kemp Puts Blame on Pierce for HUD Troubles," *The Los Angeles Times*, July 8, 1989.

34. William J. Eaton, "Rents Doubled After Project Got Big Subsidy," *The Los Angeles Times*, Oct. 3, 1989.

35. William J. Eaton, "Made $500,000 By Using Political Clout at HUD, Republican Party Official Brags," *The Los Angeles Times*, July 25, 1989.

36. Marlene Cimons, "Kemp Puts Blame on Pierce for HUD Troubles," *The Los Angeles Times*, July 8, 1989.

37. "Pierce's Friend Got $350,000 From HUD," *The Los Angeles Times*, Dec. 4, 1989.

38. James J. Kilpatrick, "Reagan Responsible for HUD Debacle," *Chicago Tribune*, Aug. 13, 1989.

39. William J. Eaton, "House Probe Focusing on Fraud in HUD Co-Insurance Program," *The Los Angeles Times*, June 29, 1989.

40. Douglas Frantz, "HUD Aided Plan to Sell the Poor $85,000 Condos," *The Los Angeles Times*, July 1, 1989.

41. Ronald J. Ostrow and William J. Eaton, "Areas Most in Need May Be Real HUD Scandal Victims," *The Los Angeles Times*, July 2, 1989.

42. "Indictment in Theft Names 'Robin HUD'", *The Los Angeles Times*, Nov. 22, 1989.

43. William J. Eaton, "Pierce Invokes 5th, Says Probers Prejudged Him," *The Los Angeles Times*, Sept. 27, 1989.

44. Quoted in Ronald J. Ostrow and William J. Eaton, "Areas Most in Need May Be Real HUD Scandal Victims," *The Los Angeles Times*, July 2, 1989.

45. William J. Eaton, "HUD Reforms Clear Congress After Hearings Reveal Abuses," *The Los Angeles Times*, Feb. 2, 1990.

46. Ronald J. Ostrow, "Thornburgh Asks Special HUD Probe Counsel," *The Los Angeles Times*, Feb. 2, 1990.

47. Robert A. Rosenblatt, "Conferees Agree to Catastrophic Care's Repeal," *The Los Angeles Times*, Nov. 18, 1989.

48. James Gerstenzang and Robert A. Rosenblatt, "Calling It 'Charade', Bush Attacks Moynihan's Plan to Cut Payroll Tax," *The Los Angeles Times*, Jan. 19, 1990.

49. Janny Scott, "Many Believe They Can't Afford Good Health Care," *The Los Angeles Times*, Feb. 5, 1990.

50. Edwin Chen, "AMA Officials Urge Insurance Coverage for All," *The Los Angeles Times*, May 14, 1991.

51. Stanley and Niemi, p. 348.

52. Robert H. Haveman, "The War on Poverty and the Poor and Non-poor," *Political Science Quarterly* (Spring 1987), 65.

53. Hugh Heclo, "General Welfare and Two American Political Traditions," *Political Science Quarterly* 2 (1986), 194; and Tom Redburn, "Are You Better Off? Yes, if You're Female or Elderly," *The Los Angeles Times*, Oct. 29, 1988.

54. Robert M. Hayes, "Homeless Children" in Frank J. Macchiarola and Alan Gartner, eds., *Caring for America's Children*, (New York: Academy of Political Science, 1989), pp. 62-63.

55. Don Irwin, "Those Under 30 Found to Be in Economic Bind," *The Los Angeles Times*, Sept. 5, 1989.

56. Tom Redburn, "Are You Better Off? Yes, if You're Female or Elderly," *The Los Angeles Times*, Oct. 29, 1988.

57. Hayes, p. 58.

58. John E. Jacob, "The Government and Social Problems," in Herbert M. Levine, ed., *Point Counter-Point*, 3rd ed. (New York: St. Martin's Press, 1989), pp. 280-281.

59. Lee May, "Blacks Look Back With Anger at Reagan Years," *The Los Angeles Times*, Jan. 20, 1989.

60. George Gilder, *Wealth and Poverty* (New York: Basic Books, 1981), p. 68.

61. Glenn C. Loury, "Internally Directed Action for Black Community Development: The Next Frontier for 'The Movement'", in Herbert M. Levine, ed., *Point Counter-Point*, 3rd ed. (New York: St. Martin's Press, 1989), p. 287.

62. "Hunger in America," KPBS, Dec. 19, 1989.

63. Hayes, pp. 58-67.

64. Hayes, p. 64.

65. Quoted in *The Washington Post*, Dec. 10, 1983, p. A8.

66. Quoted in "Reagan Says Some Homeless Sleep on Grates From "Own Choice'", *The Los Angeles Times*, Dec. 23, 1988.

67. James L. Sundquist, "How American Lost Its Social Conscience—And How Will It Get It Back," *Political Science Quarterly* 4 (1986), 520-524.

68. James Gerstenzang, "Bush Proposes $6.8 Billion Housing Plan," *The Los Angeles Times*, Nov. 11, 1989.

69. Jacob, p. 278

70. "Hunger in America," KPBS, Dec. 19, 1989.

71. Michael Lipsky and March A. Thibodeau, "Feeding the Hungry with Surplus Commodities, "*Political Science Quarterly* (Summer 1988), 226.

72. Hayes, p. 68.

73. Maria L. LaGanga, "Surplus Food Cuts Starve Lunch Programs in Schools," *The Los Angeles Times,* Jan. 31, 1990.

74. Lipsky and Thibodeau, pp. 243~244.

75. Jacob, p. 281.

76. Michael J. Ybarra, "Federal Ruses Assailed as Denying Aide to Up to 75% of Disabled Children," *The Los Angeles Times,* Sept. 3, 1989.

77. *Sullivan* v. *Zebley,* 110 S. Ct. 885, (1989).

78. Art Pine, "Darman Likens Long-Term Federal Commitments to 'Hidden Pac-Men,'" *The Los Angeles Times,* Jan. 30, 1989.

79. Haveman, p. 77, and Lipsky and Thibodeau, p. 225.

Suggestions for Further Reading

Bell, Daniel, and Lester Thurow. *The Deficit: How Big? How Long? How Dangerous?* New York: New York University Press, 1985.

Berry, Jeffrey M. *Feeding the Hungry: Rulemaking in the Food Stamp Program.* New Brunswick: Rutgers University Press, 1984.

Birnbaum, Jeffrey H., and Alan S. Murray. *Showdown at Gucci Gulch.* New York: Random House, 1987.

Block, Fred, Richard A. Cloward, Barbara Ehrenreich, and Frances Fox Piven. *The Mean Season: The Attack on the Welfare State.* New York: Pantheon, 1987.

Cherlin, Andrew J., ed. *The Changing American Family and Public Policy.* Lanham, MD: Urban Institute Press, 1988.

Chubb, John E. *Interest Groups and the Bureaucracy: The Politics of Energy.* Menlo Park: Stanford University Press, 1983.

Derthick, Martha. *Policymaking for Social Security.* Washington, DC: Brookings Institution, 1979.

Derthick, Martha, and Paul J. Quirk. *The Politics of Deregulation.* Washington, DC: Brookings Institution, 1985.

Edsall, Thomas B. *The New Politics of Inequality.* New York: Norton, 1985.

Friedman, Benjamin. *Day of Reckoning: The Consequences of American Economic Policy Under Reagan and After.* New York: Random House, 1988.

Garfinkel, Irwin, and Sara S. McLanahan. *Single Mothers and Their Children: A New American Dilemma.* Lanham, MD: Urban Institute Press, 1986.

Gilder, George. *Wealth and Poverty.* New York: Basic Books, 1981.

Heilbroner, Robert, and Peter Bernstein. *The Debt and the Deficit: False Alarms/Real Possibilities.* New York: Norton, 1989.

Klamer, Arjo. *Conversations with Economists.* Lanham, MD: Rowan and Littlefield, 1984.

Marmor, Theodore, ed. *Political Analysis and American Medical Care*. New York: Cambridge University Press, 1983.

Macchiarola, Frank J., and Alan Gartner, eds. *Caring for America's Children*. New York: Academy of Political Science, 1985.

McKenna, George, and Stanley Feingold, eds. *Taking Sides* (4th ed.). Guilford, CT: Duskin, 1985.

Moynihan, Daniel Patrick. *Came the Revolution: Argument in the Reagan Era*. San Diego: Harcourt Brace Jovanovich, 1988.

————. *Family and Nation*. New York: Harcourt Brace Jovanovich, 1986.

Murray, Charles. *Losing Ground: American Social Policy, 1950–1980*. New York: Basic Books, 1984.

Pechman, Joseph A. *Federal Tax Policy* (4th ed.). Washington, DC: Brookings Institution, 1984.

Rogers, Tom, and Cheryl Rogers. *By the Few for the Few*. Lexington, MA: Lexington Books, 1985.

Rosenbaum, Walter A. *Energy, Politics, and Public Policy* (2nd ed.). Washington, DC: Congressional Quarterly Press, 1987.

Schlesinger, Arthur M. *The Crisis of the Old Order*. Boston: Houghton Mifflin, 1956.

Spulber, Nicholas. *Managing the American Economy from Roosevelt to Reagan*. Bloomington: Indiana University Press, 1989.

Stein, Herbert. *Presidential Economics: The Making of Economic Policy from Roosevelt to Reagan and Beyond*. New York: Simon & Schuster, 1984.

Stockman, David. *The Triumph of Politics: How the Reagan Revolution Failed*. New York: Harper & Row, 1986.

Weicher, John C. *Maintaining the Safety Net: Income Redistribution Programs in the Reagan Administration*. Washington, DC: American Enterprise Institute, 1984.

White, Joseph, and Aaron Wildavsky. *The Deficit and the Public Interest*. New York: Russell Sage Foundation, 1989.

Chapter 12

FOREIGN POLICY

PREVIEW

The basic format for international relations is the nation-state system, in which each country, or state, is recognized as sovereign—the ultimate legal authority within its territory—and national self-interest is the criterion upon which foreign policy is developed and measured. The United States, like all states, has used national self-interest to guide its foreign policy.

For the first century of our existence we maintained a unilateral foreign policy and our principal focus was on the Western Hemisphere. The Monroe Doctrine warned European states to stay out of our sphere of influence as we concentrated on expanding across the continent. As the nineteenth century closed, however, we found ourselves a leading economic power, ruling a far-flung empire. Yet with the exception of World War I we remained content to ignore European affairs, and to become the self-proclaimed policeman of Latin America.

The events of World War II shifted the balance of power to a bipolarization between the United States and the Soviet Union. Nuclear weapons and the Cold War dislodged us from our traditional unilateral posture to become the leader of the Western bloc. The lessons of the interwar period led us to aid in the recovery of Western Europe with the Marshall Plan, and the North Atlantic Treaty Organization (NATO) was created to enforce our containment of communist expansion. Violent confrontations with communism in Korea and Vietnam ensued, and the two nuclear giants came close to a general war over Cuba.

President Richard M. Nixon, formerly a consummate cold warrior, managed to develop warmer relations with the People's Republic of China and with the Soviet Union, but American-Soviet relations soon abandoned détente and a new arms race began. Pursuing a foreign policy more adroit than his rhetoric implied, however, President Ronald Reagan was also able to overcome his cold-war inclinations and he reestablished closer relations with the Soviets. Yet the United States seems to have abandoned Franklin D. Roosevelt's Good Neighbor Policy, and to have reverted to interventionism in Latin America. At the same time, the United States finds itself drawn deeper and deeper into the quagmire of Middle East politics.

Although Congress plays an important role, the president controls foreign policy. The secretary of state is technically the president's chief adviser on foreign policy, but the national security adviser has often eclipsed the Cabinet official in recent years. In pursuit of foreign policy objectives, presidents use the foreign service as principal representatives to other countries and to international organizations. Their efforts are augmented by intelligence organizations that gather information and implement certain policies. Presidents also use economic means, military force, and the United Nations to conduct foreign policy.

The Department of Defense (DOD), led by the secretary of defense and other civilians, is a huge bureaucracy—where politics is certainly no stranger.

The destructiveness of modern weapons, however, brings the efficacy of warfare increasingly into question. After years of confrontation, the Western and Eastern blocs are reconfiguring: liberalization in Eastern Europe and economic developments in the West have caused reevaluations of the post–World War II bipolarity.

Since World War II the United States and the Soviet Union have built vast arsenals of conventional and nuclear weapons, until the economies of the adversaries weakened from the strain. Finally, for the first time in history, an agreement reduced the number of nuclear warheads in Europe, raising hope that more reductions will follow. Although negotiating disarmament is an extremely complicated process, people in the United States looked forward to savings from the defense budget creating a peace dividend and being spent on social and economic items at home, until events on the Arabian Peninsula consumed any savings we might otherwise have enjoyed.

The patience, secrecy, and clandestine operations required in formulating and implementing sound foreign policy cause difficulty for open governments based on popular control. To guard against the potential abuse of these necessary but menacing techniques, citizens of a democracy must remain knowledgeable about the issues of the day and committed to the principles of a free, self-governing society.

It is not easy to change the approaches on which East-West relations have been built for fifty years. But the new is knocking at every door and window.

Mikhail S. Gorbachev

Each nation-state is a sovereign entity in international affairs, which means that each country's government is the highest legal authority within its territory. The guiding principle in international affairs is *national self-interest*. Although there is considerable controversy about the proper definition of the national self-interest, the United States, like all other countries, has been motivated in its foreign policy by what it perceives as its self-interest. This singular focus in foreign policy has at times led us to noble deeds, while at other times our foreign policy has fallen short of our constitutional ideals.

History of United States Foreign Policy

In his 1796 farewell address, George Washington advised his compatriots to actively pursue their commercial interests with foreign lands, but to avoid all political entanglements not necessitated by an emergency. In giving this advice, Washington was counseling protection of the national self-interest as he understood it. Washington's policy of neutrality and his later advice that the United States remain aloof from European politics has been termed by some historians as **isolationist**. In fact, however, Washington did not intend for the United States to become disassociated from the rest of the world, and the country never behaved that way. What Washington advised and what the United States practiced for more than a century was a **unilateral foreign policy**. That is to say, the United States did not avoid external politics, but it carefully abstained from entering political alliances with other states. (See Table 12.1.)

In the earliest years of the republic, remaining neutral and pursuing policy uni-

Table 12.1

MAJOR EVENTS IN AMERICAN FOREIGN POLICY

American Revolution	1775–1783	Marshall Plan	1948
Unilateral foreign policy	1789–1949	NATO founded	1949
Louisiana Purchase	1803	End of unilateral foreign	
War of 1812	1812–1814	policy	1949
Monroe Doctrine	1823	Communists take China	1949
Manifest destiny	throughout 1800s	Korean War	1950–1953
Mexican-American War	1845–1848	Iran coup by CIA	1953
Japan forced to trade	1852	Guatemala coup by CIA	1954
Civil War	1861–1865	Warsaw Pact founded	1955
Spanish-American War	1898	Fidel Castro takes Cuba	1959
Open door policy	1899	Berlin Wall built	1961
Boxer Rebellion	1900	Cuban Missile Crisis	1962
Roosevelt Corollary and		Vietnam War	late 1950s–1975
the Panama Canal	1903	Gulf of Tonkin	
Dollar Diplomacy begins	1908	Resolution	1964
Platt Amendment	1908–1934	Dominican Republic	
Mexico incursion	1916	invasion	1965
Cuban occupation	1898–1903,	Tet Offensive	1968
	1900–1909,	Détente	1972–1979
	1912	Coup in Chile with CIA	
World War I	1914–1918	support	1973
Haiti occupation	1915–1934	Camp David accords	1978
Nicaragua occupation	1918–1933	American hostages in	
Intervention in Russia	1918	Iran	1978–1981
Kellogg-Briand Pact	1928	Sandinista-Contra War	1981–1989
Good Neighbor policy		Marines killed in	
begins	1933	Lebanon	1983
World War II	1939–1945	Invasion of Grenada	1983
American participation	1941–1945	American bombing of	
Cold War	1945–1990	Libya	1986
United Nations founded	1946	American Navy in	
Iron Curtain speech	1946	Persian Gulf	1987
Truman Doctrine	1947	Invasion of Panama	1989
Berlin blockade/airlift	1948–1949	Persian Gulf War	1990–1991

laterally was difficult because the French Revolution quickly widened into global war. Attempting to protect our right to trade with whomever we wished led us to an undeclared naval war with France during the John Adams presidency, and we fought a full-scale war with Britain between 1812 and 1814. In the meantime, President Thomas Jefferson shrewdly negotiated a treaty with France for the purchase of the Louisiana Territory—straining the bounds of the Constitution in the process.

As the Napoleonic wars ended, it became

possible for American attention to turn away from the Atlantic toward the Western frontier, and to give vent to imperialistic impulses. Hence, the United States articulated its unilateralism explicitly and implied its imperialist intentions by enunciating the **Monroe Doctrine**. Monroe's statement, in his 1823 State of the Union Address, asserted that the United States would stay out of European politics and that Europe must not establish any more colonies in the Americas. Although this bold position by such a weak power was greeted with contempt in Europe, the Monroe Doctrine expressed a deep-set American belief that the United States was to dominate the Western Hemisphere, and when the United States became powerful enough to back up its words, it did so with scarcely a qualm.[1]

Throughout the rest of the century, the United States focused its attention on domestic issues (tariffs, slavery, and industrial development) and on expansion across the continent. By the 1840s, the people of the United States were fully caught up in expansionist hysteria. American citizens had colonized Texas at the invitation of Mexico, and in 1836 they rebelled, creating the Republic of Texas and hoping for annexation to the United States. Wagon trains had begun to head out across the "great American desert" (the middle West) for Oregon and California. Our expansionist impulses were rationalized by the belief that God had bestowed upon us a **manifest destiny** to settle the continent, spreading the "blessings" of American values to the shores of the Pacific. Fired by the notion of America's special place in history, Herman Melville wrote, "We Americans are the peculiar chosen people—the Israel of our time; we bear the ark of the liberties of the world."

In 1846 a treaty with Britain gave us the Oregon Territory. The year before we had annexed Texas and started a war with Mexico for its northwestern territories (now the states of New Mexico, Colorado, Arizona, Nevada, and California). "Poor Mexico," it is said by the Mexicans, "so far from God yet so close to the United States." With the end of the Mexican War (1845–1848), the United States had managed to wrench away half of the territory of that hapless country. Not long afterwards, William Henry Seward, Lincoln's Secretary of State, mused that the capital of the United States should be located in Mexico City, because so situated, it would be closer to the center of the American empire.[2]

Having reached the Pacific in the late 1840s, Americans linked foreign policy to their commercial interests. In 1852 Admiral Matthew C. Perry used the threat of naval bombardment to force the Japanese to trade with the United States, and an unsuccessful attempt was made to annex Hawaii. Another attempt to annex Hawaii failed in the 1860s, but American arms finally "persuaded" it to seek annexation in the 1890s. Seward brought the Midway Islands under United States control and purchased Alaska from the Russian Empire in the 1860s. Cuba and the isthmus of Central America were also coveted by U.S. expansionists, but these areas remained free of U.S. control until the turn of the century.

THE UNITED STATES EMERGES AS A WORLD POWER

As the century drew to a close, U.S. expansionism gained new impetus. Decrying the colonial abuses of monarchist Spain in Cuba, American expansionists engineered a war in 1898 that quickly brought the United States into control of the Caribbean. Cuba and Puerto Rico were ceded by Spain, and the Philippine Islands gave us a solid foothold in the Orient from which to pursue our interests in China.

By 1898, the coast of China was being partitioned by the other imperialist powers

(Britain, France, Germany, Russia, and Japan) and the United States feared losing its markets there. Accordingly, McKinley's Secretary of State, John Hay, in the tradition of unilateralism, sent notes to these countries proposing an **Open Door Policy**, thus allowing all nations to trade with China. Eventually, the other colonialist states reluctantly agreed, but almost immediately afterwards, Chinese nationalists rose in rebellion. Following the Order of Literary Patriotic Harmonious Fists (called *Boxers* in the West), thousands of Chinese united to cast out the foreign devils. Joining the other imperialists in asserting our "right" to stay in China, the United Staes sent 5,000 troops to suppress the Boxer Rebellion in 1900.

By 1900 the United States could claim the status of a great power. Although our military complement was small, we had filled out our continental boundaries, dominated the Caribbean, possessed a Pacific empire, and had a toehold in China. We had also become one of the world's largest industrial producers and a major player in world trade. At the same time, a change had begun to occur in domestic political relationships. As long as the United States remained focused upon its domestic affairs, Congress usually dominated the American political scene. As it became increasingly involved in foreign affairs, however, the presidency began to emerge as the most prominent institution.[3]

Although the United States had become progressively involved in external matters, its foreign policy remained focused basically on the Western Hemisphere and the Orient. When European governments in 1903 threatened to take over the customs house of the Dominican Republic in order to be repaid for bad debts, Theodore Roosevelt expanded the Monroe Doctrine. He warned Europe to stay out of the Western Hemisphere, but so that the debts would be repaid, he sent United States forces to seize the customs house and collect the arrears. The **Roosevelt Corollary to the Monroe Doctrine** proclaimed for the United States the "right" to exercise "an international police power" in Latin America. Meanwhile on the continental mainland Roosevelt used American troops to aid a revolution to make Panama, a Colombian province, independent. Then Roosevelt quickly negotiated a treaty giving the United States a ten-mile strip across the isthmus in perpetuity. These two events gave the Latin Americans abundant cause to suspect the good will of the "Colossus of the North."

More subtle than military usurpation was **dollar diplomacy,** which found expression in William Howard Taft's Administration. Once described as imperialism without colonialism, dollar diplomacy refers to the practice of American commercial interests, supported by the U.S. government, developing heavy financial commitments in foreign economies. These investments expand the view of our national self-interest among American leaders, and American troops have often been used to enforce our will on weaker neighbors. Our main interest was to encourage stable governments in Latin America, even if they might be repressive of their own people.

Woodrow Wilson was perhaps our most aggressive "peacekeeper" of the Western Hemisphere. He not only meddled deeply in the affairs of the Mexican Revolution, finally sending an expeditionary force against Pancho Villa in 1916, but he also sent troops to take over the Dominican Republic, Nicaragua, and Haiti. These invasions established and maintained governments that were more malleable to American wishes than their predecessors had been, and American troops were kept in these countries for long periods to assure that American interests were "respected."

Although Wilson's interventionist policies continued after 1917, in that year U.S. attention was diverted by our entrance into World War I. Even during the war, however, the

American troops in Mexico in 1916.

United States insisted on a unilateral posture. Wilson refused to allow American troops to be commanded by Allied generals, and he articulated goals for the war ("a war to make the world safe for democracy" and "national self-determination") in ways that contradicted the less idealistic objectives of the Europeans. Taking a leading role in the peace negotiations, Wilson enunciated his Fourteen Points, which included the principle of national self-determination and the League of Nations.

By war's end, the crowns of Russia, Germany, Austria, and Turkey had collapsed, and the economic and political resources of Britain, France, Belgium, and Italy were exhausted, their societies in disarray. The United States was easily the most impressive political and economic power in the world, and unless it

exerted leadership, a power vacuum would occur. Within the United States, however, people longed for the simpler prewar times. They wanted to return to what Warren G. Harding called "normalcy." Consequently, the United States drew back from Wilson's idealism, refused to enter the League of Nations, and once again tried to ignore the politics in Europe that were popularly regarded as draconian and unworthy of our attention.

During the 1920s, American foreign policy took a back seat to our attempts to increase prosperity and to deal with the growing social problems associated with urbanization, increased industrialization, and a depressed agricultural market. Although we continued our "policeman's" role in Latin America, Europe was pretty much left to fend for itself. We insisted, however, that our former allies Britain and France repay their war debts in full, which encouraged them to demand full war reparations from Germany*—a ruinous set of economic dominoes. The abysmal economic circumstances in Europe during the interwar period went far toward causing the Great Depression, giving rise to fascism, and ultimately ending in World War II.

The 1930s saw the United States, as well as most other countries, grappling with the deprivations of the Great Depression. With regard to Latin America, however, the United States began to mend some fences, when Franklin D. Roosevelt announced the **Good Neighbor Policy**. In 1933 the United States joined the Latin American countries in asserting that no state had a right to intervene in the affairs of another, and by 1934, United States troops had been withdrawn from the Dominican Republic and Haiti. Furthermore, the United States renounced the Platt Amendment, which since 1902 had given the United States the right to intervene militarily in Cuban affairs.

Matters were not so sanguine in Europe or Asia, however. Social and economic problems mounted, causing political weakness and turmoil, and the unwillingness of the United States to assume international leadership was eventually followed by the rise of fascism in Italy, Nazism in Germany, and expansionist militarism in Japan. Although Roosevelt attempted to play a more active part in world affairs, American public opinion continued to demand that the United States remain politically disengaged outside the hemisphere.

* The war reparations imposed upon Germany amounted to twice the amount of monetary gold extant at the time and simply could not have been paid.

THE UNITED STATES BECOMES A MAJOR PLAYER IN WORLD AFFAIRS

The United States's aloofness from European affairs, together with Britain and France's exhaustion from the ravages of World War I and their desire to see a buffer state between themselves and the Bolshevik Soviet Union, combined to encourage them to follow a policy of **appeasement** toward Mussolini and Hitler in the 1930s. Time and again the Nazis and fascists used military force to expand their territories in Europe and Africa, and each time the West did little to oppose them. Finally, Hitler's invasion of Poland on September 1, 1939, proved that trying to appease Hitler was disastrous, and World War II was begun.

Regardless of these momentous events, American public opinion was still firmly opposed to entering the war. Gradually, however, Roosevelt was able to extend to Britain some military assistance under the guise of an executive agreement called **lend-lease**, but it was not until Japan attacked Pearl Harbor on December 7, 1941, that the United States entered the war on the side of the Allies. Meanwhile, Hitler's invasion of the Soviet Union in June of 1941 meant that the United States and the USSR would be allies. Germany's defeat ushered in a new era in world affairs, with most countries divided: The West was led by the United States and the East followed the Soviet lead.

The Cold War Relations between the United States and the Soviet Union had long been strained. The truculent and bellicose foreign policy of Vladimir Lenin, together with his communist policies at home, alarmed the West. In 1918, the United States, together with the Allies, invaded Russian ports in an unsuccessful effort to aid the counterrevolutionary White Armies in the destruction of the Bolsheviks. Failing that, the West attempted to strangle the fledgling socialist country with

Surrounded by congressmen of the day, President Franklin Delano Roosevelt signs the declaration of war in December 1941. The many donkeys and other memorabilia on the president's desk suggest his strong association with the Democratic Party that was discussed in an earlier chapter.

economic and political sanctions. Although the United States finally recognized the Soviet Union in 1933, Soviet-American relations never really became warm, and during World War II they remained tenuous.

Although the United States provided the Soviets with about $11 billion in critically needed aid during the war, the United States and Britain failed to open a second front in France until June of 1944.* In 1942 Britain and the United States invaded North Africa, but Stalin watched this move with suspicion. With two-thirds of the Nazi military machine locked in desperate combat in the Soviet Union, an Allied invasion of North Africa seemed an unconvincing attempt to relieve the beleaguered Red Army. Rather, Stalin saw the Allied maneuver as an opportunistic step to reestablish the British empire in the Mediterranean while the Soviets held the Nazis at bay. Furthermore, Winston Churchill had been a declared opponent of the Soviet Union since its creation, and he made no bones about wishing to deny it the fruits of victory following the war's end. Indeed, he openly proposed that the Allies invade Yugoslavia and drive north so that they could deny the Soviets access to Eastern Europe. This "soft underbelly of Europe" strategy, an open suggestion that the West should try to deny the Soviets security on their western flank after having been invaded twice from that direction within a quarter-century, left Stalin with profound suspicions to feed his already exaggerated paranoia about the capitalist states. For the West's part, the Soviet Union was seen as an international pariah that had actively tried to subvert the capitalist states, attempting to set off workers' rebellions that would make the world socialist. Stalin's bloody purges in the late 1930s had also alarmed the West, and Stalin's nonaggression pact with Hitler in 1939 was roundly condemned in the West as an unforgivable betrayal.†

The mutual dislike and suspicion between the United States and the Soviet Union set the tone for an inauspicious beginning to the postwar era. Each side tended to suspect the worst about the behavior of the other. The United

---

* By June of 1944 the Soviet Union had forced the Nazis to retreat across Russia and the Ukraine, and was fighting in Romania. Hence, the Soviets believe that they won the European theater of World War II virtually single-handedly and that the Allies finally invaded France only to gather spoils from the defeated Reich, denying the full fruits of victory to the Soviet Union.

† The Soviets viewed their pact with Hitler differently. In 1938 Britain and France agreed in Munich to allow Hitler to take the Sudatenland from Czechoslovakia, and Hitler went on to take the rest of the country as well. Viewing the Munich agreement as a Western invitation to Hitler to attack the Soviet Union, Stalin quickly turned the tables with the 1939 nonaggression pact.

States saw Stalin's postwar abrogation of wartime agreements as proof of his aggressive tendencies. Even when the Soviet Union entered the war against Japan on the exact day it had promised, the United States greeted its move as a cynical attempt to capitalize on the victory we had won by fighting our way to Japan's shores and obliterating Hiroshima and Nagasaki with atomic bombs. For their part, the Soviets objected to the United States's landing troops in northern China, keeping it from falling to the forces of Mao Zedong and giving it to Chiang Kai-shek. The Soviets were also intimidated by the sheer magnitude of the U.S. advantages. At war's end, the United States held two-thirds of the world's monetary gold, half of its manufacturing capacity, almost half of its shipping, and a monopoly on atomic weapons. United States territory had suffered no damage from the war, and lost only about 350,000 people.* By contrast, the Soviet Union had lost over 26 million dead[4] and suffered untold physical and psychological wounds; its European portion (where most of the population lived) lay in ruins, and half of its industrial capacity was destroyed.[5]

As the war drew to a close, the United States and the Soviet Union had different objectives. Weakened, still smarting from the West's prewar anti-Soviet policies and appeasement tactics, and bitterly aware that it had been invaded from the West twice within a quarter-century, the Soviet Union resolved to assure that the states on its western frontier would be friendly. The United States, on the other hand, still hoped to remain aloof from European affairs as much as possible. Accordingly, it sought to create international political

and economic organizations (e.g., the United Nations, the World Bank, and the International Monetary Fund) through which the world's problems could be addressed indirectly.

Bipolarization The world had been transformed by the war, however. The new reality insisted that two great camps would emerge: the West, captained by the United States; and the East, led by the Soviet Union. United States foreign policy, previously focused on enhancing its economic interests, was transformed to include guaranteeing the security of Western Europe and punctuated with an emotional strain of anticommunism, but the United States only reluctantly moved toward a wider involvement in world affairs, insistently prodded by Western Europe and compelled by a Soviet policy viewed as aggressive.

In March of 1946, Winston Churchill eloquently framed the new circumstances with his **Iron Curtain** speech in Fulton, Missouri. In the same year, the Soviet Union tried to occupy northern Iran and supported communist insurgencies in Turkey and Greece. As a result, Britain communicated to the United States early in 1947 that it could no longer maintain its traditional responsibilities in those countries and invited the United States to take up the cudgels for the West. President Truman responded quickly with the **Truman Doctrine**, which declared the United States willing to help "free peoples" to resist the forceful imposition of totalitarianism. The Truman Doctrine is significant because it essentially breaks with George Washington's rejoinder against U.S. involvement in the political affairs of other nations.

Later in the same year, an article entitled "The Sources of Soviet Conduct" appeared in *Foreign Affairs,* signed simply by Mr. X, but actually written by an experienced American observer of the Soviet Union, George Kennan. In this insightful article, Kennan analyzed Soviet history from its historical and ideological

---

* During World War II, the United States lost more people from pneumonia and tuberculosis than it did in combat. At the same time, more Soviet war dead are buried in Leningrad's Piskarevskoye cemetery than the United States lost in the entire war.

perspectives. He concluded that Soviet expansionist foreign policy was motivated by a need to secure its borders and consolidate its power. Kennan prophetically speculated that the Soviet system might not be able to survive in a long-term coexistence with the West. Accordingly, Kennan counseled a "patient but firm and vigilant *containment* of Russian expansive tendencies"[6] (emphasis added). Kennan's analysis was accepted by the Truman Administration, and **containment** of Soviet expansion as opposed to destruction of the Soviet Union became the policy of the United States. Recent events in Eastern Europe and the Soviet Union illustrate the acuity of Kennan's vision.

Kennan's prediction that "we are going to continue for a long time to find the Russians difficult to deal with,"[7] of course, also proved to be true. The West interpreted Soviet dominance in Eastern Europe as proof of its aggressive intentions, so Britain and France pressed the United States to develop an alliance structure that guaranteed their security. Still, however, the United States remained reluctant to enter multilateral agreements until 1948. In that year the Soviets engineered the overthrow of an independent Czech government and it hoped to force the Allies out of West Berlin by blockading the city. Although the blockade was finally lifted after a massive U.S. airlift to relieve the city, the West became increasingly alarmed by growing Soviet assertiveness. Hence, in 1949 the United States finally agreed to the establishment of the North Atlantic Treaty Organization (NATO) to ensure Western Europe against further Soviet gains.* Thus, the United States, under the

---

* The NATO treaty was preceded by the *Rio Pact* of 1947, which asserted that an armed attack on any country in the Western Hemisphere would be regarded as an attack on all of them. Also, in 1951 the United States signed the ANZUS accords, espousing the mutual security of Australia, New Zealand, and the United States.

Truman Administration, became in deed as well as in word the leader of a willing Western bloc. "In short," political scientist G. John Ikenberry wrote, "U.S. hegemony in Europe was largely an empire by invitation."[8] The long era of United States unilateralism in foreign policy was ended, not because of an American wish to dominate directly, but more because Britain was incapable of continuing its preeminent role in European affairs.[9]

In the meantime, the United States had learned the harsh economic lessons of the interwar period. It realized the folly of pursuing its own economic policies at the expense of European prosperity. Accordingly, Truman concluded that the United States must help Europe rebuild, and he hoped that a European recovery would stabilize the political situation, furthering the cause of peace. Hence, the European Recovery Program (the **Marshall Plan**) was born. Tens of billions of dollars in outright aid and in purchasing credits in the United States were given to Europe.[10]

The Marshall Plan and NATO proved successful in stabilizing the situation in Europe. But American interests were also involved in Asia, of course, and the political situation appeared threatening on that continent as well. Although Japan was demilitarized and rebuilt with remarkable speed, matters turned sour in China. The Chinese Revolution, which began in 1911, culminated in 1949 with a communist victory over Chiang Kai-shek's nationalist forces. Chiang's defeat occurred as an anticommunist hysteria was building in the United States, eventually resulting in the **McCarthy era** and the denigration of American civil liberties on a vast scale. Then, in 1950, North Korean forces broke across the 38th parallel, invading South Korea, and the United States led a United Nations effort to push the aggressors back.

The Korean conflict was unpopular in the United States. Public opinion was impatient with its limited objectives. As it turned out, however, Truman's limited goal of containing the aggressor and restoring the 38th parallel between the North and South proved wise. A brilliant soldier but an insubordinate general, Douglas MacArthur outmaneuvered the North Koreans and drove hard toward the Chinese border, a policy that eventually cost him his command. The People's Republic of China warned the UN forces to stay away from its frontiers and attacked with a crushing blow when the warning was ignored. The war eventually drew to a stalemate, and a peace was finally negotiated.

In the meantime, Dwight D. Eisenhower replaced Truman in the White House, and his Secretary of State, John Foster Dulles, articulated a foreign policy line much more bellicose than those of his predecessors. Claiming that the policy of containment was insufficient and that the United States could not morally abide a *bipolar world,* Dulles pledged to struggle for the elimination of communism rather than accept its coexistence. Rhetoric aside, however, the Eisenhower Administration did not jettison containment; it appeared impotent and a bit ridiculous when, after encouraging Eastern Europe to throw off its Soviet shackles, the United States did nothing to aid uprisings in Poland and East Germany in 1953 or Hungary in its revolt of 1956.

Equally absurd was the Dulles threat of **massive nuclear retaliation** against the Soviet Union for the slightest incursion beyond its sphere. Not only was the threat not credible, but Nikita Khrushchev, the new Soviet leader, was at the same time calling for **peaceful coexistence** between East and West. The contrast of the two policies made the United States appear reckless and trigger-happy, especially since the Eisenhower Administration, in an attempt to economize, began to rely increasingly upon nuclear weapons for defense. "More bang for the buck," critics called it.

The Third World The 1950s also witnessed the emergence of a new theater for So-viet-American competition: The Third World. As the empires of Britain, France, Belgium, and the Netherlands began to collapse and new independent countries emerged, the United States and the Soviet Union each tried to attract them to its side of the bipolar equation. In most cases, however, these new states sought to avoid becoming too closely identified with either superpower, even as they angled for economic aid from the two bloc leaders.

Although bellicose, Eisenhower's overt foreign policy was fairly conventional. The turmoil in the Third World, however, encouraged the administration to engage in an uncharacteristically aggressive covert foreign policy. The Central Intelligence Agency (CIA) was run by Allen Dulles, John Foster's brother, and it became deeply involved in the affairs of several underdeveloped states. In 1953, for example, it engineered a coup, placing the Shah of Iran back on the throne, and it trained and supported Savat, the deadly Iranian secret police. The next year the CIA helped overthrow the legally elected but leftist Arbenz government in Guatemala, thus inaugurating a long and bloody era of military rule.

Overtly, Eisenhower built upon Truman's policy of negotiating collective security agreements. He signed the multilateral Southeast Asia Treaty Organization (SEATO), a now-moribund accord among the United States, Britain, France, and several states in Southeast Asia. Eisenhower also followed Truman's precedent of forging bilateral treaties. In 1951 Truman had signed a mutual defense treaty with the Philippines, which had gained its independence from the United States in 1946, and Eisenhower later negotiated treaties with South Korea, Taiwan, and Japan. The administration's interest in Asia reflected the growing instability in that area. Eisenhower decided not to help the French defeat local insurgents, so in the mid-1950s Indochina was divided into Laos, Cambodia, North Vietnam, and South Vietnam. Eisenhower and Dulles were concerned that communism not be allowed to spread from China and North Vietnam throughout the rest of Southeast Asia, and American officials began to talk about the **domino theory**, which anticipated that a communist victory in any Southeast Asian country would trip off the collapse of all the others.[11] The stage was thus set for U.S. involvement in South Vietnam, to which Eisenhower had dispatched a handful of advisors.

John F. Kennedy was also a product of his times and therefore was a cold warrior of the first order. In his brief presidency, Kennedy confronted the Soviets in Berlin, and the world was brought to the verge of a nuclear war over the *Cuban Missile Crisis* in October of 1962.[12] Two years earlier Kennedy had agreed to an inherited Eisenhower plan to support an invasion of Cuba by CIA-trained anti-Castro exiles. The result was that the invaders were cut down at the Bay of Pigs. The subsequent international condemnation of the United States was muted, however, by Kennedy's establishment of the **Alliance for Progress**, a program to give economic aid to Latin American countries, and by his renunciation of the United States policy of supporting right-wing dictatorships solely because they were anticommunist. While the Alliance for Progress was sustained, soon after Kennedy's death the United States returned to supporting repressive regimes if they were anticommunist.

Kennedy also placed emphasis on increasing our nuclear military capacity, but feeling that Eisenhower's reliance on nuclear weapons limited U.S. options in the "brush wars" in the Third World, the president also called on the United States to develop a "flexible response" to communism's challenge. Accordingly, a new priority was placed on counterinsurgency tactics and personnel as well as on nuclear weapons. The focus on a flexible response led to a deeper involvement in Vietnam. By the time of his death, Kennedy had increased the number of American advisers in South Vietnam to over 500.

Lyndon B. Johnson, so progressive in domestic policy and civil rights, had a mentality regarding foreign policy more suitable to the 1950s than the late 1960s. Seeing the Vietnam conflict as a struggle between communism and the free world, he used fraudulent evidence of North Vietnamese aggression to persuade Congress to pass the **Gulf of Tonkin Resolution** in 1965. The president then used the resolution as a blank check, virtually making the conflict an American war. Quickly escalating the American presence in that shattered country, Johnson had by 1968 sent over half a million American troops to Vietnam. In 1968, Johnson and the American commander, General William Westmoreland, said they "saw the light at the end of the tunnel," thus raising American expectations that victory was near. However, the **Tet Offensive** of that year, in which communist troops engaged American and South Vietnamese forces throughout the country, disheartened many previously nominal supporters of the war, and Johnson's popularity, already badly damaged, was destroyed. Meanwhile congressional opposition to the war, which was largely centered in the president's own party, grew.

Johnson was not concerned solely with fighting communism in Asia. In 1965, when an uprising occurred in the Dominican Republic against its right-wing military dictatorship, restoring power to the democratically elected but leftist-leaning government of President Juan Bosch, Johnson concluded that the insurgents were communist-infiltrated. Ignoring the **Organization of American States (OAS)**, which had been created in 1948 to collectively manage security in the Western Hemisphere, Johnson sent 25,000 troops to the Dominican Republic to quash the rebellion. Expounding what became known as the **Johnson Doctrine**, the president asserted the "right" of the United

States to prevent "the establishment of another Communist government in the Western Hemisphere."[13] Thus Johnson had reasserted the "policeman" role claimed by the Roosevelt Corollary and later renounced by the Good Neighbor Policy.

Johnson's policy also had an important impact on the Soviet Union. By openly claiming that the United States had the right to unilaterally decide the ideological appropriateness of governments in its sphere, it implicitly invited the Soviet Union to do the same. Consequently, when the Czechs rose up against Soviet domination in 1968, the Soviets felt little restraint in crushing it. Declaring the **Brezhnev Doctrine**, the Soviet Union asserted its "right" to intervene when a socialist government was threatened by insurgencies dominated by "capitalist-imperialists." Indeed, political scientists Thomas Franck and Edward Weisband point out, "the Johnson and Brezhnev doctrines were virtually identical."[14]

Although Richard M. Nixon did not send troops to foil Marxism in Latin America, he did, reminiscent of the Eisenhower years, use the CIA to support a 1973 military coup against President Salvador Allende, resulting in Allende's death and the brutal suppression of the Chilean people. Nixon also inherited the Vietnam War and the public turmoil accompanying it. While during the 1968 presidential campaign he claimed to have a secret plan to end the war, as president he tried to end it by a military victory, just as Johnson had. To that end, he widened the war, bombing North Vietnam and mining its ports and secretly bombing and invading Cambodia. Meanwhile, domestic opposition to the war mounted, resulting in the 1970 wholesale arrest of thousands during a war protest in Washington, D.C., and the shooting of several students at Kent State University in Ohio. Eventually, the futility of American Vietnam policy became evident, so the United States withdrew during the Ford Administra-

tion. Although Vietnam was subsequently quickly taken by the communist forces, the rest of the dominoes did not come crashing down as predicted.

Détente   Other aspects of Nixon's foreign policy, however, were quite successful as he deemphasized ideology in favor of a more pragmatic view of American national self-interests. Improving U.S. relations with both China and the U.S.S.R., Nixon deftly played the two mutually suspicious communist states against each other to U.S. advantage. American-Soviet relations entered a period of **détente** (relaxing tensions), during which the United States hoped to encourage the Soviets to increase trade and contacts with the West until it became so completely integrated with the capitalist world that it would see continued friendly relations to be in its best interests.

Détente, however, did not fulfill its potential. While President Gerald Ford completed negotiations with the Soviets on the Strategic Arms Limitation Talks (SALT) and Jimmy Carter agreed to a second phase of SALT, although Congress did not ratify it, Soviet-American relations gradually cooled. Finally, in December of 1979, the Soviet Union invaded Afghanistan and the last vestiges of détente vanished. Carter's response was to stop exports of American grain and other commodities to the Soviet Union and to boycott the 1980 Moscow Olympic games.

In other areas, Carter was more successful. He completed Nixon's overtures with China by exchanging ambassadors and full diplomatic recognition, and he played an important role in helping the black majority of Rhodesia come to power in the country they later renamed Zimbabwe. His most impressive accomplishment, however, was the Camp David accords. The Arab-Israeli conflict had vexed the United States and other states since the 1940s. Several wars were fought in the region, but the problem continued to fester. In a feat of exquisite statesmanship, Carter negotiated a peace settlement between Israeli's Menachem Begin and Egypt's Anwar Sadat.

Just as the Middle East represents Carter's greatest foreign policy success, it also became the location of his most singular failure. After the CIA returned the Shah of Iran to power in 1953, the United States supported his efforts to modernize his country. Iran's strategic location and its vast oil reserves made it a valuable asset for American national interests. The Shah's policies were enforced by repressive measures that eventually evoked a rebellion and brought the religious fundamentalists to power under the leadership of the Ayatollah Khomeini. Shortly after Khomeini's rise to power, the American embassy was occupied by the fundamentalists and 52 American hostages were taken.

The inability of Carter to free the hostages, together with the Soviet military buildup and invasion of Afghanistan, conjured strong feelings in the American public that the United States had become weak. Thus, Ronald Reagan's call to stand up to terrorism, rebuild American military might, and get tough with the Soviets struck a responsive cord in the American body politic.

Reagan's Foreign Policy Iran released the American hostages on Reagan's inauguration day, a gesture that has caused serious speculation that Reagan campaign officials may have agreed to sell Iran arms if it delayed the release until Reagan took office.[15] Whatever the case, Reagan's policy toward Iran was no more successful than Carter's, and his Middle East policy was considerably less fruitful. Throughout Reagan's presidency, the Middle East continued to fester. His efforts to develop a peace plan were largely ignored, and his deployment of United States forces as peacekeepers in Lebanon ended with the terrorist murder of 241 Marines and the embarrassing withdrawal of American forces. Terrorism also

increased, with more American hostages being taken, and despite Reagan's repeated criticism of Carter's impotence in securing the release of the Iranian hostages, he left office without freeing the Americans abducted on his watch. The president solemnly pledged not to deal with terrorists, yet behind the scenes he sold weapons to Iran without getting the desired payback of securing the release of Americans held by terrorists in Lebanon.

Responding to evidence linking Libya to terrorist bombings of American servicemen in Europe, Reagan ordered an air strike on the headquarters of Colonel Muammar Qaddafi of Libya in an open attempt to assassinate the leader of a foreign country—a terrorist act in itself. The result of this belligerence was the killing of several innocent people including Qaddafi's adopted infant daughter and the wounding of two of his small sons. To deal with the threat that the long and bloody Iran-Iraq war posed to oil shipments, the United States deployed its navy in the Persian Gulf to escort oil tankers. During the course of the operation the USS *Stark* was attacked by an Iraqi fighter, killing several American sailors; and the United States shot down an Iranian airliner in the mistaken belief that it was attacking the fleet. Over 260 innocent lives were lost.

Events in Southern Africa also demanded U.S. attention. A civil war in Angola, the Union of South Africa's policies toward its territory of Namibia, and **apartheid** (racial segregation and the denial of civil and political rights to the black majority) unsettled the area. U.S. support of Jonas Savimbi, a right-wing revolutionary, was meant to pressure the Cuban government to remove its troops from Angola. The policy showed little success, however, until Mikhail Gorbachev also supported Cuba's withdrawal as part of a broader agreement to secure the independence of Namibia from South Africa. The Cuban troops withdrew in 1989.

In South Africa itself, the United States pursued a policy of **constructive engagement** during the 1980s. Essentially, this policy urged the South Africans to modify their suppression of their black majority and "colored" people, but no provisions were made to exert pressure through trade embargoes. In fact, the United States government encouraged American trade and investment in South Africa. Finally, Congress insisted on changing the policy by passing strong economic sanctions over President Reagan's veto. It is, of course, impossible to know whether the economic sanctions had the desired effect, but South African policy has relaxed its repression considerably since the sanctions were passed.

President Reagan, a staunch conservative, reinfused American foreign policy with an ideological content it had not had since before the Nixon Administration. Also, he brought attention back to Latin America. In 1983, fearing that Grenada was becoming a military base for Cuba and the Soviet Union, he launched an invasion of the tiny Caribbean island-state. The invasion caused an uproar in Latin America and fed the already growing fear that once again the United States was going to impose its ideological will on the hemisphere. The Grenadians, however, generally welcomed the American intervention, and the controversy soon abated.

The major American focus in Latin America, however, was in Central America. Here, in the neighboring countries of El Salvador and Nicaragua, socialist and antisocialist forces struggled. In El Salvador, a leftist insurgency battled a pro-United States government. Although that government did little to stop rightwing squads that murdered people by the thousands, the United States pumped billions of dollars into its defense. To the south, in Nicaragua, the Sandinista government had thrown off the repressive, American-supported Somoza dynasty. The Sandinistas, led by Daniel Or-

tega, had their own record of violating human rights, however. In any event, the United States embargoed the Nicaraguan economy, illegally mined Nicaraguan ports, and provided aid to the insurgent forces (called the *Contras*), all while maintaining diplomatic relations with the Sandinista government. Congress vacillated on this difficult problem, but ultimately it halted further military aid to the Contras. Denied official support for its policy, elements of the Reagan Administration illegally sought private support and diverted to the Contras some of the profits (the lion's share was pocketed by intermediaries in the ruse) from the secret sale of arms to Iran. Eventually, these policies were repudiated by Congress, but the Sandinista regime suffered its own repudiation when it was handed a decisive defeat in the Nicaraguan elections of 1989.

The United States also had difficulty with Panamanian strongman Manuel Noriega. For about two decades, Noriega, who had been trained for the Panamanian military in the United States, had been a valued informant for United States intelligence organizations and, ironically, for the Drug Enforcement Administration (DEA). By 1980, Noriega was one of the most important people in the American intelligence network in Latin America. Even though his own involvement in drug trafficking became well known during the early 1980s, he continued to receive preferential treatment by the United States government, and he even received commendations and letters of appreciation from the DEA. Finally, in 1987 Noriega was indicted by a Florida grand jury for alleged involvement in illegal drug trading. Following the indictment, the Reagan Administration brought economic and political pressure on Noriega to relinquish power, but without success, so the matter was left to the Bush Administration to resolve.[16]

Plagued by failure in Latin America and the Middle East, Reagan's foreign policy concerning the Soviet Union was much more successful. Where Carter had vacillated from détente to confrontation with the Soviets, Reagan's policies ran from confrontation to creating a new, warmer relationship with the world's other superpower.[17]

During the late 1970s United States authorities had highly exaggerated the Soviet military buildup, and Reagan vowed to make America strong again through a massive military upgrading; his administration even began to talk about winning a nuclear war. Furthermore, the president assumed a near-belligerent stance toward the USSR, making speeches that harked back to the 1950s and the depths of the Cold War. He spoke of an "evil empire" and complained that the Soviets were violating the SALT II agreement, but he did not disavow the agreement, as he had promised during his 1980 presidential campaign.

Reagan's emphasis on the military and his bellicose rhetoric caused deep concern in the Soviet Union; it also alarmed our NATO allies as well as many people in the United States.[18] Sensing the absence of public support for his aggressive stance, Reagan introduced the Strategic Defense Initiative (SDI, or Star Wars) as a new kind of defense that might make the United States impervious to a nuclear attack. Meanwhile, changes in the Soviet leadership brought Mikhail S. Gorbachev to office. Gorbachev called for "**new thinking**" in foreign affairs and better relations between the superpowers. To back up his rhetoric, Gorbachev initiated a series of astonishing unilateral concessions, including the withdrawal of Soviet troops from Afghanistan and a 10 percent reduction of Soviet conventional military forces. After some hesitation, the Reagan Administration adroitly moved away from its previous truculence. Reagan attended five summit meetings with Gorbachev, and an unprecedented disarmament treaty—the Intermediate-Range Nuclear Force (INF) treaty—reducing the number of nuclear missiles and warheads in Europe was signed with the USSR in May 1988.

Evolving Positions in Foreign Affairs
The changes in the Soviet foreign policy stance were not motivated by Gorbachev's new thinking alone. Rather, the Soviet Union is in serious economic decline, necessitating reduced military spending. The United States also finds its relative position in foreign affairs changing for economic reasons. The fiscal policies of the 1980s not only resulted in record national budget deficits but also ended in massive foreign trade deficits, until today the United States is the world's greatest debtor nation, causing us economic impairment.[19] While the United States and the Soviet Union remain the world's dominant military powers, increasingly it appears that economics will become the focal point of international competition in the twenty-first century, and neither the United States nor the Soviet Union is well positioned to maintain its accustomed political preeminence in the new international environment. The post–World War II bipolarity is rapidly disintegrating, and the ideological impetus for foreign policy is vanishing. At the same time, social and political differences among nations seem less important as the world turns to combat mutual problems of air and water pollution, denigration of the atmosphere, overpopulation, poverty, and hunger.

The American economic decline has not occurred in absolute terms. Indeed, the economy has rather steadily increased since World War II, but our economic position relative to many other states has declined because the economic advances of Western Europe and Japan have been more rapid than our own. In 1955, for example, the United States exported 35 percent of the world's high-tech manufactures, but by 1984 its share had slipped to 25 percent. At the same time, the United States devoted between 6.5 and 13 percent of its GNP to defense, while the NATO allies spent about 4.5 percent and Japan committed less than 1 percent of its GNP to defense. The heavy American defense expenditures meant that less of its GNP went toward capital investment, which resulted in slower economic growth.[20] Also, both American dependence on foreign capital to sustain the national budget and foreign trade deficits accrued during the 1980s have severely jeopardized our independence in foreign policy.[21] Meanwhile, the European Economic Community is scheduled to unite economically in 1992, which will create an economic entity enjoying a GNP of approximately 5.3 trillion dollars, higher than the American GNP.

The political changes afoot, together with current economic realities, mean that the infrastructure of international politics is in flux and that the United States, while still a major player, is now forced to share with its allies the power levers of foreign policy. This new relationship is certain to cause some difficulty as necessary adjustments and accommodations are made. Perhaps even more vexing is the curious position in which the United States finds itself militarily. Although it is depleting its resources by heavy commitments to defense, thus weakening further its economic position, the alternative—seeing Germany and Japan become nuclear powers—is unpalatable given the militarist tendencies of those societies earlier in this century. In effect, we hold the tail of a tiger, fearing the consequences of letting go, yet feeling ourselves become weaker as long as our grasp is fast. It is this paradoxical situation to which President Bush has fallen heir.

Bush's Foreign Policy George Bush is perhaps more experienced in foreign policy than any other person to become president in this century, and he carefully surrounded himself with people of experience in key foreign policy positions. Hence, it came as something of a surprise that Bush assumed a very cautious

and even dilatory posture on foreign policy early in his presidency, eschewing initiatives for a six-month reassessment of changing world political conditions. This respite was perhaps necessary since Bush, a moderate Republican, was following to office a much more ideological but popular Republican president.

Toward the end of Bush's first year in office, however, events began to take their own course. Late in 1989 the Eastern Bloc began to disintegrate. Poland, Hungary, East Germany, Czechoslovakia, Bulgaria, and Romania—with Gorbachev's encouragement—each ousted their hard-line leaders and created governments independent of Soviet dominance. At the same time, some of the national groups within the Soviet Union began to struggle for more autonomy within the Union or independence from it. Careful not to appear to be aggravating these challenges and restrained by its own fiscal weakness, the Bush Administration offered but a pittance of economic aid to the newly independent East European governments, while France and West Germany took the lead in encouraging their movements. This was the first time since World War II that the United States was not the major Western player in important international events.

In direct relations between the two superpowers, a lackluster summit at Malta was followed by rapidly changing events primarily motivated by declining economic conditions in the Soviet Union. Bush rejected Gorbachev's proposal that NATO and the Warsaw Pact be dismantled, countering with a proposal that each side reduce its troop level in Central Europe to 195,000, with the United States allowed to keep an additional 30,000 troops in Western Europe. To the astonishment of almost every observer, the Soviets quickly agreed. This accord gave new impetus to the talks about reducing strategic nuclear weapons. These rapid changes have brought forward new questions about the continued efficacy of

NATO and the Warsaw Pact. The Soviet Union has unilaterally removed all its troops from Hungary and Czechoslovakia, and finally the Warsaw Pact was dissolved in 1991. For its part, NATO has begun to move away from its military emphasis to more purely political concerns, and Germany, France, and the United States sent economic aid to the Soviet Union in 1990–1991 to avert a famine when Soviet food supplies were in jeopardy.

Matters relating to the second communist giant, the People's Republic of China (PRC), have been less sanguine. Having once been the American envoy to the PRC, Bush feels a special relationship with that society and believes he knows best how to deal with it. So far, however, Chinese-American relations have not been smooth. In the late spring of 1989, protesting Chinese students were brutally cut down in Beijing's Tienanmen Square. The American public's outrage at this wanton slaughter of Chinese youth demanding democratic reforms was palpable. The mild response to these events by the Bush Administration disappointed many Americans, and later, when it was learned that President Bush had sent National Security Adviser Brent Scowcroft on a secret mission to Beijing only a month after the Tienanmen massacre, the public voiced furious condemnation. At the same time, Bush vetoed a law that would have guaranteed tens of thousands of Chinese students in the United States that they would not have to return to a country in which they might be persecuted for having supported their fellow students at Tienanmen. President Bush correctly pointed out that he had already given the students sanctuary by administrative fiat, but Congress was reluctant to leave the safety of the students to the whim of a president so anxious to please the PRC. Undaunted by Congress's caution or by China's refusal to liberalize its domestic policies, Bush insisted in 1991 that China continue to benefit from favorable trade agreements with the United States in hopes that increased contacts with the West will eventually encourage the Chinese to moderate their policies.

Bush has also been sympathetic to South Africa. Gradually yielding to the economic pressures of the United States and other Western countries, South Africa has modified many of its most offensive racial policies, and it finally released Nelson Mandela in 1990 (who, as it turns out, was arrested in 1962 as a result of a tip-off by the American CIA), after 27 years in prison. In response, President Bush lifted the economic sanctions in 1991 that Congress had earlier imposed over President Reagan's veto. This revocation has caused some controversy since Democratic congressional leaders argue that South Africa has not yet fully complied with the conditions set down by Congress' resolution.

Bush's generous, sensitive policies have not applied to Latin America, however. After our failure to support an attempted military coup against Noriega in October of 1989, the strained relations between Panama and the United States became even more heated, as American citizens were threatened by elements of the Panamanian Defense Force. Suddenly, in late December, American troops invaded Panama, and after several days of fighting, a new government was installed and Noriega was extradited to the United States for trial on drug trafficking charges. Although public opinion polls in Panama and in the United States revealed the invasion to be a popular policy, the intervention aroused widespread condemnation throughout Latin America. The Latin American governments had little sympathy for Noriega, but they were outraged that the United States would so cavalierly trifle with the government of a sovereign state. Fuel was added to the fire when, shortly after the invasion of Panama, the president sent warships to the coast of Colombia to intercept drug traffickers. The ships were deployed without consultation with the Colombian government, and the maneuver met with a renewed chorus of disapproval and recrimination until the ships were withdrawn.[22]

Matters went more smoothly for the administration's policy in Nicaragua. Since the early 1980s the United States had funded insurgents in a civil war there. Then in 1990, because of pressure from the Soviet Union, the Sandinista government agreed to hold elections. The opposition presidential candidate, Violeta Barrios de Chamorro, received heavy support from the United States, and the elections were supervised by representatives of the United Nations, the Organization of American States (OAS), and other interested parties, including former President Jimmy Carter. The people of Nicaragua voted overwhelmingly for Chamorro, and President Bush celebrated the emergence of a Nicaraguan government more acceptable to the United States.

Just as matters with Nicaragua and the Soviet Union improved, however, a new crisis arose in the Middle East. Claiming that Kuwait was properly part of Iraq, President Saddam Hussein sent Iraqi forces, in August of 1990, to overrun that desert kingdom, thus threatening Saudi Arabia—the location of half the world's known oil reserves. Likening Hussein (a leader the United States supported in his war with Iran [1980–1988]) to Adolf Hitler, President Bush dispatched over one-half million American troops to Saudi Arabia and deftly secured several United Nations resolutions and international financial and military support for Operation Desert Storm to oppose the aggressor. On January 16, 1991, after a United Nations deadline for Hussein's withdrawal had elapsed, the United States and its allies unleashed massive air strikes on Iraq and Kuwait. Finally, on February 23, 1991, the allies launched a ground invasion, easily driving the Iraqis back into their homeland. In the process, Bush repeatedly called for an uprising against Hussein, but

when the Shiite Muslims in southern Iran and the Kurds in northern Iran rebelled, the United States refused to help them: thousands died as a result. Ironically, after the brief war against the Iraqi "Hitler," it seems that the United States returned to its previous policy of supporting Hussein at the expense of his people, hoping to stabilize the international politics of the oil-rich Gulf region. In fact, the hapless Iranian Kurds were betrayed by the United States on two previous occasions: In 1976, when, after being encouraged by the Nixon Administration in a rebellion against Hussein, the United States abruptly stopped its aid because a deal was struck with the Iraqi dictator; and, in 1988 when Hussein cynically killed 5000 Kurds with a gas attack on Halabja, a Kurdish village. The United States Senate took up legislation to impose economic sanctions on Hussein, but the Reagan Administration quashed it because of the administration's support for Hussein's war with Iran.[23]

A final concern about U.S. foreign policy should be considered here. With the Soviet Union withdrawing from its role as a superpower, President Bush speaks of the emergence of a "new world order." His speeches describe a world devoted to peace, democracy, and human rights, but, as the paragraphs above indicate, his actions have sometimes been less noble. Indeed, in his first two years of office, Bush used military force more often than any other president in this century. Besides Panama and Iraq, in 1989 Bush sent troops to Columbia to combat drug trafficking, commandos to El Salvador to rescue American military advisers who were being held by radical insurgents, and U.S. fighter planes to give air cover to loyalist troops putting down an attempted coup in the Philippines.[24] No doubt, this unusual willingness to use force to solve international problems is motivated by many reasons, but one wonders if the "new world order" is to be enforced around the globe by U.S. arms. Put differently, without the Soviet Union as a check, will the United States go unrestrained in world affairs?

Instruments of Foreign Policy

There are several instruments used in the development and implementation of foreign policy. Which factor is most important depends upon the issue and the players involved.

THE PRESIDENT, THE CONGRESS, AND THE COURTS

The president is perhaps less encumbered by the checks and balances in foreign policy than in any other field. The president is the nation's chief foreign policy developer and administrator, as well as being its leading diplomat. Additionally, the authority of commander-in-chief of the armed forces gives the president the power to enforce foreign policy. Yet the checks and balances deny the chief executive total discretion.

As mentioned previously, the courts are reluctant to rule in cases involving foreign policy, but they have defined somewhat the parameters of treaties and executive agreements.[25] Otherwise, however, the Supreme Court has refused to rule on important foreign policy questions. It ducked challenges to the legality of the Vietnam War on grounds that the matter was not justiciable because it was a political question, and it refused to hear a case challenging the U.S. invasion of Cambodia for the same reason.[26]

By and large, however, Congress exercises the greatest restraint on the president in foreign policy, albeit even these checks are limited. Congress declares war, ratifies treaties and presidential appointments to foreign policy posi-

tions, appropriates money, oversees intelligence operations, and debates foreign policy. Taken at face value, these powers are formidable, but in reality they have been less effective at checking the president in foreign policy than some critics might wish. In almost 200 instances where American troops have been deployed in belligerent conditions, Congress has declared war only 5 times (the War of 1812, the Mexican-American War, the Spanish-American War, World War I, and World War II); treaty ratification has often been circumvented by executive agreements; Congress rarely fails to ratify presidential appointments; and its oversight of intelligence operations has been sporadic at best. It has frequently used the appropriations power to modify foreign policy, but this control is indirect, controversial, and awkward. Presidents have become increasingly secretive about the details of their foreign policy administration and complain that they cannot effectively operate if Congress insists on acting like a panel of 535 secretaries of state. The Congress also suffers internal problems impeding its foreign policy role. Its leadership structure has been weakened since the congressional reforms of the early 1970s diffused power among several standing and subcommittees, and the public is usually much more concerned with domestic policy, distracting Congress's attention from foreign affairs.

As mentioned in Chapter 10, the emergence of the imperial presidency, the Vietnam War, and the Watergate scandal forced Congress into a more active role in foreign affairs. In 1972 it passed the **Case Act** requiring the president to inform Congress within 60 days of signing an executive agreement, and it passed the **War Powers Act** the following year in an attempt to check the president's authority to send troops into harm's way. Neither of these steps have been more than partially successful, however.

Stung by criticisms that it was too intrusive

during the Ford and Carter administrations and faced with the popularity of Ronald Reagan, Congress relaxed its strictures on foreign policy in the early 1980s. However, the loss of 241 marines to a 1983 terrorist attack in Lebanon, the revelations of the Iran-Contra affair, and the strident ideological position of the administration persuaded Congress that it should assert itself once more. In 1984 the Senate voted overwhelmingly to condemn the CIA for illegally mining Nicaragua's harbors, and in 1986 Congress voted over Reagan's veto, imposing economic sanctions on South Africa, an unprecedented challenge to the president's authority in foreign policy.[27] Congress also took the lead in pursuing encouraging talks between the Nicaraguan combatants, and, smarting from inconsistencies in Reagan Administration interpretations of long-standing agreements with the Soviet Union, the Senate held up consideration of the INF treaty until it was assured that the treaty's meaning could not be reinterpreted by the Administration without Senate approval.[28] While Congress has enjoyed a better working relationship with President Bush, it insisted that the president's policy in the Persian Gulf be debated and voted on.

Clearly, the Congress's role in foreign policy is unsettled and depends on the circumstances, the issues, and the people involved. The value of congressional involvement in foreign affairs cannot be disputed, however. The Congress provides an important forum in which foreign policy can be publicly debated. Its opposition to administration policies on Vietnam, Iran, Central America, and South Africa was critical in exposing the issues to a full public airing.

THE FOREIGN POLICY ESTABLISHMENT

The State Department Technically, the secretary of state, who heads the State Department, is the president's principal advisor on foreign policy and is resonsible to the president for its administration. In the nineteenth and early twentieth centuries, the secretaries of state usually were left to perform their role with little interference. In this century, however, the president has more often played an active role in foreign policy, and other institutions such as the National Security Council, the Department of Defense, and the intelligence community have sometimes dwarfed the status of the secretary of state.

The role played by the secretary of state is, of course, up to the president. Bush's Secretary of State, James A. Baker, is given a significant voice in foreign affairs, but Bush is in many ways his own secretary of state. Bush's administrative style has also greatly reduced the insidious infighting that characterized the previous administration.[29]

As important as the state department is, it is the smallest Cabinet-level department in government, employing only about 25,000 people and having a budget of less than $2 billion. The heart of the State Department is the **Foreign Service**, comprising about 4500 career diplomats. It is staffed by people who have passed rigorous examinations certifying their knowledge of social and political matters and foreign language competence. The usual tour of duty in foreign countries is two years.

Essentially, the United States maintains two kinds of offices in foreign countries. **Embassies** house the ambassador and the political and military personnel. The embassy's principal function is to represent the interests of the United States to the host government. **Consulates** house social and economic personnel. Their job is to see to the needs of American tourists and visitors who run afoul of the host country's laws, and to encourage trade and commerce with the United States. Of course, the United States has intelligence personnel in virtually every country where it has offices. They may be located in the embassy, the consulate, or both, as well as being located elsewhere.

Besides representing United States political interests, mediating for American travelers and commerce, and gathering intelligence in foreign countries, the State Department represents the United States in dozens of international organizations, including the United Nations, NATO, and the OAS. It also loosely coordinates the activities of the **United States Information Agencies (USIA)**. The USIA administers radio and television broadcasts such as Worldnet, Radio Free Europe, and Voice of America. Its mission is to portray the news "from the American perspective," a euphemism for propaganda.

National Security Council The National Security Council has already been discussed in Chapter 8. As mentioned, its membership comprises the president, the vice president, and the secretaries of state and defense. The director of the National Security Council heads a small staff but has become important in the formulation of foreign policy. The function of the National Security Council is to coordinate information from the various agencies that deal in foreign policy, and it offers the president options and alternatives on policy. Nevertheless, the national security adviser (NSA) has become so prominent in foreign policy formulation as to vie with the secretary of state. Although the NSA is not supposed to implement policy, during the Reagan Administration the National Security Council, or elements thereof, together with the cooperation of the CIA, entered into the operation of a secret and independent foreign policy resulting in the Iran-Contra affair, complete with surreptitious funds and even a cargo vessel at its command.

Intelligence Gathering intelligence about foreign countries, even friendly countries, is a standard procedure for any government in developing foreign policy. Intelligence agencies use agents, of course, but much of their data is gleaned by analysis from published documents. Additionally, intelligence organizations surreptitiously employ nationals to feed them information about their own country. In recent years, Americans have been convicted of selling information about the United States to the Soviet Union, Israel, Taiwan, and South Korea.

Not unlike other states, the American intelligence apparatus engages in four basic roles. It *gathers information* by surveying foreign publications, photographing foreign countries from overflights or satellites, paying informants for information, and assigning agents to spy. The information is then *analyzed* by experts, assessed for its veracity and importance, and *forwarded* to appropriate agencies of the American government.

There is, of course, a fourth function. *Operatives may be dispatched* to carry out foreign assignments that are less benign than simple information-gathering. In the past, American agents have sabotaged energy facilities, mined harbors, and destroyed agricultural production; they have attempted political assassinations (Castro, for example) and participated in the overthrow of governments (in Iraq, Iran, Guatemala, and Chile). Assassinations by United States intelligence agencies are currently illegal, but such prohibitions can and have been set aside. In 1981 and again in 1984, President Reagan signed authorization directing American agents to pursue "aggressive covert operations" against terrorists in the Middle East. This language was viewed by authorities as "a license to kill."[30]

The American intelligence apparatus is relatively complex. The Department of Defense houses two agencies, the **Defense Intelligence Agency**, which, among other things, operates overflights and satellite reconnaissance missions, and the **National Security Agency**, an ultra-secret institution that engages in cryptography (working with codes). Together, these two units enjoy the lion's share of the annual sum spent on intelligence. The State Department includes its own intelligence group called the **Bureau of Intelligence and Research**.

The various intelligence organizations of the United States are legally prohibited from engaging in information-gathering within the United States—although the CIA was found to have kept files on thousands of people living in the United States during the 1970s—so the **Federal Bureau of Investigation (FBI)** is empowered to do intelligence work within the nation's borders.

By far, the best-known American intelligence organization is the **Central Intelligence Agency (CIA)**. Created in 1947, the CIA was originally intended to act as a central clearing house for data from the various other intelligence institutions; its operative role was slight. Soon, however, it began to engage in its own efforts to gather information. Called "the Company" by its employees, the CIA became a major arm of American foreign policy implementation. In efforts to advance the security of the United States, it has helped overthrow several governments, trained the invaders of the Bay of Pigs, and trained troops in Southeast Asia to fight communism. It runs schools that train foreign nationals in counterinsurgency tactics and it trains elements of the military and police in foreign countries—some of which are accused of participating in "death squads" in their countries.

Senate investigations of the CIA in the 1970s* revealed a grisly record of intervention and spying at home and abroad, so Congress clamped down, prohibiting it from carrying out political assassinations, subverting democratically elected governments, and supporting

* George Bush was director of the CIA during the Ford Administration.

police and military units that systematically violate human rights.[31] It also required the president to report to Congress all covert activities engaged in by the United States. By the 1980s, however, Congress began to relax its oversight, fearing that it was unduly impeding the intelligence community and thus jeopardizing the national security.

During the Reagan Administration, with William Casey as director, the CIA once again began to engage in operations that were at best questionable. These policies culminated in the heavy involvement of the CIA in the Iran-Contra affair, with the result that Congress has increased its oversight of the Company again. It has created—over the objections of the Bush Administration—an inspector general to oversee its activities and to report to Congress. Also, Congress has reached agreement with the White House on rules by which Congress will be informed about covert activities.

In related matters, the Reagan Administration ran a covert propaganda operation to manipulate American public opinion, the media, and Congress in support of its Central America policies. Organized by the National Security Council, a "public diplomacy" apparatus was created and modeled after CIA covert operations. Among other things it sponsored newspaper articles ostensibly written by independent scholars, sent letters to congresspersons who were vulnerable to constituent pressure on the Central American issue, and conducted other subterfuges paid for by public funds. A General Accounting Office report labeled the effort "covert propaganda" to illegally manipulate American public opinion.[32]

For its part, the Bush Administration has also taken questionable steps. The Justice Department has issued an opinion that the FBI can enter a foreign country, apprehend fugitives from the United States, and bring them back for trial without the knowledge or permission of the host government. This new "right" is called "the president's snatch authority,"[33] and U.S. agents kidnapped a physician in Mexico suspected in the 1985 killing of United States Drug Enforcement Agency agent Enrique S. Camarena.[34] An appellate court has since ruled such abductions illegal.

In another ruling, the Justice Department said U.S. troops can be used to apprehend terrorists and drug traffickers abroad. This judgment interprets the 1878 Posse Comitatus Act prohibiting American forces from being used for civil police duties as applying only within the borders of the United States.[35] And, in a third finding, the Justice Department said it is legal for United States intelligence agencies to recruit people to overthrow their governments.[36] Each of these self-granted "rights" is a clear violation of international law, and one wonders what complications might arise if we try to exercise these "rights" and what chaos might occur if all governments assumed for themselves the same authority.

Presumably separate from our intelligence operations is another effort to meddle in the internal affairs of foreign countries. These policies, however, are quite open and aboveboard, although questionable as to their wisdom or ethics. In 1984 Congress established the **National Endowment for Democracy (NED)** to foster democracy in other nations. Most of its funds are administered by one of four groups: the Republican party, the Democratic party, the Chamber of Commerce, and the AFL-CIO. Although most NED funds have been used to support democratic institutions abroad, the Republican party has spent much of its share to support the candidacies of right-of-center political candidates. The specter of United States funds being spent to influence elections abroad is disturbing enough, but much of the money has been spent to defeat governments with which we have friendly relations. For example, $433,000 from NED accounts were given to a right-wing opponent of the government of Costa Rican President Oscar Arias Sanchez.

Even many Republicans object to such use of the funds. Representative James Leach (R-IA) complains,

> I think it's unseemly, both politically and constitutionally. Here you have the Republican Party involved with the opposition to the government in power, in a country that is the strongest democracy in Latin America and where the head of state won the Nobel Peace Prize.[37]

ECONOMIC POLICY

The United States has, since World War II, used its economic power to influence other states. There are basically three economic tools in foreign policy: economic sanctions, economic aid, and foreign trade. When *economic sanctions* are used, they usually take the form of trade embargoes and have had mixed results. The U.S. trade embargo of Cuba began in the 1960s, persists to this day, and has forced the Latin American state toward greater and greater reliance on economic aid from the Soviet Union—but it has not brought Castro to his knees. Similarly, in 1980 the Carter Administration refused to sell the Soviet Union grain in retribution for its invasion of Afghanistan. The policy caused such havoc among American farmers, however, that it was abandoned early in the Reagan Administration. Also, in 1990–1991 the United States and most other countries brought severe economic sanctions against Iraq, but the results of this effort failed and force had to be used.

Economic pressure seems to have been more successful in South Africa, Panama, and Nicaragua. Apparently, the recent relaxation of South Africa's policies toward its black majority was at least partially induced through economic pressure from the United States and other countries. The economic embargoes of the Panamanian and Nicaraguan economies seem to have played a part in the public's welcoming the 1989 U.S. invasion of the former and the 1990 anti-Sandinista vote in the latter.

A more positive use of economics to influence other countries is *foreign aid.* The largest single foreign aid program of the United States, the **Marshall Plan**, was initiated in 1947 to help rebuild the shattered European countries. Significant aid was also given to Japan. The belief was that prosperity was conducive to political stability and democracy. As the European and Japanese economies recovered, American aid to its allies became increasingly military rather than economic, but the United States began to offer economic aid to the Third World, the Alliance for Progress in Latin America being among the most intense programs. Besides direct aid, the United States makes contributions to United Nations aid programs as well as capital investments in the World Bank and the International Monetary Fund (IMF), which make loans to developing countries.

Foreign economic aid, however, has many domestic opponents and few supporters. Hence, the level of our contributions has steadily declined over the years until now Japan, with half our GNP, gives more to developing countries than we do. For many years now, almost half of our total foreign aid budget has gone to two countries, Israel and Egypt, in an effort to stabilize the political situation in the Middle East and, in Israel's case, to satisfy a domestic political constituency. (See Table 12.2.)

As military power becomes less important vis-à-vis economic power in foreign affairs, eco-

Table 12.2
UNITED STATES FOREIGN AID IN 1986 (IN BILLIONS)

LOCATION	AID FOR REGION	INDIVIDUAL COUNTRIES[a]	PERCENTAGE OF REGION'S AID	PERCENTAGE OF TOTAL AID[b]
Near East & So. Asia	$3728			**59.4%**
Egypt[a]		$1069	28.7%	17.0%
Israel		$1898	50.9%	30.3%
Pakistan		$263	6.2%	4.2%
Turkey		$120	3.2%	1.9%
East Asia	$518			**8.3%**
Philippines		$351	57.4%	5.6%
Europe	$131			**2.1%**
Latin America	$1124			**17.9%**
Costa Rica		$139	12.4%	2.2%
El Salvador		$268	23.8%	4.3%
Honduras		$112	10.0%	1.9%
Africa	$766			**12.2%**
Oceania and others	$8			**0.1%**
Total	$6275			

[a] Only states that receive $100 million or more are listed by name.
[b] Region totals in boldface.

Source: Extrapolated from Stanley and Niemi, *Vital Statistics on American Politics,* 2nd ed.

nomic aid will be more significant in maintaining our international influence, and certain leaders are urging the United States to step up its foreign aid commitment so that its leadership position in the world can be sustained. Even the fiscally conservative former head of the Federal Reserve System, Paul A. Volcker, urges an increase in our foreign aid expenditures.[38]

Foreign trade is a third method used to exert economic influence in foreign affairs. Until the twentieth century, the United States spent and borrowed more money abroad than it collected; thus it was a debtor nation. By the 1900s, however, it had reversed the situation. Prior to World War II, the United States and other major economic powers followed a seemingly logical but, as it turned out, shortsighted policy of attempting to make consistent profits from their international trading partners. These policies were generally recognized as major contributions to the Great Depression and to the emergence of fascism in Europe.

Following World War II the United States advocated low tariffs and reciprocal (evenended) trade agreements. To suppress protective tariffs it supported the General Agreement on Tariffs and Trade (GATT) in 1947 and the Kennedy Round of tariff reductions in the 1960s. The idea was to enhance domestic economic well-being by encouraging international trade. The United States remained an economic leader and the world's greatest creditor nation through the 1960s, but in the late 1970s demand for United States products declined while our imports from abroad increased. The 1980s' economic policies of incurring huge national budget deficits and maintaining a tight money supply exacerbated the problem terribly. Foreign investment flowed in; the dollar rose in value against foreign currency, so demand for our exports declined; yet the United States increased its imports using borrowed money, and matters continue to grow worse.[39]

As political tensions with the Soviet Union relaxed, economic tensions—especially with Japan—grew, and a popular demand for protectionist tariff retaliations swept the country. President Carter had already agreed to raising tariffs on several goods, and although President Reagan tried to maintain a free market policy, eventually he too was forced to accept tariffs on a large number of goods. One danger of protectionism, however, is that it may trip off retaliation, thus diminishing international commerce and threatening world prosperity. A second problem is that we Americans tend to seek refuge in seemingly painless protectionism rather than biting the bullet and getting our own economic house in order.[40]

THE UNITED NATIONS

The United Nations has long been controversial in American politics. Conservatives view it as an expensive, politically ineffective organization and a center for spies and foreign agents. Liberals, on the other hand, generally support it as a useful tool in foreign policy. Normally, however, the United States remained supportive of the organization until the 1980s. Reagan's first Ambassador to the United Nations, Jeane J. Kirkpatrick, was openly critical of the organization, claiming that its proceedings tend to worsen international problems rather than ameliorating conflict. Also, the United States objected to the organization's efforts to combat overpopulation through the use of abortions and ultimately withheld a portion of the United States contribution to the world body.

The United States contributes about 25 percent of the UN budget, more than double that paid by the Soviets, the next heaviest contributor. The issue of the American contribution to the United Nations is a matter of some concern. Opponents to the U.S. assessment argue that since nations have an equal vote in the General Assembly, the United States should either reduce its payment or be given votes proportionate to its contribution. Supporters point out that the United States GNP is by far the largest in the world and that its economy consumes about 25 percent of the world's resources. Furthermore, the United States has the veto power in the Security Council together with the other four permanent members.

For his part, President Bush, a former United States Ambassador to the United Nations, has taken a more benevolent and hopeful view of the United Nations than his conservative predecessor. Furthermore, he skillfully encouraged international support for his policy to stop Iraqi aggression in the Persian Gulf by using United Nations Security Council resolutions as justification for deploying troops in Saudi Arabia and eventually driving Hussein's troops out of Kuwait.

In any event, although the United Nations has not fulfilled the expectations of its most idealistic supporters, it remains an important instrument in world affairs, and the United States will undoubtedly continue to participate in it in pursuit of American foreign policy objectives.

Defense

Obviously, military power is the ultimate instrument by which foreign policy can be implemented. The founders were careful to provide civilian control of the military because they knew that whenever a society arms a portion of its number, it becomes a potential captive. In the current arrangement, the military is capped by several layers of civilian superiors: the president as commander-in-chief; the secretary of defense; the secretaries of the Army, Navy, and Air Force; and so on. Yet the _De-_

From left to right: General Norman Schwarzkopf, commander of Operation Desert Storm; Secretary of Defense Dick Cheney; President Bush; and Joint Chiefs of Staff Chairman, General Colin Powell.

partment of Defense (DOD) is the largest institution in the United States government, and its uniformed members have enormous power.

DEPARTMENT OF DEFENSE

Twenty percent of the national budget, about 5 percent of the GNP, is currently spent on defense. The DOD employs over 3 million civilian and uniformed people, and thus constitutes a powerful bureaucracy and an important element in the national economy.

Controlling such a large and expensive bureaucracy presents major problems for the administration. Although military personnel are supposed to be nonpartisan, that does not mean that they are nonpolitical. Indeed, DOD is rife with politics. The **Joint Chief of Staff (JCS)** is composed of a Chair, Colin Powell (Powell is the first African-American to reach the highest level of military command); a Vice Chair; and the military heads of the Army, Navy, Air Force, and Marine Corps. It is their task to advise the Secretary of Defense, the National Security Council, and the president on military affairs. Until 1986, the joint chiefs had to agree unanimously to a recommendation before it could be passed on, but recent legislation has given the chair much more authority in an effort to make JCS operations more efficient. Still, however, the various branches of the service operate independently of one another as much as possible. When the defense budget is growing there is a tendency for each service to get what it can for itself, but not to oppose programs for the other branches. This policy leads to duplication and waste. On the other hand, when the budget is shrinking, as it now is, a fiercely competitive atmosphere develops in which each branch tries to save as much of its own program as possible.

Another problem arising from the rivalry of the services is that they tend to focus on certain roles—those that are more glamorous than others—at the expense of other functions, thus causing waste. When the Army Air Corps separated from the Army and became the Air Force, it entered a protocol that prohibited the Army from developing a fleet of fixed-wing airplanes for ground support. Yet the Air Force downplays its role of providing ground support in favor of its strategic bombers. To protect its troops, the Army has amassed a fleet of helicopters whose numbers now almost equal the number of aircraft in the Air Force. Not only is this wasteful duplication, but helicopters are very vulnerable to enemy fire and are thus dangerous.[41] In another case, differences in communications systems between the Army and Navy made it impossible for soldiers in the 1983 Grenada invasion to communicate with naval support vessels. The Pentagon's own report on the invasion described a frustrated soldier telephoning Fort Bragg asking that word be passed through Naval headquarters to the deployed vessels for a request for support fire on the island. The narrow, self-serving focus of the military services reduces our military preparedness and threatens unnecessary loss of life in the event of war. Even such a strong supporter

of defense as Senator Barry Goldwater decried it. "I am saddened that the services are unable to put the national interest above parochial interests," he told the press in 1985.[42]

The bureaucratic tendency for growth also affects the military. In 1985 Senator Warren Rudman (R-NH) complained that there were more clerks in the military than combat personnel and that there were more generals and admirals in the armed forces than there were during World War II, with only one-sixth as many personnel to command.[43]

The civilian sector of DOD has similar problems. John Lehman, Reagan's politically astute Secretary of the Navy, observed that at a time when the administration claimed to be reducing the number of people in government, 100,000 bureaucrats were added to DOD. The massive increase in defense expenditures during the 1980s brought more than just new personnel and weapons; it also encouraged corruption and scandal.

Although waste and corruption in defense spending certainly far predates the Reagan administration, the scope of fraud reached unprecedented levels between 1981 and 1988. Various Justice Department and congressional investigations have exposed massive overcharges, fraud, bribery, and duplicity, falsification of test data on weapons systems, and illegal purchase of government secrets so that corporations could use the inside information to win lucrative government contracts. Dozens of the nation's major defense contractors are under investigation; several have plead guilty to criminal charges; and dozens more consultants and Defense Department employees, including a former Assistant Secretary of the Navy, are under criminal investigation, have pled guilty to collusion and bribery, or have been convicted in court.[44] Hence, much of the money spent on defense was wasted. For example, while in its first four years, the Reagan Administration spent 75 percent more than Carter had on new aircraft, it bought only 9 percent more airplanes.[45]

Besides the enormous amount of money diverted to defense during the Reagan years, the president's lax administration of policy greatly contributed to the defense procurement corruption, as it did to several other scandals mentioned in preceding chapters. Furthermore, Reagan's approach was duplicated by his Secretary of Defense, Caspar Weinberger, whom Senator Robert Dole (R-KS) once described as "the first person in history to overdraw a blank check."[46] Weinberger forcefully resisted congressional efforts to create stronger, more independent checks on DOD spending. The practice of hiring outside consultants and of encouraging competitive bidding for defense contracts also constituted for some an open, if unintended, invitation to cheat.[47] Furthermore, the clubbish atmosphere within DOD discourages whistle-blowers. In 1968 Ernest Fitzgerald, a civilian employee of the Air Force, told Congress that the C-5A transport had serious difficulties. Fitzgerald was promptly fired; when he successfully sued to get his job back, he was banished to the backwaters and given insignificant assignments.[48] More recently, after he left government service, Lawrence J. Korb, a former Pentagon official, criticized elements of Reagan's defense policy. Pressure from Navy Secretary Lehman ended in his being fired at Raytheon Corporation, a major defense contractor.[49] Perhaps the reason Korb waited until he left government service to make his criticisms is that apparently many inspectors general, who are supposed to ferret out government waste and corruption, often instead try to cover up improprieties and even report whistleblowers to their superiors.[50]

The Bush Administration is apparently turning up the heat on potential whistle-blowers. In 1989 the Justice Department reversed a Carter Administration policy designed to protect those who informed about DOD waste and corruption. Instead, the Justice Department announced that people who leak certain kinds of information to the press will be prosecuted.[51]

To the government's credit, however, when waste and corruption in the defense establishment became evident, the Reagan and Bush administrations vigorously pursued the cases legally. Until 1983, no defense contractor had been convicted of a felony since World War II, but by mid-1990 over half of the nation's major defense contractors had been investigated and 20 convictions were brought against such firms as Sperry, Northrop, General Dynamics, General Electric, TRW, and Rockwell International.[52]

That DOD and the military are political and difficult to manage should not detract from the fact that their role is essential in foreign policy. Nor should it imply that the United States has been poorly served by the military. Indeed, the United States has been fortunate; historically it has been served by a dedicated military, one that has usually honored the tradition for civilian control of both the military and the government. So far, the United States has not suffered a military coup, a fate not uncommon in many other societies. Furthermore, many of the embarrassments of the Grenada invasion were apparently overcome, and the military performed with admirable precision in the Persian Gulf War.

THE MILITARY AND FOREIGN POLICY

Karl von Clausewitz, the famous Prussian military philosopher, wrote that warfare is but the pursuit of political objectives by another means.[53] The emphasis Clausewitz placed on politics as related to warfare is generally regarded as correct, since a war for its own sake is senseless. Attitudes about the efficacy of war itself, however, have changed greatly over the years. The development and use of nuclear weapons have raised serious doubts about the continued utility of warfare. While some authorities, such as Paul Nitze, an influential foreign policy advisor to presidents since Harry S. Truman, believe that winning a nuclear war is accomplished by ending it in better shape than one's adversary, many other people have concluded that such a destructive encounter would make victory meaningless.[54]

The United States has used diplomatic, economic, and political pressure to accomplish its goal of containment, but it has also used conventional weapons for this purpose. The Korean and Vietnam wars, as well as a number of smaller engagements, were justified as efforts to contain communist expansion. Nuclear weapons are also a part of the strategy, but since their use is abhorrent, a formula had to be devised to discourage it. The strategy eventually developed and applied equally by the United States and the Soviet Union is **deterrence**.

The objective of deterrence is to develop such overwhelming nuclear force that an opponent realizes that initiating a nuclear strike would be futile because the opponent can absorb the attack and still be able to retaliate with enough force to destroy the aggressor's society. Hence, nothing is to be gained from starting a nuclear war. For this reason, deterrence is referred to as **mutually assured destruction**, with the discomforting acronym **MAD**. Its critics have also referred to it as the *balance of terror*.

The existence of abundant nuclear weapons (the United States and the Soviet Union are estimated to possess a total of over 50,000 nuclear warheads), together with their implicit finality, causes certain changes in the logic of international relations. Deterrence is fundamentally based on psychology. If your opponents believe you have enough weapons to destroy them in retaliation for an attack (whether or not you really do) and if the opponents believe you will use the weapons if at-

tacked (whether or not you will), then the opponent will probably be deterred. If, on the other hand, the opponent is not convinced of one or both of these factors, the deterrent is weakened. Hence deterrence demands a great deal of posturing as well as defense spending to communicate each factor.

Moreover, deterrence depends upon the ability to respond at a moment's notice, when prior to World War II the United States basically ignored its peacetime military, expecting to have a year or two lead-time into any war. Now, the lead-time is only a few minutes. Deterrence also requires that there be no secret weapons. There are, of course, secrets about weapons, but since the whole idea is to threaten possible opponents, each side is careful to inform the other about its capability and its resolve. Military allies have also lost a good deal of their importance in that each superpower has enough nuclear warheads deployed to destroy the other many times over. Finally, the concepts of defensive strategy have changed. Previously it was thought that a civilized state wars against its opponent's military, sparing civilians. Now, however, the side that ignores an opponent's military and threatens only its cities is thought to have a defensive, nonbelligerent posture, since its inability to destroy the opponent's retaliatory weapons assures that it will not initiate a nuclear strike. A **first-strike capacity** is understood to be the ability to launch an attack so quickly and so devastatingly that the opponent's retaliatory power would be destroyed unused. This is thought to be an aggressive or offensive strategy. A **second-strike capacity** is the ability to absorb a full blow and still be able to retaliate with enough force to destroy the opponent's society. This is considered a defensive strategy. The two strategies are mutually exclusive. If country A has a first-strike capacity, country B does not have a second-strike capacity and thus has no deterrent. On the other hand, if each adversary has a second-strike capacity, neither has a first-strike capacity. Playing this dangerous game, each party has assured the other that it has only a second-strike capacity since one side's trying to develop a first-strike capacity would destabilize the situation and perhaps trip off a preemptive strike by the other. Yet each side is also cautious and suspicious that the other is developing a first-strike force—and thus the arms race.

As frightening as deterrence is, it seems to have worked so far. Although the United States and the Soviet Union have come dangerously close to a general nuclear exchange (over Cuba in 1962, for example), they have managed to avoid it, and one may assume that the mutually assured destruction had a significant influence because nuclear weapons were used by the United States against Japan when no deterrent existed.

In pursuing our foreign policy, the United States has, as mentioned, committed itself to a number of bilateral defense agreements and collective security treaties. Of these obligations, by far the most important, and the one demanding the greatest commitment, is NATO. It was created in 1949 to prevent any further Soviet encroachment in Europe, and as a response, in 1955 the Warsaw Pact was created in the Eastern Bloc. (See Table 12.3.)

For years these adversaries stood poised and confrontational, but the economic problems of the Soviet Union ultimately led to the demise of the Eastern alliance in 1991. The collapse of the Warsaw Pact as a meaningful military threat has brought to the fore doubts about the continued need for NATO itself. The entire *raison d'être* of NATO is at issue since the Soviet Union is no longer seen as an immediate threat to the freedom of Western Europe. What the future holds for NATO is, of course, impossible to foresee at this point. It is clear, however, that changes are occurring that will modify the relationship among its members.

Table 12.3

NATO AND THE WARSAW PACT

NATO	WARSAW PACT
Belgium	Albania[a]
Canada	Bulgaria
Denmark	Czechoslovakia
Federal Republic of Germany[c]	German Democratic Republic
France[b]	Hungary
Greece	Poland
Iceland	Romania
Italy	Union of Soviet Socialist Republics
Luxembourg	
Netherlands	
Norway	
Portugal	
Turkey	
United Kingdom	
United States	

[a] In 1961 Albania broke off relations with the Soviet Union, and formally withdrew from the Warsaw Pact in 1968.
[b] Withdrew its forces in 1967, but remains a member.
[c] The GDR united with West Germany and is now in NATO.

The most important of these transformations, outside of the collapse of the Warsaw Pact and the reunification of Germany, are the growing importance of economics, even as the United States suffers an economic decline relative to its allies, and the prospect of European economic unity in 1992. This modification offers a compelling parodox.

Formerly, military prominence declined with reduced economic strength, but matters are different today. Nuclear weapons are unmatched in destructive capacity, and they are relatively inexpensive to build and maintain. Neither the United States nor the Soviet Union is likely to wish to see its nuclear preeminence challenged, so we may witness a curious situation in which societies with ailing economies remain first-rate military powers. Such an eventuality will likely cause awkwardness, anxiety, and perhaps instability in international affairs.

STRATEGIC NUCLEAR WEAPONS

The United States has a full complement of **strategic nuclear weapons**, weapons that can strike the Soviet Union or another adversary from American territory or from international waters. The basic instrument in American strategic defense is called the **Triad** and is composed of long-range bombers, submarine-based missiles, and **intercontinental ballistic missiles (ICBMs)**. The ICBMs and **submarine-launched ballistic missiles (SLBMs)** are equipped with **multiple independently targeted reentry vehicles (MIRVs)**. That is, a single missile is fitted with between 3 and 16 warheads, each of which can be programmed to strike an individual target when it separates from the missile and enters the atmosphere. (See Table 12.4.)

The ICBMs are fast and accurate. Authorities claim that they need only 30 minutes from launch in the United States to impact in the Soviet Union, and that they can accurately target a space the size of a tennis court in Moscow. Conceivably, these weapons could be used in a first strike. The SLBMs are less accurate and are designed for retaliatory attacks, although the new Trident 2 missiles will have an accuracy rivaling that of the ICBMs, so presumably they too could be used in a first strike. Bombers from the **Strategic Air Command (SAC)** are slow by comparison with missiles, so they are also viewed as retaliatory weapons. The newer bombers (B-1s and B-2s), however, have advanced capabilities and conceivably might also be used in a first strike.[55]

Most of these weapons have been immersed in controversy. The MX missile deployment mode has been debated vigorously for years. The problem is that MIRV'ed missiles are inviting targets in that knocking out one destroys several warheads at once. Several plans were considered for deploying these missiles, from housing them on subterranean railroads to clustering them in "dense packs" to protect them from Soviet attack. Ultimately, however, these ideas were abandoned, and the MX missiles were deployed in silos that previously housed the aging Minuteman missiles. Fearing that the MX was still too vulnerable, the Bush Administration persuaded Congress

Table 12.4
UNITED STATES STRATEGIC NUCLEAR WEAPONS

DELIVERY SYSTEM	PAYLOAD
1000 ICBMs (MX missiles)	2450 warheads
608 SLBMs (launched from Trident nuclear-powered submarines)	5312 warheads
318 Bombers (B-52s, B-1s, and B-2s)	2500 bombs and 1600 air-launched cruise missiles

Source: Adapted from information by Jay Peterzell and Bruce von Voorst, in "How Much Is Too Much?", *Time,* Feb. 12, 1990; and Robert C. Toth, "Planners Split on How to Meet Nuclear Threat," *Los Angeles Times,* July 24, 1989.

to permit 50 MX missiles, each with 10 war-heads, to be deployed on railroad cars. Currently, they are located on Air Force bases in Arkansas, Louisiana, Michigan, North Dakota, Texas, and Washington. In times of crisis they will be moved onto the public rail lines and hauled on random itineraries, poised for launch if need be.[56]

The new bomber fleets are also mired in controversy. The B-1 bomber, first deployed in 1985, has suffered numerous problems. A fleet of 100, at the cost of $30 billion, is unable to perform some of its tasks against the Soviet Union because of unsolved problems with its sophisticated electronics system. Even more difficulty has been experienced with the B-2, the **Stealth bomber**. Designed to elude Soviet radar detection so as to strike Soviet mobile missiles and bunkers protecting the Soviet leadership, the B-2 was kept extraordinarily secret. Finally, in the summer of 1989 the cost of the program was made public, as was information about its capacity. Each was equally shocking to Congress and to the public. The Air Force proposed building 132 bombers at a staggering cost of $564.4 million per copy, for a total of $75.4 billion. It urges that production go full speed ahead even though the craft has not been fully tested and appears to be incapable of avoiding detection by certain kinds of Soviet radar.[57] The ambiguities surrounding the weapon have alarmed Congress, and it is unwilling to buy more than a fraction of the 100 planes the Air Force wants.[58]

Equal controversy surrounds the government's program to develop the **Strategic Defense Initiative (SDI)**. Sharing the concern of most presidents before him that the superpowers could deter one another only by holding the other's population hostage to nuclear incineration, and distressed that no effective defense against a nuclear attack was possible, President Reagan announced in 1983 a plan to explore the possibility of creating a shield against nu-

U.S. Army Captain Joan Conley wore a button with a picture of her 2-year-old daughter Stephanie, while serving in the Saudi Arabian desert during the Gulf War.

clear attack and sharing the technology with the Soviet Union so as to make nuclear weapons irrelevant. The proposal, which envisioned satellites shooting down Soviet missiles with lasers, particle beams, rail guns, and kinetic energy, was greeted by some people with support and enthusiasm, but others ridiculed it as impossibly complex, enormously expensive, and easily foiled by relatively inexpensive Soviet defensive measures.

Because of the enormous cost of this program; its destabilizing influence on the Soviet Union, which believes SDI may give the United States enough protection to launch a first strike; and the system's still highly questionable efficacy, many members of Congress balk at funding it further. Debate about the weapon has been spirited, rancorous, and at times humorous. In 1989, Rep. Jon Kyl (R-AZ) compared the cost of SDI favorably with what he implied were more frivolous consumer purchases. He pointed out that more money is spent annually in the United States on pantyhose than on the SDI. Rising to the challenge, Rep. Barbara Boxer (D-CA) retorted,

Believe me, pantyhose is affordable; "Star Wars" is not. Pantyhose has a clear function; "Star Wars" does not. Pantyhose has a mission that does not change every day; "Star Wars"' mission has changed from a protective shield to military defense installations to accidental launch protection to 'brilliant pebbles' to terrorist deterrence. "Star Wars"' [mission] has changed more times than Imelda Marcos has changed her shoes.[59]

By the end of the Reagan tenure, the United States had spent $17 billion on SDI research only to abandon notions of laser and particle beam defense as impractical, and concluding that a "leak-proof" defense against incoming Soviet warheads is impossible. Hence, the hope that nuclear weapons will be rendered useless is gone. The Bush Administration, however, favors continued research and development of the project, and planned to spend $33 billion on it between 1991 and 1996. The need to reduce the annual budget deficits, however, proved compelling and SDI spending was severely cut back in the 1991 and 1992 budgets. With the success of the Patriot surface-to-air antimissile (a missile that destroys short-range missiles) in the Persian Gulf war, however, Bush has once again stridently called for more funds for antimissile defense. In doing so, he has ordered that emphasis be shifted from defending against a superpower missile attack to "providing protection from limited ballistic missile strikes whatever their source." He has called for Global Protection Against Limited Strikes (GPALS). This scaled-down version of the SDI would deploy antimissile missiles capable of destroying incoming long-range missiles. Such a capability would violate the 1972 Anti-Ballistic Missile Treaty, however.[60] By early 1991 the government had spent $24 billion on SDI–GPALS projects, but serious doubt persists in the scientific community as to the efficacy of such weapons.[61]

DISARMAMENT

In less than a half-century the world has come from total dependence on conventional weapons to relying for its security on a hair-trigger deterrence. In this evolution, each major category of weapon was first developed and deployed by the United States, with the Soviets eventually duplicating it. As you can see from Table 12.5, over the years the adversaries were able to agree on some limitations, but they failed to agree on terms of disarmament until 1988. Now, however, the potential for militarily significant reductions is recognized even by military leaders on the right wing. General John Galvin, the American Commander of NATO, told *Time* magazine:

> If you're looking for the personification of the Cold War, here I am.
>
> I'm seeing now the possibility that we can bring all of this to a close. If we can get 35 nations to sign on the dotted line on something that is irreversible and verifiable, and bring down the levels of armaments to a mere fraction of what they are today, then we really have achieved something that's worth all the sacrifices.[62]

It must be cautioned, however, that because of mutual anxieties and because Soviet and American weapons systems are so dissimilar, it is very difficult to negotiate major disarmament agreements.

The **Strategic Arms Reduction Talks (START)** have resulted in a 1991 agreement to reduce American and Soviet nuclear warheads by about 30 percent, and it is hoped that future agreements will bring the combined arsenals down by a total of 50 percent. Even so great a reduction in nuclear weapons, while significant, will still leave enough for each side to easily destroy the other, however. It must be recognized that nuclear weapons will probably never be eliminated entirely. The United

Table 12.5
THE EVOLUTION OF NUCLEAR WEAPONS

	WEAPON/TREATY	ORIGINATOR/SIGNATORIES
1945	First atomic bomb exploded	U.S.
1952	First hydrogen bomb exploded	U.S.
1956	First nuclear-powered submarine launched	U.S.
1959	First ICBM tested	U.S.
1960	First SLBMs deployed	U.S.
1962	Cuban Missile Crisis	U.S. and USSR
1963	Limited Nuclear Test Ban Treaty	127 states
1968	Nonproliferation (of nuclear weapons) Treaty	136 states
1969	SALT talks began	U.S. and USSR
1970	First MIRVs deployed	U.S.
1972	Antiballistic Missile (ABM) Treaty	U.S. and USSR
1972	SALT I Treaty	U.S. and USSR
1974	SALT II agreement	U.S. and USSR
1983	SDI research began	U.S.
1984	Air-launched cruise missiles deployed	U.S.
1988	INF disarmament treaty	U.S. and USSR
1989	First Stealth bomber tested	U.S.
1991	Significant reductions of conventional arms in Europe and the reduction of about one-third of the number of strategic warheads	U.S., NATO, USSR, and Warsaw Pact

States and the Soviet Union will insist upon keeping enough weapons to defend themselves against each other and to deter any third party, for despite efforts to limit the spread of nuclear weapons, several states have developed them. (See Table 12.6)

Another problem, of course, is whether the superpowers can trust one another and can adequately verify compliance with disarmament treaties. Problems with INF treaty compliance have already been encountered. In March of 1990 it was revealed that before the treaty was signed, the Soviet Union secretly transferred dozens of SS-23 missiles to East Germany, Czechoslovakia, and Bulgaria so that they were not part of the agreement.[63]

The current trend toward disarmament has also affected conventional forces. Gorbachev feels that money must be moved from the military budget to investment in the production of Soviet consumer goods. Accordingly, he has already implemented a unilateral 10 percent reduction of the armed forces, including deep cutbacks in Eastern Europe, and he plans much heavier cuts, perhaps totaling 50 percent by the end of the century. Large reductions in conventional arms make sense under the current circumstances because conventional forces are far more expensive to maintain than are nuclear weapons.

Much the same kind of pressure is bearing upon the United States. Long-neglected domestic issues cry out for attention. In the face of economic pressures and the reduced Soviet threat, President Bush is being pushed hard for major reductions in defense expenditures. After initial hesitation, the administration is now engaged in executing a 25 percent cut in mili-

Table 12.6
STATES WITH NUCLEAR WEAPONS

CONFIRMED	PROBABLE	SUSPECTED	CAPABLE OF PRODUCING
United States	Israel	Pakistan	Syria
Soviet Union	South Africa	Brazil	Iran
France		Argentina	Libya
United Kingdom			North Korea
China			
India			

Source: CBS news station KFBM San Diego, March 31, 1990.

tary personnel by 1997. This amounts to closing about 10 percent of our military bases and reducing the number of people in uniform by about 500,000.[64]

Major cutbacks in military expenditures, however, are likely to trip off a number of controversies. The *draft*, for example, will undoubtedly be questioned again. First used during the Civil War, it was reinstated during World War I and again during World War II. United States international commitments after World War II caused the country to continue the draft, but finally, disenchantment with the military resulting from the Vietnam War caused conscription to be abandoned in the early 1970s. However, as part of his administration's reaction to the Soviet invasion of Afghanistan, Carter reestablished registration for the draft in 1980. Congress, however, refused to agree to women being required to register along with men, and this position was sustained by the Supreme Court.[65]

A significant number of women have joined the armed services voluntarily, however. About 11 percent of the 2.1 million current troop level is composed of women, and women constitute 13 percent of the nation's reserves. Although military regulations and national law prohibit women from being assigned to combat duty, recent experience indicates that in com-

bat situations it will be next to impossible for women to be kept out of the line of fire. About 6 percent (27,000) of the American troops in Operation Desert Storm were women, and they performed very well. While none of them were intentionally committed to combat, 13 were killed: 8 in accidents and 5 of wounds received in combat.

Women are allowed to perform in 88 percent of all military job classifications, but critics of the noncombat policy charge not only that in combat situations the distinction is meaningless but also that the denial of combat jobs to women constitutes a form of suppression. Combat duty, they contend, is the surest route to promotion in the military, and this discriminatory policy prevents women from advancing.[66] A 1990 poll indicates that seven of every ten Americans think that women should serve in combat roles, and encouraged by public acceptance of female casualties in Desert Storm, Congress is seriously considering rescinding its prohibition of women in combat roles.[67]

Since the all-volunteer military was created, ethnicity and social class have also become sources of controversy in the military. While the draft called to service young men in approximate proportion to the national ethnic and social percentages, following its elimina-

Table 12.7
ETHNIC COMPOSITION OF THE MILITARY

ETHNICITY	PERCENTAGE OF POPULATION	PERCENTAGE OF MILITARY
White	73.6%	67.7%
Black	12.1%	23.0%
Latino	8.3%	4.9%
Other minorities	6.0%	4.4%
Total minorities	26.4%	32.3%

Note: Whites are 5.9 percent underenlisted to a ratio of 0.92, and the minorities are 5.9 percent overenlisted to a ratio of 1.2. See text for further explanation.

Source: Department of Defense and U.S. Census Bureau.

tion, well-to-do whites have enlisted in smaller percentages, while poor whites and ethnic minorities have volunteered in greater numbers than is proportionate to their respective national averages. (See Table 12.7.) Hence, as the Persian Gulf crisis heated up in 1991, some people wondered out loud whether the president and Congress might be less willing to engage in war with Iraq if their sons and daughters were also in the military.[68]

As funds begin to tighten for the military and as superpower tensions relax, the military has begun to scramble to keep its favorite weapons systems. The Air Force wants to take over some functions for which previously only navy aircraft carriers were used, the Army wants the Marine Corps reduced, and so forth. The Navy contends that since the United States remains a sea power, with or without a Soviet threat its role will remain unchanged. Soviet reductions in its naval operations, however, will undoubtedly result in corresponding reductions for the United States Navy, and Secretary of Defense Cheney has already decided to eliminate the $52 billion project to produce the A-12 navy carrier attack plane because of huge cost overruns. For its part, the Air Force was quick to offer its F-117A Stealth fighter for service in the Panama invasion to prove that its weapons can be used on missions previously monopolized by the Navy. Also, after selling its troubled B-2 Stealth bomber to Congress as a weapon against the Soviet Union, the Air Force quickly expanded its mission, contending that Stealth could also be very effective in combat in Third World countries. So far the Army appears to be the big loser, taking 48 percent of the proposed cuts for the 1991 and 1992 budgets. Not only are its forces being reduced in Europe and the United States, but they are also being brought home from Japan, the Philippines, and South Korea. (See Table 12.8.) By 1995, according to Bush Administration projections, Army troops will be reduced by 17.6 percent.

President Bush's 1992 budget proposed a 3.3 percent cut in military spending. This figure does not count expenditures for the Persian Gulf war.[69] Cutting the military budget is an exceedingly difficult task politically. Theoretically it may look like a good idea, but the prospect of major cutbacks can be wrenching. Members of Congress who may support reductions in general will fight strenuously to keep military bases from closing in their districts. Cities and other local communities will com-

Table 12.8
AMERICAN TROOP REDUCTION ABROAD

	CURRENT NUMBER	1990–1991 PROPOSED REDUCTION	REMAINDER
NATO	305,000	80,000	225,000
Japan	59,000	7,000	52,000
Philippines	17,800	2,000	15,800
South Korea	43,700	6,700	37,000
Total	425,500	95,700	329,800

Source: Robert C. Toth, "Soviets Accept U.S. Ceiling on Europe Forces, "*Los Angeles Times,* Feb. 14, 1950; and John M. Broder, "U.S. Plans 10% Troop Cut in 3 Asian Nations," *Los Angeles Times,* Feb. 14, 1990.

plain about Naval vessels no longer berthed in their ports because, as with welfare checks, much of the money spent on defense quickly filters into local economies. Powerful defense contractors will forcefully resist any proposed cuts to their potential earnings, and thousands of military personnel and civilian DOD employees will be laid off. The roar from disgruntled people will be deafening, and if history is any judge, when the smoke clears from the political battle ahead, fewer dollars will have been saved than might have been.

Peace Dividend   The prospects of cutting the defense budget and applying the savings—known as the **peace dividend**—to other areas, briefly caused great excitement. Supply-siders wanted to use the savings to cut taxes; some foreign policy experts wanted to apply it in a Marshall Plan for Eastern Europe; other people wanted to divert it to capital investment, to the poor, to the homeless, to education, to state and local governments, to roads, to mass transit, and to the environment. Even President Bush proposed that $800 million of it be sent as aid to the Panamanian and Nicaraguan economies, which were shattered largely by United States policies.

The potential savings had been spent 20 times over in the minds of people anxious to

realize increased government spending on their pet projects. In perspective, however, the potential savings are only modest when compared with those of past eras. (See Table 12.9.) Whatever the case might have been, until the cost of the Persian Gulf war is calculated (estimates range up to $100 billion), it is too early to count on the peace dividend to address our problems.[70]

The Dilemma of Democracy

Before closing this final chapter, a word must be said about the dilemma democracies face in pursuing foreign policy. In the early 1800s Alexis de Tocqueville observed that while democracies were efficient on domestic issues, they were devoid of the two qualities necessary for developing and implementing sound foreign policies: secrecy and patience. It is true that much of foreign policy must be developed in secret (treaty negotiations, for example) and that some of it must be implemented in camera. It is also true that politicians whose jobs depend upon popular satisfaction feel pressure to show results quickly—something a sound foreign policy may not afford. Foreign affairs are also complex and a bit arcane to the public. Responsible policies and agreements are often sub-

Table 12.9
PREVIOUS "PEACE DIVIDENDS"

EVENT AND YEAR	PERCENTAGE OF GNP SPENT IN DEFENSE	PEACE DIVIDEND AS A PERCENTAGE OF GNP
End of World War II, 1945	39.1%	
Peacetime, 1948	3.7%	35.4%[a]
End of Korean War, 1953	14.4%	
Peacetime, 1958	10.4%	4.0%[a]
Vietnam War, 1968	9.6%	
Peacetime, 1978	4.8%	4.8%[a]
U.S.-USSR reduced tension, 1991	5.5%	
Peacetime, 1994	5.1%	0.4%[b]
U.S.-USSR reduced tension, 1991	5.5%	
Peacetime, 1994	4.8%	0.7%[c]
U.S.-USSR reduced tension, 1991	5.5%	
Peacetime, 1994	4.1%	1.4%[d]

[a] Figures from Richard Hornk, "The Peaceful Dividend: Myth and Reality," *Time,* Feb. 12, 1990.
[b] Figures from *Budget of the U.S. Government 1990* (Washington, D.C.: U.S. Government Printing Office, 1989).
[c] Figures were calculated by assuming a 12.5% reduction in the defense budget.
[d] As in note c but with a 25% reduction.

tle and oblique, as is diplomatic language, to the extent that the public is often either frustrated or bored with its ambiguities.

Democracy is also uncomfortable with certain instruments of foreign policy implementation. Intelligence agents who lie, cheat, steal, and even kill to further foreign policy objectives have always been a problem in democratic societies. Not only is this behavior abhorrent, albeit perhaps necessary, but the very existence of secret agents empowered by society to spy and commit extraordinary acts may, in an effort to serve democracy, actually threaten it.

A professional military is another source of embarrassment. Inherently undemocratic, the military is pledged to defend values and lifestyles it does not itself practice and may not fully appreciate. The founders were quite right to be suspicious of the military, for even in their time it had the capacity to end the very system it was supposed to defend. Almost every military dictatorship created in this century was founded in the name of bringing democracy to its citizens.

So where does that leave us? We cannot rely solely on the military for protection of our political system. Each citizen must take responsibility for it. In the last analysis, the preservation of democracy depends upon a people devoted to its principles, who are knowledgeable on the issues and actively participate in the process. No political system dependent upon its citizen for justification and commitment can long survive public ignorance or apathy. People who take democracy for granted play a fool's game.

Summary

- The basic premise for American foreign policy is to protect the national self-interest, although that is defined differently by various people.

- The early part of our history was taken up with expanding over the continent and dominating the Western Hemisphere.

- After World War II the United States emerged as a superpower, juxtaposed to the Soviet Union.

- As the Cold War receded into irrelevance, the United States found itself consumed with problems in the Third World: specifically in Korea, Vietnam, Central America, and the Middle East.

- The United States has many devices at its disposal to effect foreign policy, including diplomacy, economic aid, and economic sanctions.

- The military is also a major instrument of United States foreign policy and has been employed numerous times.

- A major dilemma for the United States, as well as for any democracy, is how to control its clandestine and martial forces so as to maintain a democratic and free society.

Notes

1. John A. Garraty, *The American Nation,* 2nd ed., Vol. I (New York: Harper & Row, 1971), pp. 252–254.

2. Walter LaFeber, "The 'Lion in the Path': The U.S. Emergence as a World Power," *Political Science Quarterly* 5 (1986), 709.

3. Woodrow Wilson, *Constitutional Government in the United States* (New York: Columbia University Press, 1908), pp. 77–80.

4. "Soviet Wartime Toll Reported," *The Los Angeles Times,* Feb. 17, 1990.

5. Melvin C. Wren, *The Course of Russian History,* 3rd. ed. (London: Macmillan, 1968), pp. 664–665.

6. X, "The Sources of Soviet Conduct," in Robert A. Goldwin and Harry M.Clor, eds., *Readings in American Foreign Policy* (New York: Oxford University Press, 1971), pp. 337–355.

7. X, p. 344.

8. G. John Ikenberry, "Rethinking the Origins of American Hegemony," *Political Science Quarterly* (Fall 1989), 344.

9. Ikenberry, p. 400.

10. George Kennan, *Memoirs: 1925–1950* (Boston: Little, Brown, 1967), p. 336.

11. John T. Rourke, *International Politics on the World Stage,* 2nd ed. (Sluice Dock, CT: Dushkin, 1989), p. 46.

12. See Robert F. Kennedy, *Thirteen Days* (New York: Norton, 1971).

13. Thomas M. Franck and Edward Weisband, *Word Politics* (New York: Oxford University Press, 1972), p. 79.

14. Franck and Weisband, p. 6.

15. Michael Ross, "Democrats Plan to Study Alleged Hostage Deal," *The Los Angeles Times*, May 3, 1991.

16. Robin Wright and Ronald J. Ostrow, "Noriega's U.S. Intelligence Ties Could Vex Prosecution," *The Los Angeles Times*, Jan. 16, 1990.

17. Raymond L. Garthoff, "American-Soviet Relations in Perspective," *Political Science Quarterly* (Winter 1985–1986), 543.

18. James J. Sundquist, "Has America Lost Its Social Conscience—And How Will It Get It Back," *Political Science Quarterly* 4 (1986), 528.

19. Lester Thurow, "Budget Deficits," in Daniel Bell and Lester Thurow, eds., *The Deficits: How Big? How Long? How Dangerous?* (New York: New York University Press, 1985), p. 123.

20. Aaron L. Friedberg, "The Strategic Implications of Relative Economic Decline," *Political Science Quarterly* (Fall 1989), 401–431.

21. Robert Gilpin, "American Policy in the Post-Reagan Era," *Daedalus* (Summer 1987), 49.

22. John M. Broder and Melissa Healy, "U.S. Pulls Back on Navy Patrols Off Colombia," *The Los Angeles Times*, Jan. 9, 1990.

23. David Wise, "A People Betrayed," *The Los Angeles Times*, Apr. 14, 1991.

24. Jack Nelson, "Willingness to Use Force Marks Bush's 1st 2 Years," *The Los Angeles Times*, Mar. 15, 1991.

25. *Missouri v. Holland*, 252 U.S. 416 (1920); *United States v. Belmont*, 301 U.S. 324 (1937); *United States v. Pink*, 315 U.S. 203 (1942); *United States v. Guy W. Capps, Inc.*, 328 U.S. 298 (1955); and *Reid v. Covert*, 354 U.S. 1 (1957).

26. Quoted in John T. Rourke and Russell Farnen, "War, Presidents, and the Constitution," *Presidential Studies Quarterly* (Summer 1988), 518.

27. David McKay, "Presidential Strategy and the Veto Power: A Reappraisal," *Political Science Quarterly* (Fall 1989), 459.

28. Rudy Abramson, "Pact Delay Threatened by Senators," *The Los Angeles Times*, Feb. 7, 1988.

29. Doyle McManus, "Call It Luck, Skill or Both: Baker Rides a Win Streak," *The Los Angeles Times*, March 26, 1990.

30. Bob Woodward and Walter Pincus, "CIA Reportedly Got 'License to Kill' Terrorists," from *The Washington Post* as reported in the *Los Angeles Times*, Oct. 5, 1988.

31. Donna M. Schlagheck, "The Superpowers, Foreign Policy, and Terrorism," in Charles W. Kegley, Jr., ed., *International Terrorism* (New York: St. Martin's Press, 1990), pp. 176–177.

32. Robert Parry and Peter Kornbluh, "Misleading Americans," *The Los Angeles Times*, Sept. 11, 1988.

33. Ronald J. Ostrow, "FBI Gets OK for Overseas Arrests," *The Los Angeles Times*, Oct. 13, 1989.

34. David Lauter, "Mexico Leader Scolds Quayle Over Abduction," *The Los Angeles Times*, April 27, 1990.

35. Ronald J. Ostrow, "Ruling Backs U.S. Forces' Police Role," *The Los Angeles Times*, Dec. 17, 1989.

36. Robin Wright, "U.S. in New Bid to Oust Noriega," *The Los Angeles Times*, Nov. 16, 1989.

37. Quoted in Doyle McManus, "U.S. Fund Gives $433,000 to Opponents of Costa Rica Leader's Policies," *The Los Angeles Times*, Oct. 14, 1989.

38. Art Pine, "Political Changes Abroad Creating Heavy Demand for U.S. Aid," *The Los Angeles Times*, Dec. 23, 1989.

39. Friedberg, pp. 408–409.

40. Pietro S. Nivola, "The New Protectionism: U.S. Trade Policy in Historical Perspective," *Political Science Quarterly* 4 (1986), 577–600.

41. Hedrick Smith, *The Power Game* (New York: Random House, 1988), p. 199.

42. Quoted in Smith, pp. 196–197.

43. Smith, p. 213.

44. John M. Broder, "Pentagon Probe Figure Admits Bribing Paisley," *The Los Angeles Times*, March 29, 1990.

45. David Halberstam, *The Next Century* (New York: William Morrow and Company, 1991), p. 70.

46. Quoted in Smith, p. 208.

47. Daniel M. Weintraub and Melissa Healy, "Scandal's Roots Traced to Basic Reagan Policy Goals," *The Los Angeles Times*, July 4, 1988.

48. Charles Peters, *How Washington Really Works* (Reading, MA: Addison-Wesley, 1980), p. 78.

49. Weintraub and Healy, "Scandal's Roots Traced to Basic Reagan Policy Goals," *The Los Angeles Times*, July 4, 1988.

50. Ronald J. Ostrow and Robert L. Jackson, "U.S. Agency 'Watchdogs' More Like 'Lap Dogs,' Senators Say," *The Los Angeles Times*, Sept. 9, 1990.

51. Thomas B. Rosenstile, "Rule May Curb Press's Use of Secret Sources," *The Los Angeles Times*, Aug. 4, 1989.

52. Ralph Vartabedian, "Under the Gun: Arms and Fraud," *The Los Angeles Times*, May 9, 1990.

53. See Karl von Clausewitz, *On War*, edited by Anatol Rapoport (Harmondsworth, England: Pelican 1974).

54. Robert Jervis, "The Nuclear Revolution and the Common Defense," *Political Science Quarterly* 5 (1986), 692–694.

55. Robert C. Toth, "Planners Split on How to Meet Nuclear Threat," *The Los Angeles Times*, July 24, 1989.

56. "MX Missiles to be Placed on Trains, Kept in Six States," *The Los Angeles Times,* Nov. 30, 1989.

57. Ralph Vartabedian, "Why Did AF End Stealth on Stealth?" *The Los Angeles Times,* Aug. 2, 1989.

58. Paul Houston, "House Rejects Bush's Plan on B-2 Bomber, 'Star Wars,'" *The Los Angeles Times,* May 22, 1991.

59. Sara Fritz, "Stealth Bomber Funding Backed," *The Los Angeles Times,* July 26, 1989.

60. Melissa Healy, " 'Star Wars' Program Gets New Focus," *The Los Angeles Times,* Jan. 30, 1991.

61. Ralph Vartabedian, "Old Troubles Cast Shadow on New 'Star Wars' Image," *The Los Angeles Times,* Mar. 10, 1991.

62. Jay Peterzell and Bruce van Voorst, "How Much Is Too Much?" *Time,* Feb. 12, 1990, p. 21.

63. Robert C. Toth, "Soviets Also Sent Banned Missiles to Bulgaria," *The Los Angeles Times,* March 27, 1990.

64. John M. Broder, "Cheney Proposes Cutting Costs by Closing 31 Bases," *The Los Angeles Times,* Apr. 13, 1991.

65. *Rostker* v. *Goldberg,* 453 U.S. 57 (1981).

66. Marlene Cimons, "Women in Combat: Panama Stirs Debate," *The Los Angeles Times,* Jan. 11, 1990.

67. John M. Broder, "House Panel OKs Combat Role for Women," *The Los Angeles Times,* May 9, 1991.

68. Ronald Brownstein, "Volunteer Force: Is It Truly Fair?" *The Los Angeles Times,* Dec. 6, 1990.

69. Melissa Healy, "1992 Defense Budget to Continue Military Cutbacks Despite Gulf War," *The Los Angeles Times,* Feb. 1, 1991.

70. Melissa Healy, "Putting a Price Tag on War Proves to Be a Battle in Itself," *The Los Angeles Times,* May 31, 1991.

Suggestions for Further Reading

Bell, Daniel, and Lester Thurow. *The Deficits: How Big? How Long? How Dangerous?.* New York: New York University Press, 1985.

Bialer, Seweryn, and Michael Mandelbaum. *The Global Rivals.* New York: Knopf, 1988.

Cohen, Eliot. *Citizens and Soldiers.* Ithaca: Cornell University Press, 1985.

Dougherty, James, and Robert Pfaltzgraff. *American Foreign Policy: FDR to Reagan.* New York: Harper & Row, 1986.

Franck, Thomas M., and Edward Weisband. *Word Politics.* New York: Oxford University Press, 1972.

Goldwin, Robert A., and Harry M. Clor. *Readings in American Foreign Policy* (2nd ed.). London: Oxford University Press, 1971.

Hadley, Arthur T. *The Straw Giant.* New York: Random House, 1986.

Hilsman, Roger. *The Politics of Policymaking in Defense and Foreign Affairs.* Englewood Cliffs, NJ: Prentice-Hall, 1987.

Kegley, Charles W. *International Terrorism.* New York: St. Martin's Press, 1990.

Kennedy, Paul. *The Rise and Fall of the Great Powers.* New York: Random House, 1987.

Kennedy, Robert F. *Thirteen Days: A Memoir of the Cuban Missile Crisis.* New York: Norton, 1971.

Kim, Young Hum. *The Central Intelligence Agency: Problems of Secrecy in a Democracy.* Lexington, MA: Heath, 1968.

Levy, Frank. *Dollars and Dreams: The Changing American Income Distribution.* New York: Basic Books, 1987.

McCormick, James M. *American Foreign Policy and American Values.* Itasca, IL: F. E. Peacock, 1985.

Payne, Keith B. *Strategic Defense: "Star Wars" In Perspective.* Lanham, MD: Hamilton Press, 1986.

Rourke, John T. *International Politics on the World Stage* (2nd ed.). Sluice Dock, CT: Dushkin, 1989.

Scheer, Robert. *With Enough Shovels: Reagan, Bush and Nuclear War.* New York: Random House, 1982.

Woodward, Bob. *Veil: The Secret Wars of the CIA: 1981-1987.* New York: Simon & Schuster, 1987.

APPENDIX

The Declaration of Independence

The Articles of Confederation

The Constitution of the United States

The Federalist Papers

THE DECLARATION OF INDEPENDENCE

IN CONGRESS, JULY 4, 1776

The unanimous Declaration of the thirteen united States of America,

When in the Course of human events, it becomes necessary for one people to dissolve the political bands which have connected them with another, and to assume among the Powers of the earth, the separate and equal station to which the Laws of Nature and of Nature's God entitle them, a decent respect to the opinions of mankind requires that they should declare the causes which impel them to the separation.

We hold these truths to be self-evident, that all men are created equal, that they are endowed by their Creator with certain unalienable Rights, that among these are Life, Liberty and the pursuit of Happiness. That to secure these rights, Governments are instituted among Men, deriving their just powers from the consent of the governed. That whenever any Form of Government becomes destructive of these ends, it is the Right of the People to alter or to abolish it, and to institute new Government, laying its foundation on such principles and organizing its powers in such form, as to them shall seem most likely to effect their Safety and Happiness. Prudence, indeed, will dictate that Governments long established should not be changed for light and transient causes; and accordingly all experience hath shown, that mankind are more disposed to suffer, while evils are sufferable, than to right themselves by abolishing the forms to which they are accustomed. But when a long train of abuses and usurpations, pursuing invariably the same Object evinces a design to reduce them under absolute Despotism, it is their right, it is their duty, to throw off such Government, and to provide new Guards for their future security.—Such has been the patient sufference of these Colonies; and such is now the necessity which constrains them to alter their former Systems of Government. The history of the present King of Great Britain is a history of repeated injuries and usurpations, all having in direct object the establishment of an absolute Tyranny over these States. To prove this, let Facts be submitted to a candid world.

He has refused his Assent to Laws, the most wholesome and necessary for the public good.

He has forbidden his Governors to pass Laws of immediate and pressing importance, unless suspended in their operation till his Assent should be obtained; and when so suspended, he has utterly neglected to attend to them.

He has refused to pass other Laws for the accommodation of large districts of people, unless those people would relinquish the right of Representation in the Legislature, a right inestimable to them and formidable to tyrants only.

He has called together legislative bodies at places unusual, uncomfortable, and distant from the depository of their Public Records, for the sole purpose of fatiguing them into compliance with his measures.

He has dissolved Representative Houses repeatedly, for opposing with manly firmness his invasions on the rights of the people.

He has refused for a long time, after such dissolutions, to cause others to be elected; whereby the Legislative Powers, incapable of Annihilation, have returned to the People at large for their exercise; the State remaining in the meantime exposed to all the dangers of invasion from without, and convulsions within.

He has endeavoured to prevent the population of these States; for that purpose obstructing the Laws for Naturalization of Foreigners; refusing to pass others to encourage their migrations hither, and raising the conditions of new Appropriations of Lands.

He has obstructed the Administration of Justice, by refusing his Assent to Laws for establishing Judiciary Powers.

He has made Judges dependent on his Will alone, for the tenure of their offices, and the amount and payment of their salaries.

He has erected a multitude of New Offices, and sent hither swarms of Officers to harass our people; and eat out their substance.

He has kept among us, in times of peace, Standing Armies without the Consent of our legislatures.

He has affected to render the Military independent of and superior to the Civil Power.

He has combined with others to subject us to a jurisdiction foreign to our constitution, and unacknowledged by our laws; giving his Assent to their acts of pretended Legislation:

For quartering large bodies of armed troops among us:

For protecting them, by a mock Trial, from Punishment for any Murders which they should commit on the inhabitants of these States:

For cutting off our Trade with all parts of the world:

For imposing taxes on us without our Consent:

For depriving us in many cases, of the benefits of Trial of Jury:

For transporting us beyond Seas to be tried for pretended offences:

For abolishing the free System of English Laws in a neighboring Province, establishing therein an Arbitrary government, and enlarging its Boundaries so as to render it at once an example and fit instrument for introducing the same absolute rule into these Colonies:

For taking away our Charters, abolishing our most valuable Laws, and altering fundamentally the Forms of our Governments:

For suspending our own Legislatures, and declaring themselves invested with Power to legislate for us in all cases whatsoever.

He has abdicated Government here, by declaring us out of his Protection and waging War against us.

He has plundered our seas, ravaged our Coasts, burnt our towns, and destroyed the lives of our people.

He is at this time transporting large armies of foreign mercenaries to compleat the works of death, desolation and tyranny, already begun with circumstances of Cruelty & perfidy scarcely paralleled in the most barbarous ages, and totally unworthy the Head of a civilized nation.

He has constrained our fellow Citizens taken Captive on the high Seas to bear Arms against their Country, to become the executioners of their friends and Brethren, or to fall themselves by their Hands.

He has excited domestic insurrections amongst us, and has endeavoured to bring on the inhabitants of our frontiers, the merciless Indian Savages, whose known rule of warfare, is an undistinguished destruction of all ages, sexes and conditions.

In every stage of these Oppressions We have Petitioned for Redress in the most humble terms: Our repeated Petitions have been answered only by repeated injury. A Prince, whose character is thus marked by every act which may define a Tyrant, is unfit to be the ruler of a free people.

Nor have We been wanting in attentions to our British brethren. We have warned them from time to time of attempts by their legislature to extend an unwarrantable jurisdiction over us. We have reminded them of the circumstances of our emigration and settlement here. We have appealed to their native justice and magnanimity, and we have conjured them by the ties of our common kindred to disavow these usurpations which, would inevitably interrupt our connections and correspondence. They too have been deaf to the voice of justice and of consanguinity. We must, therefore, acquiesce in the necessity, which denounces our Separation, and hold them, as we hold the rest of mankind, Enemies in War, in Peace Friends.

We, therefore, the Representatives of the united States of America, in General Congress, Assembled, appealing to the Supreme Judge of the world for the rectitude of our intentions, do, in the Name, and by authority of the good People of these Colonies, solemnly publish and declare, That these United Colonies are, and of Right ought to be Free and Independent States; that they are Absolved from all Allegiance to the British Crown, and that all political connection between them and the State of Great Britain, is and ought to be totally dissolved; and that as Free and Independent States, they have full power to levy War, conclude Peace, contract Alliances, establish Commerce, and to do all other Acts and Things which Independent States may of right do. And for the support of this Declaration, with a firm reliance on the Protection of Divine Providence, we mutually pledge to each other our Lives, our Fortunes and our sacred Honor.

John Hancock
(Massachusetts)

New Hampshire
Josiah Bartlett
William Whipple
Matthew Thornton

Massachusetts
Samuel Adams
John Adams
Robert Treat Paine
Elbridge Gerry

Delaware
Caesar Rodney
George Read
Thomas McKean

New York
William Floyd
Philip Livingston
Francis Lewis
Lewis Morris

New Jersey
Richard Stockton
John Witherspoon
Francis Hopkinson
John Hart
Abraham Clark

North Carolina
William Hooper
Joseph Hewes
John Penn

Maryland
Samuel Chase
William Paca
Thomas Stone
Charles Carroll
  of Carrollton

South Carolina
Edward Rutledge
Thomas Heywood, Jr.
Thomas Lynch, Jr.
Arthur Middleton

Rhode Island
Stephen Hopkins
William Ellery

Connecticut
Roger Sherman
Samuel Huntington
William Williams
Oliver Wolcott

Pennsylvania
Robert Morris
Benjamin Rush
Benjamin Franklin
John Morton
George Clymer
James Smith
George Taylor
James Wilson
George Ross

Virginia
George Wythe
Richard Henry Lee
Thomas Jefferson
Benjamin Harrison
Thomas Nelson, Jr.
Francis Lightfoot Lee
Carter Braxton

Georgia
Button Gwinnett
Lyman Hall
George Walton

THE ARTICLES OF CONFEDERATION
AND PERPETUAL UNION

BETWEEN THE STATES OF NEW HAMPSHIRE, MASSACHUSETTS BAY, RHODE ISLAND AND PROVIDENCE PLANTATIONS, CONNECTICUT, NEW YORK, NEW JERSEY, PENNSYLVANIA, DELAWARE, MARYLAND, VIRGINIA, NORTH CAROLINA, SOUTH CAROLINA, GEORGIA.

ARTICLE 1   The stile of this confederacy shall be "The United States of America."

ARTICLE 2   Each State retains its sovereignty, freedom and independence, and every power, jurisdiction, and right, which is not by this confederation expressly delegated to the United States, in Congress assembled.

ARTICLE 3   The said states hereby severally enter into a firm league of friendship with each other for their common defence, the security of their liberties and their mutual and general welfare; binding themselves to assist each other against all force offered to, or attacks made upon them, or any of them, on account of religion, sovereignty, trade, or any other pretence whatever.

ARTICLE 4   The better to secure and perpetuate mutual friendship and intercourse among the people of the different states in this union, the free inhabitants of each of these states, paupers, vagbonds, and fugitives from justice excepted, shall be entitled to all privileges and immunities of free citizens in the several states; and the people of each State shall have free ingress and regress to and from any other State, and shall enjoy therein all the privileges of trade and commerce, subject to the same duties, impositions, and restrictions, as the inhabitants thereof respectively; provided, that such restrictions shall not extend so far as to prevent the removal of property, imported into any State, to any other State of which the owner is an inhabitant; provided also, that no imposition, duties, or restriction, shall be laid by any State on the property of the United States, or either of them.

If any person guilty of, or charged with treason, felony, or other high misdemeanor in any State, shall flee from justice and be found in any of the United States, he shall, upon demand of the governor or executive power of the State from which he fled, be delivered up and removed to the State having jurisdiction of his offence.

Full faith and credit shall be given in each of these states to the records, acts, and judicial proceedings of the courts and magistrates of every other State.

ARTICLE 5   For the more convenient management of the general interests of the United States, delegates shall be annually appointed, in such manner as the legislature of each State shall direct, to meet in Congress, on the 1st Monday in November in every year, with a power reserved to each State to recal its delegates, or any of them, at any time within the year, and to send others in their stead for the remainder of the year.

No State shall be represented in Congress by less than two, nor by more than seven members; and no person shall be capable of being a delegate for more than three years in any term of six years; nor shall any person, being a delegate, be capable of holding any office under the United States, for which he, or any other for his benefit, receives any salary, fees, or emolument of any kind.

Each State shall maintain its own delegates in a meeting of the states, and while they act as members of the committee of the states.

In determining questions in the United States, in Congress assembled, each State shall have one vote.

Freedom of speech and debate in Congress shall not be impeached or questioned in any court or place out of Congress: and the members of Congress shall be protected in their persons from arrests and imprisonments, during the time of their going to and from, and attendance on Congress, *except for treason,* felony, or breach of the peace.

ARTICLE 6   No State, without the consent of the United States, in Congress assembled, shall send any embassay to, or receive any embassy from, or enter into any conference, agreement, alliance, or treaty with any king, prince, or state; nor shall any person, holding any office of profit or trust under the United States, or any of them, accept of any present, emolument, office or title, of any kind whatever, from any king, prince, or foreign state; nor shall the United States, in Congress assembled, or any of them, grant any title of nobility.

No two or more states shall enter into any treaty, confederation, or alliance, whatever, between them, without the consent of the United States, in Congress assembled, specifying accurately the purposes for which the same is to be entered into, and how long it shall continue.

No state shall lay any imposts or duties which may interfere with any stipulations in treaties entered into by the United States, in Congress assembled, with any king, prince, or state, in pursuance of any treaties already proposed by Congress to the courts of France and Spain.

No vessels of war shall be kept up in time of peace by any State, except such number only as shall be deemed necessary by the United States, in Congress assembled, for the defence of such State or its trade; nor shall any body of forces be kept up by any State, in time of peace, except such number only as, in the judgment of the United States, in Congress assembled, shall be deemed requisite to garrison the forts necessary for the defence of such State; but every State shall always keep up a well regulated and disciplined militia, sufficiently armed and accoutred, and shall provide, and constantly have ready for use, in public stores, a due number of field pieces and tents, and a proper quantity of arms, ammunition and camp equipage.

No State shall engage in any war without the consent of the United States, in Congress assembled, unless such State be actually invaded by enemies, or shall have received certain advice of a resolution being formed by some nation of Indians to invade such State, and the danger is so imminent as not to admit of a delay till the United States, in Congress assembled, can be consulted; nor shall any State grant commissions to any ships or vessels of war, nor letters of marque or reprisal, except it be after a declaration of war by the United States, in Congress assembled, and then only against the kingdom or state, and the subjects thereof, against which war has been so declared, and under such regulations as shall be established by the United States, in Congress assembled, unless such State be infested by pirates, in which case vessels of war may be fitted out for that occasion, and kept so long as the danger shall continue, or until the United States, in Congress assembled, shall determine otherwise.

ARTICLE 7   When land forces are raised by any State for the common defence, all officers of or under the rank of colonel, shall be appointed by the legislature of each State respectively, by whom such forces shall be raised, or in such manner as such State shall direct; and all vacancies shall be filled up by the State which first made the appointment.

ARTICLE 8   All charges of war and all other expences, that shall be incurred for the common defence or general welfare, and allowed by the United States, in Congress assembled, shall be defrayed out of a common treasury, which shall be supplied by the several states, in proportion to the value of all land within each State, granted to or surveyed for any person, as such land and the buildings and improvements thereon shall be estimated according to such mode as the United States, in Congress assembled, shall, from time to time, direct and appoint.

The taxes for paying that proportion shall be laid and levied by the authority and direction of the legislatures of the several states, within the time agreed upon by the United States, in Congress assembled.

ARTICLE 9   The United States, in Congress assembled, shall have the sole and exclusive right and power of determining on peace and war, except in the cases mentioned in the 6th article; of sending and receiving ambassadors; entering into treaties and alliances, provided that no treaty of commerce shall be made, whereby the legislative power of the respective states shall be restrained from imposing such imposts and duties on foreigners as their own people are subjected to, or from prohibiting the exportation or importation of any species of goods or commodities whatsoever; of establishing rules for deciding, in all cases, what captures on land or water shall be legal, and in what manner prizes, taken by land or naval forces in the service of the United States, shall be divided or appropriated; of granting letters of marque and reprisal in times of peace; appointing courts for the trial of piracies and felonies committed on the high seas, and establishing courts for receiving and determining, finally, appeals in all cases of captures; provided, that no member of Congress shall be appointed a judge of any of the said courts.

The United States, in Congress assembled, shall also be the last resort on appeal in all disputes and differences now subsisting, or that hereafter may arise between two or more states concerning boundary, jurisdiction or any other cause whatever; which authority shall always be exercised in the manner following:

whenever the legislative or executive authority, or lawful agent of any State, in controversy with another, shall present a petition to Congress, stating the matter in question, and praying for a hearing, notice thereof shall be given, by order of Congress, to the legislative or executive authority of the other State in controversy, and a day assigned for the appearance of the parties by their lawful agents, who shall then be directed to appoint, by joint consent, commissioners or judges to constitute a court for hearing and determining the matter in question; but, if they cannot agree, Congress shall name three persons out of each of the United States, and from the list of such persons each party shall alternately strike out one, the petitioners beginning, until the number shall be reduced to thirteen; and from that number not less than seven, nor more than nine names, as Congress shall direct, shall, in the presence of Congress, be drawn out by lot; and the persons whose names shall be so drawn, or any five of them, shall be commissioners or judges to hear and finally determine the controversy, so always as a major part of the judges who shall hear the cause shall agree in the determination; and if either party shall neglect to attend at the day appointed, without shewing reasons which Congress shall judge sufficient, or, being present, shall refuse to strike, the Congress shall proceed to nominate three persons out of each State, and the secretary of congress shall strike in behalf of such party absent or refusing; and the judgment and sentence of the court to be appointed, in the manner before prescribed, shall be final and conclusive; and if any of the parties shall refuse to submit to the authority of such court, or to appear or defend their claim or cause, the court shall nevertheless proceed to pronounce sentence or judgment, which shall, in like manner, be final and decisive, the judgment or sentence and other proceedings being, in either case, transmitted to Congress, and lodged among the acts of Congress for the security of the parties concerned: provided, that every commissioner, before he sits in judgment, shall take an oath, to be administered by one of the judges of the supreme or superior court of the State where the cause shall be tried, "well and truly to hear and determine the matter in question, according to the best of his judgment, without favour, affection, or hope of reward:" provided, also, that no State shall be deprived of territory for the benefit of the United States.

All controversies concerning the private right of soil, claimed under different grants of two or more states, whose jurisdictions, as they may respect such lands and the states which passed such grants, are adjusted, the said grants, or either of them, being at the same time claimed to have originated antecedent to such settlement of jurisdiction, shall, on the petition of either party to the Congress of the United States, be finally determined, as near as may be, in the same manner as is before prescribed for deciding disputes respecting territorial jurisdiction between different states.

The United States, in Congress assembled, shall also have the sole and exclusive right and power of regulating the alloy and value of coin struck by their own authority, or by that of the respective states; fixing the standard of weights and measures throughout the United States; regulating the trade and managing all affairs with the Indians not members of any of the states; provided that the legislative right of any State within its own limits be not infringed or violated; establishing and regulating post offices from one State to another throughout all the United States, and exacting such postage on the papers passing through the same as may be requisite to defray the expences of the said office; appointing all officers of the land forces in the service of the United States, excepting regimental officers; appointing all the officers of the naval forces, and commissioning all officers whatever in the service of the United States; making rules for the government and regulation of the said land and naval forces, and directing their operations.

The United States, in Congress assembled, shall have authority to appoint a committee to sit in the recess of Congress, to be denominated "a Committee of the States," and to consist of one delegate from each State, and to appoint such other committees and civil officers as may be necessary for managing the general affairs of the United States, under their direction; to appoint one of their number to preside; provided that no person be allowed to serve in the office of president more than one year in any term of three years; to ascertain the necessary sums of money to be raised for the service of the United States, and to appropriate and apply the same for defraying the public expences; to borrow money or emit bills on the credit of the United States, transmitting, every half year, to the respective states, an account of the sums of money so borrowed or emitted; to build and equip a navy; to agree upon the number of land forces, and to make requisitions from each State for its quota, in proportion to the number of white inhabitants in such State; which requisitions shall be binding; and, thereupon, the legislature of each State shall appoint the regimental officers, raise the men, and cloathe, arm, and equip them in a soldier-like manner, at the expence of the United States; and the officers and men so cloathed, armed, and equipped, shall march to the place appointed and within the time agreed on by the United States, in Congress assembled; but if the United States, in Congress assembled, shall, on consideration of circumstances, judge proper that any State should not raise men, or should raise a smaller number than its quota, and that any other State should raise a greater number of men than the quota thereof, such extra number shall be raised, officered, cloathed, armed, and equipped in the same manner as the quota of such State, unless the legislature of such State shall judge that such extra number cannot be safely spared out of the same, in which case they shall raise, officer, cloathe, arm, and equip as many of such extra number as they judge can be safely spared. And the officers and men so cloathed, armed, and equipped, shall march to the place appointed and within the time agreed on by the United States, in Congress assembled.

The United States, in Congress assembled, shall never engage in a war, nor grant letters of marque and reprisal in time of peace, nor enter into any treaties or alliances, nor coin money, nor regulate the value thereof, nor ascertain the sums and expences necessary for the defence and welfare of the United States, or any of them: nor emit bills, nor borrow money on the credit of the United States, nor appropriate money, nor agree upon the number of vessels of war to be built or purchased, or the number of land or sea forces to be raised, nor appoint a commander in chief of the army or navy, unless nine states assent to the same; nor shall a question on any other point, except for adjourning from day to day, be determined, unless by the votes of a majority of the United States, in Congress assembled.

The Congress of the United States shall have power to adjourn to any time within the year, and to any place within the United States, so that no period of adjournment be for a longer duration than the space of six months, and shall publish the journal of their proceedings monthly, except such parts thereof, relating to treaties, alliances or military operations, as, in their judgment, require secrecy; and the yeas and nays of the delegates of each State on any question shall be entered on the journal, when it is desired by any delegate; and the delegates of a State, or any of them, at his, or their request, shall be furnished with a transcript of the said journal, except such parts as are above excepted, to lay before the legislatures of the several states.

ARTICLE 10   The committee of the states, or any nine of them, shall be authorized to execute, in the recess of Congress, such of the powers of Congress as the United States, in Congress assembled, by the consent of nine states, shall, from time to time, think expedient to vest them with; provided, that no power be delegated to the said committee, for the exercise of which, by the articles of confederation, the voice of nine states, in the Congress of the United States assembled, is requisite.

ARTICLE 11   Canada acceding to this confederation, and joining in the measures of the United States, shall be admitted into and entitled to all the advantages of this union; but no other colony shall be admitted into the same, unless such admission be agreed to by nine states.

ARTICLE 12   All bills of credit emitted, monies borrowed and debts contracted by, or under the authority of Congress before the assembling of the United States, in pursuance of the present confederation, shall be deemed and considered as a charge against the United States, for payment and satisfaction whereof the said United States and the public faith are hereby solemnly pledged.

ARTICLE 13   Every State shall abide by the determinations of the United States, in Congress assembled, on all questions which, by this confederation, are submitted to them. And the articles of this confederation shall be inviolably observed by every State, and the union shall be perpetual; nor shall any alteration at any time hereafter be made in any of them, unless such alteration be agreed to in a Congress of the United States, and be afterwards confirmed by the legislatures of every State.

These articles shall be proposed to the legislatures of all the United States, to be considered, and if approved of by them, they are advised to authorize their delegates to ratify the same in the Congress of the United States, which being done, the same shall become conclusive.

Signatories of the Articles of Confederation

New Hampshire
Josiah Bartlett
John Wentworth, Junr

Massachusetts
John Hancock
Samuel Adams
Elbridge Gerry
Francis Dana
James Lovell
Samuel Holten

Rhode Island
William Ellery
Henry Marchant
John Collins

Connecticut
Roger Sherman
Samuel Huntington
Oliver Wolcott
Titus Hosmer
Andrew Adams

New York
Jas. Duane
Fra. Lewis
Gouv. Morris
Wm. Duer

New Jersey
Jno. Witherspoon
Nathl. Scudder

Pennsylvania
Robert Morris
Daniel Roberdeau
Jno. Bayard Smith
William Clingan
Joseph Reed

Delaware
Thos. M'Kean
Nicholas Van Dyke
John Dickinson

Maryland
John Hanson
Daniel Carroll

Virginia
Richard Henry Lee
John Banister
Thomas Adams
Jno. Harvie
Francis Lightfoot Lee

North Carolina
John Penn
Corns. Harnett
Jno. Williams

South Carolina
Henry Laurens
William Henry Drayton
Jno. Matthews
Thos. Heyward Junr

Georgia
Edward Telfair
Jno. Walton
Edwd. Langworthy

THE CONSTITUTION OF THE UNITED STATES

WE THE PEOPLE OF THE UNITED STATES, IN ORDER TO FORM A MORE PERFECT UNION, ESTABLISH JUSTICE, INSURE DOMESTIC TRANQUILITY, PROVIDE FOR THE COMMON DEFENSE, PROMOTE THE GENERAL WELFARE, AND SECURE THE BLESSINGS OF LIBERTY TO OURSELVES AND OUR POSTERITY, DO ORDAIN AND ESTABLISH THIS CONSTITUTION FOR THE UNITED STATES OF AMERICA.

ARTICLE 1

Section 1. All legislative Powers herein granted shall be vested in a Congress of the United States, which shall consist of a Senate and House of Representatives.

Section 2. The House of Representatives shall be composed of members chosen every second Year by the People of the several States, and the Electors in each State shall have the Qualifications requisite for Electors of the most numerous Branch of the State Legislature.

No person shall be a representative who shall not have attained to the Age of twenty five Years, and been seven Years a Citizen of the United States, and who shall not, when elected, be an Inhabitant of that State in which he shall be chosen.

Representatives and direct Taxes shall be apportion among the several States which may be included within this union, according to their respective Numbers, which shall be determined by adding to the whole Number of free Persons, including those bound to Service for a Term of Years, and excluding Indians not taxed, three fifths of all other Persons. The actual Enumeration shall be made within three Years after the first Meeting of the Congress of the United States, and within every subsequent Term of ten Years, in such Manner as they shall by Law direct. The Number of Representatives shall not exceed one for every thirty Thousand, but each State shall have at Least one Representative; and until such enumeration shall be made, the State of New Hampshire shall be entitled to chuse three, Massachusetts eight, Rhode-Island and Providence Plantations one, Connecticut five, New York six, New Jersey four, Pennsylvania eight, Delaware one, Maryland six, Virginia ten, North Carolina five, South Carolina five, and Georgia three.

When vacancies happen in the Representation from any State, the Executive Authority thereof shall issue Writs of Election to fill such Vacancies.

The House of Representatives shall chuse their speaker and other Officers; and shall have the sole Power of Impeachment.

Section 3. The Senate of the United States shall be composed of two Senators from each State, chosen by the Legislature thereof, for six Years; and each Senator shall have one Vote.

Immediately after they shall be assembled in Consequence of the first Election, they shall be divided as equally as may be into three Classes. The Seats of the Senators of the first Class shall be vacated at the Expiration of the second Year, of the second Class at the Expiration of the fourth Year, and of the third Class at the Expiration of the sixth Year, so that one third may be chosen every second Year; and if Vacancies happen by Resignation, or otherwise, during the Recess of the Legislature of any State, the Executive thereof may take temporary Appointments until the next Meeting of the Legislature, which shall then fill such Vacancies.

No Person shall be a Senator who shall not have attained to the Age of thirty Years, and been nine Years a Citizen of the United States, and who shall not, when elected, be an Inhabitant of that State for which he shall be chosen.

The Vice President of the United States shall be President of the Senate, but shall have no Vote, unless they be equally divided.

The Senate shall chuse their other Officers, and also a President pro tempore, in the Absence of the Vice President, or when he shall exercise the Office of the President of the United States.

The Senate shall have the sole Power to try all Impeachments. When sitting for that Purpose, they shall be on Oath of Affirmation. When the President of the United States is tried, the Chief Justice shall preside: And no Person shall be convicted without the Concurrence of two thirds of the Members present.

Judgment in Cases of Impeachment shall not extend further than to removal from Office, and disqualification to hold and enjoy any Office of honor, Trust or Profit under the United States: but the Party convicted shall nevertheless be liable and subject to Indictment, Trial, Judgment and Punishment, according to law.

Section 4.   The Times, Places and Manner of holding Elections for Senators and Representatives, shall be prescribed in each State by the Legislature thereof; but the Congress may at any time by Law make or alter such regulations, except as to the Places of chusing Senators.

The Congress shall assemble at least once in every Year, and such Meeting shall be on the first Monday in December, unless they shall by Law appoint a different Day.

Section 5.   Each House shall be the Judge of the Elections, Returns and Qualifications of its own Members, and a Majority of each shall constitute a Quorum to do Business; but a smaller Number may adjourn from day to day, and may be authorized to compel the Attendance of absent Members, in such Manner, and under such Penalties as each House may provide.

Each House may determine the Rules for its Proceedings, punish its Members for disorderly Behaviour, and, with the Concurrence of two thirds, expel a Member.

Each House shall keep a Journal of its Proceedings, and from time to time publish the same, excepting such Parts as may in their Judgment require Secrecy; and the Yeas and Nays of the Members of either House on any question shall, at the Desire of one fifth of those Present, be entered on the Journal.

Neither House, during the Session of Congress, shall, without the Consent of the other, adjourn for more than three days, nor to any other Place than that in which the two Houses shall be sitting.

Section 6. The Senators and Representatives shall receive a Compensation for their Services, to be ascertained by Law, and paid out of the Treasury of the United States. They shall in all Cases, except Treason, Felony and Breach of the Peace, be privileged from Arrest during their Attendance at the Session of their respective Houses, and in going to and returning from the same; and for any Speech or Debate in either House, they shall not be questioned in any other Place.

No Senator or Representative shall, during the Time for which he was elected, be appointed to any civil Office under the Authority of the United States, which shall have been created, or the Emoluments whereof shall have been encreased during such time; and no Person holding any Office under the United States, shall be a Member of either House during his Continuance in Office.

Section 7. All Bills for raising Revenue shall originate in the House of Representatives; but the Senate may propose or concur with Amendments as on other Bills.

Every Bill which shall have passed the House of Representatives and the Senate, shall, before it become a Law, be presented to the President of the United States; If he approve he shall sign it, but if not he shall return it, with his Objections to that House in which it shall have originated, who shall enter the Objections at large on their Journal, and proceed to reconsider it. If after such Reconsideration two thirds of that House shall agree to pass the Bill, it shall be sent, together with the Objections, to the other House, by which it shall likewise be reconsidered, and if approved by two thirds of that House, it shall become a Law. But in all such Cases the Votes of both Houses shall be determined by Yeas and Nays, and the Names of the Persons voting for and against the Bill shall be entered on the Journal of each House respectively. If any Bill shall not be returned by the president within ten Days (Sundays excepted) after it shall have been presented to him, the Same shall be a Law, in like Manner as if he had signed it, unless the Congress by their Adjournment prevent its Return, in which Case it shall not be a Law.

Every Order, Resolution, or Vote to which the Concurrence of the Senate and House of Representatives may be necessary (except on a question of Adjournment) shall be presented to the President of the United States; and before the Same shall take Effect, shall be approved by him, or being disapproved by him, shall be repassed by two thirds of the Senate and House of Representatives, according to the Rules and Limitations prescribed in the Case of a Bill.

Section 8. The Congress shall have Power To lay and collect Taxes, Duties, Imposts and Excises, to pay the Debts and provide for the common Defence and general Welfare of the United States; but all Duties, Imposts and Excises shall be uniform throughout the United States;

To borrow Money on the credit of the United States;

To regulate Commerce with foreign Nations, and among the several States, and with the Indian Tribes;

To establish an uniform Rule of Naturalization, and uniform Laws on the subject of Bankruptcies throughout the United States;

To coin Money, regulate the Value thereof, and of foreign Coin, and fix the Standard of Weights and Measures;

To provide for the Punishment of counterfeiting the Securities and current Coin of the United States;

To establish Post Offices and post Roads;

To promote the Progress of Science and useful Arts, by securing for limited Times to Authors and Inventors the exclusive Right to their respective Writings and Discoveries;

To constitute Tribunals inferior to the supreme Court;

To define and punish Piracies and Felonies committed on the high Seas, and Offences against the Law of Nations;

To declare War, grant Letters of Marque and Reprisal, and make Rules concerning Captures on Land and Water;

To raise and support Armies, but no Appropriation of Money to that Use shall be for a longer Term than two Years;

To provide and maintain a Navy;

To make Rules for the Government and Regulation of the land and naval Forces;

To provide for calling forth the Militia to execute the Laws of the Union, suppress Insurrections and repel Invasions;

To provide for organizing, arming, and disciplining, the Militia, and for governing such Part of them as may be employed in the Service of the United States, reserving to the States respectively, the Appointment of the Officers, and the Authority of training the Militia according to the discipline prescribed by Congress;

To exercise exclusive Legislation in all Cases whatsoever, over such District (not exceeding ten Miles square) as may, by Cession of particular States, and the Acceptance of Congress, become the Seat of the Government of the United States, and to exercise like Authority over all Places purchased by the Consent of the Legislature of the State in which the Same shall be for the Erection of Forts, Magazines, Arsenals, dock-Yards, and other needful Buildings;-And

To make all Laws which shall be necessary and proper for carrying into Execution the foregoing Powers, and all other Powers vested by this Constitution in the Government of the United States, or in any Department or Officer thereof.

Section 9. The Migration or Importation of such Persons as any of the

States now existing shall think proper to admit, shall not be prohibited by the Congress prior to the Year one thousand eight hundred and eight, but a Tax or duty may be imposed on such Importation, not exceeding ten dollars for each Person.

The Privilege of the Writ of Habeas Corpus shall not be suspended, unless when in Cases of Rebellion or Invasion the public Safety may require it.

No Bill of Attainder or ex post facto Law shall be passed.

No Capitation, or other direct, Tax shall be laid, unless in Proportion to the Census or Enumeration herein before directed to be taken.

No Tax or Duty shall be laid on Articles exported from any State.

No Preference shall be given by any Regulation of Commerce or Revenue to the Ports of one State over those of another: nor shall Vessels bound to, or from, one State be obliged to enter, clear, or pay Duties in another.

No money shall be drawn from the Treasury, but in Consequence of Appropriations made by Law; and a regular Statement and Account of the Receipts and Expenditures of all public Money shall be published from time to time.

No Title of Nobility shall be granted by the United States: And no Person holding any office of Profit or Trust under them, shall, without the Consent of the Congress, accept of any present, Emolument, Office, or Title, of any kind whatever, from any King, Prince, or foreign States.

Section 10. No State shall enter into any Treaty, Alliance, or Confederation; grant Letters of Marque and Treaty; Alliance, or Confederation; grant Letters of Marque and Reprisal; coin Money; emit Bills of Credit; make any Thing but gold and silver Coin a Tender in Payment of Debts; pass any Bill of Attainder, ex post facto Law, or Law impairing the Obligation of Contracts, or grant any Title of Nobility.

No State shall, without the Consent of the Congress, lay any Imposts or Duties on Imports or Exports, except what may be absolutely necessary for executing its inspection Laws: and the net Produce of all Duties and Imposts, laid by any State on Imports and Exports, shall be for the Use of the Treasury of the United States; and all such Laws shall be subject to Revision and Control of the Congress.

No State shall, without the Consent of Congress, lay any Duty of Tonnage, keep Troops, or Ships of War in time of Peace, enter into any Agreement or Compact with another State, or with a foreign Power, or engage in War, unless actually invaded, or in such imminent Danger as will not admit of delay.

ARTICLE II

Section 1. The executive Power shall be vested in a President of the United States of America. He shall hold his Office during the Term of four Years, and, together with the Vice President, chosen for the same term, be elected, as follows

Each State shall appoint, in such Manner as the Legislature thereof may direct, a Number of Electors, equal to the whole Number of Senators and Representatives to which the State may be entitled in the Congress: but no

Senator or Representative, or Person holding an office of Trust or Profit under the United States, shall be appointed an Elector.

The Electors shall meet in their respective States, and vote by Ballot for two Persons, of whom one at least shall not be an Inhabitant of the same State with themselves. And they shall make a List of all the Persons voted for, and of the Number of Votes for each; which List they shall sign and certify, and transmit sealed to the Seat of the Government of the United States, directed to the President of the Senate. The President of the Senate shall, in the Presence of the Senate and House of Representatives, open all the Certificates, and the Votes shall then be counted. The Person having the greatest Number of Votes shall be the President, if such Number be a Majority of the whole Number of Electors appointed; and if there be more than one who have such Majority, and have an equal Number of Votes, then the House of Representatives shall immediately chuse by Ballot one of them for President: and if no Person have a Majority, then from the five highest on the List the said House shall in like Manner chuse the President. But in chusing the President, the Votes shall be taken by States, the Representation from each State having one Vote; A quorum for this Purpose shall consist of a Member or Members from two thirds of the States, and a Majority of all the States shall be necessary to a Choice. In every Case, after the Choice of the President, the Person having the greatest Number of Votes of the Electors shall be the Vice President. But if there should remain two or more who have equal Votes, the Senate shall chuse from them by Ballot the Vice President.

The Congress may determine the Time of chusing the Electors and the Day on which they shall give their Votes; which Day shall be the same throughout the United States.

No Person except a natural born Citizen, or a Citizen of the United States, at the time of the Adoption of this Constitution, shall be eligible to the Office of President; neither shall any person be eligible to that Office who shall not have attained to the Age of thirty five Years, and been fourteen Years a Resident within the United States.

In case of the Removal of the President from Office, or of his Death, Resignation, or Inability to discharge the Powers and Duties of the said Office, the Same shall devolve on the Vice President, and the Congress may by Law provide for the Case of Removal, Death, Resignation or Inability, both of the President and Vice President, declaring what Officer shall then act as President, and such Officer shall act accordingly, until the Disability be removed, or a President shall be elected.

The President shall, at stated Times, receive for his Services a Compensation, which shall neither be encreased nor diminished during the Period for which he shall have been elected, and he shall not receive within that Period any other Emolument from the United States, or any of them.

Before he enter on the Execution of his Office, he shall take the following Oath or Affirmation:- "I do solemnly swear (or affirm) that I will faithfully execute the Office of President of the United States, and will to the best of my Ability, preserve, protect and defend the Constitution of the United States."

Section 2. The President shall be Commander in Chief of the Army and Navy of the United States, and of the Militia of the several States, when called into the actual Service of the United States; he may require the Opinion, in writing, of the principal Officer in each of the executive Departments, upon any Subject relating to the Duties of their respective Offices, and he shall have power to grant Reprieves and Pardons for Offences against the United States, except in Cases of Impeachment.

He shall have Power, by and with the Advice and Consent of the Senate, to make Treaties, provided two thirds of the Senators present concur; and he shall nominate, and by and with the Advice and Consent of the Senate, shall appoint Ambassadors, other public Ministers and Consuls, Judges of the supreme Court, and all other Officers of the United States, whose Appointments are not herein otherwise provided for, and which shall be established by Law; but the Congress may by Law vest the Appointment of such inferior officers, as they think proper, in the President alone, in the Courts of Law, or in the Heads of Departments.

The President shall have Power to fill up all Vacancies that may happen during the Recess of the Senate, by granting Commissions which shall expire at the end of their next Session.

Section 3. He shall from time to time give to the Congress Information of the State of the Union, and recommend to their Consideration such Measures as he shall judge necessary and expedient; he may, on extraordinary Occasions, convene both Houses, or either of them, and in Case of Disagreement between them, with Respect to the Time of Adjournment, he may adjourn them to such Time as he shall think proper; he shall receive Ambassadors and other public Ministers; he shall take Care that the Laws be faithfully executed, and shall Commission all of the officers of the United States.

Section 4. The President, Vice President and all civil Officers of the United States, shall be removed from Office on Impeachment for, and Conviction of, Treason, Bribery, or other High Crimes and Misdemeanors.

ARTICLE III

Section 1. The judicial Power of the United States, shall be vested in one supreme Court, and in such inferior Courts as the Congress may from time to time ordain and establish. The Judges, both of the supreme and inferior Courts, shall hold their offices during good Behaviour, and shall, at stated Times, receive for their Services, a Compensation, which shall not be diminished during their Continuance in Office.

Section 2. The judicial Power shall extend to all Cases, in Law and Equity, arising under this Constitution, the Laws of the United States, and Treaties made, or which shall be made, under their Authority;-to all Cases affecting Ambassadors, other public Ministers and Consuls;-to all Cases of admiralty and maritime Jurisdiction;-to Controversies to which the United States shall be a party;-to Controversies between two or more States; between a State and Citizens of another State;-between Citizens of different States;-between Citizens of the same State claiming Lands under Grants of different States, and between a State, or the Citizens thereof, and foreign States, Citizens or Subjects.

In all Cases affecting Ambassadors, other public Ministers and Consols, and those in which a State shall be Party, the supreme Court shall have original Jurisdiction. In all the other Cases before mentioned, the supreme Court shall have appellate Jurisdiction, both as to Law and Fact, with such Exceptions, and under such Regulations as the Congress shall make.

The Trial of all Crimes, except in Cases of Impeachment, shall be by Jury; and such Trial shall be held in the State where the said Crimes shall have been committed; but when not committed within any State, the Trial shall be at such Place or Places as the Congress may by Law have directed.

Section 3. Treason against the United States, shall consist only in levying War against them, or in adhering to their Enemies, giving them Aid and Comfort. No Person shall be convicted of Treason unless on the Testimony of two Witnesses to the same overt Act, or on Confession in open Court.

The Congress shall have Power to declare the Punishment of Treason, but no Attainder of Treason shall work Corruption of Blood, or Forfeiture except during the Life of the Person attainted.

ARTICLE IV

Section 1. Full Faith and Credit shall be given in each State to the public Acts, Records, and judicial Proceedings of every State. And the Congress may by general Laws prescribe the Manner in which such Acts, Records, and Proceedings shall be proved, and the Effect thereof.

Section 2. The Citizens of each State shall be entitled to all Privileges and Immunities of Citizens in the several States.

A Person charged in any State with Treason, Felony, or other Crime, who shall flee from Justice, and be found in another State, shall on Demand of the executive Authority of the State from which he fled, be delivered up, to be removed to the State having Jurisdiction of the Crime.

No Person held to Service or Labour in one State, under the Laws thereof, escaping into another, shall, in Consequence of any Law or Regulation therein, be discharged from such Service or Labour, but shall be delivered up on Claim of the Party to whom such Service or Labour may be due.

Section 3. New States may be admitted by the Congress into this Union; but no new State shall be formed or erected within the Jurisdiction of any other State; nor any State be formed by the Junction of two or more States, or Parts of States, without the Consent of the Legislatures of the States concerned as well as of the Congress.

The Congress shall have Power to dispose of and make all needful Rules and Regulations respecting the Territory or other Property belonging to the United States; and nothing in this Constitution shall be so construed as to Prejudice any Claims of the United States, or of any particular State.

Section 4. The United States shall guarantee to every State in this Union a Republican Form of Government, and shall protect each of them against Invasion; and on Application of the Legislature, or of the Executive (when the Legislature cannot be convened) against domestic Violence.

ARTICLE V

The Congress, whenever two thirds of both Houses shall deem it necessary, shall propose Amendments to this Constitution, or, on the Application of the Legislatures of two thirds of the several States, shall call a Convention for proposing Amendments, which, in either Case, shall be valid to all Intents and Purposes, as Part of this Constitution, when ratified by the Legislatures of three fourths of the several States, or by Conventions in three fourths thereof, as the one or the other Mode of Ratification may be proposed by the Congress; Provided that no Amendment which may be made prior to the Year One thousand eight hundred and eight shall in any Manner affect the first and fourth Clauses in the Ninth Section of the first Article; and that no State, without its Consent, shall be deprived of its equal Suffrage in the Senate.

ARTICLE VI

All Debts contracted and Engagements entered into, before the Adoption of this Constitution, shall be as valid against the United States under this Constitution, as under the Confederation.

This Constitution, and the Laws of the United States which shall be made in Pursuance thereof; and all Treaties made, or which shall be made, under the Authority of the United States, shall be the supreme Law of the Land; and the Judges in every State shall be bound thereby, any Thing in the Constitution of Laws of any State to the Contrary notwithstanding.

The Senators and Representatives before mentioned, and the Members of the several State Legislatures, and all executive and judicial Officers, both of the United States and of the several States, shall be bound by Oath or Affirmation, to support this Constitution; but no religious Test shall ever be required as a Qualification to any Office or public Trust under the United States.

ARTICLE VII

The Ratification of the Conventions of nine States shall be sufficient for the Establishment of this Constitution between the States so ratifying the Same.

Done in Convention by the Unanimous Consent of the States present the Seventeenth Day of September in the Year of our Lord one thousand seven hundred and Eighty seven and of the Independence of the United States of America the Twelfth. In witness whereof We have hereunto subscribed our Names.

[The first 10 Amendments were ratified December 5, 1791, and form what is known as the Bill of Rights.]

AMENDMENT 1

Congress shall make no law respecting an establishment of religion, or prohibiting the free exercise thereof; or abridging the freedom of speech, or of the press; or the right of the people peaceably to assemble, and to petition the Government for a redress of grievances.

AMENDMENT 2

A well regulated Militia, being necessary to the security of a free State, the right of the people to keep and bear Arms, shall not be infringed.

AMENDMENT 3

No Soldier shall, in time of peace be quartered in any house, without the consent of the Owner, nor in time of war, but in a manner to be prescribed by Law.

AMENDMENT 4

The right of the people to be secure in their persons, houses, papers, and effects, against unreasonable searches and seizures, shall not be violated, and no Warrants shall issue, but upon probable cause, supported by Oath or affirmation, and particularly describing the place to be searched and the persons or things to be seized.

AMENDMENT 5

No person shall be held to answer for a capital, or otherwise infamous crime, unless on a presentment or indictment of a Grand Jury, except in cases arising in the land or naval forces, or in the Militia, when in actual service in time of War or public danger; nor shall any person be subject for the same offence to be twice put in jeopardy of life or limb; nor shall be compelled in any criminal case to be a witness against himself, nor be deprived of life, liberty, or property, without due process of law; nor shall private property be taken for public use, without just compensation.

AMENDMENT 6

In all criminal prosecutions, the accused shall enjoy the right to a speedy and public trial, by an impartial jury of the State and district wherein the crime shall have been committed, which district shall have been previously ascertained by law, and to be informed of the nature and cause of the accusation; to be confronted with the witnesses against him; to have compulsory process for obtaining witnesses in his favor, and to have the Assistance of Counsel for his defense.

AMENDMENT 7

In Suits at common law, where the value in controversy shall exceed twenty dollars, the right of trial by jury shall be preserved, and no fact tried by a jury, shall be otherwise reexamined in any Court of the United States, than according to the rules of the common law.

AMENDMENT 8

Excessive bail shall not be required, nor excessive fines imposed, nor cruel and unusual punishments inflicted.

AMENDMENT 9

The enumeration in the Constitution, of certain rights, shall not be construed to deny or disparage others retained by the people.

AMENDMENT 10

The powers not delegated to the United States by the Constitution, nor prohibited by it to the States, are reserved to the States respectively, or to the people.

AMENDMENT 11

[Ratified February 7, 1795]

The Judicial power of the United States shall not be construed to extend to any suit in law or equity, commenced or prosecuted against one of the United States by Citizens of another State, or by Citizens or Subjects of any Foreign State.

AMENDMENT 12

[Ratified July 27, 1804]

The Electors shall meet in their respective states and vote by ballot for President and Vice-President, one of whom, at least, shall not be an inhabitant of the same state with themselves; they shall name in their ballots the person voted for as President, and in distinct ballots the person voted for as Vice-President, and they shall make distinct lists of all persons voted for as President, and of all persons voted for as Vice-President, and of the number of votes for each, which lists they shall sign and certify, and transmit sealed to the seat of the government of the United States, directed to the President of the Senate;-The President of the Senate shall, in the presence of the Senate and House of Representatives, open all the certificates and the votes shall then be counted;-The person having the greatest number of votes for President, shall be the President, if such number be a majority of the whole number of Electors appointed; and if no person have such majority, then from the persons having the highest numbers not exceeding three in the list of those voted for as President, the House of Representatives shall choose immediately by ballot, the President. But in choosing the President, the votes shall be taken by states, the representation from each state having one vote; a quorum for this purpose shall consist of a member or members from two-thirds of the states, and a majority of all the states shall be necessary to a choice. And if the House of Representatives shall not choose a President whenever the right of choice shall devolve upon them, before the fourth day of March next following, the Vice-President shall act as President, as in the case of the death or other constitutional disability of the President.-The person having the greatest number of votes as Vice-President, shall be the Vice-President, if such number be a majority of the whole number of Electors appointed, and if no person have a majority, then from the two highest numbers on the list, the Senate shall choose the Vice-President; a quorum for the purpose shall consist of two-thirds of the whole number of Senators, and a majority of the whole number shall be necessary to a choice. But no person constitutionally ineligible to the office of President shall be eligible to that of Vice-President of the United States.

AMENDMENT 13
[Ratified December 6, 1865]

Section 1. Neither slavery nor involuntary servitude, except as a punishment for crime whereof the party shall have been duly convicted, shall exist within the United States, or any place subject to their jurisdiction.

Section 2. Congress shall have the power to enforce this article by appropriate legislation.

AMENDMENT 14
[Ratified July 9, 1868]

Section 1. All persons born or naturalized in the United States, and subject to the jurisdiction thereof, are citizens of the United States and of the State wherein they reside. No State shall make or enforce any law which shall abridge the privileges or immunities of citizens of the United States; nor shall any State deprive any person of life, liberty, or property, without due process of law; nor deny to any person within its jurisdiction the equal protection of the laws.

Section 2. Representatives shall be appointed among the several States according to their respective numbers, counting the whole number of persons in each State, excluding Indians not taxed. But when the right to vote at any election for the choice of electors for President and Vice President of the United States, Representatives in Congress, the Executive and Judicial Officers of a State, or the members of the Legislature thereof, is denied to any of the male inhabitants of such State, being twenty-one years of age, and citizens of the United States, or in any way abridged, except for participation in rebellion, or other crime, the basis of representation therein shall be reduced in the proportion which the number of such male citizens shall bear to the whole number of male citizens twenty-one years of age in such State.

Section 3. No person shall be a Senator or Representative in Congress, or elector of President and Vice President, or hold any office, civil or military, under the United States, or under any State, who, having previously taken an oath, as a member of Congress, or as an officer of the United States, or as a member of any State legislature, or as an executive or judicial officer of any State, to support the Constitution of the United States, shall have engaged in insurrection or rebellion against the same, or given aid or comfort to the enemies thereof. But Congress may by a vote of two-thirds of each House, remove such disability.

Section 4. The validity of the public debt of the United States, authorized by law, including debts incurred for payment of pensions and bounties for services in suppressing insurrection or rebellion, shall not be questioned. But neither the United States nor any State shall assume or pay any debt or obligation incurred in aid of insurrection or rebellion against the United States, or any claim for the loss or emancipation of any slave; but all such debts, obligations and claims shall be held illegal and void.

Section 5. The Congress shall have power to enforce, by appropriate legislation, the provisions of this article.

AMENDMENT 15
[Ratified February 3, 1870]

Section 1.   The right of citizens of the United States to vote shall not be denied or abridged by the United States or by any State on account of race, color, or previous condition of servitude.

Section 2.   The Congress shall have power to enforce this article by appropriate legislation.

AMENDMENT 16
[Ratified February 3, 1913]

The Congress shall have power to lay and collect taxes on incomes, from whatever source derived, without apportionment among the several States, and without regard to any census or enumeration.

AMENDMENT 17
[Ratified April 8, 1913]

The Senate of the United States shall be composed of two Senators from each State, elected by the people thereof for six years; and each Senator shall have one vote. The electors in each state shall have the qualification requisite for electors of the most numerous branch of the State legislatures.

When vacancies happen in the representation of any State in the Senate, the executive authority of such State shall issue writs of election to fill such vacancies; *Provided,* That the legislature of any State may empower the executive thereof to make temporary appointments until the people fill the vacancies by election as the legislature may direct.

This amendment shall not be so construed as to affect the election or term of any Senator chosen before it becomes valid as part of the Constitution.

AMENDMENT 18
[Ratified January 16, 1919]

Section 1.   After one year from the ratification of this article the manufacture, sale, or transportation of intoxicating liquors within, the importation thereof into, or the exportation thereof from the United States and all territory subject to the jurisdiction thereof for beverage purposes is hereby prohibited.

Section 2.   The Congress and the several States shall have concurrent power to enforce this article by appropriate legislation.

Section 3.   This article shall be inoperative unless it shall have been ratified as an amendment to the Constitution by the legislatures of the several States, as provided in the Constitution, within seven years from the date of the submission hereof to the State by the Congress.

AMENDMENT 19
[Ratified August 18, 1920]

The right of citizens of the United States to vote shall not be denied or abridged by the United States or by any State on account of sex. Congress shall have the power to enforce this article by appropriate legislation.

AMENDMENT 20
[Ratified January 23, 1933]

Section 1.   The terms of the President and Vice President shall end at noon on the 20th day of January, and the terms of Senators and Representatives at noon on the 3d day of January, of the years in which such terms would have ended if this article had not been ratified; and the terms of their successors shall then begin.

Section 2. The Congress shall assemble at least once in every year, and such meeting shall begin at noon on the 3d day of January, unless they shall by law appoint a different day.

Section 3. If, at the time fixed for the beginning of the term of the President, the President elect shall have died, the Vice President elect shall become President. If a President shall not have been chosen before the time fixed for the beginning of his term, or if the President elect shall have failed to qualify, then the Vice President elect shall act as President until a President shall have qualified; and the Congress may by law provide for the case wherein neither a President elect nor a Vice President elect shall have qualified, declaring who shall then act as President, or the manner in which one who is to act shall be selected, and such person shall act accordingly, until a President or Vice President shall have qualified.

Section 4. The Congress may by law provide for the case of the death of any of the persons from whom the House of Representatives may choose a President whenever the right of choice shall have devolved upon them, and for the case of the death of any of the persons from whom the Senate may choose a Vice President whenever the right of choice shall have devolved upon them.

Section 5. Sections 1 and 2 shall take effect on the 15th day of October following the ratification of this article.

Section 6. This article shall be inoperative unless it shall have been ratified as an amendment to the Constitution by the legislatures of three-fourths of the several states within seven years from the date of its submission.

AMENDMENT 21
[Ratified December 5, 1933]

Section 1. The eighteenth article of amendment to the Constitution of the United States is hereby repealed.

Section 2. The transportation or importation into any State, Territory, or Possession of the United States for delivery or use herein of intoxicating liquors, in violation of the laws thereof, is hereby prohibited.

Section 3. This article shall be inoperative unless it shall have been ratified as an amendment to the Constitution by conventions in several States, as provided in the Constitution, within seven years from the date of the submission hereof to the States by the Congress.

AMENDMENT 22
[Ratified February 27, 1951]

Section 1. No person shall be elected to the office of the President more than twice, and no person who has held the office of President, or acted as President, for more than two years of a term to which some other person was elected President shall be elected to the office of the President more than once. But this Article shall not apply to any person holding the office of President when this Article was proposed by the Congress, and shall not prevent any person who may be holding the office of President, or acting as President, during the term within which this Article becomes operative from holding the office of President or acting as President during the remainder of such term.

Section 2.   This article shall be inoperative unless it shall have been ratified as an amendment to the Constitution by the legislatures of three-fourths of the several States within seven years from the date of its submission to the States by the Congress.

AMENDMENT 23
[Ratified March 29, 1961]

Section 1.   The District constituting the seat of Government of the United States shall appoint in such manner as the Congress may direct:

A number of electors of President and Vice President equal to the whole number of Senators and Representatives in Congress to which the District would be entitled if it were a state, but in no event more than the least populous State; they shall be in addition to those appointed by the States, but they shall be considered, for the purposes of the election of President and Vice President, to be electors appointed by a State; and they shall meet in the District and perform such duties as provided by the twelfth article of amendment.

Section 2.   The Congress shall have power to enforce this article by appropriate legislation.

AMENDMENT 24
[Ratified January 23, 1964]

Section 1.   The right of citizens of the United States to vote in any primary or other election for President or Vice President, for electors for President or Vice President, or for Senator or Representative in Congress, shall not be denied or abridged by the United States or by any State by reason or failure to pay any poll tax or other tax.

Section 2.   The Congress shall have power to enforce this article by appropriate legislation.

AMENDMENT 25
[Ratified February 10, 1967]

Section 1.   In case of the removal of the President from office or of his death or resignation, the Vice President shall become President.

Section 2.   Whenever there is vacancy in the office of the Vice President, the President shall nominate a Vice President who shall take office upon confirmation by a majority vote of both Houses of Congress.

Section 3.   Whenever the President transmits to the President pro tempore of the Senate and the Speaker of the House of Representatives his written declaration that he is unable to discharge the powers and duties of his office, and until he transmits to them a written declaration of the contrary, such powers and duties shall be discharged by the Vice President as Acting President.

Section 4.   Whenever the Vice President and a majority of either the principal officers of the executive department or of such other body as Congress may by law provide, transmit to the President pro tempore of the Senate and the Speaker of the House of Representatives their written declaration that the President is unable to discharge the powers and duties of his office, the Vice President shall immediately assume the powers and duties of the office as Acting President.

Thereafter, when the President transmits to the President pro tempore of the Senate and the Speaker of the House of Representatives his written declaration that no inability exists, he shall resume the powers and duties of his office unless the Vice President and a majority of either the principle officers of the executive department or of such other body as Congress may by law provide, transmit within four days to the President pro tempore of the Senate and the Speaker of the House of Representatives their written declaration that the President is unable to discharge the powers and duties of his office. Thereupon Congress shall decide the issue, assembling within forty-eight hours for that purpose if not in session. If the Congress, within twenty-one days after receipt of the latter written declaration, or, if Congress is not in session, within twenty-one days after Congress is required to assemble, determined by two-thirds vote of both Houses that the President is unable to discharge the powers and duties of his office, the Vice President shall continue to discharge the same as Acting President; otherwise, the President shall resume the powers and duties of his office.

AMENDMENT 26
[Ratified June 30, 1971]

Section 1.   The right of citizens of the United States, who are eighteen years of age or older, to vote shall not be denied or abridged by the United States or by any State on account of age.

Section 2.   The Congress shall have the power to enforce this article by appropriate legislation.

DELEGATES WHO ATTENDED THE CONSTITUTIONAL CONVENTION†

George Washington*
President and Deputy from Virginia

New Hampshire
*John Langdon**
*Nicholas Gilman**

Massachusetts
Elbridge Gerry
*Nathaniel Gorham**
*Rufus King**
Caleb Strong

Connecticut
*William Samuel Johnson**
*Roger Sherman**
Oliver Ellsworth

New York
Robert Yates
*Alexander Hamilton**
John Lansing, Jr.

New Jersey
*David Brearley**
William Churchill Houston
*William Paterson**
*William Livingston**
*Johnathan Dayton**

†*Rhode Island was not represented.*
Signatories of the Constitution.

Pennsylvania
Thomas Mifflin*
Robert Morris*
George Clymer*
Jared Ingersoll*
Thomas Fitzsimons*
James Wilson*
Gouverneur Morris*
Benjamin Franklin*

Delaware
George Reed*
Gunning Bedford, Jr.*
John Dickinson*
Richard Bassett*
Jacob Broom*

Maryland
James McHenry*
Daniel of St. Thomas Jenifer*
Daniel Carroll*
John Francis Mercer
Luther Martin

Virginia
Edmund Randolph
John Blair*
James Madison, Jr.*
George Mason
George Wythe
James McClurg

North Carolina
Alexander Martin
William Richardson Davie
Richard Dobbs Spaight*
William Blount*
Hugh Williamson*

South Carolina
John Rutledge*
Charles Pinckney*
Chas. Cotesworth Pinckney*
Pierce Butter*

Georgia
William Few*
Abraham Baldwin*
William Pierce
William Houstoun

*Signatories of the Constitution.

During 1787 and 1788 James Madison, Alexander Hamilton, and John Jay wrote a series of 85 essays for the New York press encouraging ratification of the Constitution. The articles were simply signed Publius, *and they have become collectively known as the* Federalist Papers. *They are considered the most authoritative analyses of the weaknesses of the Articles of Confederation and the strengths of the Constitution. Three of the most important essays are presented here.*

THE FEDERALIST NO. 10
(MADISON)

To the People of the State of New York:

Among the numerous advantages promised by a well-constructed Union, none deserves to be more accurately developed than its tendency to break and control the violence of faction. The friend of popular governments never finds himself so much alarmed for their character and fate, as when he contemplates their propensity to this dangerous vice. He will not fail, therefore, to set a due value on any plan which, without violating the principles to which he is attached, provides a proper cure for it. The instability, injustice, and confusion introduced into the public councils, have, in truth, been the mortal diseases under which popular governments have everywhere perished; as they continue to be the favorite and fruitful topics from which the adversaries to liberty derive their most specious declamations. The valuable improvements made by the American constitutions on the popular models, both ancient and modern, cannot certainly be too much admired; but it would be an unwarrantable partiality, to contend that they have as effectually obviated the danger on this side, as was wished and expected. Complaints are everywhere heard from our most considerate and virtuous citizens, equally the friends of public and private faith, and of public and personal liberty, that our governments are too unstable; that the public good is disregarded in the conflicts of rival parties; and that measures are too often decided, not according to the rules of justice and the rights of the minor party, but by the superior force of an interested and overbearing majority. However anxiously we may wish that these complaints had no foundation, the evidence of known facts will not permit us to deny that they are in some degree true. It will be found, indeed, on a candid review of our situation, that some of the distresses under which we labor have been erroneously charged on the operation of our governments; but it will be found, at the same time, that other causes will not alone account for many of our heaviest misfortunes; and, particularly, for that prevailing and increasing distrust of public engagements, and alarm for private rights, which are echoed from one end of the continent to the other. These must be chiefly, if not wholly, effects of the unsteadiness and injustice with which a factious spirit has tainted our public administrations.

By a faction, I understand a number of citizens, whether amounting to a majority or minority of the whole, who are united and actuated by some common impulse of passion, or of interest, adverse to the rights of other citizens, or to the permanent and aggregate interests of the community.

There are two methods of curing the mischiefs of faction: the one, by removing its causes; the other, by controlling its effects.

There are again two methods of removing the causes of faction: the one, by destroying the liberty which is essential to its existence; the other, by giving to every citizen the same opinions, the same passions, and the same interests.

It could never be more truly said than of the first remedy, that it is worse than the disease. Liberty is to faction what air is to fire, an aliment without which it instantly expires. But it could not be less folly to abolish liberty, which is essential to political life, because it nourishes faction, than it would be to wish the annihilation of air, which is essential to animal life, because it imparts to fire its destructive agency.

The second expedient is as impracticable as the first would be unwise. As long as the reason of man continues fallible, and he is at liberty to exercise it, different opinions will be formed. As long as the connection subsists between his reason and his self-love, his opinions and his passions will have a reciprocal influence on each other; and the former will be objects to which the latter will attach themselves. The diversity in the faculties of men, from which the rights of property originate, is not less an insuperable obstacle to a uniformity of interests. The protection of these faculties is the first object of government. From the protection of different and unequal faculties of acquiring property, the possession of different degrees and kinds of property immediately results; and from the influence of these on the sentiments and views of the respective proprietors, ensues a division of the society into different interests and parties.

The latent causes of faction are thus sown in the nature of man; and we see them everywhere brought into different degrees of activity, according to the different circumstances of civil society. A zeal for different opinions concerning religion, concerning government, and many other points, as well of speculation as of practice; an attachment to different leaders ambitiously contending for preeminence and power; or to persons of other descriptions whose fortunes have been interesting to the human passions, have, in turn, divided mankind into parties, inflamed them with mutual animosity, and rendered them much more disposed to vex and oppress each other than to co-operate for their common good. So strong is this propensity of mankind to fall into mutual animosities, that where no substantial occasion presents itself, the most frivolous and fanciful distinctions have been sufficient to kindle their unfriendly passions and excite their most violent conflicts. But the most common and durable source of factions has been the various and unequal distribution of property. Those who hold and those who are without property have ever formed distinct interests in society. Those who are creditors, and those who are debtors, fall under a like discrimination. A landed interest, a manufacturing interest, a mercantile interest, a moneyed interest, with many lesser interests, grow up of necessity in civilized nations, and divide them into different classes, actuated by different sentiments and views. The regulation of these various and interfering interests forms the principal task of modern legislation, and involves the spirit of party and faction in the necessary and ordinary operations of the government.

No man is allowed to be a judge in his own cause, because his interest would certainly bias his judgment, and not improbably, corrupt his integrity. With equal, nay with greater reason, a body of men are unfit to be both judges and parties at the same time; yet what are many of the most important acts of legislation, but so many judicial determinations, not indeed concerning the rights of single persons, but concerning the rights of large bodies of citizens? and what are the different classes of legislators but advocates and parties to the causes which they determine? Is a law proposed concerning private debts? It is a question to which the creditors are parties on one side and the debtors on the other. Justice ought to hold the balance between them. Yet the parties are, and must be, themselves the judges; and the most numerous party, or, in other words, the most powerful faction must be expected to prevail. Shall domestic manufactures be encouraged, and in what degree, by restrictions on foreign manufactures? are questions which would be differently decided by the landed and the manufacturing classes, and probably by neither with a sole regard to justice and the public good. The apportionment of taxes on the various descriptions of property is an act which seems to require the most exact impartiality; yet there is, perhaps, no legislative act in which greater opportunity and temptation are given to a predominant party to trample on the rules of justice. Every shilling with which they overburden the inferior number is a shilling saved to their own pockets.

It is in vain to say that enlightened statesmen will be able to adjust these clashing interests and render them all subservient to the public good. Enlightened statesmen will not always be at the helm. Nor, in many cases, can such an adjustment be made at all without taking into view indirect and remote considerations, which will rarely prevail over the immediate interest which one party may find in disregarding the rights of another or the good of the whole.

The inference to which we are brought is, that the *causes* of faction cannot be removed, and that relief is only to be sought in the means of controlling its *effects*.

If a faction consists of less than a majority, relief is supplied by the republican principle, which enables the majority to defeat its sinister views by regular vote. It may clog the administration, it may convulse the society; but it will be unable to execute and mask its violence under the forms of the Constitution. When a majority is included in a faction, the form of popular government, on the other hand, enables it to sacrifice to its ruling passion or interest both the public good and the rights of other citizens. To secure the public good and private rights against the danger of such a faction, and at the same time to preserve the spirit and the form of popular government, is then the great object to which our inquiries are directed. Let me add that it is the great desideratum by which this form of government can be rescued from the opprobrium under which it has so long labored, and be recommended to the esteem and adoption of mankind.

By what means is this object attainable? Evidently by one of two only. Either the existence of the same passion or interest in a majority at the same time must be prevented, or the majority, having such coexistent passion or interest, must be rendered by their number and local situation unable to concert and carry into effect schemes of oppression. If the impulse and the opportunity be suffered to coincide, we well know that neither moral nor religious motives can be relied on as an adequate control. They are not found to be such on the injustice and violence of individuals, and lose their efficacy in proportion to the number combined together, that is, in proportion as their efficacy becomes needful.

From this view of the subject it may be concluded that a pure democracy, by which I mean a society consisting of a small number of citizens, who assemble and administer the government in person, can admit of no cure for the mischiefs of faction. A common passion or interest will, in almost every case, be felt by a majority of the whole; a communication and concert result from the form of government itself; and there is nothing to check the inducements to sacrifice the weaker party or an obnoxious individual. Hence it is that such democracies have ever been spectacles of turbulence and contention; have ever been found incompatible with personal security or the rights of property; and have in general been as short in their lives as they have been violent in their deaths. Theoretic politicians, who have patronized this species of government, have erroneously supposed that by reducing mankind to a perfect equality in their political rights, they would, at the same time, be perfectly equalized and assimilated in their possessions, their opinions, and their passions.

A republic, by which I mean a government in which the scheme of representation takes place, opens a different prospect, and promises the cure for which we are seeking. Let us examine the points in which it varies from pure democracy, and we shall comprehend both the nature of the cure and the efficacy which it must derive from the Union.

The two great points of difference between a democracy and a republic are: first, the delegation of the government in the latter to a small number of citizens elected by the rest; secondly, the greater number of citizens and greater sphere of country over which the latter may be extended.

The effect of the first difference is, on the one hand, to refine and enlarge the public views, by passing them through the medium of a chosen body of citizens, whose wisdom may best discern the true interest of their country, and whose patriotism and love of justice will be least likely to sacrifice it to temporary or partial considerations. Under such a regulation, it may well happen that the public voice, pronounced by the representatives of the people, will be more consonant to the public good than if pronounced by the people themselves, convened for the purpose. On the other hand, the effect may be inverted. Men of factious tempers, of local prejudices, or of sinister designs, may by intrigue, by corruption, or by other means, first obtain the suffrages, and then betray the interests of the people. The question resulting is, whether small or extensive republics are more favorable to the election of proper guardians of the public weal; and it is clearly decided in favor of the latter by two obvious considerations.

In the first place, it is to be remarked that, however small the republic may be, the representatives must be raised to a certain number in order to guard against the cabals of a few; and that, however large it may be, they must be limited to a certain number in order to guard against the confusion of a multitude. Hence, the number of representatives in the two cases not being in proportion to that of the two constituents, and being proportionally greater in the small republic, it follows that, if the proportion of fit characters be not less in the large than in the small republic, the former will present a greater option and consequently a greater probability of a fit choice.

In the next place, as each representative will be chosen by a greater number of citizens in the large than in the small republic, it will be more difficult for unworthy candidates to practise with success the vicious arts by which elections are too often carried; and the suffrages of the people being more free, will be more likely to centre in men who possess the most attractive merit and the most diffusive and established characters.

It must be confessed that in this, as in most other cases, there is a mean, on both sides of which inconveniences will be found to lie. By enlarging too much the number of electors, you render the representative too little acquainted with all their local circumstances and lesser interests: as by reducing it too much, you render him unduly attached to these, and too little fit to comprehend and pursue great and national objects. The federal Constitution forms a happy combination in this respect; the great and aggregate interests being referred to the national, the local and particular to the State legislatures.

The other point of difference is, the greater number of citizens and extent of territory which may be brought within the compass of republican than of democratic government; and it is this circumstance principally which renders factious combinations less to be dreaded in the former than in the latter. The smaller the society, the fewer probably will be the distinct parties and interests composing it; the fewer the distinct parties and interests, the more frequently will a majority be found of the same party; and the smaller the number of individuals composing a majority, and the smaller the compass within which they are placed, the more easily will they concert and execute their plans of oppression. Extend the sphere, and you take in a greater variety of parties and interests; you make it less probable that a majority of the whole will have a common motive to invade the rights of other citizens; or if such a common motive exists, it will be more difficult for all who feel it to discover their own strength and to act in unison with each other. Besides other impediments, it may be remarked that, where there is a consciousness of unjust or dishonorable purposes, communication is always checked by distrust in proportion to the number whose concurrence is necessary.

Hence, it clearly appears that the same advantage which a republic has over a democracy in controlling the effects of faction is enjoyed by a large over a small republic,—is enjoyed by the Union over the States composing it. Does the advantage consist in the substitution of representatives whose enlightened views and virtuous sentiments render them superior to local prejudices and to schemes of injustice? It will not be denied that the representation of the Union will be most likely to possess these requisite endowments. Does it consist in the greater security afforded by a greater variety of parties, against the event of any one party being able to outnumber and oppress the rest? In an equal degree does the increased variety of parties comprised within the Union, increase this security. Does it, in fine, consist in the greater obstacles opposed to the concert and accomplishment of the secret wishes of an unjust and interested majority? Here, again, the extent of the Union gives it the most palpable advantage.

The influence of factious leaders may kindle a flame within their particular States, but will be unable to spread a general conflagration through the other States. A religious sect may degenerate into a political faction in a part of the Confederacy; but the variety of sects dispersed over the entire face of it must secure the national councils against any danger from that source. A rage for paper money, for an abolition of debts, for an equal division of property, or for any other improper or wicked project, will be less apt to pervade the whole body of the Union than a particular member of it; in the same proportion as such a malady is more likely to taint a particular county or district, than an entire State.

In the extent and proper structure of the Union, therefore, we behold a republican remedy for the diseases most incident to republican government. And according to the degree of pleasure and pride we feel in being republicans, ought to be our zeal in cherishing the spirit and supporting the character of Federalists.

Publius

THE FEDERALIST NO. 51

(Madison)

To the People of the State of New York:

To what expedient, then, shall we finally resort for maintaining in practice the necessary partition of power among the several departments as laid down in the Constitution? The only answer that can be given is, that as all these exterior provisions are found to be inadequate, the defect must be supplied by so contriving the interior structure of the government as that its several constituent parts may, by their mutual relations, be the means of keeping each other in their proper places. Without presuming to undertake a full development of this important idea, I will hazard a few general observations, which may perhaps place it in a clearer light, and enable us to form a more correct judgment of the principles and structure of the government planned by the convention.

In order to lay a due foundation for that separate and distinct exercise of the different powers of government, which to a certain extent is admitted on all hands to be essential to the preservation of liberty, it is evident that each department should have a will of its own; and consequently should be so constituted that the members of each should have as little agency as possible in the appointment of the members of the others. Were this principle rigorously adhered to, it would require that all the appointments for the supreme executive, legislative, and judiciary magistracies should be drawn from the same fountain of authority, the people, through channels having no communication whatever with one another. Perhaps such a plan of constructing the several departments would be less difficult in practice than it may in contemplation appear. Some difficulties, however, and some additional expense would attend the execution of it. Some deviations, therefore, from the principle must be admitted. In the constitution of the judiciary department in particular, it might be inexpedient to insist rigorously on the principle: first, because peculiar qualifications being essential in the members, the primary consideration ought to be to select that mode of choice which best secures these qualifications; secondly, because the permanent tenure by which the appointments are held in that department must soon destroy all sense of dependence on the authority conferring them.

It is equally evident, that the members of each department should be as little dependent as possible on those of the others for the emoluments annexed to their offices. Were the executive magistrate or the judges not independent of the legislature in this particular, their independence in every other would be merely nominal.

But the great security against a gradual concentration of the several powers in the same department, consists in giving to those who administer each department the necessary constitutional means and personal motives to resist encroachments of the others. The provision for defence must in this, as in all other cases, be made commensurate to the danger of attack. Ambition must be made to counteract ambition. The interest of the man must be connected with the constitutional rights of the place. It may be a reflection on human nature, that such devices should be necessary to control the abuses of government. But what is government itself, but the greatest of all reflections on human nature? If men were angels, no government would be necessary. If angels were to govern men, neither external nor internal controls on government would be necessary. In framing a government which is to be administered by men over men, the great difficulty lies in this: you must first enable the government to control the governed; and in the next place oblige it to control itself. A dependence on the people is, no doubt, the primary control on the government; but experience has taught mankind the necessity of auxiliary precautions.

This policy of supplying, by opposite and rival interests, the defect of better motives might be traced through the whole system of human affairs, private as well as public. We see it particularly displayed in all the subordiante distributions of power, where the constant aim is to divide and arrange the several

offices in such a manner as that each may be a check on the other—that the
private interest of every individual may be a sentinel over the public rights.
These inventions of prudence cannot be less requisite in the distribution of the
supreme powers of the State.

But it is not possible to give to each department an equal power of self-de-
fence. In republican government the legislative authority necessarily
predominates. The remedy for this inconveniency is to divide the legislature
into different branches; and to render them, by different modes of election and
different principles of action, as little connected with each other as the nature
of their common functions and their common dependence on the society will
admit. It may even be necessary to guard against dangerous encroachments by
still further precautions. As the weight of the legislative authority requires that
it should be thus divided, the weakness of the executive may require, on the
other hand, that it should be fortified. An absolute negative on the legislature
appears, at first view, to be the natural defence with which the executive magistrate should be armed. But perhaps it would be neither altogether safe nor alone
sufficient. On ordinary occasions it might not be exerted with the requisite
firmness, and on extraordinary occasions it might be perfidiously abused. May
not this defect of an absolute negative be supplied by some qualified connection
between this weaker department and the weaker branch of the stronger department, by which the latter may be led to support the constitutional rights of the
former, without being too much detached from the rights of its own department?

If the principles on which these observations are founded be just . . . and
they be applied as a criterion to the several State constitutions and to the
federal Constitution, it will be found that if the latter does not perfectly corres-
pond with them, the former are infinitely less able to bear such a test.

There are, moreover, two considerations particularly applicable to the
federal system of America, which place that system in a very interesting point of
view.

First. In a single republic, all the power surrendered by the people is submitted to the administration of a single government; and the usurpations are
guarded against by a division of the government into distinct and separate departments. In the compound republic of America, the power surrendered by the
people is first divided between two distinct governments, and then the portion
allotted to each subdivided among distinct and separate departments. Hence a
double security arises to the rights of the people. The different governments will
control each other, at the same time that each will be controlled by itself.

Second. It is of great importance in a republic not only to guard the society
against the oppression of its rulers, but to guard one part of the society against
the injustice of the other part. Different interests necessarily exist in different
classes of citizens. If a majority be united by a common interest, the rights of
the minority will be insecure. There are but two methods of providing against
this evil: the one by creating a will in the community independent of the ma-

jority—that is, of the society itself; the other by comprehending in the society so many separate descriptions of citizens as will render an unjust combination of a majority of the whole very improbable, if not impracticable. The first method prevails in all governments possessing an hereditary or self-appointed authority. This, at best, is but a precarious security; because a power independent of the society may as well espouse the unjust views of the major, as the rightful interests of the minor party, and may possibly be turned against both parties. The second method will be exemplified in the federal republic of the United States. Whilst all authority in it will be derived from and dependent on the society, the society itself will be broken into so many parts, interests and classes of citizens, that the rights of individuals or of the minority will be in little danger from interested combinations of the majority. In a free government the security for civil rights must be the same as that for religious rights. It consists in the one case in the multiplicity of interests and in the other in the multiplicity of sects. The degree of security in both cases will depend on the number of interests and sects; and this may be presumed to depend on the extent of country and number of people comprehended under the same government. This view of the subject must particularly recommend a proper federal system to all the sincere and considerate friends of republican government, since it shows that in exact proportion as the territory of the Union may be formed into more circumscribed Confederacies or States, oppressive combinations of a majority will be facilitated; the best security under the republican forms for the rights of every class of citizens will be diminished; and consequently the stability and independence of some member of the government, the only other security, must be proportionally increased. Justice is the end of government. It is the end of civil society. It ever has been and ever will be pursued until it be obtained, or until liberty be lost in the pursuit. In a society under the forms of which the stronger faction can readily unite and oppress the weaker, anarchy may as truly be said to reign as in a state of nature, where the weaker individual is not secured against the violence of the stronger; and, as in the latter state even the stronger individuals are prompted, by the uncertainty of their condition, to submit to a government which may protect the weak as well as themselves; so, in the former state will the more powerful factions or parties be gradually induced by a like motive to wish for a government which will protect all parties, the weaker as well as the more powerful. It can be little doubted that if the State of Rhode Island was separated from the Confederacy and left to itself, the insecurity of rights under the popular form of government within such narrow limits would be displayed by such reiterated oppressions of factious majorities that some power altogether independent of the people would soon be called for by the voice of the very factions whose misrule had proved the necessity of it. In the extended republic of the United States and among the great variety of interests, parties, and sects which it embraces, a coalition of a majority of the whole society could seldom take place on any other principles than those of justice and the general good; whilst there being thus less danger to a minor from the will of a major party, there must be less pretext, also, to provide for the security of the former, by introducing into the government a will not dependent on the latter, or, in other words, a will independent of the society itself. It is no less certain than it is important, notwithstanding the contrary opinions which have been entertained, that the larger the society, provided it lie within a practical sphere, the more duly capable it will be of self-government. And happily for the *republican cause*, the practicable sphere may be carried to a very great extent by a judicious modification and mixture of the *federal principle*.

PUBLIUS

THE FEDERALIST NO. 78
(HAMILTON)

To the People of the State of New York:

We proceed now to an examination of the judiciary department of the proposed government.

In unfolding the defects of the existing Confederation, the utility and necessity of a federal judicature have been clearly pointed out. It is the less necessary to recapitulate the considerations there urged, as the propriety of the institution in the abstract is not disputed; the only questions which have been raised being relative to the manner of constituting it, and to its extent. To these points, therefore, our observations shall be confined.

The manner of constituting it seems to embrace these several objects: 1st. The mode of appointing the judges. 2d. The tenure by which they are to hold their places. 3d. The partition of the judiciary authority between different courts, and their relations to each other.

First. As to the mode of appointing the judges; this is the same with that of appointing the officers of the Union in general, and has been so fully discussed in the two last numbers, that nothing can be said here which would not be useless repetition.

Second. As to the tenure by which the judges are to hold their places: this chiefly concerns their duration in office; the provisions for their support; the precautions for their responsibility.

According to the plan of the convention, all judges who may be appointed by the United States are to hold their offices *during good behavior;* which is conformable to the most approved of the State constitutions, and among the rest, to that of this State. Its propriety having been drawn into question by the adversaries of that plan, is no light symptom of the rage for objection, which disorders their imaginations and judgments. The standard of good behavior for the continuance in office of the judicial magistracy is certainly one of the most valuable of the modern improvements in the practice of government. In a monarchy it is an excellent barrier to the despotism of the prince; in a republic it is a no less excellent barrier to the encroachments and oppressions of the representative body. And it is the best expedient which can be devised in any government to secure a steady, upright, and impartial administration of the laws.

Whoever attentively considers the different departments of power must perceive, that, in a government in which they are separated from each other, the judiciary, from the nature of its functions, will always be the least dangerous to the political rights of the Constitution; because it will be least in a capacity to annoy or injure them. The Executive not only dispenses the honors, but holds the sword of the community. The legislature not only commands the purse, but prescribes the rules by which the duties and rights of every citizen are to be regulated. The judiciary, on the contrary, has no influence over either the sword or the purse, no direction either of the strength or of the wealth of the society; and can take no active resolution whatever. It may truly be said to have neither FORCE nor WILL, but merely judgment; and must ultimately depend upon the aid of the executive arm even for the efficacy of its judgments.

This simple view of the matter suggests several important consequences. It proves incontestably that the judiciary is beyond comparison the weakest of the three departments of power [sic]; that it can never attack with success either of the other two; and that all possible care is requisite to enable it to defend itself against their attacks. It equally proves that though individual oppression may now and then proceed from the courts of justice, the general liberty of the people can never be endangered from that quarter; I mean so long as the judiciary remains truly distinct from both the legislature and the Executive. For I agree, that "there is no liberty, if the power of judging be not separated from the legislative and executive powers." And it proves, in the last place, that as liberty can have nothing to fear from the judiciary alone, but would have every thing to fear from its union with either of the other departments; that as all the effects of such a union must ensue from a dependence of the former on the latter, notwithstanding a nominal and apparent separation; that as, from the natural feebleness of the judiciary it is in continual jeopardy of being overpowered, awed, or influenced by its coordinate branches; and that as nothing can contribute so much to its firmness and independence as permanency in office, this quality may therefore be justly regarded as an indispensable ingredient in its constitution, and, in great measure, as the citadel of the public justice and the public security.

The complete independence of the courts of justice is peculiarly essential in a limited Constitution. By a limited Constitution, I understand one which contains certain specified exceptions to the legislative authority; such, for instance, as that it shall pass no bills of attainder, no *ex-post-facto* laws, and the like. Limitations of this kind can be preserved in practice no other way than through the medium of courts of justice, whose duty it must be to declare all acts contrary to the manifest tenor of the Constitution void. Without this, all the reservations of particular rights or privileges would amount to nothing.

Some perplexity respecting the rights of the courts to pronounce legislative acts void, because contrary to the constitution, has arisen from an imagination that the doctrine would imply a superiority of the judiciary to the legislative power. It is urged that the authority which can declare the acts of another void must necessarily be superior to the one whose acts may be declared void. As this doctrine is of great importance in all the American constitutions, a brief discussion of the ground on which it rests cannot be unacceptable.

There is no position which depends on clearer principles than that every act of a delegated authority, contrary to the tenor of the commission under which it is exercised, is void. No legislative act, therefore, contrary to the Constitution, can be valid. To deny this would be to affirm that the deputy is greater than his principal; that the servant is above his master; that the representatives of the people are superior to the people themselves; that men acting by virtue of powers may do not only what their powers do not authorize, but what they forbid.

If it be said that the legislative body are themselves the constitutional judges of their own powers, and that the construction they put upon them is conclusive upon the other departments, it may be answered that this cannot be the natural presumption where it is not to be collected from any particular provisions in the Constitution. It is not otherwise to be supposed that the Constitution could intend to enable the representatives of the people to substitute their *will* to that of their constituents. It is far more rational to suppose that the courts were designed to be an intermediate body between the people and the legislature, in order, among other things, to keep the latter within the limits assigned to their authority. The interpretation of the laws is the proper and peculiar province of the courts. A constitution is, in fact, and must be regarded by the judges, as a fundamental law. It therefore belongs to them to ascertain its meaning, as well as the meaning of any particular act proceeding from the legislative body. If there should happen to be an irreconcilable variance between the two, that which has the superior obligation and validity ought, of course, to be preferred; or, in other words, the Constitution ought to be preferred to the statute, the intention of the people to the intention of their agents.

Nor does this conclusion by any means suppose a superiority of the judicial to the legislative power. It only supposes that the power of the people is superior to both; and that where the will of the legislature, declared in its statutes, stands in opposition to that of the people, declared in the Constitution, the judges ought to be governed by the latter rather than the former. They ought to regulate their decisions by the fundamental laws, rather than by those which are not fundamental.

This exercise of judicial discretion, in determining between two contradictory laws, is exemplified in a familiar instance. It not uncommonly happens that there are two statutes existing at one time, clashing in whole or in part with each other, and neither of them containing any repealing clause or expression. In such a case, it is the province of the courts to liquidate and fix their meaning and operation. So far as they can, by any fair construction, be reconciled to each other, reason and law conspire to dictate that this should be done; where this is impracticable, it becomes a matter of necessity to give effect to one in exclusion of the other. The rule which has obtained in the courts for determining their relative validity is, that the last in order of time shall be preferred to the first. But this is a mere rule of construction, not derived from any positive law but from the nature and reason of the thing. It is a rule not enjoined upon the courts by legislative provision but adopted by themselves, as consonant to truth and propriety for the direction of their conduct as interpreters of the law. They thought it reasonable, that between the interfering acts of an *equal* authority, that which was the last indication of its will should have the preference.

But in regard to the interfering acts of a superior and subordinate authority, of an original and derivative power, the nature and reason of the thing indicate the converse of that rule as proper to be followed. They teach us that the prior act of a superior ought to be preferred to the subsequent act of an inferior and subordinate authority; and that accordingly, whenever a particular statute contravenes the Constitution, it will be the duty of the judicial tribunals to adhere to the latter and disregard the former.

It can be of no weight to say that the courts, on the pretence of a repugnancy, may substitute their own pleasure to the constitutional intentions of the legislature. This might as well happen in the case of two contradictory statutes; or it might as well happen in every adjudication upon any single statute. The courts must declare the sense of the law; and if they should be disposed to exercise WILL instead of JUDGMENT, the consequence would equally be the substitution of their pleasure to that of the legislative body. The observation, if it prove any thing, would prove that there ought to be no judges distinct from that body.

If, then, the courts of justice are to be considered as the bulwarks of a limited Constitution against legislative encroachments, this consideration will afford a strong argument for the permanent tenure of judicial offices, since nothing will contribute so much as this to that independent spirit in the judges which must be essential to the faithful performance of so arduous a duty.

This independence of the judges is equally requisite to guard the Constitution and the rights of individuals from the effects of those ill humors, which the arts of designing men or the influence of particular conjunctures sometimes disseminate among the people themselves; and which, though they speedily give place to better information and more deliberate reflection, have a tendency, in the meantime, to occasion dangerous innovations in the government, and serious oppressions of the minor party in the community. Though I trust the friend of the proposed Constitution will never concur with its enemies in questioning that fundamental principle of republican government, which admits the right of the people to alter or abolish the established Constitution whenever they find it inconsistent with their happiness; yet it is not to be inferred from this principle that the representatives of the people, whenever a momentary inclination happens to lay hold of a majority of their constituents, incompatible with the provisions in the existing Constitution, would, on that account, be justifiable in a violation of those provisions; or that the courts would be under a greater obligation to connive at infractions in this shape, than when they had proceeded wholly from the cabals of the representative body. Until the people have by some solemn and authoritative act annulled or changed the established form, it is binding upon themselves collectively, as well as individually; and no presumption, or even knowledge, of their sentiments, can warrant their representatives in a departure from it, prior to such an act. But it is easy to see that it would require an uncommon portion of fortitude in the judges to do their duty as faithful guardians of the Constitution, where legislative invasions of it had been instigated by the major voice of the community.

But it is not with a view to infractions of the Constitution only that the independence of the judges may be an essential safeguard against the effect of occasional ill humors in the society. These sometimes extend no farther than to the injury of the private rights of particular classes of citizens by unjust and partial laws. Here also the firmness of the judicial magistracy is of vast importance in mitigating the severity and confining the operation of such laws. It not only serves to moderate the immediate mischiefs of those which may have been passed, but it operates as a check upon the legislative body in passing them; who, perceiving that obstacles to the success of iniquitous intention are to be expected from the scruples of the courts, are in a manner compelled by the very motives of the injustice they meditate to qualify their attempts. This is a circumstance calculated to have more influence upon the character of our governments, than but few may be aware of. The benefits of the integrity and moderation of the judiciary have already been felt in more States than one; and though they may have displeased those whose sinister expectations they may have disappointed, they must have commanded the esteem and applause of all the virtuous and disinterested. Considerate men of every description ought to prize whatever will tend to beget or fortify that temper in the courts; as no man can be sure that he may not be tomorrow the victim of a spirit of injustice by which he may be a gainer today. And every man must now feel that the inevitable tendency of such a spirit is to sap the foundations of public and private confidence, and to introduce in its stead universal distrust and distress.

That inflexible and uniform adherence to the rights of the Constitution and of individuals, which we perceive to be indispensable in the courts of justice, can certainly not be expected from judges who hold their offices by a temporary commission. Periodical appointments, however regulated or by whomsoever made, would, in some way or other, be fatal to their necessary independence. If the power of making them was committed either to the Executive or legislature, there would be danger of an improper complaisance to the branch which possessed it; if to both, there would be an unwillingness to hazard the displeasure of either; if to the people or to persons chosen by them for the special purpose, there would be too great a disposition to consult popularity, to justify a reliance that nothing would be consulted but the Constitution and the laws.

There is yet a further and a weightier reason for the permanency of the judicial offices, which is deducible from the nature of the qualifications they require. It has been frequently remarked, with great propriety, that a voluminous code of laws is one of the inconveniences necessarily connected with the advantages of a free government. To avoid an arbitrary discretion in the courts, it is indispensable that they should be bound down by strict rules and precedents, which serve to define and point out their duty in every particular case that comes before them; and it will readily be conceived from the variety of controversies which grow out of the folly and wickedness of mankind, that the records of those precedents must unavoidably swell to a very considerable bulk, and must demand long and laborious study to acquire a competent knowledge of them. Hence it is, that there can be but few men in the society who will have sufficient skill in the laws to qualify them for the stations of judges. And making the proper deductions for the ordinary depravity of human nature, the number must be still smaller of those who unite the requisite integrity with the requisite knowledge. These considerations apprise us that the government can have no great option between fit character; and that a temporary duration in office, which would naturally discourage such characters from quitting a lucrative line of practice to accept a seat on the bench, would have a tendency to throw the administration of justice into hands less able, and less well qualified, to conduct it with utility and dignity. In the present circumstances of this country and in those in which it is likely to be for a long time to come, the disadvantages on this score would be greater than they may at first sight appear; but it must be confessed that they are far inferior to those which present themselves under the other aspects of the subject.

Upon the whole, there can be no room to doubt that the convention acted wisely in copying from the models of those constitutions which have established *good behavior* as the tenure of their judicial offices, in point of duration; and that so far from being blamable on this account, their plan would have been inexcusably defective if it had wanted this important feature of good government. The experience of Great Britain affords an illustrious comment on the excellence of the institution.

PUBLIUS

GLOSSARY

administration, the Composed of a large assortment of advisers to the president and agencies that implement the president's policies. It includes the executive office of the president, the Cabinet, the independent regulatory agencies, the independent regulatory boards and commissions, and the government corporations, foundations, and institutes.

adversarial system The procedure used in our courts in which attorneys for the defense and prosecution try to persuade judges and juries of the rightness of their causes.

affirmative action Efforts to actively seek and employ minorities.

Aid to Families with Dependent Children (AFDC) A federal program to give payments to the poor. This is the most costly and controversial program of government assistance to the poor. It is commonly called welfare.

Alien and Sedition Acts Passed in 1798 during the country's first scare about foreign subversion. These laws made it illegal to criticize government officials.

Alliance for Progress An economic aid program for Latin America initiated by President John F. Kennedy.

American Federation of Labor-Congress of Industrial Organizations (AFL-CIO) A labor federation forged in 1955 from two previously separate labor federations, the AFL and the CIO.

amicus curiae briefs Also called *friend of the court briefs*, these statements are sent to the court favoring or opposing one side of a case by parties who are not involved in the suit but who have an interest in its resolution.

Amnesty See *clemency power*.

Antifederalists A political party that opposed ratificatiion of the United States Constitution because the proposed national government was perceived to be too strong and a threat to individual liberty.

apartheid Severe racial segregation in the Union of South Africa.

appeasement The policy followed by England and France of trying to satisfy Hitler with concessions. The failure of this policy resulted in World War II.

appellate jurisdiction See *original jurisdiction*.

apportionment The process of drawing the boundaries of districts from which representatives are elected. The practice of drawing boundaries so as to give someone or some party the advantage is called _gerrymandering_.

Articles of Confederation The first written national constitution in history. Adopted in 1781, they provided for a compact of sovereign states. The government failed and was replaced by the federal Constitution of the United States in 1789.

bad tendency doctrine A Supreme Court doctrine adopted in 1919 giving the Congress the power to determine how grave political expression must be in order to be banned. This formula was later abandoned for the clear and present danger doctrine, oriented more toward free speech.

bicameral A body with two houses. Congress is bicameral, with the lower house being the House of Representatives and the upper house being the Senate.

bill of attainder A law that makes someone guilty of a crime without a trial. This power was used by the king's government before the Revolution, but the Constitution prohibits it.

Bill of Rights The first ten amendments of the United States Constitution. They enumerate many of the personal liberties we enjoy.

block grants Federal monetary grants given to states for use in broadly defined areas.

Brezhnev Doctrine In 1968, Soviet leader Leonid Brezhnev claimed it a Soviet "right" to put down "capitalist-imperialist" movements in the Soviet sphere of influence. This statement was patterned after the 1965 Johnson Doctrine. See _Johnson Doctrine_.

brokered conventions Nominating conventions in which party bosses, who control huge blocks of delegates, determine in back-room negotiations who will be nominated. Since most states now choose delegates for the national convention by indirect primaries, there are few brokered national nominating conventions anymore.

Brown v. Board of Education (1954 and 1955) In 1896 the Supreme Court ruled that racial segregation was constitutional as long as the "separate facilities were equal." In fact, however, the facilities for African-Americans and other minorities were almost always inferior to those for whites, so when school segregation was challenged in the Brown case, the Supreme Court ruled that "separate facilities were inherently unequal" and that schools must be integrated "with all deliberate speed." The Brown decisions were followed in the 1950s and 1960s with other rulings ordering the integration of all public facilities and accommodations.

Budget and Impoundment Act Passed in 1974, this act requires the president to notify Congress of any funds impounded and requires that they be spent unless Congress within 45 days approves the return of the funds to the Treasury.

bully pulpit A term first used by President Theodore Roosevelt to describe the influence over public policy enjoyed by the presidency.

bureaucracy A term derived from the French word for office. It is understood to mean a public or private agency that uses standard procedures to administer policy. Bureaucracies are also sometimes viewed as cumbersome, slow, and insensitive.

Bureau of Intelligence and Research An intelligence agency attached to the State Department; it gathers social, economic, and political information.

Cabinet An informal body of presidential advisors made up primarily of the heads of government departments. The exact membership and importance of the Cabinet is determined by the president. In recent years the Cabinet has been of little significance.

calendars, congressional Bills are placed on lists called calendars, waiting for their turn to reach the floor. House calendars are

Union, for all fiscal bills;

House, for all public, nonfiscal bills;

Private, for private bills;

Consent, for policy bills expected to pass without dissent;

Wednesday, for bills given privilege by committee chairs;

Discharge, for bills brought to the floor by discharge petitions. See *discharge petition*.

Senate Calendars are

Business, for all bills and resolutions, and

Executive, for presidential appointments and treaties.

Case Act Passed in 1972, it requires the president to notify Congress within 60 days of signing an executive agreement.

case law Law made by judicial rulings.

categorical grants Grants of federal money given to states to fund specific purposes. The states must also contribute their own money to these programs.

caucus Local meetings of citizens, used in some states as part of the nominating procedure. The term is also used to signify a private political meeting.

caucus, congressional Each house has a majority caucus and a minority caucus. Democrats and Republicans join different caucuses. The caucuses elect leaders, adopt rules by which they govern themselves, and assign their members to standing committees.

Caucus, King Originally, candidates for president were nominated in meetings of congressional leaders. Criticized as undemocratic, King Caucus was replaced in the 1830s by national nominating conventions.

censure A form of congressional discipline in which a house votes to punish members for unethical or illegal behavior. Punishment ranges from limiting members' expense accounts to removing them from committee assignments.

Central Intelligence Agency (CIA) Originally created in 1947 to be a central clearinghouse for information from the other United States intelligence agencies, the CIA, an independent agency, soon became involved in intelligence operations itself. Its activities have been the most controversial among all American intelligence operations.

certiorari, writ of A court order from a higher court to a lower court demanding that a case be sent up. Most cases reaching the Supreme Court arrive under a writ of certiorari.

charter colonies A type of British colony in which the rights of the citizens were outlined vis-à-vis the corporations that operated the colonies. They became the models for the practice of adopting written constitutions when the United States became independent.

checks and balances The authority of the legislative, executive, and judicial branches of government to contradict and override one another. This authority is thought to impede any single branch from becoming too powerful or repressive. James Madison also inserted checks against people by making it difficult for them to easily come into control of the government.

civil law Law regulating the rights of inividuals relative to one another.

civil liberties Freedoms that derive from the

belief that people are essentially equal and have a right to freedom of speech, press, religion, and so on.

civil rights   Individual rights recognized because of belief in human equality.

civil service   Government employment, which operates according to a merit system. Employment and promotion are awarded by use of objective standards and examinations. Civil servants are protected against political pressure in that they can be fired only for cause, not for political reasons.

Clayton Antitrust Act (1914)   A law to discourage monopolies, passed to strengthen the antimonopoly provisions of the Sherman Antitrust Act of 1890.

clear and present danger doctrine   The Supreme Court ruled that expression could not be restrained by the government unless it presented a clear and present danger to society.

clemency power   The authority of the president to modify prison sentences. They include
   amnesty, a group pardon;
   commutation, reduction of a sentence;
   pardon, forgiveness of a sentence;
   reprieve, postponement of a sentence.

Closed shop   Labor contracts that require employers to hire only people from particular unions. Closed shops are now illegal. See *Taft-Hartley Act.*

Cloture rules   The House sets strict time limits on the debate of each bill. To end debate is called the cloture. In the Senate, however, cloture takes an extraordinary majority (60 members) to pass. Thus, debate is seldom limited in the Senate, making the filibuster possible. See *filibuster.*

coattail effect   When the popularity of a candidate for high office (president or governor, for example) encourages people to vote also for candidates from the ticket-leader's party who are running for lower offices.

cognitive Madisonianism   The term given by political scientist Everett Carll Ladd to the contemporary phenomenon of the voters' deliberately electing a president from one party and the majority of Congress from the other.

Cold War   An era of strained relations between the Soviet Union and the United States and other Western powers. The Cold War is thought to have began as early as the late 1910s, with the founding of the Soviet Union. Its modern era began at the end of World War II and continued until the 1980s, when the policies of Mikhail S. Gorbachev caused tensions to relax to the point that some people believe that the Cold War has ended.

Commerce and Slave Trade Compromise   The Constitutional Convention of 1787 agreed that the national government would control interstate commerce but that exports could not be taxed, all federal ports taxes would be identical, treaties would be ratified by a two-thirds' vote of the Senate, and the slave trade would not be prohibited for 20 years.

Common Cause   A public interest group organized in 1970 to advocate clean, democratic government.

common law   From the British legal tradition, this legal system tends to protect the individual from abuse by the state. Its presumption of innocence, grand juries, and petit juries were developed as safeguards against government oppression. The concept of precedent in the common law also gives consistency and stability to the legal system by requiring all lower courts to honor interpretations of higher courts.

commutation   See *clemency.*

comparable worth   This principle goes beyond equal pay for equal work. Comparable worth holds that comparable jobs should receive equal pay. Proponents contend that male-dominated jobs are often higher paid than female-dominated jobs, even though the skill levels required for the tasks are comparable.

concurrent powers Powers that the national and state governments may each exercise. Taxation is a concurrent power. When state law contradicts national statute in a concurrent power, the state law is void because the Constitution's supremacy clause makes state law subordinate to federal law.

concurring opinions Opinions written by Supreme Court justices that agree with the Supreme Court opinion but give different reasons for a justice's voting with the majority.

confederacy A compact between sovereign states that agree to cooperate on defense, trade, and other matters. The United States has spawned two confederacies: the Articles of Confederation, 1781–1789, and the Confederate States of America, 1860–1865.

conference committee A joint congressional committee that meets to reconcile bills that have passed with different particulars in each house.

Congressional Budget Office (CBO) A staff service for Congress that analyzes fiscal legislation and reports to Congress on the projected impact of fiscal bills.

Congressional Research Service (CRS) A staff service for Congress attached to the Library of Congress. The CRS researches questions in which Congress is interested and reports its findings.

Connecticut Compromise A compromise at the 1787 Constitutional Convention between the Virginia Plan and the New Jersey Plan. The compromise created a national executive and a court system, and it gave states representation according to their populations in the lower house of Congress and equal representation in the Senate.

conservative coalition Conservative Republicans and Democrats unite in Congress in support or opposition to legislation that interests them. They often win.

conservatives They believe people are self-oriented and aggressive; thus, they tend to rely on police and military power to deal with social deviance. They tend to believe that people who have money deserve it, and they wish to protect people with property against those who they believe want to take it from them.

conspiratorial theory The belief that the society is secretly controlled by a single, small group of powerful people.

constitutional courts Those courts created by Congress under the authority of Article III of the Constitution. The Supreme Court, the appellate courts, and most of the district courts are constitutional courts.

constructive engagement The Reagan Administration policy toward the Union of South Africa in which the United States encouraged a relaxation of South Africa's racist policies but, at the same time, encouraged American firms to trade with South Africa.

consulate A diplomatic office that oversees the commercial interests of a state in a foreign country. Consulates also try to accommodate the needs of travelers from their home countries.

containment The post–World War II policy of attempting to limit communist expansion.

convention, nomination by Some states nominate candidates in party meetings called conventions. Candidates for president are also nominated in party national nominating conventions.

Council of Economic Advisers (CEA) Created by the Employment Act of 1946, the CEA is composed of three economists who advise the president on the state of the economy.

criminal law Law regulating the conduct of individuals vis-à-vis the interests of society.

critical period (1781–1789) The period during which the Articles of Confederation were in effect. The weakness of the central government during this period caused a crisis resulting in the drafting of the Constitution of the United States.

cyclical deficit A policy of borrowing no more money in a year than could be raised in taxes if all people were employed. This procedure limits borrowing to the level of the economy's potential. See *structural deficit* and *deficit*.

damage control Efforts by politicians to minimize news that will do them political harm.

Dean of the Senate See *President of the Senate*.

Declaration of Independence A statement asserting the right of people to be free from government suppression and declaring the American right to sever from the British empire because of Britain's alleged suppression of American liberties. Its principal author was Thomas Jefferson, and it was adopted by the Second Continental Congress on July 4, 1776.

Defense Intelligence Agency An intelligence agency in the Department of Defense that operates overflights and satellite reconnaissance.

deficit The amount by which annual spending exceeds revenues. Usually, deficits are covered by government borrowing. See *structural deficit* and *cyclical deficit*.

delegated powers Powers belonging to the national government. They include *express powers*, those mentioned word for word in the Constitution; *implied powers*, those powers that are necessary and proper for the exercise of the express powers; and *inherent powers*, those that by tradition belong to government regardless of whether they are listed in the Constitution.

democracy A political system that is in some way controlled by the people.

democratic republic See *republic*.

détente A French term currently used to describe the warming of tensions between the United States and the Soviet Union during the 1970s.

deterrence The nuclear strategy employed by the United States and the Soviet Union. If both sides have enough nuclear strength to be able to absorb a nuclear attack by the other and still retaliate with extreme devastation, it is hoped that neither side will initiate a nuclear strike against the other. See *mutually assured distruction (MAD)*.

direct democracy When the people themselves legislate by popular vote. No such system exists at the national level, but many states allow procedures by which the people can pass law directly, without their legislative representatives.

direct election When the results of the popular vote determine who shall win office. An indirect election is a procedure in which the people choose electors—as with the electoral college—to elect the officer.

direct taxes Taxes that people are aware they are paying, as opposed to indirect taxes, which are included in the purchase price of an item. Sales taxes, income taxes, and property taxes are direct taxes, while tariffs and most excise taxes are indirect taxes.

Discharge petition A petition requiring a standing committee in the House of Representatives to send a bill to the Discharge Calendar. To require this disposition, 218 members must sign the petition.

discount rates The interest rate charged by the Federal Reserve banks for loans it makes to member banks of the Federal Reserve System.

dissenting opinions Opinions by justices of the Supreme Court that give reasons for dissenting from the majority opinion.

divided government When the presidency and the majority of Congress are held by different political parties.

division of powers Describes federalism. See *federalism*.

dollar diplomacy The policy of American business investing heavily in poor countries and American troops being used to protect American economic interests.

domino theory A theory prevalent in the 1950s and 1960s that suggested if one country in Southeast Asia fell to the communists, the others would quickly fall as well.

double jeopardy Retrying persons on counts for which they have already been legally acquitted. The Fifth Amendment prohibits this.

Dred Scott case This 1857 Supreme Court decision held that Congress could not deny people the right to take their property wherever they wished. This was only the second time the Court ruled a federal statute unconstitutional. It was hoped that the decision would settle the question of slavery, but actually the Court's opinion exacerbated the controversy.

Due process *Procedural due process* assures that the government follows a specified procedure in criminal law. *Substantive due process* assures that the law is fairly worded.

electoral college The institution that elects the president of the United States. The people elect electors in their states, and the electors vote for president. A candidate must receive a majority of the electoral vote to be elected president.

elite theorists Political scientists, sociologists, and others who believe the society is controlled by the economic elite in the country.

embassy The political headquarters of one state on the territory of another state. Embassies are usually headed by an ambassador.

eminent domain A legal principle allowing government to compel appropriate private property for public use. The law requires that owners be paid a fair price for their property.

Employment Act of 1946 A pivotal law that formally adopted moderate socialist practices by authorizing the government to manipulate the economy in order to promote economic well-being.

Equal Rights Amendment (ERA) A proposed amendment to the Constitution to expressly prohibit discrimination based on gender. Although the ERA appeared to be on its way to easy passage in the early 1970s, it fell three states short of ratification when the deadline elapsed.

equity Law applied when the letter of the common law might result in an unjust settlement.

Era of Good Feeling Lasting from 1816 to 1824, this period of American history is unique as the only time when there was but one major political party extant (the Democratic-Republican Party, today's Democratic Party).

establishment clause A constitutional provision prohibiting the government from engaging in policies that either enhance or persecute particular religions.

exclusionary rule A rule by the Supreme Court in *Mapp* v. *Ohio* (1961) establishing that illegally obtained evidence may not be used to convict criminal defendants.

exclusive committees Standing committees in the House of Representatives (Rules, Ways and Means, and Appropriations) that are so powerful that their members are prohibited from serving on any other standing committees.

exclusive powers Powers in our federal system that only the state governments or the national government may exercise. A given exclusive power may not be exercised by both levels jointly. The power to make war is exclusive to the national government, and the right to empower local governments is exclusive to the states.

executive agreements Agreements between the president of the United States and chief executives of other states. While these agreements are not treaties and thus need no Senate ratification, they are legally binding.

Executive Office of the President (EOP) Created in 1939, this body is composed of several agencies whose principal task is to advise the president on policy. The EOP includes the White House Office, the Office of Management and Budget, the National Security Council, the Council of Economic Advisers, and the Vice President's Office.

executive orders The act of the president's promulgating law in satisfaction of the legislated intent of Congress. These laws are also called *ordinances*.

executive privilege The right of the president to withhold certain information from Congress because of the separation of powers.

exit polling When public opinion pollsters ask people how they voted as they leave the voting booth.

ex post facto law A law making an act illegal after it is committed. This power was used by the king's government before the Revolution, but it is now prohibited by the Constitution.

express powers See *delegated powers*.

expulsion The most severe form of congressional discipline in which a house votes to expel a member for engaging in unethical or illegal behavior.

extradition See *horizontal federalism*.

factions The constitutional founders used this term to refer to political parties.

fairness doctrine A policy of the Federal Communications Commission requiring that broadcasters give vent to all sides of an issue if one side is broadcast. The rule was abandoned in 1987.

faithless electors Members of the electoral college who vote for people other than those to whom they are pledged.

Federal Bureau of Investigation (FBI) Attached to the Justice Department, the FBI is the major police agency for the United States government and it also engages in domestic intelligence.

Federal Deposit Insurance Corporation (FDIC) A government corporation that collects premiums from member banks and, in return, guarantees the deposits of the banks' depositors.

federalism Developed in the United States, federalism divides governmental power between the national government and the state governments. The interrelationship between the two levels of government (vertical federalism) is a complex matter, as are relations among the states (horizontal federalism).

Federalist Papers Eighty-five essays written for publication in the New York state newspapers by James Madison, Alexander Hamilton, and John Jay, these essays are the most authoritative statement about the weaknesses of the Articles of Confederation and the virtues of the Constitution of the United States. The *Federalist Papers* are considered a masterpiece in political literature.

Federalists A political party that favored

ratification of the United States Constitution. This conservative party was led by Alexander Hamilton, but its only president was John Adams. In the 1810s the party made serious tactical errors and eventually collapsed as a national power.

Federal Reserve System A group of 12 banks created in 1913 to regulate the value of credit and the amount of currency in the economy.

Federal Savings and Loan Insurance Corporation (FSLIC) A government corporation that insured deposits in savings and loan institutions. When the savings and loan industry collapsed in 1989, the FSLIC was abolished and replaced by the Resolution Trust Corporation (RTC).

Federal Trade Commission (FTC) Created in 1914 to regulate trade practices and to promote competition.

felony A serious criminal violation.

filibuster There are few limitations to time or subject senators can discuss on the floor; thus when the minority wishes to block passage of a bill, it can take the floor and talk (for weeks sometimes), using up floor time until the majority relents. Filibusters are impossible in the House because of strict time limits for debate and because of the House germane rule on subject matter. See *germane rules*.

filibuster, post-cloture Even when the Senate has voted to close debate on a bill, in attempts to kill bills, senators in the minority can use up valuable floor time by proposing amendments and making numerous points of order.

first strike In nuclear weapons strategy a first-strike capacity is the ability to strike one's opponent with such destruction that it would be unable to retaliate (launch a second strike). Deterrence depends on each side's having a second-strike capacity. The first-strike capacity is considered dangerous because it may encourage a nuclear strike.

fiscal policy Government policies of taxing, borrowing, and spending.

flat tax A tax assessed in equal percentages on everyone regardless of their ability to pay.

floor leader Each house has a majority and minority floor leader. Their job is to lead their party's efforts in supporting or opposing legislation. The majority floor leader of the Senate is the most powerful person in the Senate, while the majority floor leader of the House is second in authority to the Speaker of the House.

food stamps Coupons given to the poor that can be redeemed in food purchases.

Foreign Service About 4500 professional diplomats who are assigned by the State Department to American legations throughout the world.

free exercise clause A constitutional provision prohibiting government from interfering with individuals' religious beliefs.

Freedom of Information Act of 1966 The belief that government tended to make too many things secret motivated this law, which requires that government, upon request, provide citizens with all but the most sensitive information.

full faith and credit See *horizontal federalism*.

General Accounting Office (GAO) A staff service for Congress headed by the Comptroller General of the United States. The GAO reports to Congress on the efficacy of government expenditures.

general election The election that occurs on the first Tuesday following the first Monday in the month of November of even years. These elections are held to fill seats in Congress and to elect the president and vice president. State ballots may include other offices as well.

germane rules   The House has two germane rules; the Senate has none. In the House, all amendments must be germane (relevant) to the legislation on the floor, thus prohibiting riders (see *riders*) and all debate must be germane to the bill on the floor, thus discouraging filibusters in the House. See *filibuster*.

gerrymandering   See *apportionment*.

Gideon v. Wainwright   A 1963 Supreme Court ruling that required states to provide a defense attorney to criminal defendants if they cannot afford to pay for one.

Gitlow v. New York   A 1925 Supreme Court ruling that used language in the Fourteenth Amendment to determine that states are obliged to give their citizens the free speech protections of the First Amendment. Subsequent cases brought almost all Bill of Rights provisions to bear on the states.

Good Neighbor Policy   Franklin D. Roosevelt's policy of respecting the rights of the Latin American states.

government foundations   Agencies created to enhance culture, they fund and foster the arts and education. Some of these agencies are the Smithsonian Institution, the National Science Foundation, and the National Foundation for the Arts and the Humanities.

Gramm-Rudman-Hollings Act   Passed in 1985, this law required reductions in the annual budget deficits until the budget is balanced in 1993. Prospects for accomplishing this goal are not good.

grandfather clause   A law used in certain southern states that waived poll taxes and literacy tests if voters' ancestors were able to vote before 1866. This law effectively prohibited African-Americans from voting but allowed poor whites to cast ballots. It was declared unconstitutional in 1915.

grand jury   A panel of citizens who hear evidence to determine whether suspects should be tried for alleged crimes. If so, the grand jury hands down a true bill of indictment.

Great Society   A term used to indicate the social objectives of the presidency of Lyndon B. Johnson.

Gulf of Tonkin Resolution   A congressional resolution that was used by presidents Lyndon B. Johnson and Richard M. Nixon to increase American involvement in the Vietnam War.

habeas corpus   A legal principle requiring that the government bring to trial in a reasonable time persons arrested for crimes.

Hatch Acts   Passed in 1939 and 1940, these laws prohibit civil servants from participating in political activities except for voting.

horizontal federalism   Refers to the relationships among the state governments in our federal system. States are obliged by the Constitution to extradite wanted people to other states, to give the judicial opinions of other states "full faith and credit," and to give to citizens of other states the same "privileges and immunities" citizens of their own states enjoy.

House Rules Committee   A standing committee that determines the placement of bills on the calendars and suggests the rules of debate for each bill. It is the most powerful committee in Congress.

impeachment   When the House of Representatives formally votes to bring charges before the bar of the Senate against a public official, the official has been impeached. The House also prosecutes the case before the Senate. The Senate must vote by two-thirds to convict.

imperial presidency From the title of a book by historian Arthur Schlesinger, Jr., who used the term to describe the presidencies of Lyndon B. Johnson and Richard M. Nixon, which were unfettered by many of the traditional congressional checks and balances.

implied powers See *delegated powers.*

independent agencies Administrative agencies that, for various reasons, have not been attached to one of the government departments, so they report directly to the president. Among the independent agencies are the Peace Corps and the Office of Drug Control.

independent regulatory boards and commissions These agencies have administrative, legislative, and judicial powers and regulate specific areas of the economy. Their members are appointed by the president and confirmed by the Senate, but they may be removed only for cause. Among these agencies are the Securities and Exchange Commission, the Federal Reserve Board, and the National Labor Relations Board.

indirect election When the popular vote elects electors who then vote to elect the officer. Presidential elections are indirect.

indirect taxes See *direct taxes.*

individual contract theory Until collective bargaining was made legal the dominant theme in employee-employer relations was that each party bargained as an individual. Thus, theoretically the worker had as much authority as the employer in negotiating the conditions of labor. Actually, since the industrialists were so much more powerful than their individual workers, this approach worked much to their advantage.

inherent powers See *delegated powers.*

intercontinental ballistic missiles (ICBMs) Missiles that can carry warheads to targets on other continents. The MX missile is the most modern ICBM in the American arsenal. It carries ten warheads, can reach the Soviet Union from the United States in 30 minutes, and is very accurate.

interest groups Groups of people organized to influence the political process.

interstate Between states.

Interstate Commerce Commission (ICC) Established in 1887 to regulate trade that crosses state lines.

intrastate Within a state.

Iran-Contra affair An episode during the Reagan Administration in which elements of the National Security Council and the CIA secretly sold arms to Iran and illegally diverted some of the proceeds to the Contra insurgents in Nicaragua.

Iron Curtain A term coined by Winston Churchill in 1946 to describe the borders of the Soviet bloc countries.

Iron Law of Oligarchy A theory by Robert Michels suggesting that all groups are controlled by only a tiny percentage of activist members.

iron triangle Refers to a powerful union among private lobbyists, congressional staff, and bureaucrats in government. When key people from each segment unite, it is very difficult to defeat them. Iron triangles are also sometimes called *subgovernments.*

isolationism When a country eschews having relations with other states.

Jim Crow laws Laws that were once used in the South to suppress African-Americans. Discrimination in voting, housing, and public accommodations were among the Jim Crow laws.

Johnson Doctrine Proclaimed by President Lyndon B. Johnson, this doctrine claimed for the United States the "right" to use American troops to put down communist insurgents in the Western Hemisphere. This statement became the model for the Brezhnev Doctrine. See *Brezhnev Doctrine*.

Joint Chiefs of Staff (JCS) Created in 1947 to coordinate military affairs and to advise the president, the JCS is composed of the ranking military officers of the Army, Navy, Air Force, and Marine Corps. It is headed by a chairman appointed by the president and confirmed by the Senate. The chair of the Joint Chiefs of Staff is the highest ranking military person in the country. Currently, General Colin Powell is chair of the JCS. He is the first African-American to rise to the pinnacle of the American military establishment.

Joint committees Committees composed of members of both houses of Congress.

judicial activism When the courts apply broad interpretations to the Constitution, thus ruling on its spirit—as the jurists read it—as well as on its letter. Judicial activism can be applied by conservatives or liberals, although currently it is associated with liberal jurists.

Judicial Act of 1789 Established the basic court structure of the United States.

judicial restraint When the courts restrict their opinions to the letter of the Constitution. Judicial restraint can be used by either conservatives or liberals, although it is currently associated with conservative jurists.

judicial review The power of the courts to void laws or executive actions because they violate the Constitution. Judicial review was originated in the United States in the Supreme Court decision of *Marbury* v. *Madison* (1803).

jurisdictional strikes Labor strikes brought on by disagreements between unions over whose members are to be hired to perform certain jobs in a given industry.

Keynesian economics A theory advanced by the British economist, John Maynard Keynes, suggesting that government should use its power to tax, borrow, and spend in ways that help assure economic prosperity.

King Caucus See *Caucus, King*.

Ku Klux Klan A white supremist organization founded after the Civil War. It ceased to exist in the late nineteenth century but reemerged in 1915 and became prominent in some states during the 1920s. The Klan enjoyed something of a comeback in the 1980s, but its political strength has not been great except in a few local areas.

Laffer curve A theory developed by economist Arthur Laffer that purports to demonstrate that people will produce less as taxes increase.

laissez-faire The capitalist principle that government should not interfere in the economy.

Landrum-Griffin Act (1959) Officially called the Labor Reforms Act, it mandates secret ballots in union elections and prohibits felons from becoming union officers. The law also requires unions to report their financial status and to file their constitutions and rules of procedure with the Labor Department.

leadership, congressional A term referring to the Speaker of the House and the majority and minority floor leaders, whips, and steering and policy committees. Important standing committee chairs are also often considered to be part of the leadership.

leaks Government information that is surreptitiously given to the media.

legislative council A staff service of Congress

that writes bills in appropriate language. Legislative Council also gives nonbinding opinions as to the constitutionality of bills.

legislative courts Also called special courts, they are created by Congress to adjudicate matters not covered in Article III of the Constitution. For example, the United States Tax Court, the Court of Military Appeals, and the Administrative Law judges are legislative courts.

legislative veto Laws that held executive action subject to Congressional approval. The legislative veto was declared an unconstitutional violation of the separation of powers in 1983.

lend-lease A procedure by which the United States gave aid to countries fighting Nazi Germany and fascist Italy during World War II.

libel Deliberate, false statements appearing in print. Because the statements must be published with the knowledge that they are false and with intent to do someone harm, libel is very difficult to prove.

liberal democracy A system of government committed to individual liberty, in which the people elect their representatives.

liberals On the left of the political spectrum, liberals believe that people are rational and moral; thus liberals tend to be optimistic about human potential. They tend to rely on persuasion rather than police or military force to get their way politically, and they use government to guard against potential abuses by the well-to-do and to redistribute wealth.

limited government The idea that government should be limited in power so as not to abuse the rights of the individual.

lobbying A process by which people approach legislators and executives to advocate for policies they support.

Locke, John (1632–1704) A British political philosopher whose ideas were used as a basis for limited government in both England and the United States.

logrolling When members of Congress vote for their colleagues' bills in exchange for support on their own legislation.

loyal opposition When opposition parties are allowed to criticize the governing party's policies and contest it for power without being suppressed. This concept is essential to a democratic system.

majority Any number over half.

mandamus, writ of A court order requiring a public agency to carry out a particular act.

manifest destiny The nineteenth-century belief that Americans were destined by God to rule the North American continent.

Mapp v. Ohio See *exclusionary rule.*

***Marbury v. Madison* (1803)** The most important Supreme Court decision in that it gave the Supreme Court, and all lower courts, the power of judicial review. See *judicial review.*

marking-up The process by which congressional committees amend legislation and draft new bills.

Marshall, John (1755–1835) Chief Justice of the Supreme Court from 1801 to 1835, Marshall may be considered one of the founders of our government in that his judicial decision gave the courts the power of judicial review and defined the line between state and national government powers.

Marshall Plan A post–World War II program in which the United States gave massive amounts of economic aid to the Western European states in an effort to help rebuild their economies.

massive nuclear retaliation The policy of the Eisenhower Administration that threatened the Soviet Union with a nuclear strike if it attempted to expand at the expense of the West.

Mayflower Compact A document establishing the Plymouth Colony in 1620. Some historians consider it the first written constitution in history.

McCarthy era During the 1950s the people of the United States were afraid of communist subversion. Led by Senator Joseph McCarthy (R-WI), the people cooperated in wholesale intimidation of those suspected of being communists. American civil liberties were severely curtailed during this period.

***McCulloch* v. *Maryland* (1819)** A Supreme Court decision establishing the implied powers doctrine and ruling that the state and national governments may not tax each other. This Marshall Court decision strengthened the national government vis-à-vis the states.

Medicaid A government welfare program that provides medical coverage to people who receive Aid to Families with Dependent Children. See *Aid to Families with Dependent Children*.

Medicare A health program paid for by workers and covering people aged 65 and over.

merit system A system in which qualifications for government employment and promotion are determined by objective standards and examinations. People employed in a merit system are protected from political pressure in that they may be fired only for cause rather than for political reasons. See *civil service*.

minority president A person who receives only a minority of the popular vote but receives a majority of the electoral vote and thus is elected president.

minority rights Liberal democratic theory holds that the rights of the individual are to be protected even when the majority may wish to deny them.

Miranda* v. *Arizona A 1966 Supreme Court ruling that among the individual rights is the right to know what one's rights are. Hence, before suspects can be questioned by police, they must be warned by the police of their rights to remain silent and to have an attorney present.

misdemeanor An infraction of minor criminal law.

monetarist policies A theory associated with economist Milton Friedman suggesting that economic prosperity can best be accomplished by the government's assuring that the money supply grows no faster than the rate of production.

monopolistic mercantilism The economic practice of the British Empire that worked to the disadvantage of the colonies. Opposition to its discriminatory policies eventually alienated large numbers of colonists and helped fuel the fire of revolution.

Monroe Doctrine The policy first enunciated in 1824 that warned Europe not to colonize the Western Hemisphere further and pledged that the United States would stay out of European affairs. Also see *Roosevelt Corollary to the Monroe Doctrine*.

multimember districts Electoral districts in which more than one legislative seat is to be won. Winners in multimember districts are often determined by proportional representation. This kind of electoral district encourages multiparty systems. See *proportional representation*.

multiple independently targeted reentry vehicles (MIRVs) Several warheads housed at the tip of a single missile. The warheads are released from the missile at a certain point in its trajectory, and each is programmed to hit its own target.

mutually assured destruction (MAD) Also called the balance of terror by its critics, this policy is the basis of deterrence. The United States and the Soviet Union each intend to destroy the other's society if attacked by nuclear weapons. See *deterrence*.

National Association for the Advancement of Colored People (NAACP) Founded in 1909, the NAACP lobbies Congress, state legislatures, and local governments on issues of interest to it. Perhaps its most effective work, however, has been in litigation before the Supreme Court. For example, the NAACP brought *Brown* v. *Board of Education* to the Supreme Court.

national committee Each political party is served by a national committee that organizes its national nominating conventions, offers services and funds to candidates, and cooperates in the presidential campaigns of its candidates.

national debt The amount of money owed from government borrowing. Essentially the national debt amounts to the total of all accumulated budget deficits, less the amount that has been paid off.

National Endowment for Democracy (NED) Created by Congress to foster democracy across the world, the NED has become controversial because some of its funds have been given to opposition parties in countries with which the United States has friendly relations.

National Labor Relations Act (1935) Also called the Wagner Act, this statute legalized collective bargaining and strikes. It also created the National Labor Relations Board to regulate union elections and to adjudicate contract disputes.

National Security Agency An intelligence unit in the Defense Department that works with codes and electronic surveillance.

National Security Council (NSC) Composed of the president, the vice president, the secretary of state, and the secretary of defense, this agency is supposed to gather data and advise the president on foreign policy. Created in 1947, the NSC has become very influential, and its chief staff aide, the National Security Advisor, fre-

quently has become the principal foreign policy adviser to the president.

natural law A theory that there is a set of absolute truths by which human conduct should be governed.

natural rights Rights that each human being has by virtue of the natural law. These rights include life, liberty, and the pursuit of happiness. Some people also believe property is among the natural rights.

New Deal A term given to the reforms of President Franklin Delano Roosevelt, which brought about Keynesian economic policies, collective bargaining, social security, welfare programs, government regulation of business and finance, and many other programs.

New Jersey Plan Proposed in the Constitutional Convention of 1789 as a counterproposal to the Virginia Plan, in an effort to secure equal voting rights for each state in Congress. Most of its provisions were abandoned, but equal state representation in the United States Senate was adopted in response to the small states' concerns about the more populated states' dominating the federal government.

news management Efforts by presidents and other politicians to assure that the media reports them in a favorable light.

"new thinking" A nonconfrontational approach to world affairs advocated by Mikhail S. Gorbachev, president of the Soviet Union.

Nonaggression Pact of 1939 An agreement between Hitler and Stalin in which they divided Europe into spheres of influence.

Office of Management and Budget (OMB) Responsible for drafting the budget and for analyzing the efficiency of the government, it reports directly to the president.

Office of Personnel Management (OPM) An independent agency that administers the merit system in the United States government. See *merit system* and *civil service*.

Old Age Survivors and Disability Insurance (OASDI)   See *social security*.

open door policy   A policy enunciated by the United States at the turn of the nineteenth century, calling upon the European colonial powers and Japan to keep China open to trade with all nations.

ordinance   Law promulgated by the president. These laws must satisfy the legislated intent of Congress. See *executive orders*. Local governments also pass ordinances because their legislative powers are delegated to them by the state governments, which maintain ultimate control over local governments' powers.

Organization of American States (OAS)   A mutual security treaty among the nations in the Western Hemisphere.

original jurisdiction   Cases can arrive before courts under original or appellate jurisdiction. The first time a case is heard it is heard under original jurisdiction. If someone wishes to appeal a judgment from a lower court, the case can be heard by a higher court under appellate jurisdiction.

pardon   See *clemency*.

partisan elections and offices   Elections and offices in which political parties formally run candidates and for which they develop policy platforms. President, senators, and members to the House of Representatives are examples of partisan offices. Usually local offices such as city council, sheriff, and state judges are nonpartisan elected offices, although some locales make these offices partisan as well.

peace dividend   An amount of money, yet to be established, which will be saved by reductions in defense expenditures. Many interest groups are hoping that these savings will be rechanneled to the programs they favor.

peaceful coexistence   A policy announced by the leader of the Soviet Union in the late 1950s and early 1960s. Nikita Khrushchev said that nuclear war would destroy the world, so the East and West would have to coexist peacefully.

Pendleton Act of 1883   Created the civil service. See *civil service*.

Pentagon Papers   Leaked to the media in the 1960s, these secret documents implied that American involvement in the Vietnam War was encouraged by deception and duplicity of the Lyndon B. Johnson Administration.

periodic registration   A system requiring voters to reregister every few years in order to remain qualified to vote.

permanent registration   Persons remain registered to vote without having to reregister, provided they remain qualified otherwise. Usually one need reregister only after a change of address or name, or if one fails to vote in a general election. See *general election*.

petition, nomination by   When candidates must get a required number of registered voters to sign a petition supporting their candidacies in order for their names to be placed on the ballot.

petit jury   A trial jury.

pluralists   Political scientists who believe that the democratic process is fueled by various groups with conflicting interests. Public policy, therefore, is almost always the result of compromises among the powerful interest groups.

plurality   The largest number of votes when no majority occurs. If more than two candidates run for the same office, it is possible that no candidate will receive a majority. In such a case, the winner will be the person who receives the plurality (the most votes).

political action committees (PACs)   Committees established by corporations and other organizations that contribute funds to election campaigns. In the past 20 years the PACs have become very numerous and account for a large portion of the money spent in each election.

political culture Fundamental attitudes, assumptions, values, and psychology of people within a society, group, or political party.

political parties Groups of people who unite for the purpose of winning elections and taking control of government.

politicos Usually used to signify persons who behave in an overtly political manner, "politicos" is also used by political scientists to signify members of Congress who vote on legislation based upon a balance between their constituents' wishes and their own best judgment. See *tribunes* and *trustees*.

poll tax A tax assessed as a qualification for voting. Poll taxes were made illegal when the Twenty-Fourth Amendment was adopted in 1964.

popular sovereignty, theory of The foundation of democratic government, this theory holds that people are equal and that they may be governed only by their consent. The people are considered the repository of ultimate political power.

popular vote The vote of the people.

pork barrel Legislation that includes government spending in enough states and congressional districts to assure its passage.

precedent (*stare decisis*) The common law principle that binds lower courts to the opinions and interpretations of higher courts.

precinct The smallest, most local political jurisdiction. Polling places are located in each precinct to facilitate voting, and because the names, addresses, and party affiliation of the voters are given on precinct lists, the precinct is the logical place to mount election campaigns.

presidential-congressional system The American system of government, featuring the separation of powers and the checks and balances. The executive and the legislature are elected separately, and the judges are appointed for life terms, thus enhancing their independence. This system evolved from the governmental structure of the royal colonies as well as from the theories of Charles de Montesquieu.

President of the Senate The Constitution makes the vice president of the United States the President of the Senate. Because the vice president is not an elected member of the Senate, however, the Senate gives very little power to its presiding officer. Hence, the vice president, who may vote only to break a tie, seldom attends Senate meetings. In the absence of the vice president, the President Pro Tempore presides. The President Pro Tempore is elected by the Senate from its membership. The position is usually given to the Dean of the Senate, the person from the majority party in the Senate who has the greatest seniority.

President Pro Tempore See *President of the Senate*.

privacy, right of Not mentioned specifically in the Constitution, the right of privacy was recognized as constitutionally protected by the Warren Court in *Griswold* v. *Connecticut* (1966).

progressive tax A tax whose percentage increases with the ability to pay.

project grants Grants of federal funds to states that must be used in certain restricted areas but may be spent as the state sees fit within the areas.

proportional representation A system by which parties are given electoral victories in multimember electoral districts in proportion to the votes they receive. See *multimember district*.

proprietary colonies British colonies given as

land grants to favorites of the king. Several of these colonies first developed many of the individual liberties that United States citizens now enjoy.

primary, nomination by   Elections that somehow nominate candidates for office. Most states now use some form of primary election. Among the kinds of primaries are the following:

> **closed primaries**   allow people to vote in the primary only for the party in which they are registered;
>
> **open primaries**   allow people to choose which party primary they wish to vote in on the day of election;
>
> **wide-open primaries,**   also called blanket primaries, allow people to vote to nominate one candidate from any party for each office;
>
> **direct primaries**   are elections in which the person receiving the highest number of votes is nominated;
>
> **indirect primaries**   elect delegates who go to conventions to nominate candidates for office.

prior restraint   Legal terminology for censorship. It is prohibited by the First Amendment except in extreme cases.

privileges and immunities   See *horizontal federalism*.

quorum   The minimum number of members of Congress or other bodies necessary to conduct official meetings.

raiding   When people from one party who are sure their candidate will win their party's primary nomination vote in the opposition party's primary, hoping to nominate the weakest candidate so that their party's candidate will face a weak opponent and easily win election to office.

realigning election   An election that results in a new majority party.

reasonable basis test   A formula used by the courts to determine whether someone has illegally discriminated. The courts try to determine whether there is a reasonable basis for an alleged discrimination. Disallowing blind people from driving is an example of a reasonable basis for discrimination; segregating schools is unreasonable discrimination.

regressive tax   A tax whose percentage increases as the ability to pay decreases.

remedy   The judgment plaintiffs seek in lawsuits.

reprieve   See *clemency*.

reprimand   A form of congressional discipline in which a house votes to publicly chastise members who have erred ethically or legally, and to caution them to refrain from such behavior.

republic   Technically a republic is a government with an executive other than a monarch. In the United States the term has come to be understood as representative government in which the people elect the representatives. The term *democratic republic*, however, would more accurately describe what is meant by *republic* in America.

Republicans, Jeffersonian   The political party founded by Thomas Jefferson. Today's Democratic party descends from the Jeffersonian Republicans.

reserved powers   Powers that the Constitution grants to the states, such as education, marriage and divorce, and business licensing.

Resolution Trust Corporation (RTC)   Created in 1989 to liquidate the properties of savings and loan institutions that went bankrupt in the late 1980s and early 1990s.

revenue   Income to the government. Revenues can come from taxes and from nontax sources such as fees, interest, and borrowing.

revenue sharing Between 1972 and 1987 the federal government returned to the states a portion of its revenues, and the states were given almost total discretion about how the money was spent.

revolving door A term used to describe the movement of people from executive positions in business to government employment and back again. Critics argue that the revolving door gives corporate America undue influence in government.

riders Amendments attached to bills in the Senate that have nothing to do with the original bill. The House germane rule (see *germane rules*) prohibits the House from attaching riders to bills.

right to work laws State laws that proscribe union shops. See *union shop*.

Roe v. Wade The 1973 case that established abortion as legal. Abortion was deemed appropriate on grounds that the decision to abort pregnancy is a private matter and should not be encroached upon by government.

Roosevelt Corollary to the Monroe Doctrine Theodore Roosevelt proclaimed that the United States had the "right" to police the Western Hemisphere to assure that Latin American countries honored their international commitments.

royal colonies British colonies governed directly by the monarch through an appointed governor. The tradition of separation of powers and checks and balances evolved from the royal colony experience, the theories of Charles de Montesquieu, and other sources.

rule of four If four justices of the Supreme Court vote to hear a case, it must be brought to the Court for review.

Salutary Neglect (1607–1763) A period of time in which the British did not govern the Anglo-American colonies with great rigor. As a result, the Americans became proficient at governing themselves. When the British began to take a keener interest in the colonies, the Americans regarded their activities as unnecessary, intrusive, and oppressive.

secondary boycott A boycott by one union against its employer to pressure another employer to settle with its union.

Second Continental Congress Meeting in 1775, after the American Revolution had begun, the Congress organized the army and appointed George Washington its commander. As the war progressed, the Congress declared independence from Britain, acted as the first government of the United States, and drafted the Articles of Confederation.

second strike See *first strike*.

select committees Congressional committees created to study issues such as drug abuse, economics, and the Iran-Contra affair.

selective perception A common phenomenon, it takes place when people are receptive only to ideas with which they agree and ignore contrary information.

selective recall When people remember information with which they agree and forget that with which they disagree.

self-announcement, nomination by A form of nomination in which, to have their names placed on the ballot, candidates simply fill out an application form.

senatorial courtesy The tradition in the Senate not to approve presidential appointments within states unless the president first clears the appointments with senators from the president's party in the states involved.

Senior Executive Service Created in 1978 to give the president more flexibility in the administration of policy. It is composed of 7000 senior bureaucrats who can be moved from one assignment to another at the president's will.

seniority rule Each caucus in Congress has adopted a rule that awards positions and stature on standing committees according to their members' seniority. No caucus any longer uses seniority as the only criterion, however.

Shays' Rebellion In 1786 a group of Massachusetts farmers rose in rebellion against economic conditions that threatened to cause them to lose their farms. Although suppressed, the rebellion alarmed many Americans, persuading them that a stronger national government was necessary.

Sherman Antitrust Act (1890) The nation's first law attempting to discourage monopolies. The law was not very effective until the Clayton Antitrust Act was passed in 1914 and the Supreme Court became less probusiness in the 1930s.

single-issue voting When people ignore the multitude of issues in elections and choose candidates based upon their views about only a single issue such as abortion, school busing, defense policy, taxes, and so on. Single-issue voting is becoming increasingly common in American elections, resulting in office-holders whose political perspectives are very narrow.

single-member district An electoral district in which only one legislative seat can be won regardless of how many candidates run. This electoral technique discourages minor parties and favors a single- or a two-party system.

Smith, Adam (1723–1790) The founder of modern economics, this Scottish philosopher enunciated the principles of capitalism in his famous book *The Wealth of Nations*, which criticized the uncompetitive practices of monopolistic mercantilism.

social contract A theory suggesting that the state is created and legitimated by an agreement among the individuals it comprises.

socialization The process by which people adopt the dominant values of society. Formal socialization takes place in school and during parental instruction. Informal socialization takes place among peers, by watching television, or by other such incidental means.

social security Formally called Old Age Survivors and Disability Insurance (OASDI), it was created in 1935. This program taxes workers and then pays them premiums when they retire, or provides for their survivors.

sovereign The highest legal authority within a state. In a democracy, the people are sovereign according to the theory of popular sovereignty. See *popular sovereignty, theory of.*

Speaker of the House The presiding officer of the House of Representatives and invariably the leader of the majority of the House. The Speaker is the most powerful person in Congress.

spoils system The practice of removing the appointees of the previous administration and replacing them with people loyal to the new president. The spoils system was largely eliminated when the civil service and other merit systems were established. See *civil service* and *merit system.*

standing committees The chief legislative committees in Congress. They may amend bills, kill them, table them, or send them to the floor with a recommended disposition.

stare decisis See *precedent.*

state central committees Each political party in each state is headed by a state central committee that is responsible for party affairs.

states' rights A view held first by liberals but now generally a conservative belief that local and state governments should be allowed to address most of the problems of government and that the national government should stay out of their affairs. In the 1950s and 1960s, states' rights positions were used to oppose desegregation and the civil rights movement.

statutes Laws made by legislatures.

Stealth bomber (B-2) A manned bomber supposed to be impervious to Soviet radar.

straight-ticket voting See *ticket splitting*.

Strategic Air Command (SAC) One of three legs of the triad deployment, SAC is composed of manned bombers. The strategic bombers are the aging B-52 and the newer B-1. The air force is hoping to add the B-2 Stealth bomber to its fleet.

Strategic Arms Limitation Talks (SALT) Discussions between the United States and the Soviet Union that resulted in two agreements to slow the building of nuclear weapons.

Strategic Arms Reduction Talks (START) Talks between the United States and the Soviet Union about reducing the number of strategic weapons they hold.

Strategic Defense Initiative (SDI) Popularly known as "Star Wars," this proposed system is supposed to make the United States impervious to a nuclear attack by ICBMs. President Reagan initiated a research and development program to see whether a defensive shield of laser beams, particle beams, and kinetic energy could be used to shoot down ICBMs launched at the United States. Since the system was never designed to defend against cruise missiles, submarine-launched missiles, or bombers, it never really could have made the United States completely safe from a nuclear attack. After several years of research the government has concluded that the most optimistic hopes for the SDI were unrealistic. Research continues on a defensive system much reduced from the original plan, however.

strategic nuclear weapons Bombers and missiles that can attack targets on other continents with nuclear warheads and bombs.

structural deficit When the government borrows so much money in a year that even if everyone was employed, its spending would still exceed revenues. See *cyclical deficit* and *deficit*.

Subcommittee Bill of Rights A reform of the majority (Democratic) caucus of the House that gave many powers formerly held by standing committee chairs to the subcommittees. Similar reforms were also adopted in the Senate and, while they have diversified the power in Congress, they have weakened party discipline and the leadership.

subcommittees Composed of members of congressional standing committees, these bodies investigate bills in detail and recommend disposition to the standing committees.

subgovernments See *iron triangles*.

submarine-launched ballistic missiles (SLBMs) Missiles launched from submarines. Missiles on Trident submarines can carry as many as 16 warheads. They are fast, but so far they lack the accuracy of ICBMs.

Supplemental Security Income (SSI) A government program that gives economic assistance to the blind, disabled, and aged poor.

supply-side economics Advocated by Ronald Reagan, this model has government giving large subsidies, tax breaks, and other advantages to business in order to promote prosperity.

supremacy clause See *concurrent powers*.

Supreme Court opinion The formal opinion of the Supreme Court. These opinions establish the interpretation of the Constitution and of other law.

suspect classifications   Areas in which unreasonable discrimination has frequently occurred are given very strict scrutiny by the courts when discrimination is alleged. These areas include race, national origin, and religion.

Taft-Hartley Act (1947)   This law makes closed shops illegal, provides that states can make union shops illegal, and forbids jurisdictional strikes and secondary boycotts. It also requires a cooling-off period before strikes can be held in industries that are important to the national welfare. See *closed shops*, *union shops*, *jurisdictional strikes*, and *secondary boycotts*.

Tet Offensive   A 1968 communist offensive in Vietnam so powerful that it disheartened many Americans, who subsequently opposed further American involvement in the war.

Third World   Developing countries in Latin America, Asia, and Africa.

Three-fifths Compromise   The Constitutional Convention of 1789 agreed that only three of every five slaves were to be counted in determining the number of seats each state would receive in the House of Representatives.

ticket splitting   When voters vote for persons from different parties for various offices. The opposite would be straight-ticket voting, in which voters vote for all the candidates running from a single party.

Tienanmen Square   The central square in Beijing, China. In May and June of 1989 a massive student protest took place there, but it was ultimately dispersed by Chinese troops at great loss of life.

tort   A civil lawsuit in which the plaintiff attempts to recover a monetary settlement for alleged damage done by the defendant.

Triad   The deployment of strategic nuclear weapons used by the United States. It depends upon intercontinental ballistic missiles (ICBMs), manned bombers, and submarine-launched ballistic missiles (SLBMs). About half of the U.S. warheads are in submarines; the other half are divided between the ICBMs and bombers. See *intercontinental ballistic missiles*, the *strategic air command*, and *submarine-launched ballistic missiles*.

trial balloons   Occasionally a politician will publicize an idea to see what public reaction it evokes. If the reaction is positive, the politician will pursue the idea.

tribunes   A term used to signify congresspersons who believe their duty is simply to reflect in Congress their constituents' wishes. See *politicos* and *trustees*.

Truman Doctrine   The formal end to the United States' unilateral approach to foreign policy. After World War II, President Harry S. Truman pledged American help to societies threatened by communist subversion.

trustees   A term used to signify members of Congress who believe it their duty to vote based on their judgment about the best interests of their district, paying little attention to their constituents' wishes. See *politicos* and *tribunes*.

two-party system   When a political system is dominated by two major parties, each of which has a good chance to win control of the government.

unemployment insurance   A government program funded by employer contributions and collected by people who have been laid off from their jobs.

unilateral foreign policy   When a country refuses to ally with other states, preferring to remain independent in foreign policy. The United States used this approach, except for during emergencies, from its founding until after World War II.

union shop Industries with labor contracts that require workers to join particular unions within a certain time after being hired. State law may now make union shops illegal. See *Taft-Hartley Act* and *right to work laws*.

unitary system A system of government in which all legitimate political power belongs to the central government, and local governments are delegated powers from the center. Britain uses a unitary system. In the United States the states enjoy unitary control over county, city, and special district governments.

United Nations (UN) An international organization created at the end of World War II to foster peace and to address world social and economic problems such as poverty, hunger, disease, and illiteracy.

United States Information Agency (USIA) Loosely connected to the State Department, USIA runs the foreign propaganda broadcasts of the United States such as Worldnet, Voice of America, and Radio Free Europe.

vertical federalism Refers to the relationship between the national government and the state governments in a federal system.

veto, line item When an executive can veto a portion of a bill while allowing the rest to become law. Although most state governors have the line item veto, the president does not.

veto, pocket If Congress adjourns while the president is considering legislation and the bill is not signed by the president, it is vetoed. Since Congress is adjourned, pocket vetoes cannot be overridden.

veto, regular If within ten days (Sundays excluded) of Congress's passing a law the president formally rejects it, it is vetoed.

Congress can override a regular veto by a two-thirds' vote in each house.

Vice President's Office Housing the vice president and a small staff, its location in the White House since the Kennedy Administration is a measure of the importance the vice presidency has recently achieved.

Virginia Plan Drafted by James Madison and proposed at the Constitutional Convention of 1789, this provided for an executive, a legislature, and a judiciary in the national government. Although its provisions giving the populous states control of the strengthened national government were modified, most of its other features were ultimately adopted, forming the basic structure of the government of the United States.

Voting Rights Act of 1965 A major civil rights act that substantially increased the number of African-American voters. Since its passage, thousands of African-Americans have been elected to public office.

Wagner Act See *National Labor Relations Act*.

War on Poverty A series of programs initiated in the 1960s by President Lyndon B. Johnson to eliminate poverty in the United States.

War Powers Act Passed in 1973, this law requires the president to notify Congress within 48 hours of sending troops into combat. Congress may require a withdrawal of the troops at any time by passing a joint resolution to that effect. The law further provides that the president must withdraw the troops within 60 days unless Congress expressly approves their continued deployment.

Watergate affair During the 1972 presidential election, five people from the committee to reelect Richard M. Nixon broke into the Democratic headquarters at the Watergate building in Washington D.C. Subsequent investigations revealed widespread corruption and criminal acts in the administration, some of which the president was involved in himself, and ultimately caused his resignation in the face of impeachment proceedings.

Webster v. Reproductive Health Services A 1989 case in which the Supreme Court ruled that a state may prohibit abortions from being performed in publicly supported hospitals.

welfare A number of government programs created to give assistance to the poor.

Whigs A prominent second party in the mid-1800s. It was noted for its opposition to Andrew Jackson.

whips Each caucus in each house has assistants to the floor leaders. They are traditionally called Whips although in the Senate they are called Assistants to the Floor Leaders. Their job is to help plan party strategy and to get commitments from members for votes on legislation.

White House Office A segment of the Executive Office of the President, this agency includes clerical and housekeeping staff as well as numerous press aides, advisers, liaison personnel, and the chief of staff. Because these people are physically closest to the president, they are often among the most powerful in the government.

white primary Some southern states prohibited African-Americans from voting in their primaries. Since Democratic candidates usually won every election in states with such restrictions, the white primary effectively denied African-Americans any impact in choosing their representatives. The white primary was declared unconstitutional in *Smith* v. *Allwright* (1944).

written constitution A document that specifies in writing the structure and powers of government and the rights of citizens. The first written national Constitution was the Articles of Confederation. The tradition for written constitutions evolved from the charters given to some Anglo-American colonies. The United States Constitution is the oldest existing written national constitution in the world.

GENERAL SUGGESTIONS FOR FURTHER READING

BELLAH, ROBERT, ET AL.
  Habits of the Heart. Berkeley, CA:
  University of California Press, 1985.

CORDS, NICHOLAS, AND
PATRICK GERSTER, EDS.
  Myth and the American Experience (Vol I).
  New York: Glencoe Press, 1973.

DAHL, ROBERT A.
  *Who Governs? Democracy and Power in an
  American City.* New Haven: Yale
  University Press, 1961.

DOWNS, GEORGE W., AND PATRICK D.
LARKEY
  The Search for Government Efficiency.
  Philadelphia: Temple University Press,
  1986.

GOODWIN, RICHARD N.
  Remembering America. Boston: Little,
  Brown, 1988.

HAMILTON, ALEXANDER, JAMES MADISON,
AND JOHN JAY
  The Federalist Papers 1788. Various
  editions.

KENNEDY, JOHN F.
  Profiles in Courage. New York: Cardinal,
  1957.

KILIAN, MICHAEL, AND ARNOLD SAWISLAK
  Who Runs Washington? New York:
  St. Martin's, 1982.

MAYHEW, DAVID R.
  Placing Parties in American Politics.
  Princeton: Princeton University Press,
  1986.

PROXMIRE, WILLIAM
  Uncle Sam: Last of the Big Spenders. New
  York: Simon & Schuster, 1972.

SCHWARZ, JOHN E.
  *America's Hidden Success: A Reassessment
  of Public Policy from Kennedy to Reagan*
  (rev. ed.). New York: Norton, 1988.

SMITH, HEDRICK
  *The Power Game: How Washington
  Works.* New York: Random House, 1988.

STANLEY, HAROLD W., AND RICHARD G.
NIEMI
  Vital Statistics on American Politics (2nd
  ed.). Washington, DC: Congressional
  Quarterly Press, 1990.

TOCQUEVILLE, ALEXIS DE
  Democracy in America (2 vols). New
  York: Knopf, 1951. Originally published
  in 1835.

CREDITS

PHOTOGRAPHS

INDEX